ENGINEERED MASONRY DESIGN

Limit States Design

Glanville
Hatzinikolas
Ben-Omran

TEXTBOOK
DESIGN MANUAL
CSA STANDARD S304.1

WINSTON HOUSE

ENGINEERED MASONRY DESIGN
Limit States Design

John I. Glanville
Professor of Civil Engineering
University of Manitoba
Winnipeg

Michael A. Hatzinikolas
Executive Director
Canadian Masonry Research Institute
Adjunct Professor of Civil Engineering
University of Alberta
Edmonton

Hamza A. Ben-Omran
GB Engineering
Adjunct Professor of Civil Engineering
University of Manitoba
Winnipeg

WINSTON HOUSE
WINNIPEG

Engineered Masonry Design
Limit States Design

Note: Although every effort has been made to ensure that the information and data in the book is factual and accurate to a degree consistent with current design practice, neither the authors nor the publisher can assume responsibility for errors or omissions, nor for engineering designs and plans based on it. Where products are shown in diagrams through the text it is for illustrative purposes only and not intended to promote a specific product over others available on the market.

Printed in Canada   Imprimé au Canada

WINSTON HOUSE ENTERPRISES
264 Wildwood Park
Winnipeg
Manitoba, R3T 0E4   ISBN 1-55056-441-2

PREFACE

Although masonry has been used in the construction of buildings for millennia, it is only within the past few decades that its structural design procedures have been developed into a rational form familiar to structural engineers. The early empirical design rules evolved into working stress design which in turn is now being replaced, in this country, by limit states design - a method already familiar to structural designers of steel, concrete and timber structures. The Canadian Standards Association has developed and, in 1994, published a limit states design standard for masonry buildings that is referenced in the 1995 National Building Code of Canada. While the standard provides the rules that govern the structural design of masonry and the minimum requirements for an acceptable level of safety and durability, there is still the need for a textbook explaining the theory behind the clauses in the standard.

This book has been written with the needs of both the novice and the practising structural designer in mind. It is divided into three parts. *Part 1* is a textbook in which the aim has been a clear treatment of fundamental principles. Once mastered, these principles can be applied to more complex situations, and in the later chapters we have attempted to illustrate this application through representative building designs, and to inject some of the "flavour" of the design process. Problem sets with answers have been included so that the book may be used for self-study. *Part 2* provides much of the factual information necessary to structural design, and includes tables and charts that will spare the designer tedious calculations. *Part 3* is a reprint of the Canadian Standards Association Standard S304.1-94 *Masonry Design for Buildings (Limit States Design)*, the standard that governs the structural design of masonry. Système International (SI) units have been used throughout the book.

This book is an expanded version of the earlier working stress design book: the eight chapters of that book have been expanded and rewritten for limit states design, and three chapters dealing with seismic resistance, veneer and cavity walls, and masonry details have been added. We have tried to be as complete as possible within a reasonable space and believe that this book meets the designers' needs. There is no question that more information about masonry exists and a bibliography for further reading is provided at the back of *Part 1*, which also lists a limit states design computer program written to conform to S304.1.

A number of people have provided valuable assistance in the preparation of this book. John W. Glanville was responsible for computer graphics, formatting and layout: David Laird P.Eng., of Halsall and Associates Toronto, interrupted his busy schedule for a detailed review: and Gary Sturgeon P.Eng., of the Masonry Council of Canada Calgary, during a very difficult period in his life painstakingly checked a draft of the book. We are sincerely grateful for their efforts and for their constructive suggestions.

This book could not have been undertaken without the generous support of the masonry industry in Canada. We are grateful to them.

Finally, we would like to thank Winston House for their patient cooperation during the development of this book.

July 1996

Note *Throughout this book reference has been made to the* **Supplement** *to the* **National Building Code of Canada.** *This supplement is being replaced in the near future by a document referred to as* **Structural Commentaries** *on the NBCC.*

CONTENTS

PART 2 - DESIGN MANUAL

PART 3 - CSA STANDARD S304.1-94

NOTATION

The following is a list of basic nomenclature used throughout the text.

a depth of equivalent rectangular stress block

A effective tension area of masonry surrounding the flexural tension reinforcement and having the same centroid as that reinforcement, divided by the number of bars

A'_s cross-sectional area of compression reinforcement

A_b cross-sectional area of reinforcement corresponding to balanced strain conditions

A_e effective cross-sectional area

A_g gross cross-sectional area

A_s cross-sectional area of reinforcement

A_{s1} area of tension reinforcement balancing the compression force in the compression reinforcement

A_{s2} area of tension reinforcement balancing the compression force in the masonry in a beam with compression reinforcement

A_v cross-sectional area of shear reinforcement

b width of beam or column

b_w width of beam web (normally beam width)

c distance of the extreme fibre of the section from the neutral axis

C_e exposure factor

C_{ge} external gust factor

C_{gi} internal gust factor

C_m factored compressive resistance of masonry in a section with compression; or, coefficient for equivalent uniform bending

C_{pe} external pressure coefficient

C_{pi} internal pressure coefficient

C_r total factored compressive resistance in a section

C_s factored compressive resistance of compression reinforcement

d effective depth of flexural member

D overall depth of flexural member; or, dead loads

d' distance from extreme compression fibre to centroid of compression reinforcement

d_b nominal diameter of bar

d_c thickness of masonry cover measured from extreme tension fibre to centre of the closest bar

e virtual eccentricity

E earthquake load

e_1 the smaller virtual eccentricity at top or bottom of member

e_2 the smaller virtual eccentricity at top or bottom of member

E_m modulus of elasticity of masonry

E_s modulus of elasticity of steel

E_v modulus of rigidity of masonry

F foundation factor

f'_m compressive strength of masonry

f'_s calculated stress in compression reinforcement

f_{cs} axial compressive stress, (unfactored axial load P/A_e)

f_m compressive stress in masonry

f_s calculated stress in tension reinforcement

f_t flexural tensile strength of masonry; or, limiting tensile stress in masonry

f_y yield strength of reinforcement

h effective height of a wall or column

I moment of inertia of the net section; or, seismic importance factor

I_{cr} moment of inertia of cracked section

I_e effective moment of inertia

I_g moment of inertia of gross masonry section

I_o moment of inertia of the effective area section about its centroidal axis

I_p weight of a part or portion of the structure

j_d distance between the resultants of the internal compressive and tensile forces on a cross-section

k ratio of the depth of compression zone in flexural member to the effective depth, d; or, effective height factor for compression member

K constant in the expression $M = kbd^2$

K_i relative stiffness of wall i

L length of wall; or, live loads

l_a additional embedment length at support or at point of inflection

l_d required development length

l_{db} basic development length

l_{dh} required development length of standard hook

l_{hb} basic development length of standard hook

M bending moment

M_a maximum moment due to unfactored loads

M_{cr} cracking moment

M_f factored moment

M_p primary moment

M_r resisting moment of a section

n modular ratio

N	number of ties
N_f	axial tension force
N_r	resistance of cross-section to tensile cracking
P	axial load in wall or column
P_D	axial dead load
p_e	external pressure
p_f	factored wind pressure
P_f	factored applied axial load
p_i	internal pressure
P_L	axial live load
P_r	factored resistance in compression
q	reference velocity pressure
R	force modification factor; or, thermal resistance
R_t	shear resistance multiplier to account for axial force
s	stirrup spacing
S	elastic section modulus; or, seismic response factor; or, time dependent factor related to duration of load
S_p	seismic response factor for portion of a building
s'	crack spacing
t	effective thickness of wall or column
T	resultant force; or, torque; or, loads due to expansion and contraction; or, fundamental period; or, temperature
T_r	factored tensile resistance of steel
u	bond stress per unit surface area of bar
U	calibration factor
u_u	ultimate average bond stress
v	shear stress; or, zonal velocity ratio
V	total shear force; or, minimum lateral seismic force at the base of the structure
V_e	equivalent lateral seismic force at the base of elastic structure.
v_f	average or nominal shear stress
V_f	factored shear force
V_m	shear resistance provided by masonry
V_r	factored shear resistance of a section
V_s	shear resistance provided by shear reinforcement
v_u	ultimate shear stress
w	flexural crack width; or, intensity of uniform loading
W	wind load; or, total load
y_t	distance from centroid to extreme fibre in tension
$\bar{y}$	centroid of section
z	quantity limiting distribution of flexural reinforcement
Σo	sum of perimeters of bars
α_D	dead load factor
α_L	live load factor
α_t	coefficient of thermal expansion

α_T	expansion or contraction load factor
α_w	wind load factor
αW	combined factored load
β_1	ratio of depth of rectangular stress block, a, to depth to neutral axis, c
β_d	ratio of factored dead load moment to total factored moment
γ	importance factor
δ	deflection
ϵ	strain
ϵ'_s	strain in compression steel
ϵ_m	strain in masonry
ϵ_{mu}	compressive strain at crushing of masonry
ϵ_s	strain in steel
ϵ_y	yield strain in steel
λ	modification factor related to unit weight of masonry unit
ρ	ratio of area of tension reinforcement to effective masonry area, A_s/bd
ρ'	ratio of area of compression reinforcement to effective masonry area, A'_s/bd
ρ_b	reinforcement ratio corresponding to balanced strain conditions
ϕ_e	resistance factor for member
ϕ_m	resistance factor for masonry materials
ϕR	factored resistance
ϕ_s	resistance factor for reinforcing steel
χ	width modification factor
Ψ	load combination factor

PART 1

TEXTBOOK

J. I. Glanville
M. A. Hatzinikolas

CHAPTER 1

STRUCTURES, LOADING AND CODES

1-1   INTRODUCTION

The term *masonry* applies to that type of construction wherein a large number of small modular units are mortared together to produce a structure or structural elements. Typically, these small units are brick, concrete block or cut stone. The main structural element is the wall, but masonry, when suitably reinforced, can also be used for columns and beams. Structural or load-bearing masonry is normally constructed from brick and concrete blocks. Non load-bearing masonry veneers are usually of brick or cut stone.

Inherent to any building or structure is the characteristic that neither it nor any of its components collapses - that is, it should have sufficient strength and stability to ensure *safety*. Also, it should continue to be safe for a reasonable period of time - that is, the quality of the materials used and the details of the construction should be sufficient to ensure *durability*. If cost were not a factor, it would be relatively simple to meet these two requirements; but to plan, design and construct a building with the additional constraint of *economy* requires considerably more skill. While the architect/ client/ engineer team work together to meet the requirements of aesthetics, form and function, with the constraints imposed by the client's purse, the principal responsibility of the structural designer is *safety*, *durability* and *economy*.

With the great variety of units available and the versatility of the masonry producers, contractors and designers, a wide range of elegant and functional masonry buildings can be constructed that are safe, durable and economical. In Canada, the design of masonry buildings is governed by the *National Building Code of Canada* 1995, and structural design, more specifically, by the *Canadian Standards Association* standard *CSA-S304.1-94 Masonry Design for Buildings*.

1-2   HISTORICAL BACKGROUND

People have been building significant masonry structures for about ten millennia, the earliest evidence of this method of construction coming from, not surprisingly, the Cradle of Civilization - the Middle East. The first city walls were of rubble, carefully stacked, several metres thick. By about five thousand years ago man had attained a surprising degree of sophistication in megalithic construction (for example, the pyramids of Egypt), and in sun-dried clay brick construction (for example, the Tower of Babel in Mesopotamia, and in Mohenjo-Daro in the Indus valley).

Through the Classical Greek period and into the Roman Empire examples of masonry structures of great beauty and utility abound - temples, palaces, houses, warehouses, docks and sea walls, aqueducts and bridges. It is interesting to note that the Romans, about two thousand years ago, had a knowledge of concretes and mortars which surpassed in strength and durability anything that was produced subsequently until the eighteenth century. Their knowledge was recorded by Vitruvius in his manuscript *De Architectura*, which was lost for several centuries. The Romans had developed the use of the arch, which appears to have originated in Syria, and the dome to a high degree of utility and sophistication, and were constructing in brick and stone masonry.

Although for several centuries there was a general decline in the quality of mortar, masonry continued to be used as the principal construction material. There are many superb examples of cathedrals, castles and bridges through the so-called Dark Ages, the Middle Ages and the Renaissance. New structural forms, such as the arch with flying buttresses and the vaulted roof appeared.

The development of structural steel and reinforced concrete about one hundred years ago led to a general decline in the use of masonry. Burgeoning knowledge about the elastic behaviour of structures was put to use in the development of design theories for the newer materials. Steel and reinforced concrete, being able to resist both tension and compression (and consequently bending) were seen as being more versatile and led to lighter and taller structures than was possible with masonry, which could only resist compression and which relied upon its mass for stability. In general, rather than keeping pace with developments in structural steel and reinforced concrete, the use of masonry declined and, to a great extent, took the form of infill walls and veneers. Furthermore, while rational design methods and building codes were developing for other construction materials, masonry was being designed by very conservative "rules of thumb."

Only when the concept of reinforcing with steel rods to resist tension was applied could masonry be re-established as a competitive construction material. Although sporadic attempts were made to reinforce brick masonry from 1825 onwards, it was not until about one hundred years later, when engineers in India and Japan realized that steel reinforcing would enhance the resistance of masonry structures to earthquake forces, that masonry entered the modern era. Since that time, through the use of reinforcement, the number of stories in masonry buildings has increased substantially while bearing wall thicknesses have decreased similarly, and masonry is also being used for beams, columns and arches.

1-3 STRUCTURAL APPLICATIONS

Structural masonry is produced by laying a large number of modular units - bricks or blocks - on beds of mortar in successive courses, one above the other, to produce a particular structural component; and these units may be concrete or fired clay products. Fig. 1-1 shows the details of two typical blocks, a standard hollow block and a lintel block. Note that the actual dimensions of the blocks, 390 mm by 190 mm, are each 10 mm less than the nominal dimensions, thereby allowing for 10 mm thick mortar joints. Once mortared into place, the actual modular dimensions become 400 mm long by 200 mm high. The width of the block, representing the thickness of the wall, will be determined by the intensity of loading. A typical block wall could have a nominal thickness of 200 mm, the actual thickness being 190 mm.

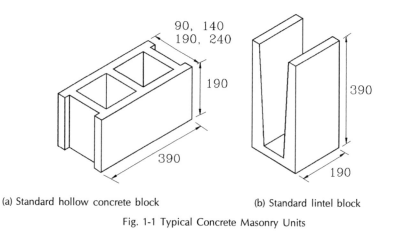

(a) Standard hollow concrete block   (b) Standard lintel block

Fig. 1-1 Typical Concrete Masonry Units

The standard block wall may be used plain, that is, unreinforced, or reinforced. To reinforce a wall, reinforcing bars are placed in selected cores, which line up vertically, and the cores are filled with grout (a high-slump concrete with a maximum aggregate size less than 14 mm). A concrete block wall with vertical reinforcement is shown in Fig. 1-2. The shape of the lintel block permits the placement of horizontal reinforcing steel and grout fill and is used specifically for spanning openings, as shown in Fig. 1-3.

Bricks, whether produced from clay or concrete, can also be used in structural, load-bearing applications, either as plain or reinforced elements. While being available in a variety of sizes, the standard metric brick is 190 mm long, 57 mm high and 90 mm wide. Allowing for 10 mm joints, the nominal dimensions in a wall then become 200 mm long, three courses high in 200 mm and 100 mm width or thickness. This is described in more detail in Chapter 2. Bricks are perhaps more frequently used as veneer where they may or may not function structurally.

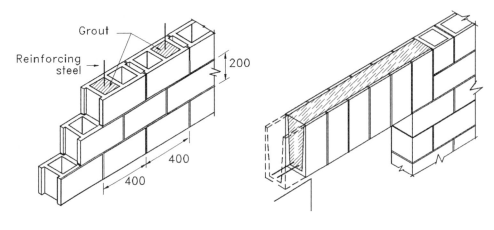

Fig. 1-2 Reinforced Masonry Wall   Fig. 1-3 Lintel Beam

Since it is difficult to reinforce stone to resist tension, its primary use is as veneer. Any load-bearing applications rely on gravity and mass for stability and resistance to tension, and the structural use of stone is restricted to massive, monumental types of structures.

In many ways reinforced masonry is similar to reinforced concrete in that it can be reinforced with steel bars and filled with concrete grout. When properly placed, the grout fills the cores and bonds to the masonry unit for a mutual sharing of the load. *The main advantage of masonry in comparison with reinforced concrete is that the need for formwork is eliminated.*

Although reinforced masonry can be used in such flexural applications as retaining walls (Fig. 1-4), it is more frequently used as load-bearing walls, that is, walls with in-plane compression loading. Typically, it will be supporting steel joists (Fig. 1-5) or precast hollowcore (Fig. 1-6) floor and roof units.

In high-rise construction, the masonry walls, in addition to supporting the gravity loads, can also serve effectively as shear walls in resisting horizontal forces due to wind and earthquake. These applied forces impose further in-plane loading (compression, tension and shear) on the walls. Fig. 1-7 shows a typical masonry wall layout in a high-rise building. In addition to resisting gravity loading, walls A resist transverse forces H_A, and stairwells and elevator shaft B resists longitudinal forces H_B.

Although there are numerous applications for structural masonry, including prestressing, these few examples should serve to illustrate its uses.

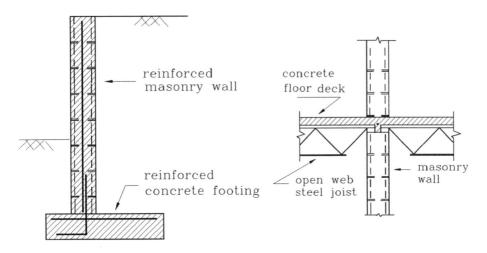

Fig. 1-4 Reinforced Masonry Retaining Wall   Fig. 1-5 Cross-Section at Steel Joist Support

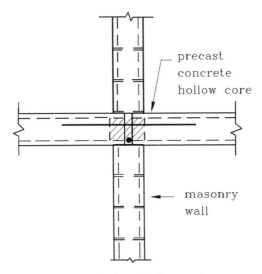

Fig. 1-6 Cross-Section at Hollowcore Support

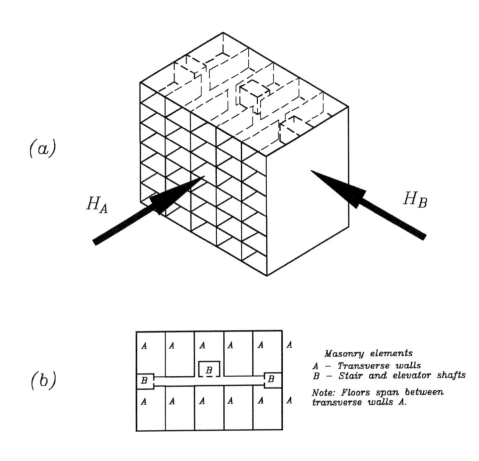

(a)

H_A H_B

(b)

Masonry elements
A — Transverse walls
B — Stair and elevator shafts

Note: Floors span between transverse walls A.

Fig. 1-7 Typical Masonry Bearing wall Building
(a) perspective of building   (b) floor plan layout

1-4 STRUCTURAL LOADS

While the function of a building is to house some sort of human activity or service, that of its structure is to support the building. This means that the structure should safely resist all anticipated loads, or physical forces, to ensure that the building remains serviceable during a reasonable "service life", or expected period of usefulness. This section of the book considers the topic of *loads*, and Section 1-5 introduces the concept of safety.

The types of loading on a structure are numerous and vary widely in the predictability of their levels of intensity. There are permanent and transitory static loads due to gravitational forces, hydrostatic fluid pressure and earth pressures, dynamic forces caused by people, machinery, wind, earthquake and blast, and there are the forces induced by factors such as the expansion and contraction caused by changes in temperature and humidity. Also, the intensity of many of these loads depends on the type of occupancy, geographic location and other factors such as building configuration.

To relieve the structural designer of the very formidable task of wading through this morass of variables, the National Building Code of Canada (NBC 1995), in Part 4.1 *Structural Loads and Procedures*, provides very specific guidelines to determine the maximum anticipated intensities of loads which a particular structure must resist. These loads can most conveniently be covered in six categories: *dead loads (D)* caused by gravitational forces, *live loads (L)* due to use and occupancy, loads caused by *wind (W)*, earthquake loads *(E)*; loads due to *expansion and contraction (T)*, and other effects such as blast.

In the following discussion, *D, L, W, E* and *T* loads are introduced, as is the probability of these loads occurring simultaneously in combination.

a) *Dead Loads (D)*

Dead load refers to the weight of all permanent materials in a building, including the weight of the structure itself and of all permanent fixtures. Generally, dead loads are the most predictable of loads since the majority of the weights are known in advance. One exception is the self-weight of the structural members, whose cross-section is frequently governed by the worst combination of loads. In such instances cross-sections are assumed, and these in turn are checked in the final design. The *Design Information* section of Part 2 of this book includes a table of dead loads of materials used in floors, ceilings, roofs, and walls.

b) *Live Loads (L)*

Live load is the term given to the loads that are due to *use and occupancy* and, although they are for the most part transitory, their maximum intensity must be anticipated and allowed for in design. They include the weight and dynamic effect of people, vehicles, and other machines and moveable objects. While live loads are difficult to define and quantify precisely, they are generally simplified to equivalent static loads. For the most part, they are expressed as vertical loading, but in the case of machinery moving horizontally, acceleration and braking forces should be considered. The *Design Information* section of Part 2 includes a table of recommended minimum floor and roof live loads that has been taken from Part 4 of the *National Building Code of Canada 1995* (NBC).

The gravity loads caused by maximum expected accumulation of snow, ice and rain are generally assumed to be in the live load *(L)* category. The determination of such loads depends on factors such as geographic location, exposure, building configuration and roof slope; and detailed information for the determination of this loading is included in Part 4 of the NBC and in the *structural commentaries on the NBC*.

c) *Wind Loads (W)*

The loads due to wind and earthquake are dynamic loads and, although for the most part transitory, they can cause great devastation if their effects are not given due consideration. The effect of wind load is generally horizontal, or *lateral*, and the intensity depends on a number of factors including geographic location. Since it is highly improbable that an earthquake will occur at the peak of a hurricane or tornado, the more severe of the two loadings is the one that governs the design.

Wind load is a dynamic force caused by the deceleration of a mass of air changing direction as it is diverted around and over a building. The result is a positive pressure on the windward face and suction, or negative pressure, on the leeward face and roof. Due to its change in direction around corners, wind tends to separate from the building and normally imposes negative pressures on exterior wall and roof surfaces that are parallel to the wind. Openings on the windward face of the building lead to positive internal pressure, and to negative internal pressure if the openings are on the lee. Wind speed, overall and local intensity and frequency of gusting, degree of exposure, building configuration and location of openings all contribute to the wind load and the response of the building to wind. Although the design of slender structures such as the CN Tower and tall buildings requires a rigorous analysis based on aerodynamic principles, wind load on the majority of masonry and other buildings can be modelled more simply, and quite adequately, as equivalent static loads. The commentaries on the NBC outline both the detailed and the simplified methods.

The simplified method consists of calculating external and internal pressures, both positive and negative, as follows:

external pressure $\qquad p_e = qC_eC_{ge}C_{pe}$ $\qquad\qquad$ (1-1)

internal pressure $\qquad p_i = qC_eC_{gi}C_{pi}$ $\qquad\qquad$ (1-2)

The reference velocity pressure, q, is based on the probability of not being exceeded in any one year of the subscripted number of years, according to the relative importance of the element or building. Thus, q_{10}, q_{30}, and q_{100} apply to localized surfaces such as cladding, most buildings, and buildings for post-disaster service, respectively. The exposure factor, C_e, is taken as 1.0 at ground level and increases with height. For example, at 50 m C_e has a value of about 1.4. The external gust factor, C_{ge}, has a value of 2.5 for cladding and 2.0 for the building, while the internal gust factor, C_{gi}, is normally taken as 1.0. Finally, the external and internal pressure coefficients, C_{pe} and C_{pi} respectively, depend on the building configuration and surface involved. The C_p values are generally less than or equal to one, but can have higher local values at corners.

d) *Earthquake Loads (E)*

Earthquake loads on a building are inertial forces induced by ground motions that cause the building and its components to accelerate and move and, of course, the resulting forces are the product of mass and acceleration. The forces experienced by the building and its components depend on the nature of the seismic activity and on the various properties of the building, such as its fundamental frequency and the degree of damping (that is, energy dissipation) available. During an earthquake, building accelerations are generally lower than the ground accelerations, but in certain instances can be greater. Since acceleration over a very brief period of time causes less damage than over a more extended period, two main ground motion parameters, peak horizontal acceleration and peak horizontal velocity, are important. Because the horizontal ground motions exceed those in the vertical direction, and since structures are normally designed to sustain substantial vertical loads with an appropriate margin of safety, only the horizontal earthquake forces need to be considered in design. The purpose of seismic design is to ensure that the building will resist moderate earthquakes without significant damage and will survive a major earthquake without collapse.

The earthquake-induced forces or loads (*E*) for which a building should be designed depend on its rigidity, damping characteristics and fundamental frequency, the nature of the foundation material, and on the maximum expected ground motions. The determination of these loads is covered in Chapter 7 *Earthquake Resistance*.

e) *Loads due to Expansion and Contraction (T)*

All construction materials undergo small volumetric changes as the result of environmental factors such as changes in ambient temperature and relative humidity. Expansion or contraction, for example, results from an increase or a decrease in temperature; concrete products shrink after initial hydration as the material dries; fired clay products that are free from moisture when they emerge from the kiln swell as they absorb moisture; and both clay and concrete products swell or shrink with an increase or decrease in moisture content.

While the volumetric strains involved are relatively small, they can accumulate over an extended distance, and if provision is not made to allow for this movement, or to take into account the internal load, *T*, caused by restraint, localized failures can take place. For example, the well-known phenomenon of frame shortening due to shrinkage and creep in tall concrete buildings can, if not properly detailed, result in the failure of cladding and infill panels.

f) *Loads in Combination*

Of the four loads *D*, *L*, *W* and *T*, only *D* is permanent. The other loads are transient and the probability that they will occur simultaneously at their maximum intensity is reflected in a *load combination factor*, Ψ. The maximum expected *service* load on a building can then be expressed as

$$D + \Psi(L + W + T) \tag{1-6}$$

The NBC specifies that when only one of L, W, or T acts in combination with D, $\Psi = 1.0$; for two of L, W or T, $\Psi = 0.70$; and when all three act at their maximum intensity with D, $\Psi = 0.60$.

Earthquake effects are evaluated by considering $D + E +$ an appropriate portion of L.

g) *Summary of Loads*

The loads discussed in this section include dead, live, wind and earthquake, and loads due to the restraint of environmentally-related volumetric strains, and the manipulation of some of the numbers at this point may appear confusing. They are, however, explained in more detail in Chapters 6 through 9 which present examples of building design.

1-5   DESIGN METHODS AND CODES

There are two basic interpretations of safety in structural design that lead to two fundamentally different design methods. These are *working stress design* and *strength design*. A third method, *limit states design*, that combines significant features of the preceding two methods, is now the standard in Canada for all construction materials. Briefly, these three methods can be described as follows.

a) *Working stress design*

In working stress design, safety is provided by ensuring that nowhere in the structure do the stresses produced by the maximum service or working loads exceed some specified safe value. The stresses are normally evaluated for the actual or service loading by an elastic analysis and compared with some specified percentage of a critical stress, such as yielding stress for steel, or compressive strength for concrete or masonry. The structure is therefore designed to prevent over-stressing under service loads.

b) *Strength design*

In strength design, safety is provided by ensuring that at no point in the structure is the resistance of that element exceeded by the effect of the service loads magnified by some factor, referred to as the load factor. The structure is therefore designed to prevent collapse under some specified overloading.

c) *Limit states design*

The intent of limit states design is to ensure that various limiting states are not exceeded during the reasonable life of the structure. Because these limiting states include stability and strength at specified overload and performance or serviceability (stress levels, cracking, deflections and vibrations) under service loading, limit states design, in essence, encompasses the other two methods, although the bulk of the design is more akin to strength design.

There are numerous building codes and standards throughout the world for the design and construction of masonry. In Canada, the principal building code, to which provincial and municipal codes make reference, is the National Building Code of Canada 1995 (NBC). This code is serviced by and makes reference to a series of Canadian Standards Association (CSA) standards. While masonry materials and construction are governed by a number of these standards, the most recent CSA structural design standard for masonry is S304.1-M94 *Masonry Design for Buildings (Limit States Design)*(referred to for the remainder of the text as S304.1). The previous edition of the standard S304-M84 *Masonry Design for Buildings*, the working stress design version, while destined for obsolescence, will remain valid until the year 2000.

It is important to note here that the structural designer should not use S304.1 and the earlier S304 in combination. S304.1 magnifies the maximum expected service loads by a load factor, whereas S304 does not. To mismatch loads and design methods might very well ensure collapse. The designer should also note that part 16 *Empirical Design for Unreinforced Masonry* of S304.1 uses working stress design principles and should not, for the same reasons, be used in conjunction with the remainder of the standard. Part 16 is a relic of the past, dealing with "rules of thumb" and, while it contains some useful practical rules, it should be avoided by the inexperienced structural designer.

1-6 RESISTANCE UNDER FACTORED LOAD

Structural design for safety consists of ensuring a high probability that the strength or resistance to failure under load (the *ultimate limit state*) of a structure and its components exceeds the maximum expected loading by a reasonable margin of safety. Although, in general, reasonable mathematical models are available for calculating this resistance, S304.1 requires that the calculated resistance be modified by a resistance factor ($\phi < 1.0$) to take into account uncertainties such as variations of dimensions and material properties. This modified resistance is referred to as the *factored resistance*, ϕR. The reasonable margin of safety, on the other hand, is assured through the application of *load factors*, α, to the maximum expected service loads, W. This leads to a *factored load*, αU and, for loads in combination, Equation (1-5) is modified by load factors to yield a factored load

$$\alpha U = \alpha_D D + \Psi(\alpha_L L + \alpha_W W + \alpha_T T) \tag{1-7}$$

where

α_D = 1.25 except

= 0.85 when dead load contributes to stability or strength

α_L = 1.5

α_W = 1.5 for wind, and

α_T = 1.25

As noted in Section 1-4 f), the load combination factor, Ψ, assumes values of 1.0, 0.70 or 0.60 when one, two or three respectively, of loads L, Q and T act in combination simultaneously.

Actually, Clause 7.1.2 of S304.1 gives the factored load as

$$\alpha U = \alpha_D D + \gamma\Psi(\alpha_L L + \alpha_W W + \alpha_T T) \tag{1-8}$$

where γ is an importance factor, generally taken as 1.0. γ may be taken as less than 1.0 "where it can be shown that collapse is not likely to cause injury or other serious consequences", in which case the minimum value is 0.80. Throughout the book γ will be assumed to have a value of 1.0.

When maximum earthquake effects are being evaluated for seismic design (which anticipates substantial damage but not collapse), the factored load is determined from the worst of

$$\alpha U = 1.0D + \gamma(1.0E)$$

and $\quad = 1.0D + \gamma(1.0L + 1.0E)$ for storage and assembly occupancies,

or $\quad = 1.0D + \gamma(0.5L + 1.0E)$ for all other occupancies $\tag{1-9}$

The factored resistance, ϕR, is calculated by applying separate resistance factors to the individual materials. Thus $\phi_m = 0.55$ is used for masonry materials, and $\phi_s = 0.85$ for reinforcing steel.

In summary, the factored resistance should be at least equal to the effect of the factored worst expected loading combination. That is,

$$\phi R \geq \alpha W \tag{1-10}$$

1-7   DESIGN AND ANALYSIS

Structural design and analysis, although based on the same principles of mechanics and material behaviour, differ considerably in execution. Design in the broadest sense starts from no more than the client's basic requirements and culminates in a set of detailed drawings from which a *safe, functional* and *economical* building can be constructed. Analysis on the other hand is used to check whether the building, as designed, meets those criteria; and should the criteria not be satisfied, another cycle of design is undertaken. Analysis is therefore part of an iterative design process.

The total design procedure includes planning to satisfy functional requirements, structural layout and selection of construction materials, determination of structural member sizes and their details, analysis to ensure that the structure is safe and economical, and the preparation of construction drawings. Inspection of construction might also be considered part of the design, for it is only through inspection that it can be determined whether the construction conforms to the details of the structural design - more specifically to the requirements for safety.

The planning phase, the structural layout and the selection of the type of construction materials (masonry, structural steel, reinforced concrete, wood, etc.) require a background of experience from the designer, and is certainly beyond the scope of this book. The ability to determine member sizes and their details, on the other hand, follows directly from an understanding of the principles of analysis outlined in subsequent chapters. In the treatment of design it will be assumed that such key data as wall heights, beam spans, and loadings are generally known; and that the design must produce such information as wall thicknesses, beam depths, reinforcement etc.

Codes and standards clearly cannot cover all situations in design, and, although S304.1 is a vast improvement over previous versions of S304, the designer will still encounter situations not covered by the standard which tax the imagination. In such instances a sound understanding of fundamental principles can prove invaluable in interpreting the intent of the code.

Without a handbook structural design can become a tedious process wherein the designer selects a trial section through approximate methods and then performs an analysis to check its efficiency, performing another cycle, if required, to improve the design. This book reduces the drudgery of trial-and-error by providing design charts and tables in Part 2 from which a direct design selection can be made.

CHAPTER 2

MASONRY MATERIALS

2-1   COMPONENT MATERIALS

Masonry is a multi-component structural material. In the case of plain masonry there are the masonry units themselves and the mortar; and for reinforced masonry there are in addition the reinforcing steel and the grout fill.

In order to understand better the structural behaviour of masonry, it is important for the designer to have some knowledge of the component materials. While a complete treatment of all the properties is beyond the scope of this book and not essential to performing the mechanics of structural design, the designer should have an appreciation of the significance of these properties to structural performance, serviceability and durability. For example, although the absorbtivity of the masonry unit is not considered in structural design calculations, it has an essential bearing on the bonding of mortar and grout fill to the unit and is, consequently, an important factor in construction; and a qualitative appreciation of the relationship between strength, absorbtivity and moisture content is helpful in understanding resistance to freeze-thaw deterioration. This chapter, then, deals not only with those properties that are used in structural design calculations, but also introduces other properties for a broader appreciation of the performance of masonry. For a thorough study of these properties and for other aspects of masonry, such as architectural considerations, thermal and acoustic properties, and construction methods, the reader is referred to the bibliography at the end of the book.

CSA Standard S304.1 Clause 3.5 *Reference Publications* provides a listing of the CSA Standards to which masonry construction and masonry materials must conform.

2-2   MASONRY UNITS

Masonry units are used in buildings not only as an attractive protection from the elements but also as effective structural load-bearing components. The exterior of the building may be constructed from load-bearing masonry, or the building may be clad with a non load-bearing masonry veneer. The units from which the masonry is constructed may be concrete or fired clay (or shale) bricks or blocks, or cut stone; and while concrete or clay units can be used in either load-bearing or non load-bearing applications, the use of stone is normally confined to non load-bearing veneer.

While the most obvious properties of masonry significant to the structural designer are its strength and its deformational behaviour under load (that is, its stress-strain relationship), there are other properties with which the designer should have some familiarity. These include creep under sustained load, expansion and contraction resulting from temperature change or from changes in moisture content, the extent to which a unit can absorb moisture and the initial rate of absorption, its density, durability, thermal conductivity, fire resistance, acoustic characteristics and appearance.

Similar to the situation in reinforced concrete, *compressive strength* is the most important structural property of masonry since it is the property most intimately related to resistance under load, and to serviceability and durability. Compressive strength, stress-strain behaviour and *modulus of elasticity* are obtained by direct compression testing through to failure. The compressive strength of units mortared together, f'_m, generally differs from the strength of individual units because of the presence of the mortar, and of the grout if the assemblage is grouted. The tensile strength of the unit is generally about 10% of the compressive strength but, if required, can also be tested, whereas tensile strength normal to the mortar joint depends on the bond between the mortar and the unit. *Creep* deformation under sustained load is of importance since it is responsible for the redistribution of internal forces within a structural element and for increased deflections, phenomena that are discussed in more detail in Chapters 3 and 4. With time, the creep deformation may be as great or greater than the initial deformation when service load is applied. *Thermal expansion and contraction*, if restrained, lead to internal forces that can cause material failure, most notably tensile cracking; and the same is true for swelling and *shrinkage* due to changes in moisture content.

For adequate bonding of mortar and grout to the masonry unit, the unit requires a capability to *absorb moisture*. On the other hand, if moisture is absorbed too rapidly from the mortar, insufficient moisture remains for proper curing and strength development, the rate at which moisture is absorbed being referred to as the *initial rate of absorbtion* (IRA). Also, the use of a unit that absorbs too much moisture (assessed by measuring *absorbtion* through immersion, drying and weighing) can lead to moisture migration through a wall and to potential deterioration from the expansive forces resulting from cycles of freezing and thawing. *Density* is important in that the weight of the unit and the productivity of the mason laying the unit are affected. The *durability* of masonry depends on its resistance to deterioration, primarily that due to cycles of freezing and thawing, a factor that is generally controlled through the selection of units of adequate strength, and proper design, detailing and construction. A knowledge of *thermal conductivity* is important to design for energy efficiency; and *acoustic characteristics* relate to sound transmission through walls. Regarding appearance, masonry units are available in a wide variety of shapes, colours and surface textures providing architects with considerable scope in designing for aesthetics, and designers can obtain further information about the range of products available from local producers.

A factor that can have a negative effect on appearance is *efflorescence*, that is, a white staining of the masonry by soluble salts being leached out of the masonry materials by moisture migration and subsequent evaporation of the moisture leaving the salt deposit. Efflorescence may also be a sign that salts are accumulating beneath the surface of the masonry which, in turn, may lead to expansive forces that may cause deterioration of low-quality materials. Since the essential contributing factors are soluble salts in the materials, moisture migration and evaporation, efflorescence can generally be avoided through the use of good quality materials conforming to the appropriate CSA standards, by proper detailing to avoid moisture migration, and by following good construction practice to ensure proper hydration of mortar and grout and to prevent the ingression of moisture through improperly tooled joints. Efflorescence can be removed through dry brushing or light sandblasting followed by rinsing with clean water or, for more persistent cases, by washing with a dilute solution of muriatic acid. However, the reader is cautioned that this paragraph presents no more than a brief discussion of efflorescence and that more detailed advice should be sought in determining the cause, potential effect, and the appropriate means of and caution to be exercised in removal.

Clay Units
Clay units, whether standard brick or "giant" brick, sometimes referred to as "jumbo" brick or hollow clay brick (similar to hollow concrete block), are initially formed from a stiff mix of clay and water. The material is then either extruded through a die and cut to length, or is pressed into steel moulds. Allowance is made during the forming process for shrinkage during drying and firing. Following forming, the bricks must first be dried and then fired in a kiln at a temperature that depends on the material, generally between 900°C and 1300°C. These processes are carefully controlled to attain strength, reduce defects and control colour.

Bricks are available in a variety of shapes, sizes, textures and colours for their various uses. The common brick, shown in Fig. 2-1, is used mostly as veneer, while the giant brick emulates the half standard height hollow concrete block shown in Fig. 2-2 and is frequently used in load-bearing construction. As can be seen from the figures the actual dimensions are 10 mm less than the nominal modular dimensions, allowing for 10 mm thick mortar joints.

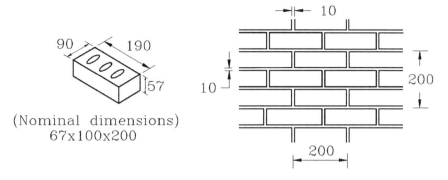

Fig.2-1 Common Brick Construction

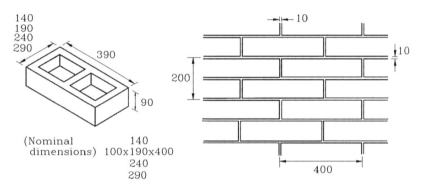

Fig. 2-2 Giant Brick Construction

The compressive strength of brick is obtained by capping the top and bottom surface of the unit to obtain a plane surface and subjecting it to increasing compressive load in a testing machine until failure takes place. The failure load (Newtons) is then divided by the cross-sectional area (mm²) of the unit to yield the compressive strength (MPa). For hollow units, the actual rather than the gross cross-sectional area is used. Because of the different configuration of standard brick and hollow giant brick, namely the aspect ratio, and due to the lateral confining effect of the loading plates, standard bricks normally fail at a higher stress than giant bricks of comparable material. The compressive strength of bricks available in Canada ranges from about 15 MPa to 70 MPa, a specified minimum value of 20 MPa being typical. The modulus of elasticity of clay masonry is much the same as that of concrete masonry of comparable strength, but clay masonry exhibits less creep under sustained load. The amount of creep strain may eventually equal the initial elastic strain.

After the firing stage of production, bricks begin to absorb moisture from the air and hydrates of the compounds developed in the kiln begin to form. This leads to a gradual and irreversible expansion that may reach about 0.2 mm/m in one year, and eventually about 0.5 mm/m. For example, a wall 10 m high may eventually gain about 5 mm in height. The *coefficient of thermal expansion* (α_t) of clay masonry is in the order of $6.0(10)^{-6}$ mm/mm/$^\circ$C, and the 10 m high wall noted earlier, if subjected to a seasonal temperature change of say 80°C, will have a seasonal height fluctuation of about 5 mm.

Absorption can be quantified by two properties: *initial rate of absorbtion* (IRA) and *percentage absorbtion*. IRA values that fall within the range of 0.25 kg/mm/m^2 and 1.5 kg/mm/m^2 are generally considered acceptable for construction; and units that absorb less moisture than 20% of their own weight after five hours of immersion in boiling water are considered to have adequate resistance to moisture migration.

More information on the specified requirements for physical properties of burned clay brick is outlined in CSA standards A82.1 and A82.8 for solid and hollow units respectively.

Concrete Units

Concrete masonry units are produced from a very dry, no-slump concrete mixed from sand, fine gravel, portland cement and water in predetermined proportions. Lightweight aggregate may be used in place of the gravel to reduce the weight of the unit. Admixtures to improve durability or to alter the colour may also be used in the mix, and fly ash is sometimes used as a partial replacement for cement. The concrete mix is then forced into moulds, using pressure and vibration, after which the mould is removed and the unit steam cured at temperatures of 50°C to 80°C for about sixteen hours. In some instances *autoclaving* (high-pressure steam curing) over a shorter period of time is used. The units are then stored to reduce the moisture content and consequently to reduce subsequent shrinkage. The configuration and dimensions of a standard 200 mm block are shown in Fig. 2-3 and the relevant geometric properties of the various widths of standard units are given in Table 2-1. It can be seen that the modular widths available are 100, 150, 200, 250 and 300, and actual dimensions are 10 mm less. The most commonly used load-bearing elements are 200 and 250, and in certain instances 100, 150 and 300 may be used. Fig. 2-4 shows a sampling of the wide variety of masonry unit shapes available, more complete information being available from local block producers.

The strength of concrete masonry units depends primarily on the mix proportions, but also on the degree of compaction and the curing process. The compressive strength is obtained in the same manner as described above for clay units. Typically, compressive strengths can range from 15 MPa to 35 MPa. Two values of compressive strength are important: the 24-hour strength should be sufficient to allow removal from steam curing and subsequent stockpiling without spoilage, and the 28-day strength to meet job specifications. There is, of course, a further strength gain beyond 28 days, especially for units containing fly-ash. The tensile strength is approximately 10% of the compressive strength. The modulus of elasticity of concrete units can be

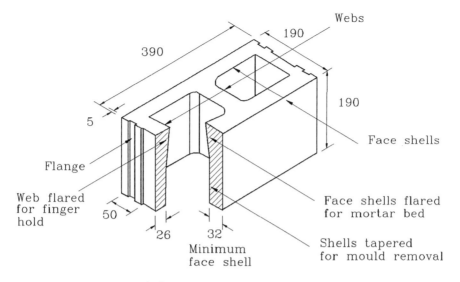

Fig. 2-3 Standard 200 x 200 x 400 mm Concrete Masonry Unit

TABLE 2-1
Properties of Standard Concrete Masonry Units

Modular size (mm)*	100	150	200	250	300
Actual overall width (mm)*	90	140	190	240	290
Minimum web thickness (mm)*	26	26	26	26	26
End flange width (mm)*	N/A	N/A	50	50	50
Equivalent thickness (mm)	66	80	103	121	141
Percentage solid	74	57	54	51	50
Approximate mass of wall in place					
Normal weight kg/m² **	140	170	215	255	300
Lightweight kg/m² **	110	130	165	195	230

* Refer to Fig. 2-3
** Based on material densities of: normal weight = 2100 kg/m³
                              lightweight = 1600 kg/m³

obtained by test, but may more generally be taken as the product of 850 and the compressive strength. Creep strain under sustained load may eventually reach twice the initial elastic strain.

While burned clay products experience some expansion over time, concrete masonry units undergo some drying shrinkage after steam curing. To some extent drying shrinkage is reversible on re-wetting and shrinkage will resume with further drying. Although a total linear shrinkage strain of about 0.0004 can be expected (autoclaved units shrink less and units with lightweight aggregate more), the age of the unit and its moisture content at the time of construction will determine how much shrinkage remains. Generally, to minimize adverse effects due to shrinkage, the moisture content of the units being laid should not exceed about 40% of maximum water absorbtion. More detailed recommendations are outlined in the CSA Standard A165 *Series on Concrete Masonry Units*. The coefficient of thermal expansion for concrete masonry units is about $8.0(10)^{-6}$ mm/mm/°C.

While absorption is as important for concrete masonry units as it is for clay masonry, there is no test for IRA. Absorbtion is measured as mass of water absorbed per unit volume by an oven-dried unit immersed in water at room temperature for 24 hours. CSA Standard A165 sets maximum limits on absorbtion varying from 175 kg/m^3 for normal weight units (density $\geq$ 2000 kg/m^3) to 300 kg/m^3 for lightweight units (density $<$ 1700 kg/m^3).

CSA Standard A82 and A165 refer to a series of standards that govern the quality of production of burned clay and concrete masonry units respectively. While the structural designer does not require a thorough knowledge of these standards, an appreciation of the principles on which the standards are based is essential. Also, because of the wide variety of units, colours and textures, the designer should obtain information from local producers to ensure that both architectural and structural requirements are met.

2-3   MORTAR AND GROUT

Mortar
The purpose of *mortar* is to provide a uniform bed for laying the masonry units, and to bond the units together to produce a weatherproof composite material capable of safely resisting the applied loading.

Mortar is produced by mixing together portland cement, hydrated lime and sand in specified portions with water. *Masonry cements* containing premixed portland cement and other components in appropriate proportions may be used in place of the individual cementious components. The purpose of the portland cement is to provide strength. The lime, which does not contribute significantly to strength, is used to give the fresh mortar the degree of plasticity or workability desired by the mason for ease in laying masonry. The sand is, of course, an inert and inexpensive filler. The amount of water to be used

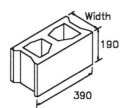

Width
190
390

Regular stretcher

One end plain
(Single corner)

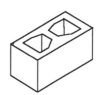

Both ends plain
(Pier)

Standard two—core width 200 x 400 units

Three—core unit

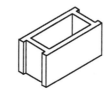

"O" Block

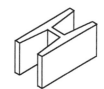

"H" Block

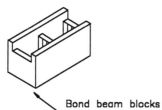

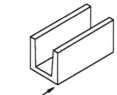

Bond beam blocks

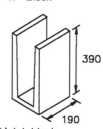

390

190

Lintel block

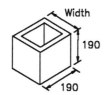

Width
190
190

Half block

Ribbed split face unit

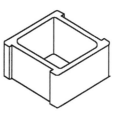

Pilaster block

Fig. 2-4 Typical Concrete Masonry Unit

in the mix will be determined by the absorption of the masonry unit and the weather conditions. Traditionally, there have been five types of mortar used in masonry construction, namely, types M, S, N, O and K (taken from the words **MaSoN wOrK**), each with its own particular use. These types, in the order listed, contain increasing lime and decreasing portland cement. Thus, type M is the strongest and least workable and type K is the weakest and most workable. Since type M, although the strongest, tends to be brittle and susceptible to shrinkage cracking, and types O and K are relatively weak and highly susceptible to weathering, types S and N are those permitted by S304.1 for structural applications. Of these two types of mortar, type S is more resistant to weathering and should be used for exterior masonry, and is commonly used for all engineered masonry. Specifications for the production of types S and N mortar are given in CSA Standard A179 *Mortar and Grout for Unit Masonry*.

As mortar is frequently mixed on the job site, it is more liable to variations in quality than other materials. The mortar should be sampled frequently and formed into 50 mm steel cube moulds for curing and compression strength testing at 7 and 28 days. Typically, type S mortar will have a 28-day cube strength in excess of 10 MPa. It should be noted that this test may not represent the strength of the mortar in the wall, which is placed in a 10 mm thickness on an absorptive surface. Absorption of moisture from the mortar reduces its water/cement ratio and potentially increases its strength. The purpose of the cube tests is to check the consistency of quality of mortar being used on the job.

Grout

The purpose of grout in masonry construction is to fill the cores, thereby increasing the effective cross-sectional area of the masonry for load resistance, and providing a bonding medium for reinforcing bars. This is illustrated in Fig. 1-2 and Fig. 1-3. Although brick is primarily applied as veneer, it may also be used in reinforced masonry. One possible arrangement for brick construction would be as shown in Fig 2-5, where reinforcement and grout are placed between two wythes of brick. A *wythe* is defined as a continuous vertical section of a masonry wall, one unit in thickness.

Grout is essentially a high-slump concrete with a maximum aggregate size of about 10 mm, though the maximum aggregate size will depend on the size of the void to be filled and on the amount of reinforcement impeding the grout flow. A high slump of about 200 mm to 250 mm is used to ensure a very workable mix capable of flowing into the voids and to ensure bonding of the grout to the masonry units through the absorption of excess water in the mix. As a result of this absorption, the water/cement ratio of the grout is reduced below that of the original mix, thereby increasing its strength. While S304.1 requires that grout have a 28-day compressive strength of not less than 10 MPa when cast in non-absorbent cylinder moulds, the *in-situ* strength of the grout is likely to be significantly greater. Generally, the *in-situ* grout strength should be no less than the specified 28-day strength of the hollow masonry unit, and a realistic estimate of the *in-situ* grout strength can be obtained from a prism test. In this test, compressive strength specimens are prepared as shown in Fig. 2-6 to simulate the absorption of moisture in the actual masonry, the paper towel liner being used to prevent bonding of the grout to the masonry units. The importance in construction of having a highly workable grout mix for a through filling of voids is reiterated. Vibration during placement of grout is also recommended.

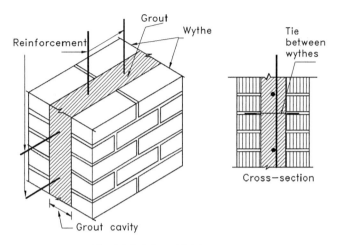

Fig. 2-5 Reinforced Brick Masonry

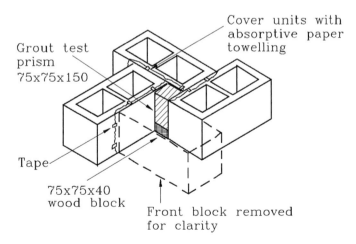

Fig. 2-6 Preparation of Grout Test Specimen

The specification governing mortar and grout is CSA-A179 which, in recognition of the fact these materials may be job-site mixes, gives proportioning for volume batching.

2-4   MASONRY STRENGTH

The previous two sections dealt briefly with the strength of the masonry units, mortar and grout. Although the actual strength of assembled masonry is obviously related to the strength of the component materials, the relationship is not a simple one. The main purpose of the strength testing of the component materials is to ensure that the specified quality is being maintained. This section discusses the strength of the assembled masonry.

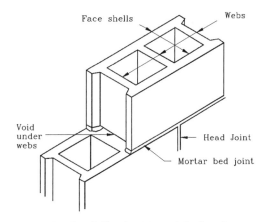

Fig. 2-7 Detail Showing Mortar Joint Location

When masonry is being constructed, the units are laid on beds of mortar in successive horizontal layers, referred to as *courses*. The mason normally places the mortar for both the bed and head joints, that is, the horizontal and vertical joints respectively, over the face shells only, and not on the cross webs. As a result, a void is created under the webs (see Fig. 2-7) and, for plain masonry, loading is transferred only through the face shells. In grouted masonry, CSA-A371 requires that webs adjacent to grouted cores be fully mortared. Under compressive loading, any discontinuity of material leads to stress concentrations and the full potential of the unit is rarely realized. The mortar, on the other hand, tends to exhibit an enhanced strength. This is due to the fact that mortar, normally being weaker than the material in the unit, has a lower modulus of elasticity and a higher Poisson's ratio. As a result, mortar tends to strain laterally more than the material in the unit, but being placed in a thin 10 mm layer, it is laterally restrained by the unit. The mortar is then in triaxial compression and has a higher apparent compressive strength. The lateral compression in the mortar is balanced by lateral tension in the masonry unit, which further reduces the ability of the unit to resist compression. As a consequence of these two factors, that is, discontinuities and lateral tension, masonry assemblages have a compressive strength lower than that of the individual units.

As in reinforced concrete, the criteria used in the structural design of masonry are, for the most part, related to the compressive strength. Clause 9.2 of S304.1 outlines two methods that may be used in the determination of the compressive strength of masonry, f'_m, to use in structural design.

The first method (Clause 9.2.2 *Prism Test*) permits the determination of f'_m from tests on masonry assemblages, such as the prism test specimens shown in Fig. 2-8. The test procedure is outlined in CSA standard A 369.1. The compressive strength of each specimen is calculated by dividing the failure load by the *effective area*, an area that includes the area of voids filled with grout (see Section 2-8). At least five specimens must be tested and the value of f'_m is taken as 1.5 times the standard deviation less than the mean.

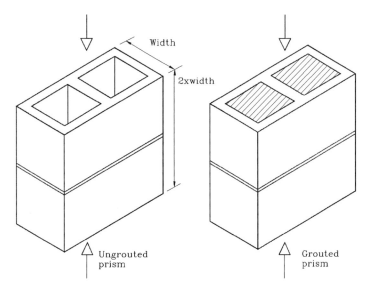

Width

2xwidth

Ungrouted
prism

Grouted
prism

Fig. 2-8 Compression Test Prisms

The second method (Clause 9.2.3 *Unit and Mortar Tests*) permits the determination of f'_m from a knowledge of the strength of the unit and the type of mortar. Tables 3, 4 and 5 in S304.1 list values of f'_m for brick masonry and for concrete block masonry, (hollow, solid or grouted units). For example, for concrete block units with a compressive strength of 20 MPa and type S mortar, Table 5 gives values of $f'_m = 13$ MPa and $f'_m = 10$ MPa respectively for use in the structural design of hollow and grouted masonry. Note that Section 4 *Field Control Tests* of S304.1 requires that control specimens be taken during construction and subsequently tested to ensure conformity with specified strengths. Note that f'_m for hollow clay brick must be determined using prism tests.

Although S304.1 requires that the 28-day compressive strength of grout cast in non-absorbent moulds be not less than 10 MPa, the in-situ strength is likely to be significantly greater if the grout is properly placed, and is likely to be at least as great as the specified strength of the unit. Since the grouting of the cores increases the cross-sectional area substantially, it follows that the load-carrying capacity of masonry should be increased substantially by grouting.

There has been a considerable amount of research work done on the strength of ungrouted and grouted masonry. Generally it has been found that, although grouting results in increased load-carrying capacity, the value of f'_m obtained for grouted masonry is less than that obtained for ungrouted masonry. This is reflected in Tables 4 and 5 of S304.1 and is attributable partly to the voids that inevitably exist in grouted masonry, and to the debonding of grout from blocks that may result from grout shrinkage, but more significantly to differential shrinkage and creep between the masonry materials and to differences in the stress-strain behaviour of unit, grout and mortar. It is interesting to note that, whereas concrete shrinks, clay brick expands with time, and the effect of differential shrinkage on strength is greater. Some typical stress-strain curves are shown schematically in Fig. 2-9.

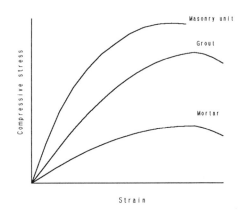

Fig. 2-9 Typical Stress Strain Curves for Masonry Unit, Grout and Mortar

The strength of masonry depends not only on the quality of the component materials, but also on the quality of construction. Consequently, proper inspection during construction is essential, especially during grouting, to ensure that the quality of masonry conforms to the intent of the structural design. CSA Standard A371 *Masonry Construction for Buildings* outlines the requirements for construction.

2-5   MASONRY DEFORMATIONS

A knowledge of deformations that can take place in masonry is essential to an understanding of its structural behaviour. Furthermore, as masonry frequently supports, or is supported by, or is tied to other structural materials, an estimate of the relative deformations that may occur is essential to an evaluation of building performance. The deformations of significance to a structural designer are those due to loading, namely elastic strain and creep, and those due to such environmental factors as humidity and temperature change.

The deformation of masonry under load is related to the stress-strain properties of the component materials but, as was the case with strength, the relationship is not a simple one. The most important property in assessing elastic deformations is the modulus of elasticity, E_m, which, as noted in Clause 8.3.1 of S304.1, may be obtained from load testing or may be taken as $850 f'_m$ with the provision that a value E_m greater than 20 000 MPa should not be used. Testing has indicated that, in general, $E_m = 850 f'_m$ is a reasonable value for masonry. However, because of the variability of the materials available, an accurate estimate of deformations in a structure requires that masonry specimens be constructed from representative materials and tested. This degree of accuracy is normally required only in research.

Whereas elastic strain is that which takes place instantaneously upon load application, creep is the increase in that strain which occurs over a period of time. The amount of creep depends on the composition of the component materials in masonry, on environmental conditions, and on the magnitude and duration of loading. It would appear that under long-term continuous loading, creep in concrete masonry will be in the order of twice the elastic strain. Creep in brick masonry is likely to be less than that in concrete masonry, with the bulk of the creep occurring in the mortar joint.

Concrete block units, mortar and grout, having water as an essential ingredient in the mix and being moist cured, undergo a period of drying after construction. This loss of moisture results in shrinkage, the amount of which depends upon the composition of the component materials and upon environmental humidity. Shrinkage can be reduced by dry storage of the blocks prior to construction.

Concrete block masonry can be expected to undergo, after construction, a linear shrinkage of the order of 0.02% to 0.03%. This value will be greater for lightweight concrete blocks made with expanded shale aggregates, and less for concrete blocks that have been *autoclaved* or steam cured at high pressure. Subsequent wetting and drying results in lesser amounts of expansion and contraction. Bricks, on the other hand, having been fired in a kiln, experience expansion over an extended period of time. This is due to hydration of amorphous materials that are formed during burning of the bricks, on environmental humidity and on time. While there is some shrinkage taking place in the mortar at the same time, there is generally a resultant expansion. A typical value of brick masonry linear expansion after two years would be 0.015% to 0.025%. The shrinkage of concrete block masonry and the expansion of brick masonry should be borne in mind, especially when the two materials are used in close proximity. Stone masonry is relatively unaffected by changes in humidity.

As for other structural materials, masonry expands when heated and contracts when cooled. This will lead to differential deformations between interior walls in a building, which are at a relatively constant temperature, and exterior walls exposed to the weather. The coefficients of linear thermal expansion are of the order of $8(10)^{-6}$ mm/mm/°C for normal concrete masonry and stone masonry, and about $6(10)^{-6}$ mm/mm/°C for clay masonry. These values are, of course, approximate and will vary with materials available locally.

2-6   REINFORCEMENT

There are two types of steel reinforcement used in masonry construction: standard reinforcing bars, as used in reinforced concrete, and joint reinforcing.

Normal reinforcing bars were developed for use in reinforced concrete and have surface deformations to enhance the bond between concrete and steel. They have a similar use in reinforced masonry, being embedded in the grout fill. The commonly used sizes in masonry construction are #10, #15, and #20 with cross-sectional areas of 100, 200, and 300 mm² respectively. These are used for grouted masonry walls and beams, and are commonly available in steel with yield strengths of $f_y=300$ MPa and $f_y=400$ MPa. The use of this type of reinforcement is illustrated in Fig. 1-2, 1-3, 1-4 and 2-5. Table 2-2 lists the relevant properties of normal deformed reinforcing steel.

Table 2-2
Properties of Standard Deformed Reinforcing Bars

Bar No.*	Nominal Dimensions**			
	Sectional Area (mm²)	Diameter (mm)	Perimeter (mm)	Unit Mass (kg/m)
10	100	11.3	35.5	0.785
15	200	16.0	50.1	1.570
20	300	19.5	61.3	2.355
25	500	25.2	79.2	3.925
30	700	29.9	93.9	5.495
35	1000	35.7	112.2	7.850
45	1500	43.7	137.3	11.775
55	2500	56.4	177.2	19.625

* Bar numbers are based on the number of millimetres included in the nominal diameter of the bar.
** Nominal dimensions of a deformed bar are equivalent to those of a plain round bar having the same mass per meter as the deformed bar.

Joint reinforcement consists of steel wires about 4 mm in diameter [No. 8 A.S.W.G. (4.1 mm) or No. 9 A.S.W.G. (3.7 mm)], interconnected by welded cross wires, that are placed in the mortar joints between courses. They are proprietary products that are available in a variety of configurations, some of which are shown in

Fig. 2-10, and are normally galvanized. Joint reinforcement may be included in structural design (see Clause 5.2.4 of S304.1), where it can be used to resist bending due to lateral wind loads on walls. However, the main purpose of this reinforcement is to provide a continuous tie along the wall, as shown in Fig. 2-11, to control shrinkage cracking, or to provide a tie between two wythes, as shown in Fig. 2-11(b). Joint reinforcement may be placed at one, two or three-course spacings, that is at 200, 400, 600 mm respectively, depending on a number of factors, prominent among which is the designer's judgement. Generally spacings greater than 400 mm are not recommended.

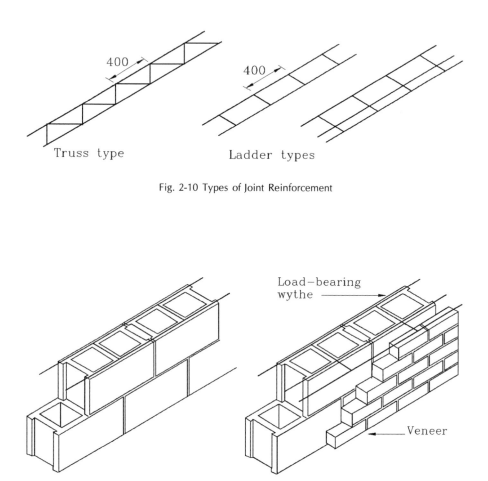

Truss type   Ladder types

Fig. 2-10 Types of Joint Reinforcement

Load–bearing wythe

Veneer

(a) Single wythe   (b) Two wythes

Fig. 2-11 Joint Reinforcement in Place

2-7   CONNECTORS

Whether the components of a building are of masonry, structural steel, reinforced concrete, or prestressed concrete or timber, each must be securely fastened to its adjacent components to ensure safety and serviceability. For example, structural steel components are generally connected with welding and bolting, timber with gluing, nailing, screwing and bolting, and architectural components (windows, doors, veneers, etc...) with a variety of fasteners. Also, each connection must safely transmit loading and, in some instances, allow for differential movement between adjacent components. In masonry construction, these connection devices are collectively known as *connectors*, the requirements for which are governed by CSA Standard A370 *Connectors for Masonry*, which provides the following definitions:

- *Connectors* -   a general term for ties, anchors and fasteners.

- *Tie* -   a device for connecting two or more wythes, or for connecting a masonry veneer to its structural backing.

- *Anchor* -   a device used to connect masonry walls at their intersections, or to attach them to their supports or to other structural members or systems.

- *Fastener* -   a device used for securing equipment, fixtures, or parts of connectors to buildings.

Connectors are normally fabricated from steel and, in common with all connections, those for masonry should have adequate protection against corrosion so that they function effectively for the intended life of the wall system. This is normally provided by a coating of zinc through hot-dip galvanizing, the thickness of the coating depending on the type of connector and the aggressiveness of the exposure environment. In severe exposures, stainless steel connectors are required.

While connectors must have an appropriate cross-sectional area and stiffness to safely transmit loads, there are some dimensional limitations on those that are placed in mortar joints. This is because the steel connector represents a rigid inclusion in a relatively soft material and, where the mortar joint is load-bearing, may lead to stress concentrations. A370 requires that round stock have a diameter no greater than two-thirds of the thickness of the mortar joint, and flat stock and longitudinal continuous wires (such as joint reinforcement) no greater than half the thickness of the mortar joint.

Ties

These are the connectors that attach a masonry veneer to its structural backing, essentially *tying* the veneer to the building. They are generally used in *cavity wall* construction where there is a space between the veneer and the structural backing. In energy-efficient buildings the space normally includes a 25 mm air space and a 50 mm - 100 mm layer of insulation, as shown in Fig. 2-12. Also, since the veneer as the final finish on the building, is constructed to more rigorous tolerances than the structural framework, the actual cavity may be significantly greater than that shown in drawings. Ties are required to transmit horizontal tensile or compressive forces (due to wind and earthquake) across the cavity and need to be well anchored at each end, and require sufficient strength and stiffness to transmit those forces safely across the cavity. Note that the insulation in the cavity is structurally ineffectual in providing resistance to buckling in compression of slender ties.

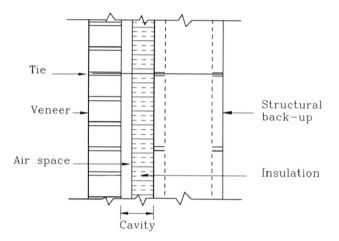

Fig.2-12 Cavity Wall Construction

Ties are normally expected to accommodate some differential vertical movement between the veneer and its structural backup. This is accomplished through the use of flexible ties, or adjustable ties, such as those shown in Fig. 2-13, which permit vertical movement while conveying horizontal forces. While the conventional corrugated tie shown has a good configuration for mechanical bonding in the mortar, it is not recommended for cavities greater than 25 mm; and since construction tolerance specifications frequently lead to substantially greater cavities, this tie is generally not suitable. The conventional Z and rectangular wire ties, provided the mortar joints in veneer and masonry backup line up, transmit compressive forces more effectively. If the mortar joints do not line up, ties are frequently bent on-site to accommodate the difference in elevation and, consequently, carry greater load and lose much of their effectiveness.

On the other hand, adjustable ties can be properly placed in the mortar joints and convey the horizontal forces across the cavity, However, care should be exercised in the selection of adjustable ties such as that shown in Fig. 2-13(d) since one leg is a relatively flexible cantilever. Slotted ties, such as those shown in Fig. 2-13(e) are preferable since they do not have this potential deficiency.

Recent developments include a tie that has sufficient flexibility to accommodate some differential movement while providing a significant degree of vertical shear force transfer between the veneer and the backup wythe. This leads to a partial composite action between the two wythes which, in turn, results in a stronger and stiffer wall. Where a large differential movement between wythes is expected, a slotted version of this connector is available. This connector, shown in Fig. 2-14, holds the insulation firmly in place, and the varying air space thickness resulting from construction tolerances is accommodated through varying lengths of V-ties.

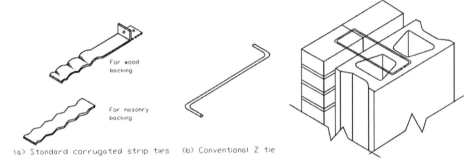

(a) Standard corrugated strip ties   (b) Conventional Z tie

(c) Conventional rectangular tie

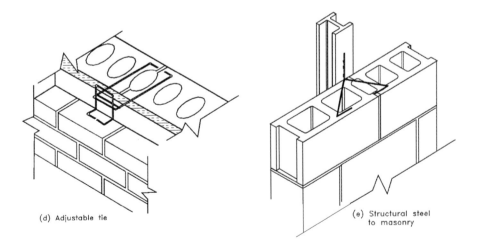

(d) Adjustable tie

(e) Structural steel to masonry

Fig. 2-13 Examples of Adjustable Ties

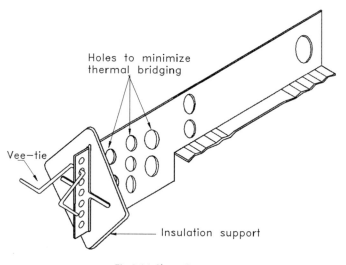

Holes to minimize
thermal bridging

Vee-tie

Insulation support

Fig.2-14 Shear Connector

Anchors

Anchors used to attach masonry walls at their intersection are frequently required to allow differential vertical movement, especially where a temperature differential is expected. Typical details are shown in Fig 2-15. A few other types of anchor are shown in Fig. 2-16.

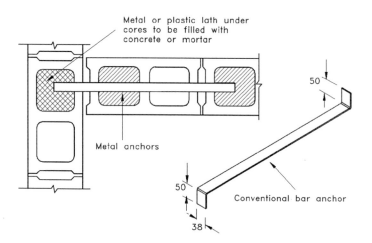

Metal or plastic lath under
cores to be filled with
concrete or mortar

50

Metal anchors

50

38

Conventional bar anchor

Fig. 2-15 Typical Details of Walls Attachment

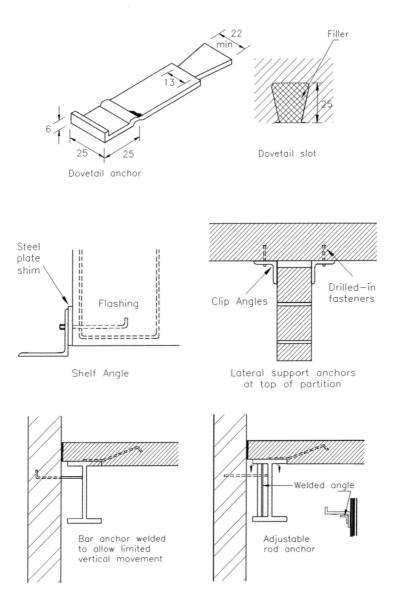

Fig. 2-16 Types of Anchor

Fasteners

The term fastener covers a wide range of nails, screws and bolts, depending on the equipment, fixture or component being secured, and on the structural material to which it is being secured. For example, nails may be used to fasten veneer ties to wood stud walls, screws where steel studs are used as the structural backup, or drilled-in expansion bolts when fastening to concrete. In all instances, of course, the fastener should safely carry whatever forces to which it may be subjected.

Connectors, then should be designed and detailed for safety, serviceability and durability. They are required to have sufficient resistance to loading, to prevent movements that result in mortar cracking and, as required, to accommodate differential movement between wythes. Since this may appear a formidable task to the novice, connector design is incorporated into later chapters of this book.

2-8   EFFECTIVE AREA

Early issues of S304, in common with American and other standards, used the *net cross-sectional area* at the mid height of the unit as the reference area for strength and other calculations. In recognition of the fact that this net area is not the minimum cross-sectional area in the direction of the load, S304-M84 introduced the concept of *mortar bedded area*, an area that is now referred to as *effective area*, A_e, in S304.1.

Effective area is the minimum area of continuous contact between unit and mortar from one course to the next. In hollow block or hollow brick construction, only the face shells (see Fig. 2-3) are mortared and the effective area is less than the area of the unit. In any case, there is little point in placing mortar on the cross-webs since these rarely line up in successive courses. Fig. 2-17 shows the area common to the unit below and the unit above for ungrouted standard two-core concrete block units. This area is the *effective area*. The reader will note that the top surfaces of a unit are wider than the bottom surfaces. The reason for this is illustrated in Fig. 2-3.

Fig. 2-17 also shows the extent to which cores line up vertically, thereby permitting grouting for the purpose of increasing strength. When cores are grouted the effective area increases to include the cross-sectional area of grout. For a fully grouted wall the effective area is essentially the same as the gross cross-sectional area. However, Fig. 2-17 illustrates the fact that the cross-webs of units can impede the flow of grout to voids directly below, and the need for a high slump, as noted in Section 2-3, and vibration during grouting must be emphasized. Effective area and other section properties for standard concrete block walls are given in Table 4.1, and also in Part 2.

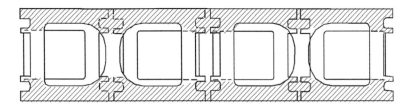

Fig.2-17 Effective Area

CHAPTER 3

ANALYSIS OF FLEXURAL MEMBERS

3-1   BASIC ASSUMPTIONS

As discussed in Section 1-5, structural masonry is designed by the *limit states method*, the intent of which is to ensure that various limiting states are not exceeded during the reasonable life of the structure. The limit states considered are strength, or resistance, under specific overload, and serviceability, or performance, under service loading. The limit state of stability, since it is related to overturning or collapse, is generally considered as resistance.

The stress-strain behaviour of masonry in a standard compression test is reasonably linear and elastic up to about 50% of f'_m, and that of reinforcing steel is known to be linearly elastic up to f_y (see Fig. 3-1). Since masonry is rarely strained beyond these values under service loading, much of the method of analysis for serviceability, particularly for bending, is based on the assumption of linear elasticity. However, as discussed in Section 2-5, masonry under sustained loading will continue to strain, or *creep*, leading in certain instances to a stress redistribution. This fact is acknowledged in S304.1 by applying a creep adjustment factor to the modulus of elasticity. On the other hand, when evaluating resistance, that is, strength under overload, the individual materials are strained to critical values causing stress redistribution, and linear elasticity can no longer be assumed.

As the structural designer is aware, the processes of design and analysis, although different, are closely related, and each designed structure must lend itself to analysis to ensure that nowhere in the structure have the design criteria been violated. In fact, the design method is developed from the method of analysis. Also, since both serviceability and strength limit states require evaluation, there are essentially two methods of analysis to consider.

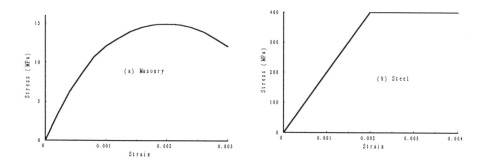

Fig. 3-1 Typical Stress-Strain Curves

Although the present chapter deals primarily with bending of walls and beams, a short treatment of axial load is given in Section 3-2 as an introduction to the theory of behaviour in masonry. Two types of bending are considered: out-of-plane bending due to loads acting perpendicular to the wall surface (such as wind loads), and in-plane bending due to loads acting in the plane of the member (such as loads on beams). The analysis in each case is similar, and only differs between unreinforced and reinforced members. The analysis for bending, or *flexure*, is based on a number of assumptions, as listed in Clause 10.2.3.1 of S304.1.

1.   A section that is plane before bending remains plane after bending.
2.   Masonry is assumed to fail when the compressive strain reaches a limiting value of 0.003.
3.   The stresses in masonry and reinforcement can be computed from the strains using stress-strain curves for masonry and steel.
4.   In reinforced masonry tensile forces are resisted only by the tensile reinforcement. This assumption acknowledges the fact that, for the tensile reinforcement to be effective, the masonry will have to suffer some minor cracking.
5.   The strain in the reinforcement is equal to the strain in the masonry at the same location. This assumption implies that reinforcement is completely surrounded by and bonded to masonry material, and full composite action between the two materials is assured.

6.   The compressive stress-strain relationship for masonry may be assumed to be parabolic, trapezoidal, or any other shape that results in a prediction of strength in substantial agreement with the results of compressive tests.

The effect of transverse loading on a structural member (see Fig. 3-2) is to produce internal bending moments, M, and shear forces, V. The magnitude of these effects at any cross-section x-x can be calculated by considering equilibrium of the forces acting on the *free body* taken to one side of that section, as shown in Fig. 3-2(b). If the material is linearly elastic and capable of withstanding both tension and compression, the distribution of bending stresses due to M is as shown in Fig. 3-2(c). The analysis for the determination of these stresses is given in Section 3-3. When the moment exceeds some critical value (governed in masonry by its ability to resist tension), reinforcing steel is placed in the beam to improve its flexural resistance, a case that is analyzed in Sections 3-4 and 3-6. The effects of shear and bond are considered in Sections 3-7 and 3-8 respectively, and serviceability is discussed in Section 3-9.

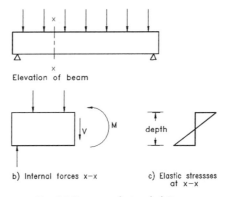

Elevation of beam

b) Internal forces x—x

c) Elastic stressses at x—x

Fig. 3-2 Transversely Loaded Beam

This chapter deals largely with analysis based on the assumptions given above. Although new symbols or notations are defined as they appear, there is a full listing under *Notation* at the beginning of the book.

3-2   AXIAL COMPRESSION

This section considers the behaviour of *short* axially-loaded compression members as a preliminary to the theory for bending. The more complex cases of eccentric loading and slenderness are considered in Chapter 5.

Unreinforced members

The *compressive stress, f_m*, in an unreinforced masonry wall subjected to axial loading is given by the equation

$$f_m = P/A_e \qquad (3\text{-}1)$$

where

P = axial load; A_e = area in compression, effective area, as shown in Fig. 3-3

The use of A_e in determining compressive stress is consistent with the determination of f'_m based on the same value of A_e, as discussed in Section 2-4. In the following worked examples, rather than using the tabulated value of A_e and other section properties from Table 4-1, calculations are based on a mean width of mortar bed.

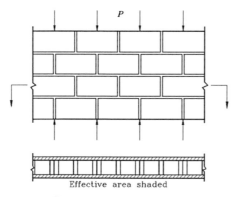

Fig. 3-3 Effective Area of Hollow Block Masonry

EXAMPLE 3-1 *A short 200 mm hollow concrete block wall is subjected to an axial load of 150 kN/m. If the mean mortar bed width per face shell is 37.7 mm, what is the compressive stress in the wall?*

Consider a unit length, that is, 1.0 m of wall. Then, since there are two face shells,

$$A_e = 2(37.7)(1000) = 75.4(10)^3 \text{ mm}^2/\text{m}$$

$$P = 150 \text{ kN/m} = 150(10)^3 \text{ N/m}$$

and

$$f_m = P/A_e = \frac{150(10)^3}{75.4(10)^3} = 1.99 \text{ MPa} \qquad \underline{\text{Ans.}}$$

EXAMPLE 3-2 *What would be the compressive stress if the wall in Example 3-1 had every fourth core grouted, that is, filled with concrete, as shown in Fig. 3-4?*

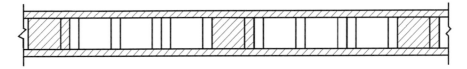

Fig. 3-4 Partially Grouted Wall

In Example 3-1 the area of voids would be the gross cross-sectional area, A_g, minus A_e, or

$$190(10)^3 - 75.4(10)^3 = 114.6(10)^3 \text{ mm}^2/\text{m}$$

Now, since 25% of the voids have been filled with grout,

$$A_e = 75.4(10)^3 + 0.25(114.6)(10)^3 = 104(10)^3 \text{ mm}^2/\text{m}$$

and

$$f_m = P/A_e = \frac{150(10)^3}{104(10)^3} = 1.44 \text{ MPa} \qquad \underline{\text{Ans.}}$$

Reinforced members

Although the assumption of linear elasticity is reasonably valid for service load flexure, creep of masonry under sustained loading renders the theory invalid for compression members. However, for the purpose of introducing the interaction of steel and masonry it will be assumed that the service loading is of short duration and that linear elasticity is valid. Note that it is normally assumed that the grout and block have a common modulus of elasticity E_m.

Consider the short axial-loaded masonry columns of length L shown in Fig. 3-5, reinforced with bars having cross-sectional area A_s and fully grouted. Under the loading P the column shortens by the amount δ and the resulting strain is

$$\epsilon = \delta/L$$

As the steel, grout, and block are all bonded together,

$$\epsilon(\text{masonry}) = \epsilon(\text{steel}) = \epsilon$$

and, recalling that the modulus of elasticity E = stress/strain, the compressive stress in the reinforcement, f_s, and in the masonry, f_m, are

$$f_s = E_s\epsilon \; ; \quad f_m = E_m\epsilon$$

which gives

$$f_s/f_m = E_s/E_m = n$$

where n is referred to as the *modular ratio*. Therefore,

$$f_s = nf_m$$

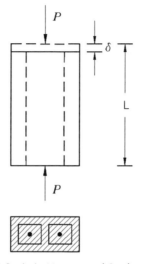

Fig. 3-5 Strain in Masonry and Steel are Equal

This indicates that at service loads the reinforcement is n times as effective as masonry in resisting stress due to the applied loading. The applied load P is now found as

$$P = \Sigma[(\text{stress})(\text{area})]$$
$$= f_m(A_g - A_s) + f_s A_s = f_m(A_g - A_s) + nf_m A_s$$

or,

$$P = f_m[A_g + (n\text{-}1)A_s]$$

The term $[A_g + (n\text{-}1)A_s]$ is referred to as the *transformed area* of the column since the steel area A_s has been transformed into an equivalent masonry area nA_s. Thus, if A_g, A_s, n and P are known, the stresses in the masonry and the steel can be found as

$$f_m = \frac{P}{A_g + (n\text{-}1)A_s} \tag{3-2}$$

$$f_s = nf_m \tag{3-3}$$

Example 3-3 *A short 200 mm hollow concrete block wall is reinforced with #15 bars at 200 mm centres and fully grouted. If E_m = 10 000 MPa and E_s = 200 000 MPa, what are the stresses produced in the materials by an applied service load of short duration of 300 kN/m?*

$$P = 300 \text{ kN/m} = 300(10)^3 \text{ N/m}$$

$$A_m = A_g = 190(1000) = (190)(10)^3 \text{ mm}^2/\text{m}$$

The cross-sectional area of one #15 bar is A_s = 200 mm². Therefore,

$$A_s/\text{m} = \frac{200(10)^3}{200} = 1000 \text{ mm}^2/\text{m}$$

The modular ratio is found as

$$n = E_s/E_m = \frac{200(10)^3}{10(10)^3} = 20$$

and the transformed area becomes

$$[A_g + (n\text{-}1)A_s] = [190(10)^3 + (20 - 1)(1000)] = 209(10)^3 \text{ mm}^2/\text{m}$$

The stress in the masonry is found as

$$f_m = P/(\text{transformed area}) = \frac{300(10)^3}{209(10)^3} = 1.435 \text{ MPa} \qquad \underline{\text{Ans.}}$$

and

$$f_s = nf_m = 20(1.435) = 28.7 \text{ MPa} \qquad \underline{\text{Ans.}}$$

If the load is applied for an extended period of time, as would be the case for the dead load, creep will take place in the blocks, mortar and grout. The masonry is then less stiff than is indicated by the modulus of elasticity E_m and a stress redistribution takes place, the reinforcement now carrying a greater share of the load. S304.1 Clause 8.2 specifies that E_m should be modified to allow for load duration, and the value to use in calculating stresses due to service load is

$$\frac{E_m}{(1+0.5\beta_d)} \qquad (3\text{-}4)$$

where β_d = dead load/total load.

If all of the service load in the preceding example were dead load, then β_d = 1.0 and the value of E_m is reduced to two-thirds its previous value. It is left as an exercise for the reader to show that the resulting stresses in masonry and steel are 1.37 MPa and 41.1 MPa respectively.

As the load is further increased, both materials are strained further and, since the steel and masonry materials are bonded together, the strain in each material has the same value, that is, $\epsilon_s = \epsilon_m$. Once the strain in the masonry reaches a value of 0.003, the steel has already yielded and the masonry materials fail in compression. Since the stress in the masonry has now reached f'_m and f_y in the steel, the probable failure load is

$$P_{\text{failure}} = A_e f'_m + A_s f_y \qquad (3\text{-}5)$$

However, because of the variability in the quality of materials, performance (or confidence) factors, $\phi < 1.0$, are applied to the strength of the materials and the resistance in compression is expressed as

$$P_r = \phi_m A_e f'_m + \phi_s A_s f_y \qquad (3\text{-}6)$$

In this expression, S304.1 dictates that $\phi_m = 0.55$ and $\phi_s = 0.85$. This compares with $\phi_c = 0.60$ and $\phi_s = 0.85$ currently being used for reinforced concrete.

When evaluating strength, limit states design assumes factored service loads and compares with factored resistance. This can be illustrated by reworking the previous example as follows.

EXAMPLE 3-4 *A short 200 mm hollow concrete block wall is reinforced with #15 bars at 200 mm centres and is fully grouted. If $f'_m = 10$ MPa, $f_y = 400$ MPa and the applied axial load is 50% dead load and 50% live load, what is the maximum safe live load?*

The factored section resistance is

$$
\begin{aligned}
P_r &= \phi_m A_e f'_m + \phi_s A_s f_y \\
&= 0.55(190)(10)^3(10) + 0.85(1000)(400) \\
&= 1385 \text{ kN/m}
\end{aligned}
$$

and the factored applied load is

$$P_f = \alpha_L P_L + \alpha_D P_D$$

where P_L and P_D are the live and dead loads, respectively.

Since $P_L = P_D$

$$
\begin{aligned}
P_f &= (\alpha_L + \alpha_D)P_L \\
&= (1.25 + 1.5)P_L \\
&= 2.75 P_L
\end{aligned}
$$

Safety requires $P_r \geq P_f$
or, $2.75P_L \leq 1385$ kN/m
Therefore, the maximum safe axial load = $1385/2.75 = 503.64$ kN/m. <u>Ans.</u>

3-3   FLEXURE OF UNREINFORCED MASONRY

When masonry walls are subjected to transverse loading, such as wind pressure, bending takes place and, in the absence of significant axial compression, tensile stresses are introduced into the wall. If the wall is not reinforced, the tensile stresses must be resisted by the component that is weakest in tension - namely the bond between mortar and unit. Consequently, the effective area governs flexural calculations.

Because masonry is many times stronger in compression than in tension, the compressive stress is relatively low and likely to be within the linear range of the stress/strain relationship. Consequently, the flexural stresses are calculated from the well known elastic expression

$$f = \pm Mc/I = \pm M/S \qquad (3\text{-}7)$$

where

M = bending moment;
I = moment of inertia of the net section;
c = distance of the extreme fibre of the section from the centroid of the net section
  = $1/2t$, where t = wall thickness;
S = elastic section modulus = I/c

If axial compression P is also present in the wall, the stresses become

$$f = P/A_e \pm M/S \qquad (3\text{-}8)$$

Bending can take place in one of two directions:

a)   the wall can span vertically, as in Fig. 3-6 where it is laterally supported at the top and bottom, and tensile stresses are perpendicular to the bed (that is, horizontal) joints, as is evident from the failure mode; or,

b)   the wall can span horizontally, as shown in Fig. 3-7 where it is laterally supported by vertical columns (or masonry pilasters), and tensile stresses are parallel to the bed joints. In this case the tensile effects result in a shearing action, as shown in the failure mode.

S304.1 recognizes that tensile resistance is greater in b) than in a). Table 6 of the standard gives the flexural tensile strength, both normal and parallel to the bed joints, for clay and concrete units with type S or N mortar.

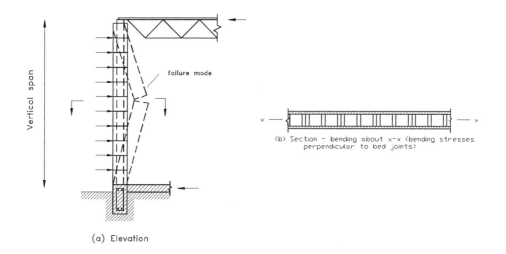

Vertical span

failure mode

(b) Section - bending about x-x (bending stresses perpendicular to bed joints)

(a) Elevation

Fig. 3-6 Wall With Vertical Span

Note that in the calculation of *M*, simple spans are normally assumed. This is because vertical control joints (discussed in later chapters), which do not transmit moments, are likely to be present.

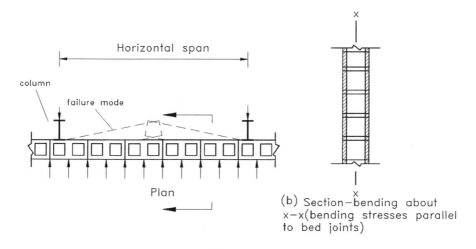

Horizontal span

column

failure mode

Plan

(b) Section—bending about x—x(bending stresses parallel to bed joints)

Fig. 3-7 Wall With Horizontal Span

EXAMPLE 3-5 *The unreinforced, ungrouted 200 concrete block wall shown in Fig. 3-8, spans horizontally between vertical columns spaced 4 m apart, and is subjected to a wind load of p = 1.0 kN/m². If type S mortar has been used and if the mean mortar bed width is 37.7 mm, what are the stresses developed in the wall by the factored load?*

A 1.0 m strip of wall is analyzed (see Fig. 3-8) and the section effective in resisting bending is shown in Fig. 3-9, *x-x* being the axis of bending.

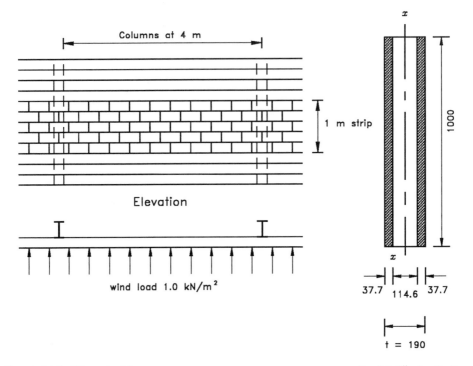

Fig. 3-8 Wall of Example 3-5   Fig. 3-9 Effective Section

For a 1.0 m strip

Recalling that the load factor $\alpha_L = 1.5$ for wind, then the factored wind is
$$w_f = \alpha_L p = 1.5 \times 1.0 \text{ kN/m}^2 \times 1 \text{ m} = 1.5 \text{ kN/m};$$
span $L = 4.0$ m

Assuming simple spans, the moment is found as

$$M_x = \frac{w_f L^2}{8} = \frac{1.5(4.0)^2}{8} = 3.0 \text{ kN-m} = 3.0(10)^6 \text{ N-mm}$$

$$I_x = \frac{1000(190)^3}{12} - \frac{1000(114.6)^3}{12} = 446.2(10)^6 \text{ mm}^4$$

$$S_x = 2I_x/t = \frac{2(446.2)(10)^6}{190} = 4.70(10)^6 \text{ mm}^3$$

Therefore the bending stress is

$$f = M_x/S_x = \frac{3.0(10)^6}{4.70(10)^6} = 0.64 \text{ MPa} \qquad \underline{\text{Ans.}}$$

Note that since the wind can act in any direction, the wind stresses in the wall are $= \pm 0.64$ MPa. From Table 6, S304.1, the limiting flexural tensile strength for this wall is $f_t = 0.9$ MPa and the factored tensile strength is $\phi_m f_t = 0.55(0.9) = 0.50$ MPa. *Therefore the spacing of the columns should be reduced.*

EXAMPLE 3-6 *The free-standing 200 mm concrete block wall shown in Fig. 3-10 is unreinforced and ungrouted. If Type S mortar has been used and if the mean mortar bed width for the block is 37.7 mm, what wind pressure p, in kN/m², will produce limiting tensile stresses in the wall: (a) neglecting the self weight of the wall, and (b) including the self weight of the wall?*

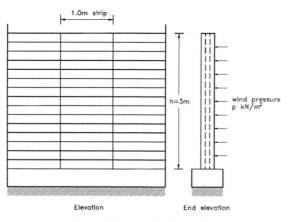

Fig.3-10 Wall analyzed in Example 3-6

Note 1. *The Notes on Table 6 of S304.1 limits the tensile strength f_t for free-standing cantilever walls to 0.1 MPa.*
2. *The unit weight of solid concrete masonry may be taken as 21.0 kN/m³ and the blocks may be assumed to be 50% solid.*

Since the wall is acting as a vertical cantilever, tensile stresses produced by the wind will be normal to the bed joints. The limiting tensile stress is $\phi_m f_t = 0.55(0.1) = 0.055$ MPa.

For a 1.0 m strip

The effective section will be the same as that shown in Fig. 3-9.

$$A_e = 2(37.7)(1000) = 75.4(10)^3 \text{ mm}^2$$

$$S_x = 4.70(10)^6 \text{ mm}^3 \quad \text{(from Example 3-5)}$$

The maximum moment occurs at the base of the wall and is

$$M_x = 1/2\alpha_l ph^2 = 1/2(1.5)p(3)^2 = 6.75p \text{ kN-m}$$

where p = wind pressure in kN/m²

The flexural stress is found as

$$f = M_x/S_x = \frac{6.75(10)^6 p}{4.70(10)^6} = 1.436p \text{ MPa}$$

a) Neglecting wall self weight:

The tensile stress f_t should be less than 0.055 MPa, or

$$f_t = 1.436p \leq 0.055 \text{ MPa}$$

or

$$p = 0.038 \text{ kN/m}^2 \qquad \qquad \text{Ans.}$$

b) Including wall self weight

The self weight of a 1.0 m strip at the base of the wall, that is, at the critical section, is found as

$$P = \alpha_D[\text{unit weight(percent solid)(thickness)(height)}]$$

Since the dead load resists overturning, $\alpha_D = 0.85$

$$= 0.85(21.0)(0.5)(0.19)(3.0) = 5.09 \text{ kN} = 5.09(10)^3 \text{ N}$$

From Equation (3-5), considering tensile stresses as positive, the tensile stress is found as

$$f_t = -P/A_e + M_x/S_x \leq 0.055 \text{ MPa}$$

that is,

$$f_t = \frac{-5.09(10)^3}{75.4(10)^3} + 1.436p \leq 0.055 \text{ MPa}$$

Solution of this equation gives the maximum value of the wind pressure as

$$p_{(max)} = 0.086 \text{ kN/m}^2 \qquad \underline{\text{Ans.}}$$

Note that although the self weight of the wall enhances its resistance to wind load, the pressure it can safely sustain is not very great, a more likely value being 1.0 kN/m². In practice, the wall of Example 3-6 would be reinforced with vertical bars extending from the foundation.

3-4   FLEXURE OF SINGLY-REINFORCED SECTIONS

When the loading is such that flexural tensile stresses in masonry exceed their prescribed limit, or where shrinkage cracks or control joints eliminate any tensile resistance, the masonry should be reinforced.

If the limiting tensile stresses, f_t, for reinforced masonry were the same as those in unreinforced masonry, the corresponding tensile stresses in the reinforcement (being bonded to masonry) would be in the order of nf_t, or about $20(0.50) = 10.0$ MPa. This would be an excessive penalty to impose upon a material with a yield stress of 300 MPa or more. In the interest of economy, reinforced masonry is allowed to crack so that the reinforcement is utilized efficiently. This, of course, is consistent with practice in reinforced concrete design.

Reinforcement can be used to enhance the flexural resistance of a wall, such as that shown in Fig. 3-6, through the provision of vertical bars in grouted cores, as shown in Figs. 1-2 and 1-4, or to span openings, as shown in Fig. 1-3. Furthermore, if the span and the loading are considerable, the beam can be more than one course in depth, as shown in Fig. 3-11.

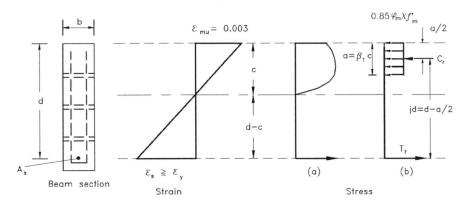

Fig. 3-11 Masonry Beam Reinforced for Tension Only

The bottom course of multi-course beams is constructed from lintel or bond beam units (see Fig. 2-4) in which the longitudinal bars are placed, and subsequent courses generally consist of standard hollow blocks. The beam is then normally fully grouted.

Recalling the basic assumptions for flexure outlined in Section 3-1, it is evident from the assumption of plane sections that the strain diagram is linear, and from the assumption of linear elasticity that the stress diagram at service loads also is linear. As the load increases, strain increases, and the materials become non-linear. Provided that the area of steel is not so great that yielding does not take place, the steel will eventually yield in tension and the masonry stress will be curved, with a maximum value of f'_m. As in reinforced concrete, the rather complicated curved masonry stress diagram can be effectively represented by an equivalent rectangular compressive stress diagram. This is shown in Fig. 3-11, where the rectangular stress distribution can be defined as:

- A masonry stress of $0.85\phi_m\chi f'_m$ uniformly distributed over the compression zone to a depth of $a = \beta_1 c$, where c is the depth to the neutral axis.

- A factor β_1 that has a value of 0.80 for values of f'_m up to 20 MPa. For greater masonry strengths, β_1 reduces continuously by 0.10 for each 10 MPa above 20 MPa. For example, if $f'_m = 25$ MPa, $\beta_1 = 0.75$.

- A factor χ that depends on the direction of the compressive stress relative to the direction in prism testing. For compressive forces applied horizontally and normal to the head joint $\chi = 0.5$, whereas for compressive forces applied vertically and normal to the bed joint $\chi = 1.0$. The χ factor, in effect, represents that portion of the width of the beam that is stressed in compression.

To further explain the χ factor, if a beam is made up of hollow units and is fully grouted, unless special care is taken to grout the *frog*, or space between units (see Fig. 2-17), that space may not be filled and flexural compression is then transmitted only through the face of the shells. In general, then, the effective width of the compression zone is only about 50% of the width of the beam. In actual calculation, the full width of the beam is used but modified by χ.

Fig. 3-11 shows the cross-section of a beam reinforced for tension only and loaded to develop its resistance. This is reflected in the strain diagram where the ultimate strain of 0.003 has been reached in compression and for now it will be assumed that the steel has yielded ($\epsilon_s \geq \epsilon_y$). The stress diagram (a) shows the probable shape of the compressive stress block at failure, while (b) illustrates the equivalent rectangular stress block with the various factors applied.

The moment of resistance is calculated by first determining the resultant resisting forces in compression and tension, C_r and T_r respectively. These forces are calculated by multiplying the factored stresses by the respective areas being stressed, as follows.

Defining the steel ratio ρ as

$$\rho = A_s/bd \qquad\qquad (3\text{-}9)$$

the factored tensile resistance of the steel is

$$T_r = \phi_s A_s f_y = 0.85 A_s f_y = 0.85 \rho b d f_y \tag{3-10}$$

The factored compressive resistance of the masonry is

$$C_r = 0.85 \phi_m \chi f'_m ba = 0.85(0.55) \chi f'_m ba \tag{3-11}$$

and since, for equilibrium, $T_r = C_r$, the depth, a, of the rectangular stress block is

$$a = \frac{\rho f_y d}{0.55 \chi f'_m} \tag{3-12}$$

Since the moment arm

$$jd = d - a/2 \tag{3-13}$$

the moment of resistance becomes

$$M_r = T_r jd = C_r jd \tag{3-14}$$

It should be noted that the reinforcement in flexural members should be checked against a maximum value and a minimum value. If too much reinforcement is present, the steel does not yield and brittle failure may result from overload. Setting the steel strain at $\epsilon_y = f_y/E_s$ in the strain diagram of Fig. 3-11 and applying the principle of similar triangles,

$$c/d = \frac{0.003}{0.003 + f_y/E_s}$$

Using a value of $E_s = 200(10)^3$ MPa, the expression is obtained which forms the basis of Clause 10.2.3.2 of S304.1 requiring that the area of reinforcement in flexural members with no axial load shall be such that

$$c/d \leq \frac{600}{600 + f_y} \tag{3-15}$$

Clause 10.2.3.4 of S304.1 requires that the steel ratio should also be checked against a lower limiting value, $\rho_{min} = 0.8/f_y$. If ρ is less than ρ_{min}, it should be one-third greater than that required by analysis. In other words, if a beam is being designed and the required area of steel gives a value of $\rho(\text{calculated}) \leq \rho_{min}$, then use $1.333 \times \rho(\text{calculated})$ in the design; or, when analyzing a beam in which $\rho \leq \rho_{min}$, use only 0.75ρ in the analysis. The main reason for this required increase in steel is that when masonry first cracks, the tensile force is transferred abruptly from the masonry to the steel, with greater effect on small quantities of reinforcement.

EXAMPLE 3-7 *The 200 mm wide, four-course concrete masonry beam shown in Fig. 3-12 is reinforced with 2 - #15 bars located 100 mm above the bottom of the beam and is fully grouted. If $f'_m = 10$ MPa and $f_y = 400$ MPa, what is the resisting moment of the beam?*

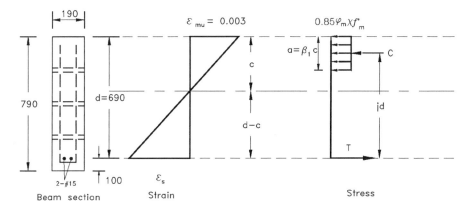

Fig. 3-12 Analysis of the Beam of Example 3-7

The steel reinforcement area is

$$A_s = 2(200) = 400 \text{ mm}^2$$

Check

$$\rho = A_s/bd = \frac{400}{190(690)} = 0.0031 > 0.002 = \frac{0.8}{400} = \rho_{min} \qquad \underline{\text{OK}}$$

Assuming that the stress, f_s, in the tension reinforcement is equal to the yield strength, f_y.

$$T_r = \phi_s A_s f_y = 0.85(400)(400) = 136(10)^3 \text{ N}$$

$$C_r = (0.85\phi_m \chi f'_m)ba, \text{ and } \chi \text{ is taken as } 0.5$$
$$= (0.85 \times 0.55 \times 0.5 \times 10)(190)a$$
$$= 444a$$

For equilibrium,

$$C_r = T_r$$
$$444a = 136(10)^3$$
$$a = 306$$
$$c = a/\beta_1$$
$$= 306/0.8 = 382 \text{ mm}$$

Check whether $f_s = f_y$.

By similar triangles

$$\frac{\epsilon_s}{d - c} = \frac{0.003}{c}$$

$$\epsilon_s = 0.003(\frac{690 - 382}{382}) = 0.0024$$

$$\epsilon_y = \frac{400}{200(10)^3} = 0.0020$$

Therefore, $\epsilon_s > \epsilon_y$ and $f_s = f_y$ <u>OK</u>

$$M_r = C_r jd = T_r jd$$

$$jd = d - a/2$$

$$M_r = \phi_s A_s f_y(d - a/2)$$
$$= 0.85(400)(400)(690 - 306/2)$$
$$= 73.0(10)^6 \text{ N-mm} = 73 \text{ kN-m.}$$

$$M_f \leq M_r = 73 \text{ kN-m.}$$

Therefore, the maximum factored moment for the beam is 73 kN-m. <u>Ans.</u>

3-5 "BALANCED" REINFORCEMENT

In the limit states design of masonry, balanced reinforcement is defined as the amount of reinforcement that permits the masonry to start crushing as the steel starts to yield. S304.1 assumes the maximum usable strain at the extreme masonry compression fibre to be equal to 0.003 and, using $\epsilon_y = f_y/E_s$ as the steel strain, the S304.1 upper limit on the area of tensile reinforcement is characterized by Equation (3-15).

EXAMPLE 3-8 *If $f'_m = 10$ MPa and $f_y = 400$ MPa, calculate the balanced steel ratio for the beam in Fig. 3-13.*

The yield strain in steel is

$$\epsilon_y = f_y/E_s = \frac{400}{200(10)^3} = 0.002$$

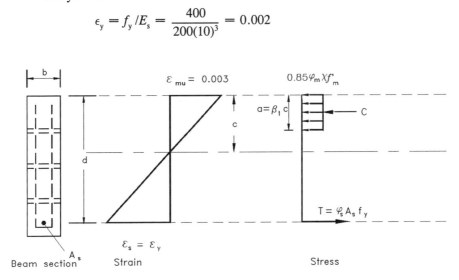

Fig. 3-13 The Balanced Case

From the linear strain condition, the depth to the neutral axis, c, can be determined by similar triangles

$$\epsilon_{mu}/\epsilon_y = \frac{c}{d - c}$$

or,

$$c = d\left(\frac{\epsilon_{mu}}{\epsilon_{mu} + \epsilon_y}\right) = d\left(\frac{0.003}{0.003 + 0.002}\right) = 0.6d$$

and the depth of the equivalent rectangular block becomes

$$a = \beta_1 c = 0.8c = 0.48d$$

Thus, the resultant tensile force is

$$T_r = \phi_s A_s f_y = \phi_s \rho_b b d f_y = 0.85\rho_b b d(400)$$

and the resultant compression is

$$C_r = (0.85\phi_m \chi f'_m)ba$$
$$= (0.85)(0.55)(0.5)(10)b(0.48d) = 1.122bd$$

For equilibrium, $T_r = C_r$, or

$$0.85\rho_b bd(400) = 1.122bd \; ; \; \rho_b = 1.122/340 = 0.0033 \qquad \underline{Ans.}$$

For these materials, the balanced steel ratio is therefore 0.0033.

When masonry beams are tested in bending, the type of failure falls into one of two categories as follows, and as shown in Fig. 3-14.

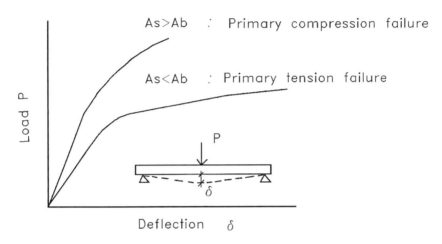

Fig. 3-14 Masonry Beam In Bending

Primary tension failure: when the area of steel, A_s, is less than the balanced steel area, A_b, the steel yields in tension before the masonry crushes and the beam fails. This type of failure is characterized by ductile behaviour and some warning of failure.

Primary compression failure: when $A_s > A_b$, the masonry crushes and the beam fails before the steel yields. The behaviour is characteristically brittle, with no warning of failure. When analyzing a beam that contains more than balanced reinforcement, only A_b can be used in calculating the moment of resistance, and any surplus reinforcement is ignored.

3-6   FLEXURE OF DOUBLY-REINFORCED SECTIONS

In addition to tensile reinforcement, steel bars may also be placed in the compression zone of a beam to enhance the compressive resistance of the masonry, or to inhibit creep and thereby to reduce deflections.

The use of compression reinforcement, A'_s, is illustrated in Fig. 3-15, where its depth from the compression face of the beam is d'.

Following an analysis similar to that of Section 3-4 and, for now, ignoring the fact that a small area of masonry is displaced by the compression steel, the factored compressive resistance of the masonry is

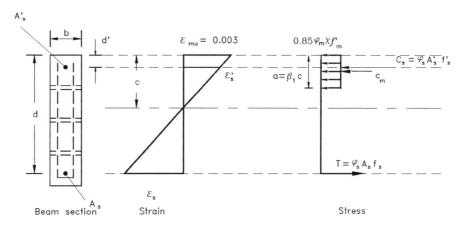

Fig. 3-15 The Doubly Reinforced Section

$$C_m = (0.85\phi_m\chi f'_m)ba = 0.85(0.55)\chi f'_m ba = 0.4675\chi f'_m ba \quad (3\text{-}16)$$

Not knowing at this stage whether the compression steel yields, its factored compressive resistance becomes

$$C_s = \phi_s\, A'_s\, f'_s = 0.85A'_s\, f'_s \quad (3\text{-}17)$$

Since C_m has been overestimated by including the area A'_s displaced by the steel, the resistance C_s should, for completeness, be reduced by $0.4675\chi f'_m A'_s$. However, since C_s is normally considerably less than C_m, and since $0.4675\chi f'_m A'_s$ is normally considerably less than $0.85A'_s f'_s$, this refinement is unnecessary.

Assuming the tensile steel yields, its factored resistance is

$$T_r = \phi_s\, A_s\, f_y = 0.85A_s\, f_y \quad (3\text{-}18)$$

For equilibrium
$$C_r = C_m + C_s = T_r$$

$$C_r = 0.85(0.55)\chi f'_m ba + 0.85A'_s\, f'_s = 0.85A_s\, f_y = T_r$$

and the depth of the rectangular block is

$$a = \frac{A_s f_y - A'_s f'_s}{0.55\chi f'_m b} \quad (3\text{-}19)$$

and, $c = a/\beta_1$

To determine the stress in the compression steel, its strain is obtained by similar triangles from the strain diagram as

$$\epsilon'_s = 0.003(\frac{c-d'}{c})$$

and, for the purpose of confirming yield of the tension steel, its strain is

$$\epsilon_s = 0.003(\frac{d-c}{c})$$

The moment arm for C_m is $jd - a/2$

The moment arm for C_s is $d - d'$, and

$$M_r = C_m(d - a/2) + C_s(d - d') \tag{3-20}$$

The analysis of a doubly-reinforced beam is illustrated in the following example.

EXAMPLE 3-9 *A four-course masonry beam is constructed from standard 200 mm concrete blocks. The beam is reinforced with 1-#20 top and 1-#30 bottom located as shown in Fig. 3-16 and is fully grouted. If $f'_m = 10$ MPa and $f_y = 400$ MPa and $E_s = 200,000$ MPa, calculate the flexural strength of the beam.*

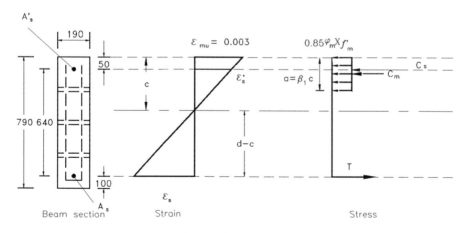

Fig. 3-16 Doubly Reinforced Beam of Example 3-9

The factored compressive resistance of the masonry is

$$C_m = 0.85\phi_m\chi f'_m ba = 0.85(0.55)(0.5)(10)a(190) = 444a$$

It is convenient to assume that all steel yields, and then to check that assumption. The factored resistance of the compression steel, then, is

$$C_s = \phi_s A'_s f_y = 0.85(300)(400) = 102(10)^3 \text{ N}$$

and that of the tension steel

$$T_r = \phi_s A_s f_y = 0.85(700)(400) = 238(10)^3 \text{ N}$$

For equilibrium, $C_m + C_s = T_r$

$$444a + 102(10)^3 = 238(10)^3$$

Therefore, $a = 306$ mm

and,
$$c = a/\beta_1 = \frac{306}{0.8} = 382.5 \text{ mm}$$

The yield strain is

$$\epsilon_y = f_y/E_s = \frac{400}{200(10)^3} = 0.0020$$

and the steel can be checked for yielding. From the strain diagram, using similar triangles

$$\epsilon'_s = 0.003(\frac{c-d'}{c}) = 0.003(\frac{382.5-50}{382.5}) = 0.0026 > 0.002 = \epsilon_y \quad \underline{OK}$$

Therefore, $f'_s = f_y$
and,
$$\epsilon_s = 0.003(\frac{d-c}{c}) = 0.003(\frac{690-382.5}{382.5}) = 0.0024 > 0.0020 = \epsilon_y$$

Therefore, $f_s = f_y$, and all steel yields. $\underline{OK}$

$$M_r = C_m(d-a/2) + C_s(d-d')$$
$$= (444)(306)(690 - 306/2) + 102(10)^3(690 - 50)$$
$$= 138.2 \text{ kN-m} \qquad\qquad\qquad \underline{Ans.}$$

Had the compression steel in this example been found not to yield (as would be the case if the same steel areas been used top and bottom, that is, $A_s = A'_s$), a lower value of f'_s could be tried with a subsequent calculation of ϵ'_s and f'_s to check the validity of the new value. For example, if the beam in the preceding example had been reinforced with 1-#30 top and bottom, A'_s would be found not to yield and successive trials would show $f'_s = 335$ MPa and $M_r = 152.5$ kN-m. On the other hand, if both sets of steel are assumed to yield, one direct calculation leads to

$$M_r = \phi_s A_s f_y (d - d') = 0.85(700)(400)(690 - 50)$$
$$= 152.3 \text{ kN-m}$$

very little different from the more "correct" value.

Generally, then, it may be assumed that the compression steel yields. If the compression steel ratio, ρ', is defined as $\rho' = A'_s/bd$, then yielding of the tension steel can be checked by ensuring that

$$\rho - \rho' \leq \rho_b \tag{3-21}$$

Tension steel is more efficient, and more economical, than compression steel in resisting bending. When calculations indicate that A'_s is required for strength reasons the quantity of tension steel is probably too great for the limited space in the beam and the designer will select a deeper beam. In the event that compression steel is used, it should be tied to prevent buckling, the requirements for which are given in Clauses 12.2.3.4 of S304.1.

The reader should note, if it is not already obvious, that throughout Sections 3-4, 3-5 and 3-6 only positive bending has been considered. In regions of negative bending the situation is inverted, with the top steel becoming the tensile reinforcement.

3-7   SHEAR

The development of internal bending moments and shear forces was discussed in Section 3-1 and subsequent sections considered the mechanics of resistance to bending. However, a beam should be analyzed not only for its resistance to bending but also for its resistance to shear forces. Although the mechanics of shear resistance in masonry is complex and not fully understood, a workable method of analysis based on simple principles is available to the structural designer. The method is similar to that used for reinforced concrete and the clauses in S304.1 governing shear are contained in the requirements of Clause 12.3 for flexural members.

Shear and diagonal tension

Fig. 3-17 shows a reinforced masonry beam with transverse loading. The shear forces, V_f, due to applied factored loading reach a maximum value at the supports and the shear stress, v, at any cross-section has its maximum value at the neutral axis where the flexural stresses are zero. The stresses acting on a unit element at the neutral surface are shown in Fig. 3-17(b), the stresses v on the vertical faces being calculable from V_f, while those on the horizontal faces are the *complementary shear stresses*, also v, required to establish equilibrium of the element.

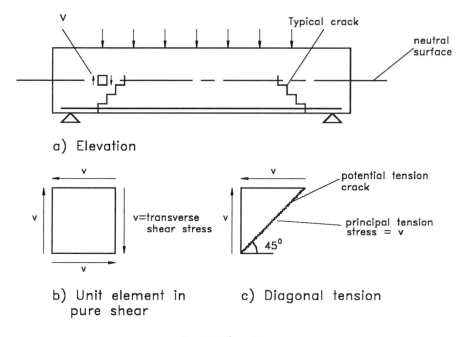

Fig. 3-17 Shear Stresses

It can readily be shown that the condition of pure shear in Fig. 3-17(b) can also be represented by a system of principal compressive and tensile stresses acting on the unit element rotated through $45°$ (in the plane of the paper). As masonry, like concrete, is weaker in tension than in compression or shear, it is the principal tension that causes failure due to shear. This critical tensile stress, referred to as *diagonal tension*, is shown in Fig. 3-17(c). When a masonry beam is overloaded in shear it will develop cracks due to the diagonal tension, generally inclined at 45 degrees at the neutral axis. The cracking will follow the path of least resistance, which may be through the masonry units, but more frequently along the mortar joints, as shown in Fig. 3-17(a).

As the element has unit sides, the horizontal and vertical shear forces in Fig. 3-17(c) are $v \times 1 = v$, and the resultant of the two shear forces is a tensile force of $v\sqrt{2}$ at $45°$. This force is acting on a diagonal of length $\sqrt{2}$ and dividing force by area, the diagonal tensile stress is v, the same value as the shear stress.

While the distribution of shear stress under factored load in the cross-section of a masonry beam is complex, it is adequate to assume an average, or nominal shear stress:

$$v_f = V_f/bd \tag{3-22}$$

where the maximum value of shear force, V_f, is normally calculated at a distance d (the effective depth of the beam) from the face of the support. This is in recognition of the fact that compression introduced by the support reaction enhances shear strength in that vicinity. This value of V_f at d from the face of the support is assumed to apply from that point to the support.

S304.1 requires that the calculated shear force under factored loads, V_f, does not exceed the factored shear resistance of the masonry member, V_r. The factored shear resistance is determined as the sum of two parts,

$$V_r = V_m + V_s \tag{3-23}$$

in which V_m is the shear resistance of the masonry and V_s is that provided by the shear reinforcement.

The factored shear resistance of masonry, V_m, is essentially the product of an average ultimate shear stress, v_u, and the nominal cross-sectional area, $b_w d$, modified by a performance factor, ϕ_m. That is, $V_m = \phi_m v_u b_w d$. However, the ultimate shear stress is not a constant: its value depends on f'_m, on beam depth, and whether the units are normal or lightweight. In recognition of this, S304.1 (Clause 12.3.5.4) gives the value of the factored shear resistance of a continuously grouted beam as

$$V_m = 0.2\lambda\phi_m\sqrt{f'_m}(1.0 - \frac{d-400}{1500})b_w d \tag{3-24}$$

$$\geq 0.12\lambda\phi_m\sqrt{f'_m}b_w d$$

$$\leq 0.2\lambda\phi_m\sqrt{f'_m}b_w d$$

where b_w is the width of the beam web (normally the beam width), λ is a modification factor that varies from 1.0 for normal weight units to 0.75 for light-weight units (Clause 12.3.4), and $\phi_m = 0.55$. A simple calculation shows that the upper limit to V_m of $0.20\lambda\phi_m(\sqrt{f'_m})b_w d$ applies to beams less than 400 mm in depth, and the lower limit of $0.12\lambda\phi_m(\sqrt{f'_m})b_w d$ to beam depths greater than 1000 mm, with a linear variation between the two depths. To simplify calculations, the designer might decide to use the upper value for all continuously grouted lintel beams, and the lower value for all deeper beams.

For the shear resistance of flexural members to be calculated according to Equation (3-24), S304.1 requires that the member be continuously grouted. This implies that beams are formed with lintel or U-shaped block. If the grout is interrupted by webs, the shear resistance provided by masonry derived from Equation (3-24) is multiplied by 0.6.

Since axial forces affect the resistance to shear they should be considered in the design. Shear resistance is enhanced by axial compression and reduced by axial tension. While S304.1 specifically requires that any improvement due to axial compression is neglected, when axial tension, N_f, is present the shear resistance is multiplied by a factor $R_t < 1.0$ (Clause 12.3.5.4).

$$R_t = 1 - N_f/N_r < 1.0$$

where $N_r = \phi_m f_t b_w d$ is the resistance of the cross-section to tensile cracking, values of f_t being obtained from Table 6 of S304.1.

When the shear force due to the factored load exceeds the shear resistance (that is, $V_f > V_m$), shear reinforcement is required to provide resistance, V_s, for the surplus shear (that is, $V_s \geq V_f - V_m$). However, in recognizing the complexity of the mechanism of shear and the uncertainties in the simplifications that are made, S304.1 requires that when $V_f > 0.50V_m$ (except for beams 200 mm or less in depth) a nominal amount of shear reinforcement be provided (12.3.5.7.1).

Shear reinforcement

Where shear reinforcement (also referred to as web reinforcement) is required it is normally provided in the form of single or two-legged stirrups, at a spacing s, as shown in Fig. 3-18(a) and (b). Inclined stirrups and bent-up bars are rarely used, and would be impossible in a multi-course concrete block beam where the cores in which the stirrup must be placed line up vertically.

Since in this discussion it is assumed that $V_f > V_m$, shear reinforcement is required to resist the surplus shear, $V_s = V_f - V_m$. Fig. 3-18(c) shows that for a stirrup or tie spacing s, a typical $45°$ crack will be transversed by a number of ties, $N = d/s$, and these N ties are required to resist V_s. Thus, the resistance of each tie must be at least equal to V_s/N.

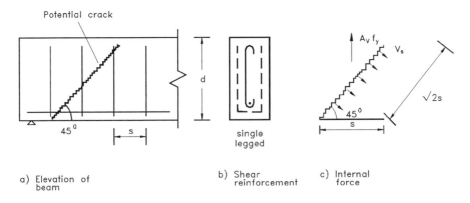

Fig.3-18 Shear Reinforcement

The resistance of one tie is

$$\phi_s A_v f_y \geq V_s/N \qquad (3-25)$$

where A_v is the cross-sectional area of the one or two legs of the tie, and f_y is its yield strength.

Now, since $N=d/s$, $V_s/N=V_s s/d$

$$\phi_s A_v f_y \geq V_s s/d$$

Then, $$V_s = \phi_s A_v f_y d/s \tag{3-26}$$

$$A_v \geq \frac{V_s s}{\phi_s f_y d} \tag{3-27}$$

and, $$s \leq \phi_s A_v f_y d/V_s \tag{3-28}$$

Equation (3-26) is used to find the actual resistance of the ties, Equation (3-27) can be used to find the required tie area if the spacing is known, and Equation (3-28) can be used to find the spacing if the tie size has been determined (for example, a single-legged #10 tie).

To prevent failure before yielding of shear reinforcement, S304.1 limits the total shear on the section by limiting the shear resistance to be provided by the web reinforcement to

$$V_s = V_f - V_m \leq 0.36 \phi_m \sqrt{f'_m}\, b_w d$$

S304.1 further requires that a minimum amount of shear reinforcement be provided to prevent sudden failure due to the spread of diagonal cracking. A minimum area of shear reinforcement should be provided in beams with a depth greater than 200 mm if the factored shear force, V_f, exceeds one half of the shear strength provided by the masonry, V_m, that is, $V_f \geq 0.5 V_m$, and the minimum area of shear reinforcement to be provided is

$$A_v = 0.35 \left(\frac{b_w s}{f_y} \right) \tag{3-29}$$

Since a potential diagonal tension crack extends along the beam a distance approximately equal to the effective depth, d, and to ensure that each potential crack contains at least one stirrup, the spacing should not exceed the lesser of $d/2$ or 600 mm.

EXAMPLE 3-10 *The four-course fully-grouted and reinforced 200 mm, normal concrete block beam shown in Fig. 3-19 is required to support a uniform dead load of 25 kN/m (including self weight) over a clear simple span of 4.0 m. If $f'_m = 10$ MPa, determine whether the beam requires shear reinforcement.*

The maximum shear force to be considered is calculated at the distance $d = 690$ from the face of the support, as shown in Fig. 3-19:

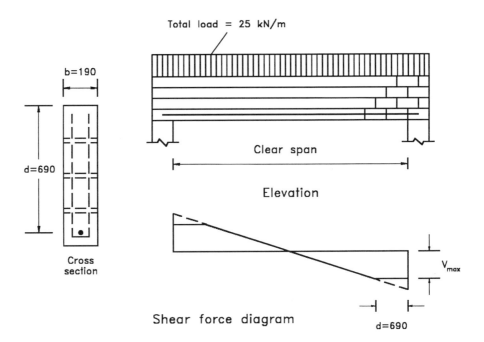

Fig. 3-19 Reinforced Masonry Beam of Example 3-10

$$\text{Max. } V_f = 1.25\,(25)(\frac{4.0}{2} - 0.69) = 40.94 \text{ kN}$$

and, from Equation (3-24), the factored shear resistance provided by masonry is

$$V_m = 0.2(1.0)(0.55)(\sqrt{10}\,)[1.0 - \frac{690 - 400}{1500}](190)(690)$$
$$= 36.79 \text{ kN}$$
$$> 0.12(1.0)(0.55)(\sqrt{10})(190)(690) = 27.36 \text{ kN} \qquad \underline{\text{OK}}$$
$$< 0.2(1.0)(0.55)(\sqrt{10})(190)(690) = 45.6 \text{ kN} \qquad \underline{\text{OK}}$$

Since $V_f = 40.94 > 18.4 = 0.5V_m$, shear reinforcement is required.

EXAMPLE 3-11 *If the beam of Example 3-10 is provided with #10 single-legged stirrups spaced at 200 mm centres, that is, one stirrup per core of two-core blocks, and if $f_y=300$ MPa, determine whether the beam is adequately reinforced for shear.*

Since, from Example 3-10, $V_f>0.5V_m$, shear reinforcement is required. The resistance provided by the shear reinforcement should not be less than

$$V_f - V_m = 40.94 - 36.79 = 4.15 \text{ kN},$$

The cross-section of the tie should be at least $A_v = 0.35b_ws/f_y$ and the shear resistance required from the steel $V_f - V_m \leq 0.36\phi_m(\sqrt{f'_m})b_wd$

Check: $A_v=100\text{mm}^2>44.33\text{mm}^2=0.35(190)(200)/300=0.35b_ws/f_y$ OK

Check: $V_f - V_m=4.15<126.86\text{kN}=0.36(0.55)(\sqrt{10})(190)(690)(10)^{-3}$

$$=0.36\phi_m(\sqrt{f'_m})b_wd$$ OK

and the actual shear provided

$$V_s = \phi_sA_v f_yd/s = 87.98 \text{ kN} > 4.15 \text{ kN} = V_f - V_m$$ OK

Therefore the beam is adequately reinforced for shear.   Ans.

3-8   BOND, DEVELOPMENT AND ANCHORAGE

Reinforced masonry is effective only if the reinforcement is bonded to the grout, and the grout to the masonry units. Generally, if the grouting operation is properly carried out, the absorption by the masonry units and the large area of contact ensures adequate grout-to-unit bond. On the other hand, the bond between reinforcement and grout is more critical, the area of contact being comparatively small.

A shear-type *bond stress* acting along the surface of a reinforcing bar is the mechanism whereby force is transferred from grout to the bar. If the resistance to bond stress is exceeded, slip between bar and grout takes place and the reinforcing steel loses its effectiveness. Although standard deformations on the surface of normal reinforcement provide substantial resistance through the mechanical interlocking of bar with grout, bond must be checked.

There are two basic ways of considering bond. One is to recognize that localized bond stress is directly related to the rate of increase of the tensile force in the reinforcement of a flexural member. This is referred to as *flexural bond stress*. The other is to assume that the bond stress is uniform along the bar, and to ensure that the bar has sufficient embedment length to develop the required strength of bar, this length being referred to as the *development length*, l_d. The anchorage of the bar can be further improved through the provision of hooks at the ends of the bars.

Flexural bond stress

Fig. 3-20 shows a beam subjected to transverse loads, and therefore to bending moments and shear forces. The forces acting on a small element of length Δx are shown in Fig. 3-20(b). The change in bar force from a value of T to $(T + \Delta T)$ must be transmitted by the bond stress, u, acting on the contact area between the bar and grout.

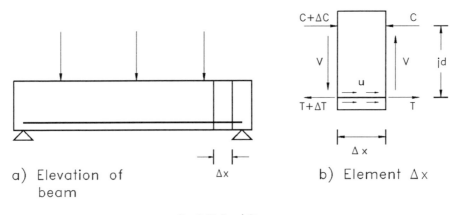

a) Elevation of beam

b) Element Δx

Fig. 3-20 Bond Stresses

A summation of forces along the bar gives

$$(T + \Delta T) - T = \Delta T = u\Sigma o\Delta x$$

where Σo is the summation of bar perimeters.

From a consideration of equilibrium of moments,

$$(T + \Delta T)jd - Tjd = V\Delta x; \quad \Delta Tjd = V\Delta x$$

or

$$\Delta T = V\Delta x/jd$$

and substituting $\Delta T = u\Sigma o\Delta x$ yields the relation for flexural bond stress u as

$$u = V/\Sigma ojd \tag{3-30}$$

Note that the maximum bond stress occurs at the location of maximum shear which in this case is taken at the centreline of the support, where the rate of change of moment has its greatest value.

Development

Unless a bar is provided with a hook at the end, the length of embedment beyond the point of maximum stress in the bar should be sufficient to develop the strength of the bar.

If the yield stress in a bar is f_y, the bar force that must be developed by a length of embedment is

$$T = f_y \times \pi d_b^2/4$$

where d_b is the bar diameter. If l_d is the required embedment, or development length, and u_u is the ultimate average bond stress, then the maximum force that can be delivered to the bar by bond is $\pi d_b u_u l_d$ and, equating these forces,

$$f_y \times \pi d_b^2/4 \;=\; \pi d_b u_u l_d$$

The required development length is therefore

$$l_d = f_y d_b/4u_u \tag{3-31}$$

The ultimate average bond stress, however, is difficult to quantify. The actual bond stress is not uniform: stress concentrations develop at the ribs of deformed bars, the degree of stress concentration depending on the size of the deformation and, therefore, on bar size; and even in regions of constant moment, where the bond stress is apparently zero, the presence of flexural cracking in a beam leads to bond stresses between cracks. Also, the bond strength in tension differs significantly from that in compression.

A substantial body of research over the past two decades has shown that, whereas Equation (3-30) describes an ideal situation, the presence of deformations on reinforcing bars renders the flexural bond stress calculation, a mainstay in working stress design, relatively ineffectual. In limit states design, the development length, that is, the length of embedment required to develop the strength of the bar, is of paramount importance. Also, although the equation shown above for l_d is generally valid, the ultimate average bond stress is almost inversely related to bar size for bars in tension, and relatively unaffected by bar size for those in compression.

In recognition of these facts, and based on confirmatory testing, Clauses 5.5.2.3 and 5.5.3.3 of S304.1 define basic development lengths for deformed bars as:

bars in tension $l_{db} = 0.004d_b^2 f_y$ (3-32a)

bars in compression $l_{db} = 0.07d_b f_y$ (3-32b)

and, for deformed wire, in tension or compression

embedded in grout $l_{db} = 0.10d_b f_y$ (3-32c)

embedded in mortar $l_{db} = 0.14d_b f_y$ (3-32d)

and the *required development length*, l_d, is the product of l_{db} and modification factors that allow for the situation in which the bar is placed. For example, because of the stress concentrations noted earlier, closely spaced bars required a greater development length than if they were spaced farther apart. Also, when the area of reinforcement provided is greater than that required by analysis, the required development length is reduced accordingly. These modification factors are described in detail in Clauses of 5.5 of S304.1 and are provided in Part 2 of this book. A summary is also provided in Table 3-1 below. This then gives the required development length

$$l_d = l_{db} \times \text{modification factors} \qquad (3\text{-}33)$$

The development length provided should not, of course, be less than the calculated required l_d, and should also not be less than the minimum values shown in Table 3-1.

As noted earlier, bond stress is likely to be greater in regions of high shear and, in recognition of this fact, Clause 5.5.7.3 of S304.1 requires that at simple supports and points of inflection the following relation be satisfied unless the reinforcement is terminating by a standard hook or an equivalent mechanical anchorage.

$$M_r/V_f + l_a \geq l_d \qquad (3\text{-}34)$$

where at a support l_a is the embedment length beyond the centreline of the support, and at a point of inflection l_a is the greater of d (effective depth) and $12\,d_b$ (d_b is the bar diameter). The calculated value of M_r/V_f may be increased by 30% when the ends of the reinforcement are confined by a compression reaction (Clause 5.5.7.3)

Table 3-1
Development Length

Modification Factors	
Situation	Factor
Bars in Tension a) top bars b) bars spaced laterally $<$ 75 mm o.c. c) bars spaced laterally $>$ 150 mm o.c. d) A_s provided $>$ A_s required by analysis e) the product of c) and d) $\geq$ 0.6 Bars in Compression a) bars spaced laterally $<$ 75 mm o.c. b) A_s provided $>$ A_s required by analysis	1.3 1.6 0.7 $A_{s_{req}}/A_{s_{prov}}$ 1.3 $A_{s_{req}}/A_{s_{prov}}$ $\geq$ 0.6

Minimum l_d
a) deformed bars   - tension
                  - compression
 	
b) deformed wires   - tension
                  - compression
	300 mm
	200 mm
	
	150 mm
	150 mm

Smooth Bars and Wires	2.0
Hooks a) yield strength other than f_y=400 MPa b) bars with side cover $\geq$ 60 mm c) 90° hooks d) cover $\geq$ 60 mm plus enclosure by ties d) A_s provided $>$ A_s required by analysis After modification, l_{dh} should not be less than the greater of $8d_b$ and 150 mm.	$f_y/400$ 0.7 0.7 0.8 $A_{s_{req}}/A_{s_{prov}}$

EXAMPLE 3-12 *A five-course 200 mm concrete block beam is singly reinforced with one #30 bar at an effective depth of 900 mm, and carries a total factored load of 80 kN/m over a span of 4m, as shown in Fig. 3-21. If $f'_m = 13$ MPa, $f_y = 400$ MPa and if the bar is 4200 long, determine whether the bond requirements of S304.1 are satisfied.*

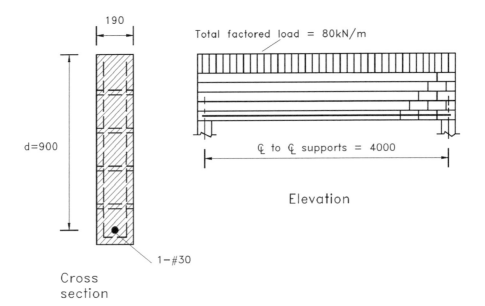

Fig. 3-21 Beam of Example 3-12

Since $w_f = 80$ kN/m, the factored moment, M_f, is

$$M_f = w_f L^2/8 = 80.0(4.0)^2/8 = 160 \text{ kN-m}$$

An analysis similar to that of Example 3-7 shows that the moment of resistance of the section is 165 kN-m and, since $M_r > M_f$, the beam is adequately reinforced for flexure. The question now is whether the reinforcement is adequately anchored.

The basic development length, $l_{db} = 0.004d_b^2 f_y$
$$= 0.004(30.0)^2(400) = 1440 \text{ mm}$$

Since $M_r > M_f$, the area of steel provided is greater than that required, and l_{db} can be modified by $A_{s_{req}}/A_{s_{prov}}$

Now, $A_{s_{req}}/A_{s_{prov}} \approx M_f/M_r = 160/165 = 0.97$ (> 0.6, OK)

The required development length is now $l_d = 0.97(1440) = 1397$ mm

Since the bars are 4200 long, they are anchored 2100 mm each side of the section of maximum moment, and

anchorage $= 2100 > 1397 = l_d$ OK

Now, however, the requirement of Equation (3-34), that is, $M_r/V_f + l_a \geq l_d$, also must be checked at the centreline of the support.

$M_r =$ moment of resistance at section $= 165$ kN-m
$V_f =$ factored shear force at section $= w_f L/2 = 160$ kN
$l_a =$ bar extension beyond centreline of support $= (4200-4000)/2$
$\quad = 100$ mm

$1.3 \, M_r/V_f + l_a = 1.3(165)(10)^6/160(10)^3 + 100 = 1440 > 1397 = l_d$ OK

Therefore the bar is adequately anchored.

Hooks

If required, the anchorage of a reinforcing bar in tension can be greatly enhanced by providing a hook at the end of the bar. The hook then provides additional development length, l_{dh}, and the basic development length starting at the point of tangency (see Fig. 3-22), for a standard hook is given in S304.1 as

$l_{hb} = 25d_b$ for $f_y = 400$ MPa   (3-35)

This basic development length is modified by factors rather similar to those for bars to give the development length, l_{dh}, of the hook. These factors are also included in Table 3-1. Once l_{hb} is modified to give l_{dh}, l_{dh} should not be less than the greater of $8d_b$ and 150 mm. Note that because of tension they would cause in the grout hooks are not used to anchor bars in compression.

EXAMPLE 3-13 *What would be the effect of adding a standard 90° hook (see Fig. 3-22) to the ends of the #30 bar in Example 3-12?*

The effect of adding a hook to the bar is to extend the anchorage for the bar by the development length of the hook, l_{dh}.

The basic development length of a standard hook is $l_{hb}=25d_b=25(30)=750$ mm

The modification factor for a 90° hook is 0.7 and, from Example 3-12, the factor $A_{s_{req}}/A_{s_{prov}} = 0.97$.

Thus, $l_{dh} = 0.7(0.97)l_{hb} = 0.7(0.97)(750) = 509$ mm ($>8d_b$ and > 150)OK

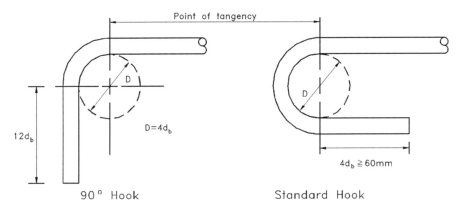

Point of tangency

$D=4d_b$

$12d_b$

$4d_b \geq 60$mm

90° Hook   Standard Hook

Fig. 3-22 Standard Hook

One can now say that the bar has been extended by an equivalent length of 509 mm and

$$1.3 \ M_r/V_c + l_d = 1.3(165)(10)^6/160(10)^3 + 100 + 509 = 1950 > 1397 = \text{QK}$$

The hook, then, has the effect of providing additional anchorage.   Ans.

Finally, because the tensile stresses that would develop in the grout, hooks are not used as anchorage for bars in compression.

Splices

Requirements for splices are not unlike those for reinforced concrete; and are contained in Clause 5.5.10 of S304.1.

3-9   SERVICEABILITY

As noted in Section 1-5, the intent of limit states design is to ensure that various limiting states are not exceeded during the reasonable life of the structure. These limiting states are *safety* (strength and stability) under specific overload, and *serviceability* (durability, stress level, cracking, deflections and vibration) under service loading. Now that flexural strength has been covered, this section deals with serviceability.

Durability is assured through the appropriate selection of materials for the aggressiveness of the environment, sufficient cover on materials that can corrode, the appropriate selection and anchorage of connectors, proper construction and subsequent maintenance, all of which do not lend themselves to the type of analysis familiar to structural designers. Stress levels, cracking, deflections and vibration are more quantifiable and, since they are being evaluated at service (that is, working) loads, analysis follows the principles familiar to working stress designers. The serviceability limit states of prime concern are deflection and crack control. Stresses at service load, where required, are readily calculated from the *transformed section* analysis outlined below, and vibration, as required, can be evaluated from the flexural stiffness derived from that analysis.

Deflections

Deflections under service load are normally calculated assuming that the materials are being stressed within the linear elastic range, and that elastic theory may be used. The deflection so calculated is of the general form

$$\delta = k\frac{WL^3}{EI} \tag{3-36}$$

where W is the total load on the span, L is the span, EI is the effective stiffness of the cross-section, and k is a factor that depends on the distribution of the load and on the support conditions. S304.1 Clause 12.4.1 requires the beam deflection to be checked if the span length exceeds $15d$.

The main problem with reinforced masonry, as with reinforced concrete, is that members in flexure generally crack in tension (an essential factor in assuring that the reinforcing steel works effectively), so there is the stiffness at the cracked section to consider as well as the stiffness at the uncracked section between cracks. The value of the modulus of elasticity of masonry is taken as $E_m = 850f'_m$ MPa ($\leq 20,000$ MPa) or is obtained by testing; and, as noted below, the effective moment of inertia, I_{eff}, is obtained from that of the cracked and uncracked sections, I_{cr} and I_o respectively.

Where the loading is of short duration, elastic analysis gives a reasonable estimate of deflection, but an estimate of deflection under sustained load should take the effects of creep into account. Also, since concrete masonry materials shrink but reinforcing steel does not, the effects of shrinkage on deflection may require consideration. The procedure adopted by S304.1 (Clause 8.3.2.4) to account for the additional deflection due to creep and shrinkage and to allow for the presence of compressive steel is to multiply the immediate deflection by the factor

$$\frac{S}{1+50\rho'} \tag{3-37}$$

Where S is a factor that varies from 0.5 for loads of up to three months duration to 1.0 for loads applied for five years or more.

Cracked Section Analysis

As was noted earlier, for tension reinforcement to be effective, tensile cracking must take place in the masonry and, once a crack starts, it is reasonable to assume that it extends to the neutral axis of the cross-section. Furthermore, if linear elastic behaviour is assumed at service loads, the situation shown in Fig. 3-23 results.

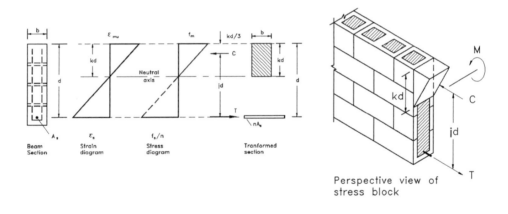

Fig. 3-23 Cross-Section of Singly Reinforced Multi-Course Masonry Beam

Fig 3-23 shows the cross-section of a singly reinforced multi-course masonry beam, the strain diagram, the stress diagram and the transformed section. Since plane sections remain plane during bending, the strain diagram is linear. It is reasonable to assume that the stress-strain relationships are linear at service loads, which leads to a linear stress diagram in which f_m is the maximum compressive stress in the masonry, f_s is the stress in the steel and no tensile stress exists in the masonry.

The ratio $n = E_s/E_m$ has previously been defined as the modular ratio, indicating that steel is n times as stiff as masonry. It is now convenient to consider the transformed section where the effective cracked section is converted to equivalent areas of masonry. In this case, the steel area is converted to an equivalent masonry area of nA_s which is stressed at f_s/n. Here it can be verified that *area* $\times$ *stress* = *force* gives the force $f_s A_s$ at the level of reinforcement.

To determine the depth to the neutral axis, moments of the areas can be taken about the neutral axis:

$$bkd(kd)/2 = nA_s(d-kd)$$

Then, dividing by bd^2 and substituting $\rho = A_s/bd$

$$0.5k^2 = n\rho(1-k)$$

and the solution to this quadratic is

$$k = \sqrt{(np)^2 + 2np} - np$$

Then $\qquad\qquad I_{cr} = b(kd)^3/3 + nA_s(d-kd)^2$ $\qquad\qquad\qquad$ (3-38)

If the designer wishes to calculate the stress at service loads, this can be done as follows: since the stress block is triangular, the resultant compressive force C is located at $kd/3$ and the moment arm jd is

$$jd = d - kd/3$$

The resultant compressive force is

$$C = 0.5f_m bkd$$

and the tensile force

$$T = A_s f_s = \rho f_s bd$$

The moment M becomes

$$M = Cjd = 0.5f_m kjbd^2 = Tjd = \rho f_s jbd^2$$

and the stresses at service load are

$$f_m = \frac{2M}{kjbd^2} \qquad\qquad\qquad (3\text{-}39)$$

$$f_s = \frac{M}{\rho jbd^2} \qquad\qquad\qquad (3\text{-}40)$$

EXAMPLE 3-14 *A five-course 190 masonry beam is reinforced with one #25 bar at an effective depth of 900 mm. If $f'_m = 10$ MPa, what is the moment of inertia of the cracked section?*

Since E_m may be taken as $850f'_m$

$$E_m = 850(10) = 8500 \text{ MPa } (< 20{,}000 \text{ } \underline{OK})$$

and $E_s = 200(10)^3$ MPa

Thus, the modular ratio

$$n = E_s/E_m = \frac{200(10)^3}{8.5(10)^3} = 23.5$$

Since $A_s = 500$ mm^2, the transformed area of steel is

$$nA_s = 23.5(500) = 11750 \text{ mm}^2$$

and taking moments of areas about the neutral axis (see Fig. 3-24)

$$190kd(kd)/2 = 11750(900-kd)$$

that is, $(kd)^2 + 123.7kd - 111.3(10)^3 = 0$

the solution to which is $kd = 277$ mm

and $I_{cr} = 190(277)^3/3 + 11750(900-277)^2 = 5907(10)^6 \text{ mm}^4$ <u>Ans.</u>

Alternatively, the equation previously derived may be used:

$$\rho = A_s/bd = 500/[190(900)] = 0.00292$$

$$k = \sqrt{(n\rho)^2 + 2n\rho} \ -n\rho = \sqrt{(23.5\times0.00292)^2 + 2(23.5)(0.00292)}$$
$$- 23.5(0.00292) = 0.308$$

$$\begin{aligned} I_{cr} &= b(kd)^3/3 + nA_s(d-kd)^2 \\ &= 190(0.308\times900)^3/3 + 23.5(500)[900-0.308(900)]^2 \\ &= 5907(10)^6 \text{ mm}^4 \end{aligned}$$ <u>Ans.</u>

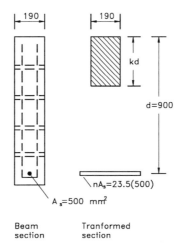

Fig. 3-24 Masonry Beam of Example 3-14

The moment of inertia of the cracked section of a doubly-reinforced beam such as that shown in Fig. 3-25 may be obtained by a similar analysis to yield:

$$k = \sqrt{(n\rho +(n-1)\rho')^2 +2[n\rho +(n-1)\rho'd'/d]} \; -[n\rho +(n-1)\rho']$$

and

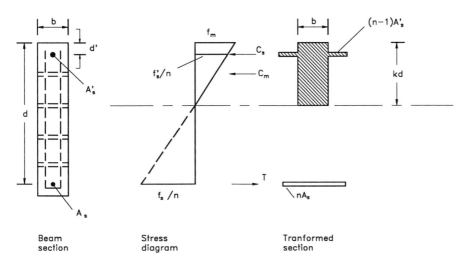

Fig. 3-25 Doubly Reinforced Beam Section

$$I_{cr} = b(kd)^3/3 + (n-1)A'_s(kd-d')^2 + nA_s(d-kd)^2 \qquad (3-39)$$

Uncracked Section Analysis

The calculation of the uncracked moments of inertia, I_o, of reinforced sections can follow an analysis similar to those for cracked sections. However, the actual calculations can be unnecessarily tedious and reasonably simplifying assumptions may be made. One assumption is to use the moment of inertia of the gross-section, $I_g = bh^3/12$, in lieu of I_o. Since the presence of steel is not taken into account, $I_g < I_o$ and deflections will be slightly overestimated. A more reasonable assumption to make is that the centroid of the section lies at the mid-depth of the cross-section, and then to calculate I_o from that point. These assumptions are illustrated in the following example.

EXAMPLE 3-15 *A five-course 190 masonry beam is reinforced with one #25 bar at an effective depth of 900 mm. If $f'_m = 10$ MPa, find the moment of inertia of the gross-section, I_g, and the uncracked moment of inertia.*

Gross moment of inertia, I_g,

$$I_g = bh^3/12 = 190(990)^3/12 = 15.4(10)^9 \text{ mm}^4 \qquad \underline{\text{Ans.}}$$

Uncracked moment of inertia, I_o,

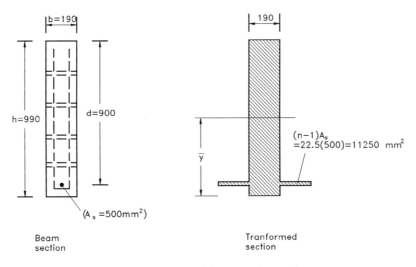

Fig. 3-26 Cross-Section of the Beam of Example 3-15

Referring to Fig. 3-26 and taking moments of areas about the base, the centroid of the section is located at

$$\bar{y} = \frac{bh^2/2 + (n-1)A_s(h-d)}{bh + (n-1)A_s}$$

$$= \frac{190(990)^2/2 + (23.5-1)(500)(990-900)}{190(990) + (23.5-1)(500)} = 472 \text{ mm}$$

$$I_o = bh^3/12 + bh(h/2-\bar{y})^2 + (n-1)A_s[\bar{y}-(h-d)]^2$$

$$= 190(990)^3/12 + 190(990)(990/2 - 472)^2$$
$$+ (23.5 - 1)(500)[472 - (990 - 900)]^2 = 17.1(10)^9 \text{ mm}^4 \quad \underline{\text{Ans.}}$$

As noted earlier, if the assumption is made that the centroid lies at the mid-depth of the section, that is, $\bar{y} = 990/2 = 495$ mm, the calculation simplifies to

$$I_o \approx bh^3/12 + (n-1)A_s(d-h/2)^2$$
$$\approx 190(990)^3/12 + (23.5-1)(500)(900-990/2)^2 = 17.2(10)^9 \underline{\text{ Ans.}}$$

In this example I_g underestimates I_o by about 10%, and the approximate value of I_o is less than 1% different than the "true" value. Since deflection calculations are approximate at best, the approximation is justified.

Effective Moment of Inertia, I_{eff}

Based on research, primarily stemming from work in reinforced concrete, the effective moment of inertia to be used in the calculation of deflection of reinforced masonry beams is obtained by combining the moments of inertia of cracked and uncracked sections as follows (Clause 8.3.2.2 of S304.1):

$$I_{eff} = (M_{cr}/M_a)^3 I_0 + [1 - (M_{cr}/M_a)^3]I_{cr}$$

where

M_{cr} = cracking moment = $(\phi_m f_t + f_{cs})I_o/y_t$
f_t = flexural tensile strength (Table 6, S304.1)
f_{cs} = unfactored axial load P/A_e
y_t = distance from centroid to extreme fibre in tension
M_a = maximum moment due to unfactored loads

and, if axial compression is also present in the beam, the bending moment resulting from the position of the axial load P relative to the centroid of the cracked section is included in the determination of I_{cr}. For the most part, of course, beams are not subjected to calculable axial load.

EXAMPLE 3-16 *A five-course 190 hollow block beam is reinforced with one #25 bar at an effective depth of 900 mm and is fully grouted. The beam is simply-supported at its ends over a span of 6.0 m, and carries a service dead load (including self weight) of 10 kN/m and a live load of 10 kN/m. If $f_y=400$ MPa, $f'_m=10$ MPa, and Type S mortar is used, estimate the maximum deflection.*

The maximum deflection of a uniformly-loaded beam simply supported over a span L is

$$\delta = 5wL^4/(384EI)$$

and, for this beam

$$w = w_D + w_L = 10.0 + 10.0 = 20.0 \text{ kN/m}$$
$$L = 6.0 \text{ m}$$
$$E_m = 850f'_m = 8,500 \text{ MPa} < 20,000$$
$$I_{eff} = (M_{cr}/M_a)^3 I_0 + [1 - (M_{cr}/M_a)^3]I_{cr}$$

In the expression for I_{eff}, I_0 and I_{cr} are obtained from the previous examples as

$$I_0 = 17.1(10)^9 \text{ mm}^4$$
$$I_{cr} = 5.91(10)^9 \text{ mm}^4$$

and $M_{cr} = (\phi_m f_t + f_{cs})I_0/y_t$

$f_t = 0.70$ MPa (Table 6, S304.1), $\phi_m = 0.55$, $y_t = 472$ mm
and since there is no axial load $f_{cs} = 0.0$

Therefore

$$M_{cr} = [0.55(0.70) + 0.0](17.1)(10^9)/472 = 13.95 \text{ kN-m}$$
and $M_a = (w_D + w_L)L^2/8 = 20.0(6.0)^2/8 = 90.0 \text{ kN-m}$
Then $I_{eff} = (M_{cr}/M_a)^3 I_0 + [1 - (M_{cr}/M_a)^3]I_{cr}$
$$= (13.95/90.0)^3(17.1)(10)^9 + [1 - (13.95/90.0)^3](5.91)(10)^9$$
$$= 5.95(10)^9 \text{ mm}^4$$

Recalling from Equation 3-37 that allowance must be made for creep and, since there is no compression steel, and using $S=0.5$ for live load and $S=1.0$ for dead load, the maximum expected deflection due to service loads now becomes

$$\delta_{max} = 5(1+0.5)w_{LL}L^4/(384EI) + 5(1+1)w_{DL}L^4/(384EI)$$
$$= 5(1.5)(10.0)(6000)^4/[384(8500)(5.95)(10)^9]$$
$$+ 5(2.0)(10.0)(6000)^4/[384(8500)(5.95)(10)^9] = 11.7 \text{ mm}$$

Maximum deflection = 11.7 mm   <u>Ans.</u>

It is important that the designer keep close track of units. In the final calculation above, units involving N and mm were used exclusively (note that 20.0 kN/m is also 20.0 N/mm) so that the final deflection is obtained in mm. Since calculations for deflection are rather tedious, Chapter 4, which deals with design rather than analysis, simplifies the process. It should be noted that deflection calculations are generally not as critical for beams as they are for slender walls, where the *Pδ effect* may predominate. Slender walls are considered in detail in Chapter 5.

Control of Cracking

Like reinforced concrete structures, masonry structures crack. Cracking may be the result of volume changes (shrinkage, creep and thermal effects), support movement, and flexural stresses. Since excessive cracking can allow the ingress of corrosive elements and/or can affect the aesthetics of masonry, a measure of control on crack width must be exercised. The control of cracking due to volume changes and support movement is the subject of other discussions. This section deals with the control of cracking resulting from flexural tension.

Based on substantial research in reinforced concrete, cracking is controlled by ensuring that the quantity

$$z = f_s \sqrt[3]{d_c A}(10)^{-3} \tag{3-41}$$

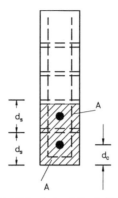

Fig. 3-27 Analysis of Crack Control

does not exceed 30 kN/mm for interior exposure and 25 kN/mm for exterior exposure (Clause 12.2.3.2.of S304.1), and 50 kN/mm for walls subjected to wind load (Clause 11.9). S304.1 notes that in especially aggressive environments, such as in coastal regions subjected to high winds and rain, this requirement may not be sufficiently restrictive.

In Equation (3-41), f_s is the stress in the reinforcing steel, which may be computed directly, or may be assumed as 60% of the yield stress; d_c is the cover on the tension steel measured from the centroid of the outermost bar; and A is the area of masonry surrounding the tensile reinforcement, having the same centroid as the tensile reinforcement and divided by the number of bars. This is illustrated in Fig. 3-27.

EXAMPLE 3-17 *Considering control of cracking, is the masonry beam of the previous example adequate for an interior use?*

Referring to Fig. 3-28(a)

$$d_c = 90 \text{ mm}$$
$$A = 190(180) = 34.2(10)^3 \text{ mm}^2$$
$$f_s = 0.6f_y = 0.6(400) = 240 \text{ MPa}$$
$$z = f_s\sqrt[3]{d_cA}(10)^{-3} = 240\sqrt[3]{90(34.2)(10)^3}(10)^{-3}$$
$$= 34.9 > 30.0 \hspace{3cm} \underline{\text{NG}}$$

The beam is not suitable for interior use.   <u>Ans.</u>

In the absence of a more rigorous analysis to determine the tensile stress in the steel, the designer at this point may choose to select two #20 bars ($A_s=2(300)$

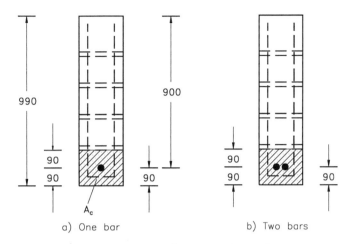

Fig. 3-28 Cross-Section of the Beam of Example 3-17

= 600mm^2), as shown in Fig. 3-28, instead of one #25 (A_s=500mm^2), in which case the steel stress will be reduced to 5/6 of its former value, and A is divided by the number of bars. That is, f_s = 5(240)/6 = 200 MPa. In that case

$$z = 200\sqrt[3]{90(34.2/2)(10)^3}\ (10)^{-3} = 23.1 < 30$$

and the beam is suitable for interior use.   Ans.

3-10   CLOSURE

This chapter has covered the analysis for flexure considering both strength and serviceability. This has involved, for strength (or resistance), theories that allow for the redistribution of stress and, for serviceability, analysis based on elastic principles that are considerably more complex. It was noted earlier that analysis is part of an iterative design process - namely, to try one section to see if it is adequate and, if not, to analyze another section - and, although the process may appear daunting, Chapter 4, dealing with the design for flexure, shows that the process is much simpler. The principal purpose of this chapter is to give the reader an understanding of the principles of the structural behaviour of masonry in flexure. With this in mind, it is important that the reader work through the problem section at the end of the chapter.

PROBLEMS 3

(The reader is reminded that actual masonry dimensions, which are 10 mm less than nominal dimensions, should be used in the calculations.)

(3-1)   A 200 x 600 (actual 190 x 590) masonry column is constructed of standard hollow concrete blocks and supports an axial service load of 150 kN. If the mean mortar bed width is 37.7 mm, what is the compressive stress in the masonry due to the service load when the column is (a) ungrouted? (b) fully grouted?

ANS. (a) f_m = 3.37 MPa (b) f_m = 1.34 MPa

(3-2)   A masonry wall is constructed of 200 mm standard hollow concrete blocks and carries an axial service load of 500 kN/m for a short period of time. If the mean mortar bed width is 37.7 mm, E_m = 10 000 MPa and E_s = 200 000 MPa, what are the stresses in the masonry and reinforcing steel due to the service load when the wall is:
(a) ungrouted?
(b) unreinforced but fully grouted?
(c) reinforced with #20 bars @400 mm on centres with only the reinforced cores grouted?
(d) reinforced with #20 bars @400 mm on centres and fully grouted?

ANS. (a) f_m = 6.63 MPa   (b) f_m = 2.63 MPa
        (c) f_m = 3.40 MPa, f_s = 68.0 MPa (d) f_m = 2.45 MPa, f_s = 48.96 MPa

(3-3)   If the load on the wall in problem 3-2 is of long duration and assuming that all of the service load were dead load, what are the compressive stresses?

ANS. (a) f_m = 6.63 MPa   (b) f_m = 2.63 MPa
        (c) f_m = 3.24 MPa, f_s = 97.12 MPa
        (d) f_m = 2.36 MPa, f_s = 70.84 MPa

(3-4)   A short 200 mm concrete block wall is subjected to a service dead load of 100 kN/m, live load of 50 kN/m and a wind load of p = 1.0 kN/m². What are the factored loads used in the design of the wall?
ANS. Factored dead load = 125 kn/m, factored live load = 75 kN/m, and factored wind load = 1.5 kN/m²

(3-5)   The wall in a warehouse is 6.0 m high and is constructed of 250 mm standard concrete masonry units which have a mean mortar bed width of 40.9 mm. If the wall is laterally supported top and bottom by the roof and floor, and if the axial loading, including self weight, on the wall is negligible, and if the wind

pressure is 1.0 kN/m^2, what is the maximum tensile stress in the wall due to the factored wind pressure
(a) when the wall is ungrouted?
(b) when the wall is unreinforced but fully grouted?

ANS. (a) $f_t = 0.99$ MPa (b) $f_t = 0.70$ MPa

(3-6)   If the wall of problem 3-5 supports an axial load of 40 kN/m (including self weight of wall), and if the wind pressure is 1.0 kN/m^2, what are the maximum tensile stresses in the wall due to the factored wind pressure.

ANS. (a) $f_t = 0.38$ MPa   (b) $f_t = 0.49$ MPa

(3-7)   A five-course 250 mm concrete masonry beam is reinforced with 2-#25 bars at an effective depth of 920 mm and fully grouted. If $f'_m = 10$ MPa, and $f_y = 400$ MPa, what is the resisting moment of the beam?

ANS. $M_r = 130.6$ kN-m

(3-8)   A singly-reinforced masonry beam is constructed from three courses of 200 mm concrete blocks and is fully grouted. If $f'_m = 10$ MPa and $f_y = 400$ MPa, and if the effective depth $d = 520$ mm,
(a) what steel area A_s gives a "balanced" beam?
(b) If precisely 326 mm^2 of reinforcement were used what would be the value the maximum safe resisting moment for the beam?

ANS. (a) $A_s = 326$ mm^2 (b) $M_r = 43.8$ kN-m

(3-9)   What is the maximum safe moment for the beam of Problem 3-8 if the reinforcement consists of 1-#15 bar.

ANS. $M_r = 30.2$ kN-m

(3-10)   Comparing Problem 3-9 where $A_s < A_{sb}$, with Problem 3-8, where the balanced steel area A_{sb} is used, comment on the effectiveness of additional tensile reinforcement in increasing the capacity of the beam.

ANS.   Increase in A_s (ΔA_s)   Increase in M (ΔM) $\Delta M / \Delta A_s$
              63 %   45%   71.4%

(3-11)   The free-standing masonry wall shown is constructed of 200 mm standard concrete block and is vertically reinforced with #15 bars @ 400 mm on centres at the centre of the block. It is fully grouted. If the unit strength is 20 MPa and f_y = 400 MPa, what is the maximum wind pressure p on the wall? Assume that the weight of the wall can be neglected.

ANS.   max. p = 1.93 kN/m²
        Note: Compare this results with Example 3-6 of Chapter 3

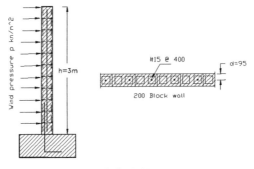

Prob. 3-11

(3-12) The five course 250 mm concrete masonry beam shown is simply-supported over a 5.0 m span and carries a central point load P. If the unit strength is 20 MPa and f_y = 400 MPa, and if the unit weight of masonry is 21.0 kN/m³, determine:
(a) the factored self weight of the beam
(b) the moment of resistance of the section
(c) the maximum value of the service live load P that may be placed on the beam.

ANS.   (a) 6.2 kN/m
        (b) M_r = 195 kN-m
        (c) max. P = 93.7 kN

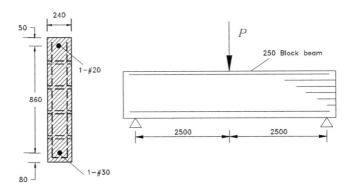

Prob. 3-12

(3-13) If the beam of Problem 3-12 were constructed to overhang one support a
distance of 3 m to carry a uniform superimposed live load of w kN/m as shown
below, what is the maximum safe value of w.

ANS.   max. $w = 12.6$ kN/m. Note that as the problem considers negative
bending, the top steel is in tension and the bottom steel in compression
at B.

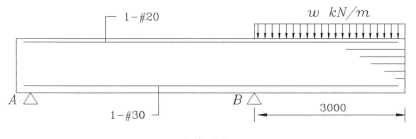

Prob. 3-13

(3-14) A four-course 250 mm concrete masonry beam is simply supported over a clear
span of 6.0 m and carries a central point service live load as shown. It may be
assumed that the beam is adequately reinforced for bending with steel at an
effective depth of 720 mm, and is fully grouted. If the unit strength is 20 MPa,
$f_y = 400$ MPa, and the unit weight of masonry is 21 kN/m³:
(a) What is the factored self weight of the beam?
(b) What is the maximum factored design shear force, and where does it occur?
(c) Is shear reinforcement required?
(d) What is the calculated required spacing of single-legged #10 stirrups, and the
actual spacing that would be used?

ANS.   (a) 4.98 kN/m
(b) max. $V_f = 78.85$ kN from support to 720 mm from support
(c) yes, max. $V_m = 47.3$ kN $< V_f = 78.85$ kN
(d) max. spacing calculated for max. V_f is $s = 582$, actual $s = 200$ mm
Note: remember to check that $s < d/2$.

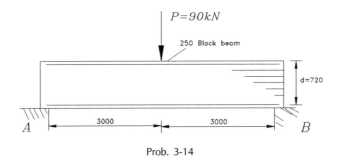

Prob. 3-14

(3-15)   If the point live load on the beam in Problem 3-14 is moved to the location
         shown:
         (a) What are the design shear force at the left and right ends of the beam, V_A and
             V_B?
         (b) Select a suitable arrangement of #10 shear reinforcement.

ANS.   (a) V_A = 101.35 kN V_B = 56.35 kN
        (b) use #10 single-legged stirrups @ 200 0.c.

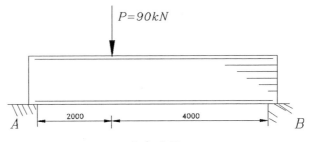

Prob. 3-15

CHAPTER 4

DESIGN OF FLEXURAL MEMBERS

4-1   DESIGN AND ANALYSIS

Structural design and analysis, although based on the same principles of mechanics and material behavior, differ considerably in execution. Design in the broadest sense starts from no more than the client's basic requirements and culminates in a set of detailed drawings from which a *safe, functional* and *economical* building can be constructed.   Analysis on the other hand is used to check whether a building, as designed, meets those criteria; and should the criteria not be satisfied, another cycle of design is undertaken. Analysis is therefore part of an iterative design process.

The total design procedure includes planning to satisfy functional requirements, structural layout and the selection of construction materials, determination of structural member sizes and their details, analysis to ensure that the structure is safe and economical, and the preparation of construction drawings. Inspection of construction might also be considered part of design, for it is through inspection that it can be determined whether the construction conforms to the details of the structural design - more specifically, to the requirements for safety.

The planning phase, the structural layout and the selection of the type of construction materials (masonry, structural steel, reinforced concrete etc.) require a background of experience from the designer, and are certainly beyond the scope of this book. The ability to determine member sizes and their details, on the other hand, follows directly from an understanding of the principles of analysis outlined in Chapter 3. In the present treatment of design it will be assumed that such key data as wall heights, beam spans, and loading are generally known; and that the design must produce such information as wall thicknesses, beam depths, reinforcement etc.

Without a handbook structural design can become a tedious process wherein the designer selects a trial section through approximate methods and then performs an analysis to check its efficiency, performing another cycle, if required, to improve the design. Design handbooks, in general, reduce the drudgery of trial-and-error by enabling the designer to make a more direct selection. However, it is not the intent of this book to emphasize handbook usage, a skill that can be acquired independently by the designer. Nevertheless the structural designer requires basic information regarding the geometry of standard masonry units, and for that purpose the section properties of standard two-core concrete block construction are given in Table 4-1. Once the principles of this chapter have been mastered, the designer can make effective use of Part 2, the design manual section, of this book.

4-2   FLEXURE OF UNREINFORCED MASONRY

Masonry walls are usually used to carry substantial in-plane compressive loads, a structural condition that is considered in Chapter 5. However, in the absence of significant axial compression the design for flexure of plain (unreinforced) masonry is governed by the tensile stresses, f_t. Since compression stresses are comparatively low, linear stress/strain behaviour can be assumed and the equation $f = M/S - P/A$ is used to calculate tensile stress. It was explained in Section 3-3 that for out-of-plane bending these tensile stresses develop either normal to or parallel with bed joints, and are calculated on the basis of *the section properties at the mortar joint*. This was also demonstrated in Examples 3-6 and 3-7 where a mean mortar bed width was used. More accurately, based on the actual geometry of the units, Table 4-1 gives a summary of the relevant section properties for standard concrete masonry walls with various amounts of grouting.

The following examples illustrate design for out-of-plane bending of unreinforced masonry.

EXAMPLE 4-1 *A free-standing plain concrete block wall, similar to that of Fig. 3-10, is 1.0 m high and is required to resist safely a wind pressure of 1.0 kN/m². Design a suitable wall using type S mortar.*

The factored wind pressure is

$$p_f = \alpha_L p = 1.5(1.0) = 1.50 \text{ kN/m}^2$$

and the maximum factored moment for a one metre width of wall is

Table 4-1
Properties of Concrete Masonry Walls per Metre Length*

Nominal Wall Thickness (mm)	Percent Solid	Min. Face Shell	Number of Grouted Cores/m	Weight** of Wall (kN/m²)	Properties at Bed Joint ***		
					A_e (mm²x10³)	I_x (mm⁴x10⁶)	S_x (mm³x10⁶)
200	54	32	0	2.11	75.4	442	4.66
			1	2.47	98.3	468	4.93
			2	2.83	121.2	494	5.20
			3	3.19	144.2	520	5.48
			4	3.55	167.1	546	5.75
			5	3.91	190.0	572	6.02
250	51	35	0	2.52	81.7	816	6.80
			1	3.00	113.4	883	7.36
			2	3.49	145.0	950	7.92
			3	3.97	176.7	1018	8.48
			4	4.46	208.3	1085	9.04
			5	4.94	240.0	1152	9.60
300	50	38	0	2.99	88.3	1341	9.25
			1	3.59	128.6	1479	10.20
			2	4.19	169.0	1617	11.15
			3	4.78	209.3	1756	12.11
			4	5.38	249.7	1894	13.06
			5	5.98	290.0	2032	14.01

*   Based on standard concrete blocks of Fig. 2-3 and Table 2-1.
** Based on mass density for both block and grout of 2100 kg/m³
    (note that lightweight block is also available).
*** These properties include the head joint and assume thorough grouting.

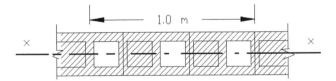

$$M_f = p_f h^2/2 = 1.50(1.0)^2/2 = 0.75 \text{ kN-m/m} = 0.75(10)^6 \text{ N-mm/m}$$

Referring to the *Notes* of Table 6 of S304.1, the flexural tensile strength, f_t, in a free-standing cantilever is limited to 0.1 MPa and the factored strength is $\phi_m f_t$ = 0.55(0.10) = 0.055 MPa.

If the self weight is not included in the calculations, the required section modulus is

$$S_x = M_f/f_t = \frac{0.75(10)^6}{0.055} = 13.6(10)^6 \text{ mm}^3/\text{m}$$

It can be seen from Table 4-1 that a fully grouted 300 wall would be required. However, as the self weight enhances the stability of the wall, it may be included in the calculations, but since the self weight is not known, a trial section must be analyzed.

Trial 1

Try a 250 ungrouted wall:

$$A_e = 81.7(10)^3 \text{ mm}^2/\text{m}, \quad S_x = 6.80(10)^6 \text{ mm}^3/\text{m}$$

Self weight = 2.52 kN/m² × height = 2.52(1.0) = 2.52 kN/m

It should be noted that S304.1 requires that where dead load is used to enhance the stability of a structure only 85% of the estimated dead load should be used in the calculations.

Factored self weight = 0.85(2.52) = 2.14 kN/m = 2.14(10)³ N/m

The maximum tensile stress then becomes

$$f_t = M_f/S - P_f/A_e = \frac{0.75(10)^6}{6.80(10)^6} - \frac{2.14(10)^3}{81.7(10)^3} = 0.084 \text{ MPa}$$

Since 0.084 MPa > 0.055 MPa, *the section is not adequate.*

Trial 2

Try a 300 ungrouted wall:

$$A_e = 88.3(10)^3 \text{ mm}^2/\text{m} \quad S_x = 9.25(10)^6 \text{ mm}^3/\text{m}$$

Factored self weight $= 0.85(2.99)(1.0) = 2.54$ kN/m

$$f_t = \frac{0.75(10)^6}{9.25(10)^6} - \frac{2.54(10)^3}{88.3(10)^3} = 0.052 \text{ MPa}$$

which is less than 0.055 MPa. Thus, *a 300 ungrouted wall is adequate.*

EXAMPLE 4-2   *If the wall in Example 4-1 is to be built from ungrouted and unreinforced 200 concrete blocks, devise a means whereby this can be accomplished satisfactorily.*

It is evident from Example 4-1 that the 200 block wall requires strengthening. This might be accomplished

a) by grouting in vertical reinforcement as shown in Fig. 4-1 (a), or
b) by providing vertical beams or pilasters, as shown in Fig. 4-1(b).

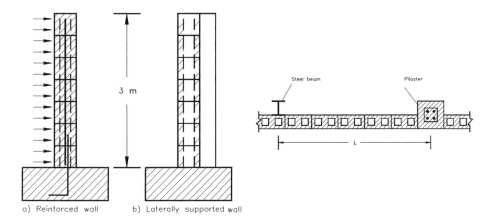

a) Reinforced wall   b) Laterally supported wall

Fig. 4-1 Strengthening of Masonry Wall

As grouting and reinforcement are excluded from the design, vertical steel supports could be provided and it then becomes a question of determining the spacing of the supports. The wall now supports a wind load over a horizontal span of L metres. Considering a 1.0 metre horizontal strip of wall and allowing for vertical control joints (which give a break in wall continuity) at the vertical supports, the moment in the masonry becomes

$$M_f = p_f L^2/8 = 1.50L^2/8 = 0.188L^2 \text{ kN-m/m}$$

Since the wall is no longer considered a free-standing cantilever and the wind is producing tension parallel with the mortar bed, the tensile strength for type S mortar (see Table 6, S304.1) is taken as 0.90 MPa. Noting from Table 4-1 that

$$S_x = 4.66(10)^6 \text{ mm}^3/\text{m}$$

the moment of resistance is

$$M_r = \phi_m f_t S_x = 0.55(0.90)(4.66)(10)^6 \text{ N-m/m} = 2.31 \text{ kN-m/m}$$

Equating the above value to the applied moment of $0.188L^2$ kN-m/m, the maximum spacing of vertical supports becomes

$$L = (\frac{2.31}{0.188})^{1/2} = 3.51 \text{ m}$$

Therefore, to retain the 200 modular nature of the masonry, *provide vertical supports at 3400 centres*. Note that since the wall is now designed to span horizontally it can be built as high as the vertical pilasters allow.

4-3   FLEXURE OF REINFORCED MASONRY

Masonry being considerably weaker in tension than in compression must be reinforced if significant bending is anticipated. This situation was analyzed in Sections 3-4, 3-5 and 3-6. The general case in the detailed design of beams is that the sizes of the opening to be spanned and the superimposed loads will be known, and the width, depth and detail of reinforcement must be determined. In many instances the beam is part of a masonry wall whose thickness has already been selected and consequently the width of the beam is frequently known.

Determination of masonry strength

Before proceeding with the detailed design the value of f'_m for the masonry should be determined. Given the compressive strength of the units and the mortar to be used (normally type S) values of f'_m for use in the design are obtainable from S304.1, Table 3 (for solid brick masonry), Table 5 (for concrete block), with the value of f'_m for hollow clay brick masonry to be determined by prism testing. Typical concrete block or hollow clay brick construction might use a unit with a compressive strength of 15 or 20 MPa and type S mortar, and reinforcement with specified yield strengths of 300 MPa or 400 MPa. The following example illustrates the determination of masonry strength.

EXAMPLE 4-3 *A masonry construction is to utilize concrete blocks with a unit compressive strength not less than 20 MPa, type S mortar, and grout conforming to S304.1. Determine the value of f'_m to be used in reinforced masonry design.*

From Table 5 of S304.1, for a unit strength of 20 MPa and type S mortar:

> *hollow masonry compressive strength f'_m* = 13 MPa
> *grouted masonry compressive strength f'_m* = 10 MPa

As noted in Chapter 2, S304.1 requires that the compressive strength of grout cylinders prepared in non-absorbent moulds should not be less than 10 MPa. Since masonry absorbs moisture from grout, the actual grout strength will be substantially higher - probably not less than the specified strength of the unit.

Determination of loading

Although the determination of loading in a building is a relatively straight-forward procedure, a reasonable estimate of loading on some beams may not be so simple. Frequently lintel beams are used to span openings in masonry walls, as shown in Fig. 4-2. In this instance, to design the beam for the total accumulated loading above the beam would impose an undue penalty, for if the lintel were removed, only a portion of the structure immediately above would collapse. In other words the masonry will form an *arch* over the opening. Arches, of course, require horizontal reactions and for this *arching action* to be effective, there must be sufficient masonry wall on each side of

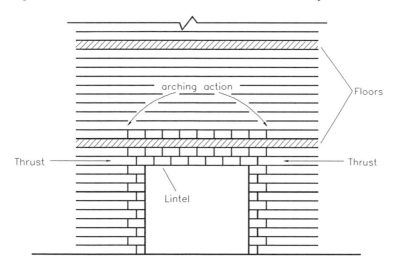

Fig. 4-2 Arching Action Over Openings

the opening to provide these reactions, or an appropriate tension tie must be provided. Although the situation is not covered by S304.1, it is frequently assumed by designers that where arching action is anticipated lintel beams should be designed to support any uniform loading that lies within the 45 degree triangle shown in Fig. 4-3(a), and the effects of concentrated loads (such as beam reaction) distributed at 60 degrees, as shown in Fig. 4-3(b). Arching action is given further consideration in a later chapter.

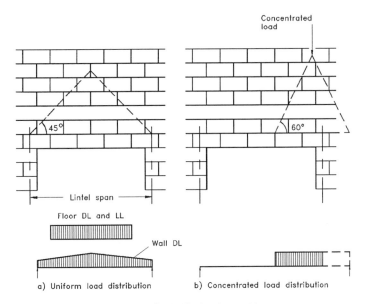

Fig. 4-3 Load Distribution by Arching

EXAMPLE 4-4 *A 200 × 200 lintel beam spans a 1600 opening in a fully-grouted 200 concrete block wall as shown in Fig. 4-3(a). The wall supports a number of 200 thick precast concrete floors, one of which is located one course above the lintel beam. If each floor imposes a uniform service load of 40kN/m ($D_L = 25\,kN/m$, $L_L = 15\,kN/m$) on the wall and if arching action may be assumed, determine the factored loading for which the beam should be designed.*

Note that the effective span is normally taken as the distance between the centres of bearing. A typical lintel bearing is 200 mm, but bearing stresses should be checked.

Effective span = 1600 + 200 = 1800 mm

From Table 4-1 the self weight of a fully grouted 200 wall is 3.91 kN/m². The calculations accompanying Fig. 4-4 are self explanatory.

Note that the significant aspect of arching in this example is not the precise determination of the loading shown in Fig. 4-4, but the fact that the loading from one floor out of several is considered in the design of the lintel. Recognizing the approximations involved in assuming 45 degree arching, and realizing that the floor load extends over most of the span, the designer would likely choose to design the beam for a uniformly distributed factored load of $53.75+4.40+0.98=59.13$ kN/m over the entire beam, thereby simplifying the calculations.

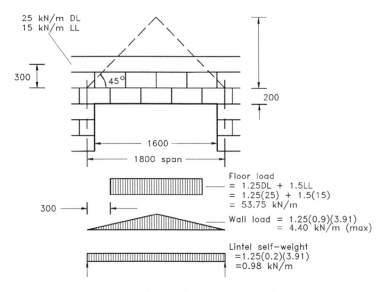

Fig. 4-4 Load Calculations of the Lintel Beam of Example 4-4

The design process

Once the span (centre-to-centre of supports) and the superimposed loading are known, the design proceeds as follows.

1. Determine the self weight of the beam, making a liberal estimate if the cross-sectional dimensions are not known, multiply each load by the appropriate load factor, and calculate the critical factored bending moment and shear forces.
2. Select a trial section (considering factored shear force and bending moment), either by an approximate method or through the use of design charts, and determine the required flexural reinforcement.
3. Check the self weight of the beam and repeat steps 1 and 2 if the total loading is significantly in error.

4.   Check the steel ratio $\rho = A_s/bd$ against the minimum value of $0.8/f_y$ (see Section 3-4) and make any required adjustment to the reinforcement. Check if the section satisfies Equation (3-15) for maximum area of tension reinforcement. Check that the reinforcement selected satisfies the bond and development requirements, and that it will fit into the rather limited space available.

5.   Check shear and design any required shear reinforcement.

6.   Check deflections and crack widths and design any miscellaneous connection hardware that may be required.

The selection of a suitable cross section can be a matter of experience, or the dimensions may have been selected previously from architectural considerations. Frequently the beam is a component part of a wall whose thickness has already been selected, in which case only the depth and reinforcement need be designed. Design charts such as the one shown in Fig. 4-5 are useful in determining suitable depths and amounts of reinforcement. Note that steel areas less than ρ_{min} are only 75% effective and that any steel area in excess of ρ_b is not considered in the calculation. Therefore, economical designs tend to be between these two values (shown in the broken lines in Fig. 4-5).

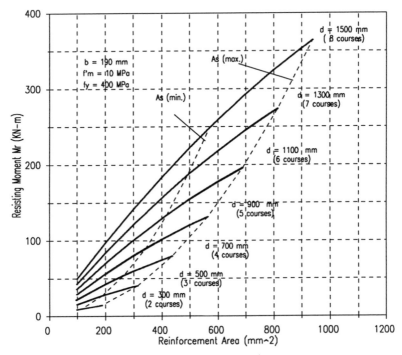

Fig. 4-5 Resisting Moment Chart

Should the designer not have access to a design handbook, approximate methods can be used effectively. It can be shown that for values of ρ between ρ_{min} and ρ_b the internal moment arm is closely approximated by $jd = 0.8d$, and a trial value of d will give a reasonable estimate of the required reinforcement. Since

$$M_r = Tjd = \phi_s A_s f_y jd, \quad M_r \geq M_f \text{ and } \phi_s = 0.85$$

and since

$$jd_{(approx.)} = 0.8d$$

the required steel area can be approximated as

$$A_s \approx \frac{M_f}{\phi_s f_y jd_{(approx.)}} = \frac{M_f}{0.85 f_y (0.8d)} \tag{4-1}$$

The value of ρ should then be checked to ensure that it falls between ρ_{min} and ρ_b, in which case the design will be adequate. If not, either a new depth is selected, or the steel area must be increased and a confirmatory analysis carried out before proceeding further.

The balanced case provides a useful reference for design, and from the principles outlined in Sections 3-4 and 3-5, it can be readily shown that the depth, a, of the equivalent rectangular stress block is

$$a = \frac{\phi_s \rho_b f_y d}{\phi_m \chi (0.85) f'_m} = \frac{0.85 \rho_b f_y d}{0.85 \phi_m \chi f'_m} = \frac{\rho_b f_y d}{\phi_m \chi f'_m} \tag{4-2}$$

Recalling that

$$M_r = \phi_s A_s f_y (d - a/2)$$

and substituting for a

$$M_r = \phi_s \rho_b f_y (1 - \frac{\rho_b f_y}{2\phi_m \chi f'_m}) bd^2$$

$$= K_b bd^2 \tag{4-3}$$

where

$$K_b = \phi_s \rho_b f_y (1 - \frac{\rho_b f_y}{2\phi_m \chi f'_m})$$

If K_b is known and a beam width has been selected a reference value of d is readily obtained.

Fig. 4-6 and 4-7, which show plots of ρ_{min}, ρ_b and K_b for two grades of steel and various masonry strengths f'_m, are included for reference. Table 4-2 gives more precise values for $f'_m = 10$ MPa and will be used in the following examples.

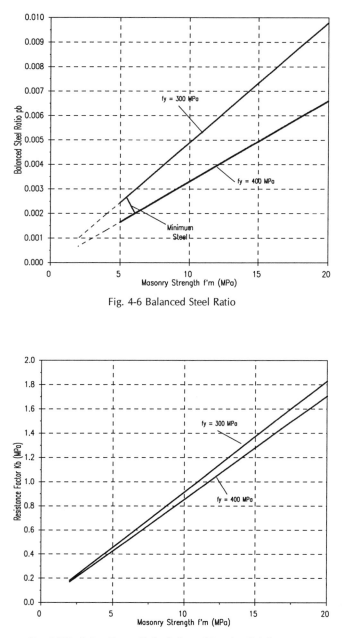

Fig. 4-6 Balanced Steel Ratio

Fig. 4-7 Resisting Factor K_b for Balanced Tension Reinforcement

Table 4-2
Limiting Values for $f'_m = 10$ MPa

χ	Steel Yield (MPa)	ϱ_{min}	ϱ_b	K_b (MPa)
0.5	300	0.00267	0.00489	0.9142
0.5	400	0.002	0.0033	0.8527
1.0	300	0.00267	0.00978	1.8284
1.0	400	0.002	0.0066	1.7054

EXAMPLE 4-5 *Perform the flexural design of a masonry beam to carry a total factored moment (inclusive of self weight) of 70 kN-m, using 200 concrete blocks with a unit compressive strength of 20 MPa, type S mortar, and reinforcement with a specific yield of 400 MPa. Assume a 90 mm cover to centre of steel.*

From Table 5 of S304.1, $f'_m = 10.0$ MPa for grouted masonry with type S mortar.

Three methods are listed below.

a) By trial-and-error

Try a 3-course beam

$$d = 590 - 90 = 500 \text{ mm}$$
$$jd \approx 0.8d$$

Assuming $\rho \leq \rho_b$

$$A_s \approx \frac{M_f(\text{N-mm})}{\phi_s f_y(0.8d)} = \frac{70(10)^6}{0.85(400)(0.8)(500)} = 515 \text{ mm}^2$$

Check: $\rho = 515/[190(500)] = 0.0054 > 0.0033 = \rho_b$ (see Table 4-2) <u>NG</u>

Try a 4-course beam

then $d = 790 - 90 = 700$ mm

$$A_s \approx \frac{70(10)^6}{0.85(400)(0.8)(700)} = 368 \text{ mm}^2$$

Check: $\rho = 368/[190(700)] = 0.00276 < 0.0033 = \rho_b$
$$> 0.002 = 0.8/f_y = \rho_{min} \qquad \underline{OK}$$

The steel area is adequate. One could therefore use a *4-course beam with 2-#15 bars* $(A_s = 400 \; mm^2)$.

b) *Using K_b*

Using the balanced case as a reference:
from Fig. 4-7 or Table 4-2, $K_b = 0.8527$

$$M_r = K_b b d^2$$

or

$$70(10)^6 = 0.8527(190)d^2$$

which gives a minimum value of $d = 657$ mm

Try a 4-course beam and, as in *a)*, 2-#15 bars are required.

Note in *a)* and *b)* that because the approximation $jd = 0.8d$ was used, the section should be analyzed.

Check:

$$\rho = \frac{400}{190(700)} = 0.00301 > 0.002 = \frac{0.8}{400} = \rho_{min} \qquad \underline{\text{OK}}$$

Since $\rho \leq \rho_b$, the steel yields and $f_s = f_y$. Therefore, from Fig. 4-8

$$a = \frac{A_s f_y}{\phi_m \chi f'_m b} = \frac{400(400)}{0.55(0.5)(10)(190)} = 306$$

$$M_r = \phi_s A_s f_y (d - a/2) = 0.85(400)(400)(700 - 306/2)$$
$$= 74.4(10)^6 \; \text{N-mm} = 74.4 \; \text{kN-m}$$

Since the resisting moment $M_r = 74.4$ kN-m is greater than the applied factored moment $M_f = 70.0$ kN-m, *use a 4-course beam with 2-#15 bars*.

Note that the use of the balanced case serves as a possible guide to an efficient section and that the 4-course beam is not the only possible solution.

c) *Using design charts*

From Fig. 4-5 it can be seen that a number of depths, of four or more courses, are possible (a complete set of beam design diagrams are provided in Part 2 of this book).

i)   Four-course beam $d = 700$ mm, $A_s = 375$ mm^2
ii) Five-course beam $d = 900$ mm, $A_s = 275$ mm^2
    In this case the steel area of 275 mm^2 is less than $\rho_{min}bd$ and should therefore be increased.

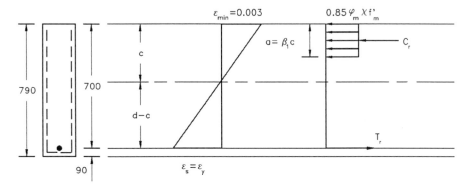

Fig. 4-8 Flexural Analysis of the Beam of Example 4-5

S304.1 dictates that the area of steel should not be less than ρ_{min} or alternatively be one third greater than that obtained from the analysis.

$$\text{Required } A_s = 1.33(275) = 366 \text{ mm}^2 > 342 \text{ mm}^2 \ (\rho_{min})$$

Similarly, a six-course beam ($d = 1100$ mm) or a seven-course beam ($d = 1300$ mm) could be used with steel ratios that satisfy the minimum requirements of S304.1. However, the use of ρ less than ρ_{min} is not recommended since it could lead to brittle failure if the computed flexural strength of the beam is less than the bending moment required to crack the section. Finally, the actual beam size may depend on shear or other considerations, but, in any case, values of ρ greater than ρ_b are not allowed by S304.1.

EXAMPLE 4-6 *Perform the flexural design of the reinforced masonry beam shown in Fig. 4-9 using normal-weight concrete blocks, $f'_m = 10$ MPa, $f_y = 400$ MPa.*

Estimate self weight

Use a unit weight of 20.5 kN/m^3 or Table 4-1.
Assuming a fully-grouted 6-course beam,

$$\text{self weight} = 20.5(0.29)(1.2) = 7.13 \text{ kN/m}$$
$$\text{(or, from Table 4-1: } (5.98)(1.2) = 7.18 \text{ kN/m)}$$

Total factored load

$$w_f = 1.5(9.0) + 1.25(7.2) = 22.5 \text{ kN/m}$$

Applied factored moment

$$M_f = w_f L^2/8 = 22.5(10.0)^2/8 = 281.3 \text{ kN-m}$$

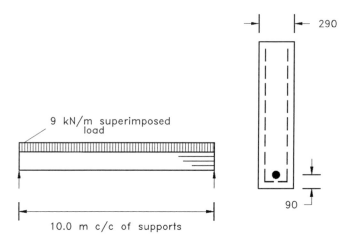

Fig. 4-9 Reinforced Masonry Beam of Example 4-6

a) By trial

Using $d = 1100$ mm for a 6-course beam and assuming $\rho \leq \rho_b$

$$A_s \approx \frac{M_f}{\phi_s f_y 0.8d} = \frac{281.3(10)^6}{0.85(400)(0.8)(1100)} = 940 \text{ mm}^2$$

Check: $\rho = 940/[290(1100)] = 0.00295 < 0.0033 = \rho_b$
$$> 0.002 = \rho_{min} \qquad \underline{\text{OK}}$$

Try 2-#25 bars ($A_s = 1000 \text{ mm}^2$).

Since A_s was calculated using an approximate value of jd, the section can now be analyzed to check whether the reinforcement selected provides an adequate resistance.

The depth of the equivalent rectangular stress block is

$$a = \frac{A_s f_y}{\phi_m \chi f'_m b} = \frac{1000(400)}{0.55(0.5)(10)(290)} = 501\,mm$$

$$M_r = \phi_s A_s f_y(d - a/2) = 0.85(1000)(400)(1100 - 501/2)$$
$$= 289 \text{ kN-m} > M_f = 281.3 \qquad\qquad \text{OK}$$

Since the resisting moment $M_r > M_f$ the beam is adequate.

b) Using charts

The chart for $b=190$ (Fig. 4-5) can also be used for this design

Assuming a 6-course beam with $M_f = 281.3$ kN-m, a 190 width of a 290 beam carries a bending moment of

$$M = 281.3(190/290) = 184.3 \text{ kN-m}$$

From Fig. 4-5 it can be seen that a 6-course beam can be used. The required steel area for 190/290 of the beam is 620 mm^2, and for the 290 beam

$$A_s = (290/190)(620) = 946 \text{ mm}^2$$

A 6-course beam with 2-#25 (A_s = 1000 mm^2) could be used.

It is left for the reader to verify that if a 7-course beam were to be used, Fig.4-5 leads to a required steel area of 790 mm^2.

EXAMPLE 4-7 *Design a free-standing 200 block wall 3.0 m high to resist safely a factored wind pressure of 2.0 kN/m^2. Use 20 MPa units, type S mortar, f_y = 300 MPa.*

Considering a 1.0 m vertical strip, and neglecting the self-weight, the maximum factored wind moment at the base is

$$M_f = \rho_f h^2/2 = (2)(3.0)^2/2 = 9.0 \text{ kN-m/m}$$

S304.1 limits the flexural tensile strength, f_t, in free-standing walls to 0.1 MPa, and if an unreinforced wall is contemplated, the required section modulus is

$$S_x = M_f/f_t = 9.0(10)^6/0.1 = 90(10)^6 \text{ mm}^3/\text{m}$$

Referring to Table 4-1, an unreinforced and fully grouted 200 mm block wall is not adequate and reinforcing steel must be used. Table 5 of S304.1 shows that the value of f'_m to be used in design can vary from 13 MPa for a hollow wall to 10 MPa for full grouting. Since some grouting is required, $f'_m = 10$ MPa may conservatively be assumed.

Assuming that $\rho \le \rho_b$ and placing the steel at the middle of the wall, the effective depth is

$$d = (190)/2 = 95 \text{ mm}$$

and

$$jd_{(approx.)} = 0.8(95) = 76.0 \text{ mm}$$

therefore, the approximate steel area is

$$A_s \approx \frac{M_f}{\phi_s f_y jd_{(approx.)}} = \frac{9.0(10)^6}{0.85(300)(76.0)} = 464 \text{ mm}^2/\text{m}$$

Check: $\rho = 464/[1000(95)] = 0.00488 < 0.00489 = \rho_b$
                                     $> 0.00267 = \rho_{min}$ <u>OK</u>

Recalling that masonry cores occur at intervals of 200 mm, a number of vertical bar arrangements are possible, and it is left to the reader to verify the steel area per meter associated with each arrangement.

> #10 bars @ 200 c/c (A_s = 500 mm^2/m)
> #15 bars @ 400 c/c (A_s = 500 mm^2/m)
> #20 bars @ 600 c/c (A_s = 500 mm^2/m)
> 2-#20 bars in 2 cores @ 1200 c/c (A_s = 500 mm^2/m)

Note that an analysis of a 1000 mm width of wall section using a steel area of 500 mm^2 shows that the depth to the neutral axis is 34 mm. Recalling that the mean mortar bed width of the 200 block is about 38 mm, then the neutral axis falls within the mortar bed, and the analysis is that of a rectangular section. Had the neutral axis fallen below the mortar bed and not all cores been filled then a tee-beam analysis would have been required. Note also that dowels to match the wall reinforcement must project from the foundation, as shown in Fig. 4-10, which also shows the wall reinforced with 2-#20 bars spaced at 1200 centres.

The reinforcing arrangement shown in Fig. 4-10 gives a series of vertical beams spaced at 1200 centres. It can be seen that the wall must be capable of spanning horizontally between the reinforced cores, a fact that was proven in Example 4-2. Note, however, that whereas the reinforcement is equivalent to 500 mm^2/m, it is in fact 600 mm^2 every 1.2 m. Note also that S304.1 Clause 5.2.1.1 limits the space between vertical reinforcement to 2.4 m along the wall and Clause 11.1.3.1 imposes a limit on the effective width of wall sections reinforced with a single reinforcing bar to the lesser of the spacing between bars or four times the wall thickness. This requirement is for walls constructed in normal running bond - that is, units overlapping in successive courses, as shown in Figs. 1-2, 2-1 and 2-2.

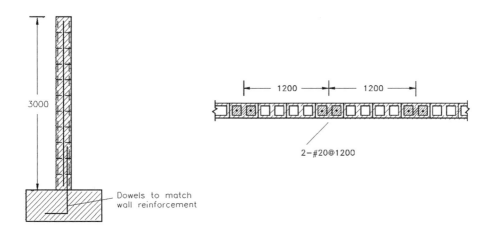

Fig. 4-10 Reinforcement Arrangement

Each vertical beam reinforced with 500 mm^2 then becomes effectively 800 mm (or more accurately, 4 × 190 = 760 mm) wide and, according to S304.1, should be analyzed as such. However, Clause 11.1.3.1 is clearly intended to cover instances of locally-applied moment (as at eccentric beam reactions) or concentrated lateral loads, and is less likely to be applicable to the more favourable conditions of wind loading.

On the other hand, Clause 11.1.3.1 requires for *stack pattern* construction that the effective width of the section in flexure be no more than the actual length of wall reinforced. The reason for this limitation is clear since stack pattern (occasionally selected by architects for its appearance) features units that are stacked directly above the units below with no overlap, and the load-sharing characteristic of running bond is, therefore, lost. The reader is cautioned that when ambiguity is encountered, and experience is lacking, it is better to err on the safe side.

Although the question of flexural crack width is considered in a later section it is worth commenting that the tensile reinforcement in Example 4-7 being closer to the neutral axis than to the tension face of the wall will produce relatively large crack widths at the surface. Flexural cracking will occur at the horizontal mortar joints and it can be shown by a relatively simple calculation that crack widths in the order of 0.3 mm can be expected at the base of the wall. While this crack width is comparatively large it should be borne in mind that peak wind loads are of short duration and moisture ingression into the joints will not be serious as if the loading were sustained. The situation could be alleviated by placing the vertical bars closer to the face shell, and while this detail is frequently shown in structural drawings it is difficult to accomplish in practice. The wall is constructed by placing concrete blocks over the dowels and then building to the full 3.0 m height. At that time the reinforcing bars are placed in the cores and the cores grouted. For 200 walls the reinforcement is likely to be, on average, at the mid-thickness. Crack widths can also be reduced by using more reinforcement, since this reduces the tensile stress in the steel. In this example large diameter dowels could have been used to control crack width.

4-4   DOUBLY-REINFORCED SECTIONS

From the analysis given in Section 3-6, it was shown that compression reinforcement can be used to add to the flexural resistance of reinforced masonry.

Compression reinforcement can be used when the depth of the beam is severely restricted and the amount of tension steel required exceeds the maximum quantity permitted by S304.1 for singly-reinforced beams. Compression reinforcement is frequently used in small lintel beams where the main purpose is to provide anchorage for the web reinforcement. If deflection problems are anticipated in a beam, the inclusion of compressive steel will inhibit masonry creep and reduce the long-term deflection.

The flexural resistance of doubly-reinforced sections can be estimated by superimposing the resistance of a singly-reinforced section having a steel area A_{s1} on the resistance of a beam having the remaining steel area A_{s2} in the tension zone and steel area A'_s in the compression zone as shown in Fig. 4-11.

Assuming the compression steel yields, equilibrium of beam 2 gives

$$A_{s2} = A'_s$$

For equilibrium in beam 1

$$\phi_s A_{s1} f_y = 0.85 \phi_m \chi f'_m ba$$

Since $\phi_s = 0.85$ and $A_{s1} = A_s - A'_s$

then $a = f_y(A_s - A'_s)/(\phi_m \chi f'_m b)$

and the total resisting moment of the section is

$$M_r = M_{r1} + M_{r2}$$

$$= \phi_s A_{s1} f_y (d - a/2) + A'_s \phi_s f_y (d - d') \qquad (4\text{-}4)$$

$$= \phi_s (A_s - A'_s) f_y [d - \frac{f_y (A_s - A'_s)}{2\phi_m \chi f'_m b}] + \phi_s A'_s f_y (d - d')$$

$$= \phi_s (\rho - \rho') f_y [1 - (\frac{\rho - \rho'}{2\phi_m \chi})(\frac{f_y}{f'_m})] bd^2 + \phi_s \rho' f_y (1 - d'/d) bd^2$$

This equation can be presented in a form similar to that of Equation (4-3) for singly-reinforced beams.

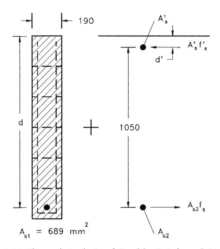

Fig. 4-11 Flexural Analysis of Doubly Reinforced Section

$$M_r = K_r bd^2 + K'_r bd^2$$

or

$$M_r = (K_r + K'_r) bd^2 \qquad (4\text{-}5)$$

where

$$K_r = \phi_s (\rho - \rho') f_y [1 - \frac{\rho - \rho'}{(2\phi_m \chi)(f'_m / f_y)}]$$

and

$$K'_r = \phi_s \rho' f_y (1 - d'/d)$$

Fig. 4-12 shows plots of K'_r and ρ' for various d'/d ratios, assuming that the compression reinforcement yields. Table 4-3 gives more precise values of compression reinforcement ratio ρ' for $f_y=400$ MPa.

This method can be used in practice in cases where the compression reinforcement does not yield since the error introduced is small. However, an exact solution can be obtained and is similar to that introduced in Section 3-6.

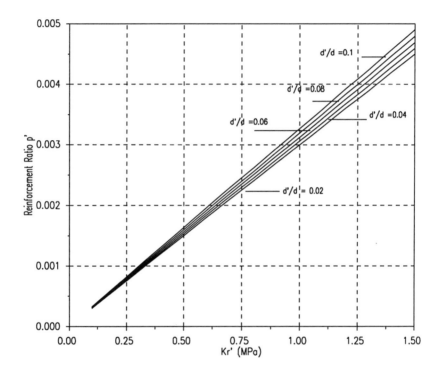

Fig . 4-12 Resistance Factor K'_r for Compression Reinforcement

EXAMPLE 4-8 *Design a six-course, 200 block masonry beam to resist a total factored moment of 225 kN-m. Use f'$_m$=10 MPa, f$_y$=400 MPa, d=1100 mm and d'=50 mm.*

It can be seen from Fig. 4-5 that $M_r = 225$ kN-m for a six-course beam falls beyond $\rho_{max} = \rho_b$ permitted by S304.1 for singly-reinforced beams. The use of compression reinforcement can now be tried to increase the moment capacity of the specified section.

Table 4-3
Compression Steel Ratio ρ' for Resistance Factor K'_r

K'_r (MPa)	d'/d				
	0.02	0.04	0.06	0.08	0.10
0.1	0.00030	0.00031	0.00031	0.00032	0.00033
0.2	0.00060	0.00061	0.00063	0.00064	0.00065
0.3	0.00090	0.00092	0.00094	0.00096	0.00098
0.4	0.00120	0.00123	0.00125	0.00128	0.00131
0.5	0.00150	0.00153	0.00156	0.00160	0.00163
0.6	0.00180	0.00184	0.00188	0.00192	0.00196
0.7	0.00210	0.00215	0.00219	0.00224	0.00229
0.8	0.00240	0.00245	0.00250	0.00256	0.00261
0.9	0.00270	0.00276	0.00282	0.00288	0.00294
1.0	0.00300	0.00306	0.00313	0.00320	0.00327
1.1	0.00330	0.00337	0.00344	0.00352	0.00360
1.2	0.00360	0.00368	0.00376	0.00384	0.00392
1.3	0.00390	0.00398	0.00407	0.00416	0.00425
1.4	0.00420	0.00429	0.00438	0.00448	0.00456
1.5	0.00450	0.00460	0.00469	0.00480	0.00490
1.6	0.00480	0.00490	0.00501	0.00512	0.00523
1.7	0.00510	0.00521	0.00532	0.00544	0.00556
1.8	0.00540	0.00552	0.00563	0.00575	0.00588
1.9	0.00570	0.00582	0.00595	0.00607	0.00621
2.0	0.00600	0.00613	0.00626	0.00639	0.00654
2.1	0.00630	0.00643	0.00657	0.00671	0.00686
2.2	0.00660	0.00674	0.00688	0.00703	0.00719
2.3	0.00690	0.00705	0.00720	0.00735	0.00752
2.4	0.00720	0.00735	0.00751	0.00767	0.00784
2.5	0.00750	0.00766	0.00782	0.00799	0.00817
2.6	0.00780	0.00797	0.00814	0.00831	0.00850
2.7	0.00810	0.00827	0.00845	0.00863	0.00882
2.8	0.00840	0.00858	0.00876	0.00895	0.00915
2.9	0.00870	0.00889	0.00907	0.00927	0.00948
3.0	0.00900	0.00919	0.00939	0.00959	0.00980

Using the balanced case as a reference, $A_{s1}=689$ mm^2 (see Fig. 4-11) which from Fig. 4-5 leads to a moment of resistance, M_{r1}, of about 195 kN-m. There is now a moment deficiency of

$$M_{r2} = M_r - M_{r1} = 225 - 195 = 30.0 \text{ kN-m}$$

The moment M_{r2} corresponds to a resistance factor

$$K'_r = M_{r2}/bd^2 = 30.0(10)^6/190(1100)^2 = 0.13 \text{ MPa}$$

By linear interpolation from Table 4-3, the compression reinforcement ratio for $K'_r=0.13$ and $d'/d=0.05$ is $\rho'=0.000402$. Therefore,

$$A'_s = \rho'bd = 0.000402(190)(1100) = 84 \text{ mm}^2$$

and since

$$A_{s2} = A'_s$$

$$A_{s2} = A'_s = 84 \text{ mm}^2$$

This gives a trial section with

$$A_s = A_{s1} + A'_s = 689 + 84 = 773 \approx 800 \text{ mm}^2$$
$$A'_s = 84 \approx 100 \text{ mm}^2$$

which, upon analysis yields

$$M_r = 233.7 \text{ kN-m} > 225 = M_f \qquad \underline{\text{OK}}$$

Use a 6 course beam with 1-#10 top bar and 1-#20 and 1-#25 bottom bars.

It is interesting to note that the same beam reinforced with 1-#20 top and 2-#20 bottom bars leads to a moment of resistance, $M_r=207.6$ kN-m, for the same amount of steel; and that 1-#25 top and bottom (total steel area = 1000 mm^2) leads to $M_r=178.5$ kN-m. This shows that compression steel contributes less than tension steel to moment of resistance.

4-5   NON-RECTANGULAR SECTIONS

Because floors do not form an integral part of beams as they do in reinforced concrete construction, non-rectangular masonry beam sections are rarely encountered. However, shear wall construction frequently utilizes tees and other shapes where walls intersect, but in this case the sections are under combined axial load and bending, a situation that is considered in a later chapter. It was noted in Example 4-7, when dealing with out-of-plane bending of masonry walls, that the compression zone might extend into the cores, and if some of the cores were unfilled a tee-beam analysis might be required. However, instances are rare as it is generally found that for $\rho < \rho_b$ the compression zone falls within the face shell, and $\rho > \rho_b$ is not permitted by S304.1. In the unlikely event that a special analysis is required it should follow the principles outlined in Section 3-4, bearing in mind that the area of the compression zone will be influenced by the shape of the cross-section, as shown in Fig. 4-13.

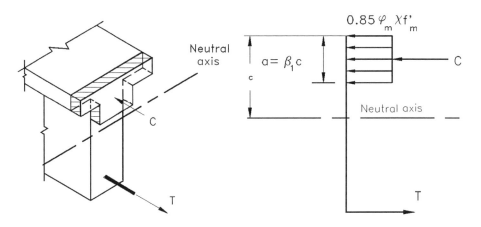

Fig. 4-13 Analysis of Non-Rectangular Section

4-6   CURTAILMENT OF FLEXURAL STEEL

It is evident that the same quantity of flexural reinforcement required at maximum moment sections is not required through sections of lesser moment, and it may be considered economical *to terminate* (*cut off* or *curtail*) some of the bars at appropriate locations. For example, the free-standing 200 concrete block wall of Example 4-7 requires 2-#20 @ 1200, as shown in Fig. 4-10, for the maximum moment at the base of the wall. However, the moment reduces rapidly above the base and at some location the reinforcement can be reduced to 1-#20 @ 1200. While the theoretical curtailment point is readily obtained by equating the applied factored moment $p_f h^2/2$ to the resisting moment $\phi_s A_s f_y jd$, bars cannot be terminated precisely at this point as other factors must be considered.

Clauses 5.5.6 to 5.5.8 inclusive, of S304.1, list the requirements for bar curtailment, which are largely self-explanatory. For example, 5.5.6.3 requires that, except for supports, a terminating bar be extended a distance at least equal to the effective depth, but not less than 12 bar diameters, beyond theoretical curtailment. This clause ensures a more favourable stress transfer from continuing bar to grout to terminated bar. Bars terminating in a tension zone represent a discontinuity that can initiate cracking, which in turn can impair the shear strength of the section. S304.1 recognizes that shear forces in beams are generally high in areas of reduced moment and imposes more stringent conditions than usual on the shear requirements at bar terminations in tension zones. That particular situation is covered by Clause 5.5.6.5.

Because of restricted space in concrete masonry beams the number of reinforcing bars is limited, more than two rarely being used. If one of these bars is terminated the number of bars, and consequently the resisting moment, is halved. For a simple beam with uniform load a moment of half the maximum moment occurs at one eighth of the span from the support. Extending the terminating bar a distance d beyond the theoretical curtailment leaves little, if any, saving in steel, and it is generally not practicable to curtail the flexural steel in these situations. However, the principles may be applicable in other situations.

Some of the principles of bar curtailment are illustrated in Example 4-9, which represents a situation different to that of the simple beam, and it is left to the reader to become familiar with the requirements of S304.1.

EXAMPLE 4-9 *The free-standing concrete block wall of Example 4-7 requires 2-#20 @ 1200 vertical reinforcement, as shown in Fig. 4-10, to resist the maximum moment at the base. Determine at what height from the top of the wall the steel may be reduced to 1-#20 @ 1200.*

The factored moment at the base of the 3.0 m wall is

$$2.0(3.0)^2/2 = 9.0 \text{ kN-m}$$

and this moment is adequately resisted by 2-#20 @ 1200. If half of the steel is curtailed the continuing steel should be checked against ρ_{min} as follows.

$$A_s = (500)/2 = 250 \text{ mm}^2/\text{m}$$

$$\rho = 250/[1000(95)] = 0.00263 < 0.00267 = 0.8/300 = \rho_{min}$$

and, as $\rho < \rho_{min}$ only $0.75A_s$ can be considered effective (see Section 3-4).

It may be stated with reasonable accuracy that the resisting moment is proportional to the effective area of reinforcement. Then

$$M/M_{max} = M/9.0 = 0.75(250)/500$$

which gives a resisting moment of $M = 3.38$ kN-m/m and, if h is the distance from the top of the wall to the theoretical curtailment

$$M = 3.38 = 2.0h^2/2 \; ; \; h = 1.84 \text{ m}$$

Recalling that terminating steel should extend at least d (95mm), but not less than 12 bar diameter ($12 \times 20 = 240$ mm), beyond theoretical curtailment, half of the 2-#20 @ 1200 may be terminated at 1840 - 240 = 1600 mm from the top of the wall.

Terminate 1-#20 @ 1200 at 1600 from the top of the wall.

Note that a shear check should be performed to ensure that the requirement of S304.1, Clause 5.5.6.5(a) has not been violated. This check is carried out in Example 4-11.

4-7   SHEAR

It will be recalled from Section 3-7 that maximum shear forces in beams are calculated at a distance equal to the effective depth of the beams from the face of the support, and that this maximum factored shear force, V_f, is assumed to apply from this point through the support. In that section it was also pointed out that when V_f exceeds the shear resistance of the masonry, V_m, shear reinforcement must be provided to carry the excess shear. The shear strength contributed by masonry for continuously grouted beams is calculated from Equation (3-24) as

$$V_m = 0.2\lambda\phi_m\sqrt{f'_m}(1.0 - \frac{d-400}{1500})b_w d$$

$$\geq 0.12\lambda\phi_m\sqrt{f'_m}b_w d$$

$$\leq 0.2\lambda\phi_m\sqrt{f'_m}b_w d$$

where λ varies from 1.0 for normal weight units to 0.75 for lightweight units and $\phi_m = 0.55$. The upper and lower limits to V_m ($0.2\lambda\phi_m(\sqrt{f'_m})b_w d$ and $0.12\lambda\phi_m(\sqrt{f'_m})b_w d$ respectively) apply to beams of depth less than 400 mm and greater than 1000 mm respectively. Thus, for 200 mm courses the factor of 0.2 applies to one and two-course beams, 0.173 and 0.146 to three and four-course beams respectively, and 0.12 to beams five or more courses.

The contribution of shear reinforcement is calculated from Equation (3-26) as

$$V_s = \phi_s f_y A_v d/s$$

and the total factored shear resistance of the masonry member is the sum of V_m and V_s

$$V_r = V_m + V_s \geq V_f$$

When $V_f > 0.5V_m$ a minimum amount of shear reinforcement, $A_v = 0.35b_w s/f_y$, must be provided; and to limit the total shear on the section

$$V_s = V_f - V_m \leq 0.36\phi_m \sqrt{f'_m}\, b_w d$$

The designer should be familiar with the requirements of Clauses 5.5.9 and 12.2 of S304.1 relating to shear reinforcement design and details, and should note that where shear reinforcement is required it shall be continued for a distance equal to the effective depth beyond the point where it is no longer required.

The reader may have inferred from Section 4-3 that cross-sectional dimensions of a beam are determined from flexural considerations alone. However, this is generally not the case and shear can also figure prominently in the selection of a section. For example, it is frequently desirable to avoid shear forces greater than one half of the shear strength provided by masonry, V_m, so that shear reinforcement is not required. In any case a violation of the factored shear resistance requires more shear reinforcement and/or the selection of a larger (b and/or d) beam section.

When shear reinforcement is required it is provided according to Equation (3-27)

$$A_v \geq \frac{V_s s}{\phi_s f_y d}$$

in the form of single or two-legged stirrups, and the bar size normally used is #10. In masonry construction using standard two-core units the spacing of the stirrups is governed by the 200 mm core spacing. Having selected a particular stirrup size the spacing can be determined from Equation (3-28) as

$$s \leq \phi_s A_s f_y d/V_s$$

and, of course, the spacing should not exceed the lesser of $d/2$ or 600 mm.

EXAMPLE 4-10 *The fully grouted eight-course 200 mm normal weight masonry beam shown in Fig. 4-14 may be considered simply supported and carries a total factored load (including self weight) of 50.0 kN/m. Assuming the beam to be adequately reinforced for flexure, design any shear reinforcement required. The masonry strength f'$_m$ = 10 MPa and f$_y$ = 400 MPa for #10 bars.*

The maximum shear force is calculated at a distance d from the face of the support, and assuming d = 1500 for an 8-course beam,

$$V_f(\text{max}) = 50[0.5(9) - 1.5] = 150.0 \text{ kN}$$

Since the beam is more than a five-course (and with the grout interrupted by cross webs a further factor of 0.6 is applied), the factored shear resistance of the masonry is

$$V_m = 0.12\lambda\phi_m\sqrt{f'_m}b_w d(0.6)$$
$$= 0.12(1.0)(0.55)(\sqrt{10})(190)(1500)(0.6)$$
$$= 35.7 \text{ kN}$$

Since $0.5V_m = 0.5(35.7) = 17.85$ kN < 150.0 kN $= V_f$, shear reinforcement is required at a spacing $s \leq d/2$ ($= 750$ mm) and, because of the 200 mm of spacing cores, the maximum spacing is 600 mm.

Try #10 single-legged stirrups, $f_y=400$ MPa

The shear reinforcement must provide a resistance of at least

$$V_s = V_f - V_m = 150.0 - 35.7 = 114.3 \text{ kN}$$

Recalling that

$$V_s = \phi_s A_v f_y d/s = 0.85(100)(400)(1500)/s = 51.0(10)^6/s \text{ N}$$

That is, $V_s = 114.3(10)^3 = 51.0(10)^6/s$
or $s = 51.0(10)^6/114.3(10)^3 = 446$ mm

Therefore, use #10 single-legged stirrups @ 400 o.c.

The spacing can be increased to the maximum of 600 mm at

$$V_s = 51.0(10)^6/600 = 85.0 \text{ kN}$$

That is,
$$V_f = V_s + V_m = 85.0 + 35.7 = 120.7 \text{ kN}$$

The minimum area of steel can now be checked as

$$A_v = 0.35b_w s/f_y = 0.35(190)(600)/400 = 99.75 < 100 \text{ mm}^2 \quad \underline{\text{OK}}$$

Shear reinforcement is theoretically no longer required at the point where $V_f=V_m=35.7$ kN. However, it should be provided for a distance of at least d beyond that point.

Fig. 4-15 shows a plot of the design shear force diagram which indicates the maximum shear force of 150.0 kN extending from the point of calculation to the

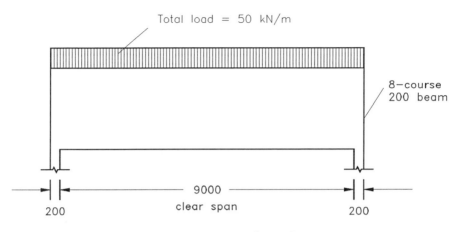

Fig. 4-14 Masonry Beam of Example 4-10

support. Also shown are the values of V_s = 85.0 kN (V_f=120.7 kN) for stirrups at 600, and V_f = 35.7 kN below which stirrups are not theoretically required. These values intersect the shear force diagram at distances that are easily calculated, or which may be scaled if the diagram is accurately drawn to scale.

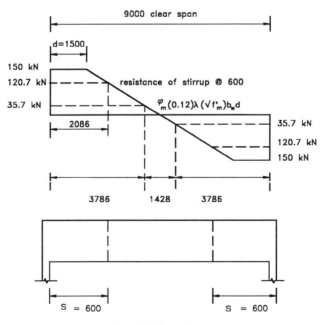

Fig. 4-15 Shear Design

The arrangement of #10 single-legged stirrups shown in Fig. 4-15 satisfies the shear requirements for the beam, and all that remains for the designer is to check that the stirrups are effectively anchored (see Section 4-8).

(The reader might note that this beam would be adequately reinforced for flexure with 2-#25 at $d = 1500$ mm.)

EXAMPLE 4-11 *Check that the 3.0 m high free-standing wall of Examples 4-7 and 4-9 satisfies the shear requirements for beams of S304.1.*

Recall that this wall is subjected to a factored wind pressure $p_f = 2.0$ kN/m^2, that it is reinforced with 2-#20 bars (in two grouted cores) at 1200 centres, and that one bar is terminated at 1.6 m from the top of the wall (that is, 1.4 m from the base).

Check shear at base of wall

The factored shear force on each vertical "beam" at the base of the wall is

$$V_f = p_f h \times \text{spacing} = 2.0(3.0)(1.2) = 7.2 \text{ kN}$$

Note that $d=95$ mm and, with two grouted cores, $b_w=400$ mm. Since normal weight units are used $\lambda=1.0$, since the "beam" is continuously grouted the factor of 0.6 does not apply, and since the "beam" is less than 400 mm in depth

$$V_m = 0.2\lambda\phi_m\sqrt{f'_m}b_w d$$

$$= 0.2(1.0)(0.55)\sqrt{10}\,(400)(95) = 13.22\text{kN} > 7.2\text{kN} = V_f \quad \underline{\text{OK}}$$

(Note also that because the beam is not greater that 200 mm in depth $V_f \leq 0.5V_m$ does not have to be checked to see if shear reinforcement is required.)

In the wall of the preceding example, shear resistance should also be checked at the point ($h = 1.4$ above the base) where one bar is terminated (Example 4-9). The abrupt termination of a bar in a tension zone represents a potential point for crack initiation and at such locations the special provisions of Clause 5.5.6.5 of S304.1 should be applied. For example, Clause 5.5.6.5(a) requires that the shear at the point of cut-off does not exceed two-thirds of that permitted, and a simple calculation in Example 4-11 will verify that adequate shear resistance is present.

The out-of-plane shear resistance of load bearing masonry walls is given in Clauses 11.5.4 and 11.5.5 of S304.1. These clauses could have been applied to the preceding example using a zero axial load - with little difference in the result. The application of these clauses is illustrated in Example 4-13.

4-8   BOND, DEVELOPMENT AND ANCHORAGE

The question of bond in beam design is largely one of performing an analytical design check. In general, the reinforcement will have been selected during the design for bending or shear, following which the bar sizes and anchorage lengths are checked to ensure that the required development lengths are available. Should they not be present then a larger number of smaller diameter bars should be selected, or greater anchorage lengths, or hooks, provided. Section 5.5 *Development and Splices of Reinforcement* of S304.1 provides the clauses that cover bond and development. It is beyond the scope of this book to give a detailed treatment of these clauses, which are for the most part self-explanatory practical rules, and it is left to the reader to become familiar with the details. In any case, since the check for development is essentially one of analysis, the principles have been discussed in Section 3-8 and are illustrated in Example 3-12. The following example examines the anchorage of web reinforcement.

EXAMPLE 4-12   *Check anchorage of the shear reinforcement of Example 4-10.*

The stirrups used in Example 4-10 were #10 single-legged with f_y=400 MPa.

Assuming that diagonal tension cracks form at approximately 45°, and with a spacing not exceeding $d/2$, some shear reinforcement may be located near the top or bottom of a crack and, consequently, rely largely on a hook for development. S304.1 recognizes that one diagonal crack may be transversed by only one tie anchored $d/2$ each side of the crack. Accordingly, S304.1 requires (Clause 5.5.9.2(a)) that each shear tie be anchored by a standard hook at each end plus $0.5l_d$ measured from the mid-depth of the beam to the point of tangency of the hook. The tie, or stirrup, should extend the full depth of the beam, with an appropriate allowance for cover.

For a #10 bar in tension

$$l_d = 0.004 d_b^2 f_y = 0.004(10)^2(400) = 160 \text{ mm}$$

Since $d/2 = 750 \text{ mm} > 80 \text{ mm} = 0.5l_d$

The anchorage of #10 single-legged stirrups hooked at each end is adequate

(Note that in this instance it is not required that stirrups be hooked around longitudinal reinforcement. Clause 5.5.9.2(b) covers the reduced development requirements for shear reinforcement hooked around longitudinal bars.)

4-9   SERVICEABILITY

Although it is essential that all structural elements possess adequate strength under the worst anticipated loadings, it is also necessary that they function satisfactorily under normal service loading. For beams and other structural masonry members the *serviceability* requirements are that deflections and flexural crack widths do not exceed reasonable limits; and conformity with the prescribed limits is assured through analytical checks following the principles outlined in Section 3-9.

Deflections

Excessive deflections can lead to such problems as cracking, buckling or crushing of non-structural components; and excessive flexibility can lead to unacceptable vibrations. For further information on deflection and vibration control the reader should refer to *The Structural Commentaries the National Building Code of Canada.* CSA S304.1 Clause, 12.4 requires that the deflection of beams be checked when the span L is greater than $15d$ in which case the immediate plus long-term service load deflection should not exceed $L/480$ (Clause 24.4.4).

Since walls as well as beams are used as flexural members it is worth noting the S304.1 requirements governing the lateral deflection of reinforced walls and columns. Clause 11.8.3. requires that the deflection due to wind not exceed

- $h/720$ when a veneer is attached;
- $h/360$ when there is a brittle finish to the wall; and
- $h/180$ for all other cases.

Reasonable estimates of deflection require reasonable values for moment of inertia, I, modulus of elasticity, E_m, and creep factors. These are provided in S304.1 and described in some detail in Section 3-9 of this book and illustrated in Examples 3-14, and 3-15. The reader is referred to those examples and to Example 4-13 at the end of this chapter that covers a number of design considerations and serviceability checks.

Crack Control

If masonry is exposed to the weather the presence of cracks encourages the ingress of moisture. This can lead to corrosion of reinforcing steel and connectors and to the disintegration of the mortar due to freeze-thaw activity. Once mortar deterioration starts, moisture can enter more freely and the problem accelerates. It should be noted that cracking due to shrinkage is an entirely different problem, one that can be solved through the judicious use of *control joints*.

As described in Section 3-9, S304.1 prescribes that cracking be controlled through ensuring that the quantity

$$z = f_s \sqrt[3]{d_c A} \, (10)^{-3}$$

does not exceed 30 kN/mm for interior exposures and 25 kN/mm for exterior exposures. For walls subjected to wind loading, the value of Z is limited to 50 kN/mm and 60 kN/mm for exterior and interior exposure, respectively. These requirements have been taken directly from CAN3-A23.3 *Code for the Design of Concrete Structures for Buildings*, where the corresponding crack widths are in the order of 0.40 mm and 0.33 mm, respectively, for interior and exterior exposures. The reader is advised, the requirements of S304.1 notwithstanding, that reinforced masonry is not reinforced concrete; also, the maximum interior crack width constraint of 0.40 mm (largely a cosmetic factor) could easily be 0.50 mm, whereas in particularly aggressive environments (wind, rain, freeze/thaw cycles) the constraint of 0.33 mm should perhaps be reduced to 0.25 mm. One of the difficulties with applying the S304.1 requirements is that the basic principles supporting it are rather obscure. The following explanation of crack width development is intended to make the mechanism of crack formation in reinforced masonry more understandable, and the two methods are compared in Example 4-13 at the end of this section.

The width of flexural cracks depends on the tensile stress in the reinforcement, on the location of the bars and on the crack spacing. In reinforced concrete the concrete is continuous and cracks form at the weak spots, generally at 100 mm to 200 mm spacings. In masonry, on the other hand, crack spacing is normally controlled by the location of the mortar joints, these being the weakest tensile component. Fig. 4-16, for example, shows two alternative arrangements for the bottom course of a masonry beam spanning an opening in a wall. On side (a) 200 high by 400 long bond beam units are used and cracking may be expected to start at 400 mm intervals, although at higher loads the influence of the second course may result in an eventual crack spacing of 200. Side (b) illustrates the use of 400 high by 200 long lintel blocks which will lead to a 200 mm crack spacing. Flexural cracks in side (a) are likely to be about twice as wide as those in side (b).

The masonry, being bonded to the steel bars, will undergo an average tensile strain equal to that in the reinforcement. As the masonry can sustain very little tensile strain the crack width at the level of the reinforcement will be only slightly less than the steel strain multiplied by the crack spacing. Plane sections remaining plane, the maximum crack width is related to the location of the steel relative to the neutral axis, and to the amount of cover, as shown in Fig. 4-17.

Crack width at the effective depth is

$$\epsilon_s s' = f_s s' / E_s$$

where

$$s' = \text{crack spacing.}$$

The maximum crack width w becomes

$$w = \frac{f_s s'(D-kd)}{E_s(d-kd)}$$

and this equation leads to a reasonable, although somewhat overestimated, value of the crack width. The equation also indicates the influence of crack spacing (that is, the head joint spacing) on crack width.

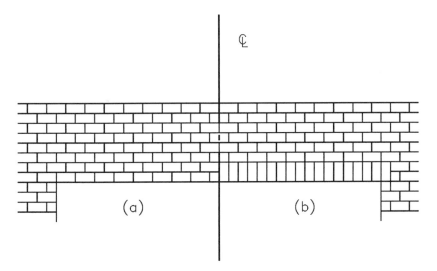

Fig. 4-16 Masonry Beam Spacing an Opening

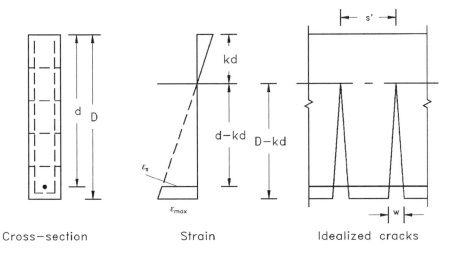

Cross−section   Strain   Idealized cracks

Fig. 4-17 Flexural Cracking

Given the maximum allowable stresses in the reinforcement and the head joint spacing, the maximum expected crack width at the level of the reinforcement can be readily calculated.

For example, if f_s=240 MPa ($0.6f_y$ where f_y = 400 MPa) and head joints are spaced at 200, the maximum expected crack width at the steel location is

$$f_s s'/E_s = \frac{240(200)}{200\,000} = 0.24 \text{ mm}$$

For deep beams the ratio $(D - kd)/(d - kd)$ is close to unity and the maximum crack width is approximately the same as that at the level of the steel. In that case the use of f_y = 400 MPa and 200 long units is acceptable for outdoor applications as $w \approx 0.25$. Generally, for outdoor exposures the use of 200 long lintel blocks for the bottom course is preferred. For shallow sections a closer estimate of crack width should be made.

Although walls are the subject of later chapters, the following example deals with a non load-bearing wall subjected to out-of-plane bending resulting from wind load. Partial grouting is involved which, for out-of-plane bending, can lead to tee-beam analysis, and, since the wall is slender compared to most beams, deflection and crack control may pose special problems. Generally, the example follows the principles outlined in Chapters 3 and 4, but where S304.1 has special provisions for walls, these are introduced in the example.

EXAMPLE 4-13 *A 6.0 m high non load-bearing wall is laterally supported top and bottom and is required to resist a maximum wind pressure of 1.0 kPa (kN/m²). Design a suitable 200 concrete block wall using a unit strength of 30 MPa, and type S mortar, and reinforcement with f_y=400 MPa.*

Note: in this example, a one metre wide strip of wall is considered as a vertical beam.

a) Strength

Considering a one-metre wide vertical strip, the factored load is

$$p_f = \alpha_L p = 1.5(1.0) = 1.5 \text{ kN/m}$$

The factored moment is

$$M_f = p_f h^2/8 = 1.5(6.0)^2/8 = 6.75 \text{ kN-m}$$

From Table 6 of S304.1, the tensile strength normal to the bed joint is 0.45 MPa for type S mortar and for an unreinforced wall the required section modulus is

$$S_x = M_f/f_t = \frac{6.75(10)^6}{0.45} = 15.0(10)^6 \text{ mm}^3/\text{m}$$

and Table 4.1 at the beginning of this chapter shows that an unreinforced 200 wall is not adequate. Vertical reinforcement is required, and this reinforcement is normally placed at the mid-thickness ($d = 190/2 = 95$ mm) which, since wind forces can be either pressure or suction, is quite appropriate.

The required steel area for the strip is

$$A_s \approx \frac{M_f}{\phi_s f_y (0.8d)} = \frac{6.75(10)^6}{0.85(400)(0.8)(95)} = 261 \text{ mm}^2/\text{m}$$

Try 1-#20 @ 1000 ($A_s = 300$ mm²) in one grouted core

(Note that 2-#15 @ 1200 gives $A_s = 333$ mm²/m and that a 1.2 metre strip with $A_s = 400$ mm² would then require analysis.)

Since the wall is only partially grouted a tee-beam analysis is required, and Clause 11.1.3.1 of S304.1 implies that no more than twice the wall thickness each side of a reinforcing bar is effective in compression. For the present example, then, the effective flange width of the 1.0 metre beam is 800 mm. Also, since the face shell of the unit forms the flange of the tee, its effective thickness can be found from the effective area in Table 4.1 as

$$t = \frac{75.4(10)^3}{2(10)^3} = 37.7 \text{ mm}$$

The tee-beam is shown in Fig. 4-18.

Check bending

Assuming that the neutral axis falls within the flange and recalling that

$$\begin{aligned} M_r &= T_r jd = \phi_s A_s f_y jd \\ &= C_r jd = 0.85\phi_m \chi f'_m bajd \end{aligned}$$

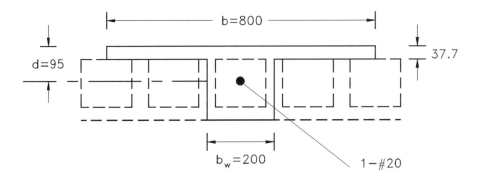

Fig. 4-18 Tee-Beam

then

$$a = \frac{\phi_s A_s f_y}{0.85 \phi_m \chi f'_m b}$$

Since the compression zone is not grouted, the higher value of $f'_m = 17.5$ MPa can be selected from Table 5 of S304.1 for 30 MPa units and type S mortar. Also, for compression normal to the bed joint, $\chi = 1.0$ (Section 3-4).

$$a = \frac{0.85(300)(400)}{0.85(0.55)(1.0)(17.5)(800)} = 15.6 \text{ mm}$$

Also, from Section 3-4, $\beta_1 = 0.70$ for 30 MPa units. Then the depth to the neutral axis is

$$c = a/\beta_1 = 15.6/0.70 = 22.3 < 37.7$$

The neutral axis falls within the flange and $jd = d - a/2$

$$M_r = \phi_s A_s f_y (d - a/2) = 0.85(300)(400)(95 - 15.6/2)$$
$$= 8.89 \text{ kN-m} > 6.75 \text{ kN-m} = M_f \qquad \underline{\text{OK}}$$

Check steel ratio

From Table 4-2 for $\chi = 1.0$, $\rho_b = 0.0066$

$$\rho = A_s/bd = 300/[800(95)] = 0.004 < \rho_b$$

[This wall actually falls into a category referred to as a *very slender wall* (Clause 11.2.4.3, S304.1 - $kh/t > 30$), which is the subject of a section in Chapter 5, and the value of ρ_{max} for very slender walls is 80% that for beams. $\rho = 0.004 < 0.8(0.0066)$ <u>OK</u>]

To check for ρ_{min}, the web of the tee is considered

$$\rho = A_s/b_w d = 300/[200(95)] = 0.016$$

$$\rho_{min} = 0.8/f_y = 0.8/400 = 0.002, \text{ and } \rho > \rho_{min} \qquad \underline{OK}$$

Check shear

The factored shear force has its maximum value at the top and bottom of the wall as

$$V_f = p_f h/2 = 1.5(6.0)/2 = 4.5 \text{ kN/m}$$

Clause 11.5.4 of S304.1 gives the out-of-plane shear resistance of walls as

$$V_r = \phi_m(v_m b_w d + 0.25P) \le \phi_m(0.4)\sqrt{f'_m} b_w d$$

where $\quad P$ = axial load in the wall = 0.0 conservatively.

$$v_m = 0.16(2 - \frac{M_f}{V_f d})\sqrt{f'_m}$$

$$M_f/V_f d \le 1.0$$
$$\ge 0.25$$

and, since the web is formed from grout, the lower value of $f'_m = 13.5$ MPa is used.

Since $M_f/V_f d = 6.75(10)^6/[4.5(10)^3(95)] > 1.0$ use 1.0

Then $\quad v_m = 0.16(2 - 1.0)\sqrt{13.5} = 0.588$ MPa
$\qquad V_r = \phi_m v_m b_w d = 0.55(0.588)(200)(95) = 6.14$ kN > 4.5 kN $= V_f$

$$< \phi_m(0.4)(\sqrt{f'_m})b_wd = 0.55(0.4)(\sqrt{13.5})(200)(95)$$
$$= 15.36 \text{ kN} \qquad \underline{\text{OK}}$$

Check development

Although it is clear that a 6000 long #20 bar is adequately anchored, development is checked here for the sake of completeness.

$$l_d = 0.004d_b^2f_y = 0.004(20)^2(400) = 640 < 3000 \qquad \underline{\text{OK}}$$

The 200 wall with 1-#20 @ 1000 has adequate strength.

b) Serviceability (service load = p = 1.0 kN/m²)

Deflection

Clause 11.8.3 limits the wind load deflection of walls to $h/720$ if there is a masonry veneer, $h/360$ if brittle finishes are attached, otherwise $h/180$.

The maximum wind load deflection of this wall is

$$\delta = \frac{5ph^4}{384E_mI_{eff}}$$

where $E_m = 850f'_m$ and, since f'_m varies from 17.5 MPa for ungrouted masonry to 13.5 MPa for fully-grouted cases, a value of $f'_m=16.7$ MPa is obtained for one core in five being grouted

$$E_m = 850(16.7) = 14.2(10)^3 \text{ MPa}$$

From Equation (3-40)

$$I_{eff} = (M_{cr}/M_a)^3I_0 + [1 - (M_{cr}/M_a)^3]I_{cr}$$

where M_{cr} = moment causing first cracking
$$= (\phi_mf_t + f_{cs})I_0/y_t$$
M_a = maximum applied moment due to unfactored loads
$$= ph^2/8$$

Since the steel is at the centre of the wall, the moment of inertia of the uncracked section, I_0, can be obtained from Table 4-1.

$$I_0 = 468(10)^6 \text{ mm}^4/\text{m}$$

From S304.1, Table 6, f_t = 0.45 MPa for tension normal to bed joints. Since the axial compressive stress, f_{cs}, enhances the cracking moment, M_{cr}, the load factor used in its calculation is 0.85. However, in this instance, since there is no applied axial load except the self-weight of the wall, f_{cs} may be taken as zero.

Thus, M_{cr} = [0.55(0.45) + 0.0](468)(10)^6/95 = 1.22 kN-m

M_a = 1.0(6.0)^2/8 = 4.50 kN-m

The moment of inertia of the cracked section, I_{cr}, is now obtained by an elastic transformed section analysis using $n = E_s/E_m = 200(10)^3/14.2(10)^3 = 14.1$. Assuming the neutral axis to lie within the flange and that the full 1000 width contributes to stiffness (compared with the 800 used for strength), and by taking moments of areas shown in Fig 4-19.

$$1000(kd)^2/2 = 14.1(300)(95 - kd)$$

which solves to give kd = 24.4 mm < 37.7 mm flange thickness, and the neutral axis lies within the flange. The cracked moment of inertia is obtained as (Equation (3-38))

$$I_{cr} = b(kd)^3/3 + nA_s(d - kd)^2$$
$$= 1000(24.4)^3/3 + 4230(95 - 24.4)^2 = 25.9(10)^6 \text{ mm}^4$$

The effective moment of inertia can now be obtained as

$$I_{eff} = (1.22/4.50)^3(486)(10)^6 + [1 - (1.22/4.50)^3](25.9)(10)^6$$
$$= 35.1(10)^6 \text{ mm}^4$$

and the maximum deflection of the wall due to wind is

$$\delta = \frac{5ph^4}{384E_m I_{eff}} = \frac{5(1.0)(6000)^4}{384(14.2)(10)^3(35.1)(10)^6} = 33.86 \text{ mm}$$

$$\delta = 33.9 \approx 33.3 = 6000/180 = h/180 \qquad \underline{OK}$$

Check crack control

In addition to the check on deflection, S304.1 (clause 11.9) requires a check on crack control. This check takes the form of requiring that the factor $z \leq 50$ kN/mm in Equation (3-41). S304.1 also cautions that in aggressive environments this requirement may not be sufficient.

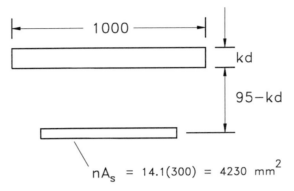

Fig. 4-19 Transformed Section Analysis

The remainder of this example discusses cracking.

From Section 3-9 and Equation (3-41)

$$z = f_s \sqrt[3]{d_c A} \, (10)^{-3} \le 50$$

for walls subject to wind load.

f_s can be taken as $0.6 f_y = 0.6(400) = 240$ MPa
$d_c = $ cover $= 95$
$A = $ area in tension $= b_w(190 - kd) = 200(190 - 24.4) = 33(10)^3$ mm^2

$$z = 240 \sqrt[3]{95(33)(10)^3} \, (10)^{-3} = 35.1 \, < 50$$

and the serviceability requirements are satisfied.

It is interesting at this point to make an estimate of the probable crack width. Assuming $f_s = 0.6 f_y = 240$ MPa and that cracks form at the bed joints (spaced at $s' = 200$) the probable crack width at the location of the steel is in the order of

$$\varepsilon_s s' = \frac{f_s}{E_s} s' = \frac{240}{200(10)^3}(200) = 0.24 \text{ mm}$$

Recalling from the transformed section analysis that $kd = 24.4$ mm, the steel is located at $95 - 25 = 70$ mm from the neutral axis and the extreme tension fibre at 190 - 25 = 165 mm. The crack width at the mortar joint is likely to be in the order of

0.24(165)/70 = 0.56 mm

While this may appear to be a rather wide crack, the reader is reminded that when the wall is subjected to positive wind pressure the crack is an interior crack. Negative wind pressure (suction) is generally less, exterior cracks will not be so wide and rain is not being driven against the wall. Also, wind is transitory in nature and the cracks soon close.

Since strength and serviceability limit states have not been exceeded, the 200 wall reinforced with 1-#20 vertical bar @ 1000 is adequate.

4-10   PRACTICAL CONSIDERATIONS

A knowledge of the method of construction is useful in design. For example, remembering that courses are laid sequentially, that only the bottom course of a concrete block beam has a continuous horizontal space, and that subsequent courses have continuous vertical cores, it will be appreciated that cages of reinforcement cannot be pre-prepared as they are for reinforced concrete (except for shallow lintel beams). Longitudinal bottom steel is placed in the bottom course before laying the next course, and stirrups are easier to place in the cores once all the courses have been laid. As a result, stirrups, and particularly two-legged stirrups, that hook around the bottom steel, are difficult to place in deep beams. In that case the lower end of the stirrup can still be hooked but anchored only by grout. Stirrups can readily be, and should normally be hooked over top reinforcement.

Furthermore, recalling the rather limited space available in concrete block beams, the designer should avoid a congested situation, selecting perhaps one large bar in preference to a number of smaller ones. But in that case bond may become a problem. It should be remembered, however, that grout is more workable than normal concrete and the maximum aggregate size smaller, and that bars can be spaced more closely than in reinforced concrete. Practical requirements for the placement of grout and reinforcement are contained in CSA Standard A371 *Masonry Construction for Buildings*.

4-11   CLOSURE

The reader, if a comparative newcomer to the study of masonry, may feel at this stage that the design of even a simple lintel is a formidable task. However, comfort is to be derived from the knowledge that the designer soon gains the experience to select beam sizes that require flexural reinforcement below p_b and that do not require web reinforcement - not because they are simpler to design (which they are) but because they are easier, and generally more economical, to construct. Nevertheless, a knowledge and understanding of all the principles is essential to the appreciation of design and to recognition of those cases that require special reinforcement.

Although this chapter has illustrated the application of basic principles to the design of masonry members in bending, and in conformity with the requirements of S304.1, not all the clauses in that document have been covered - for example, Clause 12.2.2 which gives the lateral support requirement for the compression face of a beam (a spacing not exceeding $30b$ or $120b^2/d$ for singly-supported beams, or half those values for cantilever beams). However, the designer must have an intimate knowledge of all clauses relevant to a particular design, and this requires a degree of familiarity that can only come from reading S304.1 - a task that is left to the reader.

PROBLEMS 4

(The following problems, each of which represents one of the topics from Chapter 4, are part analysis and part design. Some of the problems, like those in actual design, have a variety of structurally valid solutions, and where a number of solutions is possible some representative answer are given.)

(4-1)   A fully-grouted concrete masonry beam having a unit strength of 20 MPa is simply supported at each end over a span of 6.0 m and is required to support a superimposed live load of 20 kN/m. Assuming the beam to have adequate lateral support, select a suitable beam size and the corresponding flexural steel (f_y = 400 MPa, and 90 mm from underside of beam to centroid of steel) using
(a) 200 units;   (b) 250 units;   (c) 300 units.

ANS.   (a) 6 - course, $A_s \simeq$ 530 mm²; 7 - course, $A_s \simeq$ 420 mm²
(b) 5 - course, $A_s \simeq$ 730 mm²; 6 - course, $A_s \simeq$ 530 mm²
(c) 5 - course, $A_s \simeq$ 720 mm²
(Note that the required steel areas are shown as approximate since they were obtained from the appropriate chart of Part 2).

(4-2)   Show by analysis that the answers to Problem 4-1 are adequate.

(4-3)   Since the grid of Fig. 4-5 may not be sufficiently fine for accurate estimates of steel areas, by calculation from basic principles reproduce the chart on graph paper.

(4-4)   For b= 190 mm, f_m = 10 MPa and f_y = 400 MPa, produce a design chart of bending moment versus tensile reinforcement for two-, three- and four-course beams. That is, by calculation from basic principles enlarge the lower portion of Fig. 4-5.

(4-5)   Design a 200 mm, six-course concrete masonry beam for the span and loading of Problem 4-1. Use f_m = 10 MPa and f_y = 400 MPa, d = 1100 mm and, if required d' = 50 mm.

ANS. $A_s \simeq$ 600 mm²; $A_s \simeq$ 500 mm² $A_s' \simeq$ 100 mm²
(Note that compression steel must be tied according to clause 12.2.3.4 of S304.1)

(4-6)   Check the shear resistance in the 6-course beam of Problem 4-5 (that is, f_m = 10 MPa, f_y = 400 MPa, d = 1100, superimposed live load = 20 kN/m) assuming a clear span of 6.0 m and provide #10 single legged stirrups if required.

ANS.   Shear reinforcement is required. Use #10 single-legged stirrups @
        400 o.c.

(4-7)   The bottom course of a fully loaded concrete masonry beam consist of 400 mm
         long units. Assuming $f_s = 0.6f_y$, estimate the approximate maximum expected
         crack width when b= 190, 7-course, $A_s = 800$ mm^2, $f_y = 400$ MPa, and $f'_m =$
         10 MPa

         ANS. $w = 0.53$ mm

(4-8)   If the superimposed loading on the beam of Problem 4-5 is all of short duration
         make an estimate of the maximum expected deflection when $A_s = 600$ mm^2.

         ANS. $\delta_{max} = 5.4$ mm

(4-9)   If the superimposed loading on the beam of Problem 4-5 is all of long duration
         make an estimate of the maximum expected deflection when $A_s = 600$ mm^2

         ANS. $\delta_{max} = 7.3$ mm

CHAPTER 5

AXIAL LOAD AND BENDING - WALLS AND COLUMNS

5-1   INTRODUCTION

Masonry has been used traditionally to resist compression, and it is in this role that it is still used most extensively. In recent decades the number of stories in masonry buildings has increased substantially and bearing-wall thicknesses have decreased by an even larger factor. This has been made possible through improved methods of analysis, improved materials and the use of steel reinforcing, a development that also enables masonry to resist substantial bending. The compression elements most commonly used are *load-bearing walls* and *columns*, and while the arch is still potentially an effective compression element it is rarely used now in a structural capacity, but rather as an architectural embellishment.

The main difference between a wall and a column is one of cross-sectional dimensions. S304.1, defines a column as a vertical member having a height more than five times its thickness and a width less than three times the thickness, anything wider being a wall. This is illustrated in Fig. 5-1. Earlier working stress design editions of the standard identified another significant difference by specifying lower limiting stresses for columns than for walls. This was in recognition of the fact that a wall can arch over a weak spot and transfer the load to stronger locations, thereby producing an average resistance. On the other hand, a column, having a lesser width, will be affected more

by a localized weakness, such as cracked block or a defective mortar joint. S304.1 does
not make a comparable distinction.

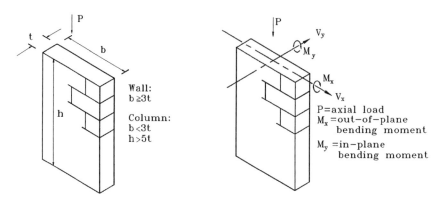

Fig. 5-1 Limiting Dimensions of Walls and Columns   Fig. 5-2 Loading on Compression Members

    In addition to the axial load, compression members are frequently required to
resist bending about either or both principal axes, as shown in Fig. 5-2. *Out-of-plane
bending* is represented by M_x (and accompanying shear, V_y) and can be produced by the
eccentric application of in-plane compressive loading, as shown in Fig. 5-3(a), and/or as
a result of transverse loading as shown in Fig. 5-3(b). *In-plane bending*, M_y (and
accompanying shear, V_x) is most frequently encountered in shear wall structures that are
subjected to horizontal wind or earthquake forces, as shown in Fig. 5-4.

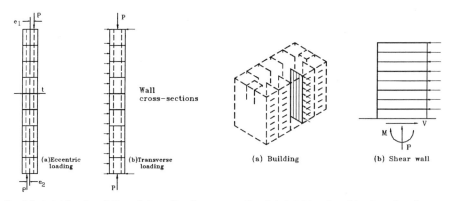

Fig. 5-3 Axial Load and Out-of-plane Bending   Fig. 5-4 Axial Load and In-plane Bending

    Design for combined axial load and bending is more difficult than for flexure
alone, especially since the effect of slenderness on strength must also be considered.
Since masonry is used primarily in wall construction, a considerable amount of research

has been directed toward the behaviour of walls. Improved understanding of this complex material has led to the developments reflected in S304.1. Nevertheless, the designer is likely to encounter situations that fall outside the strict confines of the standard, and that is where a thorough understanding of the basic principles is essential to the exercise of sound judgement.

Axial Load and Bending

The resistance of structural elements to a combination of axial load and bending is governed by the interaction of material strength and member stability. The structural design of masonry walls and columns has, in the past, been governed largely by material strength modified by semi-empirical eccentricity and slenderness coefficients, C_e and C_s respectively. This method is referred to in S304, the working stress design standard, as the *Coefficient Method*. In the 1984 edition of S304 an additional and alternative method, the *Load Deflection Method*, that considers the magnification of moments was introduced. That method has since been refined and incorporated in S304.1 as two methods, the *Pδ Method* (Clause 11.2.5.2) and the *Moment Magnifier Method* (Clause 11.2.5.3), more familiar to reinforced concrete and structural steel designers.

Typically, then, walls and columns are designed to resist a combination of factored axial load and bending moment. A primary moment due to lateral loads and the eccentric application of axial load is calculated and, since the moment produces a lateral deflection, a secondary moment is generated by the axial load acting over the deflection - that is $P\delta$. The section is then designed to resist the axial load and the total moment. The effect of slenderness, that is, the $P\delta$ effect, is therefore included rationally in the design (rather than through the use of an empirical slenderness coefficient, C_s, as in the past). Because walls and columns cannot be built and loaded without some eccentricity, S304.1 (Clause 11.2.3) requires that the primary moment be not less than the moment produced by the axial load applied at an eccentricity of $0.1t$, t being the thickness of the wall or column in the direction of bending.

With the $P\delta$ method, the procedure is to calculate the lateral deflection, δ, caused by the primary moment, M_p. A secondary moment, $P_f\delta$ (due to the factored axial load acting over δ), is generated and added to the primary moment to give a total factored moment

$$M_f = M_p + P_f\delta \tag{5-1}$$

and, since the secondary moment adds to the deflection, further iterative calculations may be necessary.

Using the moment magnifier method, the total factored moment is obtained more directly from the primary moment as

$$M_f = M_p C_m/(1 - P_f/P_{cr}) \tag{5-2}$$

where C_m is a coefficient to determine equivalent uniform bending

$$C_m = 0.6 + 0.4M_1/M_2 \geq 0.4$$

M_1 and M_2 being the lesser and greater end moments respectively, and P_{cr} is the factored version of the Euler critical load

$$P_{cr} = \pi^2 EI/(kh)^2 \qquad (5\text{-}3)$$

In these two methods when calculating δ or P_{cr}, the rigidity EI is taken as

$$\phi_e E_m I_{eff}/(1 + 0.5\beta_d) \qquad (5\text{-}4)$$

where
$\phi_e = 0.65$
$E_m = 850f'_m$
β_d = factored dead load moment/M_f, and
I_{eff} = effective moment of inertia.

Slenderness

In the limit states design standard, S304.1, the slenderness of a wall or column is defined as kh/t, where h is the height between points of lateral support and t is the thickness of the wall or the least dimension of the column cross-section. In this ratio, k is an effective length factor that can vary from 0.80 for fully fixed top and bottom to 1.0 for pin-ended walls and columns (see Appendix B of S304.1). For the majority of walls, especially if unreinforced, $k = 1.0$ is appropriate. Vertical cantilevers, that is, with no lateral support at the top, and for which $k = 2.0$, are not recommended. Shear walls are, of course, an exception to this recommendation since they function solely as vertical cantilevers.

In evaluating the slenderness and the resistance of walls and columns, the actual thickness and section properties are used. When mortar joints are raked, as opposed to flush or concave tooled (see Fig. 5-5), the thickness and the effective area are reduced by the depth of raking. The designer should be aware of the reduction in resistance, and raked joints, although they may be architecturally pleasing, should be avoided for outdoor exposures since they encourage the ingression of moisture and subsequent freeze/thaw deterioration.

Clause 11.2.4.3 of S304.1 outlines the slenderness limits that should be placed on walls and column. They are:

a)   When $kh/t < 10 - 3.5e_1/e_2$ (e_1 and e_2 being the smaller and larger of the two end eccentricities respectively), the effects of slenderness can be neglected. For a 200 wall with equal end eccentricities this leads to $kh/t = 1.0h/190 < 10 - 3.5 = 6.5$. This gives a height of 1235 mm, not a normal wall height.

b)   When $kh/t \leq 30$ (which for the 190 wall and $k=1.0$ leads to a height of 5700 mm) normal design procedures are used, and walls are referred to as *slender*.

c)   When $kh/t > 30$, the special provisions for *very slender walls* apply.

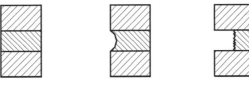

Flush   Concave   Raked

Fig. 5-5 Joint Finishes

Walls and Columns

Walls and columns may be plain (that is, unreinforced), which can include grouting, or they may be reinforced with vertical bars, as shown in Fig. 5-6. Separate columns, or pilasters, as shown in (a) and (c) may be used, or the column can be incorporated, (b) and (d), into a wall. A continuous load-bearing wall, a variety of arrangements being shown in (e), is also common.

Where the bending moment is large and the axial load small, the vertical reinforcement provides tensile resistance, and for lesser moments and higher axial loads the steel is placed in compression. S304.1 requires that the reinforcement be adequately tied to resist compression for that resistance to be evaluated. Clause 5.2 of S304.1 outlines the requirements for reinforcement, including those for lateral ties, in walls and columns, and some reinforcement arrangements are shown in Fig. 5-7.

Although unreinforced walls do not require reinforcement to provide resistance to effects of factored loads, joint reinforcement at intervals not exceeding 600 mm is recommended to control the effects of drying shrinkage and temperature differentials. In any case, horizontal reinforcement of at least 1-#15 bar should be placed in a bond beam at each floor and roof level to provide a horizontal tie at each of those levels. Also, even when not required by resistance calculations, the provision of at least 1-#15 bar vertically at corners and at the ends of walls, and around openings in walls, is recommended.

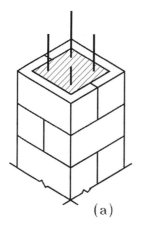

(a)

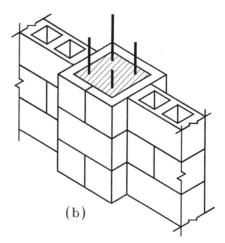

(b)

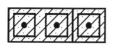

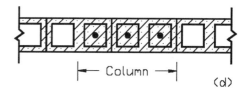

(c)

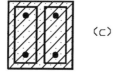

(d)

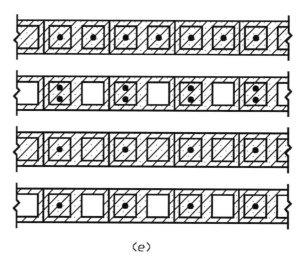

(e)

Fig. 5-6 Reinforced Columns and Walls

Construction

In reinforced concrete construction it is normal to prefabricate the reinforcement (vertical bars and lateral ties) into a cage for placement into the formwork. The same procedure can be adopted for reinforced brick columns where the encompassing wythe can be constructed around the cage [Fig. 5-7(b)], or for concrete masonry where pilaster blocks are available in open halves [Figs 5-6(a) and (b) and 5-7(a)] and can be placed around the reinforcement, or for closed units when the void is large enough for insertion of the cage after the units have been laid. However, when the columns are constructed of standard hollow blocks, or hollow clay bricks [Fig. 5-6(c), (d) and (e)] the same procedure is not feasible; and in this case ties are normally placed in the mortar joints [Fig. 5-7(c)], the vertical reinforcement then being inserted into the cores after the units have been laid. Ties for placement in the mortar joint should not have a diameter greater than 6 mm (1/4" diameter ties have been used frequently in the past) and overlapping ends should lie in the same plane. Some possible arrangements are illustrated in Fig. 5-7.

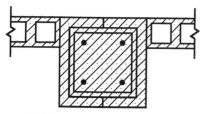

(a) Masonry block
pilaster

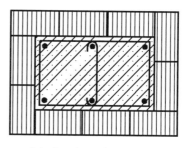

(b) Brick column

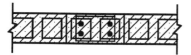

(c) Ties laid in
the mortar joint

(d) Ties for
end bar

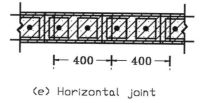

├─ 400 ─┼─ 400 ─┤

(e) Horizontal joint
reinforcement

Fig. 5-7 Column and Wall Reinforcement

In this chapter, Section 5-2 deals with the design of unreinforced walls and columns, 5-3 with the resistance of reinforced column sections, 5-4 with the resistance of reinforced wall sections to axial load and out-of-plane bending, and Section 5-5 examines the effect of slenderness. Section 5-6 deals with the special case of very slender walls ($kh/t > 30$), Section 5-7 covers the analysis and design of shear walls, that is, walls whose principal loading is in-plane bending and shear, Section 5-8 discusses serviceability and Section 5-9, Environmental loading.

5-2   UNREINFORCED WALLS AND COLUMNS - Axial Load and Bending

At the outset it should be emphasized that although S304.1 permits the use of unreinforced columns, since they normally are significant and isolated structural components, columns, for reasons of structural integrity that comes from the ductility afforded by structural steel, should be reinforced with vertical bars. Unreinforced columns, unless they are largely decorative and lightly loaded, should not be used. This section of Chapter 5, then, deals with *unreinforced* (or plain) *walls*.

In evaluating the resistance of an unreinforced wall to axial load and bending, the combination of axial load, P_f, and bending moment, M_f, can range from axial load alone to pure bending (see Example 4-13). In recognition of the fact that a wall cannot be constructed perfectly plumb, and that vertical loads are never truly applied to the centroidal axis, S304.1 (Clause 11.2.3) requires that the eccentricity of application of axial load never be less than 10% of the wall or column thickness. Thus, for a 200 wall, the minimum eccentricity of axial load is $0.1t = 0.1(190) = 19$ mm.

S304.1 (Clause 10.2.2.2) allows walls to be designed using a linear elastic analysis with some tensile stress being permitted, or (Clause 10.2.2.3) using a rectangular compressive stress block with no tension (a tensile zone is assumed to be cracked). While the rectangular stress block analysis generally leads to a marginally higher resistance, the governing equations are rather complex for hand analysis. Consequently, the simpler elastic analysis is used in this section. However, the interaction (P vs. M) design charts in Part 2 of this book have been prepared using the rectangular stress block analysis. For the elastic analysis, then, the following design criteria govern: namely, that

$$P_f/A_e \pm M_f/S_x \tag{5-5}$$

should exceed neither $\phi_m f'_m$ in compression nor $\phi_m f_t$ in tension.

As was noted in Section 5-1, walls and columns are designed for a combination of axial load and bending moment. Once the axial load is known, a primary moment, M_p, based on the axial load, the end eccentricities of the axial load, and the lateral loads, is calculated. The axial load in turn acts over the deflection produced by the primary moment to produce additional bending, or secondary moment. The wall (or column) must then be designed to resist the combined effect of the factored axial load and the total moment (primary plus secondary) due to the factored loading. In effect, once the factored axial load and the total moment due to the factored loads are known, the trial wall section can be checked for its resistance. It is important to caution the reader that axial compression can in certain instances enhance the resistance to bending and, if overestimated, can lead to a spuriously high estimate of the resistance to bending, especially where tension is the governing criterion.

In calculating δ for the $P\delta$ method or P_{cr} for the moment magnifier method, a rigidity $\phi_e E_m I_{eff}/(1 + 0.5\beta_d)$ is used. In this expression I_{eff} is given by Clause 11.2.5.4(a) for unreinforced masonry as

$$I_{eff} = 0.4I_0 \tag{5-6}$$

In this expression, I_0 is the moment of inertia of the effective cross-sectional area. The reader is cautioned that although S304.1 permits unreinforced walls to crack (Clause 10.2.2.3), such situations should generally be avoided. If flexure is likely to cause cracking the wall should be reinforced. The unreinforced wall should be designed to remain uncracked.

Rather than go through the relatively simple, separate steps of evaluating section resistance and incorporating the effects of slenderness, Examples 5-1, 5-2, and 5-3, combine these two aspects to illustrate both analysis and design.

EXAMPLE 5-1 *A 200 ungrouted wall constructed from 20 MPa units and type S mortar has a clear height of 4.0 m between lateral supports. What is the maximum factored axial load, P_f kN/m, 50% of which is factored dead load and 50% factored live load?*

Check slenderness (Clause 11.2.4.3 of S304.1)

$$kh/t = 1.0h/t = 1.0(4000)/(190) = 21.1 > 10 - 3.5e_1/e_2$$
$$< 30$$

Therefore, the $P\delta$ or moment magnifier method can be used.

Minimum end eccentricity $= 0.1t = 0.1(190) = 19$ mm
and single curvature is assumed.

Primary moment, $M_p = 0.1tP_f = 19P_f$ N-mm

To check resistance, consider a one-metre length of wall and use

$$P_f/A_e + M_f/S_x \leq \phi_m f'_m$$

where, $A_e = 75.4(10)^3$ mm^2/m $S_x = 4.66(10)^6$ mm^3/m (Table 4-1)

From Table 5, S304.1, $f'_m = 13$ MPa, and

$$\phi_m f'_m = 0.55(13.0) = 7.15 \text{ MPa}$$

For the $P\delta$ and moment magnifier method, the value of

$EI = \phi_e E_m I_{eff}/(1+0.5\beta_d)$ is required and, since the wall is loaded at minimum eccentricity, $I_0 = I_x = 442(10)^6 mm^4/m$ (Table 4-1)

$\phi_e = 0.65$

$E_m = 850f'_m = 850(13) = 11.05(10)^3$ MPa

$I_{eff} = 0.4I_0 = 0.4(442)(10)^6 = 176.8(10)^6 mm^4/m$ (Clause 11.2.5.4)

β_d = (factored dead load moment)/(factored total moment)

$= D_f/(D_f + L_f) = 0.50/(0.50 + 0.50) = 0.50$

$EI = 0.65(11.05)(10)^3(176.8)(10)^6/[1+0.5(0.5)] = 1.016(10)^{12}$ N-mm²/m

Since there is no simple direct solution for P_f, an iterative procedure has to be undertaken.

First iteration: use the primary moment to calculate P_f

$$P_f/A_e + M_f/S_x = \frac{P_f}{75.4(10)^3} + \frac{19P_f}{4.66(10)^6} \le 7.15 \text{ MPa} = \phi_m f'_m$$

which gives $P_f \le 412.3$ kN/m

a) *Pδ method* - calculate δ, $P_f\delta$ and total moment, $M_p + P_f\delta = P_f(19 + \delta)$

For a simply-supported member subject to constant moment, M

$$\delta = \frac{ML^2}{8EI} = \frac{19(412.3)(10)^3(4000)^2}{8(1.016)(10)^{12}} = 15.4 \text{ mm}$$

Since the first iteration did not include the $P\delta$ effect on moment, leading to an overestimate of P_f, further refinement is required.

Second iteration: $M_f = P_f(19 + \delta) = P_f(19 + 15.4) = 34.4P_f$

$$\frac{P_f}{75.4(10)^3} + \frac{34.4P_f}{4.66(10)^6} \le 7.15 \text{ MPa yields } P_f \le 346.3 \text{ kN/m}$$

$$\delta = \frac{M_f L^2}{8EI} = \frac{34.4(346.3)(10)^3(4000)^2}{8(1.016)(10)^{12}} = 23.5 \text{ mm}$$

Because the calculated deflection of 23.5 mm is significantly different from the 15.4 mm used in calculating M_f, another iteration is required.

Third iteration: $M_f = P_f(19 + 23.5) = 42.5P_f$

$$P_f/A_e + M_f/S_x \le 7.15 \quad \text{yields} \quad P_f \le 319.4 \text{ kN/m}$$

$$\text{and} \quad \delta = 26.7 \text{ mm}$$

Fourth iteration; $M_f = P_f(19 + 26.7) = 45.7P_f$

$$P_f \leq 309.9 \text{ kN/m}$$
$$\delta = 27.9 \text{ mm}$$

Fifth iteration: $M_f = P_f(19 + 27.9) = 46.9P_f$

$$P_f \leq 306.5 \text{ kN/m}$$
$$\delta = 28.3 \text{ mm}$$

Sixth iteration: $M_f = P_f(19 + 28.3) = 47.3P_f$

$$P_f \leq 305.4 \text{ kN/m}$$
$$\delta = 28.4 \text{ mm}$$

The process has converged sufficiently to give

Factored resistance to axial load for wall = 305 kN/m   Ans.

b) *Moment magnifier method*

If the value of P_f were known, this method would lead directly to M_f. However, because P_f is not known, an iteration procedure is followed.

Recall that $M_p = 19P_f$ and from the first iteration $P_f = 412.3$ kN/m. Then the factored moment becomes

$$M_f = M_{TOT} = M_p C_m/(1-P_f/P_{cr})$$

where $C_m = 0.6 + 0.4M_1/M_2 = 0.6 + 0.4(1.0) = 1.0$

$$P_{cr} = \frac{\pi^2 EI}{(kh)^2} = \frac{\pi^2(1.016)(10)^{12}}{4000^2} = 626.7(10)^3 \text{ N/m, and}$$

$$M_f = \frac{412.3(10)^3(19)(1.0)}{1 - [412.3(10)^3/626.7(10)^3]} = 22.9(10)^6 \text{ N-mm/m}$$

Now, since an approximate value of P_f (412.3 kN/m) was used in calculating M_f, P_f can again be calculated and the new value compared with the previous one.

Second iteration:

$$P_f/A_e + M_f/S_x = \frac{P_f}{75.4(10)^3} + \frac{22.9(10)^6}{4.66(10)^6} = 7.15 \text{ MPa}$$

gives $P_f \approx 168.6$ kN/m

Because 168.6 kN/m is very different from the 412.3 kN/m calculated in the first iteration, further refinement is required. However, rather than enter a lengthy series of iterations as before, it is more appropriate to short-cut the process by using informed estimates of P_f.

Try $P_f = 290$ kN/m (approximate mean of 412.3 and 168.6)

$$M_{TOT} = \frac{290(10)^3(19)(1.0)}{[1 - 290(10)^3/626.7(10)^3]} = 10.26(10)^6 \text{ N-mm/m}$$

$$\frac{P_f}{75.4(10)^3} + \frac{10.26(10)^6}{4.66(10)^6} = 7.15 \text{ MPa gives } P_f = 373 \text{ kN/m}$$

Try $P_f = 330$ kN/m (approximate mean of 290 and 373)

$$M_{TOT} = \frac{330(10)^3(19)}{[\,1 - 330(10)^3/626.7(10)^3\,]} = 13.2(10)^6 \text{ N-mm/m}$$

$$\frac{P_f}{75.4(10)^3} + \frac{13.2(10)^6}{4.66(10)^6} = 7.15 \text{ MPa gives } P_f = 325 \text{ kN/m}$$

Since 325 kN/m and 330 kN/m are fairly close (2%), it is reasonable at this point to take the mean of the two previous values giving $P_f \approx 327.5$ kN/m or, conservatively,

factored axial load for wall $P_f \leq 325$ *kN/m.*   <u>Ans.</u>

(Note that at this point the minimum stress $P_f/A_e - M_f/S_x$ should be checked to ensure that maximum tensile stresses are not exceeded. This is covered in Example 5-2)

It is interesting at this point to make a comparison of the two methods, and to note that whereas the $P\delta$ and moment magnifier methods give about the same estimate of factored load, the latter method is simpler to use and is more consistent with practise familiar to designers of structural steel and reinforced concrete. Also, in the preceding example, deflections were calculated from an equation that assumes a constant moment for the full height of the wall. The moment, of course, is not constant, deflections are overestimated, and the factored load is underestimated by the $P\delta$ method. To make more accurate calculations of deflection renders the $P\delta$ method more cumbersome and the moment magnifier method is preferred.

It is also interesting to make a comparison with the working stress design standard (S304) which specifies that the maximum service load for this wall is

$P = C_eC_sf_mA_e$ (C_e and C_s being eccentricity and slenderness coefficients respectively, and f_m the maximum allowable compressive stress). Application of that standard yields a maximum axial service load of 188 kN/m, which, for equal dead and live loads, gives a factored load $P_f = 1.25(94) + 1.5(94) = 258.5$ kN/m.

In design the loading is known, and the process of checking a trial wall section by the moment magnifier method is more direct than the analysis of Example 5-1. This is illustrated in Examples 5-2 and 5-3.

EXAMPLE 5-2 *A 200 wall 4.0 m high is required to carry an axial service load consisting of 200 kN/m dead and 50 kN/m live. Design the wall using 20 MPa units and type S mortar.*

Check slenderness:

$$kh/t = 1.0(4000)/190 = 21.1 > 10\text{-}3.5e_1/e_2 \text{ (Clause 11.2.4.3.2)}$$
$$< 30 \qquad\qquad \text{(Clause 11.2.4.3.2)}$$

Therefore, use the moment magnifier method.

Primary moment, $M_p = 0.1tP_f$
$P_f = 1.25D + 1.5L = 1.25(200) + 1.5(50) = 325$ kN/m
$M_p = 0.1(190)(325)(10)^3 = 6.18(10)^6$ N-mm/m
$M_f = M_pC_m/(1 - P_f/P_{cr})$
$C_m = 0.6 + 0.4M_1/M_2 = 0.6 + 0.4(1.0) = 1.0$

$$P_{cr} = \frac{\pi^2\phi_eE_mI_{eff}}{(kh)^2(1 + 0.5\beta_d)}$$

Try 200 ungrouted: $f'_m = 13$ MPa

From Table 4-1,

$A_e = 75.4(10)^3\text{mm}^2/\text{m}, S_x = 4.66(10)^6 \text{ mm}^3/\text{m}, I_x = 442(10)^6 \text{ mm}^4/\text{m},$
$\phi_e = 0.65, E_m = 850(13) = 11,050$ MPa,
$I_{eff} = 0.4I_0 = 0.4(442)(10)^6 = 176.8(10)^6 \text{ mm}^4/\text{m}$

and, since the factored moments are proportional to the factored loads

$$\beta_d = D_f/(D_f + L_f) = 1.25(200)/325 = 0.769$$

Then

$$P_{cr} = \frac{\pi^2(0.65)(11.05)(10)^3(176.8)(10)^6}{(4000)^2[1 + 0.5(0.769)]} = 565.8 \text{ kN/m}$$

and

$$M_f = \frac{6.18(10)^6}{1 - 325(10)^3/565.8(10)^3} = 14.52(10)^6 \text{ N-mm/m}$$

Check resistance

$$P_f/A_e + M_f/S_x \leq \phi_m f'_m = 0.55(13) = 7.15 \text{ MPa}$$

$$\frac{325(10)^3}{75.4(10)^3} + \frac{14.52(10)^6}{4.66(10)^6} = 7.43 \text{ MPa} > 7.15 \text{ MPa} \qquad \underline{\text{NG}}$$

(Note that this is an overstress of about 4%, which some designers would consider acceptable)

Try 200 wall, one grouted core per metre

$$A_e = 98.3(10)^3 \text{ mm}^2/\text{m}, \ S_x = 4.93(10)^6 \text{ mm}^3/\text{m}, \ I_x = 468(10)^6 \text{ mm}^4/\text{m}$$
From Table 5 of S304.1

$$f'_m = 13 - 3(1/5) = 12.4 \text{ MPa (1 out of 5 cores grouted)}$$

$$EI = \frac{\phi_e E_m I_{eff}}{1 + 0.5\beta_d} = \frac{0.65(850)(12.4)(0.4)(468)(10)^6}{1 + 0.5(0.769)} = 926(10)^9 \text{ N-mm}^2/\text{m}$$

$$P_{cr} = \frac{\pi^2 EI}{kh^2} = \frac{\pi^2(926)(10)^9}{(4000)^2} = 571.2 \text{ kN/m}$$

Then

$$M_f = \frac{M_p C_m}{1 - P_f/P_{cr}} = \frac{6.18(10)^6(1.0)}{1 - 325(10)^3/571.2(10)^3} = 14.34(10)^6 \text{ N-mm/m}$$

Check resistance

$$P_f/A_e + M_f/S_x \leq \phi_m f'_m = 0.55(12.4) = 6.82 \text{ MPa}$$

$$\frac{325(10)^3}{98.3(10)^3} + \frac{14.34(10)^6}{4.93(10)^6} = 6.21 \text{ MPa} < 6.82 \text{ MPa} \qquad \underline{\text{OK}}$$

Check minimum stress

$$P_f/A_e - M_f/S_x = 325(10)^3/98.3(10)^3 - 14.34(10)^6/4.93(10)^6 = 0.40 \text{ MPa}$$

Since this is compression the maximum tensile stress is not exceeded.   <u>OK</u>

Use a 200 wall with one grouted core per metre   <u>Ans.</u>

(Note that axial loads applied at minimum eccentricity are unlikely to produce tensile stresses and it is generally not necessary to check for tension unless lateral loads are also present.)

EXAMPLE 5-3 *The 200 exterior wall of a building is 2.4 m high between points of lateral support and is required to support an axial service load of 250 kN/m (200 kN/m dead load, 50 kN/m live load) applied at end eccentricities of 25 mm at the top and zero at the bottom, and a wind suction of 0.8 kPa (producing bending in the same direction). Using 20 MPa units and type S mortar, check whether an unreinforced wall can be used and, if so, design the wall.*

Since there are three types of load applied to this wall, namely, dead, live and wind loads, various combinations have to be considered in accordance with Equation (1-6).

$$W_f = \alpha_D D + \gamma \Psi(\alpha_L L + \alpha_Q Q)$$

where Q represents the effects of wind, $\gamma = 1.0$, and $\Psi = 1.0$ for one of L and Q and $\Psi = 0.70$ for both loads in combination. Since the effect of dead load alone is less than the effects of dead plus live loads, this case does not need to be considered.

a) *Dead load plus live load*

Although a base eccentricity of zero is given, S304.1 requires that a minimum value of $0.1t = 19$ mm be used. Since the top eccentricity is 25 mm, this gives a mean eccentricity at mid-height of $(19 + 25)/2 = 22$ mm for calculating the primary moment, M_p, for magnification.

The factored axial load is

$$P_f = 1.25D + 1.5L = 1.25(200) + 1.5(50) = 325 \text{ kN/m}$$

and the primary moment is

$$M_p = P_f e = 325(10)^3(22) = 7.15(10)^6 \text{ N-mm/m}$$

b) *Dead load plus wind load*

The primary moment consists of the factored dead load acting over a mean eccentricity of 22 mm and the moment $P_f h^2/8$ caused by the factored wind pressure $p_f = \alpha_Q Q = 1.5(0.8) = 1.2$ kN/m^2 acting over the height $h = 2400$ mm.

$$P_f = \alpha_D D = 1.25(200) = 250 \text{ kN/m}$$

$$M_p = P_f e + p_f h^2/8$$
$$= 250(10)^3(22) + 1.2(2400)^2/8 = 6.36(10)^6 \text{ N-mm/m}$$

c) *Dead load plus live load plus wind*

In this instance 70% of the live load and wind load are assumed to act. That is,

$$L_f = 0.7(1.5)(50) = 52.5 \text{ kN/m}$$
$$p_f = 0.7(1.5)(0.8) = 0.84 \text{ kN/m}^2$$
$$P_f = 1.25(200) + 52.5 = 302.5 \text{ kN/m}$$

and the primary moment is,

$$M_p = 302.5(10)^3(22) + 0.84(2400)^2/8 = 7.26(10)^6 \text{ N-mm/m}$$

A wall section must now be chosen to carry the worst of

a) $P_f = 325$ kN/m and $M_p = 7.15$ kN-m/m
b) $P_f = 250$ kN/m and $M_p = 6.36$ kN-m/m
c) $P_f = 302.5$ kN/m and $M_p = 7.26$ kN-m/m

and it would appear that a) is the governing load case.

Try a 200 ungrouted wall $f'_m = 13$ MPa

From Table 4-1,

$$A_e = 75.4(10)^3 \text{ mm}^2/\text{m}, \quad S_x = 4.66(10)^6 \text{ mm}^3/\text{m and,}$$
$$I_x = 442(10)^6 \text{ mm}^4/\text{m}$$

Check load case: a) $P_f = 325$ kN/m, $M_p = 7.15$ kN-m/m

Recall,

$$M_f = \frac{M_p C_m}{1 - P_f/P_{cr}}$$

where $\quad P_{cr} = \pi^2 EI/(kh)^2$

and

$$EI = \frac{\phi_e E_m I_{eff}}{1 + 0.5\beta_d}$$

$$\phi_e E_m = 0.65(850)(13) = 7.18(10)^3 \text{ MPa}$$

$$I_{eff} = 0.4I_0 = 0.4(442)(10)^6 = 176.8(10)^6 \text{ mm}^4/\text{m}$$

$$\beta_d = (\text{factored dead load moment})/(\text{factored total moment})$$
$$= (\text{factored dead load/factored total load})$$
$$= 1.25(200)/325 = 0.769$$

Therefore

$$EI = \frac{7.18(10)^3(176.8)(10)^6}{1 + 0.5(0.769)} = 917(10)^9 \text{ N-mm}^2/\text{m}$$

$$P_{cr} = \frac{\pi^2 EI}{(kh)^2} = \frac{\pi^2(917)(10)^9}{2400^2} = 1571 \text{ kN/m}$$

and $$C_m = 0.6 + 0.4M_1/M_2 = 0.6 + 0.4e_1/e_2 = 0.6\,(19/25) = 0.904$$

Then

$$M_f = \frac{M_p C_m}{1 - P_f/P_{cr}} = \frac{7.15(10)^6(0.904)}{1 - 325/1571} = 8.15(10)^6 \text{ N-mm/m}$$

Note that this moment of 8.15 kN-m is greater than that produced at the top of the wall ($P_f e_{max} = 0.025(325) = 8.13$ kN-m) and therefore governs this load case in evaluating section resistance to the worst effect of the factored load.

Check resistance

$$P_f/A_e + M_f/S_x \le \phi_m f'_m = 0.55(13) = 7.15 \text{ MPa}$$

$$\frac{325(10)^3}{75.4(10)^3} + \frac{8.15(10)^6}{4.66(10)^6} = 6.06 \text{ MPa} < 7.15 \text{ MPa} \underline{\text{ OK}}$$

It is left as an exercise for the reader to verify that load cases b) and c) are also satisfied.

Therefore, *use a 200 ungrouted wall*.   Ans.

Although S304.1 permits effective height factors, k, less than 1.0 (that is, kh = effective height) in calculating the critical load, P_{cr}, it is not possible to secure a significant degree of fixity at the ends of unreinforced walls, and for these walls the actual height (that is, $k = 1.0$) should be used in the calculations. Note that $k = 1.0$ was used in Examples 5-1, 5-2 and 5-3.

S304.1 defines any wall (or column) with a slenderness ratio $kh/t > 30$ as a very slender wall subject to the special provisions of Clause 11.2.5.6. Although unreinforced walls are not excluded from the clause, because of the potential for sudden brittle failure, very slender walls should be provided with some nominal vertical reinforcing. Very slender walls are the subject of Section 5-6.

This section has shown clearly that the analysis and design of unreinforced walls can be an arduous process, one that can be eased considerably through the use of the tables and charts provided in Part 2 of this book.

Finally, it should be reiterated that although unreinforced columns are permitted by S304.1, their use should be avoided. As significant load-bearing elements they should be provided with the additional structural integrity afforded by vertical reinforcement.

5-3   REINFORCED COLUMNS - Resistance to Axial Load and Bending

As noted above, columns being discrete and significant load-bearing structural elements should, in the interest of structural integrity, be reinforced. S304.1 (Clause 5.2.5.1) requires that when columns are reinforced, the area of reinforcement lie between 1% and 4% of the effective area of the column. Thus a 390 × 390 reinforced column should have vertical reinforcement with an area between $0.01(390)^2 = 1521$ mm^2 and $0.04(390)^2 = 6084$ mm^2, suitably tied to resist compression. In such instances, the tie diameter should not be less than 3.8 mmϕ (No. 9 ASWG) and the spacing should not exceed 16 bar diameters, 48 tie diameters, or the least dimension of the column (Clause 5.2.5.3.1). If the tie is placed in the mortar joint its diameter should be significantly less than the thickness (10 mm) of the joint to avoid stress concentrations. Although S304.1 (Clause 5.1.4) requires that *joint* reinforcement not exceed 5 mmϕ, a maximum size of 6 mmϕ (1/4") is acceptable for *ties* laid in mortar joints.

Since analysis and design are more complex for reinforced than for unreinforced walls and columns, the *resistance* of the cross-section to combined axial load and bending is considered separately from the effects of slenderness in the following discussion. Also, in the design of columns, both uniaxial and biaxial bending must be considered.

Axial Load and Uniaxial Bending

The resistance of a reinforced column section, where vertical reinforcement is adequately tied to resist compression, can be calculated according to the following analysis. The moment used in the analysis is the total moment (primary plus secondary), that is, the magnified moment. In developing the relationships for the resistance to axial load and bending the following principles apply.

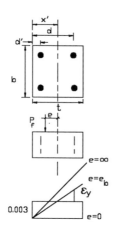

Fig. 5-8 Analysis of Reinforced Column

Section Resistance

The resistance of the section is governed by

$P_r \geq P_f$, the factored axial load
$M_r \geq M_f$, total moment due to factored load
$e = M_r/P_r$ = eccentricity (or M_f/P_f)

The following three cases are easily identified and form the basis of constructing an interaction diagram.

a) *Axial load only (e = 0, c = ∞)*

Referring to Fig. 5-8, the resistance of the section to axial load is derived as

$$P_r = \phi_m\chi(0.85f'_m)(bt - A_{s1} - A_{s2}) + \phi_s(A_{s1} + A_{s2})f_y$$

$$\approx \phi_m\chi(0.85f'_m)bt + \phi_s(A_{s1} + A_{s2})f_y \qquad (5\text{-}7a)$$

where $\chi = 1.0$ for walls and columns.

S304.1 (Clause 10.2.3.5.2) imposes a further factor of 0.8 to this expression for an upper limit of

$$P_{r(max)} = 0.8[0.85\ \phi_m f'_m(A_e - A_s) + \phi_s A_s f_y] \qquad (5\text{-}7b)$$

b) *Balanced case (e = e_b)*

That is, the tension steel is starting to yield as the masonry reaches its limiting strain in compression

$$\epsilon_m = 0.003, \ \epsilon_s = \epsilon_y$$

From the strain diagram, the depth to the neutral axis is

$$c = \frac{0.003}{\epsilon_y + 0.003}d = \frac{600}{f_y + 600}d,$$

and the depth of the rectangular stress block is

$$a = \beta_1 c$$

The stress in the compression steel is obtained from

$$\epsilon'_s = 0.003(c - d')/c, \quad f'_s = \epsilon'_s E_s \leq f_y$$

The forces in component materials are

$$C_m = \phi_m \chi (0.85 f'_m) ba, \quad \chi = 1.0$$
$$C_s = \phi_s A_{s1} [f'_s - \phi_m (0.85 f'_m)] \approx \phi_s A_{s1} f'_s$$
$$T_r = \phi_s A_{s2} f_y \tag{5-8}$$

Then
$$C_r = C_m + C_s$$
$$P_r = C_r - T_r$$

The resistance of the column to the "balanced" combination of axial load and moment is

$$P_{rb} = C_m + C_s - T_r \tag{5-9}$$

And the moment of resistance is obtained by taking a summation of the component forces about the centroid

$$M_{rb} = P_{rb} e_b$$
$$= C_m(\bar{x} - a/2) + C_s(\bar{x} - d') + T_r(d - \bar{x}) \tag{5-10}$$

Where $\bar{x}$ is the location of the centroid of the section, normally $t/2$ for a symmetrically reinforced section.

c) *Bending alone (e = ∞)*
        The procedure is that outlined in Chapters 3 and 4 for doubly-reinforced sections.

General case
        The appropriate procedure is to develop a P_r vs. M_r interaction diagram. This is done most simply by stepping the location of the neutral axis across the section from $c = t$ to c for bending alone, performing an analysis for P_r and M_r in each case.
        Note that $c > t$ is prone to error from the assumption of a rectangular stress block, and for the interaction diagram, a straight line $M_r P_r$ relationship can be assumed from $c = t$ to $c = ∞$ (axial load only). The principles are illustrated by the following example.

EXAMPLE 5-4 *A 390 × 390 masonry column is reinforced with 4-#25 vertical bars, as shown in Fig. 5-9, tied to resist compression. If f'_m = 10 MPa and f_y = 400 MPa, determine the resistance (M_r and P_r) of the section for*
a) axial load alone (M = 0)
b) the balanced case of axial load and bending
c) bending alone (P = 0), and
d) select suitable ties

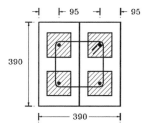

Fig. 5-9 Reinforced Masonry Column of Example 5-4

$$A_{s1} = A_{s2} = 2(500) = 1000 \text{ mm}^2$$

a) *Axial load alone (M = 0)*

Check steel ratio

$$A_s = A_{s1} + A_{s2} = 1000 + 1000 = 2000 \text{ mm}^2$$
$$\rho = A_s/bt = 2000/[390(390)] = 0.013 > 0.01$$
$$< 0.04 \qquad \underline{\text{OK}}$$

$$P_r \leq 0.8[\phi_m \chi(0.85f'_m)bt + \phi_s A_s f_y] \text{ and } \chi = 1.0 \text{ for columns}$$
$$= 0.8[0.55(1.0)(0.85)(10)(390)(390) + 0.85(2000)(400)]$$
$$= 1113(10)^3 \text{ kN} \qquad \underline{\text{Ans.}}$$

(Note that had the displacement of grout by steel been allowed for, P_r = 1105 kN - a difference of less than 1%)

b) *Balanced case (e =e_b)* - that is, tension steel starts to yield as the masonry reaches the crushing strain of 0.003.

$$c = 600d/(f_y + 600) = 600(390 - 95)/(400 + 600) = 177 \text{ mm}$$
$$a = \beta_1 c = 0.80(177) = 141.6 \text{ mm}$$
$$\epsilon'_s = 0.003(c - d')/c = 0.003(177 - 95)/177 = 0.00139$$
$$f'_s = \epsilon'_s E_s = 0.00139(200)(10)^3 = 278 \text{ MPa} < f_y \qquad \underline{\text{OK}}$$

$$C_m = \phi_m \chi(0.85f'_m)ba = 0.55(1.0)(0.85)(10)(390)(141.6)$$
$$= 258.2 \text{ kN}$$

$$C_s = \phi_s A_{s1} f'_s = 0.85(1000)(278) = 236.3 \text{ kN}$$

$$T_r = \phi_s A_{s2} f_y = 0.85(1000)(400) = 340.0 \text{ kN}$$

and $$P_r = C_m + C_s - T_r = 258.2 + 236.3 - 340.0$$
$$= 154.5 \text{ kN}$$

Since the section is symmetrically reinforced, $\bar{x} = t/2$ and

$$M_r = C_m(t/2 - a/2) + C_s(t/2 - d') + T_r(d - t/2)$$
$$= 258.2(10)^3(195-70.8) + 236.3(10)^3(195-95) + 340(10)^3(295-195)$$
$$= 89.7(10)^6 \text{ N-mm} = 89.7 \text{ kN-m}$$

and the eccentricity for the balanced case is

$$e_b = M_r/P_r = 89.7(10)^6/154.5(10)^3 = 580 \text{ mm}$$

For the balanced case then,

$$P_r = 154.5 \text{ kN}, \ M_r = 89.7 \text{ kN-m and } e_b = 580 \text{ mm} \qquad \underline{\text{Ans.}}$$

c) *Bending alone*

Since this case now involves bending only, the steel on the tension side must be checked to ensure that it is greater than $\rho_{min} = 0.8/f_y = 0.002$

$$\rho = A_{s2}/bd = 1000/[390(295)] = 0.0087 > \rho_{min} \qquad \underline{\text{OK}}$$

and, since $A_{s1} = A_{s2}$, it is not necessary to check ρ_{max}.

It is now left as an exercise for the reader to show that the moment of resistance of the doubly-reinforced section subject to pure bending is
$$M_r = 76.1 \text{ kN-m} \qquad \underline{\text{Ans.}}$$

d) *Selection of ties*

Because the ties in this column pass over webs and face shells which are only 10 mm (the thickness of the mortar joints) #10 ties cannot be used. In such instances a maximum tie diameter of 6 mm (1/4") is recommended to avoid serious stress concentrations. The maximum spacing, *s*, of 6 mm ties is

$$s \leq 16 \text{ bar diameters} = 16(25) = 400 \text{ mm}$$
$$\leq 48 \text{ tie diameters} = 48(6) = 288 \text{ mm}$$
$$\leq \text{least column dimension} = 390 \text{ mm}$$

Use 6 mm ϕ ties @ 200 centres   Ans.

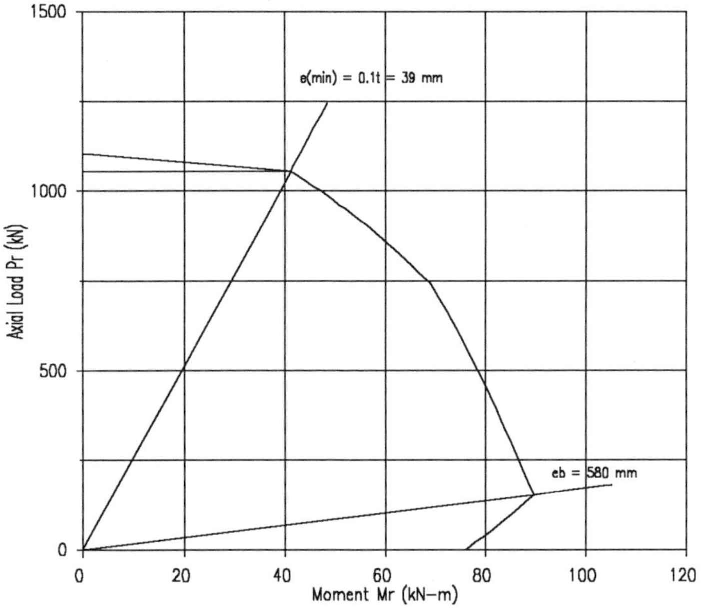

Fig. 5-10 Interaction Diagram of Reinforced Masonry Column

From an analysis of the column of Example 5-4, by stepping the neutral axis from a value of *c* for pure bending to *c* = *t* and beyond, the interaction diagram of Fig. 5-10 is obtained. Note the cut-off at $e_{min} = 0.1t$ and the peak moment at $e = e_b$. As an exercise in understanding, the reader is invited to confirm at least one point between *c* = 177 mm for the balanced case and *c* = *t* = 390 mm.

Columns that are subject to axial load and uniaxial bending, such as that in Example 5-4, are required to meet minimum eccentricity requirements about each major axis. Since the column in this example is square, with equal resistance about each major axis, that requirement is satisfied.

Axial Load and Biaxial Bending

Masonry columns may be subjected to, in addition to axial load, significant bending about both major axes. This is especially true for corner columns carrying intersecting but eccentrically supported beams. Such a situation is illustrated in Fig. 5-11 where (a) shows the factored axial load and factored moments (suitably magnified) at the section, and (b) shows the equivalent situation of the axial load applied at eccentricities e_x and e_y (that include any lateral deflection).

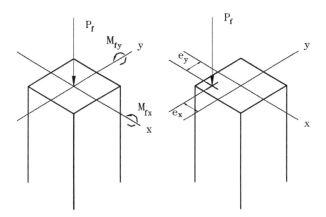

(a) Axial load and moments   (b) Axial load and eccentricities

Fig. 5-11 Axial Load and Biaxial Bending

A precise analysis of a biaxially loaded reinforced column is a complex procedure. Fortunately, S304.1 (based on research in masonry and reinforced concrete), in Clause 11.4.2, provides a criterion that satisfactorily permits the design. However, the process really requires that interaction diagrams be available to the designer. The criterion is

$$\frac{M_{fx}}{M_{rx}} + \frac{M_{fy}}{M_{ry}} \leq 1.0 \tag{5-11}$$

where M_{fx} and M_{fy} are concurrently the total factored moments (including the effects of slenderness) about the major axes, and M_{rx} and M_{ry} are the factored moments of resistance in the presence of the factored axial load, P_f. The values M_{rx} and M_{ry} are most conveniently obtained from interaction diagrams. Where the column is not identical about both axes, two diagrams are required.

EXAMPLE 5-5 *The column of Example 5-4 (that is, a 390 × 390 column with 4-#25 bars located as shown in Fig. 5-9 and suitably tied for compression) is subjected to a factored axial load $P_f = 155$ kN and total factored moments of $M_{fx} = 40$ kN-m and $M_{fy} = 45$ kN-m. If $f'_m = 10$ MPa and $f_y = 400$ MPa, determine whether the section can safely satisfy the loading.*

Since this column in this example is square and has equal resistance about each major axis, and is the subject of Fig. 5-10, that interaction diagram can be used.

From the interaction diagram of Fig. 5-10, for a factored axial load $P_f = 155$ kN, the moment of resistance about either axis is about 90 kN-m. That is, $M_{rx} = M_{ry} = 90$ kN-m.

Applying Equation (5-11)

$$\frac{M_{fx}}{M_{rx}} + \frac{M_{fy}}{M_{ry}} = \frac{40.0}{90.0} + \frac{45.0}{90.0} = 0.94 < 1.00 \qquad \underline{OK}$$

Therefore, the column can safely resist the loading.   <u>Ans.</u>

Note that the values of P_f and $M_{fx} + M_{fy}$ in this example were conveniently chosen to correspond with the balanced case. If M_{fx} and M_{fy} are due to the eccentric application of P_f, any overestimate of P_f will in turn result in an overestimate of M_{fx} and M_{fy} also, and the analysis is valid. If, however, M_{fx} and M_{fy} are largely the result of the loading (for example, wind loading), an overestimate of P_f can lead to a spuriously high value of M_r. For this reason, the elevated resistance to bending due to axial load, especially around the balanced case, should be reviewed carefully.

5-4   REINFORCED WALLS - Resistance to Axial Load and Bending

The term *load-bearing* normally applies to walls that carry vertical in-plane forces caused by gravity loading. This axial load is usually accompanied by some out-of-plane bending, whether due to lateral forces (such as wind or earthquake) or to the eccentric application of the gravity loading or from eccentricities introduced because of construction tolerances. This is exemplified in the S304.1 requirement that walls be designed for a primary moment of at least that produced by the axial load acting over an eccentricity of 0.1t. That is, $M_p \geq P_f(0.1t)$.

Reinforcement

When out-of-plane bending is sufficient to cause tensile cracking, vertical reinforcement should be provided. If the reinforcement is adequately tied then, under different loading conditions, it can be included in the calculation of resistance to compression. A reinforced wall can be subjected to load combinations ranging from pure bending (a situation considered in some detail in Example 4-13) to axial load acting over the minimum eccentricity of $0.1t$. As was the case for reinforced columns, the structural design of reinforced walls is most conveniently conducted through the medium of axial load vs. moment interaction diagrams.

When vertical reinforcement is required to resist flexural tension there should be sufficient area of steel to meet the minimum area of steel for flexure, that is $\rho \geq 0.8/f_y$. The application of that requirement was illustrated in Example 4-13. Clause 5.2.1.1 requires that the flexural steel be continuous between lateral supports, be spaced no farther apart than 2400 mm, and that it be provided at each side of each opening over 1200 mm, each side of control joints, and at corners and ends of walls, and that it be placed to ensure at least 15 mm of grout cover all around. When the wall spans horizontally and flexural cracking is anticipated, horizontal reinforcement meeting the same requirements should be provided. In this case the joint reinforcement can be considered as all or part of the horizontal steel.

When the steel is tied to resist compression the design is similar to that for columns, except for a reduction in the maximum area of steel. The minimum area of vertical reinforcement in load bearing walls and in reinforced sections of partially reinforced walls is specified in Clause 5.2.1.2 as 0.133% of the gross area of the wall. The maximum area of vertical steel, no matter what the loading circumstances, is specified in Clause 5.2.3 as 2% of the gross area of the wall, that is, for a nominal 250 wall $A_s \leq 0.02(1000)(240) = 4800$ mm²/m. Although bar sizes up to #30 are permitted in masonry, #25 is generally the maximum size used, #15 and #20 being more common.

The National Building Code and S304.1 require that in certain seismic zones a *minimum seismic reinforcement* be provided in walls. These requirements are covered in detail in Chapter 7.

Resistance

The resistance of a reinforced wall to axial load and out-of-plane bending is obtained by following the same principles outlined in Section 5-3 for reinforced columns. The main differences are that walls have the vertical steel placed at the mid-thickness and may not be fully grouted. Also, while the vertical steel can resist flexural tension, if not suitably tied it should not be relied on to resist compression. In the following analysis the wall is assumed to be fully grouted.

Considering a one-metre length of wall, the resistance of the section is governed by,

$P_r \geq P_f$, the factored axial load
$M_r \geq M_f$, the total moment due to the factored load
$e = M_r/P_r$ = eccentricity (or M_f/P_f).

The following cases are easily identified and form the basis of an interaction diagram.

a) *Axial load only* ($e = 0$, $c = \infty$)

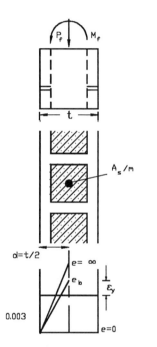

Fig. 5-12 Reinforced Walls Under Axial
Load and Bending

Referring to Fig. 5-12, the resistance of the fully grouted section to axial load is

$$P_r = \phi_m\chi(0.85f'_m)A_e \qquad (5\text{-}13a)$$

However, S304.1 (Clause 10.2.3.5.1) places an upper limit on resistance of

$$P_r = 0.8(0.85)\phi_m\chi f'_m A_e \qquad (5\text{-}13b)$$

where
A_e = effective area, mm^2/m
    = $1000t$ for a fully grouted wall
χ = 1.0

and, if the vertical steel is tied to resist compression

$$P_r = \phi_m\chi(0.85f'_m)A_e + \phi_s A_s f_y \qquad (5\text{-}14a)$$

Again, S304.1 (Clause 10.2.3.5.2) places an upper limit of

$$P_r = 0.8[0.85\phi_m\chi f'_m(A_e - A_s) + \phi_s A_s f_y] \qquad (5\text{-}14b)$$

b) *Balanced case* ($e = e_b$)

That is, the steel is starting to yield in tension as the masonry reaches its limiting strain of 0.003.

$$\epsilon_s = \epsilon_y, \; \epsilon_m = 0.003$$

From the strain diagram, the depth to the neutral axis is

$$c = \frac{0.003}{\epsilon_y + 0.003} d = \frac{0.0015t}{\epsilon_y + 0.003} = \frac{300t}{f_y + 600}$$

and the depth of the rectangular stress block is

$$a = \beta_1 c$$

The forces in the component materials are

$$C_m = \phi_m \chi (0.85 f'_m) ba, \ \chi = 1.0, \ b = 1000 \text{ mm}$$
$$T_r = \phi_s A_s f_y \qquad\qquad\qquad\qquad\qquad (5\text{-}15)$$

The resistance of the wall to the "balanced" combination of axial load and moment is

$$P_{rb} = C_m - T_r \qquad\qquad\qquad\qquad\qquad (5\text{-}16)$$

and the moment of resistance is obtained by taking a summation of the moments of the component forces about the centroid

$$M_{rb} = P_{rb} e_b = C_m(t/2 - a/2) \qquad\qquad\qquad (5\text{-}17)$$

c) *Bending alone* $(e = \infty)$

The procedure that is outlined in Chapters 3 and 4, and more specifically in Example 4-13.

There are a few points worth noting in this analysis. If the wall is only partially grouted, the accurate determination of P_r and M_r involves a rather complicated tee-beam analysis, one that is best handled by computer-generated interaction diagrams, such as those included in Part 2 of this book. Strictly speaking, if compression is confined to the face shell (which may occur if M_f has a high value and p_f a low one) the value of f'_m for an ungrouted wall can be used since the grout is not in compression, while f'_m for the grouted wall should be used for axial load alone. However, this differentiation only complicates the calculation and the lower value of f'_m can be used throughout with little loss of accuracy.

EXAMPLE 5-6 *A 250 concrete block wall is reinforced with #20 vertical bars @ 400 mm centres and is fully grouted, as shown in Fig. 5-13. If 20 MPa units and type S mortar are used, and if $f_y = 400$ MPa, determine the resistance (P_r and M_r) of the section for*
a) axial load alone (M = 0)
b) the balanced case of axial load and bending, and
c) bending alone (P = 0)

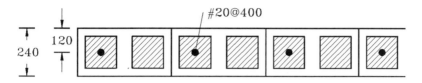

Fig. 5-13 Reinforced Masonry Wall

Considering a one-metre length of wall, the area of steel per metre is

$$A_s/m = \text{area of one bar} \times 1000/\text{spacing}$$
$$= 300(1000)/400 = 750 \text{ mm}^2/\text{m}$$

For 20 MPa units $f'_m = 13$ MPa ungrouted, 10 MPa fully grouted.

a) *Axial load alone (M = 0)*

i) If the steel is not tied to resist compression there is no need to check the steel
ratio at this point and

$$P_r = 0.8(0.85)\phi_m f'_m A_e$$
$$= 0.8(0.85)(0.55)(10)(1000)(240) = 897.6 \text{ kN}$$

ii) If the steel is tied to resist compression, the steel ratio is checked against the
maximum steel ratio for walls. That is, $A_s/A_g \leq 0.02$

$$\rho = A_s/bt = 750/[1000(240)] = 0.0031 < 0.02 \qquad \underline{\text{OK}}$$

and

$$P_r = 0.8[0.85\phi_m f'_m(A_e - A_s) + \phi_s A_s f_y]$$
$$= 0.8[0.85(0.55)(10)(240{,}000 - 750) + 0.85(750)(400)]$$
$$= 1099 \text{ kN} \qquad \underline{\text{Ans.}}$$

b) *Balanced case (e = e_b)* - steel starts to yield in tension as masonry strain
reaches 0.003

$$c = 300t/(f_y + 600) = 300(240)/(400 + 600) = 72 \text{ mm}$$
$$a = \beta_1 c = 0.80(72) = 57.6 \text{ mm}$$
$$C_m = \phi_m \chi(0.85f'_m)ba$$
$$= 0.55(1.0)(0.85)(10)(1000)(57.6) = 269.3 \text{ kN/m}$$
$$T_r = \phi_s A_s f_y = 0.85(750)(400) = 255.0 \text{ kN/m}$$

Then $P_{rb} = C_m - T_r = 269.3 - 255.0 = 14.3$ kN/m

and $M_{rb} = C_m(t/2 - a/2) = 269.3(10)^3(120 - 57.6/2) = 24.56$ kN-m/m

and the eccentricity for the balanced case is

$$e_b = M_{rb}/P_{rb} = 24.56(10)^6/14.3(10)^3 = 1717 \text{ mm}$$

$$P_{rb} = 14.3 \text{ kN/m}, \quad M_{rb} = 24.56 \text{ kN-m/m} \qquad \underline{\text{Ans.}}$$

c) *Bending alone*

Since this case involves bending alone, the steel ratio must be checked.

From Table 4-2,

$$\rho_{max} = 0.0066 \text{ for } \chi = 1.0, \text{ and}$$
$$\rho_{min} = 0.8/f_y = 0.8/400 = 0.002$$

$$\rho = A_s/bd = 750/[1000(120)] = 0.00625 > \rho_{min}$$
$$< \rho_{max} \qquad \underline{\text{OK}}$$

Again, it is left as an exercise for the reader to verify that the resistance of the section to pure bending is

$$M_r = 23.65 \text{ kN-m/m} \qquad \underline{\text{Ans.}}$$

The P_r vs. M_r interaction diagram for the wall section of Example 5-6 is shown in Fig. 5-14, and the reader should note that, since the steel ratio in bending of 0.00625 is close to the maximum value of 0.0066, the "balanced" case and that of pure bending are in close proximity. The peak moment in the interaction curve does not occur at the "balanced" situation (that is, the steel on the point of yielding in tension) - as was the case for the column in Example 5-4 - but at some location of neutral axis that places the steel in compression.

As before, the appropriate way to construct an interaction diagram is by stepping the neutral axis across the section from the value of c for pure bending to $c = 240$ mm, and by using a straight line relationship from that point to the values for axial load only. As an exercise, the reader may wish to verify some of the points on the iteraction diagram shown in the following table.

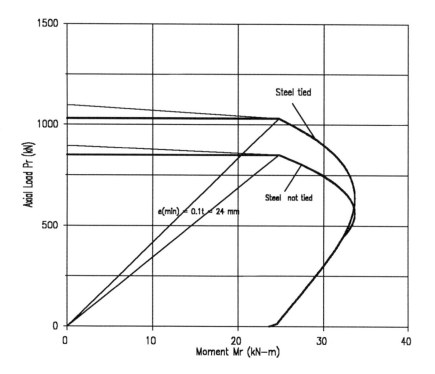

Fig. 5-14 Interaction Diagram of Reinforced Masonry Wall

Table 5-1
Resistance Values for Fig. 5-14

Depth to NA c (mm.)	P_r (kN/m)		M_r (kN-m/m)	Comments
	A_s not tied	A_s tied		
68.2	0	0	23.65	Pure bending
72.0	14.3	14.3	24.56	"balanced" case
120	448.8	448.8	32.30	NA @ centre
150	561.0	637.5	33.66	Peak moment
175	654.5	774.7	32.70	
200	748.0	901.0	29.90	
225	841.5	1020	25.25	
240	898.0	1089	21.54	NA @ edge
	897.6	1099	0.00	Axial load

There is no doubt that vertical reinforcement enhances the resistance of a wall to compression - research has proven it. However, if the steel is not adequately tied, or, more accurately, if the masonry materials are not adequately confined, failure under axial load tends to be of a brittle, rather than a ductile, nature. The extent to which joint reinforcement provides lateral constraint is a moot point. Standard No. 9 joint reinforcement consists of two longitudinal wires 3.7 mmϕ (#9 ASWG) with 3.7 mmϕ cross-wires spaced at 400 mm. This joint reinforcement placed in every course, that is, at a spacing of 200 mm, does not meet the maximum spacing requirement of 48 tie diameters (48 $\times$ 3.7 = 177.6 mm < 200 mm). No.8 joint reinforcement (4.1 mmΦ) approximately meets the spacing requirement, but is not currently available in Canada. However, with a cross-wire spacing of 400 mm, it is likely that some vertical reinforcement will be more than the maximum distance of 150 mm from a corner, specified by S304.1. It might be noted that, since ties in mortar joints represent a rigid inclusion that can lead to stress concentrations, S304.1 limits the tie size to a maximum size of 5.0 mmϕ. However, bearing in mind the e_{min} cut-off in the interaction diagram, a section will not be designed for the case of axial load alone and the use of No. 8 joint reinforcement is probably justifiable as lateral reinforcement.

One relatively common practice among structural designers is to design the reinforced cores as reinforced concrete columns, having specified the compressive strength of the grout, neglecting the resistance to compression of the masonry unit, but including the increased stiffness afforded by the unit. This is a practice that should be avoided. Because the grout shrinks more than the unit, the unit carries the load until the differential shrinkage strain is overcome. Beyond that point, the grout picks up load. If tested under axial load to failure, the unit always fails first and the grout is relatively intact. While this may appear to justify the use of the "grout column" concept, the stiffness of the column decreases immediately, severely reducing the load-carrying capacity of the column.

5-5   EFFECT OF SLENDERNESS - Reinforced Walls and Columns

Since unreinforced walls are relatively simple to analyze, both resistance and the effect of slenderness were covered in Section 5-2 for this type of wall. The analysis of reinforced columns and walls, however, is more complex, and Sections 5-3 and 5-4 deal solely with *resistance*. This section covers the effects of slenderness and the magnification of moment that results. The special case of *very slender walls*, that is, $kh/t > 30$, is the subject of Section 5-6.

As noted previously, Clause 11.2.4.3 of S304.1 outlines slenderness limits as follows:

a)   When $kh/t < 10 - 3.5e_1/e_2$ the effect of slenderness can be neglected.
b)   When $kh/t < 30$, normal design procedures are used.
c)   When $kh/t > 30$, the specified provisions for very slender walls apply.

The following discussion covers b).

The effect of slenderness on a reinforced masonry column or wall subjected to axial load and bending is to produce a magnified moment due to the axial load acting over the deflection produced by bending, or the $P\delta$ *effect*. However, as was noted earlier, rather than use the $P\delta$ *method* (Clause 11.2.5.2 of S304.1), the more direct *moment magnifier method* (Clause 11.2.5.3) is the appropriate method of analysis.

The moment magnifier method requires that the column or wall section be designed to resist a combination of the factored axial load, P_f, and the primary moment, M_p, magnified by the factor $C_m/(1 - P_f/P_{cr})$, that is,

$$M_f = M_{TOT} = M_p C_m/(1 - P_f/P_{cr}) \tag{5-18}$$

where $\quad C_m = 0.6 + 0.4M_1/M_2$ as defined earlier

$\qquad\qquad P_{cr} = \pi^2 \phi_e E_m I_{eff}/[(1 + 0.5\beta_d)(kh)^2]$

and $\qquad\quad \phi_e = 0.65$

$\qquad\qquad E_m = 850f'_m \leq 20,000$ MPa, or the value obtained from testing

$\qquad\qquad I_{eff} = $ effective moment of inertia

$\qquad\qquad \beta_d = $ factored dead load moment/M_f

The effective moment of inertia is that given by Clause 11.2.5.4 of S304.1, that is,

$$I_{eff} = 0.25I_0 - (0.25I_0 - I_{cr})(e - e_k)/(2e_k) \tag{5-19}$$

where $\quad I_0 = $ moment of inertia of the uncracked section

$\qquad\qquad I_{cr} = $ moment of inertia of the cracked section

$\qquad\qquad e = M_p/P_f$

$\qquad\qquad e_k = S/A_e$

$\qquad\qquad S = $ section modulus of the uncracked section

Clause 11.2.5.4 notes that I_{eff} should not be taken greater than $0.25I_0$ but need not be less than I_{cr}. When I_{cr} is greater than $0.25I_0$, I_{cr} may be used in calculating P_{cr}. It is interesting to note that although $0.25I_0$ is used to calculate I_{eff} for reinforced masonry walls and columns, $I_{eff} = 0.4I_0$ is used for unreinforced masonry. As noted in S304.1, the higher value may be used for reinforced walls provided the reinforcement is not considered in the design.

The appropriate way to illustrate the magnification of moment and design for resistance is through examples.

EXAMPLE 5-7 *A 390 × 390 masonry column is 5.0 m high and is reinforced with 4-#25 bars and 6 mmϕ ties @ 200. The loading on the column is entirely due to dead load and consists of an axial service load of 400 kN and end moments due to service loads of*

*20 kN-m about each of the major axes and at each end of the column. If $f'_m = 10$ MPa
and $f_y = 400$ MPa, determine whether the column section has sufficient resistance.*

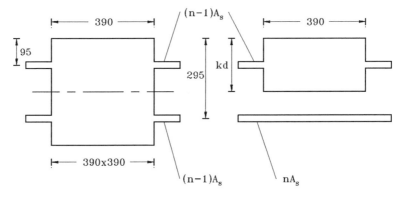

a) Uncracked section   b) Cracked section

Fig. 5-15 Transformed Section of Masonry Column of Example 5-7

Since this is the column section of Example 5-4, the interaction diagram of
Fig. 5-10 can be used. Also, because biaxial bending is involved, the principles
of Example 5-5 apply.

Check slenderness

Since k is not specified, use $k = 1.0$

$$kh/t = 1.0(5000)/(390) = 12.8 < 30 \qquad\qquad \underline{OK}$$

and the moment magnifier method can be used.

The factored axial load is

$$P_f = \alpha_D P_D = 1.25(400) = 500 \text{ kN}$$

and the primary end moments are

$$M_{px} = M_{py} = \alpha_D M = 1.25(20) = 25 \text{ kN-m}$$

In this column, the primary moments should not be less than the axial load
applied at the minimum eccentricity of $0.1t$, that is,

$$P_f e_{min} = 500(10)^3(0.1)(390) = 19.5(10)^6 \text{ N-mm} = 19.5 \text{ kN-m}$$

and

$$M_{px} = M_{py} = 25 \text{ kN-m} > 19.5 \text{ kN-m} \qquad \text{OK}$$

Check reinforcement

$$\rho = A_s/bt = 4(500)/[390(390)] = 0.013 > 0.01$$
$$< 0.04 \qquad \text{OK}$$

and the tie spacing of 200 mm

$$s < 48 \text{ tie diameters} = 48(6) = 288 \text{ mm}$$
$$< 16 \text{ bar diameters} = 16(25) = 400 \text{ mm}$$
$$< \text{least column dimension} = 390 \text{ mm} \qquad \text{OK}$$

Having the values of P_f, M_{px} and M_{py}, it is now required that the moments are magnified to obtain the total moment and then check section resistance. The primary moment about each axis is then magnified to give the total moment.

$$M_f = M_{TOT} = M_p C_m/(1 - P_f/P_{cr})$$

and the magnification is applied to M_{px} and M_{py}, in this expression.

$$P_{cr} = \pi^2 \phi_e E_m I_{eff}/[(1 + 0.5\beta_d)(kh)^2]$$

where $\phi_e = 0.65$
$E_m = 850f'_m = 850(10) = 8500 \text{ MPa} < 20,000 \text{ MPa} \qquad \text{OK}$
$\beta_d = M_D/M_f = 1.0$
$k = 1.0$ since fixity was not specified.

and from Equation (5-19)

$$I_{eff} = 0.25I_0 - (0.25I_0 - I_{cr})(e - e_k)/(2e_k)$$

where I_0 and I_{cr} are the moments of inertia of the uncracked and cracked sections, respectively,

$$e = M_p/P_f = 25(10)^6/[500(10)^3] = 50 \text{ mm}$$
$$e_k = S/A_e = I_0/(y_t A_e)$$

To obtain the moments of inertia of the uncracked and cracked sections, a transformed section analysis is performed. For this the value of the modular ratio ($n = E_s/E_m$) is required.

$$n = E_s/E_m = 200,000/8500 = 23.5$$

Referring to Fig. 5-15 a)

Uncracked section

$$
\begin{aligned}
I_{ox} = I_{oy} = I_o &= bh^3/12 + 2(n-1)A_s(h/2 - d')^2 \\
&= 390^4/12 + 2(23.5 - 1)(1000)(390/2 - 95)^2 = 2378(10)^6 \text{ mm}^4 \\
A_e &= 390(390) + 2(23.5 - 1)(1000) = 197.1(10)^3 \text{ mm}^2
\end{aligned}
$$

Then $e_k = 2378(10)^6/[(390/2)(197.1)(10)^3] = 61.8$ mm

Cracked section

From Fig. 5-15 b) the depth kd to the centroid of the section is found by taking moments of areas about the centroidal axis

$$390(kd)^2/2 + (23.5 - 1)(1000)(kd - 95) = 23.5(1000)(295 - kd)$$

which solves to give $kd = 128$ mm, and since $d' < kd$ the analysis is valid.

Then

$$
\begin{aligned}
I_{cr} &= b(kd)^3/3 + (n-1)A'_s(kd - d')^2 + nA_s(d - kd)^2 \\
&= 390(128)^3/3 + 22.5(1000)(128 - 95)^2 + 23.5(1000)(295 - 128)^2 \\
&= 953(10)^6 \text{ mm}^4
\end{aligned}
$$

Thus $I_o = 2378(10)^6$ mm^4 and $I_{cr} = 953(10)^6$ mm^4

Then $I_{eff} = 0.25I_0 - (0.25I_0 - I_{cr})(e - e_k)/(2e_k)$
$$
\begin{aligned}
&= 0.25(2378)(10)^6 - [0.25(2378)(10)^6 - 953(10)^6](50 - 61.8)/[2(61.8)] \\
&= 561(10)^6 \text{ mm}^4 \qquad < 595(10)^6 = 0.25\, I_o \\
&\qquad\qquad\qquad\qquad\quad < 953(10)^6 = I_{cr}
\end{aligned}
$$

and S304.1 notes that I_{eff} need not be less than I_{cr}.

Then $I_{eff} = 953(10)^6$ mm^4

The value of P_{cr} can now be calculated as

$$
\begin{aligned}
P_{cr} &= \pi^2\phi_e E_m I_{eff}/[(1 + 0.5\beta_d)(kh)^2] \text{ and } \beta_d = 1.0 \\
&= \pi^2(0.65)(8500)(953)(10)^6/[(1 + 0.5)(5000)^2] = 1386 \text{ kN}
\end{aligned}
$$

Thus $M_f = M_p C_m/(1 - P_f/P_{cr})$

$$= 25(10)^6(1.0)/(1 - 500/1386) = 39.1 \text{ kN-m}$$

That is, $M_{fx} = M_{fy} = 39.1$ kN

From the interaction diagram (Fig. 5-10) for this column, a value of $P_f = 500$ kN gives a value of $M_r \approx 78$ kN-m. That is, $M_{rx} = M_{ry} = 78$ kN-m.

For biaxial bending

$$M_{fx}/M_{rx} + M_{fy}/M_{ry} = 39.1/78 + 39.1/78 = 1.003 \approx 1.00 \qquad \underline{OK}$$

Therefore, the column has adequate resistance.   <u>Ans.</u>

It is interesting to note that for the same *M/P* ratio the working stress design standard, S304, allows an axial service load of only 200 kN compared to the 400 kN of the previous example.

EXAMPLE 5-8 *A 4.0 m high 250 masonry wall is reinforced with #20 vertical bars @ 400 and is fully grouted. The wall carries a service axial load consisting of 240 kN/m dead load and 120 kN/m live load. If f'$_m$ = 10 MPa and f$_y$ = 400 MPa, determine whether the wall can safely carry the load.*

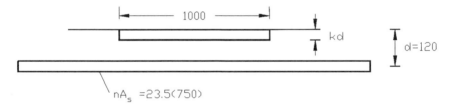

Fig. 5-16 Transformed Section of Masonry Wall of Example 5-8

Note that this is the wall of Example 5-6 and the interaction diagram shown in Fig. 5-14 can be used.

Check slenderness

Because it is not specified, use $k = 1.0$

$$kh/t = 1.0(4000)/240 = 16.7 < 30 \qquad \underline{OK}$$

Considering a one-metre length of wall, the factored axial load is

$$P_f = \alpha_D P_D + \alpha_L P_L = 1.25(240) + 1.5(120) = 480 \text{ kN/m}$$

and the primary moment that is produced by P_f acting over the minimum eccentricity of $0.1t = 24$ mm is

$$M_p = 480(10)^3(24) = 11.5(10)^6 \text{ N-mm} = 11.5 \text{ kN-m}$$

The interaction diagram shows that the steel in the wall is in compression.

Check steel ratio

$$A_s = 300 \text{ mm}^2/400 \text{ mm} = 300(1000)/400 = 750 \text{ mm}^2/\text{m}$$
$$\rho = A_s/A_g = 750/[1000(240)] = 0.0031 < 0.02 \text{ for walls} \quad \underline{\text{OK}}$$

The primary moment, M_p, should now be magnified to obtain the total factored moment. That is,

$$M_f = M_p C_m/(1 - P_f/P_{cr})$$
$$C_m = 0.6 + 0.4M_1/M_2 = 0.6 + 0.4(1.0) = 1.0$$
$$P_{cr} = \pi^2 \phi_e E_m I_{eff}/[(1 + 0.5\beta_d)(kh)^2]$$

where $\phi_e = 0.65$ and $E_m = 850f'_m = 8500$ MPa
              $\beta_d = M_{fdead}/M_f = P_{fdead}/P_f = 1.25(240)/480 = 0.625$
              $k = 1.0$

and $I_{eff} = 0.25I_0 - (0.25I_0 - I_{cr})(e - e_k)/(2e_k)$
I_0 and I_{cr} being the uncracked and cracked moments of inertia.

Since the reinforcement is at the centre of the wall

$$I_0 = 1000(240)^3/12 = 1152(10)^6 \text{ mm}^4/\text{m}$$

and I_{cr} is found by considering the transformed section of Fig. 5-16

$$n = E_s/E_m = 200,000/8500 = 23.5$$

Then taking moments of areas

$$1000(kd)^2/2 = 23.5(750)(120 - kd)$$

which gives $kd = 49$ mm

and $I_{cr} = 1000(kd)^3/3 + nA_s(120 - kd)^2$

$$= 1000(49)^3/3 + 23.5(750)(120 - 49)^2 = 128(10)^6 \text{ mm}^4/\text{m}$$

Thus $I_o = 1152(10)^6 \text{ mm}^4/\text{m}$ and $I_{cr} = 128(10)^6 \text{ mm}^4/\text{m}$

Also, $e = M_p/P_f = e_{min} = 0.1t = 24 \text{ mm}$
and $e_k = I_0/(y_t A_e) = 1152(10)^6/[120(240)(10)^3] = 40 \text{ mm}$

Then $I_{eff} = 0.25(1152)(10)^6 - [0.25(1152)(10)^6 - 128(10)^6](24 - 40)/[2(40)]$
        $= 320(10)^6 \text{ mm}^4/\text{m} \quad > 288(10)^6 = 0.25(1152)(10)^6 = 0.25I_0$
        $> 128(10)^6 = I_{cr}$

Therefore $I_{eff} = 288(10)^6 \text{ mm}^4/\text{m}$

Then $P_{cr} = \pi^2 \phi_e E_m I_{eff}/[(1 + 0.5\beta_d)(kh)^2]$
        $= \pi^2(0.65)(8500)(288)(10)^6/[(1 + 0.5*0.625)(4000)^2]$
        $= 748 \text{ kN/m}$

and $M_f = M_p C_m/(1 - P_f/P_{cr})$ and $C_m = 0.6 + 0.4M_1/M_2 = 1.0$
        $= 11.5(1.0)/(1 - 480/748) = 32.1$

Reference to the interaction diagram of Fig. 5-14 shows that for $P_f = 480 \text{ kN/m}$ the wall with steel tied for compression has $M_r \approx 33 \text{ kN-m/m}$.

Since $M_r > M_f$ the wall can safely carry the load   <u>*Ans.*</u>

5-6   VERY SLENDER WALLS

The lateral deflection of a wall under axial load and bending depends on the intensity of loading, the effective rigidity, $E_m I_{eff}$, of the wall section and the square of the height. If the wall is comparatively high, the $P\delta$ effect can be considerable and very sensitive to overload and to error in calculation. Because of this, S304.1 introduces a new category called *very slender walls* and makes special provisions for their design in Clause 11.2.5.6. The method is a limit states design adaptation of that outlined in the *Uniform Building Code* (U.B.C.) in the U.S.A., and the reader should note that very slender walls in S304.1 are referred to as slender walls in the U.B.C.

A very slender wall is one whose slenderness ratio, kh/t, exceeds 30. This means that for k taken conservatively as 1.0, walls higher than $30t$ are in this category.

The design principles for very slender walls are the same as those outlined earlier (Sections 5-2 to 5-5 inclusive) but with restrictions placed on the axial load, service load deflection and area of reinforcement that are intended to prevent the potential for sudden, brittle failure. The special provisions are:

a)   the axial load, P_f, should not exceed $0.1\phi_m f'_m A_e$;

b)   the mid-height deflection due to service loads and $P\delta$ effects should not exceed $h/720$ where a veneer is attached, $h/360$ where there is a brittle finish to the wall, and $h/180$ for all other cases.

c)   the area of vertical reinforcement should not exceed 80% of the maximum permitted for bending, that is, $\rho = A_s/bd \leq 0.80\rho_b$;

d)   the area of vertical reinforcement should not be less than $0.00133A_g$;

e)   the wall is to be assumed pin-ended, that is, $k = 1.0$;

f)   the wall should be at least 140 mm thick and the joints should *not* be raked; and

g)   other structural provisions, as follows.

Given that

M_s = service load moment, including $P\delta$ effects, at the mid-height of the wall;

M_n = nominal moment strength of the wall with all material resistance factors ϕ taken as 1.0;

M_{cr} = cracking moment for the section; and

δ_s = the mid-height deflection under service loads;

then, for $M_s < M_{cr}$

$$\delta_s = 5M_s h^2/(48E_m I_0) \tag{5-20}$$

and, for $M_{cr} < M_s < M_n$

$$\delta_s = 5M_{cr} h^2/(48E_m I_0) + 5(M_s - M_{cr})h^2/(48E_m I_{cr}) \tag{5-21}$$

where I_0 and I_{cr} are the moments of inertia of the uncracked and cracked sections respectively, as defined earlier. The moment causing cracking is taken as

$$M_{cr} = (\phi_m f_t + f_{cs})I_0/y_t = (\phi_m f_t + f_{cs})S \tag{5-22}$$

where f_{cs} is the axial stress due to the factored down service dead load, that is, $0.85P_D/A_e$.

The factored moment, M_{TOT}, used in evaluating the structural adequacy of the wall takes into account $P\delta$ effects. However, rather than use the moment magnifier method, the following expression that requires displacement calculations is specified by S304.1 (Clause 11.2.5.6.7).

$$M_{TOT} = w_f h^2/8 + P_{tf}(e/2) + (P_{wf} + P_{tf})\delta_f \tag{5-23}$$

where w_f = factored wind load

P_{tf} = factored roof and/or floor loads

P_{wf} = factored weight of wall tributary to the design section

δ_f = horizontal deflection at mid-height of the wall under factored lateral and axial loads, $P\delta$ effects being included

e = eccentricity of P_{tf}

While these requirements may appear rather formidable, upon closer examination the structural designer will recognize the individual terms. For example, $\delta = 5Mh^2/48EI$ is merely another way of writing the deflection of a simple beam with uniform load. In any case, application of the provisions for very slender walls will become clearer after studying Examples 5-9 and 5-10.

If the wall section used in Examples 5-6 and 5-8 (a fully-grouted 250 wall with #20 @ 400) were used in a very slender wall application, the limiting factored axial load is $P_f = 0.1\phi_m f'_m A_e$ which for $f'_m = 10$ MPa gives $P_f \leq 132$ kN/m. Fig. 5-14, the interaction diagram for this section, shows that the limiting slender wall P_f is substantially below that for the section and that any failure upon overload would be of the more ductile primary tension type.

Very slender walls are used mainly in buildings that require considerable head room but whose walls are not required to support a substantial gravity load. Buildings in this category include single storey warehouses, assembly plants, gymnasiums and arenas.

The wall in a building is likely to be subjected to dead load and live load (including snow) as axial or eccentrically applied vertical load, and to lateral wind (interior walls are often not subjected to wind load) or earthquake load. In that case, the various loading combinations must be considered for their maximum effect, as explained in Section 1-6. In the following example, rather than go through all loading combinations, the assumption is made that dead load plus wind load is the worst combination.

EXAMPLE 5-9 *An 8.0 m high 250 wall constructed from 20 MPa units and type S mortar is reinforced with 2-#15 bars ($f_y = 400$ MPa) in two grouted cores @ 1000. It carries an axial dead load of 20 kN/m and a wind load of 1.0 kPa. Determine whether the wall is suitable for this loading.*

Check slenderness

$$kh/t = 1.0 \ (8000)/240 = 33.3 > 30$$

Therefore the wall is subject to the provisions for *very slender walls*.

Check axial load

$$f'_m = 13.0 - 3.0(2/5) = 11.8 \text{ MPa for two out of five cores grouted}$$
$$A_e = 145(10)^3 \text{ mm}^2/\text{m (Table 4-1)}$$

$$P_f = \alpha_D P_D = 1.25(20.0) = 25 \text{ kN/m}$$
$$< 0.1\phi_m f'_m A_e = 0.1(0.55)(11.8)(145)(10)^3 = 94.1 \text{ kN/m} \quad \underline{OK}$$

Check reinforcement

For bending $\rho_{max} = 0.0066$

For very slender walls $\rho_{max} = 0.80 \,(0.0066) = 0.0053$

$$A_{smax} = \rho_{max}bd = 0.0053(1000)(120) = 636 \text{ mm}^2/\text{m}$$

$$A_s = 2(200) = 400 \text{ mm}^2/\text{m} < 636 \text{ mm}^2/\text{m} \qquad \underline{\text{OK}}$$

$$A_{smin} = 0.00133A_g = 0.00133(240)(10)^3 = 319 \text{ mm}^2/\text{m} < 400 \qquad \underline{\text{OK}}$$

Note that if $A_s > A_{smax}$, A_{smax} would be used in subsequent calculations.

Deflection under service load

Service loads are $p = 1.0$ kPa wind and $P = 20$ kN/m dead load, which can be assumed to act at a minimum eccentricity of 24 mm producing bending in the same direction as the wind. Then, as a first calculation, excluding $P\delta$ effects,

$$\begin{aligned} M_s &= ph^2/8 + 0.1tP \\ &= 1.0(8000)^2/8 + 0.1(240)(20)(10)^3 = 8.48(10)^6 \text{ N-mm/m} \end{aligned}$$

$$M_{cr} = (\phi_m f_t + f_{cs})S$$

where $\phi_m = 0.55$
$\quad\quad f_t = 0.45$ MPa for hollow block (Table 6 of S304.1)
$\quad\quad\;\; = 0.70$ MPa for fully-grouted units
$\quad\quad\;\; = 0.45$ MPa conservatively
$\quad\quad f_{cs} = P/A_e = 20(10)^3/145(10)^3 = 0.14$ MPa
$\quad\quad S = 7.92\,(10)^6 \text{ mm}^3/\text{m}$ (from Table 4-1)

Then $M_{cr} = [0.55(0.45) + 0.14](7.92)(10)^6 = 3.07$ kN-m /m
$$< 8.48 \text{ kN-m/m} = M_s$$

As noted earlier, if $M_{cr} < M_s < M_n$ then the lateral deflection is calculated by Equation (5-21). In almost all instanced of very slender walls under wind load, $M_{cr} < M_s$. M_n is an estimate of the flexural strength of the wall with material resistance factors taken as 1.0. Clearly, if $M_s > M_n$, the wall fails in flexure and there is no point proceeding with this section. M_n is most conveniently, and with reasonable accuracy, estimated as

$$M_n \approx 0.8A_s f_y d = 0.8(400)(400)(120) = 15.36 \text{ kN-m/m} > M_s$$

and, since $M_{cr} < M_s < M_n$

$$\delta_s = 5M_{cr}h^2/(48E_mI_0) + 5(M_s - M_{cr})h^2/(48E_mI_{cr})$$

The first term of this equation calculates the deflection of the uncracked section due to the load at cracking and adds the deflection of the cracked section due to the post-cracking load.

$$E_m = 850f'_m = 850(11.5) = 9775 \text{ MPa}$$
$$I_0 = 950(10)^6 \text{ mm}^4/\text{m (from Table 4-1)}$$

To find I_{cr} (see Example 3-14)

$$n = E_s/E_m = 200\ 000/9775 = 20.46$$

Now, taking moments of the areas of the transformed section

$1000(kd)^2/2 = nA_s(d\text{-}kd)$
$1000(kd)^2/2 = 20.46(400)(120 - kd)$ gives $kd = 36.9$ mm

and reference to Part 2 of this book will show that 36.9 mm is less than the average face shell thickness. Then,

$$I_{cr} = 1000(kd)^3/3 + nA_s(d - kd)^2$$
$$= 1000(36.9)^3/3 + 20.46(400)(120 - 36.9)^2 = 73.3(10)^6 \text{ mm}^4/\text{m}$$

Now, as a first try, excluding $P\delta$ effects,

$$\delta_s = 5h^2/(48E_m)[M_{cr}/I_0 + (M_s - M_{cr})/I_{cr}]$$
$$= 5(8000)^2/[48(9775)][3.07/950 + (8.48 - 3.07)/73.3]$$
$$= 52.5 \text{ mm} > 44.4 \text{ mm} = h/180 \qquad\qquad \underline{NG}$$

Because any further calculation of δ_s has to include a $P\delta$ effect, leading to increased deflection

since $\delta_s > 44.4$ mm = h/180 the wall section is not suitable   *Ans.*

Because the deflection criterion has not been met in the preceding example, it would be pointless to pursue further analysis, except out of academic interest. Further calculation to check strength shows that the wall violates strength criteria by about 2 - 3% The following example illustrates a complete check of a wall that does meet the loading requirements of Example 5-9.

EXAMPLE 5-10 *An 8.0 m high 250 wall constructed from 20 MPa units and type S mortar is reinforced with #20 vertical bars spaced at 400 ($f_y = 400$ MPa) and fully* *grouted. It carries an axial dead load of 20 kN/m and a wind load of 1.0 kPa. Determine whether the wall is suitable for this loading.*

Note that this is the wall of Example 5-9, more heavily reinforced and fully grouted. For clarity the complete calculations are covered.

Check slenderness

$$kh/t = 1.0(8000)/240 = 33.3 > 30$$

Therefore the wall is subject to the provisions for *very slender walls*.

Check axial load

$$f'_m = 10.0 \text{ MPa for a fully-grouted wall}$$
$$A_e = 240(10)^3 \text{ mm}^2/\text{m}$$

$$P_f = \alpha_D P_D = 1.25(20) = 25 \text{ kN/m}$$
$$< 0.1\phi_m f'_m A_e = 0.1(0.55)(10.0)(240)(10)^3 = 132 \text{ kN/m} \qquad \underline{\text{OK}}$$

Check reinforcement

For bending $\rho_{max} = 0.0066$

For very slender walls $\rho_{max} = 0.8(0.0066) = 0.0053$

$$A_{smax} = \rho_{max}bd = 0.0053(1000)(120) = 636 \text{ mm}^2/\text{m}$$
$$A_s = 300(1000/400) = 750 \text{ mm}^2/\text{m} > A_{smax}$$

Since $A_s > A_{smax}$, use $A_s = A_{smax} = 636 \text{ mm}^2/\text{m}$

Deflection under service load

Wind load $p = 1.0$ kPa
Service load $P = 20$ kN/m, which can be assumed to act at minimum eccentricity of $0.1t = 24$ mm producing bending in the same direction as the wind. As a first calculation, excluding $P\delta$ effects

$$M_s = ph^2/8 + 0.1tP$$
$$= 1.0(8000)^2/8 + 0.1(240)(20)(10)^3 = 8.48(10)^6 \text{ N-mm/m}$$

$$M_{cr} = (\phi_m f_t + f_{cs})S$$

where $\phi_m = 0.55$

$f_t = 0.70$ MPa (Table 6 of S304.1)
$f_{cs} = P/A_e = 20(10)^3/240(10)^3 = 0.083$ MPa
$S = 9.60 (10)^6$ mm^6/m (Table 4-1)

Then $M_{cr} = [0.55(0.70) + 0.083](9.6)(10)^6 = 4.50$ kN-m /m $< M_s$
$M_n \approx 0.8A_s f_y d = 0.8(636)(400)(120) = 24.4$ kN-m/m $> M_s$

and, since $M_{cr} < M_s < M_n$

$$\delta_s = 5M_{cr}h^2/(48E_m I_0) + 5(M_s - M_{cr})h^2/(48E_m I_{cr})$$

$E_m = 850f'_m = 850(10.0) = 8500$ MPa
$I_0 = 1152(10)^6$ mm^4/m (Table 4-1)

To find I_{cr} (see Example 3-14)

$$n = E_s/E_m = 200\ 000/8500 = 23.53$$

$1000(kd)^2/2 = nA_s(d-kd)$
$1000(kd)^2/2 = 23.53(636)(120 - kd)$ gives $kd = 46.8$ mm

Then $I_{cr} = 1000(kd)^3/3 + nA_s(d - kd)^2$
$= 1000(46.8)^3/3 + 23.53(636)(120 - 46.8)^2 = 114.4(10)^6$ mm^4/m

As a first try, excluding $P\delta$ effects,

$$\delta_s = 5h^2/(48E_m)[M_{cr}/I_0 + (M_s - M_{cr})/I_{cr}]$$
$$= 5(8000)^2/[48(8500)][4.50/1152 + (8.48 - 4.50)/114.4]$$
$$= 30.4 \text{ mm} < 44.4 \text{ mm} = h/180 \qquad \underline{\text{OK}}$$

Now, using $\delta = 30.4$ mm to add the $P\delta$ effect to M_s

$$M_s = 8.48(10)^6 + 20(10)^3(30.4) = 9.09 \text{ kN-m}$$

and $\delta_s = 5(8000)^2/[48(8500)][4.50/1152 + (9.09 - 4.50)/114.4] = 34.5$ mm

It is clear that another iteration is not necessary and $\delta_s < h/180$ $\underline{\text{OK}}$

Moment due to factored load $M_f = M_{TOT}$

$$M_{TOT} = p_f h^2/8 + P_{tf}e/2 + (P_{wf} + P_{tf})\delta$$

Assuming that $P = 20$ kN/m includes the weight of the wall and, conservatively, that this P_{tf} and $(P_{wf} + P_{tf})$ have the same value,

$$P_f = \alpha_D P_D = 1.25(20) = 25.0 \text{ kN/m}$$
$$p_f = \alpha_Q p = 1.5(1.0) = 1.5 \text{ kPa}$$

and, assuming as a first approximation that the factored load deflection is

$$\delta = \alpha_Q \delta_s = 1.5(34.5) = 51.8 \text{ mm}$$

then $M_{TOT} = 1.5(8000)^2/8 + 25(10)^3(24/2) + 25(10)^3(51.8) = 13.6 \text{ kN-m/m}$

Substituting M_{TOT} for M_s in the deflection calculation gives

$$\delta = 5(8000)^2/[48(8500)][4.50/1152 + (13.6 - 4.50)/114.4] = 65.5 \text{ mm}$$

Another iteration with $\delta = 70$ mm, say, gives

$$M_{TOT} = 1.5(8000)^2/8 + 25(10)^3(24/2) + 25(10)^3(70) = 14.0 \text{ kN-m/m}$$

and another deflection calculation gives $\delta = 68.2$ mm < 70 OK

Thus, conservatively, $M_f \approx 14.0$ kN-m/m

This particular wall section is the subject of the interaction diagram of Fig. 5-14 from which it can be seen that strength requirements have been met. Alternatively, if an interaction diagram is not available, and recalling that very slender walls are subject to low levels of axial load that enhance the flexural resistance, then to determine that $M_r > M_f$ is sufficient.

It was shown in Chapter 4, Equation (4-1), that the area of steel required to resist bending can be approximated as

$$A_s \approx M_f/[\phi_s f_y(0.8)d] = 14.0(10)^6/[0.85(400)(0.8)(120)] = 429 \text{ mm}^2/\text{m}$$

and, since $A_s = 636$ mm$^2 > 429$ mm^2, $M_r > M_f$. Thus strength and deflection requirements are met, and *the wall is suitable for the loading.*   *Ans.*

The reader will be relieved to be assured that much of the complexity of designing these walls is eased through the use of Part 2 of this book. It is also of interest that this wall does *not* meet the requirements of S304, the working stress design version of the standard.

5-7   SHEAR WALLS

Shear walls are used in high-rise buildings for overall stability and to provide resistance to horizontal forces resulting from wind and earthquake. These walls may be load-bearing (that is, supporting gravity loads) or non load-bearing, and can have a variety of configurations - such as straight wall, "I", "T" or box shaped cross-sections. Fig. 1-7 illustrates the use of shear walls in a masonry building where walls A, in addition to acting as load-bearing walls, behave as shear walls in resisting horizontal forces H_A; and shafts B act as shear walls in resisting horizontal forces H_B. A similar building is shown in Fig. 5-4 and the forces acting on a transverse shear wall are shown in Fig. 5-4(b).

Typically, shear walls are subjected to in-plane bending and shear combined with axial load. Although out-of-plane bending can also be present it is not commonly encountered in significant combination with in-plane bending. The distribution of forces acting on a building to the various shear walls depends on the relative stiffness of these elements, a distribution that is discussed in Chapter 6. The present discussion considers individual shear walls, the design and analysis of which must conform to the requirements of S304.1.

Shear walls, then, are subjected to uniaxial load P, and in-plane bending moment M, and a transverse shear force V, as shown in Figs. 5-17 and 5-18. The two effects that require consideration in design are the intensity of vertical force produced by P and M, and shear force V.

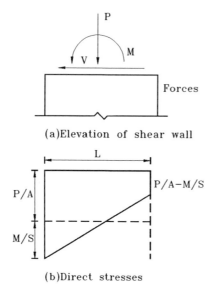

(a)Elevation of shear wall

(b)Direct stresses

Fig. 5-17 Shear Wall Forces

Axial Load and In-Plane Bending

The axial force P produces an average compressive stress P/A_m, increasing or reducing the compression by M/S at the ends of the wall. These stresses are shown in Fig. 5-17(b). Tension should not be permitted in an unreinforced shear wall, and where tension is expected vertical reinforcement should be provided.

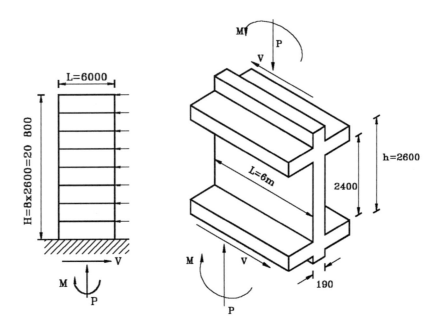

Fig. 5-18 Typical Shear Wall of an Eight-Story Building

The general result of the vertical force P and in-plane moment M is to produce vertical axial forces in the wall. In this way, then, whether the value of P is large or not, a shear wall becomes a bearing wall due to the effect of the in-plane bending. However, to allow for out-of-plane slenderness between levels of lateral support, the axial force $P/A + M/S$ is applied to an out-of-plane eccentricity $0.1t$. This produces an out-of-plane primary moment that is then magnified by the $P\delta$ effect in the manner described in Section 5-2 for plain walls, and Section 5-5 for reinforced walls. The resistance of the wall is then obtained from the interaction diagram for axial load and out-of-plane bending. For a straight wall of length L, then, the criteria for design are

$$P_f/L + 6M_f/L^2 \leq P_r \text{ kN/m} \tag{5-24}$$

and, for plain walls

$$P_f/L - 6M_f/L^2 \geq 0 \qquad (5\text{-}25)$$

That is, it is inadvisable to have tension in an unreinforced shear wall.

In these expressions, P_f (kN) is the total factored axial load on the wall, L (m) is the length of the wall, and M_f (kN-m) is the total in-plane moment due to factored loads. $6M_f/L^2$ is then the kN/m equivalent of M_f/S for a rectangular section. P_r is the resistance in kN/m. When the governing criterion is compression, as in Equation (5-24), the dead load factor is $\alpha_D = 1.25$, whereas for Equation (5-25) the dead load factor will normally be $\alpha_D = 0.85$ since the dead load reduces tensile forces.

In-Plane Shear

Although shear stresses due to the transverse shear force V may conservatively be calculated according to the expression for a homogeneous elastic section

$$v = VQ/It \qquad (5\text{-}26)$$

where Q = the first moment of the area of the cross-section, to one side of the shear stress location, about the centroidal axis of bending,

and I = the moment of inertia of the cross-section about the centroidal axis of bending,

it is more reasonable to assume that the resistance of the length of wall parallel to the shear force can be mobilized and the design criterion is then $V_r \geq V_f$.

The resistance to horizontal in-plane shear is provided by the length of the wall parallel to the shear force. That is, the flanges of I, T or L shapes do not contribute to shear resistance.

Clause 11.5.3 of S304.1 gives the factored in-plane shear resistance of a wall as

$$V_r = \phi_m(v_m bd + 0.25P)\gamma_g + \phi_s(0.60A_s f_y d/s) \qquad (5\text{-}27)$$

where

- $v_m = 0.16[2 - M_f/(V_f d)]\sqrt{f'_m}$ MPa, the shear strength of masonry
- $1.0 \geq M_f/(V_f d) \geq 0.25$
  and $M_f/(V_f d)$ can be taken conservatively as 1.0, and $v_m = 0.16\sqrt{f'_m}$
- $b = t$, the wall thickness
- d is the length of wall, L, when there is no tension, or the effective depth to the tensile steel, but need not be less than $0.8L$
- $P = 0.85$ times the total dead load

- $\gamma_g = A_e/A_g$, a factor that allows for the degree of grouting
- A_v = area of shear reinforcement/bars of vertical steel
- s = spacing of vertical shear reinforcement, and the total area of steel resisting shear $A_v d/s$.

As the structural designer knows, shear stress in one direction is accompanied by an equal and perpendicular complementary shear stress. Equation (5-27) is valid for standard running bond construction where the masonry units overlap from course to course. However, in stack pattern construction (that is, units do not overlap in successive courses) resistance to vertical shear is from the shear friction provided by horizontal reinforcement. Since the horizontal shear force is V_f/L kN/m, the complementary vertical shear force has the same value and the resistance is $\phi_s \mu A_s f_y$, where A_s is the area of horizontal reinforcement per metre and the coefficient of friction $\mu = 0.7$. However, due to the inherent weakness in its resistance to vertical shear, stack pattern construction should be avoided in significant shear walls.

Sliding Shear

In addition to the other shear requirements that must be met, a wall should have adequate resistance to sliding shear on a horizontal plane. Resistance to sliding shear is assured when $V_r \geq V_f$ using the shear-friction concept

$$V_r = \phi_m \mu C \qquad\qquad (5\text{-}28)$$

where
C = the compressive force P_f plus the factored yield strength of the vertical reinforcement, and
μ = 1.0 for masonry-to-masonry or masonry-to-concrete
= 0.7 otherwise.

EXAMPLE 5-11 *Fig 5-18 shows one shear wall from an eight-storey building such as that shown in Fig. 5-4. The wall, which supports precast concrete floors 200 mm deep with a floor-to-floor height of 2600 mm, is constructed from 200 standard concrete blocks (20 MPa units and type S mortar), and is fully-grouted to the level of the 5th floor. The accumulated loading in the lowest level of the wall (that is, between the main and 2nd floors) is:*

> *Dead load = 200 kN/m; Live load = 100 kN/m*
> *Moment due to wind = 1000 kN-m*
> *Horizontal shear due to wind = 120 kN.*

Check the adequacy of the fully-grouted wall, and determine whether reinforcing is required.

1) Loading combinations

The load combinations to be considered can be expressed as

$$\alpha_D D + \gamma \Psi(\alpha_L L + \alpha_Q Q)$$

where $\gamma = 1.0$
$\alpha_D = 1.25$ or 0.85
$\alpha_L = \alpha_Q = 1.5$
$\Psi = 1.0$ for one of L or Q
$= 0.7$ for both L and Q

The factored loads, then, are

$$\alpha_D D = 1.25(200) = 250 \text{ kN/m, or}$$
$$= 0.85(200) = 170 \text{ kN/m}$$
$$\alpha_L L = 1.50(100) = 150 \text{ kN/m}$$
$$M_f = 1.50(1000) = 1500 \text{ kN-m}$$

and
$$6M_f/L^2 = 6(1500)/6^2 = 250 \text{ kN/m}$$

a) dead plus live

$$P_f = 250 + 150.0 = 400 \text{ kN/m compression.}$$

b) dead plus wind

$$P_{fmax} = \alpha_D D + 6M_f/L^2, \text{ and } \alpha_D = 1.25$$
$$= 250 + 250 = 500 \text{ kN/m compression.}$$

$$P_{fmin} = \alpha_D D - 6M_f/L^2, \text{ and } \alpha_D = 0.85$$
$$= 170 - 250 = -80.0 \text{ kN/m (tension).}$$

c) dead plus live plus wind

$$P_{fmax} = \alpha_D D + \Psi(\alpha_L L + 6M_f/L^2), \text{ and } \alpha_D = 1.25$$
$$= 250 + 0.7(150 + 250) = 530 \text{ kN/m compression}$$

$$P_{fmin} = \alpha_D D + \Psi(\alpha_L L - 6M_f/L^2), \text{ and } \alpha_D = 0.85$$
$$= 170 + 0.7(150 - 250) = 100.0 \text{ kN/m compression}$$

d) summary of loads

The worst case for compression is *c)*: P_f = 530 kN/m
The worst case for tension is *b)*: P_f = -80.0 kN/m

2. Check compression resistance for P_f = 530 kN/m

Axial compression is required to be applied at a minimum eccentricity of 0.1*t* to produce out-of-plane bending.

For a fully-grouted wall f'_m = 10 MPa
From Table 4-1 A_e = 190(10)³ mm²/m
$\qquad\qquad\quad S_x$ = 6.02(10)⁶ mm³/m
$\qquad\qquad\quad I_x = I_o$ = 572(10)⁶ mm²/m

For out-of-plane bending

$$M_p = P_f(0.1t) = 530(10)^3(0.1)(190) = 10.07(10)^6 \text{ N-mm/m}$$
$$M_f = M_pC_m/(1 - P_f/P_{cr}), \text{ the magnified moment}$$
$$C_m = 1.0 \text{ for equal end moments } M_p$$
$$P_{cr} = \pi^2EI/(kh)^2$$
$$EI = \phi_eE_mI_{eff}/(1 + 0.5\beta_d)$$
$$\phi_eE_m = 0.65(850)f'_m = 0.65(850)(10) = 5525 \text{ MPa}$$
$$I_{eff} = 0.4I_0 = 0.4(572)(10)^6 = 229(10)^6 \text{ mm}^4/\text{m (unreinforced wall)}$$
$$\beta_d = \text{factored dead load moment/factored total moment}$$
$$\quad = \text{factored dead load/factored total load}$$
$$\quad = 250/530 = 0.472$$

$$EI = 5525(229)(10)^6/[1 + 0.5(0.472)] = 1.024(10)^{12} \text{ N-mm}^2/\text{m}$$

and $\qquad P_{cr} = \pi^2EI/(kh)^2 = \pi^2(1.024)(10)^{12}/2400^2 = 1754 \text{ kN/m}$

The magnified out-of plane moment is then

$$M_{TOT} = M_pC_m/(1 - P_f/P_{cr})$$
$$\quad = 10.07(10)^6(1.0)/(1 - 530/1754) = 14.43(10)^6 \text{ N-mm/m}$$

The compressive stress in the wall should now be checked as

$$P_f/A_e + M_{TOT}/S \le \phi_mf'_m = 0.55(10) = 5.5 \text{ MPa}$$

$$\frac{530(10)^3}{190(10)^3} + \frac{14.43(10)^6}{6.02(10)^6} = 5.19 \text{ MPa} < 5.5 \text{ MPa} \qquad \underline{\text{OK}}$$

and since $P/A_e - M_{TOT}/S > 0$ tension is not induced by the out-of-plane bending.

Therefore the wall has adequate resistance in compression   <u>Ans.</u>

3. Resistance to tension, P_f = -80.0 kN/m

At this point the tensile stress due to in-plane bending can be calculated as

$$f_t = P_f/A_e = 80.0(10)^3/190(10)^3 = 0.42 \text{ MPa}$$

which is approximately equal to ϕ_m =0.55 times the value of 0.70 MPa in Table 6 of S304.1 for tension normal to the bed joints of grouted masonry.
However, as noted earlier, it is inadvisable to allow tension in an unreinforced wall and vertical reinforcement in the tension zone is recommended, and a reasonable estimate of the required amount of steel may be obtained from the $P_f/L \pm 6M_f/L^2$ diagram for dead plus wind load (α_D = 0.85). This is shown in Fig. 5-19, where P_f = 170 $\pm$ 250 kN/m.

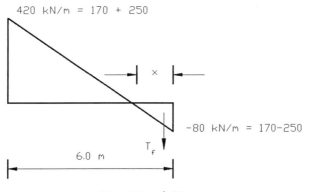

Fig. 5-19 Load Diagram

By similar triangles, the length $\varkappa$ of the tensile zone is

$$\varkappa = 6.0(80)/(420 + 80) = 0.96 \text{ m}$$

and the resultant tensile force is

$$T_f = 80.0(0.96)/2 = 38.4 \text{ kN}$$

Using f_y = 400 MPa, the required area of steel can be obtained as follows:

$$T_r = \phi_s A_s f_y = 0.85 A_s(400) \geq 38.4(10)^3 \text{ N}$$

and $A_s \geq 113 \text{ mm}^2$

Thus, 1-#15 bars (A_s = 200 mm²) could be placed in the outer core of the wall and, since the wind can blow from either direction, the reinforcement should be placed at each end of the wall. The reinforcement arrangement is shown in Fig. 5-20.

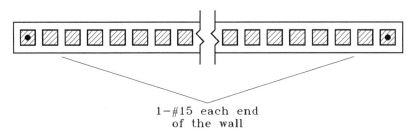

1-#15 each end
of the wall

Fig.5-20 Reinforcing Bars Arrangement

4. Shear

The shear force due to wind, V = 120 kN

Then, $V_f = \alpha_Q V = 1.5(120) = 180$ kN

and the shear resistance V_r must be at least equal to V_f, where,

$$V_r = \phi_m(v_m bd + 0.25P)\gamma_g + \phi_s(0.60A_s f_y d/s)$$
$$\gamma_g = 1.0 \text{ for a fully-grouted wall and } \phi_m = 0.55$$

While this expression is complex, it may be simplified by using actual or conservative values of variables. That is,

$$v_m \geq 0.16(\sqrt{f'_m}) = 0.16(\sqrt{10}) = 0.506 \text{ MPa}$$
$$b = 190 \text{ mm}$$
$$d \geq 0.8L = 0.8(6000) = 4800 \text{ mm}$$
$$P = 0.85DL = 0.85(200)(6.0) = 1020 \text{ kN}$$

Then $V_r \geq 0.55[0.506(190)(4800) + 0.25(1020)(10)^3] = 394.0$ kN

$$V_r \geq 394.0 \text{ kN} > 180 \text{ kN} = V_f \qquad \underline{\text{OK}}$$

The fully-grouted 200 wall with 1-#15 each end is adequate.   Ans.

Note that the calculations shown in 3. above, though adequate in Example 5-11, are approximate since the presence of steel in a cracked section will change the location of the neutral axis.   More "precise" hand calculations are lengthy, and the designer should use the appropriate sections of Part 2.

Flanged Shear Walls

Flanged shear wall configurations are encountered where the main in-plane wall intersects a transverse wall.   One example is the stairwell shaft of Figs. 1-7 and 5-4, shown in Fig. 5-21.

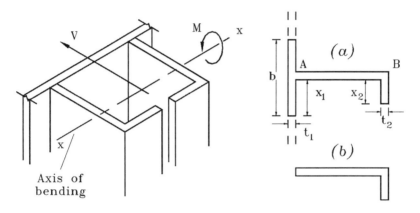

Fig.5-21 Flanged Shear Walls

Intersected walls are effective as flanges only when adequate shear transfer can take place along the vertical interface.   The vertical shear resistance can be provided through interlocking bond of the units in each wall, as would be the case in B.   However, interlocking bond is more difficult to accomplish in A, and if a shear resistance is required it would be more appropriate to provide grout keys.   When the walls are keyed together the effective section is as shown in Fig 5-21(a).   On the other hand, the designer may prefer (and the mason certainly will) to provide insulation and flexible steel ties between the two walls at A so that the outside wall can expand and contract vertically relative to the inside wall through the change of seasons, in which case the effective section is that shown in Fig. 5-21(b).

The requirements governing the flange widths that may be considered effective in design are given in Clause 11.1.3.2 of S304.1.   Referring to Fig 5-21(a) these may be summarized briefly as:

$$b \leq 1/6 \times \text{wall height above the section under consideration}$$
$$x_1 \leq 6t_1$$

$x_2 \leq 1/16 \times$ wall height above the section under consideration

$x_2 \leq 6t_2$

Once the effective section has been determined the location of the neutral axis and appropriate section properties can be calculated. The design then follows the principles outlined earlier. The principal difference to note is that the vertical shear stress at two wall interface locations should be checked. Moreover, the intersecting walls support each other laterally, thereby reducing the effective slenderness - most frequently at locations of maximum compressive stress.

EXAMPLE 5-12 *The 200 concrete block shear wall ($f'_m = 10$ MPa) of Fig 5-22 is nominally reinforced and fully grouted. If the horizontal shear force due to wind is 150 kN check the vertical shear stress at the wall interface A.*

Before analyzing the cross-section the flange width must be checked

$$x_2 = 1000 - 190 = 810 < 6t = 6(190) = 1140 \text{ mm} \qquad \underline{\text{OK}}$$

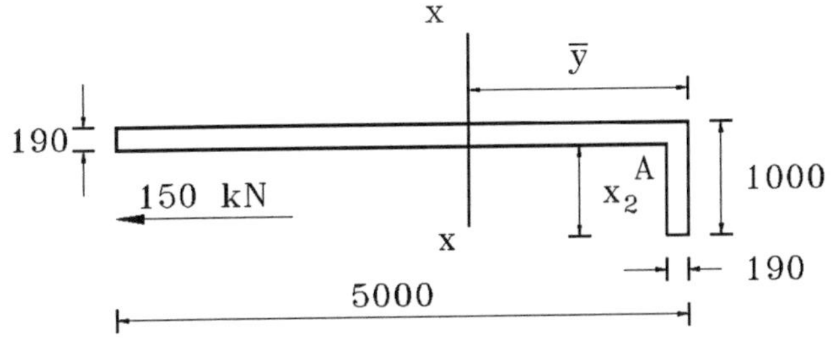

Fig. 5-22 Shear Wall of Example 5-12

and this assumes that the height of wall above this section is at least

$$16x_2 = 16(810) = 12960 \text{ mm}$$

At this point, shear can be checked by using the expression $v = VQ/It$ or by setting the vertical shear force equal to the average horizontal shear force. The two methods are compared in the following analysis.

The location of the centroid is

$$\bar{y} = \frac{5000(190)(2500) + (1000 - 190)(190)(95)}{5000(190) + (1000 - 190)(190)} = 2165 \text{ mm}$$

and the moment of inertia is

$$I_x = 190(5000)^3/12 + 190(5000)(2500 - 2165)^2 + 810(190)^3/12$$
$$+ 810(190)(2165 - 95)^2 = 2.746(10)^{12} \text{ mm}^4$$

For the interface A

$$Q = 1000(190)(2165 - 95) = 393.3(10)^6 \text{ mm}^3$$

The factored shear force is

$$V_f = 1.5(150) = 225.0 \text{ kN/m}$$

and since half of the vertical section is likely to consist of head joint and no grouting, only 50% of the vertical section is effectively resisting shear. This can be modelled by taking $t = 95$ mm rather than 190 mm. Then the shear stress is

$$v_f = V_f Q/It = \frac{225(10)^3(393.3)(10)^6}{2.746(10)^{12}(95)} = 0.34 \text{ MPa}$$

and, from Example 5-11, the limiting shear stress may conservatively be taken as $v_m = 0.16\sqrt{f'_m} = 0.16\sqrt{10} = 0.506$ MPa. Since

$$v_f = 0.34 \text{ MPa} < 0.506 \text{ MPa} = v_m \qquad \underline{\text{OK}}$$

and horizontal reinforcement and/or grout keys are not required.

An alternative approach is to set the vertical shear equal to the average horizontal shear per metre. Since the shear is resisted by the 5.0 m web, the vertical shear can be taken as

$$V_f = 225.0/5.0 = 45.0 \text{ kN/m}$$

and this value applies not only at the corner, but throughout the web. As before, only half of the section is assumed to be effective in resisting shear and for a 1.0 m height

$$V_r = v_m(1000)t(0.50) = 0.506(1000)(190)(0.50)$$
$$= 48.1 \text{ kN/m} > 45.0 \text{ kN/m} = V_f \qquad \underline{\text{OK}}$$

This second approach generally is more conservative and much simpler to apply.

EXAMPLE 5-13 *A stairwell shaft similar to that of Fig. 5-21 is shown in Fig. 5-23 and carries a horizontal factored shear force of 450 kN. Determine the vertical shear stresses at the wall interfaces A and B.*

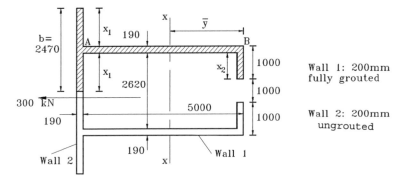

Fig. 5-23 Stairwell Shaft

Assuming that walls 1 and 2 are bonded together, the effective section must be determined.

Check: x_2 = 1000 - 190 = 810 < 6t = 6(190) = 1140 mm   OK
            x_1 = 6t = 6(190) = 1140 mm

and, since

$$x_1 < (0.5)(\text{stairwell width}) \qquad\qquad \text{OK}$$

then $b = 2x_1 + t = 2(1140) + 190 = 2470$ mm

and this assumes that height of the wall above this section is at least

$$6b = 6(2.47) = 14.82 \text{ m}$$

a) Now, following the $v = VQ/It$ procedure, the shaded portion of Fig. 5-23 is the section effective in resisting a horizontal shear force of 450/2 = 225 kN. In calculating the properties ($\bar{y}$, I and Q) it must be remembered that whereas wall 1 is fully grouted, wall 2 is ungrouted and approximately 50% solid. The location of the neutral axis is then

$$\bar{y} = \frac{0.5(2470)(190)(5095) + 5000(190)(2500) + 810(190)(95)}{0.5(2470)(190) + 5000(190) + 810(190)} = 2678 \text{ mm}$$

and

$$I_x = 0.5(2470)(190)^3/12 + 0.5(2470)(190)(5095 - 2678)^2$$
$$+ 190(5000)^3/12 + 190(5000)(2678 - 2500)^2$$
$$+ 810(190)^3/12 + 810(190)(2678 - 95)^2 = 4.408(10)^{12} \text{ mm}^4$$

Then for shear stress calculation from $v = VQ/It$

$$Q_A = 0.5(2470)(190)(5095 - 2678) = 567.1(10)^6 \text{ mm}^3$$
$$Q_B = 1000(190)(2678 - 95) = 490.8(10)^6 \text{ mm}^3$$

Because of the interlocking of units at B, the effective thickness can be taken as 50% of the actual wall thickness. On the other hand, the area resisting shear at the wall intersection A will depend on the detail of construction. For example, if wall 1 is merely butted against wall 2 the only resistance to shear is that provided by the head joints, which may be of questionable quality, or by the shear friction provided by the reinforcement crossing the intersection. Assuming for the moment that the grout keys (as described below) provide a 50% continuity, as at B, the shear stresses are

at A,

$$v_A = V_f Q_A/It = \frac{225(10)^3(567.1(10)^6}{4.408(10)^{12}(95)} = 0.305 \text{ MPa} \qquad \underline{\text{Ans.}}$$

and, at B,

$$v_B = V_f Q_B/It = \frac{225(10)^3(490.8)(10)^6}{4.408(10)^{12}(95)} = 0.264 \text{ MPa} \qquad \underline{\text{Ans.}}$$

It might be noted that the vertical shear force at A is resisted by the two sides of the flange in wall 2. Also, since the wall is not grouted, and because head joints provide little shear resistance, the effective thickness in shear is two face shells in alternative courses each side of the intersection. This is equivalent to two continuous 32 mm face shells and the vertical shear stress in wall 2 is

$$v_f = \frac{225(10)^3(567.1)(10)^6}{4.408(10)^{12}(2)(32)} = 0.452 \text{ MPa}$$

b) The simpler method referred to in Example 5-12 can be applied as follows.

The average horizontal shear in the web is

$$v_f = 225/5.0 = 45 \text{ kN/m}$$

and this is also the complementary vertical shear force. If the effective area at
A and B in wall 1 is 50% of the gross area, then the vertical shear stress is

$$v = 45.0(10)^3/[1000(95)] = 0.474 \text{ MPa}$$

and the vertical shear stress in wall 2 is

$$v = 45(10)^3/[1000(2)(32)] = 0.703 \text{ MPa}$$

As indicated earlier, the mason automatically interlocks the blocks at locations
B (Fig. 5-23). However, at A, wall 2 is likely to be built straight through with wall 1
abutting. There is then no natural bond between the two walls since head joints alone
cannot be relied upon. An effective bond can be provided by opening appropriate face
shells in wall 2, and using "H" blocks or lintel blocks on end to provide suitable voids
for an effective grout key, as shown in Fig. 5-24, steel ties are also normally being
included. However, if wall 2 is an exterior wall with insulation on the inside, it will
undergo diurnal and seasonal temperature expansion and contraction and considerable
stressing of joint A will take place. In this event it is preferable to provide a caulked or
insulated space between the two walls.

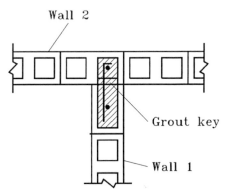

Fig. 5-24 Grout Key at Wall Intersection

Bi-Axial Bending

Bi-axial bending is not normally a significant factor in masonry wall design.
In-plane bending is of significance at the lower levels of shear walls in high-rise
buildings, whereas out-of-plane bending is significant (that is e is large) in the upper
levels of buildings. At the lower levels the accumulated axial load is normally high so

that $e = M/P$ is small. This principle is illustrated in Fig. 5-25 which shows the cross-section of the end load-bearing wall of a building. If each level adds a load ΔP to the wall at eccentricity e', as shown in (a), the maximum moment $\Delta Pe'$ occurs at the top of the building where the virtual eccentricity $e = \Delta Pe'/\Delta P = e'$. Since the wall is braced against sideways by transverse shear walls the distribution of moments $\Delta Pe'$ added to each level will be as shown in (b), the maximum value being approximately $\Delta Pe'/2$. At the lowest wall level $P = \Sigma \Delta P$ and the virtual eccentricity is $e = M/P = \Delta Pe'/\Sigma \Delta P$. For example, if the wall is 200 concrete block and $e' = 80$ mm, then at the top of the wall out-of-plane bending may be significant, whereas 10 levels lower $P = 10\Delta P$ and the moment is $\Delta Pe'/2$. At this lower level the virtual eccentricity is $e'/20 = 80/20 = 4$ mm, and the minimum eccentricity $0.1t = 19$ mm will apply.

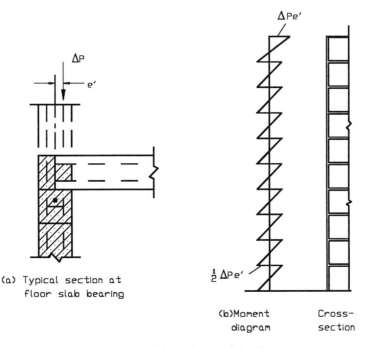

(a) Typical section at
floor slab bearing

(b)Moment
diagram

Cross-
section

Fig. 5-25 Out-of-plane Shear Wall Bending

5-8   SERVICEABILITY

Although it is essential that all structural elements possess adequate strength under the worst anticipated loadings, it is also necessary that they function satisfactorily under normal service loading. For walls and other structural masonry members the *serviceability* requirements are that deflections and flexural crack widths do not exceed reasonable limits; and conformity with the prescribed limits is assured through analytical checks following the principles outlined in Section 3-9.

Deflections

As noted in Section 4-9, excessive deflections can lead to such problems as cracking, buckling or crushing of non-structural components; and excessive flexibility can lead to unacceptable vibrations. For further information on deflection and vibration control the reader should refer to the *Supplement* to the National Building Code of Canada. The specific S304.1 deflection limitations for walls and columns under service wind load are given in Clause 11.8.3 as

a)   where masonry veneers are attached - span/720;
b)   where brittle finishes are attached - span/360; and
c)   otherwise - span/180

A representative example of deflection calculation of wall deflection is given in Example 4-13.

Crack Control

If masonry is exposed to the weather the presence of cracks encourages the ingress of moisture. This can lead to corrosion of reinforcing steel and to the disintegration of the mortar and unit due to freeze-thaw activity. Once mortar deterioration starts, moisture can enter more freely and the problem accelerates. It should be noted that cracking due to shrinkage is an entirely different problem, one that can be solved through the judicious use of *control/movement joints*.

As described in Section 3-9, S304.1 prescribes that cracking be controlled through ensuring that the quantity

$$z = f_s \sqrt[3]{d_c A}\,(10)^{-3}$$

does not exceed 30 kN/mm for interior exposures and 25 kN/mm for exterior exposures, except that for cracking due to wind loading the factor can assume the values 60 kN/mm and 50 kN/mm respectively. The more lenient requirements for wind are because of the transitory nature of the loading and the fact that cracking closes in the absence of wind.

Typical calculations regarding crack control are to be found in Example 4-13.

5-9   ENVIRONMENTAL LOADING

The preceding sections have been concerned primarily with the basic and calculable mechanics of the structural behaviour of masonry elements. Unfortunately, analysis by these simple principles does not always accurately represent the actual observed behaviour in a building. This is partly because the idealized elements used in design, and their simplified force systems, are rarely completely representative of actual conditions; and also because theories of structural behaviour are an imperfect representation of reality. Elements interact with each other, construction practices may affect design assumptions, and environmental factors may introduce unexpected effects. A complete treatment of this topic is beyond the scope of this text and a bibliography for further reading is provided at the end of the book. However, brief mention of two factors for consideration will serve to alert the reader to these problems.

Temperature Induced Loading

In addition to the more direct calculable effects of gravity, wind and earthquake loading, changes in temperature can impose loading on elements in a building. This is encountered, for example, where shear walls extend from the interior to the exterior of a building, that is, from a relatively constant temperature to a diurnally and seasonally changing temperature outside. From the point of view of energy conservation, the extension of the structure through the insulated skin of a building represents poor design since heat will be lost through the thermal bridge. However, the practice of extending the bearing walls through to support outside balconies, as shown in Fig. 5-26(a), has frequently been adopted in the past in high-rise buildings. The provision of a vertical separation in the shear wall at the insulated skin would relieve the temperature-induced stresses, and reduce heat loss, but would result in shorter shear walls and a loss of building stiffness in its resistance to horizontal loading. The temperature-induced loading in a wall without such a separation depends on the coefficient of thermal expansion of masonry ($\alpha \approx 8(10)^{-6}/°C$) and the temperature difference, and has the distribution shown in Fig. 5-26(b). The effect, if ignored in the design, can lead to tensile cracking in the upper sections of the wall and overload in compression in the lower sections. Although the effect is not fully understood, some allowance should be made for it in the design. This situation is considered again in the next chapter.

Control/Movement Joints

Vertical control/movement joints are provided in masonry walls to allow for horizontal expansion or contraction due to such environmental factors as temperature changes or wetting and drying. Brick walls expand with time, whereas newly constructed concrete masonry contracts as a result of shrinkage.

The omission of control joints can result in the buckling of brick veneers or cracking of concrete block walls. These joints, which take the form of appropriately caulked vertical discontinuities in the wall, must be suitably spaced (typically 6 to 8 m)

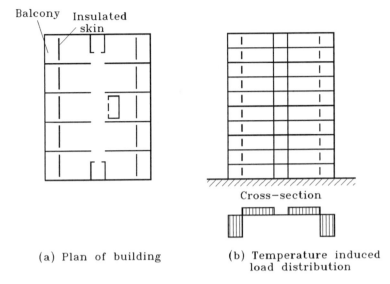

Balcony Insulated
            skin

(a) Plan of building

(b) Temperature induced
    load distribution

Fig. 5-26 Temperature-induced Loading

and judiciously located. The structural implication of control joints is that horizontal continuity in the wall cannot always be assumed. Examples 3-4 and 4-2 illustrate this principle by assuming simply-supported moments in horizontally spanning walls subjected to wind loading. Fig. 5-27 shows a typical control joint detail for a concrete block wall, where it should be noted that the vertical cores on each side of the control joint are normally reinforced and grouted, and Fig. 5-28 illustrates an example of improperly and properly located control joints. Note that, as in previous discussions on temperature effects, a continuous vertical separation, such as a control joint in a shear wall, will result in two shorter shear walls having a lesser total strength and stiffness.

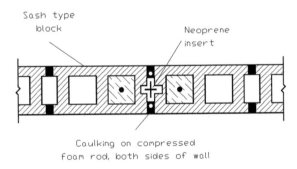

Sash type
block

Neoprene
insert

Caulking on compressed
foam rod, both sides of wall

Fig. 5-27 Control Joint Detail

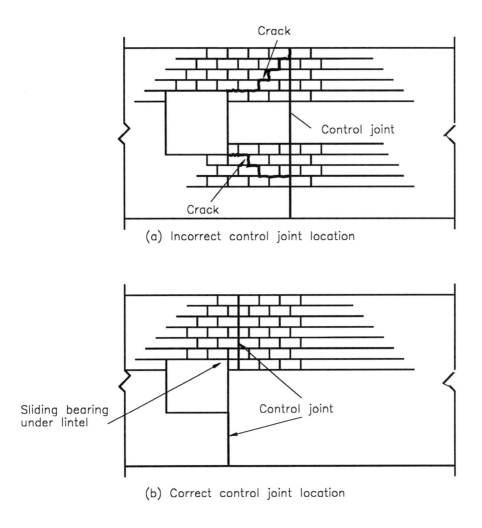

Fig. 5-28 Control Joint Location

PROBLEMS 5

(5-1)   An exterior ungrouted block wall of a building constructed from 20 MPa units
and type S mortar has a clear height of 5.0 m between lateral supports. What
is the maximum factored axial load, 40% of which is factored dead load and
60% factored live load; for a
(a) 200 wall,   (b) 250 wall,   (c) 300 wall?
Use section properties from Table 4-1.

ANS.   (a) $P_f \approx 279$ kN/m;   (b) $P_f \approx 374$ kN/m;   (c) $P_f \approx 442$ kN/m

(5-2)   A 250 wall 5.0 m high is required to carry an axial load consisting of 200 kN/m
service dead load and 100 kN/m service live load. Design the wall using 20
MPa units and type S mortar.

ANS.   Use a 250 wall with one grouted core per metre

(5-3)   A 390 x 390 masonry column is constructed from 20 MPa units, mortar type S,
and reinforced with 4-#30 vertical bars as shown. If $f_y = 400$ MPa, and if the
reinforcement is tied to resist compression, construct the moment interaction
diagram and give values to the resistance M_r and P_r of the section for
(a) axial load alone
(b) the balanced case of axial load and bending
(c) bending alone

ANS.   (a) $P_r = 1320$ kN
(b) $P_r = 113$ kN, $M_r = 112.7$ kN-m, and $e_b = 998.2$ mm
(c) $M_r = 102.9$ kN-m

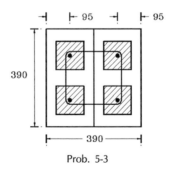

Prob. 5-3

(5-4)   A 200 concrete block wall is reinforced with # 15 vertical bars @ 600 mm
centres and is fully grouted as shown. If $f'_m = 10.0$ MPa, and $f_y = 400$ MPa,

construct the moment interaction diagram and give values to the resistance M_r and P_r of the section for
(a) axial load alone
(b) the balanced case of axial load and bending
(c) bending alone

ANS.   (a) steel tied for compression P_r = 800 kN,
             steel not tied for compression P_r = 710.6 kN
        (b) P_r = 99.85 kN, M_r = 15.4 kN-m, and e_b = 154.2 mm
        (c) M_r = 9.39 kN-m

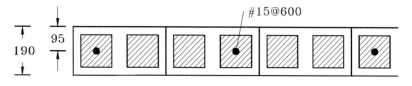

Prob. 5-4

(5-5)   A 600 x 600 column is formed from a configuration of 200 x 400 standard concrete block as shown. Six vertical bars are provided and all cores grouted, the central space being left open as a service duct, and the column is laterally supported top and bottom over a clear height of 9.0 m. If the column supports a factored axial load of P_f = 500 kN, and a factored end moment of M_f = 40 kN-m at each end, what is the required reinforcement? Use f'_m = 10.0 MPa, and f_y = 400 MPa, and remember to perform all necessary checks.

ANS.   6-#25 bars vertical, 6 mm ϕ @ 200 mm

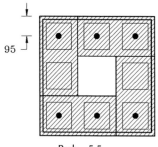

Prob. 5-5

(5-6)   A 600 x 600 concrete masonry column is provided with 6 mm ties at 200, is
reinforced with 6-#30 vertical bars located as shown and is fully grouted. Also
shown are the strain and the equivalent stress diagrams due to axial load and
bending. If the unit strength is 15 MPa, the grout strength is 20 Mpa, $f_y = 400$
and if type S mortar is used, determine for a short column the maximum
combination of P_r and M_r when
(a) a = 190 mm
(b) a = 295 mm
(c) a = 495 mm
(d) a = 590 mm

ANS.   (a) P_r = 322 kN, M_r = 350 kN-m
(b) P_r = 958 kN, M_r = 306 kN-m
(c) P_r = 1952 kN, M_r = 149 kN-m
(d) P_r = 2074 kN, M_r = 123 kN-m

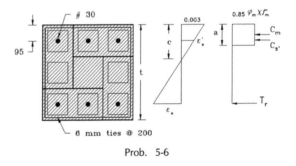

Prob. 5-6

(5-7)   Plot the P_r versus M_r interaction diagram for the column section of Problem 5-6.

(5-8)   The diagram shows a typical shear wall from a 10-storey building. The wind
loading is as shown and the axial loading to the wall consists of a service dead
load (including wall self-weight) per level of 30 kN/m and a service live load
per level which may be taken as 10 kN/m. The masonry unit has a compressive
strength of 15.0 MPa, mortar type S and the reinforcing steel yield strength f_y
= 400 MPa.
(a) What is the safe factored axial load (kN/m) for an ungrouted 200 wall?
(b) What is the safe factored axial load for a fully-grouted 200 wall reinforced
to meet the requirements of 5.2.2.2 of S304.1?
(c) What is the safe factored axial load for an ungrouted 250 wall?
(d) What is the safe factored axial load for a fully-grouted and reinforced
(5.2.2.2) 250 wall?

(e) What are the values of factored moment M_f and horizontal factored shear V_f due to wind at the 6th floor and the main floor?

(f) What are the maximum and minimum design values of the factored axial load (that is, $P/A \pm M/S$) in the wall just above the 6th floor and just above the main floor? (Remember to look at all load combinations)

(g) Is tension reinforcement required in the shear wall?

(h) Is the capacity of a fully-grouted and reinforced 250 wall [see(d)] exceeded at the main floor level? What vertical steel is suitable?

ANS.   (a) $P_f \approx 290$ kN/m
        (b) $P_f \approx 410$ kN/m
        (c) $P_f \approx 328$ kN/m
        (d) $P_f \approx 557$ kN/m
        (e) $M_f = 1267.5$ kN-m, $V_f = 195$ kN; $M_f = 5070$ kN-m, $V_f = 390$ kN
        (f) 262.5 kN/m (D.L + L.L), 82.5 kN/m (D.L. + Wind);
            525 kN/m (D.L + L.L), 210 kN/m (D.L. + Wind)
        (g) No
        (h) No. 1-#15 at each end of wall

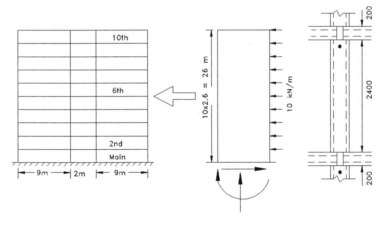

Prob. 5-8

(5-9)   For the shear wall of Problem 5-8 determine between what levels is it appropriate to use wall types (a), (b) and (d).

ANS.   wall type (a) 7th to roof level
        wall type(b) 4th to 7th
        wall type(d) main to 4th

(Note: remember to provide some vertical reinforcement for the full height at each end of the wall. The 1-#15 bar from Problem 5-8(h) would be suitable.)

CHAPTER 6

BUILDINGS

6-1   INTRODUCTION

The preceding chapters have been concerned primarily with the analysis and design of individual structural elements, acting under assumed loading and considered in isolation from any particular building. The information can now be put to use in building design. Although a complete treatment of the subject is beyond the scope of this text, the main principles of the structural design of buildings can be illustrated through some simple examples. The examples selected, rather than presenting a detailed design of all components in a building, discuss the interaction of various components and present some typical problems in building design. Section 6-4 introduces the design of low buildings, Section 6-5 discusses high-rise buildings, and Section 6-6 offers some brief comments on construction. However, before proceeding to these sections it is necessary to give further consideration to two topics that received brief mention in Chapter 5, namely the distribution of horizontal forces to lateral load-resisting elements (shear walls), and arching action. Note that Chapters 7 and 8 deal with building design in more detail.

6-2   LATERAL LOAD-RESISTING ELEMENTS

Throughout much of Chapter 5 it was assumed that walls were laterally supported top and bottom perpendicular to their plane, and this requires that structural elements are available to provide the horizontal resistance at these levels of support. In masonry structures this was shown (Section 5-7) to be provided by shear walls, and the horizontal forces are transmitted to these walls by floor and roof systems.

Horizontal forces in buildings stem from a variety of sources. Forces from within the structure itself, such as those due to expansion and contraction from changes in temperature and humidity, can be controlled through the judicious use of control joints and expansion joints. External agencies that can cause horizontal forces are wind, earthquake, blast, earth and fluid pressures. Although masonry is used in various applications to resist each of these forces, the present discussion is limited primarily to considering the effects of wind loading.

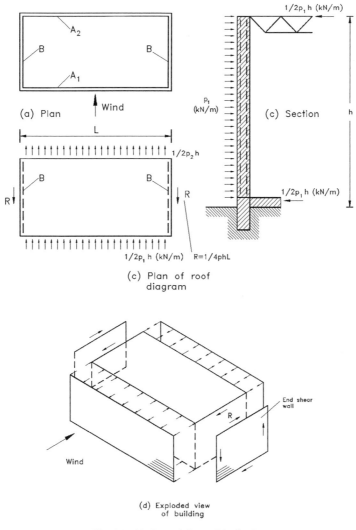

Fig. 6-1 Horizontal Force Distribution

A simple example of the transmission of horizontal forces to the ground is the rectangular single-storey building with perimeter walls A and B shown in Fig. 6-1. The actual effect of the wind on the exterior wall A_1 is a positive pressure p_1, and on wall A_2 a negative pressure p_2, for an overall pressure $p = p_1 + p_2$ on the building. Since the height of the building is h the walls A require horizontal supporting forces at floor and roof levels, as shown in Fig 6-1(b). The roof diaphragm acts as a horizontal beam [Fig 6-1(c)] simply supported between end walls B, and these end walls must then provide the shear resistance to transfer the horizontal reaction $R = 0.25phL$, where $L =$ building length, to the ground. Fig 6-1(d) is an exploded view of the building with these forces shown. In this example there is clearly the need for a roof that can span between the shear walls B as a horizontal beam, and for these walls to be strong enough to transmit the horizontal roof reactions to the ground; and, furthermore, the elements must be connected together to transmit the reactions. Without all of these components the building would be in danger of being blown over.

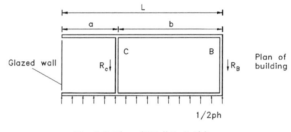

Fig. 6-2 Glazed Wall in Building

If it is required that certain walls be glazed, as shown in Fig. 6-2, the provision of an interior shear wall C will restore the resistance lost through the removal of one wall B, but in this case it can be seen that wall C is required to supply a greater resistance R_c than that of wall B. If, for example, $a = L/3$ and $b = 2L/3$ then a straightforward beam calculation will show that $R_B = phL/8$ and $R_C = 3phL/8$. However an accurate estimate of shear wall forces may not be so simple when there are more than two shear walls, as shown in Fig. 6-3. In this instance the distribution of horizontal forces to shear walls will depend on the relative in-plane stiffness of the shear walls and on that of the roof diaphragm. The problem is then similar to that of a continuous beam (the horizontal diaphragm) on elastic supports (the shear walls). However, since the loading is not known so precisely some approximations are justified. For example, in low (one- and two-storey) buildings the shear walls are not very high and are normally relatively unyielding. This being the case it is normal practice to distribute horizontal wind pressures to the walls according to wind surfaces that are tributary to individual walls. This is illustrated in Example 6-1. On the other hand for high-rise buildings the floor diaphragms are normally stiff compared to the shear walls, and since a stiff diaphragm will cause all shear walls to deflect essentially the same amount, it is normal practice to distribute horizontal forces to shear walls according to their relative stiffness. This is illustrated in Example 6-2.

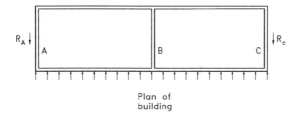

Plan of
building

Fig. 6-3 Shear Walls Forces

When the resultant horizontal force on a building passes through the *centre of rigidity*, or resistance, of the structure, the distribution of forces described in the previous paragraph represents the total effect of the horizontal agency.   However, when the resultant force does not pass through the centre of rigidity the structure is required to resist not only the distribution of forces described above but also the effect of torque. Since earthquake forces are produced by imposing accelerations on the various masses in a building, the resultant force will act through the centre of mass. Wind loads, on the other hand, act in general at the centroid of the area exposed to the wind, although the *National Building Code* does require that uneven wind distributions be considered. Forces due to torque are considered in Example 6-3.

EXAMPLE 6-1 *Fig 6-4 shows the dimensions of a one-storey 10.0 × 36.0 m building which houses five car-wash bays and an office section.   The structure consists of 200 block masonry walls A to G inclusive, with a light steel joist roof spanning between walls A, B, C, and D, and the building is 5.0 m high. For a maximum expected wind pressure (that is, positive pressure on the windward side and negative pressure on the leeward side) of 1.0 kN/m² determine the in-plane wind forces developed in each wall and evaluate their effect.*

For a strength or resistance evaluation the factored wind pressure is used. That is,

$$p_f = \propto_Q p = 1.5(1.0) = 1.5 \text{ kN/m}^2$$

Since there are masonry shear walls in both the longitudinal and transverse directions and since the roof system is attached to the tops of these walls, all exterior walls are laterally supported top and bottom in the manner shown in Fig. 6-1(b). Consequently, the horizontal wind load resisted by the roof is

$$0.5p_f h = 0.5(1.5)(5.0) = 3.75 \text{ kN/m}$$

Since the wind can blow in any direction, the effect of the wind in both the longitudinal and transverse directions should be examined.

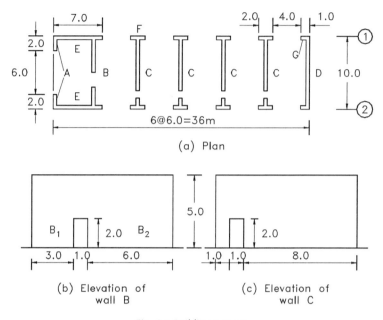

(a) Plan

(b) Elevation of
wall B

(c) Elevation of
wall C

Fig. 6-4 Building Lay-out

(a) Longitudinal Wind

Wind in the longitudinal direction is resisted by walls E, F, and G. Since the building is 10.0 m wide the load to be resisted by each of wall lines 1 and 2 is

$$3.75(10)/2 = 18.75 \text{ kN}$$

If each of the walls is anchored by dowels to the foundation it will act as a vertical cantilever with a wind force applied at the top; and since the tops of the walls are connected together by the roof each wall will deflect essentially the same amount. This means that the wind force distributed to each wall section will be in proportion to its relative stiffness K, which, since all walls are the same height, may be represented by EI. That is

$$F_i = \frac{K_i(F)}{\Sigma K_i} = \frac{E_i I_i(F)}{\Sigma E_i I_i}$$

Assuming that walls A and E, and walls D and G, are not interconnected (not generally the case) wall lines 1 and 2 each consist of one wall E, 7.0 m long, four walls F each 2.0 m long, and wall G 1.0 m long. Although a 'precise' analysis is complex, the stiffness of each wall may reasonably be taken as $EI = EtL^3/12$, and since L is the only variable the stiffness may be represented by L^3. Then,

Wall E	Stiffness $= L^3 = 7.0^3 = 343$	
Wall F	$L^3 = 2.0^3 = 8; 4(8.0) =$	32
Wall G	$L^3 = 1.0^3 = 1$	$\underline{1}$
		376

Wall E therefore resists

$$(K/\Sigma K) \times F = (343/376)18.75 = 17.52 \text{ kN}$$

Each wall F resists

$$(8/376)18.75 = 0.40 \text{ kN}$$

and each wall G resists

$$(1/376)18.75 = 0.05 \text{ kN}$$

Since wall E resists 90% of the wind load, it may be assumed that it provides the full resistance. Since E is not a bearing wall (transverse walls A to D support the roof) the only gravity load is self-weight. If the wall is 200 ungrouted concrete masonry, the self-weight is

$$\text{unit weight} \times \text{height} \times \text{length} = 2.11(5.0)(7.0) = 73.9 \text{ kN}$$

The factored dead load becomes

$$\begin{aligned}
p_f &= \alpha_D(73.9) \\
&= 1.25(73.9) = 92.4 \text{ kN for compression, or} \\
&= 0.85(73.9) = 62.8 \text{ kN for tension due to overturning, for} \\
&\quad \text{example, and the factored load on the wall is that shown in} \\
&\quad \text{Fig. 6-5.}
\end{aligned}$$

The in-plane overturning moment is

$$M_f = 18.75(5) = 93.75 \text{ kN-m}$$

and the maximum and minimum vertical forces become

$$p_f/L \pm 6M_f/L^2 = 92.4/7 + 6(93.75)/7^2 = 24.7 \text{ kN/m maximum}$$
$$= 62.8/7 - 6(93.75)/7^2 = -2.50 \text{ kN/m minimum}$$

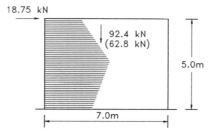

Fig. 6-5 Loading on the Wall of Example 6-1

Reference to Chapter 5 will show that 24.7 kN/m compression is very light for a 200 wall 5.0 m high. Similarly, the tensile force of 2.50 kN/m translates into $2.50\,(10)^3/75.4(10)^3 = 0.033$ MPa tensile stress, well below $\phi_m = 0.55$ times the 0.45 MPa value of Table 6 in S304.1 for tension normal to the bed joint (grouted hollow block). In any case, end cores of the walls should normally be reinforced with at least one vertical bar grouted with a matching dowel, thereby producing some additional resistance to tension.

The horizontal in-plane shear force is $V_f = 18.75$ kN which is accompanied by a complementary vertical shear force.

From Clause 11.5.3.3 v_m may be conservatively taken as $v_m = 0.16(\sqrt{f'_m}) = 0.58$ MPa for $f'_m = 13$ MPa. The shear resistance may be conservatively calculated as

$$V_r = \phi_m v_m bd\gamma_g$$
$$= 0.55(0.58)(190)(7000)(0.5) = 212 \text{ kN} > 18.75 \text{ kN} = V_f \underline{\text{ OK}}$$

and clearly the building is adequately braced in the longitudinal direction.

(b) Transverse Wind

Wind in the transverse direction is resisted by walls A, B, C and D and it is reasonable to assume that the wind force resisted by each of those walls is determined by the area tributary to each wall, and the car-wash doors are assumed to be closed.

The wind force to be resisted by each of walls A and D is

$$0.5(3.75)(6.0) = 11.25 \text{ kN}$$

and by each of walls B and C

$$= 3.75(6.0) = 22.5 \text{ kN}.$$

It is clear from a comparison with (a) that walls B, C and D are not seriously stressed by wind. If a control joint is assumed (conservatively) at the intersection of walls A and E then the wind force of 11.25 kN along wall A is applied at the top of walls each 2.0 m long. That is, a force of 5.625 kN is applied at the top of each wall, or $V_f = 5.625$ kN. Conservatively,

$$V_r = \phi_m v_m bd\gamma_g$$
$$= 0.55(0.58)(190)(2000)(0.5) = 60.6 \text{ kN} > 5.625 \text{ kN} \qquad \underline{OK}$$

An evaluation of wall A for combined axial load and in-plane bending requires further information about the structure of the wall over the glazed portion and about the roof loading. It may be assumed for the present discussion that the roof load is applied without eccentricity to the top of the wall and that a 1.0 m deep beam spans the full openings between walls A, and furthermore that the most critical factored loading for one of the 2.0 m wall sections is that shown in Fig. 6-6.

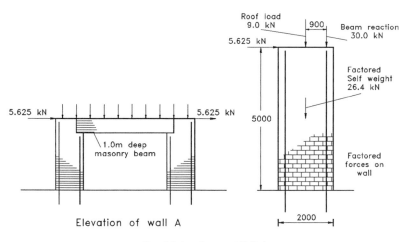

Fig. 6-6 Loading on Wall A

Referring to Fig. 6-6, the factored axial load at the base of wall A is then

$$P_f = 9.0 + 30.0 + 26.4 = 65.4 \text{ kN}$$

(when gravity loads counteract tension, α_D is 0.85 rather than 1.25, in which case P_f is about 65.4(0.85)/1.25 = 44.5 kN)

and, taking moments about the centreline of the base the in-plane factored moment at the base of the wall is

$$M_f = 30.0(0.9) + 5.625(5.0) = 55.13 \text{ kN-m}$$

Expressing in-plane forces in kN/m in the manner of Example 5-11 these forces at the base of the wall become

$$P_f/L \pm 6M_f/L^2$$

where $L = 2.0$ m. Then

$$P_f/L \pm 6M_f/L^2 = 65.4/2.0 + 6(55.13)/2.0^2 = 115.4 \text{ kN/m (compression)}$$
$$= 44.5/2.0 - 6(55.13)/2.0^2 = -60.4 \text{ kN/m (tension)}$$

as shown in Fig 6-7.

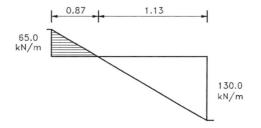

Fig. 6-7 Forces at the Base of Wall

The tensile force produced in the wall is then 0.5(60.4)(0.69) = 20.8 kN.

Since it is good practice to reinforce and grout the end core (or cores) of a section of a wall a small quantity of steel dowelled into the foundation should provide the tensile resistance required. For example, if one #15 bar with $f_y = 400$ MPa is used at each end of the wall the tensile resistance is

$$T_r = \phi_s A_s f_y = 0.85(200)(400) = 68.0 \text{ kN} > 20.8 \text{ kN}$$

and, although this analysis for tension is not precise for example, a cracked section analysis might be more appropriate), it is clearly adequate.

Strictly speaking, the axial compression due to in-plane bending should be checked at minimum out-of-plane 0.1t, according to the principles outlined in Chapter 5. However, a quick check will show that the maximum compressive stress due to a force of 115.4 kN/m is very much lower than $\phi_m f'_m$ and further calculation is unnecessary.

Therefore, the building is adequately braced for wind.

In this example a number of simplifying assumptions were made. It was assumed that walls *A* to *G* were not bonded to adjacent walls, whereas in actual fact walls *D* and *G* would be interlock bonded, as would be the case at the intersection of *A* and *E*, a control joint probably being provided in wall *E* at about 1.0 m from the intersection. Walls *B* and *C* would not be interlocked with walls *F*, but tied with flexible steel ties placed in the mortar joints. It should be noted that wall *B* consists essentially of two shear walls coupled by the portion of the wall over the door opening. They may conservatively be taken as two separate shear walls, one 3.0 m long and the other 6.0 m (the latter providing the main resistance). Similarly, walls *C* may conservatively be taken as being 8.0 m long.

Another simplifying assumption was that the relative stiffness could be represented by *EI*. This assumes that bending deflections predominate. If stiffness is defined as the inverse of the deflection produced by a unit load then relative stiffness is related to deflections due to both shear and bending. For a vertical cantilever of height *h* fixed at the base and subject to a horizontal force *P* at the top the deflection at the top may be given as

$$\delta = \delta(\text{bending}) + \delta(\text{shear})$$

$$= \frac{Ph^3}{3E_m I} + \frac{1.2Ph}{E_v A} \qquad (6\text{-}1)$$

where E_v is the *modulus of rigidity*.

Shear deflections predominate in long low walls ($L/h > 2.0$) and bending deflections in short high walls ($L/h < 1/2$), with a combination of shear and bending for walls between those limits. Since the building in Example 6-1 was found to have ample resistance to wind forces the simplifying assumption was justified. In fact, an experienced designer would realize for this low building that wind load would present a potential problem only for wall *A*, and much of the calculation would have been avoided.

EXAMPLE 6-2 *Fig. 6-8 shows a ten-storey apartment building with transverse masonry load-bearing walls A and B and stairwell and elevator shafts enclosed by masonry walls C and D which are connected by flexible steel ties to walls A. All walls are 200 concrete block. The wind pressure diagram shown in (b) includes windward and leeward pressures and can act in any direction. Determine the maximum effects of this service wind loading at ground level in each of the walls.*

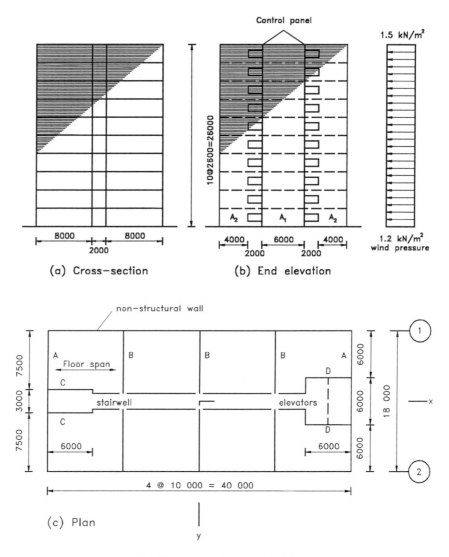

Fig. 6-8 Ten-Story Apartment Building

For a 1.0 m vertical strip of building the moment at ground level due to wind is

$$M = 0.5(1.2)(26.0)^2 + 0.3(26.0)^2/3 = 473.2 \text{ kN-m/m}$$

and the horizontal shear due to wind is

$$V = 0.5(1.2 + 1.5)(26.0) = 35.1 \text{ kN/m}$$

The effects of factored wind loading, M_f and V_f, would then be these values of M and V multiplied by $\alpha_Q = 1.5$.

(a) Transverse Wind

Since the end walls A have openings and are provided with control joints (these have been well placed), as shown in Fig. 6-8(b), each wall consists essentially of three walls: a central portion 6.0 m long and two outer portions also 6.0 m long, but because of the window openings the effective structural length of these outer portions may be taken as 4.0 m. Resistance to transverse wind is then represented by six walls B, 8.0 m long, two walls A_1, 6.0 m long, and four walls A_2, 4.0 m long. Note that the front wall of the elevator shaft provides negligible resistance.

Since the building is 40.0 m long the total moment at ground level is

$$M = 473.2(40.0) = 18,928 \text{ kN-m}$$

and the shear force at ground level is

$$V = 35.1(40) = 1404 \text{ kN}$$

Also, note that since walls A and B are symmetrically located about the central axis y the centre of rigidity and the resultant wind force coincide, and consequently there are no torsional effects to consider.

Since it will be assumed that the floor and roof each act as a rigid diaphragm, and since each wall has a value of $L/h < 1/2$ the total effect of the wind may be distributed to the walls according to their relative flexural stiffness $K \propto EI \propto L^3$.

The moments and shear in each wall can be calculated and summarized as follows:

Wall	Wall length	L^3	$K/\Sigma K = L^3/\Sigma L^3$
B	8.0 m	$512 \times 6 = 3072$	$512/3760 = 0.1362$
A_1	6.0 m	$216 \times 2 = 432$	$216/3760 = 0.0574$
A_2	4.0 m	$64 \times 4 = 256$	$64/3760 = 0.0170$

$$\Sigma L^3 = 3760$$

and, multiplying the total shear by these coefficients the moment and shear in each wall at ground level become

Wall	Wall length (m)	Coefficient	Moment (kN-m)	Shear force (kN)
B	8.0	0.1362	2578	191
A_1	6.0	0.0574	1087	80.7
A_2	4.0	0.0170	322	23.9

Again, the effects of factored wind load are the foregoing values of moment and shear multiplied by $\alpha_Q = 1.5$.

(b) Longitudinal Wind

Wind in the longitudinal direction is resisted by walls C of the stairwell and walls D of the elevator shaft and if the end returns on wall C are neglected the total effect is carried equally by four walls each 6.0 m long. Note that since the walls are symmetrical about the central axis x the centre of rigidity and the resultant load coincide and that consequently there are no torsional effects to consider.

Moment per wall = 473.2(18.0)/4 = 2129 kN-m
Shear per wall = 35.1(18.0)/4 = 158 kN

and the intensity of wind loading in the walls may be determined when required. As before, the factored effects for evaluating strength are obtained by multiplying moment and shear values by $\alpha_Q = 1.5$.

In Example 6-2 the shear walls were located in such a manner that the centre of rigidity coincided with the resultant wind force, thereby eliminating the need for torsional calculations. The *National Building Code of Canada* requires that in addition to considering maximum wind load on the building the designer should investigate 75% of the wind load on any part of the building with full load on the remainder. This load can now be applied so that a torque is introduced, and although the resultant horizontal force is reduced, the effect of torque may result in a load increase in a particular wall.

It will be recalled from Example 6-1 that a section of wall, i, with a stiffness K_i in the direction of the force F applied to the building resists that force in proportion to its relative stiffness, that is

$$F_i = K_i F / \Sigma K_i \tag{6-2}$$

Equation (6-2) applies in each of the two principal directions, as follows

$$F_{ix} = K_{ix} F_x / \Sigma K_{ix}; \quad F_{iy} = K_{iy} F_y / \Sigma K_{iy} \tag{6-3}$$

and these expressions give the force distribution to each wall only when torque is not present, that is, the resultant force passes through the centre of rigidity.

When the resultant force F is located at an eccentricity e from the centre of rigidity, a torque $T = Fe$ is applied to the building. This is illustrated in Fig. 6-9 where the force F_y located a t eccentricity e_x leads to a torque $T = F_y e_x$.

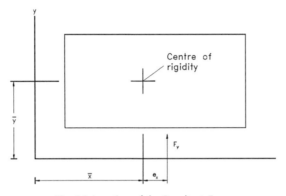

Fig. 6-9 Location of the Resultant Force

The precise analysis for stresses in an elastic section due to torsion is complex and may be found in any book on the *theory of elasticity*. However, in the present situation it may be assumed with reasonable accuracy that each floor is a rigid diaphragm and that the force induced in each shear wall is proportional to its stiffness and to its distance from the centre of rigidity. This being the case, the location $(\overline{x}, \overline{y})$ of the centre of rigidity relative to the arbitrary x- and y-axes shown in Fig. 6-9 becomes

$$\overline{x} = \Sigma K_y x / \Sigma K_y; \quad \overline{y} = \Sigma K_x y / \Sigma K_x$$

where x and y are the ordinates of the centroids of individual shear walls, and K_x and K_y are their relative stiffnesses in the x and y directions respectively. It was noted in Example 6-2 for a straight wall of the same material and thickness as other walls that $K \propto L^3$. Then referring to Fig. 6-10,

$$K_x \propto L_x^3; \quad K_y \propto L_y^3$$

Fig. 6-10 shows a simplified plan view of the shear walls in a building subjected to torque T. A rotation θ due to T will cause displacements of the walls in proportion to their distance from the centre of rigidity. For example, walls 1 and 2 are displaced by the amounts

$$\delta_{1x} = \theta y_1 \text{ and } \delta_{2y} = \theta x_2$$

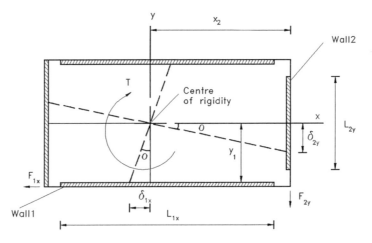

Fig. 6-10 Shear Wall Subjected to Torque

respectively. The corresponding shear wall forces will be

$$F_{1x} = K_{1x}\delta_{1x} = K_{1x}\theta y_1, \text{ and } F_{2y} = K_{2y}\delta_{2y} = K_{2y}\theta x_2$$

respectively. Since θ is not known, these forces may be expressed in a general form for wall i as

$$F_{1x} = CK_{1x}y_1 \text{ and } F_{1y} = CK_{1y}x_1 \tag{6-4}$$

where C is a constant. Furthermore, the force F_{1x} contributes to the torque by the amount

$$\Delta T_i = F_{ix}y_i$$

and in general terms, the total torque T becomes

$$T = \Sigma\Delta T_i = \Sigma(F_{ix}y_i + F_{iy}x_i) = C\Sigma(F_{ix}y_i^2 + F_{iy}x_i^2)$$

from which expression the value of constant C is found as

$$C = \frac{T}{\Sigma(K_{ix}y_i^2 + K_{iy}x_i^2)} = T/J \qquad (6\text{-}5)$$

where

$$J = \Sigma(K_{ix}y^2 + K_{iy}x^2)$$

is referred to as the *relative rotational stiffness*.

Equation (6-5) may now be substituted into Equation (6-4) and combined with Equations (6-3), and the resulting wall forces due to combined shear and torque become

$$F_{ix} = K_{ix}F_x/\Sigma K_{ix} + K_{ix}y_iT/J$$

and

$$F_{iy} = K_{iy}F_y/\Sigma K_{iy} + K_{iy}x_iT/J \qquad (6\text{-}6)$$

It should be noted that Equation (6-6) contains plus signs only, and that a force reduction due to torque is normally neglected in design.

EXAMPLE 6-3 *Determine the maximum effect of the wind load distribution shown in Fig. 6-11 on each wall of the building in Example 6-2 (see also Fig. 6-8).*

From Example 6-2 the horizontal force at the base of the building due to wind is 35.1 kN/m. For the loading shown in Fig. 6-11 the resultant wind force is

$$F_y = 0.75(35.1)(20) + 35.1(20) = 1228.5 \text{ kN}$$

and, taking moments about the centreline of the building this force F_y is located at

$$e_x = \frac{35.1(20)(10) - 0.75(35.1)(20)(10)}{1228.5} = 1.43 \text{ m}$$

as shown.

The torque can now be found as
$$T = 1228.5(1.43) = 1755 \text{ kN-m}$$

Although some walls may be grouted to higher levels than others, and therefore have a greater stiffness, all walls are constructed of 200 concrete blocks and it may reasonably be assumed that their relative stiffnesses are proportional to the

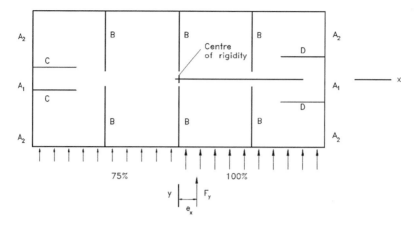

Fig. 6-11 Building Subjected to Wind Load

cubes of their lengths. That is, $K_i \propto L_i^3$. The simplest procedure for calculating the quantities for use in Equation (6-6) is through tabulation as follows:

Wall	L_y	L_y^3	x	No. of walls n_y	$n_y L_y^3$	$n_y L_y^3 x$	$n_y L_y^3 x^2$
A_1	6.0	216	20.0	1	216	4320	86 400
A_1	6.0	216	-20.0	1	216	-4320	86 400
A_2	4.0	64	20.0	2	128	2560	51 200
A_2	4.0	64	-20.0	2	128	-2560	51 200
B	8.0	512	10.0	2	1024	10 240	102 400
B	8.0	512	0	2	1024	0	0
B	8.0	512	-10.0	2	1024	-10 240	102 400
					$\Sigma=3760$	$\Sigma=0$	$\Sigma=480\,000$

Wall	L_x	L_x^3	y	No. of walls n_x	$n_x L_x^3$	$n_x L_x^3 y$	$n_x L_x^3 y^2$
C	6.0	216	1.5	1	216	324	486
C	6.0	216	-1.5	1	216	-324	486
D	6.0	216	3.0	1	216	648	1944
D	6.0	216	-3.0	1	216	-648	1944
					$\Sigma=864$	$\Sigma=0$	$\Sigma=4860$

Since $K \propto L_i^3$ the location of the centre of rigidity is found as

$$\overline{x} = \Sigma K_y x / \Sigma K_y = \Sigma n_y L_y^3 x / \Sigma n_y L_y^3 = 0/3760 = 0.0$$

$$\overline{y} = \Sigma K_x y / \Sigma K_x = \Sigma v_x L_x^3 y / \Sigma n_x L_x^3 = 0/864 = 0.0$$

and, predictably (from symmetry), the centre of rigidity is at the geometric centre of the building.

The relative stiffness may now be calculated as

$$J = \Sigma(K_x y^2 + K_y x^2) \propto \Sigma(n_x L_x^3 y^2 + n_y L_y^3 x^2)$$
$$= 4860 + 480\ 000 = 484\ 860$$

Now, recalling Equation (6-6) and the fact that $K \propto L_i^3$, the forces due to wind in each of the walls can be calculated from $F_y = 1228.5$ and $T = 1755$ kN-m as follows

Walls	$\dfrac{K_{iy}}{\Sigma K_{iy}} = \dfrac{L_y^3}{\Sigma n_y L_y^3}$	$\dfrac{K_{ix} y}{J}$	$\dfrac{K_{iy} x}{J}$	$\dfrac{K_{ix} y_i}{J} T$ (kN)	$\dfrac{K_{iy} F_y}{\Sigma K_{iy}} + \dfrac{K_{iy} x_i T}{J}$ (kN)
A_1	0.0574		0.0089		70.5+15.6 = 86.1
A_2	0.0170		0.0026		20.9+4.6 = 25.5
B	0.1362		0.0106		167.3+18.6 = 185.9
B_C	0.1362		0.0		167.3 +0.0 = 167.3
C		0.00067		1.18	
D		0.00134		2.35	

The final column of this table gives the forces in walls A and B produced by the eccentric force F_y. It might be noted from a comparison with Example 6-2(a) that for this building there is little difference in the maximum wall forces from full concentric loading to a reduced but eccentric loading. It should also be noted that although no external forces in the x-direction have been considered in this example, walls C and D receive some loading from the torque. The forces due to torque in walls C and D are predictably, because of their proximity to the x-axis, quite small. As in Example 6-2, the effects of the factored wind loads are obtained by applying the multiplying factor $\alpha_Q = 1.5$.

While the foregoing analysis determining the distribution of lateral forces to individual building components has been illustrated by examples of wind pressures, the distribution of horizontal seismic forces can be determined in the same manner. Also, it might be noted that whereas an analysis based on elastic principles may not be entirely "precise" for strength design, a reasonable distribution of lateral loads is obtained.

6-3   ARCHING ACTION

The distribution of load from a masonry wall to the supporting beam was discussed in Section 4-3, where it was explained that in many instances the wall transmits a substantial portion of the load across an opening by *arching action*. In that event the lintel beam over the opening is required to support no more than the load that falls within a 45° triangle, as was shown in Figs. 4-2 and 4-3 and in Example 4-4. However, arching action can only be effective when the horizontal restraints it requires are available. This means that either the structure on each side of the opening is strong enough to provide the resistance, or that a tension tie is provided above the opening. In the absence of suitable horizontal restraint the lintel beam over the opening should be designed to support the total load.

Fig. 6-12 shows a masonry wall supporting several floors with an opening spanned by a lintel beam. In this instance it is likely that the wall arches over the opening since (a) there is a portion of wall each side of the opening, (b) the continuous bond beam at each floor provides a number of ties over the opening, (c) the horizontal joint reinforcement provides some, albeit small, tying action, and (d) no control joint. The arching action being assured, the lintel is then designed for loading similar to that illustrated in Example 4-4. It should be noted that the lintel reinforcement is rarely extended beyond the lintel bearing and therefore it does not normally act as a tie to resist arching action. Although the working stress design standard S304 (Clause 5.8.1.3) requires a reinforced bond beam at each floor and roof level, S304.1 has no such provision. Nevertheless, reinforced bond beams should be provided at each of these levels to incorporate a complete tension tie throughout the structure at regular intervals. The selection of bar size is left to the discretion of the structural designer, who typically uses a #15 to #25 bar.

Fig. 6-13 shows an opening in a masonry wall with only a small length of wall *A* on one side of the opening. Since *A* is not likely to provide much horizontal support for arching action, approximate methods may be used to determine the size of bar in each bond beam that will serve as a tie. For instance, it could be assumed that each floor is supported by the floor-to-floor section of wall below acting as a beam spanning the opening and reinforced with the bond beam bar. For example, if the opening is 3.0 m and the load at each floor level is 40 kN/m, and if the floor-to-floor distance is 2.8 m then a simple calculation will show that a beam 2.8 m deep so loaded and spanning 3.0 m is adequately reinforced with a #15 bar. The wall now, being so reinforced, will arch effectively over the beam.

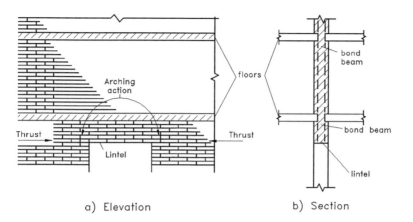

a) Elevation   b) Section

Fig. 6-12 Arching action

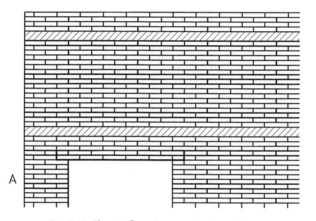

Fig. 6-13 Floor-to-floor Section Acting as Beam

Arching action is frequently called into play in the design of foundation beams that support masonry walls. Fig. 6-14 shows a pile-supported grade beam which in turn supports a load-bearing wall. The grade beam is frequently designed to carry only that load that falls within the 45° triangle discussed earlier, in which case the wall must then arch over the span between the piles. As a result, the walls are more highly stressed at pile locations, and additional vertical reinforcement, as shown, may be considered necessary. Once again, simplifying assumptions must be made about the distribution of loading to piles. For example, it may be assumed that the accumulated wall load is distributed over a length x representing a 45° transmission of load through the grade beam to the pile, as shown in Fig. 6-14.

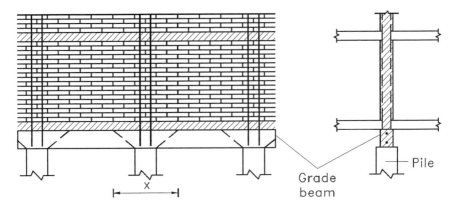

Fig. 6-14 Arching Action in Foundation

Situations involving arching action are normally highly indeterminate and any reasonable approximation conservatively applied is adequate.

6-4   ONE- AND TWO-STOREY BUILDINGS

The design of one- and two-storey buildings is rarely governed by the axial compressive capacity of the walls, except perhaps where there are short lengths of wall that support the reactions from beams over large openings. It is more likely that the design will be governed by the slenderness of the relatively high walls required in buildings such as warehouses, and by their flexural resistance to wind pressures perpendicular to their surface. Another factor requiring consideration is the resistance of the building to horizontal loads, such as wind and earthquake, and in industrial buildings to horizontal forces from cranes and hoists. This requires that not only should the walls be adequate but that the roof should act effectively as a diaphragm and be properly connected to the walls, and, furthermore, that the roof is anchored down to resist uplift due to negative wind pressures. The designer should allow for effects of changes in temperature and humidity.

EXAMPLE 6-4 *The resistance of the car-wash building shown in Fig. 6-4 to wind forces was examined in Example 6-1. Discuss other factors to be considered in the design. Assume 200 mm concrete block construction with 20 MPa units and reinforcing steel with $f_y = 300$ MPa. The roof dead load may be taken as 1.0 kN/m² and the snow load as 2.0 kN/m².*

The overall resistance of the building to wind having been assured in Example 6-1, other factors to be considered are:

(a) design of load-bearing walls B and C;

(b) design of load-bearing end wall D;
(c) design of the beam over the opening in wall A;
(d) design of the lintel beam over the double doors;
(e) design of walls along lines 1 and 2;
(f) consideration of roof connection to masonry walls;
(g) other considerations.

(a) Interior wall B and C

It will be recalled from Example 6-1 that the roof structure of this building consists of steel joists spanning between transverse masonry walls, and one typical joist support detail is shown in Fig. 6-15.

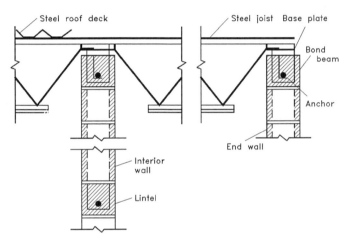

Fig. 6-15 Typical Joist Support Detail

It is clear from the diagram that gravity loading from the roof is applied to interior walls with negligible eccentricity and the minimum eccentricity can be used.

Since the height of the 200 wall is 5000 the slenderness ratio is

$$kh/t = 1.0(5000)/190 = 26.3 < 30$$

Therefore, this wall is subject to the standard provisions for slender walls.

Check Axial Load

Since the walls are spaced at 6.0 m, the maximum factored load from the roof to the wall is

$$6.0(\alpha_D D + \alpha_L L) = 6.0[1.25(1.0) + 1.5(2.0)] = 25.5 \text{ kN/m}$$

and including the self weight to mid-height

$$P_f = 25.5 + 1.25(2.11)(5.0)/2 = 32.1 \text{ kN/m}$$

Assuming an ungrouted wall (f'_m = 13.0 MPa) and following Example 5-1

$$\begin{aligned}
P_{r(max)} &= 0.8(0.85\phi_m f'_m A_e) = 0.8(0.85)(0.55)(13.0)(75.4)(10)^3 \\
&= 366 \text{ kN/m} > P_f \qquad\qquad\qquad\qquad\qquad\qquad \underline{\text{OK}}
\end{aligned}$$

The primary moment for the wall is

$$M_p = P_f(0.1)t = 32.1(10)^3(0.1)(190) = 610 \text{ N-mm/m} = 0.610 \text{ kN-m/m}$$

Recalling that $M_{TOT} = C_m M_p/(1 - P_f/P_{cr})$

where $\quad C_m = 0.6 + 0.4 M_1/M_2 = 0.6 + 0.4(1.0) = 1.0$

and $\quad P_{cr} = \pi^2 E_m I_{eff}/[(kh)^2(1 + 0.5\beta_D)]$

$$I_{eff} = 0.4 I_0 = 0.4(442)(10)^6 = 176.8(10)^6 \text{ mm}^4/\text{m}$$

$$E_m = 850 f'_m = 850(13.0) = 11,050 \text{ MPa}$$

$$\beta_D = M_D/M_{TOT} = 14.1/32.1 = 0.44$$

Then,

$$P_{cr} = \frac{\pi^2(11,050)(176.8)(10)^6}{5000^2[1 + 0.5(0.44)]} = 632.2 \text{ kN/m}$$

and $\quad M_{TOT} = 0.610/(1 - 32.1/632.2) = 0.643 \text{ kN-m/m}$

Then, to check compressive and tensile stresses

$$\begin{aligned}
P_f/A_e + M_{TOT}/S &= 32.1(10)^3/[75.4(10)^3] + 0.643(10)^6/[4.66(10)^6] \\
&= 0.56 \text{ MPa} < 0.55(13.0) = \phi_m f'_m \qquad\qquad \underline{\text{OK}}
\end{aligned}$$

Actually, the compressive force in the wall should be applied at minimum out-of-plane eccentricity in the manner of Chapter 5, but since the compressive stress is an order of magnitude smaller than that permitted that rather lengthy step can be omitted. The tension can now be checked as follows:

$$P_f/A_e - M_{TOT}/S = 32.1(10)^3/[75.4(10)^3] - 0.641(10)^6/[4.66(10)^6]$$
$$= 0.288 \text{ MPa}$$

and, since there is no tension, this wall is OK for axial load. At this point it is worth noting that the preceding rather lengthy calculations can be reduced considerably through the use of Part 2 of this book, a procedure that will be illustrated in subsequent chapters.

Check Resistance to Wind Load

Another possible load case occurs when a transverse wind is blowing and two adjacent bays have double doors open on the windward and leeward sides respectively, leading to a combination of positive and negative pressures on opposite sides of a wall. However, since the interior of the building is being considered, it is unlikely that gust effects will be significant. Recalling from Example 6-1 that the overall wind pressure on the building was 1.0 kN/m², it may be assumed for illustrative purposes that interior walls are to be designed for a total wind pressure of 0.8 kN/m². (Note that the designer should consult the Supplement to the National Building Code of Canada for more precise information on wind loading.)

The resistance of the interior walls to wind load and minimum axial load should now be considered. Note that when wind pressures are acting on the walls of a building there is also a negative vertical pressure on the roof of approximately the same magnitude. It is therefore likely that the 1.0 kN/m² roof dead load does little more than counteract the uplift due to wind. Since axial load enhances the resistance of the wall to bending, it may conservatively be taken as zero. The factored wind pressure is

$$p_f = 1.5(0.8) = 1.20 \text{ kPa}$$

and the maximum factored moment occurs at mid-height of the wall

$$M_f = p_f h^2/8 = 1.2(5000)^2/8 = 3.75 \text{ kN-m/m}$$

The tensile stress in the wall due to bending is

$$f_t = M_f/S = 3.75(10)^6/[4.66(10)^6] = 0.805 \text{ MPa}$$

and, since this is greater than ϕ_m times the value of 0.7 MPa given in Table 6 of S304.1, vertical reinforcement is required. As explained in Chapter 4 the moment of resistance of a reinforced section can be approximated as

$$M_r \approx \phi_s A_s f_y (0.8d) \quad \text{where } d = t/2 = 95 \text{ mm}$$

Then the required area of steel is

$$A_s \approx M_f / [\phi_s f_y (0.8d)]$$
$$= 3.75(10)^6 / [0.85(300)(0.8)(95)] = 193.4 \text{ mm}^2/\text{m}$$

Now, rather than go through the lengthy process outlined in Example 4-13, it will be assumed that the wall is adequately reinforced with #15 @ 1000. And it might be noted that since the ends of the interior walls are tied to and therefore receive lateral support from the exterior walls, wind pressures are of consequence only toward the mid-height of the walls.

Other factors to consider in the design of these interior walls are the lintel beams over the door openings, the bond beam at the top of the wall (see Fig. 6-15), joint reinforcement and control joints.

The lintel over the door opening carries no more than a small triangular load over a clear span of 1.0 m, and a simple calculation will show that a 200 mm deep lintel reinforced with 1-#10, located as shown in Fig. 6-15, is adequate.

Although S304.1 does not specify horizontal reinforcement in a non-seismic zone, it is sound practice to provide horizontal reinforcement in conformity with the minimum requirement of Clause 5.2.2.2. That is,

$$A_h = 0.002A_g(1 - \alpha), \quad 0.33 \le \alpha \le 0.67$$
$$= 0.002(190)(1000)(0.33) = 125 \text{ mm}^2/\text{m}$$

Recalling that No. 9 ASWG (3.8 mm diameter) joint reinforcement has a cross-sectional area of 22.7 mm^2, placement at 200 mm centres (that is, in each course) gives

$$A_h = 22.7(1000)/200 = 113.5 \text{ mm}^2/\text{m}$$

which almost satisfies the 125 mm^2/m requirement. The designer may choose to provide joint reinforcement every second course, the balance being placed in the bond beam, that is 22.7(1000)/400 = 56.7 mm^2/m is provided by joint reinforcing. The balance for the top half (2.5 m) of the wall then becomes

$$A_s = (125 - 56.7)(2.5) = 171 \text{ mm}^2$$

and 1-#15 can be used as reinforcement in the bond beam. The reinforced concrete foundation supporting the wall becomes a comparable tie at the bottom of the wall. In general the reinforcing in a bond beam should not be less than 1-#15. It is evident that there are no clear rules for reinforcing this wall; however, although there are a number of possible solutions, that shown in Fig. 6-16 is adequate.

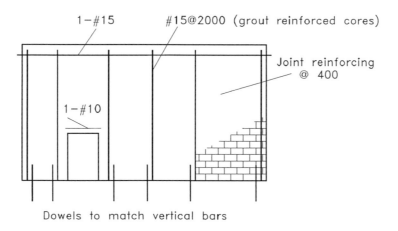

Fig. 6-16 Bond Beam Reinforcement

(b) End Wall D

Since wind load predominates, the design of wall *D* can follow the same procedure as *(a)*, and the reader can verify that for a wind pressure of 1.0 kN/m^2 , 2-#15 vertical bars at 1600 mm centres is adequate. Note that the steel joist bearing is normally centrally located - that is, with little eccentricity.

(c) Beam Over Opening in Wall A

Figs. 6-4 and 6-6 show this as a 1.0 m deep beam spanning a clear opening of 6.0 m. A five-course, fully grouted beam can be used here, and it may be assumed that any doors or windows in the opening are non-structural - that is, they do not provide vertical support for the beam. The gravity loading for the beam consists of roof load plus self-weight (from Table 4-2), and the factored load is

$$w_f = [1.25(1.0) + 1.5(2.0)]6.0/2 + 1.25(3.91) = 17.64 \text{ kN/m}$$

and, if 200 mm bearing is assumed at each support the span becomes 6.2 m. If the beam is now assumed to be simply-supported the reader can verify that 2-#20 bars are required in the bottom course - and that shear reinforcement is not required. Note that since the bond beam constitutes the top course of this beam some negative moment resistance is available at the support, and this could be used to reduce the positive moment steel. The beam reaction now becomes

$$R_f = 17.64(1/2)(6.2) = 54.7 \text{ kN}$$

and assuming a 200 bearing length, a fully-grouted bearing (which is normal practice), the bearing resistance may be calculated as (10.4.1 of S304.1)

$$R_r = 0.85\phi_m f'_m A_b$$

where A_b is the bearing area and $f'_m = 10$ MPa for a fully-grouted core. Then

$$R_r = 0.85(0.55)(10.0)(190)(200) = 177.6 \text{ kN} > 54.7 \text{ kN} = R_f \quad \underline{\text{OK}}$$

The reader is referred to Clause 10.4 for a fuller description of resistance to bearing.

It should be noted that this beam will provide lateral support for the window and door mullions below when there is a wind pressure. However, since the beam is laterally restrained at the top by the roof joists it is not required to carry the full effect of the wind in out-of-plane bending. The situation is shown in Fig. 6-17(a).

A precise analysis is out of the question since a combination of bending and torsion is involved, and an approximate design is required if these forces are to be carried by the masonry. However, it is beyond the scope of this book to consider the application of approximate methods to such special cases. A number of solutions are possible, one of which is to relieve the masonry of wind forces from the window by providing the full-height mullions shown in Fig 6-17(b).

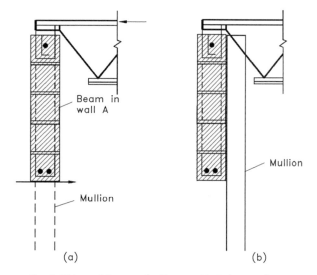

Beam in
wall A

Mullion

(a)

Mullion

(b)

Fig. 6-17 Lateral Support for Door and Window Mullions

It will be recalled that one aspect of the design of wall *A* was considered in
Example 6-1. The reader can confirm that design as being adequate for the
loading case considered in this example.

(c) Lintel Beams in Wall Lines 1 and 2

Since these walls are parallel with the roof joists they are not classed as load-
bearing. Typically the roof joists are spaced at 1.5 m to 2.0 m centres and
the wall carries little roof load. Overhead doors are frequently supported on
their own steel frame and little load is imposed on the masonry. In that event
the lintel will carry little more than its own self-weight and wind load.

(e) Walls 1 and 2

Walls *F* are only lightly loaded, and since they are laterally supported by
interior walls, wind loading does not present a problem. It is nevertheless
good practice to reinforce full height and grout at least one core at each end
of each wall *F*, especially since vehicles will be using these door openings.
Steel door frames can also be used to protect the openings. Wind loading
predominates in the design of walls *E*, but since they are laterally supported
by walls *A* and *B*, 6.0 m apart, the effect of the wind is not as serious as it
was for wall *D*. It should be noted that once again a continuous bond beam
should be provided for the full length of walls 1 and 2.

(f) Roof Connection

The roof-to-wall connection should be able not only to support the gravity loading from the roof but also resist uplift due to wind, and this uplift can be particularly severe at the corners of buildings. Fig. 6-15 shows typical joist supports where base plates are provided to prevent bearing stresses being exceeded, and anchors welded to the base plates to resist uplift. It is good practice to anchor any vertical steel in the wall into the bond beam so that more than the weight of the bond beam can be mobilized to resist uplift. In long buildings it is also necessary to provide for some thermal expansion and contraction in the joist seats. In the relatively short (36.0 m) building in this example an expansion joint is not required.

(g) Other Considerations

Other factors requiring consideration fall mainly into the category of detailing, but are nevertheless an important part of design. For example, improperly located control joints can result in unsightly cracking in the walls and can lead eventually to a deterioration of the masonry. Although a 6.0 m and 8.0 m spacing of vertical control joints was suggested in Section 5-8, the required spacing will depend largely on the amount of horizontal reinforcing in the wall (see Table 7-1 of Chapter 7). For example, if end wall *D* is provided with joint reinforcing every course, a control joint would not be required. However, the door opening towards the mid-length of wall *B* constitutes a weakness and a crack in the wall above the opening is likely if a control joint is not provided at each location. Similarly, a control joint should be provided at one end of each lintel in wall lines 1 and 2, and in wall *A*, located as shown in Fig 6-18. Another appropriate location for a control joint is in wall *E*, close to the intersection with wall *A*. This will accommodate any thermal expansion or contraction in the roof in combination with wall shrinkage.

It should also be noted that the bond beam is required to provide a continuous tie and, consequently, where walls intersect the bond beam, steel from one wall should be anchored into the adjacent beam. This may require that the face shell of one of the bond beam units be cut to accommodate the reinforcing bar and grout. This is discussed again in Section 6-5, and an appropriate detail is shown in Fig. 6-19.

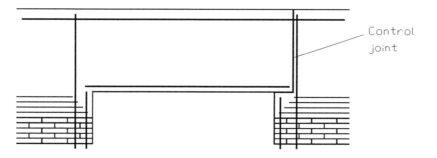

Fig. 6-18 Location of Control Joint

The function of this building should be borne in mind during design and construction. As a car-wash its interior will be continuously at a high relative humidity. There will consequently be a constant tendency for moisture to migrate outwards through the masonry, and any defects will soon become apparent. This will be especially true during severe winters when cycles of freezing and thawing will produce accelerating deterioration. Improperly designed, detailed, constructed or finished, this building will soon experience the need for continuous repair.

The bond beam at roof level can serve a more calculable structural function than providing an encompassing tie for the whole building. If, for example, the building of Example 6-4 consisted merely of four exterior walls with no interior walls then the roof joists would span in the 10.0 m direction - that is, between the longitudinal walls - and wind load distribution would be similar to that shown in Fig. 6-1.

For a 10.0 m × 36.0 m × 5.0 m high building the $0.5ph = 0.5(1.5)(5.0) = 3.75$ kN/m factored horizontal roof load must be transmitted through the roof diaphragm to the end walls. The roof then acts as a horizontal beam spanning 36.0 m between the end walls. Depending on the construction of the roof the bond beams may be required to act as tension and compression chords for the roof diaphragm. It can readily be shown that a horizontal beam spanning 36.0 m loaded with 3.75 kN/m will develop a force of 60.8 kN in each of the chords, 10.0 m apart.

The roof then transmits a factored horizontal shear force of

$$w_f L = 0.5(3.75)(36.0) = 67.5 \text{ kN}$$

to the top of each end wall. The end walls must be capable of resisting this force and furthermore, the connection between the roof deck and the end walls must transfer this force from the roof to the top of the wall. The structural requirements of the roof system, which has been assumed to act as an effective diaphragm, are beyond the scope of this text, as are the practical details of the roof-to-wall connection.

6-5   HIGH-RISE BUILDINGS

Masonry is frequently used in the construction of high-rise buildings, normally up to twelve stories in height, but which may be higher. One of the main advantages of masonry is that it performs the dual function of serving as a load-bearing structure while at the same time providing an enclosure for the building and partitions between various areas. Among its other advantages masonry construction is fast, economical and labour-intensive (each unit is mortared into place by hand), and although it performs somewhat akin to reinforced concrete the need for formwork is eliminated; and, in addition to supporting load, in its function as a partition it has good resistance to sound transmission, fire, and to agents of environmental deterioration. Masonry, both brick and concrete block, are available in a variety of textures and finishes, and can be constructed in a variety of patterns so that the wall itself can provide the appropriate architectural finish.

Masonry high-rise construction is used typically in situations where interior partitions are required, such as hotels, an apartment or an office building and these partitions can serve as bearing walls. Ideally, floor plans should be repetitive so that load bearing and shear walls are continuous for the full height of the building. However, it is frequently required that the lower one or two stories be of a different layout than the floors above - for example, reception, lobby and dining spaces in hotels - and it may be required to frame larger open spaces, and an adequate base can be provided on which to construct a masonry tower. The structural layout of a high-rise masonry building must be such that there are adequate shear walls to resist horizontal forces from any direction.   There are numerous possible floor plan arrangements, those shown earlier (Figs. 1-7, 5-4, 5-26, and 6-8) being rather simple and unimaginative examples.

High-rise masonry differs from masonry in low buildings in that its principal structural function is in resisting in-plane loading (both axial compression and shear wall bending) rather than out-of-plane bending which predominates in low buildings. Many of the details of construction are similar in both, but may assume greater importance in high-rise buildings. For example, the ties that hold an outside wythe or veneer to an exterior bearing wall (since the wind forces are greater at greater heights and the hazards of falling masonry greater); or the bond beams or ties that are provided at each floor and roof level to tie the structural elements together into an integral whole.   Fig. 6-19 shows a detail that ensures continuity of horizontal reinforcing between intersecting walls, and that accommodates vertical reinforcing. Note that it is desirable to provide vertical reinforcing not only at each end of each wall, but also in each wall at wall intersections. Although horizontal joint reinforcing may also extend across a wall intersection it does not provide a significant tie. Where an interior wall abuts an exterior wall which has thermal insulation on the inside and where a thermal break is required, steel ties should still be provided across the insulated space between the two intersecting elements, especially at the bond beam locations. These ties can take a variety of forms, from the use of one of many proprietary products available to the extension of the bond beam steel through the insulated space.

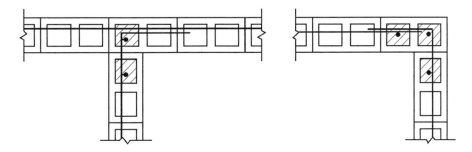

Fig. 6-19 Reinforcing Detail at Wall Intersections

Floor and roof systems that can be used in high-rise masonry construction are cast-in-place reinforced concrete, precast and prestressed concrete units, or open-web steel joists supporting a thin concrete slab poured on a fluted sheet steel deck. A variety of such systems are illustrated in Fig. 6-20. The need for structural continuity in three directions should be noted. Where vertical reinforcement is required in masonry walls it should be continuous from one level to the next; bond beam reinforcement may be provided in the wall, as shown in Fig. 6-20(b), or in a poured concrete slab (as shown in (a), (c) and (d)); and a horizontal tie is provided normal to the plane of the wall, grouted into place between precast units (Fig. 6-20(b)) or located in the poured concrete. Precast concrete floor and roof units without concrete topping should be used cautiously, especially where a sound diaphragm is essential to the distribution of horizontal forces to the shear walls. The concrete topping assists greatly in providing this diaphragm action.

It might be noted that the floor/ wall connection shown in Fig. 6-20(b) is not always constructed with the bond beam bar located below the floor slab. The problem is that the wall below a particular floor is normally grouted *after* the precast floor slabs are in place, there being a floor surface to work from, and the space available between the abutting ends of floor slabs for pouring grout is quite limited. The presence of a bar directly below this space will further impede the flow of grout. If bond beam blocks with cut-down webs, such as that shown in Fig. 2-4, are used for the bond beam course, the horizontal bar can be placed to one side of the centre line of the wall. However, these are not always available, and a common practice is to use standard blocks for the entire wall, and once the grout has been poured to the floor level the bond beam bar is pushed down manually into the grout space between the floor slabs.

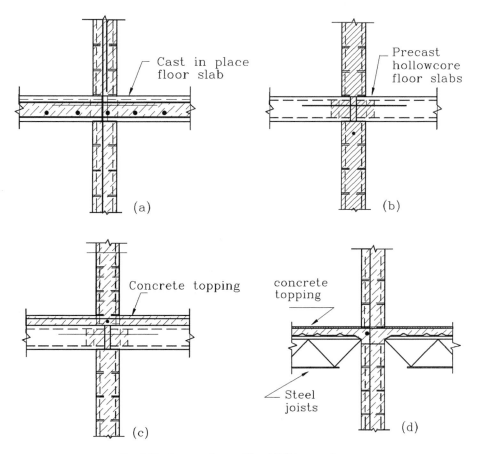

Fig. 6-20 Cross-sections at Floor/Wall Intersections

The structure of a building should be designed not only for its resistance to "primary" loads, such as those due to gravity, wind and earthquake, but consideration should be given to "secondary" effects, such as differential strains resulting from environmental changes, that may assume primary importance. For example, the exterior wall of a building may experience an annual temperature change of 80° C or more while the interior remains at a relatively constant temperature. If the building is 30.0 m high and if the thermal coefficient of linear expansion $\alpha = 8(10)^{-6}/°C$ then an exterior wall might undergo a length change of

$$\alpha \Delta Th = 8(10)^{-6}(80)(30)(10)^3 = 19 \text{ mm}$$

or more. Where intersecting interior and exterior walls are not rigidly interconnected, this differential vertical movement can lead to problems at upper levels of a building where roof and floor systems tie into both interior and exterior. On the other hand, where interior and exterior walls are interconnected the relative movement is inhibited, but both may be subjected to high stresses which if not accounted for will lead to tensile cracking in the upper levels of a building, where the accumulated compression due to gravity loading is not very great, or to compression overload at lower levels. This effect was discussed briefly in Section 5-8 and the nature of secondary load diagram is shown in Fig. 5-26. This situation is considered in the following example.

EXAMPLE 6-5 *Fig 6-21 shows the relevant dimensions of a masonry bearing wall high-rise building in which the interior walls extend through an insulated skin to support masonry balconies. Discuss the loading, in addition to gravity and wind loading, induced in the walls when the interior temperature is +20°C and the outside temperature -40°C.*

Assuming elastic behaviour, 200 mm concrete masonry, $f'_m = 10$ MPa (and consequently $E_m = 850f'_m = 8500$ MPa), $\alpha = 8(10)^{-6}/°C$, the temperature-induced stresses may be obtained as

$$\Delta T = 20 - (-40) = 60°C$$

would cause a free (or unstressed) contraction, or temperature-induced strain of

$$\epsilon_T = 8(10)^{-6}(60) = 0.00048$$

With the walls being interconnected the same free contraction can take place only if the interior portion is uniformly stressed in compression to

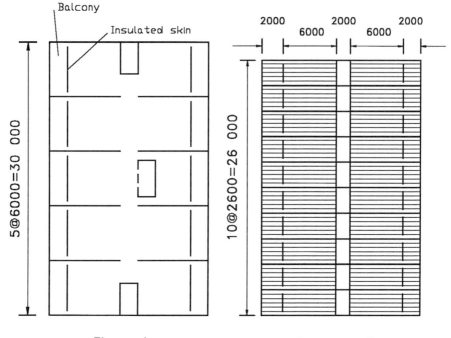

Fig. 6-21 High-rise Masonry Building

$$\sigma = \epsilon_T E_m = 0.00048(8.5)(10)^3 = 4.1 \text{ MPa}$$

and applying the load factor $\alpha_T = 1.25$

$$\sigma_f = 1.25(4.1) = 5.1 \text{ MPa}$$

as shown in Fig 6-22(b). This is equivalent to applying a force of

$$P_T = \sigma_f A = 5.1(6000)t = 30.6(10)^3 t \text{ N}$$

at the mid-length of the interior wall, as shown in Fig. 6-22(a).

This now represents an artificial situation since P_T is a hypothetical load, and the removal of P_T from the whole wall is the equivalent of superimposing a tensile stress

$$\sigma = P_T/A = 30.6(10)^3t/8000t = 3.83 \text{ MPa}$$

along the full length of wall, as shown in Fig. 6-22(c). Stresses in Figs. (b) and (c) are then combined to give the stresses shown in (d), and it can be seen that the calculated stresses are high compared to the limiting stresses for the wall.

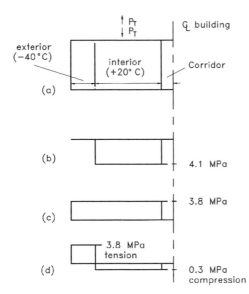

Fig. 6-22 Temperature-induced Stresses

The actual stresses are likely to be less than the calculated values since creep in the masonry will lead to some relaxation of stress, and since heat loss through the wall will ease the abrupt temperature change assumed in the calculations, and it is likely that the actual stresses will be only about half the calculated values. Nevertheless, even with the reduced stresses cracking will occur at upper levels unless the walls are reinforced for tension, and at lower levels additional compression will occur. In the hot season the stresses are reversed and less serious since the temperature differential is reversed and probably less.

In the foregoing analysis it should be noted that whereas P_T was initially applied at the centroid of the interior wall, its removal (from the same location) was not from the centroid of the full wall. This eccentric removal of load causes a tendency for in-plane bending shown in Fig. 6-23. In the present example this bending is prevented by axial forces developed in the tie beams (an extension of the bond beams) which connect both halves of the building across the corridor.

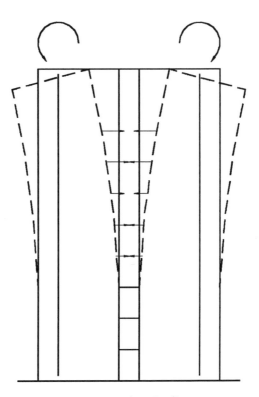

Fig. 6-23 In-plane Bending

Another problem afflicting the building of Fig. 6-21 is the continuous line of balconies for the full length of the building. Those balcony floors are likely to be precast units spanning between bearing walls and not attached to the interior floor slabs. The seasonal expansion and contraction of these balcony floors should be allowed for through the provision of a sliding bearing at each end of each unit, otherwise the walls and/or slabs will suffer some damage.

Since the extension of a warm wall through a cold exterior results in heat loss from the building, this situation should be avoided wherever possible. In instances where it may be unavoidable, some allowances in the design should be made for temperature-induced stresses through the provision of additional reinforcement, otherwise overload and cracking will occur.

Since a numerical example of the complete design of a high-rise building is not given in this section, a summary is appropriate. The main emphasis then in the structural design of high-rise masonry buildings is on ensuring

(a)   that an adequate system of shear walls provides the required resistance to horizontal forces;

(b)   that the floor and roof systems provide the structural diaphragms necessary for the distribution of horizontal shear forces to the shear walls;

(c)   that the walls can adequately resist any combination of horizontal forces and gravity loading;

(d)   that "secondary" effects, such as differential temperatures and shrinkage, have been considered in the design;

(e)   that other structural elements, such as beams and lintels, have been properly designed, and that where arching action has been assumed it is available;

(f)   that non-structural elements, such as veneers, are appropriately tied to the building, and;

(g)   that all components of the building are tied together to give an integral whole.

6-6   COMMENTS ABOUT CONSTRUCTION

Masonry construction has the deceptive outward appearance of being relatively simple - merely the laying of successive courses of bricks or concrete blocks by hand on beds of mortar. However, it is less simple for the structural designer to understand than construction in reinforced concrete or steel. This is partially because considerably less time and attention is devoted to masonry in structural design courses, but primarily because of the vast range of masonry units and hardware available, the numerous ways in which masonry can be put together and the need for appropriate hardware; and the construction may be plain or reinforced, grouted or ungrouted. In many instances details of construction are left to masonry contractors who, if responsible and competent, will generally do a good job since they are familiar with the products and techniques. However, the designer should become familiar with the problems and details of construction in order to design and detail effectively.

Masonry probably lends itself to construction problems more than reinforced concrete or structural steel, and for the most part the cause is ignorance. The designer is not always familiar with the requirements of construction and structural drawings are frequently improperly or incompletely detailed. The contractor is not always fully aware of the intent of the design and may not be able, while coping with unrealistic deadlines and adverse weather, to determine which are the critical points in the structure that require special attention.   Regular communication between the structural designer and the contractor is essential to the smooth running and successful completion of a project.   Furthermore, it is important that this communication includes frequent inspections of construction.   Unfortunately, this need for regular, competent and thorough inspection by the designer or their representative, is rarely fully appreciated; the reader is referred to CSA Standard A371 *Masonry Construction for Buildings* for construction requirements, some of which require a design decision. The design is valid only when all of its requirements have been met in the field.

Foremost among the requirements of construction relating to strength and serviceability are the sampling of materials for quality control testing, ensuring that reinforcement is in place where required, ensuring that where walls and columns are to be fully grouted this is indeed properly done, and protecting the construction from adverse weather until the mortar and grout have cured sufficiently.   It would be simplistic to leave the impression that these few items are all that require attention, and it must be pointed out that the structural designer should not only be familiar with the requirements of CSA-S304.1 but also with those of CSA-A371 *Masonry Construction for Buildings*.

6-7   CONCLUDING REMARKS

This chapter has not attempted a thorough treatment of the subject of buildings.   There are numerous topics, such as earthquake resistant design, connections and jointing to other structural materials, retaining walls, veneers, construction techniques etc., that have not been cover in detail.   The intent has been merely to introduce some of the typical problems and give some of the flavour of the design process.   Design for earthquake resistance is covered in Chapter 7 and two detailed examples of building design are covered in Chapters 8 and 9.   The remainder of Part 1 deals with the design of veneer and cavity walls and discusses some masonry construction details.

CHAPTER 7

EARTHQUAKE RESISTANCE

7-1   INTRODUCTION

All too frequently, earthquakes cause enormous devastation with great loss of human life. This results from ground movements with their accompanying large forces on buildings and, in most instances, from inappropriate design. The purpose of this chapter is to evaluate these seismic forces on masonry buildings and to consider the design procedures for adequate resistance. Section 7-2 deals with the determination of seismic loads, while the remainder of the chapter considers issues specific to masonry. These include the special provisions of S304.1 for seismic design, specifically, Clauses 5.2.2 *Minimum Seismic Reinforcement for Walls* and Appendix A *Seismic Design of Shear Walls with Nominal Ductility*. The reader should refer back to Section 1-4 for introductory comments and, in addition to the NBC and S304.1, should also have access to the *Supplement to the NBC*, which includes a *Commentary on the Effects of Earthquakes*.

7-2   SEISMIC LOADING

Earthquake loads on a building are inertial forces induced by ground motions that cause the building and its components to accelerate and move with some velocity and, of course, the resulting forces are the product of mass and acceleration. Since acceleration over a very brief period of time causes less damage than over a more extended period, two ground motion parameters, *peak horizontal acceleration* and *peak horizontal velocity*, are important. Because the horizontal ground motions exceed those in the vertical direction, and since structures are normally designed to sustain substantial vertical loads with an appropriate margin of safety, only the horizontal forces need to be considered in design. The purpose of seismic design is to ensure that the building can resist moderate earthquakes without significant damage and survive a major earthquake without collapse, *moderate* and *major* being relative terms that depend on geographic location and its potential for seismic activity.

As noted in Section 1-4, the earthquake-induced forces or loads (E) for which a building should be designed depend on its rigidity, damping characteristics and fundamental frequency, the nature of the foundation material, and on the maximum expected ground motions. Since it is virtually impossible to predict these ground motions accurately, and to avoid unnecessarily expensive overdesign, a minimum degree of seismic risk is recommended by the NBC, namely, the probability of ten percent in fifty years that peak specified horizontal ground accelerations and velocities will be exceeded.

Although earthquake motions are difficult to predict, and the response of the structure difficult to analyze precisely, Part 4 of the National Building Code of Canada (Section 4.1.9) and the *Supplement* to the NBC (Commentary J *Effects of Earthquakes*) outline fairly straightforward procedures for the determination of seismic loading. For example, these seismic loads, although multidirectional, can be considered to act horizontally and separately along each of the major axes of the building.

The reader may recall from Section 6-2 and Examples 6-2 and 6-3 that when the resultant wind force on a building does not coincide with the centre of rigidity of the structure, torsional effects are introduced, the torsional moment being the product of the resultant force and its perpendicular distance from the centre of rigidity. In the wind analysis the wind pressure is assumed to be uniform and the resultant force at the centre of area of the exposed face. In earthquake design, seismic forces act at the centre of mass (or the centres of masses) and torsional moments are calculated as the product of the seismic force and its perpendicular distance from the centre of rigidity of the structure. If the building is of a layout symmetrical about the major axes, then the centres of mass and rigidity coincide, theoretically eliminating torsion. However, the NBC requires that, in addition to calculated torsional moment, an allowance be made for torsional moment due to *accidental eccentricity*, a situation that is discussed later in this section.

The National Building Code of Canada defines seven *acceleration-related* or *velocity-related seismic zones*, Z_a and Z_v respectively, numbered from 0 to 6 in increasing order of seismic risk, this being measured by a *zonal acceleration ratio* (a is the ratio of the peak horizontal ground acceleration to the acceleration due to gravity) and a *zonal velocity ratio* (v is the ratio of the peak horizontal ground velocity to a velocity of 1m/s). These zonal ratios increase from 0.00 in zones $Z_a=0$ or $Z_v=0$ to 0.40 in zones $Z_a=6$ or $Z_v=6$. As noted above, related to these degrees of risk is that the probability of exceedance of the peak ground motion parameters is ten percent in fifty years.

Direct Seismic Shear Forces
The NBC requires that a structure be designed to resist a calculated base shear, V, that should not be less than

$$V = (V_e/R)U \tag{7-1}$$

In this relationship V_e is the *equivalent base shear* of an elastic structure, a reasonable approximation of V_e being given in Equation (7-2); U is a *calibration factor* specified as 0.6; and R is a *force modification factor* that reflects the damping characteristics of the building, a factor having values from 1.0 for rigid, brittle structures to 4.0 for ductile structures. The force modification factors for masonry from the NBC are those shown in Table 7-1.

Table 7-1
Force Modification Factors (from the NBC)

Case	Type of Lateral Load Resisting System	R
	Masonry structures designed and detailed according to CAN3-S304.1-M94	
20	reinforced masonry wall with *nominal ductility*	2.0
21	reinforced masonry	1.5
22	unreinforced masonry	1.0

The value of V_e is specified by the NBC to be

$$V_e = vSIFW \qquad (7\text{-}2)$$

In this relationship v is the zonal velocity ratio defined earlier whose value depends on the particular seismic zone and is obtained from the *Supplement* to the NBC, except that when $Z_v=0$ and $Z_a>0$ the value of Z_v is taken as 1 and $v=0.05$; S is a *seismic response factor* which generally is likely to have a value between 1.0 and 4.0; I is a *seismic importance factor* having a value of 1.5 for post-disaster buildings, 1.3 for schools and 1.0 for all other buildings; F is a *foundation factor* with values from 1.0 to 2.0 depending on whether the foundation material is dense and hard or soft; and W is the accumulated dead load plus 25% of the snow load.

Zones Z_a and Z_v are defined in the NBC *Supplement* by their peak ground motion parameters, a and v respectively, as shown in Table 7-2, with the values of a and v for a particular geographical location being obtained from the peak horizontal ground accelerations and velocities, respectively, given in the *Supplement*.

The seismic response factor S depends on the fundamental period T of the building and on the ratio Z_a/Z_v. The fundamental period may be calculated from established principles of mechanics or, more simply, using expressions given in the NBC, that for braced frames or shear wall structures such as masonry being

$$T = 0.09h_n/\sqrt{D_s} \text{ seconds} \qquad (7\text{-}3)$$

where h_n is the height in metres of the main roof level above external grade, and D_s the dimension in metres of the wall constituting the main lateral load-resisting system parallel to the seismic load. Zones Z_a and Z_v can be obtained from the *Supplement* and are reproduced in Table 7-2. Values of S are given in Table 7-3. As noted above, the seismic importance factor I is 1.5 for post-disaster buildings, 1.3 for schools and 1.0 for all other buildings. The foundation factor F depends on the soil type, and values from the NBC are given in Table 7-4.

Table 7-2
Definition of Seismic Zones (from the NBC)

Acceleration-related or velocity-related seismic zone Z_a or Z_v	Range of Peak Horizontal ground Acceleration PHA, g, or Peak Horizontal ground Velocity PHV, m/s, for 10% probability of exceedance in 50 years		Zonal acceleration ratio a zonal velocity ratio v
	Equal to	Less than	
0	0.00	0.04	0.00
1	0.04	0.08	0.05
2	0.08	0.11	0.10
3	0.11	0.16	0.15
4	0.16	0.23	0.20
5	0.23	0.32	0.30
6	0.32 or greater	-	0.40

Table 7-3
Seismic Response Factors S (from the NBC)

T sec.	Z_a/Z_v	S
≤ 0.25	> 1.0	4.2
	1.0	3.0
	< 1.0	2.1
> 0.25 but < 0.50	> 1.0	$4.2 - 8.4(T - 0.25)$
	1.0	$3.0 - 3.6(T - 0.25)$
	< 1.0	2.1
≥ 0.50	all values	$1.5/\sqrt{T}$

Since V represents the total minimum horizontal base shear at incipient collapse, an estimate of its distribution throughout the height of the building is also essential to the design. It is now assumed in the NBC that a portion of V, $F_t = 0.07TV$ (that need not exceed $0.25V$ and may be considered as zero when $T < 0.7$ s), is applied horizontally at the top of the building, the remainder of V being distributed over the height of the building in proportion to the product of the weight at each level and its height above the ground; that is, the horizontal force at any level i (including the top level) is

$$F_i = (V - F_t)W_i h_i / \Sigma(W_i h_i) \tag{7-4}$$

Alternatively, the dynamic analysis outlined in the *Supplement* to the NBC can be used to calculate the distribution of lateral forces along the height of a building.

Table 7-4
Foundation Factors F (from the NBC)

Category	Type and depth of soil measured from the foundation or pile cap level	F
1	Rock and dense and very dense coarse-grained soils, very stiff and hard fine-grained soils; compact coarse-grained soils and firm and stiff fine-grained soils from 0 to 15 m deep	1.0
2	Compact coarse-grained soils, firm and stiff fine-grained soils with a depth greater than 15 m; very loose and loose coarse-grained soils and very soft and soft fine-grained soils from 0 - 15 m deep	1.3
3	Very loose and loose coarse-grained soils with depth greater than 15 m	1.5
4	Very soft and soft fine-grained soils with depth greater than 15 m	2.0

While the preceding discussion has focussed on earthquake forces on buildings, the forces on individual components are determined in a similar manner. Parts of buildings, such as walls and parapets, and connections or attachments, are designed to be at the point of collapse when subjected to a lateral force, V_p, that should not be less than

$$V_p = vIS_p W_p \tag{7-5}$$

In this relationship v is the zonal velocity ratio as before; I is the seismic importance factor; the seismic response factor S_p has the values given in Table 7-5; and W_p is the weight of the part, or portion of the parts (such as a veneer). The lateral force acts normal to the surface of walls and parapets, and in any direction for connections, and its distribution is that of the distribution of mass in the part. For example, for a wall the mass is normally uniformly distributed and, consequently, so would be the lateral seismic load on the wall.

S304.1 has some special sections that relate specifically to seismic design, namely, Clauses 5.2.2 *Minimum Seismic Reinforcement for Walls* and Appendix A *Seismic Design of Shear Walls with Nominal Ductility*. These topics are discussed in Sections 7-3 and 7-4 of this chapter.

Table 7-5

Values of S_p for Architectural Parts or Portions of Buildings (from the NBC)

Category	Architectural Part	Direction of Force	S_p
1	All exterior and interior walls except those of categories 2 and 3	normal to flat surface	1.5
2	Cantilever parapet and other cantilever walls except retaining walls	normal to flat surface	6.5
3	Exterior and interior ornamentations and appendages	any direction	6.5
4	Connections/attachments for categories 1, 2 and 3		
	The body of connections/attachments	any direction	2.5
	All fasteners and anchors in the ductile connection, such as bolts, inserts, welds, or dowels	any direction	see NBC
	Non-ductile connections/attachments	any direction	15
5	Floors and roofs acting as diaphragms	any direction	0.7
6	Towers, chimneys, smokestacks and penthouses when connected to or forming part of a building	any direction	4.5
7	Horizontally cantilevered floors, balconies, beams, etc.	vertical	4.5
8	Suspended ceilings, light fixtures and other attachments to ceilings with independent vertical support	any direction	2.0
9	Masonry veneer connections	normal to flat surface	5.0

EXAMPLE 7-1 *The ten-storey apartment building shown in Fig. 6-8 and featured in the wind analysis of Example 6-2 is of 200 mm precast concrete hollowcore roof and floor construction supported on 200 concrete masonry walls A, B, C and D. These walls and the floor at exterior grade are supported on a reinforced concrete foundation, which in turn is founded on rock. The building is located in a seismic zone similar to that of Ottawa. Neglecting torsion due to accidental eccentricity and given the data below, determine*

a)   *the zonal acceleration and velocity ratios, a and v respectively, and the appropriate seismic zones Z_a and Z_v respectively;*
b)   *the fundamental periods of the building in the x and y directions, T_x and T_y;*
c)   *the seismic response factors in the x and y directions, S_x and S_y respectively;*
d)   *the seismic importance factor I and the foundation factor F;*
e)   *the total weight W of the building;*
f)   *the force modification factor R for the building;*
g)   *the equivalent elastic base shear forces V_x and V_y;*
h)   *the seismic base shear forces V_x and V_y;*
i)   *the distribution of horizontal seismic forces along the height of the building, and the total base moments M_x and M_y;*
j)   *in-plane seismic shear forces and moments at the base of walls A, B, C and D;*
k)   *seismic loading normal to walls A, B, C and D.*

Data
- From the *Supplement* to the NBC the specified (10% in 50 years) peak horizontal ground acceleration (PHA) and velocity (PHV) for Ottawa are 0.20g and 0.098 m/sec respectively.
- Walls A, B, C and D are fully-grouted 200 concrete block weighing 3.91 kN/m² (Table 4-1).
- 200 hollowcore floors with an allowance for light partitions and exterior walls along grid lines 1 and 2 and roof weigh 3.5 kN/m².
- Roof snow load: 1.2 kN/m².

a) Seismic ground motions and zones

From Table 7-2

| For PHA = 0.20g | $a = 0.20$ and $Z_a = 4$ | |
| For PVA = 0.098 m/s | $v = 0.10$ and $Z_v = 2$ | Ans. |

b) Fundamental periods T_x and T_y

From Equation (7-3), $T = 0.09 h_n / \sqrt{D_s}$
From Fig. 6-8, $h_n = 26.0$ m

In the x (longitudinal) direction the load-resisting system consists of walls C and D and $D_{sx} = 6.0$ m. Then $T_x = 0.09(26.0)/\sqrt{6.0} = 0.96$ s.

Because of the location of control joints in wall A, the main load-resisting system in the y (transverse) direction consists of walls B, with $D_{sy} = 8.0$ m, and $T_y = 0.09(26.0)/\sqrt{8.0} = 0.83$ s.

$$T_x = 0.96 \text{ s}, \ T_y = 0.83 \text{ s} \qquad \underline{Ans.}$$

c) *Seismic response factors S_x and S_y*

From Table 7-3, for $T > 0.5$ s and $Z_a/Z_v = 2$, $S = 1.5/\sqrt{T}$

Then $S_x = 1.5/\sqrt{T_x} = 1.5/\sqrt{0.96} = 1.53$
and $S_y = 1.5/\sqrt{T_y} = 1.5/\sqrt{0.83} = 1.65$ $\underline{Ans.}$

d) *Seismic importance and foundation factors*

Since the building is neither post-disaster nor school, the seismic importance factor I is 1.0. $I = 1.0$
From Table 7-4, for foundation on rock $F = 1.0$ $\underline{Ans.}$

e) *Weight W of the building*

The weight W includes roof, walls, floors and 25% snow.
Plan area $= 40(18) = 720$ m^2
Total wall length per floor (walls A, B, C and D)
$$L = 2A + 6B + 2C + 2D$$
$$= 2(18) + 6(8.0) + 2(6.0) + 2(6.0) = 108 \text{ m}$$
Height of wall (floor to ceiling) per floor $= 2.4$ m
Wall area per floor $= 108(2.4) = 259.2$ m^2

Weights
       25% snow $= 0.25(1.2)(720) = 216$ kN   216 kN
       Roof $= 3.5(720) = 2520$ kN   2520 kN
       Floor $= 3.5(720) = 2520$ kN
       9 floors $= 9(2520) = 22680$ kN   22680 kN
       Walls $= 3.91(259.2) = 1013.5$ kN/level
       Total walls $= 10(1013.5) = 10135$ kN   <u>10135 kN</u>
                                                               35551 kN
                         Total weight $W = 35551$ kN $\underline{Ans.}$

f) Force modification factor R

From Table 7-1, assuming reinforced masonry with nominal ductility (see discussion following this example),

$$R = 2.0 \quad \text{Ans.}$$

g) Equivalent base shears V_{ex} and V_e

From Equation (7-2), $V_e = vSIFW$
Then $V_{ex} = vS_xIFW = 0.10(1.53)(1.0)(1.0)(35550) = 5439\ kN$
and $V_{ey} = vS_yIFW = 0.10(1.65)(1.0)(1.0)(35550) = 5866\ kN$ Ans.

h) Seismic base shear forces V_x and V_y

From Equation (7-1), $V = V_eU/R$

Then $V_x = V_{ec}U/R = 5439(0.6)/2 = 1632\ kN$ $V_x = 1632\ kN$
and $V_y = V_{ey}U/R = 5866(0.6)/2 = 1760\ kN$ $V_y = 1760\ kN$ Ans.

i) Horizontal seismic force distribution

The horizontal force at the roof level is $F_t = 0.07TV \le 0.25V$
Then $F_{tx} = 0.07T_xV_x = 0.07(0.96)(1632) = 109.7\ kN < 0.25V_x$
and $F_{ty} = 0.07T_yV_y = 0.07(0.83)(1760) = 102.3\ kN < 0.25V_y$

and the remaining forces, $V_x - F_{tx} = 1632 - 109.7 = 1522\ kN$ and
$V_y - F_{ty} = 1760 - 102.3 = 1658\ kN$, are distributed through all levels (including the roof) in proportion to the weight added at each level and its height above the ground, as given in Equation (7-4), $F_i = (V - F_t)W_ih_i/\Sigma(W_ih_i)$, where F_i is the horizontal force at level i, W_i is the weight contributed at level i, and h_i is the height above external grade of level i.

Note in the following table summarizing the calculations that at the roof level the 0.25 snow has been added to the "floor" load, and in the two right-hand columns F_{tx} and F_{ty} have been added to obtain the seismic forces at the top.

Seismic forces for V_x = 1632 kN, V_y = 1760 kN					Seismic forces	
Level i	Height h_i (m)	Weight added at level (kN)			$W_i h_i$	F_{ix} (kN)	F_{iy} (kN)
		Wall	Floor	W_i			
Roof	26.0	0.0	2736	2736	71136	333.4	345.9
10	23.4	1013.5	2520	3533.5	82684	260.3	283.5
9	20.8	1013.5	2520	3533.5	73497	231.3	251.9
8	18.2	1013.5	2520	3533.5	64310	202.4	220.4
7	15.6	1013.5	2520	3533.5	55123	173.5	188.9
6	13.0	1013.5	2520	3533.5	45936	144.6	157.5
5	10.4	1013.5	2520	3533.5	36748	115.7	125.7
4	7.8	1013.5	2520	3533.5	27561	86.8	94.5
3	5.2	1013.5	2520	3533.5	18374	57.8	62.9
2	2.6	1013.5	2520	3533.5	9187	28.9	31.5
1	0.0	1013.5	0.0	1013.5	0.0	0.0	0.0
			Σ	35551	484556	1635	1763

Check ΣF_{ix} = 1635 kN ≈ 1632 = V_x, ΣF_{iy} = 1763 kN ≈ 1760 = V_y OK

The total base moments are obtained from a straightforward calculation as

$$M_y = \Sigma(F_{ix}h_i) = 30097 \ kN\text{-}m$$
$$M_x = \Sigma(F_{iy}h_i) = 32326 \ kN\text{-}m \qquad \underline{Ans.}$$

j) Distribution of seismic shear forces and moments to walls

Check building torsion - refer to Fig. 6-8

From symmetry (see also Example 6-3), centre of rigidity is at the origin.
From symmetry, centre of mass is at the origin.
Since centres of rigidity and mass coincide,   *Building torsion = 0.0 kN-m*

Since, *for the purpose of this example only*, torsion due to accidental eccentricity is being neglected, and since there is no other calculable building torsion, the direct effect of transverse seismic shear forces and moments is shared by walls A and B, and in the longitudinal direction by walls C and D. Assuming that the roof and floors act as reasonably rigid diaphragms, and using the distribution coefficients developed in Example 6-2, the base seismic shear forces and moments in each wall become

Transverse seismic action

Wall	No. walls	Wall length (m)	Distribution coefficient	Moment (kN-m)	Shear force (kN)
B	6	8.0	0.1362	4402	239.7
A_1	2	6.0	0.0574	1856	101.0
A_2	4	4.0	0.0170	550	29.9

Longitudinal seismic action

Wall	No. walls	Wall length (m)	Distribution coefficient	Moment (kN-m)	Shear force (kN)
C	2	6.0	0.25	7524	408
D	2	6.0	0.25	7524	408

k) Seismic loading normal to walls A, B, C and D

When seismic loading is along the *x*-axis, C and D are the shear walls offering in-plane resistance while walls A and B are subject to out-of-plane (that is, normal to the wall) seismic loading. Similarly, when walls A and B act as shear walls, walls C and D receive out-of-plane loading. This situation is covered by Equation (7-5) for *parts* of a building and by Table 7-5.

From Equation (7-5), $V_p = vIS_pW_p$
from   a) $v = 0.20$
from   d) $I = 1.0$
from Table 7-5 *Category 1*, $S_p = 1.5$
and from the *data*, $W_p = 3.91$ kN/m^2

Then $V_p = 0.20(1.0)(1.5)(3.91) = 1.17$ kN/m^2

Seismic loading normal to walls $V_p = 1.17$ kN/m^2   Ans.

Discussion of Example 7-1

The reader might note from Example 7-1 that torsional effects were checked after the overall seismic forces had been determined. In the example, torsion due to accidental eccentricity was neglected and since the centres of mass and rigidity coincided there was no building torsion (that is, moment about the vertical axis). Had torsion been present, then the seismic force distribution to individual shear walls would have been a combination of direct shear forces and those due to torsion. Although Example 6-3 deals with torsion due to wind, whether the forces are wind or seismic the principles of determining the effect of torsion are the same. Torsion due to seismic effects is considered later in this section.

While Example 7-1 considers seismic loading, Example 6-2 deals with the effects of a fairly representative wind load. It is interesting to make a comparison. The reader is cautioned, however, that although Ottawa is mentioned in Example 7-1 it is only for illustrative purposes, and no attempt has been made to correlate wind load, snow load and foundation type with that location. Example 6-2 lists the effects at grade level of the *service* wind loading, and the factored effects are obtained by applying the load factor for wind, $\alpha_W = 1.5$. In Example 7-1 the load factor for seismic effects is 1.0. A comparison of the effects in each of the walls is shown in Table 7-6.

For the loads used in Examples 6-2 and 7-1 there is not a great difference between the maximum factored effects of wind and earthquake in the transverse direction (walls A and B): shear forces are about the same and seismic moments are about 20% greater than wind moments. However, for loading in the longitudinal direction, seismic shear forces are about 75% greater than those due to wind, while seismic moments are about 135% greater than wind moments. This, of course, is because wind forces are related to the area of the exposed face (significantly different for transverse and longitudinal directions) while seismic effects are directly related to the weight of the building regardless of the direction of seismic loading. While this building layout might be adequate for wind or earthquake in the transverse direction, and for wind in the longitudinal direction, it is likely that more shear walls would be required in the x direction (parallel to walls C and D), probably along grid lines 1 and 2 (see Fig. 6-8), for seismic resistance.

Table 7-6
Comparison of Example 6-2 and Example 7-1

Wall	Wall length (m)	Factored wind effects		Factored seismic effects	
		Base shear (kN)	Base moment (kN-m)	Base shear (kN)	Base moment (kN-m)
A_1	6.0	121.1	1631	101.0	1856
A_2	4.0	35.9	483	29.9	550
B	8.0	286.5	3867	239.7	4402
C	6.0	237.0	3194	408	7524
D	6.0	237.0	3194	408	7524

Referring to Fig. 6-8, additional resistance to longitudinal effects could be accomplished by adding, for example, 6.0 m long masonry walls in each of the 8.0 m bays along grid lines 1 and 2. This would add eight walls the same length as walls C and D for a total of twelve 6.0 m shear walls. Since the number of walls is then increased from four to twelve, the longitudinal seismic effects are about one-third of the values noted in Table 7-6. A practical design comment: since the floors are hollowcore slabs spanning between walls A and B, the additional walls are not load-bearing but continuous full height, and the connections between wall and hollowcore should be designed to resist the seismic forces added at each level.

Also to be noted is that Example 7-1 assumed reinforced masonry with *nominal ductility* to determine the value of the force modification factor as $R = 2.0$. Had the walls been unreinforced, the structure would have been considered brittle and $R = 1.0$, leading to seismic design loads 100% greater. Shear walls with nominal ductility are defined in Appendix A of S304.1 and are the subject of a later section of this chapter.

Finally, in part k) of Example 7-1 the seismic loading normal to walls is calculated as 1.17 kN/m^2, which in this instance is about the same as the service wind load. Note that while wind load is most extreme on exterior walls, this seismic load applies to all walls. Although *Commentary J - Effects of Earthquakes* of the *Supplement* to the NBC notes that Category 1 of Table 7-5 does not include walls forming part of the main lateral force resisting system, walls A and B do not act as such when walls C and D are the resisting shear walls, and neither do C and D when A and B are the shear walls. This explains why the walls are considered as *architectural parts* for seismic loading normal to the wall. These walls then have to be designed for resistance to the appropriate axial load and out-of-plane seismic load.

Reduction of Overturning Moments

The overturning moment at any level in a building or in a shear wall is the sum of the products of the horizontal forces above that level and the height of the force from that level. The *Commentary* to the NBC notes that for modes higher than the fundamental there is a reduction in the overturning moment. Because of this the NBC [Clause 4.1.9.1.(23)] permits the overturning moment M at the base of a structure to be multiplied by a *reduction coefficient* $J \leq 1.0$, where

$$
\begin{aligned}
J &= 1.0 && \text{when } T < 0.5; \\
J &= (1.1 - 0.2T) && \text{when } 0.5 \leq T \leq 1.5; \text{ and} \\
J &= 0.8 && \text{when } T > 1.5
\end{aligned}
\tag{7-6}
$$

Similarly, the overturning moment M_i at any level i may be multiplied by a reduction coefficient

$$
J_i = J + (1 - J)(h_i/h_n)^3
\tag{7-7}
$$

where h_i is the height of level i above the base and h_n is the height of the building.

EXAMPLE 7-2 *Calculate the reduced overturning base moments due to seismic loading for the building of Example 7-1.*

From part *i)* of Example 7-1, the total base moments are $M_y = 30097$ kN-m
$M_x = 32326$ kN-m

From part *b)*, $0.5 \leq (T_x = 0.96$ and $T_y = 0.83) \leq 1.5$
Therefore, the reduction coefficients $J = 1.1 - 0.2T$ are
$$J_y = 1.1 - 0.2T_x = 1.1 - 0.2(0.96) = 0.908$$
and $J_x = 1.1 - 0.2T_y = 1.1 - 0.2(0.83) = 0.934$
Then the reduced overturning base moments for design are JM
Design base moment about y-axis $M_y = 0.908(30097) = 27328$ kN-m
Design base moment about x-axis $M_x = 0.934(32326) = 30192$ kN-m   Ans.

In this example, of course, T_x was used to determine M_y since they both apply to seismic action in the *x*-direction and, similarly, T_y for M_x.

Torsional Moments

Torsional moments about the vertical axis of a building are the result of horizontal forces acting at an eccentricity to the centre of rigidity. Example 6-3 considered torsional effects due to wind, and the reader is referred to that example, to Figs. 6-9 and 6-10, and to Equations (6-2) through (6-6) for a basic treatment of torsional effects.

As noted earlier, the NBC [Clause 4.1.9.1.(28)] requires that although calculable torsion may not be present (for example, when the centres of mass and rigidity coincide), some allowance must always be made for torsion. This is because the actual distribution of masses is not known precisely and simplifying assumptions made in the calculation of the centres of mass and rigidity frequently lead to some error in calculating their locations. Also, although seismic action is assumed to act in a specific linear direction, a torsional component may also be present.

As a result, the NBC requires that allowance be made for an *accidental eccentricity* in the application of the horizontal seismic forces. This accidental eccentricity at any level *i* is taken as $0.1D_{ni}$, where D_{ni} is the dimension of the building at level *i* normal to the assumed seismic forces. Furthermore, if the centre of mass (and therefore, of the seismic force) is calculated at level *i* at an eccentricity e_i from the centre of rigidity, the calculable torsion is increased or decreased by 50%, whichever produces the worst effect. This leads to the NBC requirement that the torsional moment T_i applied at each level *i* be calculated as the worst of

$$T_i = F_i (1.5e_i \pm 0.1D_{ni})$$
and $$T_i = F_i (0.5e_i \pm 0.1D_{ni})$$ (7-8)

where F_i is the seismic force at level *i*. Alternatively, at each level *i*, $0.1D_{ni}Fi$ can be added to the results of a more detailed three-dimensional dynamic analysis.

EXAMPLE 7-3   *For the building featured in Examples 6-2 and 7-1*

a)   *calculate the design torsional moment T_{bx} at the base of the structure due to*
          seismic forces in the x-direction;
b)   *calculate the design torsional moment T_{by} at the base of the structure due to*
          seismic forces in the y-direction; and
c)   *discuss the increased in-plane shear forces and moments in shear walls due to*
          torsion.

        a)   Design base torsional moment T_{bx} for x-direction seismic forces

From Example 7-1, part *h)*, the accumulated base shear force in the *x*-direction
is V_x = 1632 kN
Because of symmetry about the *x*-axis, centres of mass and rigidity coincide and
e_y = 0.0
The accidental eccentricity = $0.1D_y$ = 0.1(18.0) = 1.80 m
(see Fig. 6-8 for building dimensions)

Then the design base torsional moment *T_{bx} = 1632(1.80) = 2938 kN-m* <u>Ans.</u>

        b)   Design base torsional moment T_{by} for y-direction seismic forces

From Example 7-1, part *h)*, V_y = 1760 kN
Because of symmetry about the *y*-axis e_x = 0.0
The accidental eccentricity = $0.1D_x$ = 0.1(40.0) = 4.0 m (see Fig 6-8)

Then the design base torsional moment *T_{by} = 1760(4.0) = 7040 kN-m* <u>Ans.</u>

        c)   Increase in shear wall forces due to torsion

The reader may recall that Equation (6-6) describes the distribution of shear
forces to walls resulting from direct horizontal shear and torsion

$$F_{ix} = K_{ix}V_x/\Sigma K_{ix} + K_{ix}y_iT/J$$
$$F_{iy} = K_{iy}V_y/\Sigma K_{iy} + K_{iy}x_iT/J$$

Note that the first terms in the equations relate to the distribution of direct shear
and have already been calculated in Example 7-1; and the second terms have
been calculated in Example 6-3 for the same building for a wind torsion of 1755
kN-m. Note also that all walls participate in resisting torsion, whereas only
those walls in the same direction as the seismic force resist the direct shear.
Using the results from Examples 6-3 and 7-1, the in-plane shear forces are those
shown in the following table.

Direct shear and torsional forces in walls

Wall	$K_{ix}y_i/J$ (Ex. 6-3)	$K_{iy}x_i/J$ (Ex. 6-3)	Seismic forces in walls (kN)	
			x-direction $V_x = 1632$ kN $T_x = 2938$ kN-m	y-direction $V_y = 1760$ kN $T_y = 7040$ kN-m
A_1		0.0089	101.0 + 26.1 = 127.1	0.0 + 62.7 = 62.7
A_2		0.0026	29.9 + 7.6 = 37.5	0.0 + 18.3 = 18.3
B		0.0106	239.7 + 31.1 = 270.8	0.0 + 74.6 = 74.6
B_{cl}		0.0	239.7 + 0.0 = 239.7	0.0 + 0.0 = 0.0
C	0.00067		0.0 + 2.0 = 2.0	408.0 + 4.7 = 412.7
D	0.00134		0.0 + 3.9 = 3.9	408.0 + 9.4 = 417.4

This table shows the increased in-plane shear forces in the building shear walls. Walls B, for example, have the maximum shear force increased from 239.7 kN to 270.8 kN when seismic action is in the x-direction and torsion is considered. Since moments are obtained as $\Sigma F_i h_i$, the moments at the bases of the shear walls increase similarly. The results apply to half of the walls in the building since the other half experience a reduced shear due to torsion.

This section has been concerned solely with the determination of seismic loads, and with the forces induced in shear walls by these loads. However, in structural design various load combinations must be considered. While designing a building for seismic resistance the assumption is made that in a major earthquake the structure will not collapse but may be expected to sustain considerable damage, service loads generally being the factored loads. As noted in Section 1-6, the factored resistance of the structure should be at least as great as the factored loads, and the factored load cases for seismic design are

$$1.0D + \gamma(1.0E)$$
and $\quad\quad 1.0D + \gamma(1.0L + 1.0E)$ for storage and assembly occupancies
or $\quad\quad 1.0D + \gamma(0.5L + 1.0E)$ for all other occupancies $\quad\quad$ (7-9)

where E represents the distribution of horizontal forces V throughout the height of the building, and γ is generally taken as 1.0. Once the worst combination of loads has been determined and their distribution to the various structural components calculated, the design for resistance to that loading proceeds in a manner similar to that outlined in preceding chapters.

As noted earlier in this section, the seismic forces to be used in design depends on a number of factors (see Equations 7-1 and 7-2), prominent among which is the force modification factor R which varies significantly with the amount of reinforcement in the walls. The following sections discuss reinforcement for seismic resistance.

7-3   MINIMUM SEISMIC REINFORCEMENT FOR WALLS

Section 7-2 discussed in some detail the determination of seismic forces and their distribution through the building. As noted, the force modification factor R used in calculating seismic forces varies from 1.0 for plain masonry to 1.5 for reinforced masonry to 2.0 for masonry shear walls reinforced for nominal ductility. Since the seismic forces depend on the reciprocal of R [from Equation (7-1) $V = V_e U/R$], plain masonry must be designed for larger seismic forces than those used for reinforced masonry.

Depending on the severity of the seismic forces, reinforcement may or may not be required for resistance. In any case, Clauses 5.2.2 *Minimum Seismic Reinforcement in Walls* of S304.1 requires that at least some minimum amount be provided in certain seismic zones Z_a and Z_v (the higher zone governing). Horizontal joint reinforcement may be considered as contributing to horizontal steel requirement. The minimum requirements are as follows.

Load-Bearing Walls and Shear Walls

In seismic zones Z_a and Z_v of 0 or 1, provided the wall can resist the seismic forces, no minimum quantity of reinforcement is specified. If the walls are unreinforced, the force modification factor is $R = 1.0$

In seismic zones where the greater of Z_a and Z_v is 2 or higher, both vertical and horizontal steel are required. The amount must be sufficient to provide resistance to the seismic forces calculated using a force modification factor $R = 1.5$, but shall have a total area of vertical and horizontal steel of at least $0.002A_g$; and at least one-third of the reinforcement must be placed in one direction, the remainder in the other. That is, the minimum reinforcement is

$$A_v = 0.002A_g\alpha$$
$$A_h = 0.002A_g(1 - \alpha) \tag{7-10}$$

where A_g is the gross cross-sectional area of the wall, A_v and A_h are the areas of vertical and horizontal reinforcement, respectively, and α is a distribution factor between 0.33 and 0.67. The spacing of the reinforcement cannot exceed six times the wall thickness or 1.2 m, and although a maximum spacing of joint reinforcement is not specified in S304.1, it is advisable not to exceed 400 mm.

A further requirement where the greater of Z_a and Z_v is 2 or higher is for reinforcement of at least 1-#15 to be provided around each masonry panel and around each opening exceeding 1000 mm in width or height; and the steel is to be detailed to permit the yield stress of the bars to develop at corners and splices.

The following example illustrates the principles.

EXAMPLE 7-4   *A building with 200 mm masonry shear walls is located in seismic zones*
$Z_a = 1$ *and* $Z_v = 2$. *If 9 ga.(ASWG) joint reinforcement is being used*

a)   *what is the area of minimum seismic reinforcement required; and*
b)   *suggest suitable reinforcement.*

a)   Minimum seismic reinforcement
Since $Z_v = 2 > Z_a = 1$, Z_v governs, and minimum seismic reinforcement is
required. The minimum area steel is

$$A_v + A_h = 0.002A_g = 0.002(190)(10)^3 = 380 \ mm^2/m$$

b)   Suggested reinforcement

The minimum total reinforcement is 380 mm²/m and at least
        $380(0.33) = 125.4$ mm²/m
must be placed in one direction, the remainder in the other.

Assuming 9 ga. joint reinforcement ($A_s = 22.3$ mm² for the two 3.77 mm wires
- see Part 2 of this book) at 400 mm (i.e. every second course), the area A_{h1}
contributed to A_h by the joint reinforcement is
        $A_{h1} = 22.3(1000)/400 = 55.8$ mm²/m
and the remaining horizontal reinforcement should have an area A_{h2} of
        $A_{h2} \geq 125.4 - 55.8 = 69.6$ mm²/m

Try #10 bars @ 1000 ($A_{h2} = 100$ mm²/m)
Check   spacing = 1000 < 6t = 6(190) = 1140 mm and < 1.2 m   <u>OK</u>
and $A_h = 55.8 + 100 = 155.8$ mm²/m
Since $A_v + A_h \geq 380$ mm²/m
          $A_v \geq 380 - 155.8 = 224.2$ mm²/m

Try #15 bars @ 800
Check   Spacing = 800 < 6t = 1140 and < 1.2 m   <u>OK</u>
and $A_v = 200(1000)/800 = 250$ mm²/m > 224.2 mm²/m   <u>OK</u>
Check $A_h + A_v = 155.8 + 250 = 405.8$ mm²/m > 380 mm²/m   <u>OK</u>

One suggested minimum reinforcement arrangement is #10 @ 1000
horizontal, #15 @ 800 vertical & 9 ga. joint reinforcement @ 400.
Note also that the reinforcement should include 1-#15 around each wall
panel, suitably lapped at corners to provide the development length.

Non-Load-Bearing Walls

S304.1 minimum reinforcement for non-load-bearing walls depends on the greater of seismic zones Z_a and Z_v.

In seismic zones 4 or higher, the specific minimum total area of reinforcement is $0.001A_g$ distributed as for load-bearing walls in zones 2 or higher; that is, minimum reinforcement is

$$A_v = 0.001A_g\alpha$$
$$A_h = 0.001A_g(1-\alpha) \tag{7-11}$$

and, as before, α is a factor between 0.33 and 0.67. The spacing should not exceed 400 mm for joint reinforcement or 1.2 m for vertical steel. There is also a requirement for a horizontal bond beam at each floor and roof level.

In seismic zones 2 and 3, non-load-bearing walls are required to be reinforced in one or more directions with a minimum total steel area of at least $0.0005A_g$, with spacing that should not exceed 400 mm for joint reinforcement and 1.2 m for other bars. Again, there is a requirement for bond beams. There is the additional requirement that where reinforcement is placed in one direction only, it should be continuous between points of lateral support (floor-to-floor for vertical steel, for example) and located to provide resistance to lateral loading (at the mid-thickness, for example).

In seismic zones 0 and 1, no reinforcement is specified for non-load-bearing walls. In principle, joint reinforcement and bond beams at each level are advisable, as is a vertical bar and grouting at least the end core at each end of a wall panel.

7-4   SHEAR WALLS WITH NOMINAL DUCTILITY

As noted in Section 7-2, the seismic forces for which a building is to be designed depends on, among other factors, the force modification factor R, reduced design forces resulting from higher values of R. The greater the ductility of a structure, the greater its ability to absorb energy which, in turn, leads to higher values of R with a consequent reduction in the design forces.

For plain masonry $R=1.0$, for reinforced masonry $R=1.5$, and $R=2.0$ for shear walls reinforced for nominal ductility. The requirements for $R=2.0$ are outlined in S304.1, Appendix A *Seismic Design of Shear Walls with Nominal Ductility*. S304.1 notes that although the provisions of the appendix are not mandatory they can be used as part of the standard.

The main features of Appendix A are:
- shear walls are required to be of reinforced masonry;
- redistribution of moments obtained from elastic analysis is not permitted;
- both vertical and horizontal reinforcement are to be provided;
- vertical reinforcement shall be uniformly distributed over the length of the wall, with spacing not exceeding one-quarter of the wall effective depth, six times the wall thickness, or 1200 mm, whichever is less;

- no more than half the vertical steel can be lapped within a plastic hinge region;
- horizontal bars shall be continuous to the ends of walls and be provided with 180° end hooks around vertical bars; and
- other requirements relating to the plastic hinge region: these include limiting the compressive strain to 0.0025, limiting the extent of the plastic hinge region, and reducing the shear resistance within the plastic hinge region by one-half.

The intent of the appendix is to have reinforcement that is detailed for ductility, and to reduce effects within the plastic hinge region, such as shear, that can precipitate brittle failure. The minimum reinforcement required is that outlined in Section 7-3 for load-bearing and shear walls. The requirements for in-plane and out-of-plane shear resistance are those outlined is Section 5-7 of this book and in Clause 11.5 of S304.1, except that in the plastic hinge region, the in-plane shear resistance is reduced by 50%. There is also a reduction in the resistance to sliding friction in the plastic hinge region.

If the action of the shear wall is primarily bending, an analysis to determine whether a plastic hinge forms is relatively simple to manage. Since the presence of axial load is likely to enhance the resistance to bending, the axial load can frequently and conservatively be neglected. If, on the other hand, axial load predominates, a more thorough analysis involving interaction diagrams is required. The plastic hinge concept is relatively simple to manage, except that S304.1 requires in-plane compressive forces to be applied at a minimum out-of-plane eccentricity of $e=0.1t$. This introduces a further complication, one that is alleviated through the use of the design aids in Part 2.

The reader is referred to Appendix A at the back of S304.1 for a listing of all the requirements.

CHAPTER 8

DESIGN EXAMPLE - ONE-STORY INDUSTRIAL BUILDING

8-1   INTRODUCTION

This chapter outlines the principles that may be used in the structural design of the masonry components of a typical single-story industrial building. While every effort has been made to ensure the data is factual and the results accurate, the reader is cautioned that the example has been developed for illustrative purposes and is not to be used for an actual building where the design conditions and criteria will be job specific.

The example describes the design of a warehouse building incorporating at one end an office section with a mezzanine level. A perspective sketch of the building is shown in Fig. 8-1, and Figs. 8-2 and 8-3 show building elevations and sections. Floor and roof plans are shown in Fig. 8-4. The roof consists of a steel deck supported on open-web steel joists, which in turn are supported on a central steel beam and exterior masonry bearing walls. The steel beam is supported on masonry pilasters. The mezzanine floor is a steel deck with concrete topping supported on open-web steel joists. Exterior and interior walls are load-bearing concrete masonry, and the main floor is a concrete slab-on-grade. The spread footings shown are schematic only.

For illustrative purposes and to establish loading criteria the structure is assumed to be in Edmonton, Alberta.

8-2   MATERIALS

(a)   Concrete Masonry Units

Standard two-core 250 lightweight concrete blocks that satisfy the requirements of CSA Standard A165-94 are used, and the unit compressive strength is taken as 15 MPa.

(b)   Mortar

Type S mortar is used, volume batched according to CSA Standard A179-94 *Mortar and Grout for Unit Masonry*. The specified proportions are:

> 1 part normal portland cement
> 1/2 part hydrated lime
> 4.5 parts sand

(c)   Grout

Grout is used to fill cores, as required, and to construct lintel beams. The grout also can be volume batched and CSA Standard A179-94 specifies the following proportions:

> 1 part normal portland cement,
> 0-1/10 parts hydrated lime or lime putty,
> 2.25-3 times the sum of cementitious materials of fine aggregate,
> 1-2 times the sum of cementitious materials of coarse aggregate,

the aggregates being measured in the damp loose state.

The compressive strength of the grout depends on its consistency when poured, on the size of the void being filled, and on the absorptive capacity of the unit. Because of this, there is no requirement for compressive strengthusing the proportion specification of the standard. Although grout is frequently ordered as ready-mix concrete of a particular compressive strength, the reader should note that standard cylinder strength is not representative of actual poured grout strength.

(d)   Steel

The reinforcing steel used in the lintel beams and grouted cores has a yield strength of 400 MPa.

8-3   MASONRY STRENGTH

The compressive strength, f'_m, to be used in design is determined by one of two methods, namely, by testing prisms or by testing masonry units and mortar cubes. These methods are described in Chapter 2.

Since 15 MPa units and Type S mortar are used in this example, the value of f'_m, the masonry compressive strength, is obtained from Table 5 of S304.1. This value is found to be 9.8 MPa for hollow units and 7.5 MPa for grouted units.

The flexural tensile strength is obtained from Table 6 of S304.1. For hollow units, the values are found to be 0.45 MPa and 0.90 MPa for stresses normal and parallel to bed joint respectively. For grouted units, the values are 0.7 MPa and 0.90 MPa.

8-4   DESIGN LOADS

The building, described in Section 8-1 and illustrated in Figs. 8-1 to 8-4 inclusive, is loaded as follows:

Roof (roofing, insulation and steel deck)	0.72 kN/m²
Joists (@ 1800 mm o.c.)	0.14 kN/m²
Sprinkler system	0.06 kN/m²
Framing	0.11 kN/m²
Miscellaneous	0.07 kN/m²
Total roof dead load	1.10 kN/m²
Roof (snow, rain, ponding)	1.00 kN/m²
Office (2.5 dead + 2.5 live)	5.00 kN/m²
Wall self weight*	2.40 kN/m²
Wind**	0.80 kN/m²

* Approximate weight assuming one grouted core per metre
** The wind load is calculated on the probability of being exceeded in any one
   year of 1 in 30 for structural wall design.

$$p = qC_eC_gC_p + qC_eC_{pi}$$

$$= 0.4(0.9)(2.0)(0.7) + 0.4(0.9)(0.7) = 0.76 \text{ kN/m}^2$$

$$\approx 0.80 \text{ kN/m}^2$$

(1/10 for the cladding, 1/100 for special buildings)

For more information on wind loading the reader should consult *Part 4 of the National Building Code of Canada, 1995.*

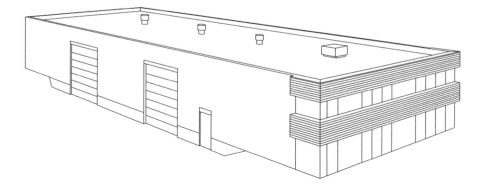

Fig. 8-1 Perspective: Proposed Office / warehouse

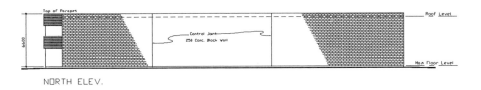

NORTH ELEV.

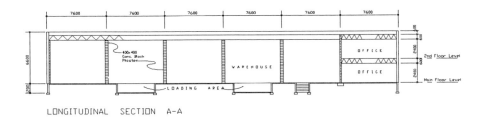

SOUTH ELEV.

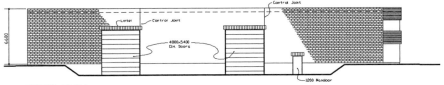

LONGITUDINAL SECTION A-A

Fig. 8-2 Elevations and Longitudinal Section

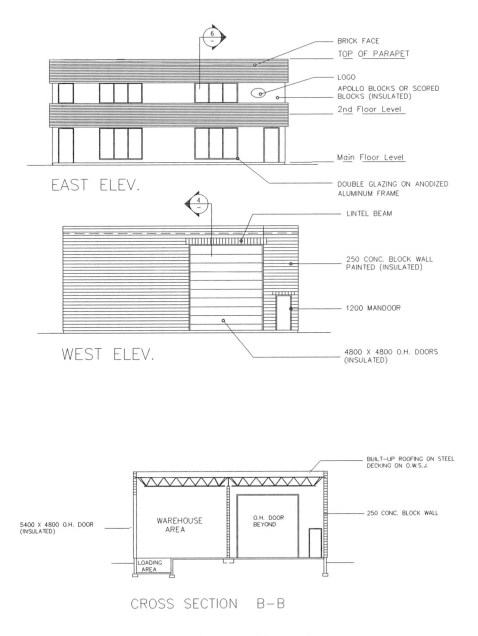

BRICK FACE
TOP OF PARAPET

LOGO
APOLLO BLOCKS OR SCORED
BLOCKS (INSULATED)
2nd Floor Level

Main Floor Level

DOUBLE GLAZING ON ANODIZED
ALUMINUM FRAME

EAST ELEV.

LINTEL BEAM

250 CONC. BLOCK WALL
PAINTED (INSULATED)

1200 MANDOOR

4800 X 4800 O.H. DOORS
(INSULATED)

WEST ELEV.

BUILT-UP ROOFING ON STEEL
DECKING ON O.W.S.J.

250 CONC. BLOCK WALL

5400 X 4800 O.H. DOOR
(INSULATED)

WAREHOUSE
AREA

O.H. DOOR
BEYOND

LOADING
AREA

CROSS SECTION   B-B

Fig. 8-3 Elevations and Cross Section

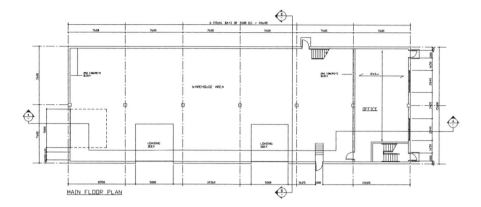

MAIN FLOOR PLAN

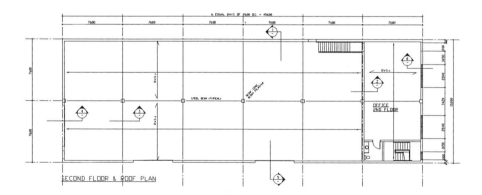

SECOND FLOOR & ROOF PLAN

Fig. 8-4 Building Plan

8-5   DESIGN OF MASONRY ELEMENTS

(a) Types of Construction

The two basic types of construction for concrete block masonry walls are stack bond and running bond. In stack bond type of construction the mortar joints line up both in the horizontal and vertical directions. In running bond there is an overlapping of blocks by 50% and the vertical joints are in alignment in every second course. For two-core blocks and running bond construction the cross webs do not line up, and as a result this type of construction should be carried out with face mortar bedding.

For the construction of load bearing walls, and especially for walls subjected to lateral loads, running bond is recommended. This type of construction provides for better resistance to lateral loads by the interlocking of blocks where stack bond has weak lines along the vertical mortar joints. Also vertical loads applied at the top of the walls are more effectively spread in running bond than in stack bond.

(b) Design of Load-Bearing Walls - Section 1-1, Fig. 8-5

Since the roof joists span 7600 and the wall height is 6000 plus 600 parapet, the gravity design loads are:

Factored roof dead load	$1.25(1.10)(7.6/2) = 5.23$ kN/m
Factored wall weight (@ mid-height)	$1.25(2.4)(6.0/2 + 0.60) = 10.8$ kN/m
Total factored dead load	$5.23 + 10.8 = 16.03$ kN/m
Factored snow load	$1.5(1.0)(7.6/2) = 5.70$ kN/m
Wind induced factored load $p_f = \alpha_w \, p =$	$1.5(1.0)(0.8) = 1.2$ kN/m

Assuming 40 mm eccentricity of the vertical load, and a minimum eccentricity of $0.1t = 0.1(240) = 24$ mm at the bottom of the wall. This gives a mean eccentricity at mid-height of $(24 + 40)/2 = 32$ mm for calculating the primary moment, M_p, for magnification.

The wall should now be checked for the factored loading conditions [dead + live], [dead + wind] and [dead +0.7(live + wind)].

Check slenderness (Clause 11.2.4.3 of S304.1)

$$kh/t = 1.0h/t = 1.0(6000)/(240) = 25 > 10\text{-}3.5e_1/e_2$$
$$> 10\text{-}3.5(24/40) = 7.9$$
$$kh/t = 1.0h/t = 1.0(6000)/240 = 25 < 30$$

Therefore, use the moment magnifier method.

From Table A-1 of Part 2, $A_e = 81.7(10^3)$ mm^2/m, and $S_x = 6.80(10^6)$ mm^3/m

From Table C-1 of Part 2, for 250 mm, and 15 MPa hollow concrete block
$$E_m I_{eff} = 2718.91(10^9) \text{ N-mm}^2$$

Dead Load + Live Load

The vertical factored load P_f at the section is then
$$P_f = 5.70 + 16.03 = 21.73 \text{ kN/m}$$

and the primary moment is
$$M_p = P_f \, e = 21.73(10^3)(32) = 0.7(10^6) \text{ N-mm/m}$$

$\beta_d =$ Factored dead load/factored total load $= 16.03/21.73 = 0.74$

From Fig. C-2 of Part 2, for $h = 6000$ mm
$$P_{cr} / E_m I_{eff} = 130(10^{-9}) \text{ /mm}^2$$

therefore,
$$P_{cr} = 130(10^{-9})(2718.91)(10^9) = 353.46 \text{ kN}$$

For $P_f / P_{cr} = 21.73/353.46 = 0.061$, and $e_1/e_2 = 40/24 = 1.67$
        From Fig. C-3 of Part 2,
        $M_f / M_p = 1.35$
therefore,
$$M_f = 1.35(0.7)(10^6) = 0.95(10^6) \text{ N-mm/m}$$

Check resistance

   Compression: $P_f / A_e + M_f / S_x \le \phi_m f'_m = 0.55(9.8) = 5.39$ MPa

$$\frac{21.73\,(10^3)}{81.70\,(10^3)} + \frac{0.95\,(10^6)}{6.80\,(10^6)} = 0.41 < 5.39 \quad \underline{ok}$$

   Tension: $P_f / A_e - M_f / S_x \le \phi_m f_t = 0.55(0.45) = 0.25$ MPa

$$\frac{21.73\,(10^3)}{81.70\,(10^3)} - \frac{0.95\,(10^6)}{6.80\,(10^6)} = 0.13\ (compression)\ \underline{ok}$$

Alternatively,

the resistance of a 250 wall with unit strength of 15 MPa can be checked using the P-M interaction diagram of Fig. E-7 of Part 2

The point $P_f = 21.73$ kN/m, and $M_f = 0.95$ kN-m/m lies within the curve for the 250 mm, 15 MPa ungrouted concrete masonry wall.

Therefore, the wall can carry the specified load.   <u>OK</u>

Dead Load + Wind Load

The primary moment consist of the factored dead load acting over a mean eccentricity of 32 mm and the moment $p_f h^2/8$ caused by the factored wind pressure p_f acting over the height h = 6000 mm.

$$P_f = 16.03 \text{ kN/m}$$

$$\begin{aligned} M_p &= P_f\, e + p_f h^2/8 \\ &= 16.03(10^3)(32) + 1.2(6000)^2/8 = 5.91(10^6) \text{ N-mm/m} \end{aligned}$$

β_d = Factored dead load/factored total load = 16.03/16.03 = 1.0

From Fig. C-2 of Part 2, for h=6000 mm
$$P_{cr} / E_m I_{eff} = 119(10^{-9}) \text{ /mm}^2$$

therefore,
$$P_{cr} = 119(10^{-9})(2718.91)(10^9) = 323.6 \text{ kN}$$

For $P_f / P_{cr} = 16.03/323.6 = 0.05$, and $e_1/e_2 = 40/24 = 1.67$
From Fig. C-3 of Part 2,
$$M_f / M_p = 1.34$$

therefore,
$$M_f = 1.34(5.91)(10^6) = 7.9(10^6) \text{ N-mm/m}$$

Check resistance

compression: $P_f / A_e + M_f / S_x \leq \phi_m f'_m = 0.55(9.8) = 5.39$ MPa

$$\frac{16.03\,(10^3)}{81.70\,(10^3)} + \frac{7.9\,(10^6)}{6.80\,(10^6)} = 1.34 < 5.39 \quad \underline{ok}$$

tension: $P_f / A_e - M_f / S_x \leq \phi_m f'_m = 0.55(0.45) = 0.25$ MPa

$$\frac{16.03\,(10^3)}{81.70\,(10^3)} - \frac{7.9\,(10^6)}{6.80\,(10^6)} = 0.97 \ (tension) > 0.25 \quad \underline{NG}$$

Alternatively,
the resistance of a 250 wall with unit strength of 15 MPa can be checked using the P-M interaction diagram of Fig. E-7 of Part 2.

The point $P_f = 16.04$ kN/m, and $M_f = 7.9$ kN-m/m lies outside the curve for the 250 mm, 15 MPa concrete masonry wall.

Therefore,
the wall cannot carry the specified load.   <u>NG</u>

[*Dead Load* + 0.7(*Live Load* + *Wind Load*)]

In this instance 70% of the live load and wind load are assumed to act. That is,

$L_f = 0.7(5.7) = 4.0$ kN/m
$p_f = 0.7(1.2) = 0.84$ kN/m
$P_f = 16.03 + 4.0 = 20.03$ kN/m

and the primary moment is,

$$M_p = 20.03(10^3)(32) + 0.84(6000)^2/8 = 4.42(10^6) \text{ N-mm/m}$$

β_d= Factored dead load/factored total load = 16.03/20.03 = 0.80

From Figure C-2 of Part 2, for h=6000 mm
$$P_{cr} / E_m I_{eff} = 127(10^{-9}) \text{ /mm}^2$$

therefore,
$$P_{cr} = 127(10^{-9})(2718.91)(10^9) = 345.3 \text{ kN}$$

For $P_f / P_{cr} = 20.03/345.3 = 0.06$, and $e_1/e_2 = 40/24 = 1.67$
From Fig. C-3 of Part 2,
$$M_f / M_p = 1.35$$
therefore,
$$M_f = 1.35(4.42)(10^6) = 6.0(10^6) \text{ N-mm/m}$$

Check resistance

compression: $P_f / A_e + M_f / S_x \leq \phi_m f'_m = 0.55(9.8) = 5.39 \text{ MPa}$

$$\frac{20.03\,(10^3)}{81.70\,(10^3)} + \frac{6.0\,(10^6)}{6.80\,(10^6)} = 1.13 < 5.39 \quad \underline{ok}$$

tension: $P_f / A_e - M_f / S_x \leq \phi_m f_t = 0.55(0.45) = 0.25 \text{ MPa}$

$$\frac{20.03\,(10^3)}{81.70\,(10^3)} - \frac{6.0\,(10^6)}{6.80\,(10^6)} = 0.64 \; (tension) > 0.25 \quad \underline{NG}$$

Alternatively,
       the resistance of a 250 wall with unit strength of 15 MPa can be checked using the P-M interaction diagram of Fig. E-7 of Part 2

       The point $P_f = 20.03$ kN/m, and $M_f = 6.0$ kN-m/m lies outside the curve for the 250 mm, 15 MPa concrete masonry wall.

Therefore,
       the wall cannot carry the specified load.   <u>NG</u>

       Assuming one grouted core per meter and using Fig. F-31 of Part 2, the required reinforcing is

$$A_s = 300 \text{ mm}^2/\text{m}$$

Therefore, *1-#20 @ 1000 o.c. vertical reinforcement is required.* This is adequate for all load cases.

Note that only one core per metre needs to be grouted and that matching dowels (that is, #20 @ 1000 o.c.) should extend vertically from the supporting concrete foundation.

Comments

The reader should note that Clause 11.1.3.1 of S304.1 states that "in walls and columns the width of section acting with a single reinforcing bar shall be taken as the lesser of the spacing between bars and either 4 times the wall thickness for running bond or the length of reinforced unit for stack pattern." In that case, a width of wall $b = 4(240) = 960 \approx 1000$ mm resist 1.0 m width of wind, and the design is valid. Had the decision been made to reinforce at intervals of 1800 o.c. to match the joist spacing, the moment for each reinforced section would be greater but the value of b would remain $960 \approx 1000$ mm. However, Clause 11.1.3.1 is clearly intended to cover instances of locally-applied moment (as at eccentric beam reactions) or concentrated lateral loads, and is not likely to be applicable to the more favourable conditions of wind loading. This limitation placed on the effective width is commented on in more detail in Chapter 4 following Example 4-7. The reader can note that the limitation $b = 4t$ on effective width applies only to flexure and that the full length of the wall is considered effective in resisting vertical loading.

When the distance between reinforced sections becomes considerable, the ability of the wall to span horizontally between vertical reinforced sections should also be checked.

Check the Effect of Wind at Door Openings

The floor plan of Fig. 8-4 shows large overhead door openings 5.0 m wide. This means that four #20 vertical bars have been interrupted by the opening with a loss in flexural resistance for the wall. Reinforced sections must now be incorporated as door jambs to resist the accumulated bending due to wind, and also the reaction for the door lintel. Each jamb is then subjected to wind and gravity load from 2.5 m of door opening plus half the distance to the next reinforced core.

A calculation similar to that for the wall will show that 3-#20 full height in three grouted cores will be adequate. However, the lintel will require 200 bearing at each end, and common practice would be to provide one reinforced and grouted core at the bearing and 3-#20 extending full height.

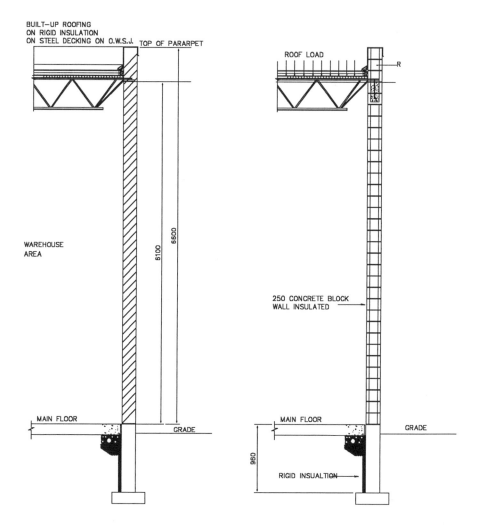

Fig. 8-5 Section 1

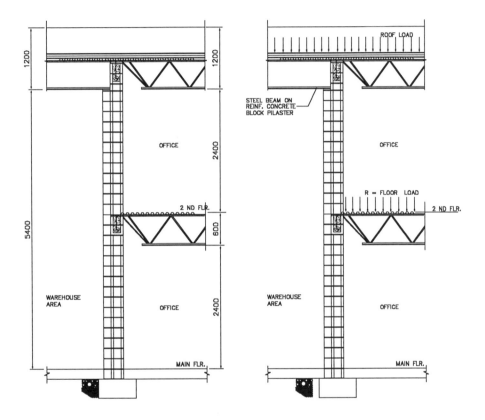

Fig. 8-6 Section 2

(c) Design of Load-Bearing Wall - Section 2, Fig. 8-6

This is an interior wall that supports half the roof load from a 7600 office bay, half of the roof load to the first warehouse roof joist 1800 from the wall, and half of the mezzanine office floor span.

Loading:

Roof factored live load	$1.5(1.0)(7.6/2 + 1.8/2) = 7.05$ kN/m
Roof factored dead load	$1.25(1.1)(7.6/2 + 1.8/2) = 6.46$ kN/m
Mezzanine office factored live load	$1.5(2.5)(7.6)/2 = 14.25$ kN/m
Mezzanine office factored dead load	$1.25(2.5)(7.6)/2 = 11.88$ kN/m
Upper wall factored self weight	$1.25(2.4)(2.4 + 0.6) = 9.0$ kN/m
Lower wall factored self weight	$1.25(2.4)(2.4 + 0.6) = 9.0$ kN/m

Total gravity factored loading $= 7.05 + 6.46 + 9.0 = 22.51$ kN/m
    (upper wall)

Total gravity factored loading $= 22.51 + 14.25 + 11.88 + 9.0 = 57.64$ kN/m
    (lower wall)

Since this is an interior wall, only the internal wind pressure will act. However, if the full design factored wind load of 1.2 kN/m² is used, the design can serve also for outside walls for the office area.

Check slenderness (Clause 11.2.4.3 of S304.1)

$$kh/t = 1.0h/t = 1.0(3000)/(240) = 12.5 > 10-3.5e_1/e_2$$
$$> 10-3.5(1) = 6.5$$
$$kh/t = 1.0h/t = 1.0(3000)/240 = 12.5 < 30$$
therefore, use the moment magnifier method

Dead Load + Live Load

The maximum factored dead load $= 6.46 + 11.88 + 9.0 + 9.0 = 36.34$ kN/m
    (lower level)

The maximum factored live load $= 7.05 + 14.25 = 21.30$ kN/m
    (lower level)

The total maximum factored load P_f $= 36.34 + 21.30 = 57.64$ kN/m
    (lower level)

Assuming a minimum eccentricity of $0.1t = 0.1(240) = 24$ mm
the primary moment is
$$M_p = P_f e = 57.64(10^3)(24) = 1.38(10^6) \text{ N-mm/m}$$

$\beta_d =$ factored dead load/factored total load $= 36.34/57.64 = 0.63$

From Fig. C-2 of Part 2, for $h = 3000$ mm
$$P_{cr} / E_m I_{eff} = 542(10^{-9}) /\text{mm}^2$$
therefore,
$$P_{cr} = 542(10^{-9})(2718.91)(10^9) = 1473.65 \text{ kN}$$

For $P_f / P_{cr} = 57.64/1473.65 = 0.039$, and $e_1/e_2 = 1.0$
From Fig. C-3 of Part 2,
$M_f / M_p = 1.04$
therefore,
$$M_f = 1.04(1.38)(10^6) = 1.44(10^6) \text{ N-mm/m}$$

Check resistance

Compression: $P_f / A_e + M_f / S_x \le \phi_m f'_m = 0.55(9.8) = 5.39$ MPa

$$\frac{57.64(10^3)}{81.70(10^3)} + \frac{1.44(10^6)}{6.80(10^6)} = 0.92 < 5.39 \quad \underline{ok}$$

Tension: $P_f / A_e - M_f / S_x \le \phi_m f_t = 0.55(0.45) = 0.25$ MPa

$$\frac{57.64(10^3)}{81.70(10^3)} - \frac{1.44(10^6)}{6.80(10^6)} = 0.49 \quad (compression) \quad \underline{ok}$$

Alternatively,
        the resistance of a 250 mm wall with unit strength of 15 MPa can be checked using the P-M interaction diagram of Fig. E-7 of Part 2

        The point $P_f = 57.64$ kN/m, and $M_f = 1.44$ kN-m/m lies within the curve for the 250 mm, 15 MPa ungrouted concrete masonry wall.

Therefore, the wall can carry the specified load.   OK

An unreinforced 250 mm block wall is adequate.

Wind load

The worst situation for wind is when uplift on the roof is assumed to remove the dead load.

$$M_w = p_f h^2/8 = 1.2(3.0)^2/8 = 1.35 \text{ kN-m/m}$$

$$M_w/S_x = 1.35(10)^6/6.80(10)^6 = 0.20 \text{ MPa} < 0.55(0.45) = 0.25 \text{ MPa } \underline{OK}$$

The walls providing the enclosure for the office section of the building do not require vertical reinforcing. However, 1-#15 vertical should be placed in a grouted core each side of each door or window opening and at each end of each wall.

d) Design of Concrete Masonry Pilasters

Section 3-3, Fig. 8-7, shows a typical interior reinforced concrete masonry pilaster. The roof area tributary to the pilaster is

$$7600(7600) = 57.8(10)^6 \text{ mm}^2 = 57.8 \text{ m}^2$$

the total factored roof dead load on the pilaster is

$$1.25(57.8)(1.1) = 79.5 \text{ kN}$$

and the total factored roof live load on the pilaster is

$$1.5(57.8)(1.0) = 86.70 \text{ kN}$$

Assuming a fully-grouted 400x400 pilaster, and the density to be 23.5 kN/m³, the factored self-weight at mid-height is

$$1.25(0.39)(0.39)(5.4/2)(23.5) = 12.1 \text{ kN}$$

to give a total factored vertical load of $79.5 + 86.7 + 12.1 = 178.3$ kN

Check slenderness
$$kh/t = 1.0h/t = 1.0(5400)/(390) = 13.8 > 10 - 3.5e_1/e_2$$
$$kh/t = 1.0(5400)/390 = 13.8 < 30$$
therefore use the moment magnifier method

Assuming a minimum eccentricity of $0.1t = 0.1(390) = 39$ mm for the axial load

the primary moment $M_p = 178.3(0.039) = 7.0$ kN-m

For the moment magnifier method, the value of
$$EI = \phi_e \, E_m I_{eff}/(1+0.5\beta_d) \text{ is required where}$$

$$I_{eff} = 0.25I_0 - (0.25I_0 - I_{cr})(e-e_k)/(2e_k)$$

As noted in Chapter 5, and in Clause 5.2.5.1 of S304.1,

$$0.01 \le \rho = A_s/A_e \le 0.04$$
and, consequently,

$$A_s(\min) = 0.01(390)(390) = 1521 \text{ mm}^2$$

Therefore assume 4#25 bars (total $A_s = 2000 \text{ mm}^2$)
$E_m = 850f'_m = 850(7.5) = 6375 \text{ MPa} < 20,000 \text{ MPa, and } E_s = 200,000$

$$n = E_s/E_m = 200,000/6375 = 31.37$$

Uncracked section (refer to Fig. 5-15 a)

$$I_x = I_0 = bh^3/12 + 2(n-1)A_s(h/2 - d')^2$$
$$= 390^4/12 + 2(31.37 - 1)(1000)(390/2 - 95)^2 = 2535(10)^6 \text{ mm}^4$$
$$A_e = 390(390) + 2(31.37 - 1)(1000) = 212.8(10)^3 \text{ mm}^2$$

Then $e_k = I/S = 2535(10)^6/[(390/2)(212.8)(10)^3] = 61.1 \text{ mm}$

Cracked section (refer to Fig. 5-15 b)

$$390(kd)^2/2 + (31.37 - 1)(1000)(kd - 95) = 31.37(1000)(295 - kd)$$

which solves to give $kd = 137.2$ mm, and since $d' < kd$ the analysis is valid.

Then

$$I_{cr} = b(kd)^3/3 + (n-1)A'_s(kd - d')^2 + nA_s(d - kd)^2$$
$$= 390(137.2)^3/3 + 30.37(1000)(137.2 - 95)^2 + 31.37(1000)(295 - 137.2)^2$$
$$= 1171(10)^6 \text{ mm}^4$$

Thus $I_0 = 2535(10)^6 \text{ mm}^4$ and $I_{cr} = 1171(10)^6 \text{ mm}^4$

Then $I_{eff} = 0.25I_0 - (0.25I_0 - I_{cr})(e - e_k)/(2e_k)$
$$= 0.25(2535)(10)^6 - [0.25(2535)(10)^6 - 1171(10)^6](39 - 61.1)/[2(61.1)]$$
$$= 537(10)^6 \text{ mm}^4 \qquad < 634(10)^6 = 0.25 \, I_0$$
$$< 1171(10)^6 = I_{cr}$$

and S304.1 notes that I_{eff} need not be less than I_{cr}.

Then $I_{eff} = 1171(10)^6$ mm^4

The value of P_{cr} can now be calculated as

$$P_{cr} = \pi^2\phi_e E_m I_{eff}/[(1 + 0.5\beta_d)(kh)^2]$$

where

$\beta_d = (79.5+12.1)/178.3 = 0.51$

$P_{cr} = \pi^2(0.65)(6375)(1171)(10)^6/[(1 + 0.5(0.51))(5400)^2] = 1309$ kN

Thus $M_f = M_p C_m/(1 - P_f/P_{cr})$
         $= 7(10)^6(1.0)/(1 - 178.3/1309) = 8.1(10)^6$ N-mm $= 8.1$ kN-m

From Fig. G-6 of Part 2, for this column(15 MPa units, $\gamma = 0.5$, and $\rho = 0.01$) a value of $P_f/A_e = 178.3(10)^3/(390x390) = 1.17$ MPa gives a value of $M_r/A_e t = 1.08$ MPa. Thus for $P_f = 178.3$ kN, $M_r = 1.08(390)^3 = 64.1(10)^6$ N-mm $= 64.1$ kN-m

Since the column is stressed to less than half of its capacity, reinforcement can be reduced to 0.5%. That is

$A_s = 0.005(390)(390) = 761$ mm^2

Use 4#15 vertical bars ($A_s = 800$ mm^2) and lateral ties should be provided in conformity with Clauses 5.2.5.3 of S304.1.

Alternatively,

S304.1 noted that the value of effective stiffness for unreinforced masonry ($EI_{eff} = 0.4E_m I_o$) may be conservatively used for reinforced walls or columns where reinforcement is not taken into account in the calculation of the walls or columns resistance.

Therefore,
$I_o = bh^3/12 = 390(390)^3/12 = 1928(10)^6$ mm^4

$S = I_o/\bar{y} = 1928(10)^6/195 = 9.9(10)^6$ mm^3, $A_e = 390(390) = 152.1(10)^3$ mm^2

$I_{eff} = 0.4I_o = 0.4(1928)(10)^6 = 771(10)^6$ mm^4

$$P_{cr} = \pi^2(0.65)(6375)(771)(10)^6/[(1 + 0.5(0.51))(5400)^2] = 861.6 \text{ kN}$$

Thus $\quad M_f = M_p C_m/(1 - P_f/P_{cr})$
$$= 7(10)^6(1.0)/(1 - 178.3/861.6) = 5.5(10)^6 \text{ N-mm} = 8.8 \text{ kN-m}$$

Check Resistance

Compression: $\quad P_f / A_e + M_f / S_x \leq \phi_m f'_m = 0.55(7.5) = 4.13$

$$\frac{178.3(10^3)}{152.1(10^3)} + \frac{8.8(10^6)}{9.9(10^6)} = 2.1 < 4.13 \quad \underline{ok}$$

Tension: $\quad P_f / A_e - M_f / S_x \leq \phi_m f_t = 0.55(0.7) = 0.39 \text{ MPa}$

$$\frac{178.3(10^3)}{152.1(10^3)} - \frac{8.8(10^6)}{9.9(10^6)} = 0.28 \ (compression) \quad \underline{ok}$$

therefore, the pilaster has sufficient capacity without reinforcement. However, some vertical reinforcement is required

$$A_s = 0.005(390)(390) = 761 \text{ mm}^2$$

Use 4#15 vertical bars ($A_s = 800 \text{ mm}^2$) and lateral ties should be provided in conformity with Clauses 5.2.5.3 of S304.1.

Fig. 8-8 shows the details of an end pilaster, the design for which, provided the total load is axial, is similar to an interior pilaster.

(e) Design of Lintel Beams

Openings for doors and windows in masonry require beams, referred to as lintels, to span over and to support the loads above the openings. The lintels are supported on the adjacent masonry each side of the opening. Lintel beams may be of precast or cast-in-place concrete, or structural steel, or masonry. Masonry lintels are the most appropriate for masonry buildings because they:
- are visually attractive,
- have low maintenance costs,
- do not require fire proofing,
- minimize differential movement between dissimilar materials.

Reinforced masonry lintels may be built with lintel blocks, bond beam masonry units or standard units with depressed, cut-out or grooved webs, and they are constructed and reinforced as described in Section 3-4 of Chapter 3.

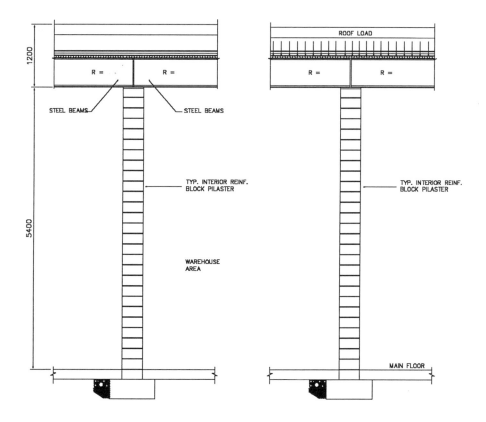

Fig.8-7 Section 3

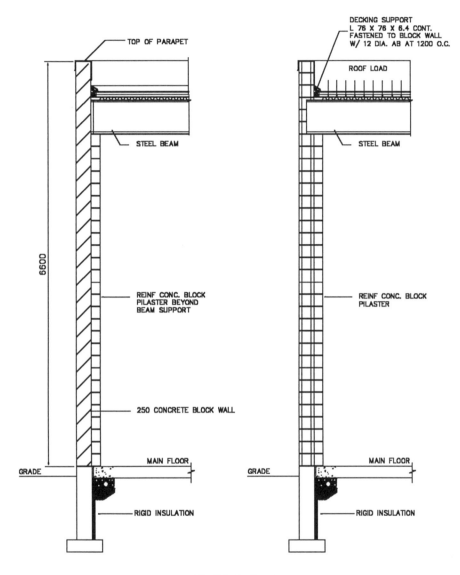

Fig. 8-8 Section 4

Loading

The loading on lintels may be distributed (as from the self-weight of the wall), or concentrated (as from joist reactions). However, if there are three or more equal concentrated loads at uniform spacing, or if the distance of the point of application of the concentrated load above the lintel is greater than one-third of the joist spacing then uniform distribution may reasonably be assumed.

Design of Lintel - Section 5-5, Fig. 8-9

The joist bearings are located at 6000 mm above the floor level (see Fig. 8-5) and the height of the opening is 5400 mm (Fig. 8-9). Since the joist bearings are located at a distance 6000 - 4200 = 1800 mm above the door opening, that is, greater than one-third of the joist spacing (1800 > 1800/3 = 600), the roof load may be assumed uniformly distributed.

From Fig. 8-9 the height of the wall above the opening is 2400 mm, and assuming eight courses (1600 mm) to be fully grouted and the remainder ungrouted, the wall factored self-weight (at 1.92 kN/m² ungrouted and 4.34 kN/m² fully grouted (see Table A-1 of Part 2) is calculated as

$$1.25[1.6(4.34) + 0.8(1.92)] = 10.6 \text{ kN/m}$$

the roof factored dead load, uniformly distributed, is

$$1.25(1.1)(7.6/2) = 5.23 \text{ kN/m}$$

and the roof factored live load, uniformly distributed, is

$$1.5(1.0)(7.6/2) = 5.70 \text{ kN/m}$$

for a total uniform factored load of 10.6 + 5.23 + 5.70 = 21.53 kN/m

Assuming a clear opening of 5000 (Fig. 8-4) and an assumed 200 mm bearing each end, the span is 5.4 m and the maximum bending moment is

$$M_f = w_f L^2/8 = 21.53(5.4)^2/8 = 78.5 \text{ kN-m}$$

Although, the design charts available in Part 2 are for 200 block (b=190 mm), they can also be used for this design (b=240 mm). For a 190 width of a 240 beam the factored moment $M_f = 78.5(190/240) = 62.1$ kN-m.

From Fig. B-2 (see Example 1) of Part 2, or from the principles outlined in Chapters 3 and 4, it can be shown that a four-course 190 beam with a tensile steel area, $A_s = 315$ mm² is adequate.

$$A_s = 315 \text{ mm}^2 \quad > A_s(\text{min.}) = 281 \text{ mm}^2 \qquad \text{OK}$$
$$< A_s(\text{max.}) = 348 \text{ mm}^2 \qquad \text{OK}$$

therefore, the required steel area for 190/240 of the beam is 315 mm², and for the 240 beam

$$A_s = 315(240/190) = 398 \text{ mm}^2$$

Use a four-course beam with 2-#15 bottom

The maximum factored shear is calculated at a distance $d = 0.74$ m from the face of the support as

$$V_f \text{ max} = 21.53(5.4/2 - 0.74) = 42.2 \text{ kN}$$

and the factored shear resistance of masonry is

$$V_m = 0.2\lambda\phi_m\sqrt{f}_m\{1.0\text{-}[(d\text{-}400)/1500]\}b_wd$$

Since the beam is not continuously grouted, S304.1 (Clause 12.3.5.4) applies a factor of 0.6 to the above equation. Therefore

$$V_m = 0.6(0.2)(0.75)(0.55)(\sqrt{7.5})\{1.0\text{-}[(740\text{-}400)/1500]\}(240)(740)$$
$$=18.6 \text{ kN}$$

$$> 0.6(0.12\lambda\phi_m\sqrt{f'}_mb_wd) = 0.6(0.12)(0.75)(0.55)(\sqrt{7.5})(240)(740)$$
$$= 14.5 \text{ kN} \qquad \text{OK}$$

$$< 0.6(0.2\lambda\phi_m\sqrt{f'}_mb_wd) = 0.6(0.2)(0.75)(0.55)(\sqrt{7.5})(240)(740)$$
$$=24.1 \text{ kN} \qquad \text{OK}$$

Alternatively,

From Table B-37 of Part 2, and applying a factor of 0.6 for discontinuity in grouting, and multiplying by 0.75 for lightweight units, the shear resistance of masonry
$$V_m = 0.6(0.75)(0.233)(240)(740) = 18.6 \text{ kN}$$

Since $V_f > V_m$ shear reinforcement is required.
$$V_s = V_{f\text{-}}V_m = 42.2 - 18.6 = 23.6 \text{ kN} \leq 0.36 \ \phi_m\sqrt{f}_mb_wd$$
$$= 0.36(0.55)(\sqrt{7.5})(240)(740)$$
$$= 96.3 \text{ kN} \qquad \text{OK}$$

Try #10 single legged stirrups, $f_y = 400$ MPa
$$V_s = \phi_sA_v f_yd/s$$
$$s = 0.85(100)(400)(740)/(23.6)(10)^3$$
$$= 1066 \text{ mm}$$

S304.1 (Clause 12.3.5.8) limit the maximum spacing of shear reinforcement to the lesser of $d/2$ or 600 mm.

$d/2 = 740/2 = 370$ mm
because of the 200 mm of spacing cores
Use #10 single-legged stirrups, $f_y = 400$ MPa @ 200 o.c.

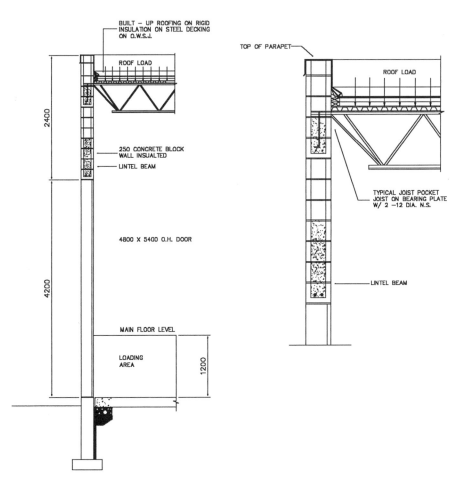

BUILT — UP ROOFING ON RIGID
INSULATION ON STEEL DECKING
ON O.W.S.J.

TOP OF PARAPET

ROOF LOAD

ROOF LOAD

2400

250 CONCRETE BLOCK
WALL INSUALTED

LINTEL BEAM

TYPICAL JOIST POCKET
JOIST ON BEARING PLATE
W/ 2 —12 DIA. N.S.

4800 X 5400 O.H. DOOR

4200

LINTEL BEAM

MAIN FLOOR LEVEL

LOADING
AREA

1200

Fig. 8-9 Section 5

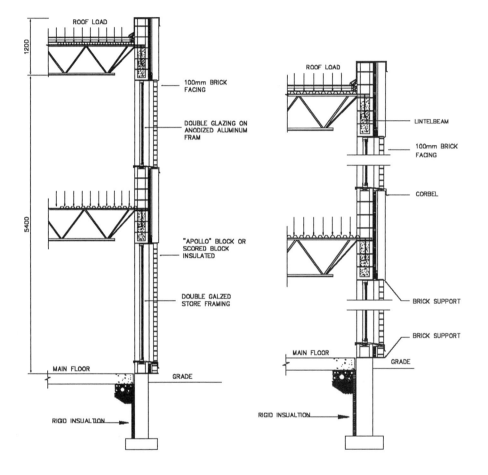

Fig. 8-10 Section 6

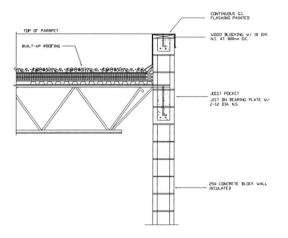

O.W.S.J. Bearing on Concrete Block Wall

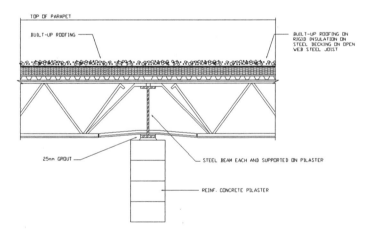

O.W.S.J. Bearing on Steel Beam

Fig. 8-11 Typical Connections

Check minimum area of shear reinforcement

$$A_v = 0.35b_w \, s/f_y = 0.35(240)(200)/400 = 42.0 \text{ mm}^2 < 100 \text{ mm}^2 \qquad \underline{\text{OK}}$$

Use a four-course beam with 2-#15 bottom with #10 single-legged stirrups @ 200 o.c.

It is interesting to note that some advantage could have been taken of arching action (as outlined in Section 4-3 of Chapter 4) to reduce the effective applied load. However, in this example the saving would have been small.

Bearing Stresses

Where concentrated loads are applied, a check should be made to ensure that the masonry is not overstressed in bearing. Such conditions exist at the support points of beams, lintels and joists.

From the lintel design above, the bearing reaction is

$$R = 21.53(5.4/2) = 58.1 \text{ kN}.$$

Allowing for a 200 bearing at each end and a grout-filled and reinforced core at the bearing point, the factored bearing resistance of masonry is:

$$
\begin{aligned}
B_r &= 0.85\phi_m f_m A_1 \qquad \text{(S304.1 Clause 10.4.1)} \\
&= 0.85(0.55)(7.5)(240)(200) \\
&= 168.3 \text{ kN} > 58.1 \text{ kN} \qquad\qquad\qquad \underline{\text{OK}}
\end{aligned}
$$

A typical joist reaction is

$$[(1.5)(1.0) + (1.25)(1.10)](7.60/2)(1.8) = 19.67 \text{ kN}$$

and the required bearing area is determined from

$$19.67(10)^3/A_1 = 0.85(0.55)(7.5)$$

which gives a required bearing, $A_1 = 5610 \text{ mm}^2$

Similar calculations are made at the beam reactions on the pilasters.

(f) Design for Lateral Loads

Wind

The total lateral load resulting from wind pressure is evaluated by multiplying the wind pressure per square metre with the exposed surface of the building. The larger area exposed is

$$45.6(6.6) = 301 \text{ m}^2$$

The wind pressure per square metre is

$$p = qC_eC_gC_p + qC_eC_{pi} = 0.4(0.9)(2.0)(0.7) + 0.4(0.9)(0.7) = 0.76 \text{ kN/m}^2$$
$$\approx 0.80 \text{ kN/m}^2$$

The total factored wind load is

$$P_f = 1.5(301)(0.80) = 390.1 \text{ kN}$$

Earthquake Force

Following the procedures of Chapter 7 and the *Commentary on the Effect of Earthquakes* in the *Supplement to the NBC* the seismic base shear force is that given in Equation (7-1)

$$V = (V_e/R)U \tag{8-1}$$

where the calibration factor $U = 0.6$, the force modification factor $R = 1.0$ for unreinforced masonry (see Table 7-1) and the equivalent elastic base shear is given in Equation (7-2) as

$$V_e = vSIFW \tag{8-2}$$

In this expression, for Edmonton $v = 0.05$. S depends on the ratio Z_a/Z_v (which for Edmonton is $0/1 = 0$) and on T, the fundamental period T which from Equation (7-3) is

$$T = 0.09h_n/\sqrt{D_s}$$
$$= 0.09(6.6)/(15.20)^{0.5} = 0.152$$

From Table 7-3, for $Z_a/Z_v < 1.0$ and $T \leq 0.25$, the seismic response factor $S = 2.1$. The importance factor $I = 1$ and the foundation factor for illustrative purposes is assumed to be 1.0. It now remains to determine W, the accumulated dead load plus 25% of the snow load.

25% snow = 0.25(1.0)(45.6)(15.2) = 173.3 kN	173.3 kN
weight of walls = 2.4(6.6)[2(45.6) + 3(15.2)] = 2166.9 kN	2166.9 kN
weight of roof = 1.1(45.6)(15.2) = 762.4 kN	762.4 kN
weight of mezzanine = 2.5(7.6)(15.2) = 288.8 kN	288.8 kN
Total weight W =	3391.4 kN

Then the seismic force for design (recall the seismic force load factor = 1.0) is

$$V_e = vSIFW = 0.05(2.1)(1.0)(1.0)(3391.4) = 356.1 \text{ kN}$$

and $V = (V_e/R)U$
         $= (356.1/1.0)(0.6) = 213.7 \text{ kN}$

Since the factored earthquake force

$$V = 213.7 \text{ kN} < 390.1 \text{ kN} = \text{factored wind force } P_f$$

wind forces govern the design. However, it should be noted that had the building been located in seismic zones Z_a or $Z_v = 2$ or greater then zone minimum wall reinforcing (see Chapter 7) would be required., in which case the force modification factor increases to 1.5 - with a consequent reduction in the calculated force.If it is assumed that the building is laterally supported only by the end walls then the wind induced factored moment at the roof level is

$$M_f = w_f L^2/8 = [1.5(0.80)(6.0/2 + 0.6)](45.6)^2/8 = 1123 \text{ kN-m}$$

This action is illustrated in Fig. 8-12.

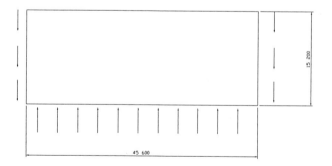

Fig. 8-12 Roof Diaphragm Action

The force required to resist this moment is

$$T_r = M_f/d = 1123/15.2 = 73.9 \text{ kN}$$

The area of bond beam tension steel required to develop this force is

$$A_s = T_r/\phi_s f_y = 73.9(10)^3/[0.85(400)] = 217 \text{ mm}^2$$

Use 2-#15 bars in the bond beam

And, since an equal compressive force occurs in the opposite bond beam, the required area in compression is

$$A_c = 73.9(10)^3/[0.85\chi\phi_m f'_m] = 73.9(10)^3/[0.85(1.0)(0.55)(7.5)] = 20886 \text{ mm}^2$$

and one grouted course $[240(200) = 48\,000 \text{ mm}^2]$ is sufficient

Distribution of Lateral Loads to Shear Walls

The distribution of lateral loads due to wind or earthquake to the shear walls of a building should always be considered. This is especially important for taller buildings, or for buildings with rather sparse or oddly arranged shear walls. A comprehensive treatment of the subject is given in Section 6-2 of Chapter 6 where a rather similar low building is examined in Example 6-1. In the discussion following that example it was noted that the experienced designer will quickly recognize potential shear wall problems and will devise simple and conservative approximations for checking their adequacy.

In the present example, the most highly stressed shear wall is the wall with the large door opening at the end of the warehouse. The structural portion of the wall is 6000 mm high (to roof level) and 8200 mm (see the main floor plan in Fig. 8-4) is the only significant length of wall.

Since half of the total wind load of 390.1 kN is resisted at the roof level (the remainder being resisted by the foundation), and if a very conservative half of the horizontal wind force at the roof level is applied to the 8.2 m length of shear wall, then the force at the top of the wall is

$$390.1/4 = 97.5 \text{ kN}$$

The self weight of the wall can be taken as

$$2.4(6.6)(8.2) = 129.9 \text{ kN}$$

The section properties for the wall are
$$A_e = 81.7(10)^3 \text{ mm}^2/\text{m}$$
and, $$S_x = tL^2/6 = 81.7(8200)^2/6 = 916(10)^6 \text{ mm}^3$$

Following the procedure given in Example 6-1, the horizontal in-plane shear force is $V_f = 97.5$ kN which is accompanied by a complementary vertical shear force of 97.5 kN

Shear strength contributed by masonry v_m may be taken conservatively from S304.1 Clause 11.5.3.3 as

$$v_m = 0.16\sqrt{f'_m} = 0.16\sqrt{9.8} = 0.5$$

The shear resistance may be calculated as
$$V_r = \phi_m v_m bd\gamma_g \quad [\text{where } \gamma_g = A_e/A_g = 81.7(10)^3/240(10)^3 = 0.34]$$
$$= 0.55(0.5)(240)(8200)(0.34) = 184 \text{ kN} > 97.5 \text{ kN} = V_f \qquad \underline{\text{OK}}$$

The moment applied at the base of the wall by the wind is $97.5(6.0) = 585.2$ kN-m and the factored vertical load from the wall self-weight is $1.25(129.9) = 162.4$ kN. Conservatively neglecting any roof loading the tensile stress at the base of the wall is

$$M/S_x - P/A_m = 585.2(10)^6/916(10)^6 - 162.4(10)^3/81.7(10)^3 < 0$$

and the shear wall is not subjected to vertical tension.

(g) Control Joints

It is well known that building materials are subject to movement that result from changes in temperature and moisture content, contraction due to carbonation and movements of other parts of the structure (foundation settlements, deflections of beams, elastic and creep, deformation of columns, etc.)

When masonry units are bonded together by mortar to form a wall, any restraint that prevents the wall from expanding or contracting freely causes stress in the wall. If a concrete block wall is restrained against thermal expansion the comparatively low compressive stresses rarely cause damage to the wall. This expansion is offset by shrinkage from carbonation and drying of the joints. As a result, expansion joints are not necessary in concrete masonry except where required by the configuration of the building. However, when concrete block wall is used as backing for clay brick veneer, expansion joints are required to accommodate expansion of the brick.

When contraction of the concrete masonry units is prevented, tensile stresses build up gradually in the wall. When the tensile stresses exceed the tensile strength of the unit, or the bond between the unit and the mortar, cracks will occur and the stresses will be relieved. These types of cracks usually disfigure the wall and cannot easily be concealed. The stability of the wall is also affected and caulking is required to inhibit water penetration. Such cracks can be prevented by control joints.

Control joints form a continuous, vertical break in a wall. If the control joints are spaced sufficiently close horizontal tensile stresses in the wall are relieved and the horizontal movements accumulate at the joint, where they are inconspicuous. A control joint must permit ready movement of the wall in a longitudinal direction and be sealed against visible movement, sound and weather. The control joint may also be required at times to provide lateral stability through shear transfer. A typical control joint detail is shown in Fig. 5-27 of Chapter 5.

Location of Control Joints

Some rules for the location of control joints have been developed from experience. Since there are many possible layouts of walls and partitions with their openings for doors, windows, and ducts, judgment must be exercised in determining where the joints should be placed. American Concrete Institute recommendations for spacing control joints in masonry are given in Table 8-1. In earthquake regions the U.S. building regulations limit the maximum spacing between control joints in reinforced masonry construction to 15 m and the distance of a joint from a corner to 7.5 m.

Control joints should also be located at the following points of weakness or high stress concentrations:

i)   at all abrupt changes in wall height;
ii)   at all changes in wall thickness, such as those at pipe or duct chases and those adjacent to columns or pilasters;
iii)   above joints in foundations and floors;
iv)   below joints in roofs and floors that bear on the wall;
v)   at a distance of not over one-half the allowable joint spacing from bonded intersections or corners; and
vi)   at one or both sides of all door and window openings unless other crack control measures are used, such as joint reinforcement or bond beams.

TABLE 8-1

Maximum spacing of joint reinforcement (mm)	Maximum spacing of control joints	
	Panel length/height	Panel length (m)
None	2.0	12 m
600 mm	2.5	14 m
400 mm	3.0	15 m
200 mm	4.0	18 m

Note that for stack bond construction, joint reinforcement should be provided no further apart than 400 mm.

All large openings in walls should be recognized as natural and desirable joint locations. Although some adjustment in the established joint pattern may be required, it is effective to use vertical sides of wall openings as part of the control joint layout. Under windows the joints usually are in line with the sides of the openings. Above doors and windows the joints must be offset to the end of the lintels. To permit movement, the bearing of at least one end of the lintel should be built to slide. This is illustrated in Fig. 5-28 of Chapter 5.

When a concrete masonry wall is reduced in thickness across the face of a column, a control joint should be placed along one or both sides of the column. Thin concrete masonry across the column face should be tied to the column by means of dovetail anchors or another suitable device.

Where bond beams are provided only for crack control, control joints should extend through them. If there is a structural reason for a bond beam, a false groove or raked joint should be provided to control the location of the anticipated crack.

A concrete masonry or cast-in-place concrete foundation having both sides backfilled does not usually require control joints. However, long concrete masonry basement walls may require control joints, continuous metal ties (joint reinforcement), or reinforcing bars.

Where concrete masonry units are used as a backing for another material with masonry bond, the control joints should extend through the facing. Control joints need not extend through the facing when using flexible metal ties.

Control joints should extend through plaster applied directly to concrete masonry units. Plaster applied on lath that is furred out from concrete masonry requires control joints over previous joints in the base.

Joint Reinforcement

Although continuous concrete masonry walls can be built essentially free from cracks, it is the infrequent crack for which joint reinforcement is provided. The function of joint reinforcement is not to eliminate cracking in concrete masonry walls but merely to prevent the formation of conspicuous shrinkage cracks. Joint reinforcement does not become effective until the concrete masonry begins to crack. At this time the stresses are transferred to and redistributed by the steel. The result is evenly distributed, very fine cracks that are barely visible to the naked eye.

The effectiveness of joint reinforcement depends on the type of mortar and the bond between the mortar and the longitudinal wires. The better the bond strength, the more efficient is the reinforcement in controlling cracking, and in-service experience has shown that only Types S, and N mortar should be considered for use with joint reinforcement.

Frequently the joint reinforcement is placed on top of the bare masonry course, the mortar then being applied to cover the face shells and joint reinforcement. It is better practice, however, to place the joint reinforcement on a bed of mortar with more mortar being placed on top: in this way, stress concentrations in the face shell are minimized. Minimum recommended mortar cover for the wire is 16 mm for the exterior wall face and 12.5 mm for the interior face.

Prefabricated or job-fabricated corner and T-type joint reinforcement should be used around corners and to anchor abutting walls and partitions. Prefabricated corners and tees are considered superior because they are more accurately formed, fully welded, and easier to install. A 150 mm lapping of side wires at splices is essential to the continuity of the reinforcement so that tensile stresses are transmitted.

As can be seen in Table 8-1 the vertical spacing of joint reinforcement is interdependent with the spacing of control joints. In addition, joint reinforcement should be located as follows:

i)   In the first and second bed joints immediately above and below wall openings. The reinforcement should extend not less than 600 mm past each side of the opening or to the end of the panel, whichever is less.

ii)   In the first two or three bed joints above floor level, below roof level, and near the top of the wall.

Joint reinforcement need not be located closer to a bond beam than 600 mm. It should not extend through control joints unless specifically called for and detailed in the plans.

CHAPTER 9

DESIGN EXAMPLE - LOW-RISE RESIDENTIAL BUILDING

9-1   INTRODUCTION

Masonry is frequently the appropriate material to select for attractive, economical apartment buildings. Foremost among its advantages are its high degree of fire safety, low sound transmission between apartment units, and low maintenance cost. Masonry bearing-wall residential buildings range in height from low-rise to twelve or more stories.

This chapter outlines the principles that may be used in the structural design of the masonry components of a typical low-rise residential building. While every effort has been made to ensure that data is factual and the results accurate, the reader is cautioned that the example has been developed for illustrative purposes and is not to be used for an actual building where the design conditions and criteria will be job specific.

The example building is a thirty-suite apartment block with ten suites on each of the basement, main and upper levels. Building elevations are shown in Fig. 9-1 and the typical floor plan in Fig. 9-2. The structure consists of 200 mm precast concrete hollow-core floor slabs supported on 200 mm concrete masonry bearing walls. The structural layout of bearing walls is shown in Fig. 9-3 and the direction of floor and roof hollow core slab framing can be seen in Fig. 9-4. The building is assumed to be clad with brick veneer and supported on reinforced concrete footings.

For illustrative purposes and to establish loading criteria the structure is assumed to be subject to a roof snow load of 1.60 kN/m², a wind load $q_{30} = 0.40$ kN/m², and to be located in an area of low seismic risk.

9-2   MATERIALS

(a) Concrete Masonry Units

Standard two-core 200 lightweight concrete blocks that satisfy the requirements of CSA Standard A165-94 are used, and the unit compressive strength is taken as 15 MPa.

(b) Mortar

Type S mortar is used, volume batched according to CSA Standard A179-94. The specified proportions are:

> 1 part normal portland cement
> 1/2 part hydrated lime
> 4.5 parts sand

(c) Grout

Grout is used to fill cores, as required, and to construct lintel beams. The grout also can be volume batched and CSA Standard A179-94 specifies the following proportions:

> 1 part normal portland cement,
> 0-1/10 parts hydrated lime or lime putty,
> 2.25-3 times the sum of cementitious materials of fine aggregate,
> 1-2 times the sum of cementitious materials of coarse aggregate,

the aggregates being measured in the damp loose state.

The compressive strength of the grout depends on its consistency when poured, on the size of the void being filled, and on the absorptive capacity of the unit. Because of this, there is no requirement for compressive strength in the standard. Although grout is frequently ordered as ready-mix concrete of a particular compressive strength, the reader should note that standard cylinder strength is not representative of actual poured grout strength. Also, the grout should have a high slump.

(d) Steel

The reinforcing steel used in the lintel beams and grouted cores has a yield strength of 400 MPa.

9-3   MASONRY STRENGTH

The compressive strength, f'_m, to be used in design is determined by one of two methods, namely, by testing prisms or by testing masonry units and mortar cubes. These methods are described in Chapter 2.

Since 15 MPa units and Type S mortar are used in this example, the value of f'_m, the masonry compressive strength, is obtained from Table 5 of S304.1. This value is found to be 9.8 MPa for hollow units and 7.5 MPa for grouted units.

The flexural tensile strength is obtained from Table 6 of S304.1. For hollow units, the values are found to be 0.45 MPa and 0.90 MPa for stresses normal and parallel to bed joint respectively. For grouted units, the values are 0.7 MPa and 0.90 MPa.

9-4   DESIGN LOADS

The building, described in Section 9-1 and illustrated in Figs. 9-1 to 9-4 inclusive, is loaded as follows:

Floor system	2.64 kN/m²
Levelling topping	0.15 kN/m²
Partition load	0.95 kN/m²
Total dead load	3.74 kN/m²
Live Load	1.90 kN/m²
Roof snow	1.60 kN/m²

The wind load is calculated on the probability of being exceeded in any one year of 1 in 30.

For wall element design the wind pressure is given by

$$p = q_{30}C_eC_gC_p + q_{30}C_eC_{pi}$$

$$= 0.4(1.0)(2.5)(0.7) + 0.4(1.0)(0.5) = 0.90 \text{ kN/m}^2$$

The wind load on the building is given by

$$p = q_{30}C_eC_gC_p$$

$$= 0.40(1.0)(2.0)(0.7 + 0.5) = 0.96 \text{ kN/m}^2$$

For further information on wind loading the reader should consult *Part 4 of the National Building Code of Canada, 1995*.

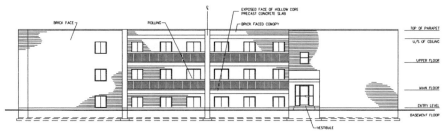

TYPICAL FRONT & REAR ELEVATION

TYPICAL SIDE ELEVATION

Fig. 9-1 Building Elevations

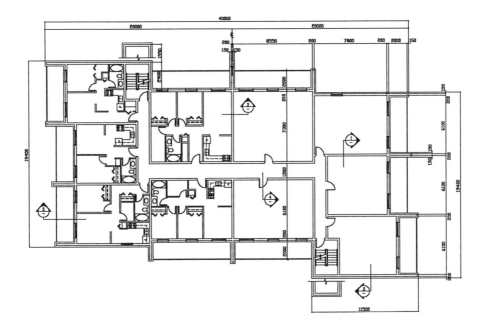

Fig. 9-2 Typical Floor Plan

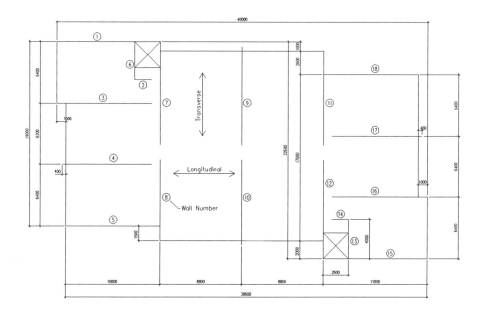

Fig. 9-3 Typical Structural Floor Plan

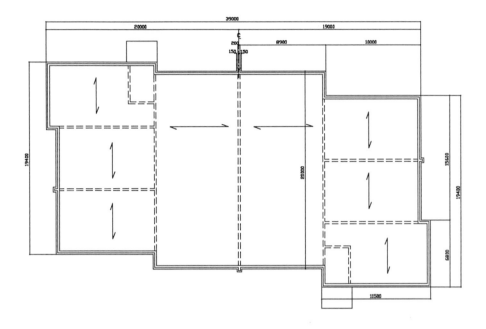

Fig. 9-4 Roof Plan

9-5   DESIGN OF MASONRY ELEMENTS

(a) Types of Construction

A description of the two basic types of construction for concrete masonry walls, namely, stack bond and running bond, and a discussion of their structural implications is given in Section 8-5. Running bond is assumed in this example.

The two main types of structural element in this building are the walls and the lintels that span openings in the walls. The design of the walls is conducted in two phases. The first is the design for their direct load-bearing capability - axial load and/or out-of-plane bending; and the second phase is to examine their action as shear walls in the overall resistance of the building to wind or earthquake.

(b)   Interior Load Bearing Walls - Section 1-1

Walls #9 and #10, shown in Figs. 9-3 and 9-5, support the greatest tributary width (8800 mm) of roof and floor and are therefore the most heavily loaded. The loading is as follows:

factored roof dead load	$1.25(2.79)(8.8) = 30.7$ kN/m
factored snow load	$1.5(1.60)(8.8) = 21.1$ kN/m
2nd floor - factored dead load	$1.25(3.74)(8.8) = 41.1$ kN/m
- factored live load	$1.5(1.90)(8.8) = 25.1$ kN/m
main floor - factored dead load	$1.25(3.74) (8.8) = 41.1$ kN/m
- factored live load	$1.5(1.90)(8.8) = 25.1$ kN/m

Assuming the weight of lightweight block wall with one core per metre grouted to be 1.97 kN/m^2, and from Fig. 9-5 the floor-to-floor distance is 2.6 m, then
factored weight of wall/floor $1.25(1.97)(2.6) = 6.4$ kN/m

Taking the load on each section of wall, the design factored loads become

upper level	$30.7 + 21.1 + 6.4 = 58.2$ kN/m
main - upper	$58.2 + 41.1 + 25.1 + 6.4 = 130.8$ kN/m
basement - main	$130.8 + 41.1 + 25.1 + 6.4 = 203.4$ kN/m

It should be noted that two simplifying and conservative assumptions have been made in these estimates of load.

    i)   The width of roof and floor tributary to the wall is taken as the centreline-to-centreline of spans whereas the actual floor tributary width would exclude the thickness. That is, 8.8 m rather than 8.8 - 0.2 = 8.6 m has been used.

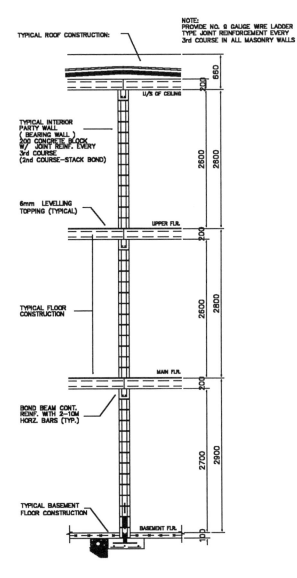

Fig. 9-5 Bearing Wall - Section 1-1

ii)   The reduction in live load permitted by the *National Building Code of Canada* for tributary areas greater than 20 m² [Clause 4.1.6.9(2)] has not been applied.

It can now be assumed that the load has been applied with minimum eccentricity of 0.1t = 0.1(190) = 19 mm both top and bottom. Hinged support conditions are also assumed at both the top and bottom of the wall and therefore, k =1.0.

Check slenderness

$kh/t = 1.0h/t = 1.0(2700)/190 = 14.2 > 10-3.5(e_1/e_2) = 6.5$
$kh/t = 1.0h/t = 1.0(2700)/190 = 14.2 <30$
therefore, use the moment magnifier method

From Table C-1 of Part 2, for 200 mm , and 15 MPa hollow concrete block
$E_m I_{eff} = 1472.74(10^9)$ N-mm²
The vertical factored load P_f at the section is
$P_f = 203.4$ kN/m in which 132.1 kN/m is factored dead load

and the primary moment is
$M_p = P_f e = 203.4(10^3)(19) = 3.9(10^6)$ N-mm/m

β_d= Factored dead load/factored total load = 132.1/203.4 = 0.65

From Fig. C-1 of Part 2, for h=2700 mm, and β_d= 0.65
$P_{cr} / E_m I_{eff} = 664(10^{-9})$ /mm²

therefore, $P_{cr} = 664(10^{-9})(1472.74)(10^9) = 977.9$ kN

For $P_f / P_{cr} = 203.4/977.9 = 0.208$, and $e_1/e_2 = 1.0$
From Fig. C-3 of Part 2,
$M_f / M_p = 1.26$
therefore, $M_f = 1.26(3.9)(10^6) =4.9(10^6)$ N-mm/m

From Table A-1 of Part 2, $A_e = 75.4(10^3)$ mm²/m, and $S_x = 4.66(10^6)$ mm³/m

Check resistance

Compression $P_f / A_e + M_f / S_x \le \phi_m f'_m = 0.55(9.8) = 5.39$ MPa

$$\frac{203.4\,(10^3)}{75.40\,(10^3)} + \frac{4.9\,(10^6)}{4.66\,(10^6)} = 3.75 < 5.39 \quad \underline{ok}$$

Tension $\qquad P_f / A_e - M_f / S_x \le \phi_m f_t = 0.55(0.45) = 0.25$ MPa

$$\frac{203.4\,(10^3)}{75.40\,(10^3)} - \frac{4.9\,(10^6)}{4.66\,(10^6)} = 1.65 \; (compression) \quad \underline{ok}$$

Therefore, the wall is adequate to carry the specified factored load

Alternatively,
the resistance of a 200 wall with unit strength of 15 MPa can be checked using the P-M interaction diagram of Fig. E-2 of Part 2
    The point P = 203.4 kN/m, and M = 4.9 kN-m/m lies within the curve for the 200 mm, 15 MPa ungrouted and unreinforced concrete masonry wall.

Therefore, the 200 ungrouted wall can carry the specified load.   <u>OK</u>

    However, it is good practice to reinforce and grout one core at each end of each wall (and each side of each door and window opening). The need to reinforce walls in seismic zones is discussed later in this chapter.

(c) Interior Load Bearing Walls - Section 2-2

            These walls, #3, #4, #16 and #17 in Fig. 9-3 and shown in Section 2-2 of Fig. 9-6, support a tributary floor and roof width of

$$(6200 + 6400)/2 = 6300 \text{ mm}$$

and the loads transmitted to these walls are

Roof	- factored dead load	= 1.25(2.79)(6.30) = 22.0 kN/m
	- factored snow load	= 1.5(1.60)(6.30) = 15.1 kN/m
2nd floor	- factored dead load	=1.25(3.74)(6.30) = 29.5 kN/m
	- factored live load	= 1.5(1.90)(6.30) = 18.0 kN/m
main floor	- factored dead load	= 1.25(3.74)(6.30) = 29.5 kN/m
	- factored live load	= 1.5(1.90)(6.30) = 18.0 kN/m
factored weight of wall/level		= 1.25(1.97)(2.6) = 6.4 kN/m

Taking the load at mid-height of each section of wall, the factored design loads become

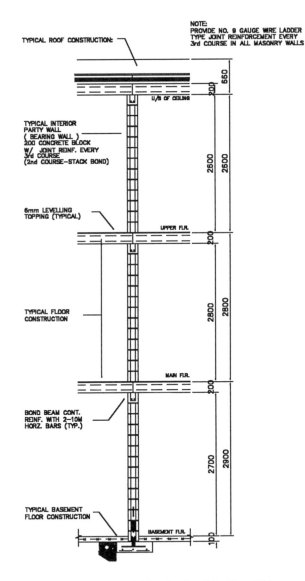

Fig. 9-6 Bearing Wall - Section 2-2 - Party Wall

upper level		$22.0 + 15.1 + 6.4/2 = 40.3$ kN/m
main - upper		$40.3 + 29.5 + 18.0 + 6.4 = 94.2$ kN/m
basement - main		$94.2 + 29.5 + 18.0 + 6.4 = 148.1$ kN/m

and, since 148.1 kN/m < 203.4 kN/m for the walls of section 1-1, similar analysis will show that no grouting is required.

(d) Exterior Walls - Section 3-3

These walls, shown in section 3-3 of Fig. 9-7 are numbered as #1, #5, #15, and #18 in Fig. 9-3. They support a tributary roof and floor width of one half of the distance between centrelines. That is,

$(6.4 - 0.1)/2 = 3.15$ m

and the gravity loads transmitted to the walls are

roof	- factored dead load	$= 1.25(2.79)(3.15) = 11.0$ kN/m
	- factored snow load	$= 1.5(1.60)(3.15) = 7.6$ kN/m
2nd floor	- factored dead load	$= 1.25(3.74)(3.15) = 14.7$ kN/m
	- factored live load	$= 1.5(1.90)(3.15) = 9.0$ kN/m
main floor	- factored dead load	$= 1.25(3.74)(3.15) = 14.7$ kN/m
	- factored live load	$= 1.5(1.90)(3.15) = 9.0$ kN/m
factored weight of wall per level		$= 1.25(1.97)(2.6) = 6.4$ kN/m
factored weight of parapet		$=1.25(2.0) = 2.5$ kN/m

The weight of the brick veneer is not carried by the concrete block wall but is supported by the foundation wall. The gravity load carried by the walls at the various levels are

upper level	$11.0 + 7.6 +2.5 + 6.4/2 = 24.3$ kN/m
main-upper	$24.3 + 14.7 + 9.0 + 6.4 = 54.4$ kN/m
basement-main	$54.4 + 14.7 + 9.0 + 6.4 = 84.5$ kN/m

and, since 84.5 kN/m < 203.4 kN/m for the walls of section 1-1, similar analysis will show that no grouting is required, and the wall is adequate for dead load plus live load.

Now, since these are exterior walls, the effect of wind must also be considered and the following load cases at each level should be considered:

i)   dead load + live load
ii)   dead load + wind load
iii)   dead load + 0.7(live load + wind load)

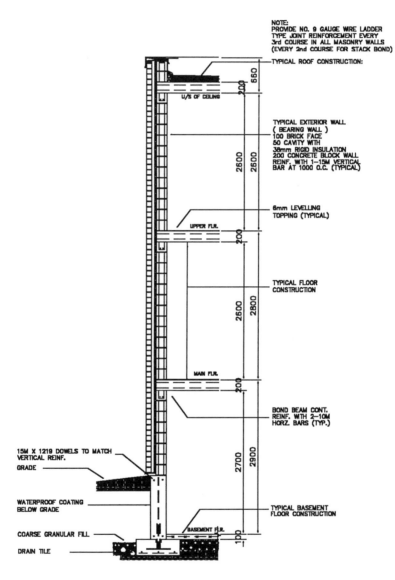

NOTE:
PROVIDE NO. 9 GAUGE WIRE LADDER
TYPE JOINT REINFORCEMENT EVERY
3rd COURSE IN ALL MASONRY WALLS
(EVERY 2nd COURSE FOR STACK BOND)

TYPICAL ROOF CONSTRUCTION:

U/S OF CEILING

TYPICAL EXTERIOR WALL
(BEARING WALL)
100 BRICK FACE
50 CAVITY WITH
38mm RIGID INSULATION
200 CONCRETE BLOCK WALL
REINF. WITH 1-15M VERTICAL
BAR AT 1000 O.C. (TYPICAL)

6mm LEVELLING
TOPPING (TYPICAL)

UPPER FLR.

TYPICAL FLOOR
CONSTRUCTION

MAIN FLR.

BOND BEAM CONT.
REINF. WITH 2-10M
HORZ. BARS (TYP.)

15M X 1219 DOWELS TO MATCH
VERTICAL REINF.

GRADE

WATERPROOF COATING
BELOW GRADE

TYPICAL BASEMENT
FLOOR CONSTRUCTION

COARSE GRANULAR FILL

BASEMENT FLR.

DRAIN TILE

Fig. 9-7 Bearing Wall - Section 3-3 - Exterior Wall

i)   *Dead load + live load*

As was shown above, the wall is adequate to support this load.

ii)   *dead load + wind load*

The primary moment consist of the factored dead load acting over a minimum eccentricity of $0.1t = 0.1(190) = 19$ mm and the moment $p_f h^2/8$ caused by the factored wind pressure p_f acting over the height 2700 mm.

the factored dead load $P_f = 58.9$ kN/m

the factored wind load $p_f = 1.5(1.0)(0.90) = 1.35$ kN/m

the primary moment is

$$M_p = P_f e + p_f h^2/8$$
$$= 58.9(10^3)(19) + 1.35(2700)^2/8 = 2.35(10^6) \text{ N-mm/m}$$

β_d = Factored dead load/factored total load = $58.9/84.5 = 0.697$

Fig. C-1 of Part 2, for h=2700 mm, and β_d=0.697

$$P_{cr} / E_m I_{eff} = 653(10^{-9}) \text{ /mm}^2$$

therefore, $P_{cr} = 653(10^{-9})(1472.74)(10^9) = 961.7$ kN

For $P_f / P_{cr} = 58.9/961.7 = 0.06$, and $e_1/e_2 = 1.0$

From Fig. C-3 of Part 2,

$$M_f / M_p = 1.06$$

therefore, $M_f = 1.06(2.35)(10^6) = 2.49(10^6)$ N-mm/m

From Table A-1 of Part 2, $A_e = 75.4(10^3)$ mm²/m, and $S_x = 4.66(10^6)$ mm³/m

Check resistance

Compression $P_f / A_e + M_f / S_x \leq \phi_m f'_m = 0.55(9.8) = 5.39$ MPa

$$\frac{58.9(10^3)}{75.40(10^3)} + \frac{2.49(10^6)}{4.66(10^6)} = 1.32 < 5.39 \quad \underline{ok}$$

Tension $P_f / A_e - M_f / S_x \leq \phi_m f_t = 0.55(0.45) = 0.25$ MPa

$$\frac{58.9(10^3)}{75.40(10^3)} - \frac{2.49(10^6)}{4.66(10^6)} = 0.25 \ (compression) \quad \underline{ok}$$

Therefore, the wall is adequate to carry the specified factored load

Alternatively,
the resistance of a 200 wall with unit strength of 15 MPa can be checked using the P-M interaction diagram of Fig. E-2 of Part 2

The point P = 58.9 kN/m, and M = 2.49 kN-m/m lies within the curve for the 200 mm, 15 MPa ungrouted and unreinforced concrete masonry wall.

Therefore, the 200 ungrouted wall can carry the specified load.   OK

iii)   *dead load + 0.7(live load + wind)*

Assuming the factored wind pressure of 1.35 kN/m to act on the full height of the basement wall, that is 2.85 m centre-to-centre of floor slabs, the primary moment due to 70% of the factored wind load is

$$M_{pw} = 0.7(ph^2/8) = 0.7(1.35)(2.85)^2/8 = 0.96 \text{ kN-m/m}$$

and the factored axial load is $P_f = P_f (DL) + 0.7(P_f (LL))$
$$= 58.9 + 0.7(25.6) = 76.8 \text{ kN/m}$$

The primary moment consists of the factored axial load acting over a minimum eccentricity of 0.1t = 0.1(190) = 19 mm and the moment M_{pw} caused by 70% of the factored wind pressure p_f acting over the height 2850 mm.
The primary moment is
$$M_p = P_f e + M_{pw}$$
$$= 76.8(10^3)(19) + 0.96(10^6) = 2.42(10^6) \text{ N-mm/m}$$

β_d= Factored dead load/factored total load = 58.9/76.8 = 0.77
Fig. C-1 of Part 2, for h=2850 mm, and β_d= 0.77
$$P_{cr} / E_m I_{eff} = 570(10^{-9}) /\text{mm}^2$$

therefore, $P_{cr} = 570(10^{-9})(1472.74)(10^9) = 839.5$ kN

For $P_f / P_{cr} = 76.8/839.5 = 0.09$, and $e_1/e_2 = 1.0$
From Fig. C-3 of Part 2,
$$M_f / M_p = 1.1$$
therefore, $M_f = 1.1(2.42)(10^6) = 2.66(10^6)$ N-mm/m

From Table A-1 of Part 2, $A_e = 75.4(10^3)$ mm^2/m, and $S_x = 4.66(10^6)$ mm^3/m

Check resistance

Compression $P_f / A_e + M_f / S_x \le \phi_m f'_m = 0.55(9.8) = 5.39$ MPa

$$\frac{76.8\,(10^3)}{75.40\,(10^3)} + \frac{2.66\,(10^6)}{4.66\,(10^6)} = 1.59 < 5.39 \quad \underline{ok}$$

Tension $P_f / A_e - M_f / S_x \le \phi_m f_t = 0.55(0.45) = 0.25$ MPa

$$\frac{76.8\,(10^3)}{75.40\,(10^3)} - \frac{2.66\,(10^6)}{4.66\,(10^6)} = 0.45 \; (compression) \quad \underline{ok}$$

Therefore, the wall is adequate to carry the specified factored load

Alternatively,
the resistance of a 200 wall with unit strength of 15 MPa can be checked using the P-M interaction diagram of Fig. E-2 of Part 2

The point P = 76.8 kN/m, and M = 2.66 kN-m/m lies within the curve for the 200 mm, 15 MPa ungrouted and unreinforced concrete masonry wall.

Therefore, the 200 ungrouted wall can carry the specified load.   OK

(e) Lintel Beams over Door Openings

Section 4-4 of Fig. 9-8 shows a typical lintel over a door opening. In this instance the tributary floor width = 6.3 m and the span is the clear opening plus 0.2 m (200 mm bearing each end). Assuming a self-weight of lintel of 2.0 kN/m, the uniform factored load becomes

$$w_f = 1.25(\,2.0) + (6.3)[1.25(3.74\,) + 1.5(1.90)] = 49.9 \text{ kN/m}$$

and for a clear opening of 1.0 m the span is 1.2 m. The factored moment is then

$$M_f = w_f L^2/8 = 49.9(1.2)^2/8 = 9.0 \text{ kN-m}$$

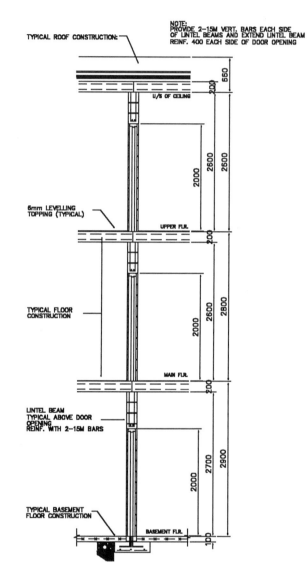

Fig. 9-8 Section 4-4 - Through Door

From Fig. B-2 of Part 2 a two-course beam with $A_s = 200$ mm^2 is adequate and there is sufficient space below the hollow-core bearing to accommodate two courses.

The shear force at a distance $d = 340$ mm from the face of support is

$$49.9(1.0/2 - 0.34) = 7.98 \text{ kN}$$

and from Table B-37 of Part 2, the shear resistance of masonry V_m is
$$V_m = v_m bd = 0.301(190)(340) = 19.4 \text{ kN}$$
However a factor of 0.6 must be applied for discontinuity in grouting (S304.1 Clause 12.3.5.4), therefore,
$$V_m = 0.6(19.4) = 11.7 \text{ kN}$$
and, since $11.7 > 7.98$, no shear reinforcement is required.

Thus, a two-course lintel reinforced with 1-#15 bottom bar is adequate and the steel should extend at least 200 mm into the supporting wall at each end of the lintel.

(f) Corridor Lintels

Corridor lintels are normally supported on double steel angles placed back-to-back, thereby maintaining a ceiling line uninterrupted by beams. The design of the supporting steel angles is not covered in this example.

(g) Masonry Support for Hollow-core

The hollow-core floor slab layout is shown in Fig. 9-4 and some suggested support details for the hollow-core are shown schematically in Fig. 9-9 where three conditions are shown. The designer might wish to use alternate details at the exterior wall support where a heat bridge is to be avoided. Fig. 9-10 illustrates one possible structural arrangement at a balcony.

(h) Design for Lateral Loads

Wind and seismic loads are transmitted through the floors (acting as rigid diaphragms) to the shear walls that are parallel to the direction of the wind or earthquake motion - the projected section is used for non-parallel walls. The greater the relative stiffness of the wall, the greater is its share of the lateral load; and depending on the length-to-height ratio, L/h, of the walls the relative stiffnesses are calculated as flexural and/or shear stiffnesses. For relatively tall buildings of irregular shear-wall layout the analysis for resistance to lateral load can become quite complex, and a detailed discussion on the topic is given in Section 6-2 of Chapter 6. However, the present building is relatively low and has a symmetric arrangement of shear walls, and a reasonably simple design check for the effect of lateral loads is possible. The effect of wind load is evaluated in the following calculations.

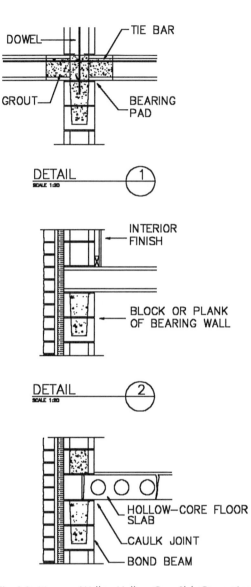

Fig. 9-9 Masonry Wall to Hollow Core Slab Connection

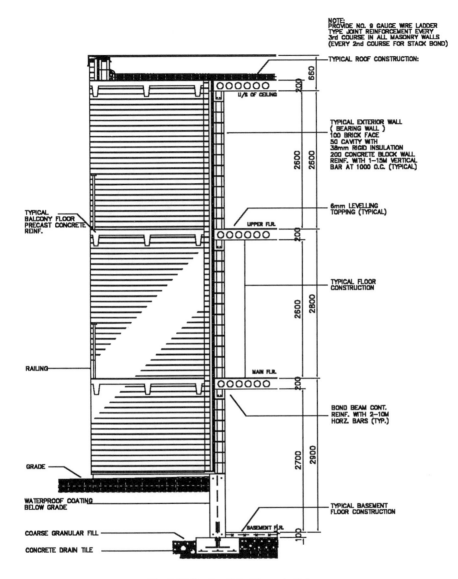

NOTE:
PROVIDE NO. 9 GAUGE WIRE LADDER
TYPE JOINT REINFORCEMENT EVERY
3rd COURSE IN ALL MASONRY WALLS
(EVERY 2nd COURSE FOR STACK BOND)

TYPICAL ROOF CONSTRUCTION:

U/S OF CEILING

TYPICAL EXTERIOR WALL
(BEARING WALL)
100 BRICK FACE
50 CAVITY WITH
38mm RIGID INSULATION
200 CONCRETE BLOCK WALL
REINF. WITH 1-15M VERTICAL
BAR AT 1000 O.C. (TYPICAL)

6mm LEVELLING
TOPPING (TYPICAL)

TYPICAL
BALCONY FLOOR
PRECAST CONCRETE
REINF.

UPPER FLR.

TYPICAL FLOOR
CONSTRUCTION

RAILING

MAIN FLR.

BOND BEAM CONT.
REINF. WITH 2-10M
HORZ. BARS (TYP.)

GRADE

WATERPROOF COATING
BELOW GRADE

TYPICAL BASEMENT
FLOOR CONSTRUCTION

COARSE GRANULAR FILL

CONCRETE DRAIN TILE

BASEMENT FLR.

Fig. 9-10 Section 5-5 - Through Balcony

Transverse Wind

The overall length of the building is 40 m and the height from basement floor to top of parapet wall is 8.96 m. Using the wind pressure of 0.96 kN/m² determined in Section 9-4 and assuming conservatively that the basement floor is at ground level, the overall factored wind moment at the foundation level is

$$M_f = 1.5(0.96)(40)(8.96)^2/2 = 2312 \text{ kN-m}$$

and the factored base shear is

$$V_f = 1.5(0.96)(40)(8.96) = 516.1 \text{ kN}$$

Reference to Figs. 9-2 and 9-3 shows that, neglecting the short stairwell walls, there are six shear walls, symmetrically arranged around the building centreline, resisting the lateral load. The lengths of these walls vary from 8.5 m to 10.8 m in length.

Assuming conservatively that all walls are 8.5 m long and share the factored wind load equally, the factored wind moment per wall becomes

$$M_f/\text{wall} = 2312/6 = 385 \text{ kN-m}$$

and the factored horizontal shear force per wall is

$$V_f/\text{wall} = 516.1/6 = 86.0 \text{ kN}$$

Now, following the procedures outlined in Section 5-7 of Chapter 5 the vertical in-plane load in the walls due to wind is

$$P_{f \text{ wind}} = \pm 6 \, M_f/L^2 = 6(385)/8.5^2 = \pm 31.97 \text{ kN/m}$$

and the factored horizontal shear force due to wind is 86.0 kN

The three load cases that must be considered are
i)   dead load + live load
ii)   dead load + wind
iii)   dead load + 0.7(live load + wind)

Load case i) has been considered earlier, and a simple calculation will show that neither of the load cases ii) nor iii) results in in-plane tension or a level of compression greater than that of load case i).

Shear strength contributed by masonry v_m may be taken conservatively from S304.1 Clause 11.5.3.3 as

$$v_m = 0.16\sqrt{f'_m} = 0.16\sqrt{9.8} = 0.5 \text{ MPa}$$

The shear resistance may be calculated as

$$V_r = \phi_m v_m b d \gamma_g \quad [\gamma_g = A_e/A_g = 75.4(10)^3/190(10)^3 = 0.4]$$
$$= 0.55(0.5)(190)(8500)(0.4) = 177.7 \text{ kN} > 86.0 \text{ kN} = V_f \qquad \underline{\text{OK}}$$

the walls are not overstressed in shear.

Longitudinal Wind

When the wind is directed along the longitudinal axis of the building the overall force is less since the narrower face is exposed to the wind. Also, because there are more longitudinal than transverse shear walls (eight compared with six, of approximately the same length), an analysis of the effects of longitudinal wind need not be undertaken.

9-6   VENEER

Buildings are frequently clad with a 90 mm thick brick veneer. The reason for using the veneer can be aesthetic and/or protection from the weather, and the veneer material can either be a clay or a concrete product. A brick veneer is not essential to a masonry building since concrete blocks are now produced in a variety of attractive colours and textures, and with appropriate detailing concrete block walls can be made energy-efficient and weatherproof. However, for the purpose of illustrating some of the factors that require consideration in design, the building in the present example is assumed to be clad with brick veneer.

The masonry veneer is not a structural component in a building and should not be required to carry any gravity load other than its own weight. Wind loads acting on the veneer are transferred directly to a backing structural system through a grid of steel ties and the only structural requirement for the veneer is to span either without cracking or with limited cracking between the ties. The load-bearing masonry walls provide an excellent backing for the veneer, and for walls that are not load bearing the structural backing can either be concrete masonry or light-gauge metal studs. Metal stud systems are more flexible than concrete masonry and, if careful attention is not paid to design and detailing, the transverse deflections can lead to excessive veneer cracking, moisture ingress into the mortar joints of the veneer leading to freeze/thaw deterioration. The present building is assumed to have a 200 concrete masonry backing system for the veneer.

Concrete Masonry Backing

The design factored wind pressure of 1.1 kN/m² [1.5(0.72) based on q_{10} for cladding] is transferred directly to the backing system, thereby placing the wall in bending, and the calculations of Section 9-5(d)(ii) show that a 200 mm masonry wall provides an adequate back-up for the veneer.

Ties

The selection of veneer ties and other details of veneer construction are governed by the requirements of the CSA Standards A370-94, *Connectors for Masonry*, and A371-94, *Masonry Construction for Buildings*, and additional useful information in the Portland Cement Association *Concrete Masonry Handbook*. Ties were discussed in Chapter 2 of this book.

9-7   OTHER REINFORCEMENT

As was noted in Section 5-4 of Chapter 5, Clause 5.2.1.3 of S304.1 requires that horizontal reinforcement be provided at certain specific locations, such as at floor and roof levels, at the top of a wall and top and bottom of openings in walls. This continuous tie at each floor and roof level is referred to as a bond beam. Placing the bond beam in the wall directly below the floor provides a suitable bearing for the hollow core slab and it is customary to provide at least 1-#15 or 2-#10 bars in the single-course bond beam. Bond beams are illustrated in Figs. 9-6, 9-7, 9-9 and 9-10, and are discussed further in Chapters 5, 6 and 8.

Clause 4.1.9.3. of the *National Building Code of Canada* requires that masonry construction in buildings located in velocity-related seismic zones 2 or greater be reinforced according to the requirements of Clause 6.3.3 of S304.1. This clause in turn requires that minimum reinforcement be provided in conformity with the requirements of Clause 5.2.2.

9-8   CLOSURE

The building design examples covered in Chapters 8 and 9 are not intended to be complete building designs. Rather, they indicate the main structural concerns in building design and illustrate how safety is assured. As was the case in Chapter 6 the intent has been to cover typical problems and to provide some of the flavour of the design process. There are other topics, such as the problems of the building envelope, that fall outside of the scope of the book and further reading is essential.

CHAPTER 10

CAVITY WALLS AND MASONRY VENEER

10-1 INTRODUCTION

A wythe is defined as a masonry wall of one masonry unit in thickness (with a minimum thickness of 75 mm). A cavity wall is a construction of masonry laid up with a continuous *cavity* between two masonry wythes. The cavity includes the thickness of the cavity insulation plus the width of the air space. The wythes in a cavity wall are tied together with (metal) ties or bonding units (headers).

When used for the construction of closures in engineered structures, cavity walls may be designed to serve either as loadbearing walls, or as non-loadbearing (infill) walls. A loadbearing cavity wall is defined as a wall designed to carry vertical loads in addition to its own dead load. A masonry infill wall is a non-loadbearing wall constructed between structural elements to provide closure and separation. Both loadbearing and non-loadbearing walls can be designed to resist lateral loads.

Loadbearing and non-loadbearing cavity walls are each further classified into two categories, non-composite and composite in structural action. Non-composite cavity walls are walls which are not capable of any measurable shear transfer between their wythes. Conversely, a composite wall is an assembly which is specifically designed to transfer shear between the two wythes. Composite action is provided by connecting the two wythes with header courses (bonding units), filling the space between the wythes (the collar joint) with grout or mortar to bond and key the wythes, by connecting the wythes with mechanical ties capable of transferring shear, or by a combination of these. The engineering properties of a composite wall are therefore determined by the properties of its components and by the extent of composite action between its wythes (full or partial action depending upon tie stiffness and tie interaction with the masonry at the location of its embedment). Composite walls, by utilizing the structural properies of the exterior wythe in resisting loads, can provide for reduced initial construction costs.

For buildings, the term *veneer* refers to a comparatively thin outer layer on the surface of an exterior wall built to improve appearance and to provide some protection against weathering to extend the service life of inner wall components. A *masonry veneer* is such a layer, usually of single wythe construction using burned clay units, concrete brick or block units, or natural stone, securely fastened to a backing wall, but not so bonded or attached as to be considered as exerting common reaction with the backing wall under lateral, out-of-plane loading.

Masonry veneer in Canada is typically 90 mm thick and is supported in the vertical direction either by resting on the main structural components of the building or on steel shelf angles attached to these structural components or to secondary support framing. Since the veneer is too slender to resist lateral loading and to stand without lateral support, horizontal (metal) ties between the veneer and the supporting backing wall are provided at regular intervals. The masonry veneer wall differs from the cavity wall in that (a) it is non-loadbearing, (b) the supporting backing wall need not be of masonry construction, but may be of steel or wood stud, or concrete, and c) composite action (shear transfer) between the veneer and the backing wall is usually not intended by design. Like the masonry cavity wall, the veneer wall usually includes an air space between the veneer and the supporting backing wall.

For both cavity walls and masonry veneer, the ties used to support the outer masonry wythe must be capable of safely transferring lateral loads due to wind or earthquake to the backing wall, and since wind and earthquake can act in any direction, these ties must be capable of effectively resisting both tension and compression loads.

The cavity in cavity and veneer walls serves a number of functions. It facilitates the incorporation of non-masonry wall components such as continuous insulation and the air/vapour barrier (to prevent or retard moisture from reaching the backing wall or entering interior spaces). The cavity provides a pathway for the drainage to the exterior of the wall of any moisture which has penetrated; it provides a chamber to effect pressure equalization or partial pressure equalization between the exterior wythe and the backing wall to help resist moisture penetration through the exterior masonry wythe into the wall assembly; and it serves to accommodate construction tolerances and differential movement between the wythes or between the veneer and its backing. The design width of the air space in a cavity or veneer wall is usually 25 mm, measured from the exterior face of the cavity insulation to the back of the exterior wythe.

Figures 10-1(a) and 10-1(b) illustrate masonry veneer and cavity wall construction, respectively.

In this chapter, the principal requirements for a rational, engineered design of masonry cavity and veneer walls are presented and design examples provided. Because these wall systems also serve as separations between internal and external environments, that is, between conditioned interior space and unconditioned exterior space, and must therefore effectively resist environmental loads, this chapter also provides the reader with some very basic information about the application of building science to masonry wall design and construction.

10.2   ELEMENTS OF BUILDING SCIENCE

Exterior wall assemblies are part of the building envelope, the function of which is to separate the conditioned, interior space of the building from the unconditioned, exterior environment. The degree of separation is a design consideration and is governed, among other things, by the cost of improving the envelope measured against the benefits to be derived by these improvements.

Often, a "life cycle cost study" is used to help quantify these benefits by considering such factors as future costs of heating and cooling, initial construction costs, and maintenance costs. An energy life cycle cost study is based upon the understanding that there exists an optimum for each component of the building envelope relating to heat loss, beyond which further increase of thermal resistance, or air and vapour tightness, does not produce savings proportional to the initial cost. Moreover, increasing the degree of separation to reduce heating/cooling costs and to provide comfort has been shown to increase the need for maintenance of, and increase the likelihood for durability related problems in wall, components and assemblies.

The energy consumption of a building, as it relates to building envelope, is determined by the configuration of the building, the size of the envelope, the thermal resistance of the various components of the envelope, air tightness, the amount of glazing, building orientation and operational procedures.

Structural components generally have low thermal resistance, and the wall assembly is usually thermally upgraded with the incorporation of insulation. Also, placement of the insulation at the appropriate location with respect to the air and vapour barrier will serve to minimize and to control the location of condensation within the wall assembly. The overall thermal performance of the wall system is greatly affected by the type thikness of insulation, and by the size and frequency of thermal bridges (penetrations by highly conductive materials) through the otherwise continuous plane of insulation. Strict reliance upon nominal insulating values stated by the manufacturer for the insulation type and thickness, without a consideration for the effects of thermal bridging (such as steel or wood stud bridging through batt insulation infill) can be misleading by representing a significantly higher thermal resistance for the wall system than is actually provided. Notwithstanding, the components of the building envelope should be selected, designed, detailed and constructed in such a way as to minimize thermal bridges since these can unnecessarily result in heat loss and energy consumption, and increase the likelihood of condensation within the wall system which can lead to deterioration of the bridge elements or of adjacent materials. Thermal bridges which penetrate a major portion of the thickness of the building envelope can be avoided or at least the number and cross-sectional area minimized through proper detailing. Chapter 11 demonstrates details for exterior wall assemblies designed for thermal efficiency.

Uncontrolled air leakage through the building envelope can result in large depositions of condensation within the exterior walls during the cold weather months and is the primary cause of deterioration, efflorescense, corrosion and failure of masonry components. For this reason a high degree of air tightness is of paramount importance for most building envelopes in extreme climates. Cavity and veneer walls, when properly

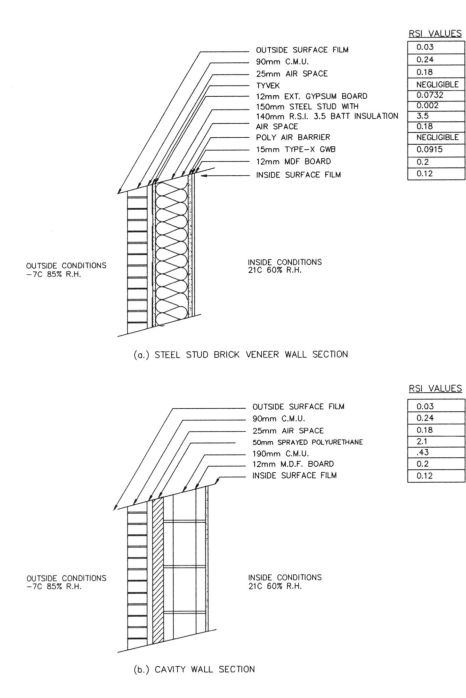

	RSI VALUES
OUTSIDE SURFACE FILM	0.03
90mm C.M.U.	0.24
25mm AIR SPACE	0.18
TYVEK	NEGLIGIBLE
12mm EXT. GYPSUM BOARD	0.0732
150mm STEEL STUD WITH	0.002
140mm R.S.I. 3.5 BATT INSULATION	3.5
AIR SPACE	0.18
POLY AIR BARRIER	NEGLIGIBLE
15mm TYPE-X GWB	0.0915
12mm MDF BOARD	0.2
INSIDE SURFACE FILM	0.12

OUTSIDE CONDITIONS
−7C 85% R.H.

INSIDE CONDITIONS
21C 60% R.H.

(a.) STEEL STUD BRICK VENEER WALL SECTION

	RSI VALUES
OUTSIDE SURFACE FILM	0.03
90mm C.M.U.	0.24
25mm AIR SPACE	0.18
50mm SPRAYED POLYURETHANE	2.1
190mm C.M.U.	.43
12mm M.D.F. BOARD	0.2
INSIDE SURFACE FILM	0.12

OUTSIDE CONDITIONS
−7C 85% R.H.

INSIDE CONDITIONS
21C 60% R.H.

(b.) CAVITY WALL SECTION

Fig. 10-1 Wall Sections showing Components and Thermal Ratings

designed and constructed, lend themselves to achieving the needed air tightness.

The incorporation of a continuous air/vapour barrier within the exterior wall assembly, at a location which will minimize the risk of accidental damage to the barrier and at a location where little or no condensation will occur, will help ensure that moisture related problems will not occur during service. The presence of insulation in a building assembly is indeed beneficial, but it can interfere with the ability of the wall assembly to dry if rain water penetrates the assembly or if condensation occurs within the assembly. Masonry cavity walls and masonry veneer walls provide for resistance to rain penetration and readily facilitate drying by incorporating an air space between the exterior wythe and the inner wythe or backing wall (to retard movement of water through to the inner backing wall) by providing flashing and drain holes over support locations and openings to redirect water to the exterior, and through the placement of vent holes in the exterior wythe or veneer to assist in drying the cavity.

Other desirable properties of the building envelope are fire and sound resistance. Masonry walls in general are well known to provide for high sound absorption and fire resistance.

The requirements for environmental separation, including the control of vapour diffusion, air leakage and moisture ingress are contained in Part 5, "Environmental Separation" of the National Building Code of Canada.

A complete and detailed evaluation and treatment of the non-structural properties of cavity and veneer walls is beyond the scope of this textbook. However, a cursory treatment of the main characteristics of the building envelope, i.e. thermal performance, condensation, moisture migration and its prevention is presented in the form of examples.

EXAMPLE 10-1 *The walls shown in Fig. 10.1(a) and (b) are termed a brick veneer/steel stud (BV/SS) wall system and a cavity wall system, respectively. The thermal resistance (RSI) for each component in these wall systems has been tabled adjacent to the Figure. Calculate the **effective** thermal resistance for each wall.*

The effective thermal resistance of a wall may be calculated using the guidelines and tabulated values contained in the National Energy Code for Buildings (NECB) or the ASHRAE Handbook of Fundamentals. In order to better understand the following calculations, the reader should be familiar with the NECB, and especially with the information provided in its Appendices B and C, which present the thermal characteristics of common building assemblies and methods for calculating the effective thermal resistance of building assemblies.

The thermal properties for wall (a) are obtained from Table C.1(a) of the NECB "Properties for Building Materials". The thermal resistance for continuous materials in series are additive:

$$RSI = 0.03 + 0.24 + 0.18 + 0.0732 + (stl.stud + insulation) + 0.0915 + 0.2 + 0.12$$
$$= 0.935 + (stl. stud + insulation)$$

To adjust for thermal bridging by the steel studs (the studs are in parallel with the insulation contained between them): from Table B8 of the NECB, the effective RSI value of the 140 mm insulation (which has a nominal thermal resistance of 3.52 RSI) when placed between 152 mm steel studs located at 406 mm centres is 1.68 (including siding, gypsum board, and sheathing paper). Hence:

(Stl. Stud + Insulation) RSI = 1.68 - 0.11 (siding) - 0.08 (gypsum) - 0.01 (sheathing paper) = 1.48 RSI

Effective RSI = 0.935 + 1.48 = 2.42

For the cavity wall (b) of Fig. 10-1, the effective thermal resistance is obtained using values from Table C1 of the NECB:

Effective RSI = 0.03 + 0.24 + 0.18 + 2.1 + 0.43 + 0.20 + 0.12 = 3.3

This value will increase to 3.86 RSI if the cores of the concrete masonry units are filled with loose fill insulation such as perlite.

EXAMPLE 10-2 *The interior temperature is 21°C, and the exterior temperature is -7° C. For each of the interior relative humidities of 65, 60, 55, 50 , 45 and 40%, determine the dew point location for the wall assemblies shown in Fig. 10-1(a) and (b).*

The temperature profile across the wall assemblies is plotted on Fig. 10.2 (a) and (b) It is obtained by using the relations:

$$T_n = T_1 - \left[R_n / R_t \right] \Delta T$$

$$\Delta T = T_1 - T_0$$

where R_n = total thermal resistance to outer edge of the nth component
             R_t = total thermal resistance of the wall
             T_n = temperature of the outer edge of the nth component
             T_i = inside temperature
             T_0 = outside temperature

For wall (a)
     R_t = 2.42 from Example 10-1
     ΔT = $T_i - T_0 = 21 - (-7) = 28°C$

The temperature at the inside face of the interior drywall is

$$T_n = 21 - [0.32/2.42] (28.0) = 21.0 - 3.707 = 17.3°C$$

Note that at this location $R_n = 0.12 + 0.2 = 0.32$

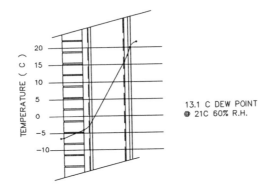

13.1 C DEW POINT
@ 21C 60% R.H.

DEW POINT TABLE

R.H.@21 (%)	DEW PT (C)
65	14.2
60	13.1
55	12.8
50	10.6
45	8.9
40	6.9

WALL TEMPERATURE GRADIENT

a) Steel Stud/Brick Veneer (SS/BV) Wall

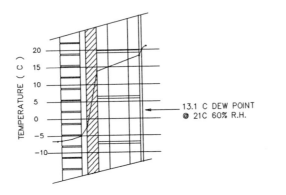

13.1 C DEW POINT
@ 21C 60% R.H.

DEW POINT TABLE

R.H.@21 (%)	DEW PT (C)
65	14.2
60	13.1
55	12.8
50	10.6
45	8.9
40	6.9

WALL TEMPERATURE GRADIENT

b) Cavity Wall

Fig. 10-2 Temperature Gradient Profile & Dew Point for Steel Stud/Brick Veneer and Cavity Wall Assemblies

Similarly the temperature at the exterior face of the exterior drywall is

$$T_n = 21.0 - [1.97/2.42]\,(28.0) = 21.0 - 22.8 = -1.8°C$$

The remaining points needed to plot the temperature gradient through wall (a), and the points needed to plot the temperatures through the wall (b) cross-section, are obtained similarly.

Relative humidity is the ratio of the mass of water vapour being held in air at a given temperature, to the maximum mass of water vapour which the air can hold at that temperature (saturated air). Warm air can hold a larger amount of water in vapour than can cold air. There exists a temperature at which air holding moisture, upon cooling, becomes saturated. At this point, if the temperature is further reduced or if more vapour is added, the excess vapour must condense. This temperature is known as the dew point temperature. It can be located along the temperature profile of the exterior wall of a building using a psychrometric chart (Fig. 10-3) which defines the relationships between air temperature, relative humidity and water vapour content. The chart shows that for an interior temperature of 21°C and relative humidity of 35%, the dew point is approximately 4°C. For the same interior temperature and 40% relative humidity, the dew point temperature shown by Fig. 10-3 is 6.9°C. Other dew point temperatures are listed in Fig. 10-2 and can be obtained in a similar manner. If the interior air is cooled below the dew point temperature condensation will occur on surfaces of wall components below that temperature. Knowing the location of the dew point, the designer is expected to take steps to ensure that interior air which contains moisture does not reach that location. The most effective way to achieve this is by placing an air/vapour barrier on the warm side of the main insulating component of the wall assembly to prevent or retard the passage of air and vapour. There are a number of commercially available air/vapour barriers; the most common ones being thermally fused membranes, peel and stick membranes, and spray-on or trowel-on membranes.

10-3   CAVITY WALLS

Fig. 10-4 shows the cross-section and components of a cavity wall. This wall was earlier defined as a construction of masonry laidup with a continuous cavity between its two adjacent, parallel wythes.
Both composite and non-composite cavity walls can economically accommodate the installation of a continuous plane of insulation, and thus, if desired, can afford very high thermal efficiency. In addition to the inclusion of an air space to retard the transverse movement of moisture from the exterior to inner components and interior space, moisture protection both from the interior and exterior can be enhanced by incorporating an air/vapour barrier membrane on the warm side of the insulation. The membrane serves three functions: as the barrier to air movement and vapour diffusion through the wall, and as the principal resistance to the ingress of precipitation. When the air space within the cavity is relied upon as the primary protection against water

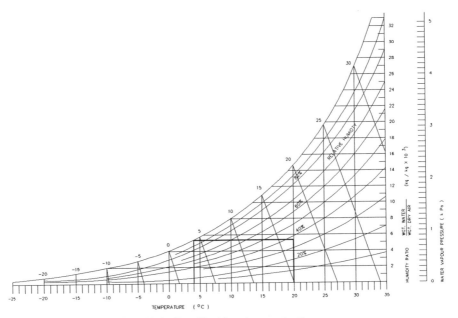

Fig. 10-3 Simplified Psychrometric Chart

penetration (for example, where a membrane is not provided on the outer face of the inner wythe), the CSA A371 construction standard requires that the air space be increased from a recommended width of 25 mm to a minimum width of 40 mm. In cavity walls, the drainage system provided by the air space can be enhanced with flashings and weep holes to redirect water to the exterior, and with wall vents to facilitate drying the air space.

For non-composite cavity walls the main structural design considerations demanded in S304.1 include the following:

a) Gravity loads from roofs, beams, girders, are assumed to act on the wythe closest to the center of the span of the member.

b) Lateral loads acting parallel to the wall are carried (resisted) by the wythe to which they are applied.

c) For lateral load effects, unless otherwise indicated by rational analysis, the cavity wall stiffness shall be taken as the sum of the stiffnesses of the two wythes acting non-compositely, the ties acting as struts, forcing the two wythes into similar curvatures, but transferring no shear across the cavity. Assuming that the interior wythe resists the total lateral load is an acceptable solution.

d) If the backing is assumed to resist the entire lateral load, for flexible interior wythes (see S304.1 Clause 13.3.2), the lateral deflection of the veneer is limited to the span of the interior wythe divided by 600. For this case it is also acceptable to limit the lateral deflection of the interior wythe to its span divided by 720, provided the requirements of S304.1-94, Clause 13.3.3, Notes (1) and (2) are satisfied.

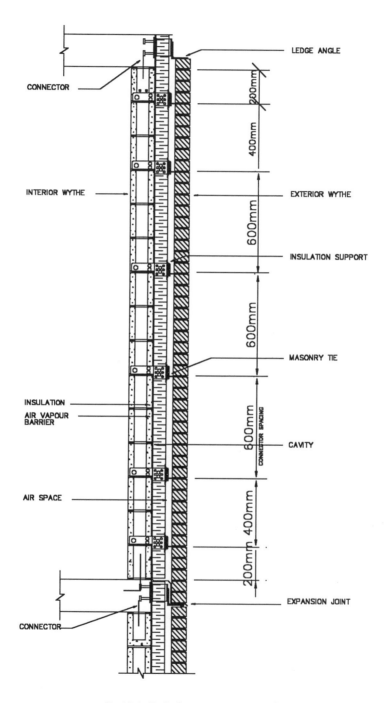

Fig 10-4 Typical Masonry Cavity Wall

Cavity wall design assumes that loads acting perpendicular to the exterior wythe are transferred to the interior wythe by masonry wall ties. The maximum tie spacing recommended by CSA S304.1-94 and A370-94 is 600 mm vertically and 800 mm horizontally. A370-94 states that at openings, ties must be spaced at not more than 300 mm from the edge and at not more than 600 mm apart. Additionally, ties must be placed at a distance not exceeding 300 mm from the top of the wall and not more than 400 mm from the bottom support where the bottom support does not provide adequate lateral resistance. With the design assumption that loads are shared (transferred) between the two wythes of the cavity wall, the design of the wall is carried out using the guidelines developed in earlier chapters.

The reader is expected to be familiar with the guidelines and requirements contained in CSA Standard A370-94 "Connectors for Masonry" and CSA Standard A371 "Masonry Construction for Buildings". Some of the requirements of these standards as they relate to ties, connectors and their performance requirements are introduced in examples 10-3 and 10-4.

Multi-component masonry members acting in composite action are designed using empirical rules in most standards. For example ACI 530-93 states that walls constructed with collar joints filled with mortar are to be designed by limiting the average shear developed in the interface between the wythes and the collar joint to 0.035 MPa. When grout is used the limiting stress is 0.07 MPa. For walls where composite action relies on header units for shear transfer, the limiting shear stress in the header unit is $\sqrt{f'}$, where f'_m is the compressive strength of the header unit.

Clause 11.2.2 of S301.4 refers to the design requirements of composite walls. Traditional composite walls, achieving composite action by using headers or grouted collar joints, are not now commonly used in Canada because of climatic conditions. The design and construction of cavity walls with mechanical ties capable of transferring shear across the cavity (while allowing for the incorporation of insulation and air/vapour barrier within the cavity), has been rapidly gaining acceptance in recent years. The design of these walls requires a rational analysis where the properties of the two wythes and those of the tie are taken into account.

Fig. 10-5 shows a mechanical tie capable of shear transfer. For an insulated composite wall, the shear stresses introduced from movements by temperature difference between the interior and exterior wythes as by well as by the material properties of the wythes, are a function of the tie stiffness, the number and spacing of ties, and the cavity width. These stresses are usually small, and for walls less than 12 metres in height, do not significantly affect the design of the wall.

Moisture expansion of the exterior burned clay wythe, in conjunction with moisture shrinkage of the interior concrete block wythe, will cause compressive stresses within the brick wythe and tensile stresses within the concrete block wythe. The compressive stresses within the brick wythe can be beneficial in reducing cracking and hence moisture penetration, while the small tensile stresses within the block wythe can be accommodated, if required, by incorporating small amounts of vertical reinforcement.

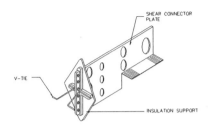

(A) SHEAR CONNECTOR COMPONENTS

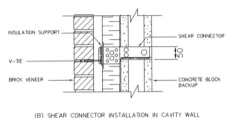

(B) SHEAR CONNECTOR INSTALLATION IN CAVITY WALL

Fig. 10-5 Shear Connected Cavity Wall

Examples of proprietary tie systems used in cavity walls are shown in Figures 10.14 (a), (b), (c). It is strongly recommended that reliable performance data to verify compliance with CSA A370 be obtained by the designer prior to design and construction.

EXAMPLE 10-3 *The wall shown in Fig. 10-4 spans 3,000 mm between supports and is acted upon by a 0.60 kPa wind load. The cavity is 75 mm (including insulation), the interior wythe is constructed with 15 MPa, 190 mm concrete masonry units with Type S mortar and the exterior wythe utilizes 40 MPa, 90 mm burned clay units with Type S mortar. For this wall*

a)   *determine maximum tie load*

b)   *provide a tie layout at a wall section with an opening*

c)   *design the inner wythe*

The properties of the concrete block wythe are (from Table 4-1):

$$A_m = 75.4 \times 10^3 \text{ mm} \quad I_x = 442 \times 10^6 \text{ mm}^4 \text{ and } S_x = 4.7 \times 10^6 \text{ mm}$$
$$f_m' = 9.8 \text{ MPa}$$

The properties of the brick wythe are calculated for a solid clay brick unit:

$$A_m = 90.0 \times 10^3 \text{ mm} \quad I_x = 60.7 \times 10^6 \text{ mm}^4 \text{ and}$$

f'_m = 13.0 MPa

The elastic modulus for both wythes is assumed to be 850 f'_m :

$$\frac{EI_{block}}{EI_{brick}} = \frac{\left(442 \text{ x } 10^6\right)\left(9.8 \text{ x } 850\right)}{\left(60.7 \text{ x } 10^6\right)\left(13 \text{ x } 850\right)} = 5.49 > 2.5$$

Thus the interior block wythe is termed a non-flexible backing by S304.1.

a) Maximum tie load
Assuming that the ties are placed at 600 mm vertical by 800 mm horizontal, the load to be transferred to the block wythe by each tie is

(0.6 m)(0.8 m)(0.6 kPa) = 0.29 kN

and the required compressive/tensile strength of the tie spanning the 75 mm cavity must be

0.29/ϕ = 0.29/0.9 = 0.32 kN

The tie will be embedded into the mortar in both the block wythe and the brick wythe, and the ties must be capable of resisting a pull-out or push-out load and buckling load of

0.29/ϕ = 0.29/0.6 = 0.48 kN

See 8.4.2.1.2 of A370-94 for ϕ factor selection.

b) Tie layout
The interaction between ties and a masonry assembly is affected by the type of units, type of mortar used, tie embedment depth, tie configuration, and the presence or absence of vertical load. The location of the tie along the height of the wall is also a factor in the expected behaviour of the tie. The most critical tie is the one at the top of the wall where the vertical load on the exterior wythe is minimum, and the load on the tie is a maximum. Fig. 10-6 shows the tie layout at a location with openings based on the guidelines provided by S304.1-94 and A370-94.

c) Design of inner wythe
The backing wythe is designed to resist a 0.6 kPa lateral :

$$M_f = p_f L^2 / 8 = 1.5(0.6)(3.0)^2 / 8 = 1.01 \text{ kN - m}$$

Neglecting the weight of the blockwork

$$f = M_f/S_x = 1.01 (10)^6/[4.7(10)^6] = 0.21 \text{ MPa} < \phi f_t = (0.55)(0.45) = 0.25 \text{ MPa}$$

No reinforcement is required. It is, however, good practice to provide reinforcement at each side of openings and at corners and wall ends. Note that the pier section shown between windows in Fig. 10-6 will carry additional loads transferred from the windows.

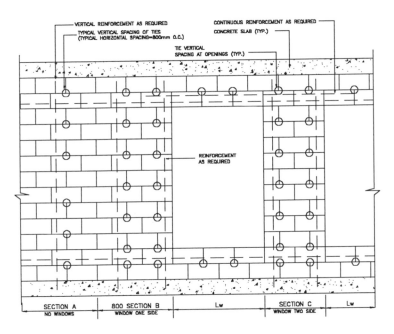

Fig. 10-6 Tie Location at Openings

10-4   MASONRY VENEER

A masonry veneer was defined earlier as a single wythe of masonry uits securely fastened to a backing wall for the purpose of providing ornamentation and protection for inner components but not so bonded or attached as to be considered as exerting common reaction under load.

A masonry veneer is commonly backed by a steel frame system or a wood frame system. Masonry veneer with wood frame backing is normally used in low rise (four storeys or less) residential structures, whereas steel frame backing is used mainly in commercial and high rise residential structures.

Fig. 10-7 shows a section through an exterior wall assembly having a masonry veneer. The components and features of the wall shown in Fig. 10-7 include provisions for accommodating movement and deformations resulting from the structure and from the physical properties of the materials from which the assembly is constructed. Column shortening of concrete frame structures, deflection of beams and slabs, movements due to thermal effects and material properties of the veneer, along with construction tolerances, must be accounted for in the design of exterior non-bearing veneer assemblies, if they are indeed to remain non-loadbearing elements under service.

The properly constructed masonry veneer wall includes many of the components discussed under cavity walls needed to effectively resist air movement and vapour diffusion through the wall, to resist the ingress of precipitation into interior space, and to resist heat loss from the building interior. As with cavity walls, these components or configurations include:

- an air barrier membrane (serves also as vapour barrier and barrier to precipitation; located within the wall where the membrane temperature is above the dew point temperature)
- a drainage system (air space, flashings, vents, weep holes)
- continuous insulation in the cavity space with few thermal bridges; insulation is so placed in the assembly to ensure that the dew point temperature is located to the exterior of the backing wall

The structural design of exterior wall assemblies incorporating a masonry veneer is based on the design requirements in Clause 13 of CSA Standard S304.1:

Loads acting perpendicular to the plane of the veneer are transferred and resisted entirely by the backing system.

When the rigidity EI of the backing system is less than 2.5 times that of the veneer (termed flexible backing), the deflection of the veneer is limited to $L/600$, where L is the height of the structural backing.

When EI of the backing system is not less than 2.5 times that of the veneer, it is acceptable to limit the bending deflection of the structural backing to $L/720$ provided certain ties are used; for these ties, deflection under a 0.45 kN load plus 1/2 of the total free play must not exceed 1.0 mm

For flexible backing, unless otherwise shown by a detailed analysis considering the tie forces before and after cracking of the veneer, all ties should be designed to resist 40% of the lateral load on a vertical line of ties, and not less than double the tributary lateral load on the tie.

The veneer must be a minimum of 75 mm in thickness and must be provided with ties spaced not more than 800 mm apart horizontally and 600 mm apart vertically.

It is recommended that the placement of the ties not be staggered. This is in order to facilitate the placement of the insulation and the air barrier.

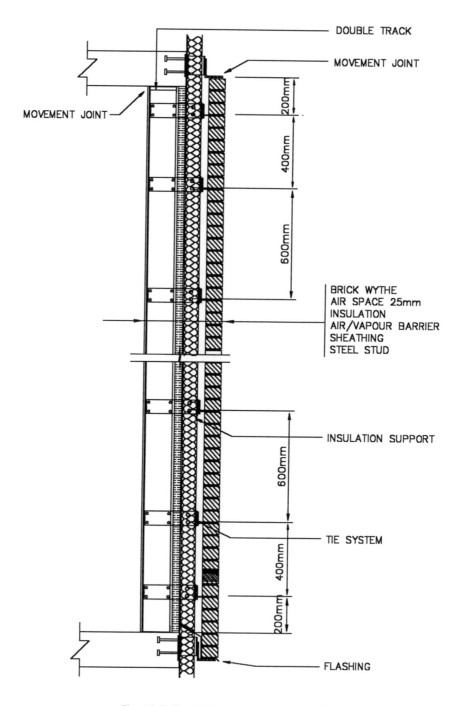

Fig. 10-7 Typical Masonry Veneered Wall

EXAMPLE 10-4 *The exterior wall of an 8-storey apartment building consists of steel stud framing finished with a burned clay (brick) veneer. A typical framing elevation incorporating an opening is shown in Fig. 10-8. Design the wall assembly based on the following assumptions: the steel stud spacing is 400 mm and the storey height is 2800 mm floor to floor; sheathing on both sides of studs provides for adequate torsional restraint for loads not applied through the shear center of the stud; the cavity width is 75 mm, the window opening is 1600 x 1800 mm, and the sill height is 400 mm. The 1 in 10 year design wind load is 1.0 kPa and the 1 in 30 year design wind load is 1.20 kPa . The design must satisfy the requirements of Clause 13 of CSA S304.1.*
Selection of a steel stud for the full height wall

The clear height is 2800 - 200 = 2600 mm. The spacing of the steel studs is 400 mm, and the framing is designed for strength using the 1 in 30 year design wind load of 1.20 kPa, and for deflection using the 1 in 10 year design wind load of 1.0 kPa (4.1.8.1(4) of the NBC). The steel framing (structural backing) is designed to resist the entire lateral load applied to the wall (Clause 13.3.1 of S304.1).

Clause 13.3.3 of CSA S304.1 states that the *veneer* shall not deflect more than $L/600$ where L is the unsupported height of the structural backing. Furthermore, Notes 1 to 3 allow the designer to use $L/720$ as the allowable deflection of the framing system and conveniently neglect secondary effects such as tie deformation and track deflection, provided that tie deflection due to one half of the total mechanical play plus deflection under a tension or compression load of 0.45 kN does not exceed 1.0 mm..

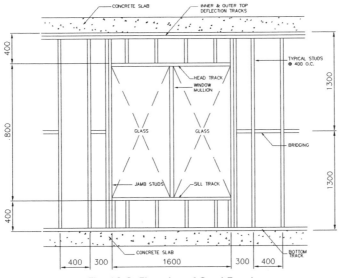

Fig. 10-8 Elevation of Steel Framing

For a clear span of 2600 mm the allowable deflection is:

$$\delta = \delta = \frac{L}{720} = \frac{260}{720} = 3.61 \text{mm}$$

The required moment of inertia for one stud is:

$$I = \frac{5wL^4}{384E\delta} = \frac{(5)(0.4 \times 1.0)(2600^4)}{(384)(2.0 \times 10^5)(3.61)} = 0.33 \times 10^6 \text{ mm}^4$$

From the manufacturer's product literature (Table 10-1), a 92 mm x 16 gauge steel stud has a moment of inertia of 0.372×10^6 mm^4. This stud will deflect 3.20 mm under service load. Use 92 mm x 16 gauge (1.52 mm thick) steel studs.

Incorporating ties capable of transferring shear across the cavity will couple the masonry veneer to the steel backing wall, resulting in bending strength and stiffness which are more than the sum of the individual values. The use of shear connectors designed by rational analysis (S304.1-94, Clauses 8.1.3, 8.3.4.1 and 11.2.2) will provide for meeting the strength and deflection guidelines of S304.1-94 with reduced steel framing stiffness requirements (stud width, thickness and spacing).

From manufacturers product literature (Table 10-1), using a 92 mm x 16 gauge stud, the allowable exterior reaction for a 25 mm bearing length is P = 2.47 kN, and thus no web stiffening is required; that is:

$$2.47 \text{ kN} > (2.6/2)(0.4)(1.0)(1.5) = 0.8 \text{ kN}$$

Window framing

The window opening is shown in Figure 10-8. The wind load acting on the glass is assumed to be transferred to the supporting members. For simplicity it is assumed that only full height studs resist lateral loads. The factored load acting on the jamb stud is

$$\begin{aligned} W_x &= [0.5\,(0.3)(1.20) + (0.5)(1.6)(1.20)]\,1.5 \\ &= (0.18 + 0.96)\,(1.5) \\ &= 1.71 \text{ kN/m} \end{aligned}$$

Factored bending moment
$$M_f = 1.71\,(2.6)^2/8 = 1.44 \text{ kN-m.}$$

Required stiffness for 3.61 mm allowable deflection, where w is the 1 in 10 year service load:

$$\begin{aligned} I &= 5wL^4/(384E\delta) \\ &= 5(1.71/1.5)(1.0/1.2)(2600)^4/[384(200)(10)^3(3.61)] = 0.78\,(10)^6 \text{ mm}^4 \end{aligned}$$

A built-up section is required: use 2 - 92 mm wide by 1.52 mm thick steel studs and a 16 gauge track arranged as shown in Fig. 10-9. These have a combined moment of inertia of 1.116×10^6 mm^4.

Table 10-1 Stud Section Properties*

Stud Designation	A (mm)	B (mm)	C (mm)	D (mm)	E (mm)	Thickness T (mm)	Weight Per Metre (kg)	P_2 (kN)	Perforated Properties Cross Sectional Area (mm²)	Local Buckling Factor Q	I_x(mm⁴) ×10⁶	S_x(mm³)	R_x (mm)	Resisting Moment Max.	P_1 (kN)
92 x 20 ga.	92.1	34.9	9.5	38.1	101.6	0.91	1.25	0.74	124.52	0.63	0.204	4424.5	40.4	0.628	1.45
92 x 18 ga.	92.1	41.3	12.7	38.1	101.6	1.22	1.82	1.30	185.82	0.83	0.305	6620.3	40.4	0.942	3.41
92 x 16 ga.	92.1	41.3	12.7	38.1	101.6	1.52	2.25	2.47	229.05	0.80	0.372	8078.8	40.4	1.74	6.64
92 x 14 ga.	92.1	41.3	12.7	38.1	101.6	1.91	2.75	3.70	280.02	0.89	0.450	9766.7	40.1	2.105	11.59
102 x 20 ga.	101.6	41.3	12.7	38.1	101.6	0.91	1.44	0.71	150.33	0.71	0.296	5817.4	44.5	0.828	1.51
102 x 18 ga.	101.6	41.3	12.7	38.1	101.6	1.22	1.90	1.27	197.43	0.80	0.385	7570.8	44.2	1.078	3.57
102 x 16 ga.	101.6	41.3	12.7	38.1	101.6	1.52	2.35	2.43	243.24	0.77	0.470	9242.3	43.9	1.992	6.96
102 x 14 ga.	101.6	41.3	12.7	38.1	101.6	1.91	2.90	3.66	298.08	0.86	0.569	11192.3	43.7	2.413	12.85
152 x 20 ga.	152.4	34.9	9.5	63.5	114.3	0.91	1.68	0.00	155.49	0.59	0.665	8734.3	65.5	1.169	1.29
152 x 18 ga.	152.4	41.3	12.7	63.5	114.3	1.22	2.40	1.10	227.76	0.70	0.989	12978.5	66.0	1.846	3.07
152 x 16 ga.	152.4	41.3	12.7	63.5	114.3	1.52	2.96	2.22	280.66	0.66	1.212	15895.4	65.8	3.426	5.99
152 x 14 ga.	152.4	41.3	12.7	63.5	114.3	1.91	3.66	3.44	345.18	0.74	1.476	19369.4	65.5	4.173	11.70
203 x 18 ga.	203.2	41.3	12.7	63.5	114.3	1.22	2.89	0.00	289.69	0.63	2.008	19762.7	83.3	2.603	2.59
203 x 16 ga.	203.2	41.3	12.7	63.5	114.3	1.52	3.57	2.00	358.09	0.58	2.467	24269.1	83.1	5.075	5.07
203 x 14 ga.	203.2	41.3	12.7	63.5	114.3	1.91	4.42	3.23	441.96	0.60	3.016	29693.2	82.6	6.385	9.95

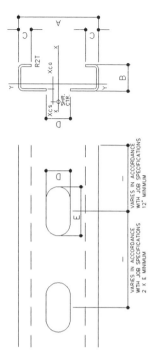

Notes:
1. See general notes.
2. Material: 0.91 mm and 1.22 mm ASTM A446 grade A (228 MPa)
   1.52 mm and 1.91 mm ASTM A446 grade A (345 MPa)
3. P_1 = allowable exterior reaction shear governs.
   P_2 = allowable exterior reaction web crippling governs with
   25.4 mm bearing length.

* Adopted from the literature of Bailey Steel Products

From Table 10-1 the resisting moment of the section is:
$$3 \ (1.74 \text{ kN}) = 5.22 \text{ kN-m} > 1.44 \text{ kN-m}$$

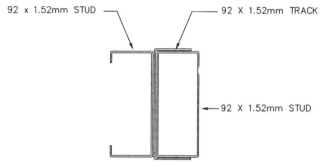

Fig. 10-9 Built Up Member

Design of sill head section
The factored load acting on the sill and head section is, approximating for the load contribution from the window:
$$W_f = [0.2(\ 1.0) + 0.25(\ 1.80)(\ 1.0)]\ 1.5 = [(0.2 + 0.45)(1.5)] = 0.975 \text{ kN/m}$$
The allowable deflection is $1600/720 = 2.22$ mm and the required moment of inertia of the sill and head is, where w is 1 the in 10 year service load:
$$I = 5wL^4/(384E\delta)$$
$$= 5(.975/1.5)(1600)^4/[384(200)(10)^3(2.22)] = 0.125 \times (10)^6 \text{ mm}^4$$
From Table 10-1, a single 18 gauge (1.22 mm) stud may be used for the construction of the head and still. Although the required moment of inertia is less than that provided by a 92 x 20 gauge stud, clause 8.5.1 of CSA A370 recommends a minimum stud thickness of 1.22 mm.

It is left to the reader to show that deflection, and not strength, governs the selection of stud cross-section.

Design of connection of the metal framing to the main structure
In order to accommodate the expected slab deflection a connection of the type shown in Fig. 10-10 (A), (B), (C) should be used. For this example type (A) is chosen. Referring to Fig. 10-10, the required space between the outer and inner track is assumed to be 20 mm (12 mm slab deflection and 8 mm tolerance).

Assuming that the inner track distributes the load uniformly to the outer track, the factored load to be used for strength design is:
$$P = 2.6(1.5)(1.2)(1/2) = 2.34 \text{ kN/m} = 2.34 \text{ N/mm}$$
The factored moment resulting from the reaction of the stud 0n the outer track is
$$M_f = 45 \times 2.34 = 105.30 \text{ N-mm/mm}$$
Note that 45 mm is the depth of the outer track.

Try a 1.52 mm (16 gauge) thick outer track, where $f_y = 345$ MPa;
$$M_r = 0.85 \ (bt^2/6) \ f_y = 0.85(1.52)^2(345)/6 = 112.9 \text{ N-mm/mm} > M_f$$

Try a 1.52 mm (16 gauge) thick outer track, where f_y = 345 MPa;
$$M_r = 0.85 \, (bt^2/6) \, f_y = 0.85(1.52)^2(345)/6 = 112.9 \text{ N-mm/mm} > M_f$$

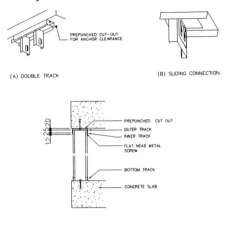

(A) DOUBLE TRACK   (B) SLIDING CONNECTION

(C) STRUCTURAL CONNECTION TO CONCRETE SLAB

Fig. 10-10 Details of Steel Structural Wall Assembly

Check deflection of outer track

    The unfactored reaction used to calculate deflection under the action of a 1.0 kPa wind load is:
$$P_f = 1.0 \, (2.6/2) = 1.3 \text{ kN/m}$$

    In order to maintain a total deflection of 3.61 mm, the outer track deflection must be limited to 3.61 - 3.2 = 0.4 mm at mid span of the vertical studs or 0.8 mm at the track location (rigid translation; similar triangles). Note that 3.2 mm is the calculated deflection for the 92 mm x 16 gauge full height stud chosen. The deflection of the upper track is calculated using the deflected shape shown in Fig. 10-11.

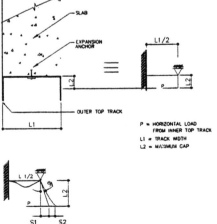

P = HORIZONTAL LOAD FROM INNER TOP TRACK
L1 = TRACK WIDTH
L2 = MAXIMUM GAP

Fig. 10-11 Deformation of Outer Track in a Double Track Connection

$$\delta = \delta_1 + \delta_2 = \frac{P}{EI}\left[\frac{L_2^2 L_1}{8} + \frac{L_2^3}{3}\right] = 0.8\text{mm}$$

For
$$\begin{aligned}
P &= 1.3 \text{ N/mm} \\
L_1 &= 92 \text{ mm} \\
L_2 &= 45 \text{ mm} \\
E &= 200{,}000 \text{ MPa}
\end{aligned}$$

$$0.8 = \frac{1.3}{200{,}000 I}\left[\frac{45^2 \times 92}{8} + \frac{45^3}{3}\right]$$

$$(0.8)(200{,}000)I = 1.30[23{,}287 + 30{,}375]$$

$$I = 0.436\text{mm}^4 / \text{mm}$$

$$I = \frac{bt^3}{12} \text{ for } b = 1\text{mm and } I = 0.436\text{mm}^4$$

$$t = \sqrt[3]{12 \times 0.436} = 1.735\text{mm}$$

From Table 10-1, a 92 x 14 gauge track (1.91 mm thick) is chosen. The moment of inertia of this section is $0.58 \text{ mm}^4/\text{mm} > 0.436 \text{ mm}^4/\text{mm}$.

The system for accommodating deflection shown in Fig. 10-10 (B) eliminates the need for double track and provides for a stiffer connection.

The design of masonry ties

The maximum tie spacing in the vertical direction permitted by S304.1 is 600 mm. Clause 6.1.2 of CSA Standard A370-94 "Connectors for Masonry" requires ties to be located not more than 300 mm from the edge of an opening. Clause 6.1.3 of the CSA A370 requires that ties be placed not lower than 300 mm from the top of the wall and not higher than 400 mm from a bearing support not having adequate lateral resistance. Fig. 10-12 shows tie locations which satisfy these requirements, and Fig. 10-13 illustrates a configuration for a masonry tie fastened to a metal stud and positioned in the mortar joint.

Brick veneer steel stud wall systems are invariably flexible backing systems by S304. Where a flexible backing is used, Clause 13.2.3 of S304.1 requires ties to be designed for 40% of the tributary lateral load on one vertical line of ties but not less than double the tributary lateral load on the tie. Thus the factored load per tie is the greater of:

$$P_{fe} = 1.5 \ (0.4)(0.4)(2.6)(1.2) = 0.75 \text{ kN}$$
$$P_{fe} = 1.5 \ (2.0)(0.4)(0.6)(1.2) = 0.864 \text{ kN}$$

The factored resistance of a tie is obtained by applying the resistance ϕ factor given by Clause 8.4.2.1.2 of A370 as follows

ϕ = 0.9 for material failure of the metal components of the tie

ϕ = 0.6 for embedment failure or fastener failure

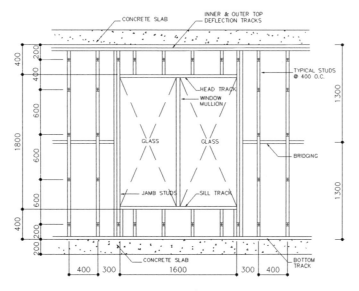

Fig. 10-12 Tie locations

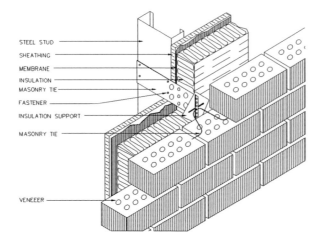

Fig. 10-13 Masonry Tie in Wall Assembly

Choose a tie with ultimate material strength of

$$0.864/\phi = 0.864/0.9 = 0.96 \text{ kN}$$

and having an ultimate mortar pullout/push-through strength, ultimate fastener to stud strength, and buckling strength greater than

$$0.864/\phi = 0.864/0.6 = 1.44 \text{ kN}$$

Additionally, clause 13.3.3 Note (2)(b) of S304.1 requires that tie deflection due to one half of the total mechanical play plus a tension or compression load of 0.45 kN not exceed 1.0 mm.

Examples of proprietary tie systems used in masonry veneer wall systems are shown in Figures 10.14 (a), (b), (c). It is strongly recommended that reliable performance data to verify compliance with CSA A370 be obtained by the designer prior to design and construction.

EXAMPLE 10-5. *Design a steel stud/brick veneer wall assembly for a commercial structure located in an earthquake zone area having a zonal velocity ratio of 0.30. The unit weight of the veneer is 2.4 kN/m² and the backing assembly is assumed to weigh 0.9 kN/m².*

The load imposed on the veneer during an earthquake is calculated using the requirements of the National Building Code of Canada 1995 Section 4.1.9.1(15) as follows:

$$V_p = vIS_p W_p$$

where v = zonal velocity ratio

I = seismic importance factor of the stucture

= 1.5 for post disaster structures

= 1.3 for schools

= 1.0 for all others

S_p = horizontal force factor for part or portion of a building and its anchorage (see Table 7-5)

= 5.0 for masonry veneer connecting

= 15.0 for non-ductile connections

= 1.5 for all exterior and interior walls

W_p = weight of a part or portion of a structure

For this example

$$V_p = vI S_p W_p$$
$$= 0.3 \, (1.0)(5.0)(2.4) = 3.60 \text{ kN/m}^2$$

Space ties at 600 mm vertical by 400 mm horizontal. The load per tie is

$$0.6 \, (0.4)(3.60) = 0.864 \text{ kN}$$

Install ties having an ultimate material strength of:

$$0.864/\phi = 0.864 = 0.960 \text{ kN}$$

and pullout/fastener/buckling strength from joints and fasteners of
$$0.864/\phi = 0.864/0.6 = 1.44 \text{ kN}$$

The ties must satisfy all other design requirements discussed herein and stated in CSA A370. The designer may choose to decrease spacing of ties in order to reduce the required ultimate strength.

Design of steel stud framing

$$V_p = vIS_pW_p = (0.3)(1.0)(1.5)(3.3) = 1.485 \text{ kN/m}^2$$

Note that the weight of the steel stud framing and sheathing is now added to the overall weight of the brick veneer. The framing is designed to resist a 1.485 kN/m² load using the procedures developed earlier.

Design of connections

$$V_p = vIS_pW_p = (0.3)(1.0)(15)(3.3) = 14.85 \text{ kN/m}^2$$

The reaction force per metre is $14.85(2.6)(1/2) = 19.30$ kN/m

The upper and lower track is fastened to the main structure by means of drilled-in inserts. Assuming a fastener spacing of 400 mm then the required strength of this connection is:

$$(19.30)(0.4)/\phi = (19.30)(0.4)/0.6 = 12.86 \text{ kN per fastener.}$$

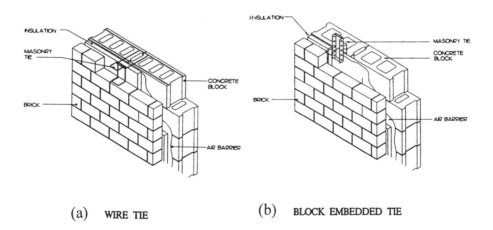

(a) WIRE TIE   (b) BLOCK EMBEDDED TIE

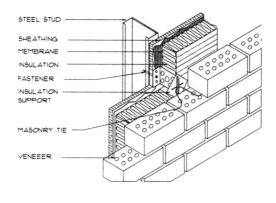

(c)   SURFACE MOUNTED TIE

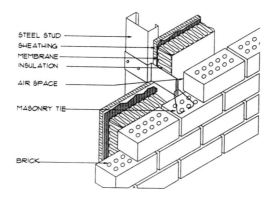

(d)   WRAP AROUND STUD TIE

Fig. 10-14   Some Propietary Tie Systems

CHAPTER 11

MASONRY DETAILS

11-1 INTRODUCTION

There are three components essential to the successful production of a building: design, detailing and construction, all of which must be of high quality. Without proper architectural design the building will not have the humanistic qualities of function and aesthetics important to the user and the public; proper structural design is essential to safety and durability; appropriate materials and details must be selected and effectively shown and described on construction drawings to avoid irritating and expensive repair and retrofit; and the designer must inspect construction regularly to ensure that the building meets the intent of the design - and all within the constraints imposed by the client's purse. If one or more of the three components falls below an acceptable standard, there will be problems, the severity of which will depend on the particular deficiencies.

The preceding chapters have been concerned largely with ensuring an understanding of the structural behaviour of masonry under load, the purpose, of course, being design by rational, calculable procedures for safe resistance to load. Additional discussion on veneer and cavity walls explained some of the principles of building science essential to design for function and durability. For the most part, structural designers have a reasonable understanding of the details required to satisfy structural requirements, but all too often are unfamiliar with details that ensure the integrity of the building envelope.

The purpose of this chapter is to provide the designer, whether structural or architectural, with some examples of the type of detailing required for good quality masonry. Since buildings provide protection from the weather, good detailing of exterior walls in regions of climatic extremes becomes especially important. The chapter illustrates a number of masonry details for single-wythe walls and block walls with brick veneer with accompanying explanations. They are a few that have been extracted from the much more thorough *State-of-the-Art Details for Masonry Construction* prepared by the *Canadian Masonry Research Institute* in Edmonton, a publication available (also on diskette in AutoCAD) from that organization. Note that although the details for walls with veneers show shear-connector ties between the veneer and back-up wall, other conventional ties may be used.

For the most part the details are for *exterior* walls of buildings, since it is there that the most serious problems normally become evident. In any case, if the designer is familiar with good details for exterior walls, those required for interior walls, being simpler, are relatively easy to devise. The details show how masonry supports other structural components such as floor and roof joists, and how masonry in turn is supported. Since exterior walls are featured, the placement of insulation for energy efficiency is important, as is the prevention of moisture migration, either in or out, through the wall system. Rainwater entering the building is obviously undesirable. In a cold climate such as that in Canada, moisture-laden vapour tends to migrate outwards in the winter, and condensation of moisture in the wall must be prevented to minimize subsequent freeze/thaw deterioration or corrosion of metal components.

The reader is expected to have a sufficient knowledge of construction to read and understand the details, and to appreciate that certain information peripheral to masonry may not be shown: for example, if masonry is shown supported by concrete without reinforcement, this does *not* mean that the concrete is unreinforced! Nevertheless, some terms may be unfamiliar to the novice. *Air/vapour barrier* (or air barrier) is a highly flexible, durable and impervious material, such as polythene, acting as an effective barrier to the passage of air and water vapour. *Flashing* is a continuous strip of durable and relatively flexible material located at the bottom of a wall (or section of wall) to collect and divert water out of the wall system. *Weep holes* are openings provided in the head (vertical) joints of the veneer, directly above the flashing, to allow any accumulated water behind the veneer to escape. Weep holes also act as *vents* to equalize air pressures inside and outside of the veneer. Although masonry veneer at the foundation level can be supported directly on the grade beam or foundation wall, it may also be supported on continuous horizontal steel *shelf angles* (sometimes referred to as ledge angles). In a multi-storey building the veneer is usually supported on shelf angles at each floor level above the third floor. This is to allow for the different expansion and contraction characteristics of the veneer and the masonry backing wall. For example, clay bricks in a veneer, having been fired in a kiln, tend to take on some atmospheric moisture and expand with time, whereas concrete blocks, having been moist-cured, tend to shrink as they dry. Also, since the two wythes may be at different temperatures, some differential thermal expansion and contraction is to be expected. To alleviate potential stress build-up, soft (that is, easily compressible) joints, rather than hard mortar joints are provided at the top of each section of veneer, just below the next shelf angle above. These principles are illustrated in the details.

Section 11-2 illustrates masonry-to-foundation support details; Section 11-3 shows some typical details for single-wythe exterior walls; Section 11-4 provides details for two-wythe (veneer plus back-up) walls; and Section 11-5 illustrates movement joints.

11-2   MASONRY TO FOUNDATION SUPPORT DETAILS

Figs. 11-1 and 11-2 show a concrete block wall with a brick veneer supported on a reinforced concrete foundation, the former having a structural floor slab while the latter has a ground floor slab-on-grade. To be noted here are the placement of insulation between the block wythe and the veneer and theair/ vapour barrier inside the insulation, and the shelf angle, flashing and weep holes. Not shown are the reinforcement in the foundation or any dowels extending from the foundation to match vertical reinforcement in the wall.

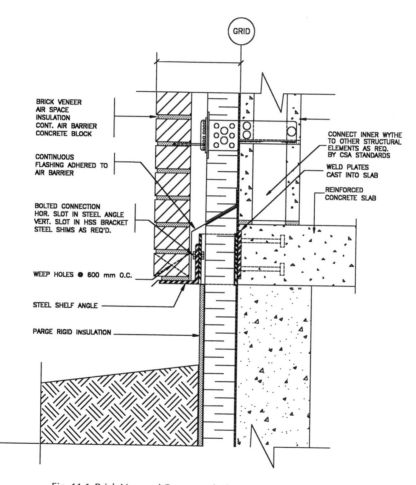

GRID

BRICK VENEER
AIR SPACE
INSULATION
CONT. AIR BARRIER
CONCRETE BLOCK

CONTINUOUS
FLASHING ADHERED TO
AIR BARRIER

BOLTED CONNECTION
HOR. SLOT IN STEEL ANGLE
VERT. SLOT IN HSS BRACKET
STEEL SHIMS AS REQ'D.

WEEP HOLES @ 600 mm O.C.

STEEL SHELF ANGLE

PARGE RIGID INSULATION

CONNECT INNER WYTHE
TO OTHER STRUCTURAL
ELEMENTS AS REQ.
BY CSA STANDARDS

WELD PLATES
CAST INTO SLAB

REINFORCED
CONCRETE SLAB

Fig. 11-1 Brick Veneer / Concrete Block Detail at Foundation

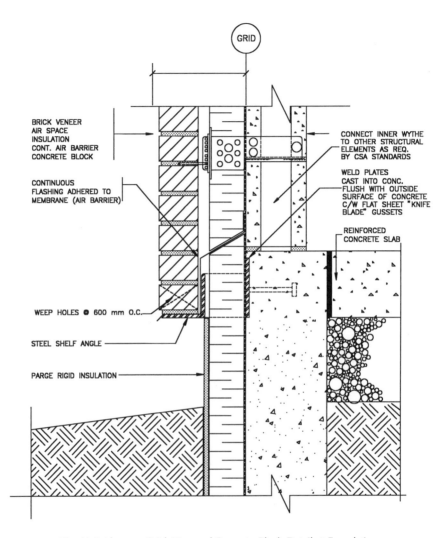

BRICK VENEER
AIR SPACE
INSULATION
CONT. AIR BARRIER
CONCRETE BLOCK

CONTINUOUS
FLASHING ADHERED TO
MEMBRANE (AIR BARRIER)

WEEP HOLES @ 600 mm O.C.

STEEL SHELF ANGLE

PARGE RIGID INSULATION

CONNECT INNER WYTHE
TO OTHER STRUCTURAL
ELEMENTS AS REQ.
BY CSA STANDARDS

WELD PLATES
CAST INTO CONC.
FLUSH WITH OUTSIDE
SURFACE OF CONCRETE
C/W FLAT SHEET "KNIFE
BLADE" GUSSETS

REINFORCED
CONCRETE SLAB

GRID

Fig. 11-2 Alternate Brick Veneer / Concrete Block Detail at Foundation

Fig. 11-3 shows an appropriate detail of the foundation support for a single-wythe load-bearing wall. Note the insulation on the inside of the wall, and the location of the air/vapour barrier on the inside of the insulation to prevent moisture condensation in the insulation.

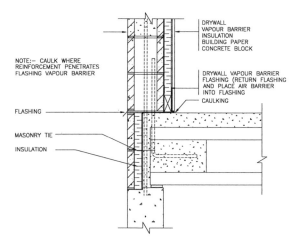

Fig. 11-3 Masonry Wall Flashing Above Floor Slab

11-3   SINGLE WYTHE MASONRY WALL DETAILS

Fig. 11.4 shows a precast concrete hollow core slab supported on a concrete masonry bearing wall. Note the presence of the bond beam providing a horizontal tension tie at the general floor level. The steel dowel is normally provided in the grout keys between adjacent hollow core slabs, and will be longer than the bar shown. The hollow core slabs may not have the concrete topping shown but instead may receive a levelling coat of grout. One additional comment: although the dowel from the floor extends vertically into the wall, the anchorage is not likely to be able to develop the full resistance of the bar; generally, though, it will not be required to do so.

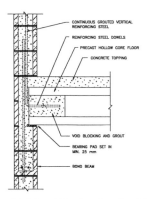

Fig. 11-4 Load Bearing Exterior Wall

Figs. 11-5 and 11-6 show the bearing details for wood and open-web steel joist floors, respectively. Note again the bond beam.

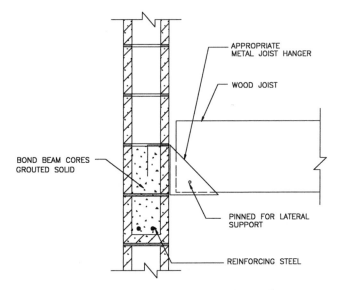

Fig. 11-5 Load Bearing Masonry Wall With Wood Joists

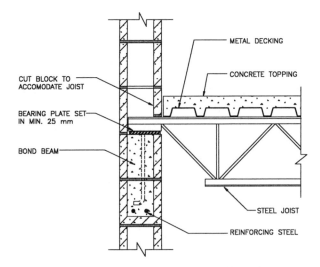

Fig. 11-6 Load Bearing Masonry Wall With Steel Joists

Figs. 11-7 and 11-8 show the details of a balcony wing wall extending out from a load-bearing interior wall. The vertical control joint permits differential vertical movement between the inside and outside walls, but because of the heat bridge, insulation is shown on both sides of the interior wall. Also to be noted are the steel plates placed above and below the balcony slabs to prevent horizontal movement of the slabs from splitting the block. The horizontal dowels in the balcony slabs will normally be longer than shown.

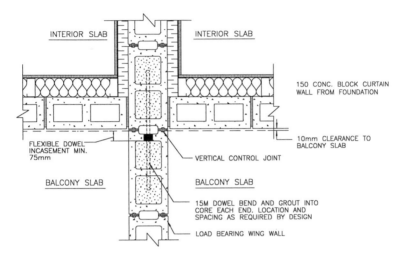

Fig. 11-7 Balcony Wing Wall Plan Detail

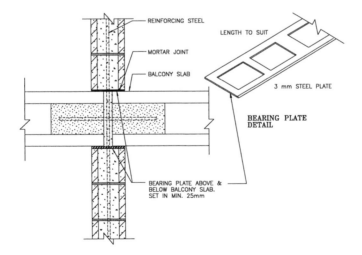

Fig. 11-8 Balcony Wing Wall Section

Fig. 11-9 shows the support for a precast concrete hollow core roof. To be noted are the dowel from the slab to wall (which will normally extend further into the slab) and the reinforcement and grouting of the masonry parapet.

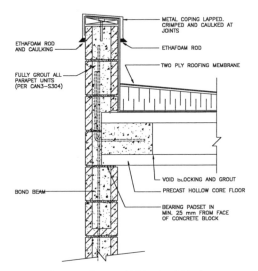

ETHAFOAM ROD
AND CAULKING

FULLY GROUT ALL
PARAPET UNITS
(PER CAN3–S304)

BOND BEAM

METAL COPING LAPPED.
CRIMPED AND CAULKED AT
JOINTS

ETHAFOAM ROD

TWO PLY ROOFING MEMBRANE

VOID BLOCKING AND GROUT
PRECAST HOLLOW CORE FLOOR

BEARING PADSET IN
MIN. 25 mm FROM FACE
OF CONCRETE BLOCK

Fig. 11-9 Parapet With Metal Coping

Fig. 11-10 shows the connection between a precast concrete hollow core slab to a non-load-bearing exterior wall. A Z-type bar is grouted into the slab and also into the wall to carry lateral wind or seismic loads. This being a single-wythe wall, the air/vapour barrier and insulation are on the inside of the block wythe.

Fig. 11-11 shows the bearing of precast concrete hollow core floor slabs on an interior masonry wall. The horizontal reinforcing dowels shown in the floor are normally placed in the grout key between the slabs and longer than shown. If concrete topping is present, as shown, reinforcement can be placed in the topping to provide a substantial tie across the bearing wall. To be noted here is that although it is simple to show the wall below grouted, it is not so simple in practice. The problem here is that the contractor finds it convenient to grout the wall *after* the floor slabs have been placed. A glance at the figure shows there is very little room between the slabs for thorough grouting, and careful inspection is clearly warranted.

11-4   TWO-WYTHE MASONRY WALL DETAILS

Fig. 11-12 shows the details of connection between block wall, reinforced concrete floor and brick veneer. To be noted here are the location of insulation and

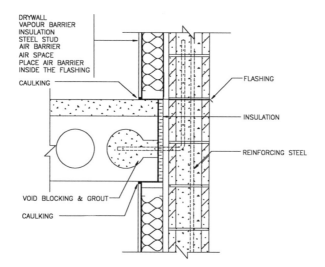

DRYWALL
VAPOUR BARRIER
INSULATION
STEEL STUD
AIR BARRIER
AIR SPACE
PLACE AIR BARRIER
INSIDE THE FLASHING

CAULKING

FLASHING

INSULATION

REINFORCING STEEL

VOID BLOCKING & GROUT

CAULKING

Fig. 11-10 Non-Load Bearing Exterior Wall

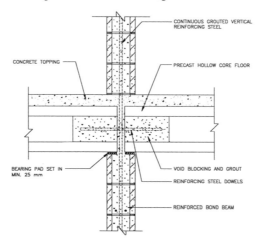

CONTINUOUS GROUTED VERTICAL
REINFORCING STEEL

CONCRETE TOPPING

PRECAST HOLLOW CORE FLOOR

BEARING PAD SET IN
MIN. 25 mm

VOID BLOCKING AND GROUT

REINFORCING STEEL DOWELS

REINFORCED BOND BEAM

Fig. 11-11 Load Bearing Interior Wall

air/vapour barrier, shelf angle support, flashing and weep holes, and the compressible joint immediately beneath the shelf angle.

Figs. 11-13 and 11-14 show the recommended air/vapour barrier detail for the connection shown in Fig. 11-12. If the masonry wythe beneath the slab is an infill panel, there is likely to be a soft joint between the top of the masonry and the underside of the reinforced concrete. In that case, provision should be made in the air/vapour barrier for some differential movement.

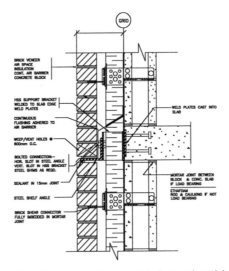

Fig. 11-12 Brick Veneer / Concrete Block Detail at Slab Edge

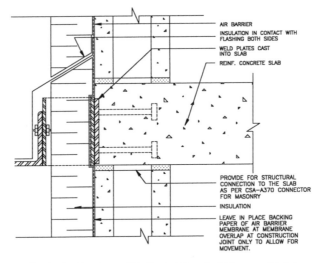

Fig. 11-13 Membrane (Air Barrier) Detail at Movement Joint

Fig. 11-15 shows the recommended detail for a low masonry parapet. Note that the roof membrane is continued *over* the parapet and lapped with and sealed to the wall air barrier. Also note the reinforcing dowel from the concrete slab into the parapet block, with accompanying grouting. A bond beam would normally be provided in the block wall below the slab, but in this instance the slab, being reinforced, may be used in place of a bond beam. If the structural roof system were of the joist type, the detail would be similar, except that a bond beam would be required, with a vertical bar extending from the bond beam into the parapet.

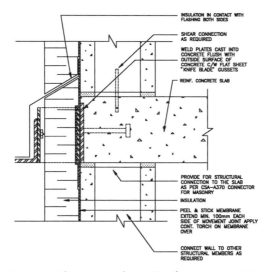

INSULATION IN CONTACT WITH FLASHING BOTH SIDES

SHEAR CONNECTION AS REQUIRED

WELD PLATES CAST INTO CONCRETE FLUSH WITH OUTSIDE SURFACE OF CONCRETE C/W FLAT SHEET "KNIFE BLADE" GUSSETS

REINF. CONCRETE SLAB

PROVIDE FOR STRUCTURAL CONNECTION TO THE SLAB AS PER CSA–A370 CONNECTOR FOR MASONRY

INSULATION

PEEL & STICK MEMBRANE EXTEND MIN. 100mm EACH SIDE OF MOVEMENT JOINT APPLY CONT. TORCH ON MEMBRANE OVER

CONNECT WALL TO OTHER STRUCTURAL MEMBERS AS REQUIRED

Fig. 11-14 Alternate Membrane Detail at Movement Joint

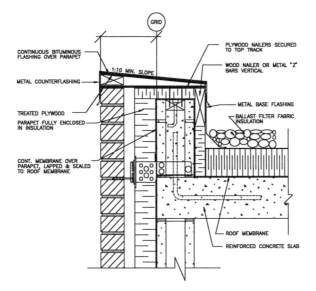

GRID

CONTINUOUS BITUMINOUS FLASHING OVER PARAPET

PLYWOOD NAILERS SECURED TO TOP TRACK

WOOD NAILER OR METAL "Z" BARS VERTICAL

1:10 MIN. SLOPE

METAL COUNTERFLASHING

METAL BASE FLASHING

BALLAST FILTER FABRIC INSULATION

TREATED PLYWOOD

PARAPET FULLY ENCLOSED IN INSULATION

CONT. MEMBRANE OVER PARAPET, LAPPED & SEALED TO ROOF MEMBRANE

ROOF MEMBRANE

REINFORCED CONCRETE SLAB

Fig. 11-15 Brick Veneer / Concrete Block Detail of Low Parapet W/ Protected Membrane Roof

Fig. 11-16 shows an appropriate detail at a high parapet.   Note the roof membrane below the roof insulation and continued over the slab to lap with the wall membrane, where it should be sealed.   If the roof structure were joists the vertical bars in the parapet wall would be anchored in the bond beam.

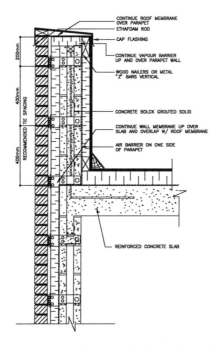

Fig. 11-16 Brick Veneer / Concrete Block Detail at High Parapet

11-5   MOVEMENT JOINTS

The joints featured in Figs. 11-17 and 11-18 are commonly referred to as *expansion* joints or *control* joints.   They run vertically in the masonry wall, their purpose being to allow relatively unrestrained horizontal expansion and contraction.   Clay brick expands with time and concrete block shrinks to some extent, so the terms *control* or *movement* are more representative of their function.   These joints extend right through the wythe, or through both wythes if there is a veneer.   As shown in Fig. 11-17, the joints are placed close to the corners of buildings to prevent movements of abutting walls from causing local cracking and spalling, and they should also be placed no further apart than about eight metres.   There should also be control joints at points of natural weakness in the wall: for example, in the vicinity of door and window openings.

Fig. 11-18 shows two acceptable movement/control joints.   Note that the joint allows in-plane movement but the joint material may be required to act as a shear key, inhibiting differential out-of-plane movement between the two sides of the joint. Note also that one vertical core on each side of the joints is reinforced and grouted.

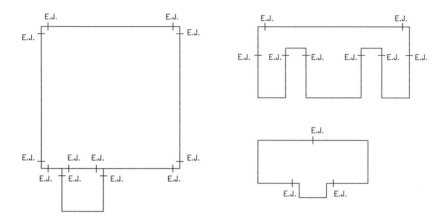

Fig. 11-17 Typical Expansion Joint Placement (will vary with size of building)

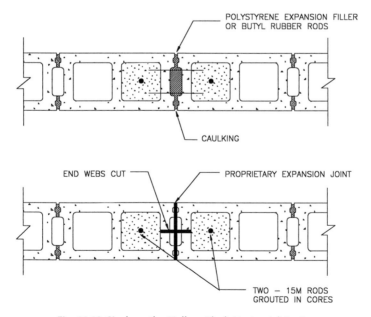

Fig. 11-18 Single-wythe Hollow Block Horizontal Section

11-6   CLOSURE

The details covered in this chapter should supplement the material in the preceding chapters. In summary, the early part of the book introduced masonry materials and structures, and discussed loading, design methods and codes and standards. This was followed by the structural analysis and design of masonry components, emphasis being placed on the basic principles of the structural behaviour of masonry. There are a couple of chapters dealing with the design of buildings and two dealing with the special problems of exterior walls, followed by the present chapter that introduces masonry details. However, these cannot be expected to cover all instances a designer will encounter. A thorough understanding of the basic material covered in the earlier chapters, supplemented by material in the later chapters, will provide most of the tools required to tackle special structural problems. However, the need for further reading is emphasized and a selected bibliography is provided at the end of Part 1.

BIBLIOGRAPHY

The books, handbooks, software and standards listed in this abbreviated bibliography contain useful information for further study and reference.

Drysdale, R.G., Hamid, A.A., and Baker, L.R., *Masonry Structures - Behavior and Design*, Prentice-Hall Inc., Englewood Cliffs, N.J., 1994

Schneider, R.R., and Dickey, W.L., *Reinforced Masonry Design*, Prentice-Hall Inc., Englewood Cliffs, N.J., 1987 (2nd Edition)

Sahlin, S., *Structural Masonry*, Prentice-Hall Inc., Englewood Cliffs, N.J. 1971

Hatzinikolas, M.A., *State of the Art Details for Masonry Construction*, Canadian Masonry Research Institute, Edmonton, Alta., 1994

Amrhein, J.E., *Reinforced Masonry Engineering Handbook*, Masonry Institute of America, Los Angeles, Calif., 1992 (5th Edition)

Masonry Council of Canada, *Guide to Energy Efficiency in Masonry and Concrete Buildings*, 1982

Panarese, W.C., Kosmatka, S., and Randall, F.A., *Concrete Masonry Handbook for Architects, Engineers, Builders,* Portland Cement Association, Skokie, Ill., 1991

MacGregor, J.G., *Reinforced Concrete Mechanics & Design*, Prentice-Hall Inc., Englewood Cliffs, N.J., 1992 (2nd Edition)

Canadian Portland Cement Association, *Concrete Design Handbook*, 1995, (2nd Edition)

Atlantic Masonry Research and Advisory Bureau Inc., *Masonry LSD 95, Windows based* software for masonry design conforming to CSA S304.1-94

Canadian Standards Association Standards

S304.1-94, *Masonry Design for Buildings (Limit States Design)*

CAN3-S304-M84, *Masonry Design for Buildings*

A371-94, *Masonry Construction for Buildings*

A370-94, *Connectors for Masonry*

A179-94, *Mortar and Grout for Unit Masonry*

NOTES

INDEX

368

PART 2

DESIGN MANUAL

H. A. Ben-Omran

CONTENTS - PART 2

Moment Capacity of a 200 Block Beam

Shear

Masonry Wall - Analysis

Unreinforced Wall Interaction Diagram

Reinforced Wall Interaction Diagram (f_y = 400 MPa)

CONTENTS

INTRODUCTION - PART 2

The purpose of Part 2 is to provide practical information for the designer. The information includes dimensions of standard two-core concrete blocks and associated section properties, structural design charts and tables that conform to the requirements of CSA S304.1, design load guidelines, standard beam information and a table of metric (S.I.)/imperial conversion factors. These design aids facilitate the design process by reducing the number of tedious calculations that would otherwise have to be carried out. The user is cautioned, however, that the use of the charts without a proper understanding of the theory is unwise since the significance of the results may not be appreciated or, worse, a fundamental error in interpretation may go undetected. The purpose, then, of Part 2 is not to assist those who do not understand the theory, but, rather, to facilitate those who do.

Part 2 starts with some design examples that illustrate the use of the subsequent design information. Not all of the information contained in Part 2 is illustrated, since some of it is self-explanatory, nor are the anomalies that crop up in some of the charts addressed in the examples - these are left to the designer for interpretation.

The design tables and charts in Part 2 are based on the standard two-core concrete blocks whose dimensions are given on pages 2-9 and 2-10. Where the designer is using masonry units with other dimensional configurations, judgement must be exercised in the interpretation of the results.

As noted in Chapter 3 of Part 1, a factor χ (either 0.5 or 1.0) is included in S304.1 for beams to allow for incomplete grouting of the compression zone (for example, where there is an unfilled space between standard units in an otherwise fully-grouted beam $\chi = 0.5$). The conservative approach has been taken in Part 2 and $\chi = 0.5$ has been assumed for the beam design charts and tables.

Finally, although every effort has been made to ensure that the data presented in Part 2 is factual and accurate to a degree consistent with current design practice, neither the authors nor the publisher can assume responsibility for errors or omissions, nor for engineering designs or plans based on it.

DESIGN EXAMPLES

Example 1   Rectangular Beam Design (tension steel only)

Given: *Unit strength = 30 MPa,   Type S mortar, f_y = 400 MPa*
50 mm clearance from bottom fibre to centre of reinforcing steel
Design factored moment, M_f = 150 kN-m

Find: *1) Beam size with tensile reinforcement only*
2) Tensile reinforcement

Solution:

(a)   - Assume b = 190 mm.
  - Enter *Moment Capacity* = 150 kN-m in Figure B-6 and it can be seen that a masonry beam from five to eight courses is possible. Choose a five-course beam for this example.
  - Extend the line horizontally from 150 kN-m to intersect the *5 courses* beam curve. Extend downward from the intersection and read
  Steel Area = 560 mm²

  Use 200 block, 5 courses, 2-#20 bars (A_s = 600 mm²)

(b)   - Following the above steps select an eight-course beam.
  - From the chart a steel area of 300 mm² is required. However, in this case 300 mm² is less than minimum steel area and should therefore be increased by 1/3.
  - Required A_s = 1.33(300) = 400

  Use 200 block, 8 courses, 2-#15 bars (A_s = 400 mm²)

(c)   - Assume 300 normal-weight concrete blocks.
  - With factored M_f = 150 kN-m, a 190 width of a 290 beam carries a bending moment of M = 190(150)/290 = 98.28 kN-m and following the above steps select a four-course beam.
  - From the chart a steel area of 470 mm² is required.
  - Required A_s = 290(470)/190 = 717.37 mm².

  Use 300 block, 4 courses, 1-#20 and 1-#25 bar (A_s = 800 mm²)

(d)   - Assume a 200 block, five course beam,
$d = 5(200) - 10 - 50$ cover $= 940$ mm.

- From Table B-36
for b=190 mm $bd^2 = 167.88(10)^6$ mm^3
- Enter K$_r$ = M/bd^2 = 150(10)^6/167.88(10)^6 = 0.893 in Table B-2
- For *Unit Strength = 30 MPa*, a steel ratio of 0.00285 is read (linear interpolation is permitted).
- Required $A_s = \rho bd = 0.00285(190)(940) = 508$ mm^2.

Use 200 block, 5 courses, 2-#20 ($A_s = 600$ mm^2)

Note: Same answer as Solution (a).

Example 2   Rectangular Beam Design (tension and compression steel)

Given: *Unit strength = 15 MPa, Type S mortar,* f_y = 400 MPa
Six course, 200 concrete block, d' = 55 mm, d = 1100 mm
Design factored moment, M_f = 200 kN-m

Find: Tension and compression reinforcement

Solution: - Assume $\rho'/\rho = 0.4$
- From given, $d' = 55$ and $d = 1100$, therefore, $d'/d = 0.05$
- From Table B-36, $bd^2 = 229.9(10)^6$ mm^3
- Calculate flexural resistance factor K$_r$
$K_r = M_f / bd^2 = 200(10)^6/ 229.9(10)^6 = 0.870$ MPa
- Look up reinforcement ratio ρ and corresponding K$_r$ in Table B-20
$\rho = 0.0029$ (linear interpolation permitted)
- $A_s = \rho \, bd = 0.0029(190)(1100) = 606$ mm^2
- $A'_s = 0.4(606) = 242$ mm^2

Use 200 block, 6 courses, 1-#20 bar ($A'_s = 300$ mm^2), d' = 55 and 2-#25 bars ($A_s = 1000$ mm^2), d = 1 000

Example 3   Rectangular Beam Design: Shear reinforcement

Given: *Unit strength = 15 MPa, Type S mortar,* f_y = 300 MPa
200 block, 8 courses, d = 1540 mm
Uniformly distributed factored load = 45 kN/m, span = 9 m

Find: Required shear reinforcement

Solution: - V_f (max) = $w[½L - d]$ = 45[½(9) - 1.54] = 133.2 kN
                      - $v_f = V_f / b_w d$ = 133.2(10)^3 / (190)(1540) = 0.455 MPa
                      - From Table B-37, v_m = 0.181 MPa
                        for discontinuity in grouting, v_m= 0.6(0.181) = 0.109 < v_f = 0.455 MPa
                        therefore *shear reinforcement is required.*

                      - $v_s = v_f - v_m$ = 0.455 - 0.109 = .346 MPa
                        ≤ $0.36\phi_m\sqrt{f_m}$ = 0.36(.55)$\sqrt{7.5}$ = 0.542
                      - Assume #10 (A_s = 100 mm^2) single legged stirrups.
                      - Calculate $1/s = vb/(0.85A_s f_y)$ = 0.346(190)/[0.85(100)(300)] = 0.00258 for entry
                        into Figure B-9
                      - From $1/s$ = 0.00258 draw a line horizontally to the right for a distance d =
                        1540 mm and join this point to intersect the horizontal axis at $L/2$ = 4500 mm.
                      - Now read, from left to right the number of vertical lines (i.e. stirrups)
                        intercepted. This gives the required number of stirups and their spacing.

                      *The number of stirrups required is 8 - #10 @ 200 and 7 - #10 @ 400 from each
                      end of the beam.*

Example 4   Wall Section Modulus - Strong Axis Bending

Given: *250 block, 6 000 mm long wall, 3 grouted cores per metre*

Find: *Section modulus about strong axis*

Solution: - Enter *Wall Length, L* = 6 m in Figure A-2.
                      - Extend the line vertically upward until it intercepts the *3 cores/m* curve.
                      - Extend the line horizontally from the intersection and read
                        Section Modulus at 1065(mm^{3}x 10^{-6}).

                      Section modulus = 1065(10)^6 mm^3

Example 5   Critical load P_{cr} - Unreinforced Masonry Wall

Given: *200 block, 2 Grouted Cores/m, 4000 mm High Wall, Unit Strength = 15 MPa, Type
                      S mortar and, Factored Dead Load = 225 kN/m, Factored Live Load = 150 kN/m*

Find: Critical Load P_{cr}

Solution: - *Total Factored Load P_f = 225+150 = 375 kN/m*
                         - β_d = *Factored Dead Load / Total Factored Load* = 225/375 = 0.6
                         - Enter Span, h = 4000 mm in Figure C-2.
                         - Extend the line vertically upward to intersect the β_d = 0.6 curve.
                         - Extend leftward from the intersection and read
                            P_{cr} / $(EI)_{eff}$ = 308 (1/mm^2) (x10^{-9})
                            P_{cr} / $(EI)_{eff}$ = 308(10^{-9}) /mm^2
                         - From Table C-1, For 200 Block, 2 Grouted Cores/m, and 15 MPa Units read
                            $(EI)_{eff}$ = 1491.48 (N-mm^2 x 10^9)
                            $(EI)_{eff}$ = 1491.48 (10^9) N-mm^2
                         - The Critical Load P_{cr} for the Wall is
                            P_{cr} = 308(10^{-9})(1491.48) (10^9) = 459375.8 N

                         Critical load P_{cr} = 459.4 kN

Example 6   Factored Moment M_f - Unreinforced Masonry Wall

Given: *Masonry Wall of Example 5*

Find: Factored Moment M_f

Solution: - Following the procedure in Example 5, obtain P_{cr} =459.4 kN/m
                         - P_f / P_{cr} = 375/459.4 = 0.82
                         - For e_1 = e_2 = 0.1t = minimum eccentricity
                            Primary moment, M_p = 0.1tP_f = 0.1(190)(375)(10)^3 = 7.13(10)^6 N-mm/m
                         - Enter P_f / P_{cr} = 0.82 in Figure C-3
                         - Extend the line vertically upward to intersect the curve e_1 /e_2 = 1.0
                         - Extend leftward from the intersection and read

                            M_f/M_p = 5.2 at the left
                         - M_f = 5.2(7.13)(10)^6 = 37.1(10)^6 N-mm/m

                         Factored moment = 37.1 kN-m/m

Example 7   Critical load P_{cr} - Reinforced Masonry Wall

Given: *250 block, 4000 mm High Wall, 4 Grouted cores/m, Unit Strength = 20 MPa,*
                         Type S mortar, Factored Dead Load = 300 kN/m, Factored Live Load = 75 kN/m,
                         Vertical Reinforcement Area = 800 mm^2, and f_y = 400 MPa

Find: *Critical Load* P_{cr}

Solution: - *Total Factored Load* $P_f = 300+75 = 375$ kN/m
                           - $\beta_d =$ *Factored Dead Load / Total Factored Load* $= 300/375 = 0.8$
                           - Enter Span, h = 4000 mm in Figure C-2.
                           - Extend the line vertically upward to intersect the $\beta_d = 0.8$ curve.
                           - Extend leftward from the intersection and read
                           $P_{cr} / (EI)_{eff} = 286(1/mm^2)$ $(x10^{-9})$
                           $P_{cr} / (EI)_{eff} = 286(10^{-9})$ /mm^2
                           - From Table D-8, For 250 Block, 20 MPa Units, 4 Grouted Cores/m, Vertical
                           Reinforcement Area = 800 mm^2, and assuming minimum eccentricity $e = 0.1t$
                           read
                           $(EI)_{eff} = 2443.96$ (N-mm^2 x 10^9)
                           $(EI)_{eff} = 2443.96$ (10^9) N-mm^2
                           - The Critical Load P_{cr} for the Wall is
                           $P_{cr} = 286(10^{-9})(2443.96)$ $(10^9) = 698972.56$ N
                           Critical load $P_{cr} = 698.97$ kN

Example 8   Factored Moment M_f - Reinforced Masonry Wall

Given: *Masonry Wall of Example 7*

Find: Factored Moment M_f

Solution: - Following the procedure in Example 7, obtain $P_{cr} = 698.97$ kN/m
                           - $P_f / P_{cr} = 375/698.97 = 0.54$
                           - For $e_1 = e_2 = 0.1t =$ Minimum Eccentricity
                           Primary Moment, $M_p = 0.1tP_f = 0.1(240)(375)(10)^3 = 9.0(10)^6$ N-mm/m
                           - Enter $P_f / P_{cr} = 0.54$ in Figure C-3
                           - Extend the line vertically upward to intersect the curve $e_1/e_2 = 1.0$
                           - Extend leftward from the intersection and read
                           $M_f/M_p = 2.3$ at the left
                           - $M_f = 2.3(9.0)(10)^6 = 20.7(10)^6$ N-mm/m

                           Factored moment = 20.7 kN-m/m

Example 9   Ungrouted Wall: Axial Load/Moment Interaction

Given: *Unit strength = 30 MPa, Type S mortar*

250 block wall
Bending Moment, M = 20 kN-m/m

Find:

The axial load that the ungrouted wall can carry

Solution:

- Enter Moment M = 20 kN-m/m in Figure E-9.
- Extending vertically from 20 to the curve for ungrouted wall and horizontally to the vertical axis gives a reading of 480 kN/m

This ungrouted wall can carry a maximum factored axial load of 480 kN/m.

Example 10   Grouted Unreinforced Wall: Axial Load/Moment Interaction

Given:

Unit strength = 20 MPa, Type S mortar
200 block wall
Factored axial compression at the ends (i.e. $e_1 = e_2 = 0$) = 300 kN/m

Find:

Maximum factored moment that may be applied to the wall.

Solution:

- Enter factored axial load $P_f = 300$ kN/m in Figure E-3 and extend the line horizontally to intersect the fully grouted wall curve.
- Extending vertically downward from the intersection to the horizontal axis and read 18.8 kN-m/m

A maximum factored moment of 18.8 kN-m/m may be applied to this wall.

Example 11   Reinforced Masonry Wall: Axial Load/Moment Interaction

Given:

Unit strength = 30 MPa, 200 mm Block, Type S mortar
Vertical Reinforcement Area $A_s = 1000$ mm^2/m, $f_y = 400$ MPa
4 Grouted Cores/m
Factored Axial Compression load = 250 kN/m

Find:

Maximum factored moment that may be applied to the wall.

Solution: - Enter factored axial load $P = 250$ kN/m in Figure F-19 and extend the line
              horizontally to intersect the $A_s = 1000$ mm^2/m curve.
              - Extending vertically downward from the intersection to the horizontal axis and
              read 23.8 kN-m/m

A maximum factored moment of 23.8 kN-m/m may be applied to this wall.

Example 12   Grouted Masonry Column: Axial Load/Moment Interaction

Given: *400 x 400 column*, $\gamma = 0.5$
              Unit strength = 15 MPa, Type S mortar
              Factored axial compression load = 450 kN
              Factored bending moment = 75 kN-m

Find: *Required reinforcement to resist the design factored axial load and moment*

Solution: - Enter $P/A_e = 450(10)^3/[(390)(390)] = 2.96$ MPa in Figure G-6 and extend the
              line horizontally.
              - Enter $M/[(A_e)(t)] = 75(10)^6/[(390)(390)(390)] = 1.26$ MPa and extend the line
              vertically to intersect the horizontal line.
              - The intersection point lies in between $\rho = 0.01$ and 0.02
              Estimate $\rho = 0.015$
              - Since $\rho = A_s/A_e = 0.015$,
              - $A_s = 0.015\, A_e = (0.015)(390)(390) = 2\,282$ mm^2.

Provide 6-#25 vertical bars with appropriate ties

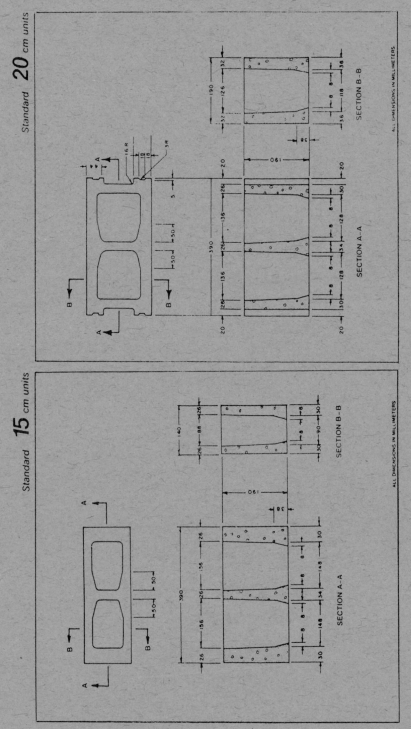

Standard **20** cm units

Standard **15** cm units

SECTION B-B

SECTION A-A

ALL DIMENSIONS IN MILLIMETERS

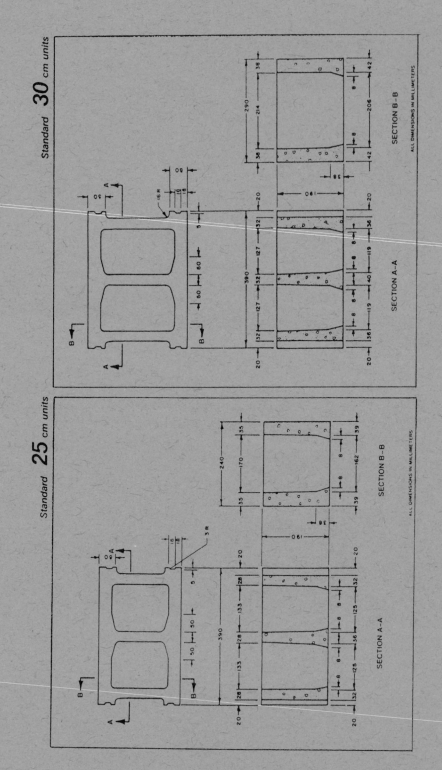

Standard **30** cm units

Standard **25** cm units

Table A-1 Properties of Concrete Masonry Walls per Metre Length*

Nominal Wall Thickness (mm)	Percent Solid	Min. Face Shell	Number of Grouted Cores/m	Weight** of Wall (kN/m²)	Properties at Bed Joint ***		
					A_e (mm²x10³)	I_x (mm⁴x10⁶)	S_x (mm³x10⁶)
150	57	26	0	1.67	52.0	172	2.46
			1	1.91	69.6	183	2.62
			2	2.15	87.2	195	2.78
			3	2.40	104.8	206	2.95
			4	2.64	122.4	217	3.11
			5	2.88	140.0	229	3.27
200	54	32	0	2.11	75.4	442	4.66
			1	2.47	98.3	468	4.93
			2	2.83	121.2	494	5.20
			3	3.19	144.2	520	5.48
			4	3.55	167.1	546	5.75
			5	3.91	190.0	572	6.02
250	51	35	0	2.52	81.7	816	6.80
			1	3.00	113.4	883	7.36
			2	3.49	145.0	950	7.92
			3	3.97	176.7	1018	8.48
			4	4.46	208.3	1085	9.04
			5	4.94	240.0	1152	9.60
300	50	38	0	2.99	88.3	1341	9.25
			1	3.59	128.6	1479	10.20
			2	4.19	169.0	1617	11.15
			3	4.78	209.3	1756	12.11
			4	5.38	249.7	1894	13.06
			5	5.98	290.0	2032	14.01

*   Based on standard concrete blocks of Fig. 2-3 and Table 2-1.

**   Based on mass density for both block and grout of 2100 kg/m³
        (note that lightweight block is also available).

***   These properties include the head joint and assume thorough grouting.

        A_e = Effective Area

        I_x = Moment of inertia about x-axis

        S_x = Section modulus about x-axis

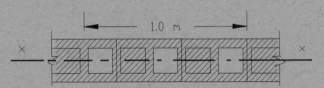

Table A-2 Properties of Reinforcing Bars

Designation	Area (mm²)	Diameter (mm)	Perimeter (mm)	Mass (kg/m)
9 ga.	* 22.3	3.77	* 23.7	* 0.175
8ga.	* 26.6	4.11	* 25.8	* 0.208
#10	100.	11.3	35.5	0.786
#15	200.	16.0	50.1	1.570
#20	300.	19.5	61.3	2.355
#25	500.	25.2	79.2	3.925
#30	700.	29.9	93.9	5.495
#35	1000.	35.7	112.2	7.850
#45	1500.	43.7	137.3	11.775
#55	2500.	56.4	177.2	19.625

* Quantities for 2-wires ladder type

Table A-3 Area of Multiple Bars (mm²)

Multiple	1	2	3	4	5	6	7	8	9	10
#10	100	200	300	400	500	600	700	800	900	1000
#15	200	400	600	800	1000	1200	1400	1600	1800	2000
#20	300	600	900	1200	1500	1800	2100	2400	2700	3000
#25	500	1000	1500	2000	2500	3000	3500	4000	4500	5000
#30	700	1400	2100	2800	3500	4200	4900	5600	6300	7000
#35	1000	2000	3000	4000	5000	6000	7000	8000	9000	10000
#45	1500	3000	4500	6000	75000	9000	10500	12000	13500	15000
#55	2500	5000	7500	10000	12500	15000	17500	20000	22500	25000

Table A-4 Perimeter of Multiple Bars (mm)

Multiple	1	2	3	4	5	6	7	8	9	10
#10	35.5	71.0	106.5	142.0	177.5	213.0	248.5	284.0	319.5	355.0
#15	50.1	100.2	150.3	200.4	250.5	300.6	350.7	400.8	450.9	501.0
#20	61.3	122.6	183.9	245.2	306.5	367.8	429.1	490.4	551.7	613.0
#25	79.2	158.4	237.6	316.8	396.0	475.2	554.4	633.6	712.8	792.0
#30	93.9	187.8	281.7	375.6	469.5	563.4	657.3	751.2	845.1	939.0
#35	112.2	224.4	336.6	448.8	561.0	673.2	785.4	897.6	1009.8	1122.0
#45	137.3	274.6	411.9	549.2	686.5	823.8	961.1	1098.4	1235.7	1373.0
#55	177.2	354.4	531.6	708.8	886.0	1063.2	1240.4	1417.6	1594.8	1772.0

Table A-5 Beam Reinforcement Ratio, $\rho = A_s/bd$ (x10^{-3})
200 Block

Effective Depth (mm)	Reinforcement Bar Area, A_s (mm^2)					
	100	200	300	500	700	1000
100	5.263	10.526	15.789	26.316	36.842	52.632
200	2.632	5.263	7.895	13.158	18.421	26.316
300	1.754	3.509	5.263	8.772	12.281	17.544
400	1.316	2.632	3.947	6.579	9.211	13.158
500	1.053	2.105	3.158	5.263	7.368	10.526
600	0.877	1.754	2.632	4.386	6.140	8.772
700	0.752	1.504	2.256	3.759	5.263	7.519
800	0.658	1.316	1.974	3.289	4.605	6.579
900	0.585	1.170	1.754	2.924	4.094	5.848
1000	0.526	1.053	1.579	2.632	3.684	5.263
1100	0.478	0.957	1.435	2.392	3.349	4.785
1200	0.439	0.877	1.316	2.193	3.070	4.386
1300	0.405	0.810	1.215	2.024	2.834	4.049
1400	0.376	0.752	1.128	1.880	2.632	3.759
1500	0.351	0.702	1.053	1.754	2.456	3.509
1600	0.329	0.658	0.987	1.645	2.303	3.289

Table A-6 Beam Reinforcement Ratio, $\rho = A_s/bd$ (x10^{-3})
250 Block

Effective Depth (mm)	Reinforcement Bar Area, A_s (mm^2)					
	100	200	300	500	700	1000
100	4.167	8.333	12.500	20.833	29.167	41.667
200	2.083	4.167	6.250	10.417	14.583	20.833
300	1.389	2.778	4.167	6.944	9.722	13.889
400	1.042	2.083	3.125	5.208	7.292	10.417
500	0.833	1.667	2.500	4.167	5.833	8.333
600	0.694	1.389	2.083	3.472	4.861	6.944
700	0.595	1.190	1.786	2.976	4.167	5.952
800	0.521	1.042	1.563	2.604	3.646	5.208
900	0.463	0.926	1.389	2.315	3.241	4.630
1000	0.417	0.833	1.250	2.083	2.917	4.167
1100	0.379	0.758	1.136	1.894	2.652	3.788
1200	0.347	0.694	1.042	1.736	2.431	3.472
1300	0.321	0.641	0.962	1.603	2.244	3.205
1400	0.298	0.595	0.893	1.488	2.083	2.976
1500	0.278	0.556	0.833	1.389	1.944	2.778
1600	0.260	0.521	0.781	1.302	1.823	2.604

ENGINEERED MASONRY DESIGN

Table A-7 Beam Reinforcement Ratio, $\rho = A_s/bd$ (x10^{-3})
300 Block

Effective Depth (mm)	Reinforcement Bar Area, A_s (mm^2)					
	100	200	300	500	700	1000
100	3.448	6.897	10.345	17.241	24.138	34.483
200	1.724	3.448	5.172	8.621	12.069	17.241
300	1.149	2.299	3.448	5.747	8.046	11.494
400	0.862	1.724	2.586	4.310	6.034	8.621
500	0.690	1.379	2.069	3.448	4.828	6.897
600	0.575	1.149	1.724	2.874	4.023	5.747
700	0.493	0.985	1.478	2.463	3.448	4.926
800	0.431	0.862	1.293	2.155	3.017	4.310
900	0.383	0.766	1.149	1.916	2.682	3.831
1000	0.345	0.690	1.034	1.724	2.414	3.448
1100	0.313	0.627	0.940	1.567	2.194	3.135
1200	0.287	0.575	0.862	1.437	2.011	2.874
1300	0.265	0.531	0.796	1.326	1.857	2.653
1400	0.246	0.493	0.739	1.232	1.724	2.463
1500	0.230	0.460	0.690	1.149	1.609	2.299
1600	0.216	0.431	0.647	1.078	1.509	2.155

Table A-8 Development Lengths, l_d, for Deformed Reinforcing Bars
$l_d = l_{db}$ x (Factors from Clause 5.5.3.4) x (Factors from Clause 5.5.3.5)

Bar Size	Rebar Grade	Basic Development Length, l_{db} (mm)	
		Tension	Compression
#10	300	153	237
	400	204	316
#15	300	307	336
	400	410	448
#20	300	456	410
	400	608	546
#25	300	762	529
	400	1016	706
#30	300	1073	628
	400	1430	837
#35	300	1529	750
	400	2039	1000
#45	300	2292	918
	400	3056	1224
#55	300	3817	1184
	400	5090	1579

Modification Factors

Tension:
     a) Top bars   1.3
     b) Bars spaced laterally < 75 mm o.c.   1.6
c) Bars spaced laterally > 150 mm o.c.0.7
     d) Excess reinforcement area is provided   x A_s required /(A_s Provided)
     e) The product of c) and d) $\geq$ 0.6
Compression:
     a) Bars spaced laterally < 75 mm o.c.   1.6
     b) Excess reinforcement area is provided   x A_s required /(A_s Provided) $\geq$ 0.6

Table A-9 Wall Reinforcement Ratio, $\rho = A_s/A_g$

Wire or Bar Size	Spacing S (mm)	Wall Thickness (mm)			
		b=140	b=190	b=240	b=290
2 - 9 ga.	@ 1200	0.00013	0.00010	0.00008	0.00006
	800	0.00020	0.00015	0.00012	0.00010
	600	0.00027	0.00020	0.00015	0.00013
	400	0.00040	0.00029	0.00023	0.00019
	200	0.00080	0.00059	0.00046	0.00038
2 - 8 ga.	@ 1200	0.00016	0.00012	0.00009	0.00008
	800	0.00024	0.00018	0.00014	0.00011
	600	0.00032	0.00023	0.00018	0.00015
	400	0.00048	0.00035	0.00028	0.00023
	200	0.00095	0.00070	0.00055	0.00046
#10	@ 1200	0.00060	0.00044	0.00035	0.00029
	800	0.00089	0.00066	0.00052	0.00043
	600	0.00119	0.00088	0.00069	0.00057
	400	0.00179	0.00132	0.00104	0.00086
	200	0.00357	0.00263	0.00208	0.00172
#15	@ 1200	0.00119	0.00088	0.00069	0.00057
	800	0.00179	0.00132	0.00104	0.00086
	600	0.00238	0.00175	0.00139	0.00115
	400	0.00357	0.00263	0.00208	0.00172
	200	0.00714	0.00526	0.00417	0.00345
#20	@ 1200	0.00179	0.00132	0.00104	0.00086
	800	0.00268	0.00197	0.00156	0.00129
	600	0.00357	0.00263	0.00208	0.00172
	400	0.00536	0.00395	0.00313	0.00259
	200	0.01071	0.00789	0.00625	0.00517
#25	@ 1200	0.00298	0.00219	0.00174	0.00144
	800	0.00446	0.00329	0.00260	0.00216
	600	0.00595	0.00439	0.00347	0.00287
	400	0.00893	0.00658	0.00521	0.00431
	200	0.01786	0.01316	0.01042	0.00862
	@ 1200	0.00417	0.00307	0.00243	0.00201
	800	0.00625	0.00461	0.00365	0.00302
#30	600	0.00833	0.00614	0.00486	0.00402
	400	0.01250	0.00921	0.00729	0.00603
	200	0.02500	0.01842	0.01458	0.01207

Table A-10 Bed Joint Section Modulus - Strong Axis Bending (mm^{3}x10^{-6})
200 Block

Wall Length (mm)	Number of grouted core(s) per metre					
	0	1	2	3	4	5
0	0	0	0	0	0	0
1000	12.67	16.47	20.27	24.07	27.87	31.67
2000	50.67	65.87	81.07	96.27	111.47	126.67
3000	114.00	148.20	182.40	216.60	250.80	285.00
4000	202.67	263.47	324.27	385.07	445.87	506.67
5000	316.67	411.67	506.67	601.67	696.67	791.67
6000	456.00	592.80	729.60	866.40	1003.20	1140.00
7000	620.67	806.87	993.07	1179.27	1365.47	1551.67
8000	810.67	1053.87	1297.07	1540.27	1783.47	2026.67
9000	1026.00	1333.80	1641.60	1949.40	2257.20	2565.00
10000	1266.67	1646.67	2026.67	2406.67	2786.67	3166.67

Table A-11 Bed Joint Section Modulus - Strong Axis Bending (mm^{3}x10^{-6})
250 Block

Wall Length (mm)	Number of grouted core(s) per metre					
	0	1	2	3	4	5
0	0	0	0	0	0	0
1000	13.60	18.80	24.00	29.60	34.80	40.00
2000	54.40	75.20	96.00	118.40	139.20	160.00
3000	122.40	169.20	216.00	266.40	313.20	360.00
4000	217.60	300.80	384.00	473.60	556.80	640.00
5000	340.00	470.00	600.00	740.00	870.00	1000.00
6000	489.60	676.80	864.00	1065.60	1252.80	1440.00
7000	666.40	921.20	1176.00	1450.40	1705.20	1960.00
8000	870.40	1203.20	1536.00	1894.40	2227.20	2560.00
9000	1101.60	1522.80	1944.00	2397.60	2818.80	3240.00
10000	1360.00	1880.00	2400.00	2960.00	3480.00	4000.00

Table A-12 Bed Joint Section Modulus - Strong Axis Bending (mm^3 x10^{-6})
300 Block

Wall Length (mm)	Number of grouted core(s) per metre					
	0	1	2	3	4	5
0	0	0	0	0	0	0
1000	14.50	21.27	28.03	34.80	41.57	48.33
2000	58.00	85.07	112.13	139.20	166.27	193.33
3000	130.50	191.40	252.30	313.20	374.10	435.00
4000	232.00	340.27	448.53	556.80	665.07	773.33
5000	362.50	531.67	700.83	870.00	1039.17	1208.33
6000	522.00	765.60	1009.20	1252.80	1496.40	1740.00
7000	710.50	1042.07	1373.63	1705.20	2036.77	2368.33
8000	928.00	1361.07	1794.13	2227.20	2660.27	3093.33
9000	1174.50	1722.60	2270.70	2818.80	3366.90	3915.00
10000	1450.00	2126.67	2803.33	3480.00	4156.67	4833.33

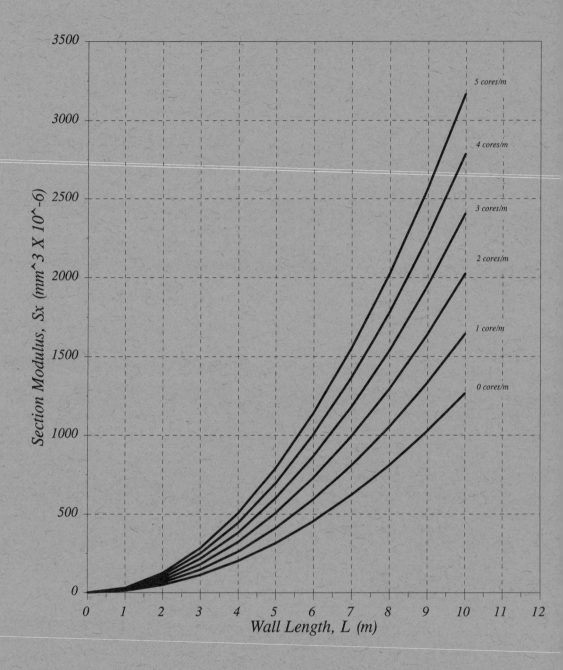

Figure A-1 Wall Section Modulus at Bed Joint
Strong Axis Bending, 200 Block

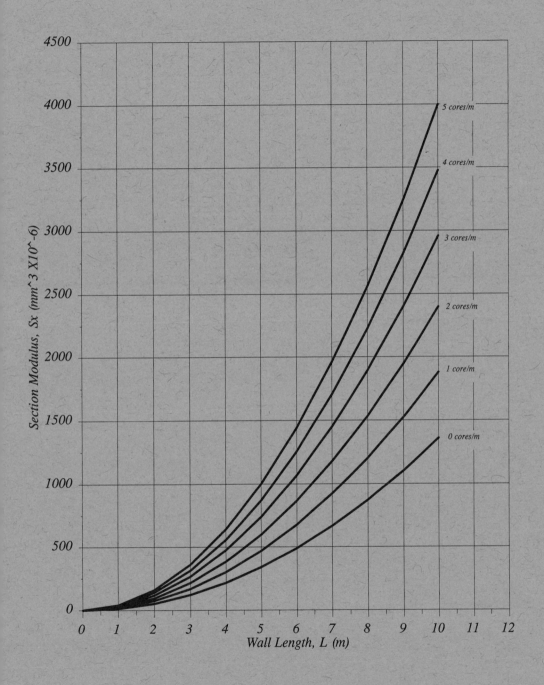

Figure A-2 Wall Section Modulus at Bed Joint
Strong Axis Bending, 250 Block

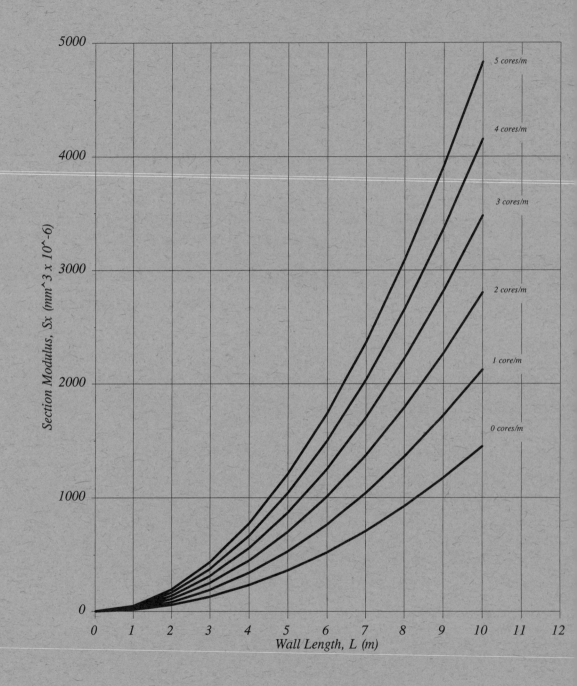

Figure A-3 Wall Section Modulus at Bed Joint
Strong Axis Bending, 300 Block

Table B-1 Beams Reinforcement Ratio ρ for Resistance Factors K_r
Reinforcement $f_y = 300$ MPa

K_r (MPa)	Unit Strength	10	15	20	30	>40
0.1		0.00040	0.00040	0.00040	0.00040	0.00040
0.2		0.00082	0.00082	0.00080	0.00080	0.00079
0.3		0.00126	0.00123	0.00122	0.00121	0.00120
0.4		0.00173	0.00167	0.00164	0.00162	0.00161
0.5		0.00223	0.00213	0.00208	0.00205	0.00203
0.6		0.00277	0.00260	0.00253	0.00248	0.00245
0.7		0.00336	0.00309	0.00299	0.00292	0.00288
0.8		0.00402	0.00361	0.00347	0.00337	0.00331
0.9		0.00477	0.00416	0.00396	0.00383	0.00376
1.0		0.00568	0.00474	0.00447	0.00429	0.00421
1.1		0.00694	0.00536	0.00499	0.00477	0.00466
1.2			0.00603	0.00554	0.00527	0.00513
1.3			0.00676	0.00612	0.00577	0.00560
1.4			0.00758	0.00672	0.00629	0.00608
1.5			0.00853	0.00736	0.00682	0.00658
1.6			0.00969	0.00804	0.00737	0.00708
1.7			0.01136	0.00876	0.00794	0.00759
1.8				0.00954	0.00853	0.00812
1.9				0.01040	0.00914	0.00865
2.0				0.01138	0.00977	0.00920
2.1				0.01249	0.01044	0.00977
2.2				0.01389	0.01113	0.01034
2.3				0.01601	0.01186	0.01094
2.4					0.01264	0.01155
2.5					0.01347	0.01219
2.6					0.01437	0.01284
2.7					0.01535	0.01352
2.8					0.01644	0.01423
2.9					0.01771	0.01497
3.0					0.01925	0.01574
3.1					0.02146	0.01655
3.2						0.01741
3.3						0.01833
3.4						0.01932
3.5						0.02041
3.6						0.02161
3.7						0.02299
3.8						0.02465
3.9						0.02692

Table B-2 Beams Reinforcement Ratio ρ for Resistance Factors K_r
Reinforcement $f_y = 400$ MPa

K_r (MPa)	Unit Strength	10	15	20	30	>40
0.1		0.00030	0.00030	0.00030	0.00030	0.00030
0.2		0.00062	0.00061	0.00060	0.00060	0.00060
0.3		0.00095	0.00092	0.00091	0.00090	0.00090
0.4		0.00130	0.00125	0.00123	0.00122	0.00121
0.5		0.00168	0.00159	0.00156	0.00153	0.00152
0.6		0.00208	0.00195	0.00190	0.00186	0.00184
0.7		0.00252	0.00232	0.00224	0.00219	0.00216
0.8		0.00301	0.00271	0.00260	0.00253	0.00249
0.9		0.00358	0.00312	0.00297	0.00287	0.00282
1.0		0.00426	0.00355	0.00335	0.00322	0.00315
1.1		0.00521	0.00402	0.00375	0.00358	0.00350
1.2			0.00452	0.00416	0.00395	0.00385
1.3			0.00507	0.00459	0.00433	0.00420
1.4			0.00568	0.00504	0.00472	0.00456
1.5			0.00639	0.00552	0.00512	0.00493
1.6			0.00727	0.00603	0.00553	0.00531
1.7			0.00852	0.00657	0.00596	0.00569
1.8				0.00716	0.00640	0.00609
1.9				0.00780	0.00685	0.00649
2.0				0.00853	0.00733	0.00690
2.1				0.00937	0.00783	0.00732
2.2				0.01042	0.00835	0.00776
2.3				0.01201	0.00890	0.00821
2.4					0.00948	0.00867
2.5					0.01010	0.00914
2.6					0.01077	0.00963
2.7					0.01151	0.01014
2.8					0.01233	0.01067
2.9					0.01328	0.01122
3.0					0.01444	0.01180
3.1					0.01610	0.01241
3.2						0.01306
3.3						0.01375
3.4						0.01449
3.5						0.01530
3.6						0.01621
3.7						0.01724
3.8						0.01849
3.9						0.02019

Table B-3 Compression Steel Ratio ρ' for Resistance Factor K'_r

K'_r (MPa)	d'/d				
	0.02	0.04	0.06	0.08	0.10
0.1	0.00030	0.00031	0.00031	0.00032	0.00033
0.2	0.00060	0.00061	0.00063	0.00064	0.00065
0.3	0.00090	0.00092	0.00094	0.00096	0.00098
0.4	0.00120	0.00123	0.00125	0.00128	0.00131
0.5	0.00150	0.00153	0.00156	0.00160	0.00163
0.6	0.00180	0.00184	0.00188	0.00192	0.00196
0.7	0.00210	0.00215	0.00219	0.00224	0.00229
0.8	0.00240	0.00245	0.00250	0.00256	0.00261
0.9	0.00270	0.00276	0.00282	0.00288	0.00294
1.0	0.00300	0.00306	0.00313	0.00320	0.00327
1.1	0.00330	0.00337	0.00344	0.00352	0.00360
1.2	0.00360	0.00368	0.00376	0.00384	0.00392
1.3	0.00390	0.00398	0.00407	0.00416	0.00425
1.4	0.00420	0.00429	0.00438	0.00448	0.00456
1.5	0.00450	0.00460	0.00469	0.00480	0.00490
1.6	0.00480	0.00490	0.00501	0.00512	0.00523
1.7	0.00510	0.00521	0.00532	0.00544	0.00556
1.8	0.00540	0.00552	0.00563	0.00575	0.00588
1.9	0.00570	0.00582	0.00595	0.00607	0.00621
2.0	0.00600	0.00613	0.00626	0.00639	0.00654
2.1	0.00630	0.00643	0.00657	0.00671	0.00686
2.2	0.00660	0.00674	0.00688	0.00703	0.00719
2.3	0.00690	0.00705	0.00720	0.00735	0.00752
2.4	0.00720	0.00735	0.00751	0.00767	0.00784
2.5	0.00750	0.00766	0.00782	0.00799	0.00817
2.6	0.00780	0.00797	0.00814	0.00831	0.00850
2.7	0.00810	0.00827	0.00845	0.00863	0.00882
2.8	0.00840	0.00858	0.00876	0.00895	0.00915
2.9	0.00870	0.00889	0.00907	0.00927	0.00948
3.0	0.00900	0.00919	0.00939	0.00959	0.00980

Table B-4 Flexural Resistance Factor K_r(MPa) for Beams With Both
Tension and Compression Reinforcement
Unit Strength = 15 MPa, f_y = 300 MPa and d'/d = 0.05

ρ	ρ'/ρ				
	0.2	0.4	0.6	0.8	1.0
0.001	0.183	0.164	0.171	0.174	----
0.002	0.355	0.363	0.335	0.346	0.352
0.003	0.651	0.690	0.715	0.728	0.729
0.004	0.820	0.893	0.942	0.967	0.971
0.005		1.083	1.163	1.205	1.213
0.006		1.259	1.377	1.442	1.455
0.007			1.586	1.677	1.697
0.008			1.789	1.911	1.940
0.009			1.986	2.143	2.182
0.010				2.374	2.424
0.011				2.603	2.666
0.012				2.831	2.909
0.013				3.057	3.151
0.014				3.282	3.393
0.015				3.505	3.635

Table B-5 Flexural Resistance Factor K_r(MPa) for Beams With Both
Tension and Compression Reinforcement
Unit Strength = 20 MPa, f_y = 300 MPa and d'/d = 0.05

ρ	ρ'/ρ				
	0.2	0.4	0.6	0.8	1.0
0.001	0.162	0.169	0.174	---	---
0.002	0.361	0.317	0.337	0.346	0.351
0.003	0.677	0.705	0.722	0.729	0.729
0.004	0.867	0.919	0.954	0.970	0.971
0.005	1.040	1.124	1.181	1.210	1.214
0.006	1.194	1.319	1.404	1.449	1.456
0.007		1.504	1.622	1.686	1.698
0.008		1.679	1.836	1.923	1.940
0.009			2.046	2.158	2.182
0.010			2.251	2.392	2.425
0.011			2.452	2.625	2.667
0.012			2.648	2.857	2.909
0.013				3.088	3.151
0.014				3.318	3.394
0.015				3.547	3.636

Table B-6 Flexural Resistance Factor K$_r$(MPa) for Beams With Both
Tension and Compression Reinforcement
Unit Strength = 30 MPa, f$_y$ = 300 MPa and d'/d = 0.05

ρ	ρ'/ρ				
	0.2	0.4	0.6	0.8	1.0
0.001	---	---	---	---	---
0.002	0.365	0.325	0.339	0.347	0.351
0.003	0.698	0.716	0.727	0.730	0.730
0.004	0.904	0.940	0.963	0.972	0.972
0.005	1.097	1.157	1.196	1.214	1.215
0.006	1.277	1.366	1.425	1.454	1.457
0.007	1.444	1.568	1.651	1.693	1.699
0.008	1.598	1.762	1.873	1.932	1.941
0.009		1.949	2.093	2.170	2.183
0.010		2.128	2.309	2.407	2.426
0.011		2.300	2.521	2.643	2.668
0.012			2.731	2.878	2.910
0.013			2.937	3.113	3.152
0.014			3.140	3.346	3.394
0.015			3.339	3.579	3.637

Table B-7 Flexural Resistance Factor K$_r$(MPa) for Beams With Both
Tension and Compression Reinforcement
Unit Strength ≥ 40 MPa, f$_y$ = 300 MPa and d'/d = 0.05

ρ	ρ'/ρ				
	0.2	0.4	0.6	0.8	1.0
0.001	---	---	---	---	---
0.002	0.311	0.332	0.343	0.349	---
0.003	0.710	0.723	0.730	0.731	0.731
0.004	0.926	0.952	0.968	0.973	0.974
0.005	1.131	1.176	1.204	1.215	1.216
0.006	1.326	1.393	1.437	1.457	1.458
0.007	1.511	1.605	1.667	1.698	1.700
0.008	1.684	1.811	1.895	1.937	1.942
0.009	1.848	2.011	2.120	2.177	2.184
0.010	2.001	2.204	2.343	2.415	2.426
0.011		2.393	2.562	2.653	2.669
0.012		2.575	2.780	2.890	2.911
0.013		2.751	2.994	3.127	3.153
0.014			3.206	3.363	3.395
0.015			3.416	3.598	3.637

Table B-8 Flexural Resistance Factor K_r(MPa) for Beams With Both
Tension and Compression Reinforcement
Unit Strength = 15 MPa, f_y = 300 MPa and d'/d = 0.1

ρ	ρ'/ρ				
	0.2	0.4	0.6	0.8	1.0
0.001	---	---	---	---	---
0.002	0.350	0.316	0.328	0.335	---
0.003	0.643	0.674	0.692	0.696	0.697
0.004	0.810	0.872	0.911	0.925	0.926
0.005		1.057	1.124	1.153	1.155
0.006		1.228	1.331	1.381	1.384
0.007			1.533	1.606	1.614
0.008			1.728	1.829	1.843
0.009			1.917	2.051	2.072
0.010				2.272	2.302
0.011				2.491	2.531
0.012				2.708	2.761
0.013				2.924	2.990
0.014				3.139	3.220
0.015				3.352	3.449

Table B-9 Flexural Resistance Factor K_r(MPa) for Beams With Both
Tension and Compression Reinforcement
Unit Strength = 20 MPa, f_y = 300 MPa and d'/d = 0.1

ρ	ρ'/ρ				
	0.2	0.4	0.6	0.8	1.0
0.001	---	---	---	---	---
0.002	0.321	0.327	0.335	---	---
0.003	0.670	0.689	0.697	0.699	0.700
0.004	0.857	0.899	0.923	0.928	0.929
0.005	1.027	1.099	1.143	1.156	1.158
0.006	1.179	1.289	1.358	1.385	1.387
0.007		1.468	1.569	1.614	1.617
0.008		1.638	1.775	1.841	1.846
0.009			1.977	2.066	2.075
0.010			2.174	2.290	2.305
0.011			2.367	2.513	2.534
0.012			2.556	2.735	2.763
0.013				2.956	2.993
0.014				3.175	3.222
0.015				3.394	3.451

Table B-10 Flexural Resistance Factor K_r(MPa) for Beams With Both
Tension and Compression Reinforcement
Unit Strength = 30 MPa, f_y = 300 MPa and d'/d = 0.1

ρ	ρ'/ρ				
	0.2	0.4	0.6	0.8	1.0
0.001	---	---	---	---	---
0.002	---	---	---	---	---
0.003	0.690	0.701	0.703	0.704	0.704
0.004	0.894	0.920	0.932	0.932	0.933
0.005	1.085	1.131	1.157	1.161	1.162
0.006	1.262	1.335	1.379	1.390	1.392
0.007	1.426	1.532	1.597	1.618	1.621
0.008	1.577	1.721	1.812	1.847	1.850
0.009		1.903	2.024	2.076	2.079
0.010		2.077	2.232	2.305	2.308
0.011		2.244	2.437	2.531	2.538
0.012			2.639	2.756	2.767
0.013			2.838	2.980	2.996
0.014			3.033	3.204	3.226
0.015			3.225	3.426	3.455

Table B-11 Flexural Resistance Factor K_r(MPa) for Beams With Both
Tension and Compression Reinforcement
Unit Strength $\geq$ 40 MPa, f_y = 300 MPa and d'/d = 0.1

ρ	ρ'/ρ				
	0.2	0.4	0.6	0.8	1.0
0.001	---	---	---	---	---
0.002	---	---	---	---	---
0.003	0.702	0.706	0.708	0.708	0.708
0.004	0.916	0.931	0.936	0.937	0.938
0.005	1.119	1.150	1.163	1.166	1.167
0.006	1.311	1.363	1.390	1.394	1.396
0.007	1.493	1.569	1.614	1.623	1.625
0.008	1.664	1.770	1.834	1.852	1.854
0.009	1.825	1.965	2.051	2.080	2.083
0.010	1.975	2.153	2.266	2.309	2.313
0.011		2.336	2.478	2.538	2.542
0.012		2.513	2.688	2.767	2.771
0.013		2.685	2.895	2.994	3.000
0.014			3.099	3.220	3.230
0.015			3.301	3.445	3.459

Table B-12 Flexural Resistance Factor K_r(MPa) for Beams With Both
Tension and Compression Reinforcement
Unit Strength = 15 MPa, f_y = 300 MPa and d'/d = 0.15

ρ	ρ'/ρ				
	0.2	0.4	0.6	0.8	1.0
0.001	---	---	---	---	---
0.002	0.310	0.321	---	---	---
0.003	0.635	0.659	0.667	0.669	0.670
0.004	0.799	0.852	0.880	0.884	0.886
0.005		1.032	1.086	1.100	1.102
0.006		1.198	1.285	1.315	1.318
0.007			1.479	1.531	1.535
0.008			1.666	1.747	1.751
0.009			1.848	1.960	1.967
0.010				2.170	2.184
0.011				2.379	2.400
0.012				2.586	2.617
0.013				2.792	2.834
0.014				2.996	3.050
0.015				3.199	3.267

Table B-13 Flexural Resistance Factor K_r(MPa) for Beams With Both
Tension and Compression Reinforcement
Unit Strength = 20 MPa, f_y = 300 MPa and d'/d = 0.15

ρ	ρ'/ρ				
	0.2	0.4	0.6	0.8	1.0
0.001	---	---	---	---	---
0.002	---	---	---	---	---
0.003	0.662	0.672	0.675	0.676	0.676
0.004	0.847	0.879	0.889	0.892	0.893
0.005	1.014	1.073	1.102	1.107	1.109
0.006	1.164	1.258	1.312	1.323	1.325
0.007		1.433	1.515	1.538	1.541
0.008		1.597	1.714	1.754	1.758
0.009			1.908	1.969	1.974
0.010			2.098	2.185	2.190
0.011			2.283	2.401	2.407
0.012			2.464	2.613	2.623
0.013				2.823	2.840
0.014				3.033	3.056
0.015				3.241	3.273

Table B-14 Flexural Resistance Factor K$_r$(MPa) for Beams With Both
Tension and Compression Reinforcement
Unit Strength = 30 MPa, f$_y$ = 300 MPa and d'/d = 0.15

ρ	ρ'/ρ				
	0.2	0.4	0.6	0.8	1.0
0.001	---	---	---	---	---
0.002	---	---	---	---	---
0.003	0.681	0.684	0.685	0.686	---
0.004	0.884	0.896	0.900	0.902	0.902
0.005	1.072	1.106	1.114	1.117	1.119
0.006	1.247	1.305	1.328	1.333	1.335
0.007	1.408	1.496	1.541	1.548	1.551
0.008	1.557	1.680	1.751	1.764	1.767
0.009		1.857	1.955	1.979	1.983
0.010		2.026	2.156	2.195	2.200
0.011		2.188	2.353	2.410	2.416
0.012			2.547	2.626	2.632
0.013			2.738	2.842	2.849
0.014			2.926	3.057	3.065
0.015			3.110	3.273	3.282

Table B-15 Flexural Resistance Factor K$_r$(MPa) for Beams With Both
Tension and Compression Reinforcement
Unit Strength ≥ 40 MPa, f$_y$ = 300 MPa and d'/d = 0.15

ρ	ρ'/ρ				
	0.2	0.4	0.6	0.8	1.0
0.001	---	---	---	---	---
0.002	---	---	---	---	---
0.003	0.694	0.695	---	---	---
0.004	0.904	0.909	0.911	0.912	0.912
0.005	1.106	1.121	1.126	1.128	1.128
0.006	1.296	1.331	1.340	1.343	1.345
0.007	1.475	1.534	1.554	1.559	1.561
0.008	1.644	1.729	1.767	1.774	1.777
0.009	1.802	1.919	1.980	1.990	1.993
0.010	1.950	2.102	2.190	2.205	2.209
0.011		2.280	2.394	2.421	2.426
0.012		2.452	2.596	2.636	2.642
0.013		2.618	2.795	2.852	2.858
0.014			2.992	3.067	3.074
0.015			3.186	3.283	3.291

Table B-16 Flexural Resistance Factor K$_r$(MPa) for Beams With Both
Tension and Compression Reinforcement
Unit Strength = 15 MPa, f$_y$ = 300 MPa and d'/d = 0.2

ρ	ρ'/ρ				
	0.2	0.4	0.6	0.8	1.0
0.001	---	---	---	---	---
0.002	---	---	---	---	---
0.003	0.628	0.641	0.645	0.646	0.647
0.004	0.789	0.832	0.845	0.849	0.850
0.005		1.006	1.045	1.051	1.054
0.006		1.167	1.240	1.253	1.257
0.007			1.425	1.456	1.460
0.008			1.605	1.658	1.664
0.009			1.779	1.861	1.867
0.010				2.063	2.071
0.011				2.266	2.274
0.012				2.464	2.478
0.013				2.659	2.681
0.014				2.853	2.885
0.015				3.046	3.089

Table B-17 Flexural Resistance Factor K$_r$(MPa) for Beams With Both
Tension and Compression Reinforcement
Unit Strength = 20 MPa, f$_y$ = 300 MPa and d'/d = 0.2

ρ	ρ'/ρ				
	0.2	0.4	0.6	0.8	1.0
0.001	---	---	---	---	---
0.002	---	---	---	---	---
0.003	0.652	0.657	0.658	0.659	---
0.004	0.837	0.854	0.860	0.862	0.862
0.005	1.001	1.048	1.060	1.064	1.066
0.006	1.148	1.227	1.260	1.267	1.269
0.007		1.397	1.459	1.469	1.472
0.008		1.556	1.653	1.671	1.676
0.009			1.839	1.874	1.879
0.010			2.021	2.076	2.083
0.011			2.199	2.278	2.286
0.012			2.372	2.481	2.489
0.013				2.683	2.693
0.014				2.886	2.896
0.015				3.088	3.100

Table B-18 Flexural Resistance Factor K_r(MPa) for Beams With Both
Tension and Compression Reinforcement
Unit Strength = 30 MPa, f_y = 300 MPa and d'/d = 0.2

ρ	ρ'/ρ				
	0.2	0.4	0.6	0.8	1.0
0.001	---	---	---	---	---
0.002	---	---	---	---	---
0.003	0.675	0.675	---	---	---
0.004	0.871	0.877	0.878	0.879	---
0.005	1.059	1.075	1.080	1.082	1.083
0.006	1.231	1.270	1.281	1.285	1.286
0.007	1.390	1.460	1.481	1.487	1.490
0.008	1.536	1.639	1.681	1.690	1.693
0.009		1.811	1.880	1.892	1.896
0.010		1.975	2.079	2.094	2.100
0.011		2.132	2.269	2.296	2.303
0.012			2.455	2.499	2.506
0.013			2.639	2.701	2.710
0.014			2.818	2.903	2.913
0.015			2.995	3.106	3.116

Table B-19 Flexural Resistance Factor K_r(MPa) for Beams With Both
Tension and Compression Reinforcement
Unit Strength $\geq$ 40 MPa, f_y = 300 MPa and d'/d = 0.2

ρ	ρ'/ρ				
	0.2	0.4	0.6	0.8	1.0
0.001	---	---	---	---	---
0.002	---	---	---	---	---
0.003	---	---	---	---	---
0.004	0.894	0.895	---	---	---
0.005	1.090	1.097	1.099	1.099	---
0.006	1.279	1.295	1.301	1.303	1.303
0.007	1.457	1.491	1.502	1.505	1.507
0.008	1.623	1.685	1.702	1.708	1.710
0.009	1.779	1.873	1.902	1.910	1.914
0.010	1.924	2.051	2.101	2.113	2.117
0.011		2.224	2.301	2.315	2.320
0.012		2.391	2.500	2.517	2.523
0.013		2.552	2.696	2.719	2.727
0.014			2.885	2.922	2.930
0.015			3.071	3.124	3.133

Table B-20 Flexural Resistance Factor K_r(MPa) for Beams With Both
Tension and Compression Reinforcement
Unit Strength = 15 MPa, f_y = 400 MPa and d'/d = 0.05

ρ	ρ'/ρ				
	0.2	0.4	0.6	0.8	1.0
0.001	0.180	0.203	0.217	0.225	0.230
0.002	0.589	0.619	0.641	0.646	0.647
0.003	0.820	0.893	0.942	0.967	0.970
0.004		1.143	1.235	1.284	1.292
0.005			1.517	1.599	1.615
0.006			1.789	1.911	1.938
0.007				2.220	2.261
0.008				2.527	2.583
0.009				2.831	2.906
0.010				3.132	3.229
0.011				3.431	3.552
0.012				3.727	3.875
0.013					4.198
0.014					4.521
0.015					4.844

Table B-21 Flexural Resistance Factor K_r(MPa) for Beams With Both
Tension and Compression Reinforcement
Unit Strength = 20 MPa, f_y = 400 MPa and d'/d = 0.05

ρ	ρ'/ρ				
	0.2	0.4	0.6	0.8	1.0
0.001	0.196	0.212	0.222	0.228	0.231
0.002	0.610	0.635	0.643	0.647	0.648
0.003	0.867	0.919	0.954	0.968	0.970
0.004	1.093	1.190	1.256	1.289	1.293
0.005		1.443	1.550	1.607	1.615
0.006			1.836	1.923	1.938
0.007			2.115	2.236	2.261
0.008			2.385	2.548	2.584
0.009				2.857	2.906
0.010				3.165	3.229
0.011				3.471	3.552
0.012				3.774	3.875
0.013				4.076	4.198
0.014				4.376	4.521
0.015				4.673	4.884

Table B-22 Flexural Resistance Factor K_r(MPa) for Beams With Both
Tension and Compression Reinforcement
Unit Strength = 30 MPa, f_y = 400 MPa and d'/d = 0.05

ρ	ρ'/ρ				
	0.2	0.4	0.6	0.8	1.0
0.001	0.212	0.222	0.228	0.231	---
0.002	0.626	0.640	0.646	0.648	0.649
0.003	0.904	0.940	0.963	0.969	0.971
0.004	1.159	1.227	1.272	1.291	1.294
0.005	1.390	1.501	1.576	1.612	1.616
0.006		1.762	1.873	1.932	1.939
0.007		2.009	2.165	2.249	2.261
0.008			2.451	2.564	2.584
0.009			2.731	2.878	2.907
0.010			3.005	3.191	3.230
0.011			3.273	3.502	3.552
0.012				3.811	3.875
0.013				4.119	4.198
0.014				4.426	4.521
0.015				4.731	4.844

Table B-23 Flexural Resistance Factor K_r(MPa) for Beams With Both
Tension and Compression Reinforcement
Unit Strength $\geq$ 40 MPa, f_y = 400 MPa and d'/d = 0.05

ρ	ρ'/ρ				
	0.2	0.4	0.6	0.8	1.0
0.001	0.224	---	---	---	---
0.002	0.636	0.644	0.648	0.650	0.650
0.003	0.926	0.952	0.967	0.971	0.973
0.004	1.197	1.249	1.282	1.292	1.295
0.005	1.450	1.535	1.591	1.613	1.617
0.006	1.684	1.811	1.895	1.934	1.940
0.007	1.900	2.076	2.195	2.256	2.262
0.008		2.330	2.489	2.574	2.585
0.009		2.575	2.780	2.890	2.907
0.010			3.065	3.206	3.230
0.011			3.346	3.520	3.553
0.012			3.622	3.833	3.876
0.013			3.894	4.145	4.198
0.014			4.161	4.456	4.521
0.015				4.765	4.844

Table B-24 Flexural Resistance Factor K_r(MPa) for Beams With Both
Tension and Compression Reinforcement
Unit Strength = 15 MPa, f_y = 400 MPa and d'/d = 0.1

ρ	ρ'/ρ				
	0.2	0.4	0.6	0.8	1.0
0.001	0.211	0.218	0.223	---	---
0.002	0.582	0.605	0.614	0.618	0.619
0.003	0.810	0.872	0.910	0.920	0.924
0.004		1.116	1.194	1.223	1.229
0.005			1.466	1.525	1.534
0.006			1.728	1.828	1.839
0.007				2.125	2.144
0.008				2.418	2.449
0.009				2.708	2.754
0.010				2.996	3.060
0.011				3.281	3.365
0.012				3.564	3.671
0.013					3.977
0.014					4.282
0.015					4.588

Table B-25 Flexural Resistance Factor K_r(MPa) for Beams With Both
Tension and Compression Reinforcement
Unit Strength = 20 MPa, f_y = 400 MPa and d'/d = 0.1

ρ	ρ'/ρ				
	0.2	0.4	0.6	0.8	1.0
0.001	---	---	---	---	---
0.002	0.603	0.614	0.619	0.622	0.623
0.003	0.857	0.899	0.918	0.925	0.927
0.004	1.080	1.163	1.214	1.227	1.232
0.005		1.409	1.499	1.529	1.537
0.006			1.775	1.832	1.841
0.007			2.043	2.134	2.146
0.008			2.304	2.437	2.451
0.009				2.735	2.757
0.010				3.029	3.062
0.011				3.321	3.367
0.012				3.611	3.672
0.013				3.899	3.978
0.014				4.185	4.283
0.015				4.469	4.589

Table B-26 Flexural Resistance Factor K_r(MPa) for Beams With Both
Tension and Compression Reinforcement
Unit Strength = 30 MPa, f_y = 400 MPa and d'/d = 0.1

ρ	ρ'/ρ				
	0.2	0.4	0.6	0.8	1.0
0.001	---	---	---	---	---
0.002	0.618	0.623	0.626	0.627	0.627
0.003	0.894	0.916	0.926	0.930	0.932
0.004	1.145	1.200	1.224	1.233	1.237
0.005	1.373	1.467	1.520	1.535	1.541
0.006		1.721	1.812	1.838	1.846
0.007		1.962	2.094	2.140	2.150
0.008			2.369	2.442	2.445
0.009			2.639	2.745	2.760
0.010			2.903	3.047	3.065
0.011			3.161	3.350	3.370
0.012				3.648	3.675
0.013				3.943	3.981
0.014				4.236	4.286
0.015				4.527	4.591

Table B-27 Flexural Resistance Factor K_r(MPa) for Beams With Both
Tension and Compression Reinforcement
Unit Strength ≥ 40 MPa, f_y = 400 MPa and d'/d = 0.1

ρ	ρ'/ρ				
	0.2	0.4	0.6	0.8	1.0
0.001	---	---	---	---	---
0.002	0.627	0.630	0.613	0.632	0.632
0.003	0.914	0.927	0.933	0.936	0.937
0.004	1.184	1.218	1.232	1.239	1.241
0.005	1.433	1.501	1.530	1.541	1.546
0.006	1.664	1.770	1.826	1.844	1.850
0.007	1.876	2.028	2.122	2.146	2.155
0.008		2.276	2.408	2.448	2.460
0.009		2.513	2.688	2.751	2.764
0.010			2.963	3.053	3.069
0.011			3.234	3.355	3.374
0.012			3.500	3.658	3.679
0.013			3.761	3.960	3.984
0.014			4.018	4.263	4.289
0.015				4.561	4.594

Table B-28 Flexural Resistance Factor K_r(MPa) for Beams With Both
Tension and Compression Reinforcement
Unit Strength = 15 MPa, f_y = 400 MPa and d'/d = 0.15

ρ	ρ'/ρ				
	0.2	0.4	0.6	0.8	1.0
0.001	---	---	---	---	---
0.002	0.574	0.587	0.593	0.595	0.597
0.003	0.799	0.851	0.871	0.880	0.884
0.004		1.088	1.147	1.164	1.170
0.005			1.415	1.447	1.457
0.006			1.666	1.731	1.744
0.007				2.015	2.032
0.008				2.299	2.319
0.009				2.583	2.607
0.010				2.860	2.895
0.011				3.132	3.182
0.012				3.400	3.470
0.013					3.758
0.014					4.047
0.015					4.335

Table B-29 Flexural Resistance Factor K_r(MPa) for Beams With Both
Tension and Compression Reinforcement
Unit Strength = 20 MPa, f_y = 400 MPa and d'/d = 0.15

ρ	ρ'/ρ				
	0.2	0.4	0.6	0.8	1.0
0.001	---	---	---	---	---
0.002	0.593	0.599	0.602	0.603	0.604
0.003	0.846	0.872	0.844	0.889	0.891
0.004	1.066	1.134	1.162	1.173	1.178
0.005		1.375	1.437	1.457	1.465
0.006			1.711	1.741	1.752
0.007			1.972	2.024	2.039
0.008			2.222	2.308	2.326
0.009				2.591	2.613
0.010				2.875	2.901
0.011				3.159	3.188
0.012				3.443	3.476
0.013				3.722	3.763
0.014				3.995	4.051
0.015				4.265	4.339

Table B-30 Flexural Resistance Factor K_r(MPa) for Beams With Both
Tension and Compression Reinforcement
Unit Strength = 30 MPa, f_y = 400 MPa and d'/d = 0.15

ρ	ρ'/ρ				
	0.2	0.4	0.6	0.8	1.0
0.001	---	---	---	---	---
0.002	0.611	0.612	0.613	0.613	0.613
0.003	0.880	0.892	0.898	0.900	0.902
0.004	1.130	1.163	1.179	1.186	1.189
0.005	1.356	1.427	1.457	1.470	1.476
0.006		1.680	1.734	1.754	1.762
0.007		1.914	2.009	2.038	2.049
0.008			2.282	2.321	2.336
0.009			2.547	2.605	2.623
0.010			2.801	2.888	2.910
0.011			3.049	3.172	3.197
0.012				3.455	3.484
0.013				3.739	3.772
0.014				4.023	4.059
0.015				4.307	4.347

Table B-31 Flexural Resistance Factor K_r(MPa) for Beams With Both
Tension and Compression Reinforcement
Unit Strength ≥ 40 MPa, f_y = 400 MPa and d'/d = 0.15

ρ	ρ'/ρ				
	0.2	0.4	0.6	0.8	1.0
0.001	---	---	---	---	---
0.002	0.623	0.623	---	---	---
0.003	0.901	0.907	0.910	0.911	0.911
0.004	1.165	1.184	1.193	1.197	1.199
0.005	1.414	1.455	1.474	1.482	1.486
0.006	1.644	1.720	1.753	1.767	1.773
0.007	1.852	1.979	2.030	2.051	2.060
0.008		2.222	2.305	2.335	2.347
0.009		2.452	2.580	2.618	2.633
0.010			2.853	2.902	2.920
0.011			3.122	3.185	3.207
0.012			3.378	3.469	3.494
0.013			3.629	3.752	3.781
0.014			3.875	4.036	4.068
0.015				4.319	4.355

Table B-32 Flexural Resistance Factor K_r(MPa) for Beams With Both
Tension and Compression Reinforcement
Unit Strength = 15 MPa, f_y = 400 MPa and d'/d = 0.2

ρ	ρ'/ρ				
	0.2	0.4	0.6	0.8	1.0
0.001	---	---	---	---	---
0.002	0.565	0.573	0.576	0.578	0.579
0.003	0.788	0.822	0.838	0.845	0.848
0.004		1.059	1.096	1.111	1.117
0.005			1.350	1.376	1.386
0.006			1.601	1.641	1.656
0.007				1.906	1.925
0.008				2.171	2.195
0.009				2.436	2.464
0.010				2.701	2.734
0.011				2.966	3.004
0.012				3.231	3.274
0.013					3.545
0.014					3.815
0.015					4.086

Table B-33 Flexural Resistance Factor K_r(MPa) for Beams With Both
Tension and Compression Reinforcement
Unit Strength = 20 MPa, f_y = 400 MPa and d'/d = 0.2

ρ	ρ'/ρ				
	0.2	0.4	0.6	0.8	1.0
0.001	---	---	---	---	---
0.002	0.587	0.589	0.590	0.591	0.591
0.003	0.831	0.848	0.856	0.860	0.861
0.004	1.051	1.096	1.118	1.127	1.131
0.005		1.335	1.375	1.393	1.400
0.006			1.631	1.658	1.669
0.007			1.884	1.923	1.938
0.008			2.135	2.188	2.207
0.009				2.453	2.477
0.010				2.717	2.746
0.011				2.982	3.016
0.012				3.247	3.286
0.013				3.512	3.555
0.014				3.777	3.825
0.015				4.042	4.095

Table B-34 Flexural Resistance Factor K_r(MPa) for Beams With Both
Tension and Compression Reinforcement
Unit Strength = 30 MPa, f_y = 400 MPa and d'/d = 0.2

ρ	ρ'/ρ				
	0.2	0.4	0.6	0.8	1.0
0.001	---	---	---	---	---
0.002	0.607	---	---	---	---
0.003	0.869	0.875	0.877	0.878	0.879
0.004	1.111	1.133	1.143	1.147	1.149
0.005	1.334	1.382	1.405	1.414	1.419
0.006		1.624	1.664	1.681	1.688
0.007		1.859	1.921	1.946	1.957
0.008			2.176	2.212	2.226
0.009			2.429	2.477	2.495
0.010			2.681	2.741	2.764
0.011			2.931	3.006	3.034
0.012				3.271	3.303
0.013				3.535	3.572
0.014				3.800	3.842
0.015				4.065	4.111

Table B-35 Flexural Resistance Factor K_r(MPa) for Beams With Both
Tension and Compression Reinforcement
Unit Strength $\geq$ 40 MPa, f_y = 400 MPa and d'/d = 0.2

ρ	ρ'/ρ				
	0.2	0.4	0.6	0.8	1.0
0.001	---	---	---	---	---
0.002	---	---	---	---	---
0.003	0.893	0.895	0.895	---	---
0.004	1.149	1.160	1.164	1.166	1.167
0.005	1.390	1.417	1.429	1.435	1.437
0.006	1.616	1.667	1.691	1.702	1.707
0.007	1.827	1.912	1.951	1.969	1.976
0.008		2.150	2.209	2.234	2.245
0.009		2.384	2.465	2.500	2.514
0.010			2.720	2.765	2.783
0.011			2.974	3.030	3.052
0.012			3.226	3.295	3.321
0.013			3.477	3.559	3.590
0.014			3.727	3.824	3.860
0.015				4.089	4.129

Table B-36 Values of $bd^2 \times 10^{-6}$ mm^3
$$M_r = K_r bd^2 \times 10^{-6}$$

Depth d (mm)	Width b (mm)			
	90	140	190	240
290	7.57	11.77	15.98	20.18
300	8.10	12.60	17.10	21.60
340	10.40	16.18	21.96	27.74
490	21.61	33.61	45.62	57.62
500	22.50	35.00	47.50	60.00
540	26.24	40.82	55.40	69.98
690	42.85	66.65	90.46	114.26
700	44.10	68.60	93.10	117.60
740	49.28	76.66	104.04	131.42
890	71.29	110.89	150.50	190.10
900	72.90	113.40	153.90	194.40
940	79.52	123.70	167.88	212.06
1090	106.93	166.33	225.74	285.14
1100	108.90	169.40	229.90	290.40
1140	116.96	181.94	246.92	311.90
1290	149.77	232.97	316.18	399.38
1300	152.10	236.60	321.10	405.60
1340	161.60	251.38	341.16	430.94
1490	199.81	310.81	421.82	532.82
1500	202.50	315.00	427.50	540.00
1540	213.44	332.02	450.60	569.18

Table B-37 Values* of v_m (MPa)

Effective Depth (mm)	Unit Strength (MPa)				
	10	15	20	30	>40
90	0.246	0.301	0.348	0.404	0.454
100	0.246	0.301	0.348	0.404	0.454
140	0.246	0.301	0.348	0.404	0.454
290	0.246	0.301	0.348	0.404	0.454
300	0.246	0.301	0.348	0.404	0.454
340	0.246	0.301	0.348	0.404	0.454
490	0.231	0.283	0.327	0.380	0.426
500	0.230	0.281	0.325	0.377	0.423
540	0.223	0.273	0.315	0.366	0.411
690	0.198	0.243	0.281	0.326	0.366
700	0.197	0.241	0.278	0.323	0.363
740	0.190	0.233	0.269	0.313	0.351
890	0.166	0.203	0.234	0.272	0.305
900	0.164	0.201	0.232	0.269	0.302
940	0.157	0.193	0.223	0.259	0.290
1090	0.148	0.181	0.209	0.242	0.272
1100	0.148	0.181	0.209	0.242	0.272
1140	0.148	0.181	0.209	0.242	0.272
1290	0.148	0.181	0.209	0.242	0.272
1300	0.148	0.181	0.209	0.242	0.272
1340	0.148	0.181	0.209	0.242	0.272
1490	0.148	0.181	0.209	0.242	0.272
1500	0.148	0.181	0.209	0.242	0.272
1540	0.148	0.181	0.209	0.242	0.272

* Values are for:
        Normal weight units
        Mortar type *S*
        Continuously grouted Beam
        Zero axial Load

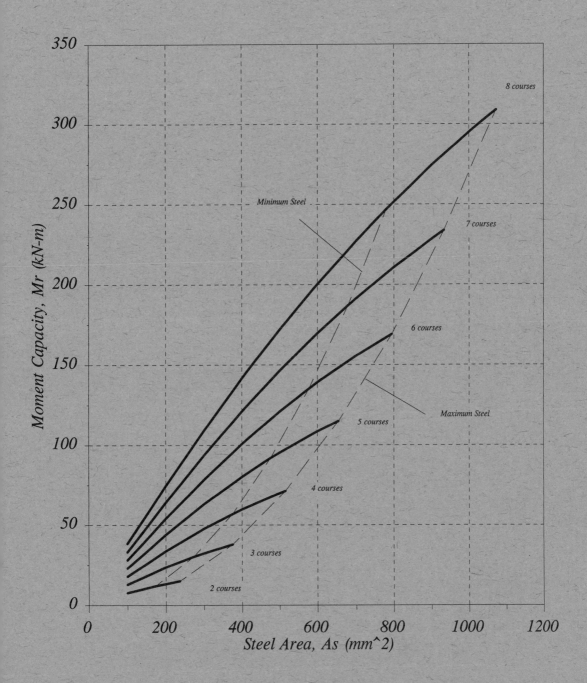

Figure B-1 Moment Capacity of a 200 Block Beam
15 MPa Unit Strength, f_y = 300 MPa

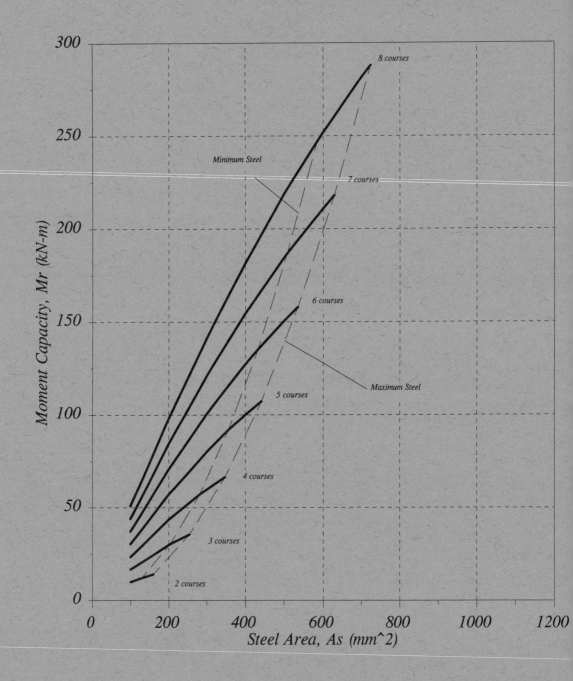

Figure B-2 Moment Capacity of a 200 Block Beam
15 MPa Unit Strength, f_y = 400 MPa

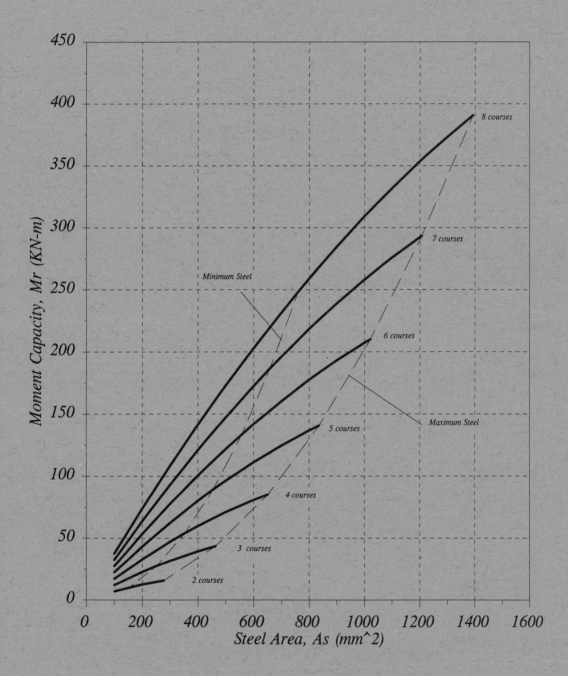

Figure B-3 Moment Capacity of a 200 Block Beam
20 MPa Unit Strength, f_y = 300 MPa

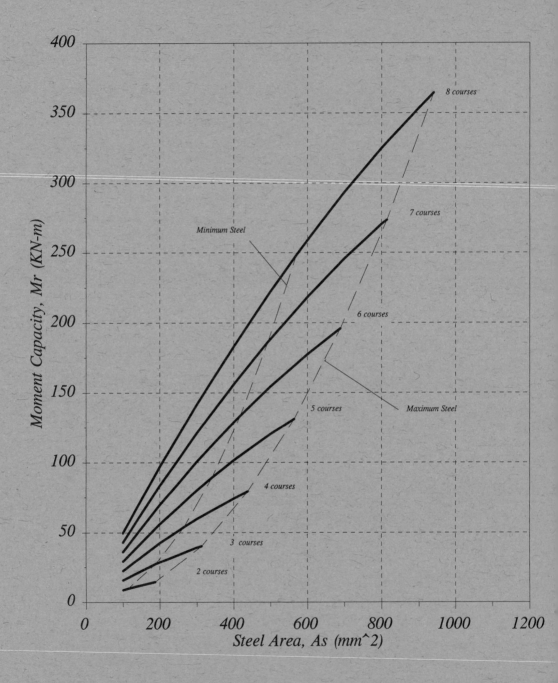

Figure B-4 Moment Capacity of a 200 Block Beam
20 MPa Unit Strength, f_y = 400 MPa

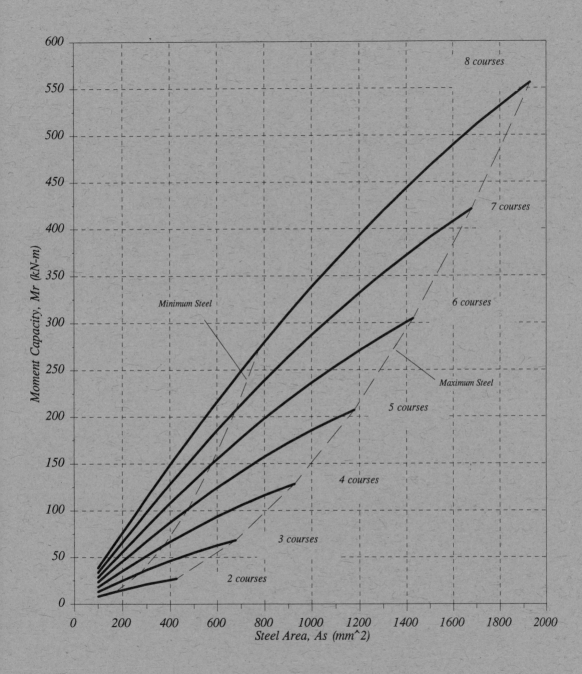

Figure B-5 Moment Capacity of a 200 Block Beam
30 MPa Unit Strength, f_y = 300 MPa

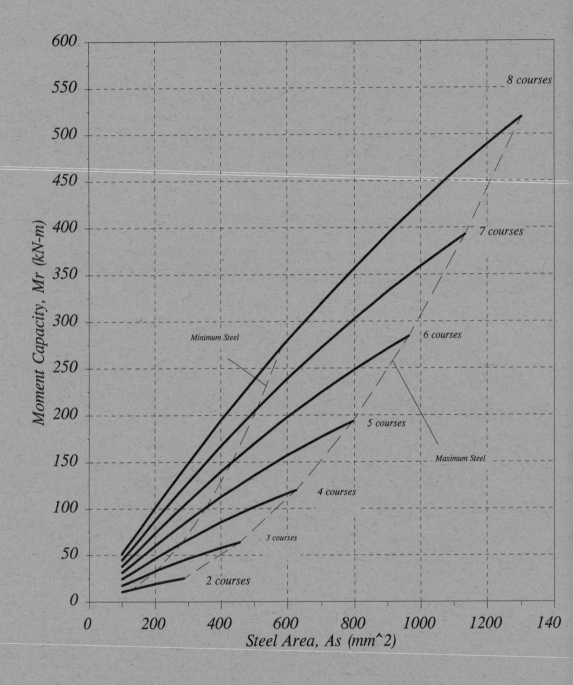

Figure B-6 Moment Capacity of a 200 Block Beam
30 MPa Unit Strength, f_y = 400 MPa

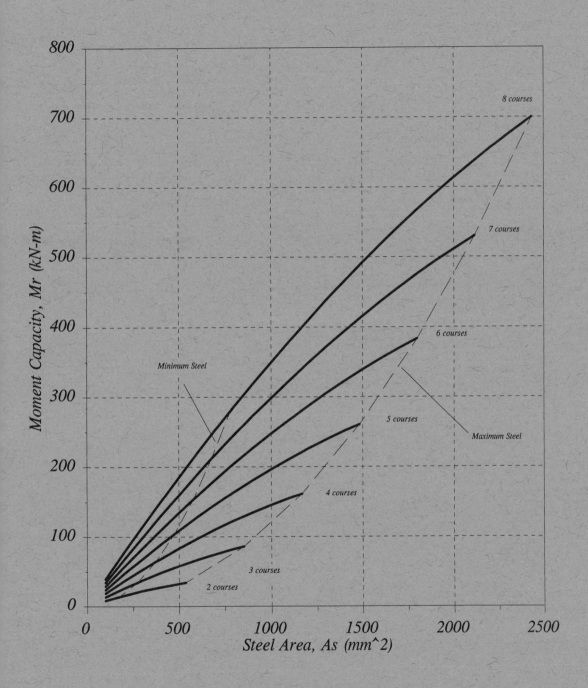

Figure B-7 Moment Capacity of a 200 Block Beam
40 MPa Unit Strength, $f_y = 300$ MPa

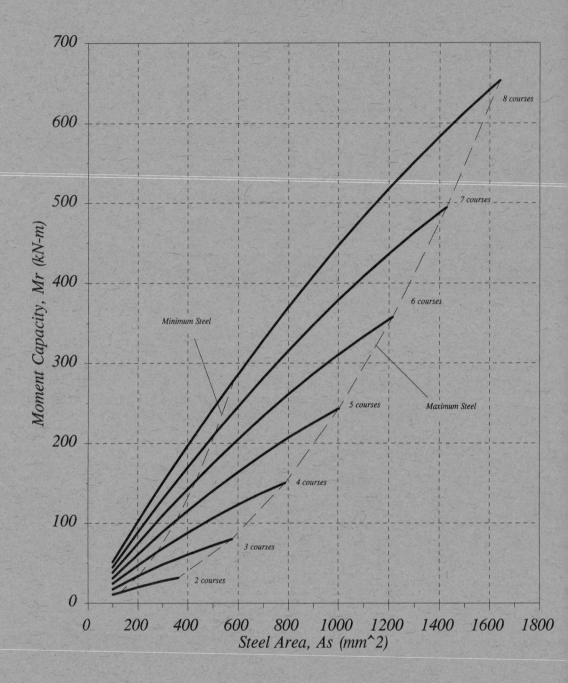

Figure B-8 Moment Capacity of a 200 Block Beam
40 MPa Unit Strength, f_y = 400 MPa

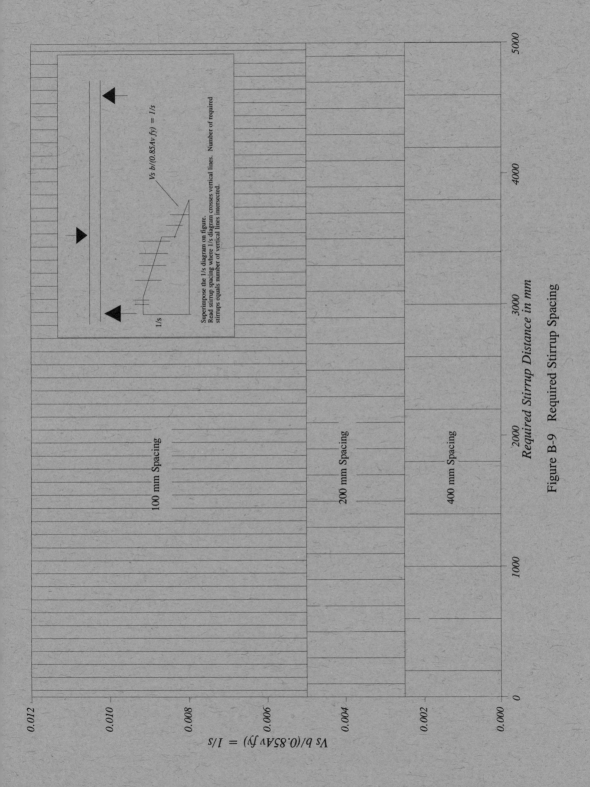

Figure B-9   Required Stirrup Spacing

Table C-1 Values of $(EI)_{eff}$ (N-mm^2 x 10^9) for Unreinforced Masonry Walls[*]

Nominal Wall Thickness (mm)	Number of Grouted Cores/m	Unit Strength (MPa)				
		10	15	20	30	>40
200	0	976.82	1472.74	1953.64	2629.90	3306.16
	1	986.54	1486.18	1973.09	2657.30	3341.52
	2	990.96	1491.48	1981.93	2670.56	3359.20
	3	990.08	1488.65	1980.16	2669.68	3359.20
	4	983.89	1477.69	1967.78	2654.65	3341.52
	5	972.40	1458.60	1944.80	2625.48	3306.16
250	0	1803.36	2718.91	3606.72	4855.20	6103.68
	1	1861.36	2804.05	3722.73	5013.67	6304.62
	2	1905.70	2868.24	3811.40	5135.70	6460.00
	3	1938.27	2914.33	3876.54	5226.41	6576.28
	4	1955.17	2936.44	3910.34	5275.27	6640.20
	5	1958.40	2937.60	3916.80	5287.68	6658.56
300	0	2963.61	4468.21	5927.22	7978.95	10030.68
	1	3117.73	4696.71	6235.46	8397.76	10560.06
	2	3243.70	4882.05	6487.40	8741.50	10995.60
	3	3343.42	5027.08	6686.85	9015.30	11343.76
	4	3412.99	5125.92	6825.98	9208.63	11591.28
	5	3454.40	5181.60	6908.80	9326.88	11744.96

[*] Mortar type *S*

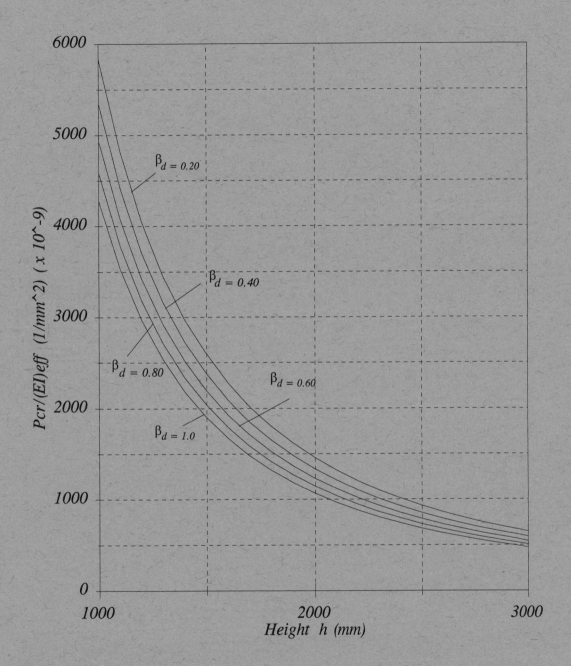

Figure C-1 $P_{cr} / (EI)_{eff}$ For Masonry Wall
(h = 1m to 3m)

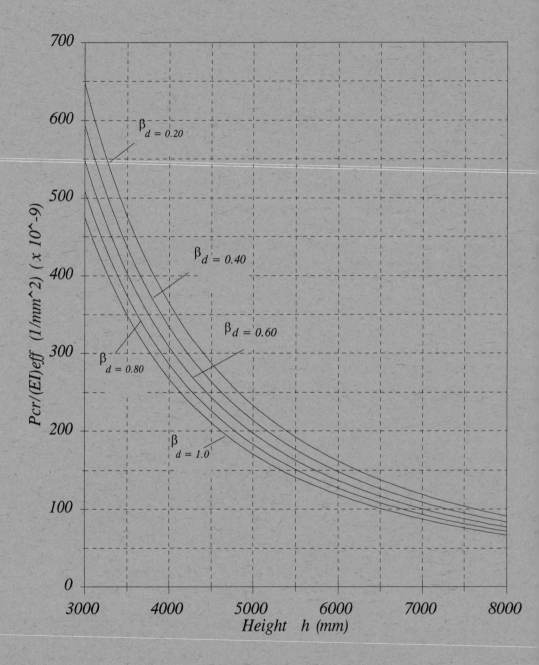

Figure C-2 $P_{cr} / (EI)_{eff}$ For Masonry Wall
(h= 3m to 8m)

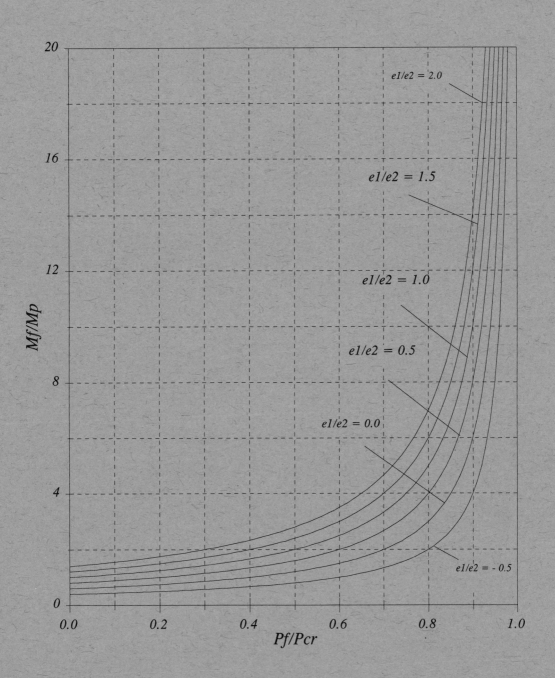

Figure C-3 Relationship Between $P_f\,/\,P_{cr}$ and $M_f\,/\,M_p$ For Masonry Walls

Table D-1 Values of $(EI)_{eff}$ (N-mm^2 x 10^9) for Reinforced Masonry 200 Block Wall[*]
Unit Strength = 10 MPa

Vertical Reinforcement Area (mm^2)	Number of Grouted Cores/m	Eccentricity e (mm)							
		0.1t	0.2t	0.3t	0.4t	0.5t	0.6t	0.7t	≥0.8t
300	1	616.59	616.59	594.35	532.63	470.91	409.19	347.47	290.76
	2	619.35	619.35	564.68	490.98	417.28	343.58	286.51	286.51
	3	618.80	618.80	534.62	450.43	366.23	282.04	282.04	282.04
	4	614.93	597.32	504.08	410.85	317.61	277.22	277.22	277.22
	5	607.75	574.30	473.67	373.03	272.40	272.12	272.12	272.12
400	1	616.59	616.59	598.69	549.00	499.32	449.64	399.96	354.31
	2	619.35	619.35	574.85	514.87	454.89	394.90	348.45	348.45
	3	618.80	618.80	549.68	480.55	411.43	342.30	342.27	342.27
	4	614.93	600.37	523.28	446.20	369.11	335.71	335.71	335.71
	5	607.75	579.94	496.29	412.64	328.98	328.75	328.75	328.75
600	1	616.59	616.59	605.82	575.94	546.06	516.19	486.31	458.85
	2	619.35	619.35	591.52	554.00	516.48	478.96	449.90	449.90
	3	618.80	618.80	574.23	529.65	485.08	440.50	440.48	440.48
	4	614.93	605.32	554.41	503.51	452.61	430.55	430.55	430.55
	5	607.75	589.04	532.77	476.49	420.22	420.06	420.06	420.06
800	1	616.59	616.59	611.55	597.55	583.55	569.56	555.56	542.70
	2	619.35	619.35	604.82	585.22	565.63	546.04	530.87	530.87
	3	618.80	618.80	593.72	568.63	543.55	518.47	518.46	518.46
	4	614.93	609.22	578.99	548.75	518.52	505.42	505.42	505.42
	5	607.75	596.18	561.39	526.59	491.79	491.70	491.70	491.70
1000	1	616.59	616.59	616.29	615.48	614.66	613.84	613.02	612.26
	2	619.35	619.35	615.81	611.03	606.25	601.46	597.76	597.76
	3	618.80	618.80	609.75	600.70	591.65	582.61	582.60	582.60
	4	614.93	612.42	599.11	585.80	572.49	566.72	566.72	566.72
	5	607.75	602.00	584.71	567.41	550.12	550.07	550.07	550.07
1500	1	745.28	745.28	745.28	745.28	745.28	745.28	745.28	616.59
	2	724.99	724.99	724.99	724.99	724.99	724.99	619.35	619.35
	3	703.90	703.90	703.90	703.90	703.90	703.90	618.80	618.80
	4	681.94	681.94	681.94	681.94	681.94	614.93	614.93	614.93
	5	659.05	659.05	659.05	659.05	659.05	607.75	607.75	607.75
2000	1	841.41	841.41	841.41	841.41	841.41	841.41	841.41	616.59
	2	816.37	816.37	816.37	816.37	816.37	816.37	619.35	619.35
	3	790.44	790.44	790.44	790.44	790.44	790.44	618.80	618.80
	4	763.56	763.56	763.56	763.56	763.56	763.56	614.93	614.93
	5	735.67	735.67	735.67	735.67	735.67	735.67	607.75	607.75
2500	1	914.84	914.84	914.84	914.84	914.84	914.84	914.84	616.59
	2	885.83	885.83	885.83	885.83	885.83	885.83	619.35	619.35
	3	855.89	855.89	855.89	855.89	855.89	855.89	618.80	618.80
	4	824.96	824.96	824.96	824.96	824.96	614.93	614.93	614.93
	5	792.98	792.98	792.98	792.98	792.98	607.75	607.75	607.75
3500	1	1020.48	1020.48	1020.48	1020.48	1020.48	1020.48	1020.48	616.59
	2	985.22	985.22	985.22	985.22	985.22	985.22	619.35	619.35
	3	949.02	949.02	949.02	949.02	949.02	949.02	618.80	618.80
	4	911.82	911.82	911.82	911.82	911.82	614.93	614.93	614.93
	5	873.56	873.56	873.56	873.56	873.56	607.75	607.75	607.75

[*]Mortar type S

Table D-2 Values of $(EI)_{eff}$ (N-mm² x 10⁹) for Reinforced Masonry 200 Block Wall[*]
Unit Strength = 15 MPa

Vertical Reinforcement Area (mm²)	Number of Grouted Cores/m	Eccentricity e (mm)							
		0.1t	0.2t	0.3t	0.4t	0.5t	0.6t	0.7t	$\geq 0.8t$
300	1	928.86	928.86	887.61	773.15	658.69	544.23	429.77	324.59
	2	932.18	932.18	831.71	696.28	560.86	425.43	320.56	320.56
	3	930.41	930.41	776.91	623.38	469.86	316.33	316.27	316.27
	4	923.56	891.65	722.72	553.80	384.87	311.69	311.69	311.69
	5	911.63	851.34	669.99	488.63	307.28	306.78	306.78	306.78
400	1	928.86	928.86	892.86	792.96	693.05	593.15	493.24	401.45
	2	932.18	932.18	844.06	725.29	606.52	487.75	395.78	395.78
	3	930.41	930.41	795.28	660.13	524.98	389.82	389.77	389.77
	4	923.56	895.38	746.25	597.11	447.97	383.36	383.36	383.36
	5	911.63	858.29	697.85	537.41	376.96	376.52	376.52	376.52
600	1	928.86	928.86	901.79	826.65	751.52	676.39	601.26	532.22
	2	932.18	932.18	865.01	774.47	683.93	593.39	523.28	523.28
	3	930.41	930.41	826.29	722.15	618.01	513.87	513.82	513.82
	4	923.56	901.67	785.78	669.89	554.00	503.79	503.79	503.79
	5	911.63	869.91	744.44	618.96	493.48	493.13	493.13	493.13
800	1	928.86	928.86	909.22	854.72	800.22	745.72	691.22	641.14
	2	932.18	932.18	882.38	815.25	748.12	681.00	629.02	629.02
	3	930.41	930.41	851.88	773.34	694.80	616.26	616.22	616.22
	4	923.56	906.82	818.24	729.66	641.08	602.71	602.71	602.71
	5	911.63	879.41	782.49	685.57	588.65	588.38	588.38	588.38
1000	1	928.86	928.86	915.58	878.74	841.90	805.05	768.21	734.35
	2	932.18	932.18	897.19	850.02	802.86	755.69	719.17	719.17
	3	930.41	930.41	873.62	816.82	760.03	703.23	703.20	703.20
	4	923.56	911.19	845.71	780.22	714.74	686.37	686.37	686.37
	5	911.63	887.40	814.53	741.66	668.79	668.59	668.59	668.59
1500	1	928.86	928.86	928.28	926.65	925.03	923.40	921.78	920.28
	2	932.18	932.18	926.58	919.04	911.50	903.96	898.12	898.12
	3	930.41	930.41	916.54	902.68	888.81	874.94	874.94	874.94
	4	923.56	919.76	899.62	879.49	859.35	850.63	850.63	850.63
	5	911.63	903.00	877.06	851.12	825.17	825.10	825.10	825.10
2000	1	1061.51	1061.51	1061.51	1061.51	1061.51	1061.51	1061.51	928.86
	2	1033.26	1033.26	1033.26	1033.26	1033.26	1033.26	932.18	932.18
	3	1003.80	1003.80	1003.80	1003.80	1003.80	1003.80	930.41	930.41
	4	973.06	973.06	973.06	973.06	973.06	923.56	923.56	923.56
	5	940.92	940.92	940.92	940.92	940.92	911.63	911.63	911.63
2500	1	1173.65	1173.65	1173.65	1173.65	1173.65	1173.65	1173.65	928.86
	2	1140.05	1140.05	1140.05	1140.05	1140.05	1140.05	932.18	932.18
	3	1105.15	1105.15	1105.15	1105.15	1105.15	1105.15	930.41	930.41
	4	1068.84	1068.84	1068.84	1068.84	1068.84	923.56	923.56	923.56
	5	1031.02	1031.02	1031.02	1031.02	1031.02	911.63	911.63	911.63
3500	1	1342.15	1342.15	1342.15	1342.15	1342.15	1342.15	1342.15	928.86
	2	1299.68	1299.68	1299.68	1299.68	1299.68	1299.68	932.18	932.18
	3	1255.78	1255.78	1255.78	1255.78	1255.78	1255.78	930.41	930.41
	4	1210.35	1210.35	1210.35	1210.35	1210.35	923.56	923.56	923.56
	5	1163.30	1163.30	1163.30	1163.30	1163.30	911.63	911.63	911.63

[*]Mortar type S

Table D-3 Values of $(EI)_{eff}$ (N-mm^2 x 10^9) for Reinforced Masonry 200 Block Wall[*]
Unit Strength = 20 MPa

Vertical Reinforcement Area (mm^2)	Number of Grouted Cores/m	Eccentricity e (mm)							
		$0.1t$	$0.2t$	$0.3t$	$0.4t$	$0.5t$	$0.6t$	$0.7t$	$\geq 0.8t$
300	1	1233.18	1233.18	1172.65	1004.68	836.71	668.74	500.77	346.43
	2	1238.71	1238.71	1091.52	893.13	694.73	496.34	342.71	342.71
	3	1237.60	1237.60	1012.94	788.24	563.54	338.85	338.75	338.75
	4	1229.87	1183.17	935.98	688.79	441.61	334.52	334.52	334.52
	5	1215.50	1127.24	861.73	596.23	330.72	329.98	329.98	329.98
400	1	1233.18	1233.18	1178.51	1026.81	875.12	723.42	571.72	432.34
	2	1238.71	1238.71	1105.38	925.66	745.94	566.22	427.05	427.05
	3	1237.60	1237.60	1033.60	829.58	625.55	421.52	421.43	421.43
	4	1229.87	1187.39	962.54	737.70	512.86	415.44	415.44	415.44
	5	1215.50	1135.12	893.32	651.51	409.71	409.04	409.04	409.04
600	1	1233.18	1233.18	1188.69	1065.25	941.81	818.37	694.93	581.51
	2	1238.71	1238.71	1129.35	981.95	834.55	687.15	573.01	573.01
	3	1237.60	1237.60	1069.24	900.85	732.47	564.08	564.00	564.00
	4	1229.87	1194.64	1008.17	821.70	635.22	554.44	554.44	554.44
	5	1215.50	1148.60	947.33	746.07	544.80	544.25	544.25	544.25
800	1	1233.18	1233.18	1197.37	1098.01	998.64	899.28	799.92	708.62
	2	1238.71	1238.71	1149.70	1029.74	909.77	789.81	696.91	696.91
	3	1237.60	1237.60	1099.36	961.11	822.85	684.59	684.53	684.53
	4	1229.87	1200.74	1046.57	892.39	738.22	671.43	671.43	671.43
	5	1215.50	1159.89	992.58	825.27	657.97	657.51	657.51	657.51
1000	1	1233.18	1233.18	1204.94	1126.57	1048.21	969.85	891.48	819.48
	2	1238.71	1238.71	1167.40	1071.28	975.17	879.05	804.62	804.62
	3	1237.60	1237.60	1125.47	1013.31	901.16	789.01	788.96	788.96
	4	1229.87	1206.01	1079.71	953.42	827.13	772.42	772.42	772.42
	5	1215.50	1169.59	1031.49	893.38	755.27	754.89	754.89	754.89
1500	1	1233.18	1233.18	1220.44	1185.08	1149.73	1114.38	1079.02	1046.54
	2	1238.71	1238.71	1203.48	1156.00	1108.52	1061.03	1024.27	1024.27
	3	1237.60	1237.60	1178.44	1119.26	1060.09	1000.92	1000.89	1000.89
	4	1229.87	1216.64	1146.64	1076.65	1006.65	976.32	976.32	976.32
	5	1215.50	1189.08	1109.61	1030.13	950.66	950.44	950.44	950.44
2000	1	1233.18	1233.18	1232.59	1230.95	1229.31	1227.67	1226.03	1224.53
	2	1238.71	1238.71	1231.61	1222.05	1212.49	1202.93	1195.53	1195.53
	3	1237.60	1237.60	1219.51	1201.41	1183.31	1165.21	1165.20	1165.20
	4	1229.87	1224.84	1198.22	1171.60	1144.98	1133.45	1133.45	1133.45
	5	1215.50	1204.00	1169.41	1134.82	1100.23	1100.13	1100.13	1100.13
2500	1	1369.46	1369.46	1369.46	1369.46	1369.46	1369.46	1369.46	1233.18
	2	1334.38	1334.38	1334.38	1334.38	1334.38	1334.38	1238.71	1238.71
	3	1297.82	1297.82	1297.82	1297.82	1297.82	1297.82	1237.60	1237.60
	4	1259.65	1259.65	1259.65	1259.65	1259.65	1229.87	1229.87	1229.87
	5	1219.74	1219.74	1219.74	1219.74	1219.74	1215.50	1215.50	1215.50
3500	1	1593.69	1593.69	1593.69	1593.69	1593.69	1593.69	1593.69	1233.18
	2	1548.14	1548.14	1548.14	1548.14	1548.14	1548.14	1238.71	1238.71
	3	1500.88	1500.88	1500.88	1500.88	1500.88	1500.88	1237.60	1237.60
	4	1451.79	1451.79	1451.79	1451.79	1451.79	1229.87	1229.87	1229.87
	5	1400.75	1400.75	1400.75	1400.75	1400.75	1215.50	1215.50	1215.50

[*]Mortar type S

Table D-4 Values of $(EI)_{eff}$ (N-mm^2 x 10^9) for Reinforced Masonry 200 Block Wall[*]
Unit Strength = 30 MPa

Vertical Reinforcement Area (mm^2)	Number of Grouted Cores/m	Eccentricity e (mm)							
		0.1t	0.2t	0.3t	0.4t	0.5t	0.6t	0.7t	≥0.8t
300	1	1660.82	1660.82	1572.55	1327.62	1082.69	837.77	592.84	367.80
	2	1669.10	1669.10	1454.78	1165.88	876.99	588.10	364.39	364.39
	3	1668.55	1668.55	1341.67	1014.75	687.82	360.90	360.76	360.76
	4	1659.16	1591.23	1231.70	872.17	512.63	356.87	356.87	356.87
	5	1640.93	1512.53	1126.28	740.02	353.77	352.70	352.70	352.70
400	1	1660.82	1660.82	1579.04	1352.13	1125.22	898.31	671.39	462.90
	2	1669.10	1669.10	1470.16	1201.99	933.83	665.66	458.01	458.01
	3	1668.55	1668.55	1364.68	1060.76	756.84	452.93	452.79	452.79
	4	1659.16	1595.95	1261.36	926.77	592.19	447.23	447.23	447.23
	5	1640.93	1521.36	1161.66	801.96	442.27	441.27	441.27	441.27
600	1	1660.82	1660.82	1590.53	1395.49	1200.46	1005.42	810.38	631.18
	2	1669.10	1669.10	1497.29	1265.69	1034.10	802.50	623.16	623.16
	3	1668.55	1668.55	1405.13	1141.68	878.23	614.77	614.66	614.66
	4	1659.16	1604.21	1313.34	1022.48	731.62	605.60	605.60	605.60
	5	1640.93	1536.77	1223.45	910.13	596.81	595.94	595.94	595.94
800	1	1660.82	1660.82	1600.52	1433.23	1265.94	1098.64	931.35	777.63
	2	1669.10	1669.10	1520.82	1320.95	1121.08	921.20	766.43	766.43
	3	1668.55	1668.55	1440.10	1211.63	983.15	754.67	754.57	754.57
	4	1659.16	1611.32	1358.11	1104.89	851.68	741.97	741.97	741.97
	5	1640.93	1549.99	1276.44	1002.88	729.32	728.57	728.57	728.57
1000	1	1660.82	1660.82	1609.40	1466.74	1324.07	1181.41	1038.75	907.66
	2	1669.10	1669.10	1541.66	1369.87	1198.08	1026.30	893.27	893.27
	3	1668.55	1668.55	1470.97	1273.37	1075.76	878.15	878.07	878.07
	4	1659.16	1617.58	1397.49	1177.40	957.31	861.96	861.96	861.96
	5	1640.93	1561.58	1322.89	1084.20	845.51	844.85	844.85	844.85
1500	1	1660.82	1660.82	1628.04	1537.11	1446.18	1355.24	1264.31	1180.76
	2	1669.10	1669.10	1585.25	1472.22	1359.18	1246.15	1158.62	1158.62
	3	1668.55	1668.55	1535.28	1401.98	1268.69	1135.39	1135.33	1135.33
	4	1659.16	1630.56	1479.16	1327.76	1176.36	1110.77	1110.77	1110.77
	5	1640.93	1585.50	1418.75	1252.01	1085.27	1084.81	1084.81	1084.81
2000	1	1660.82	1660.82	1643.11	1593.97	1544.83	1495.69	1446.55	1401.40
	2	1669.10	1669.10	1620.30	1554.51	1488.72	1422.94	1371.99	1371.99
	3	1668.55	1668.55	1586.72	1504.87	1423.03	1341.18	1341.15	1341.15
	4	1659.16	1640.88	1544.13	1447.39	1350.64	1308.73	1308.73	1308.73
	5	1640.93	1604.41	1494.57	1384.74	1274.90	1274.59	1274.59	1274.59
2500	1	1660.82	1660.82	1655.68	1641.42	1627.16	1612.90	1598.64	1585.54
	2	1669.10	1669.10	1649.43	1622.92	1596.41	1569.89	1549.36	1549.36
	3	1668.55	1668.55	1629.30	1590.05	1550.79	1511.54	1511.52	1511.52
	4	1659.16	1649.39	1597.68	1545.98	1494.27	1471.87	1471.87	1471.87
	5	1640.93	1619.93	1556.76	1493.59	1430.43	1430.25	1430.25	1430.25
3500	1	1878.83	1878.83	1878.83	1878.83	1878.83	1878.83	1878.83	1660.82
	2	1830.56	1830.56	1830.56	1830.56	1830.56	1830.56	1669.10	1669.10
	3	1780.30	1780.30	1780.30	1780.30	1780.30	1780.30	1668.55	1668.55
	4	1727.88	1727.88	1727.88	1727.88	1727.88	1727.88	1659.16	1659.16
	5	1673.13	1673.13	1673.13	1673.13	1673.13	1640.93	1640.93	1640.93

[*]Mortar type S

Table D-5 Values of $(EI)_{eff}$ (N-mm^2 x 10^9) for Reinforced Masonry 200 Block Wall[*]
Unit Strength $\geq$ 40 MPa

Vertical Reinforcement Area (mm^2)	Number of Grouted Cores/m	Eccentricity e (mm)							
		0.1t	0.2t	0.3t	0.4t	0.5t	0.6t	0.7t	0.8t
300	1	2088.45	2088.45	1972.03	1649.00	1325.97	1002.93	679.90	383.09
	2	2099.50	2099.50	1817.03	1436.27	1055.51	674.76	379.92	379.92
	3	2099.50	2099.50	1668.85	1238.14	807.43	376.72	376.53	376.53
	4	2088.45	1998.97	1525.35	1051.73	578.11	372.91	372.91	372.91
	5	2066.35	1897.18	1388.26	879.35	370.43	369.02	369.02	369.02
400	1	2088.45	2088.45	1978.99	1675.25	1371.52	1067.78	764.05	484.97
	2	2099.50	2099.50	1833.53	1475.02	1116.51	758.00	480.38	480.38
	3	2099.50	2099.50	1693.59	1287.61	881.64	475.67	475.49	475.49
	4	2088.45	2004.05	1557.31	1110.56	663.81	470.27	470.27	470.27
	5	2066.35	1906.71	1426.47	946.23	465.99	464.66	464.66	464.66
600	1	2088.45	2088.45	1991.45	1722.31	1453.16	1184.01	914.87	667.57
	2	2099.50	2099.50	1863.03	1544.28	1225.54	906.79	659.96	659.96
	3	2099.50	2099.50	1737.68	1375.80	1013.92	652.04	651.88	651.88
	4	2088.45	2013.07	1614.09	1215.11	816.13	643.27	643.27	643.27
	5	2066.35	1923.60	1494.15	1064.70	635.26	634.07	634.07	634.07
800	1	2088.45	2088.45	2002.46	1763.86	1525.25	1286.65	1048.05	828.81
	2	2099.50	2099.50	1889.00	1605.26	1321.53	1037.79	818.08	818.08
	3	2099.50	2099.50	1776.37	1453.19	1130.01	806.83	806.69	806.69
	4	2088.45	2020.97	1663.76	1306.55	949.34	794.59	794.59	794.59
	5	2066.35	1938.31	1553.12	1167.93	782.74	781.68	781.68	781.68
1000	1	2088.45	2088.45	2012.35	1801.20	1590.05	1378.90	1167.75	973.74
	2	2099.50	2099.50	1912.29	1659.94	1407.59	1155.24	959.83	959.83
	3	2099.50	2099.50	1810.97	1522.39	1233.81	945.24	945.11	945.11
	4	2088.45	2028.00	1708.04	1388.07	1068.11	929.49	929.49	929.49
	5	2066.35	1951.38	1605.53	1259.67	913.82	912.86	912.86	912.86
1500	1	2088.45	2088.45	2033.50	1881.02	1728.55	1576.07	1423.60	1283.50
	2	2099.50	2099.50	1961.88	1776.38	1590.87	1405.37	1261.73	1261.73
	3	2099.50	2099.50	1884.36	1669.19	1454.03	1238.86	1238.76	1238.76
	4	2088.45	2042.87	1801.59	1560.31	1319.03	1214.49	1214.49	1214.49
	5	2066.35	1978.88	1715.76	1452.63	1189.50	1188.78	1188.78	1188.78
2000	1	2088.45	2088.45	2050.95	1946.90	1842.84	1738.79	1634.74	1539.13
	2	2099.50	2099.50	2002.63	1872.05	1741.47	1610.90	1509.78	1509.78
	3	2099.50	2099.50	1944.39	1789.26	1634.12	1478.99	1478.92	1478.92
	4	2088.45	2054.96	1877.71	1700.46	1523.20	1446.41	1446.41	1446.41
	5	2066.35	2001.14	1804.97	1608.80	1412.62	1412.08	1412.08	1412.08
2500	1	2088.45	2088.45	2065.77	2002.84	1939.91	1876.98	1814.05	1756.22
	2	2099.50	2099.50	2037.11	1953.01	1868.91	1784.80	1719.68	1719.68
	3	2099.50	2099.50	1994.99	1890.46	1785.93	1681.40	1681.36	1681.36
	4	2088.45	2065.12	1941.61	1818.10	1694.60	1641.09	1641.09	1641.09
	5	2066.35	2019.74	1879.52	1739.31	1599.09	1598.70	1598.70	1598.70
3500	1	2109.34	2109.34	2109.34	2109.34	2109.34	2109.34	2109.34	2088.45
	2	2099.50	2099.50	2092.95	2084.11	2075.28	2066.45	2059.61	2059.61
	3	2099.50	2099.50	2076.55	2053.59	2030.64	2007.68	2007.67	2007.67
	4	2088.45	2081.40	2044.11	2006.81	1969.51	1953.35	1953.35	1953.35
	5	2066.35	2049.42	1998.47	1947.53	1896.58	1896.44	1896.44	1896.44

[*]Mortar type S

Table D-6 Values of $(EI)_{eff}$ (N-mm^2 x 10^9) for Reinforced Masonry 250 Block Wall[*]
Unit Strength = 10 MPa

Vertical Reinforcement Area (mm²)	Number of Grouted Cores/m	Eccentricity e (mm)								
		0.1t	0.2t	0.3t	0.4t	0.5t	0.6t	0.7t	0.8t	≥ 0.9t
400	1	1163.35	1163.35	1133.03	1030.48	927.93	825.38	722.83	620.28	608.70
	2	1191.06	1191.06	1096.96	967.02	837.08	707.13	599.59	599.59	599.59
	3	1211.42	1211.36	1055.96	900.57	745.17	589.95	589.95	589.95	589.95
	4	1221.98	1187.93	1010.34	832.75	655.16	579.71	579.71	579.71	579.71
	5	1224.00	1158.48	961.92	765.36	568.80	568.80	568.80	568.80	568.80
500	1	1163.35	1163.35	1138.52	1054.53	970.55	886.57	802.58	718.60	709.12
	2	1191.06	1191.06	1112.53	1004.09	895.64	787.20	697.45	697.45	697.45
	3	1211.42	1211.37	1079.77	948.17	816.57	685.12	685.12	685.12	685.12
	4	1221.98	1192.83	1040.77	888.72	736.66	672.06	672.06	672.06	672.06
	5	1224.00	1167.42	997.67	827.93	658.18	658.18	658.18	658.18	658.18
600	1	1163.35	1163.35	1143.44	1076.11	1008.78	941.45	874.12	806.79	799.19
	2	1191.06	1191.06	1126.46	1037.25	948.04	858.84	785.01	785.01	785.01
	3	1211.42	1211.38	1101.01	990.65	880.28	770.04	770.04	770.04	770.04
	4	1221.98	1197.19	1067.85	938.51	809.17	754.22	754.22	754.22	754.22
	5	1224.00	1175.35	1029.38	883.42	737.46	737.46	737.46	737.46	737.46
800	1	1163.35	1163.35	1151.98	1113.54	1075.09	1036.64	998.20	959.75	955.41
	2	1191.06	1191.06	1150.54	1094.59	1038.63	982.68	936.37	936.37	936.37
	3	1211.42	1211.39	1137.61	1063.83	990.05	916.35	916.35	916.35	916.35
	4	1221.98	1204.66	1114.32	1023.98	933.64	895.25	895.25	895.25	895.25
	5	1224.00	1188.90	1083.59	978.29	872.98	872.98	872.98	872.98	872.98
1000	1	1163.35	1163.35	1159.20	1145.16	1131.11	1117.07	1103.02	1088.98	1087.39
	2	1191.06	1191.06	1170.81	1142.85	1114.88	1086.91	1063.77	1063.77	1063.77
	3	1211.42	1211.40	1168.29	1125.18	1082.06	1039.00	1039.00	1039.00	1039.00
	4	1221.98	1210.90	1153.11	1095.32	1037.53	1012.97	1012.97	1012.97	1012.97
	5	1224.00	1200.16	1128.63	1057.10	985.57	985.57	985.57	985.57	985.57
1500	1	1346.07	1346.07	1346.07	1346.07	1346.07	1346.07	1346.07	1346.07	1163.35
	2	1312.19	1312.19	1312.19	1312.19	1312.19	1312.19	1191.06	1191.06	1191.06
	3	1276.86	1276.86	1276.86	1276.86	1276.86	1211.42	1211.42	1211.42	1211.42
	4	1239.94	1239.94	1239.94	1239.94	1239.94	1221.98	1221.98	1221.98	1221.98
	5	1224.00	1221.73	1214.92	1208.12	1201.31	1201.31	1201.31	1201.31	1201.31
2000	1	1538.50	1538.50	1538.50	1538.50	1538.50	1538.50	1538.50	1538.50	1163.35
	2	1495.89	1495.89	1495.89	1495.89	1495.89	1495.89	1191.06	1191.06	1191.06
	3	1451.62	1451.62	1451.62	1451.62	1451.62	1211.42	1211.42	1211.42	1211.42
	4	1405.57	1405.57	1405.57	1405.57	1405.57	1221.98	1221.98	1221.98	1221.98
	5	1357.60	1357.60	1357.60	1357.60	1224.00	1224.00	1224.00	1224.00	1224.00
2500	1	1688.81	1688.81	1688.81	1688.81	1688.81	1688.81	1688.81	1688.81	1163.35
	2	1638.70	1638.70	1638.70	1638.70	1638.70	1638.70	1191.06	1191.06	1191.06
	3	1586.81	1586.81	1586.81	1586.81	1586.81	1211.42	1211.42	1211.42	1211.42
	4	1533.01	1533.01	1533.01	1533.01	1533.01	1221.98	1221.98	1221.98	1221.98
	5	1477.18	1477.18	1477.18	1477.18	1224.00	1224.00	1224.00	1224.00	1224.00
3500	1	1910.51	1910.51	1910.51	1910.51	1910.51	1910.51	1910.51	1910.51	1163.35
	2	1848.23	1848.23	1848.23	1848.23	1848.23	1848.23	1191.06	1191.06	1191.06
	3	1784.06	1784.06	1784.06	1784.06	1784.06	1211.42	1211.42	1211.42	1211.42
	4	1717.87	1717.87	1717.87	1717.87	1717.87	1221.98	1221.98	1221.98	1221.98
	5	1649.56	1649.56	1649.56	1649.56	1224.00	1224.00	1224.00	1224.00	1224.00

[*]Mortar type S

Table D-7   Values of $(EI)_{eff}$ (N-mm^2 x 10^9) for Reinforced Masonry 250 Block Wall[*]
Unit Strength = 15 MPa

Vertical Reinforcement Area (mm^2)	Number of Grouted Cores/m	Eccentricity e (mm)								
		0.1t	0.2t	0.3t	0.4t	0.5t	0.6t	0.7t	0.8t	≥ 0.9t
400	1	1752.53	1752.53	1693.97	1495.92	1297.87	1099.82	901.77	703.71	681.36
	2	1792.65	1792.65	1614.47	1368.42	1122.37	876.31	672.68	672.68	672.68
	3	1821.46	1821.35	1531.79	1242.24	952.68	663.46	663.46	663.46	663.46
	4	1835.28	1772.64	1445.90	1119.17	792.43	653.61	653.61	653.61	653.61
	5	1836.00	1716.71	1358.83	1000.95	643.07	643.07	643.07	643.07	643.07
500	1	1752.53	1752.53	1700.62	1525.06	1349.50	1173.94	998.38	822.83	803.01
	2	1792.65	1792.65	1633.41	1413.51	1193.61	973.71	791.72	791.72	791.72
	3	1821.46	1821.36	1560.88	1300.40	1039.93	779.74	779.74	779.74	779.74
	4	1835.28	1778.65	1483.26	1187.87	892.48	766.98	766.98	766.98	766.98
	5	1836.00	1727.74	1402.94	1078.15	753.36	753.36	753.36	753.36	753.36
600	1	1752.53	1752.53	1706.70	1551.71	1396.71	1241.72	1086.72	931.73	914.23
	2	1792.65	1792.65	1650.69	1454.65	1258.61	1062.56	900.32	900.32	900.32
	3	1821.46	1821.37	1587.36	1353.34	1119.33	885.58	885.58	885.58	885.58
	4	1835.28	1784.10	1517.18	1250.25	983.32	869.91	869.91	869.91	869.91
	5	1836.00	1737.72	1442.88	1148.04	853.20	853.20	853.20	853.20	853.20
800	1	1752.53	1752.53	1717.51	1599.06	1480.61	1362.16	1243.72	1125.27	1111.90
	2	1792.65	1792.65	1681.31	1527.55	1373.79	1220.04	1092.79	1092.79	1092.79
	3	1821.46	1821.39	1634.13	1446.88	1259.63	1072.59	1072.59	1072.59	1072.59
	4	1835.28	1793.71	1576.91	1360.10	1143.29	1051.18	1051.18	1051.18	1051.18
	5	1836.00	1755.24	1512.97	1270.70	1028.43	1028.43	1028.43	1028.43	1028.43
1000	1	1752.53	1752.53	1726.90	1640.23	1553.55	1466.88	1380.21	1293.53	1283.75
	2	1792.65	1792.65	1707.84	1590.72	1473.61	1356.49	1259.56	1259.56	1259.56
	3	1821.46	1821.40	1674.52	1527.65	1380.77	1234.06	1234.06	1234.06	1234.06
	4	1835.28	1801.98	1628.28	1454.59	1280.90	1207.10	1207.10	1207.10	1207.10
	5	1836.00	1770.25	1573.01	1375.77	1178.53	1178.53	1178.53	1178.53	1178.53
1500	1	1752.53	1752.53	1746.06	1724.18	1702.29	1680.40	1658.52	1636.63	1634.16
	2	1792.65	1792.65	1761.69	1718.94	1676.20	1633.45	1598.07	1598.07	1598.07
	3	1821.46	1821.43	1756.10	1690.77	1625.44	1560.19	1560.19	1560.19	1560.19
	4	1835.28	1818.58	1731.50	1644.42	1557.34	1520.35	1520.35	1520.35	1520.35
	5	1836.00	1800.24	1692.94	1585.65	1478.36	1478.36	1478.36	1478.36	1478.36
2000	1	1907.38	1907.38	1907.38	1907.38	1907.38	1907.38	1907.38	1907.38	1752.53
	2	1860.55	1860.55	1860.55	1860.55	1860.55	1860.55	1792.65	1792.65	1792.65
	3	1821.46	1821.46	1818.99	1816.52	1814.05	1811.59	1811.59	1811.59	1811.59
	4	1835.28	1831.30	1810.57	1789.84	1769.11	1760.30	1760.30	1760.30	1760.30
	5	1836.00	1823.05	1784.19	1745.34	1706.48	1706.48	1706.48	1706.48	1706.48
2500	1	2128.90	2128.90	2128.90	2128.90	2128.90	2128.90	2128.90	2128.90	1752.53
	2	2072.43	2072.43	2072.43	2072.43	2072.43	2072.43	1792.65	1792.65	1792.65
	3	2013.56	2013.56	2013.56	2013.56	2013.56	1821.46	1821.46	1821.46	1821.46
	4	1952.10	1952.10	1952.10	1952.10	1952.10	1835.28	1835.28	1835.28	1835.28
	5	1887.84	1887.84	1887.84	1887.84	1836.00	1836.00	1836.00	1836.00	1836.00
3500	1	2469.90	2469.90	2469.90	2469.90	2469.90	2469.90	2469.90	2469.90	1752.53
	2	2396.91	2396.91	2396.91	2396.91	2396.91	2396.91	1792.65	1792.65	1792.65
	3	2321.19	2321.19	2321.19	2321.19	2321.19	1821.46	1821.46	1821.46	1821.46
	4	2242.55	2242.55	2242.55	2242.55	2242.55	1835.28	1835.28	1835.28	1835.28
	5	2160.78	2160.78	2160.78	2160.78	1836.00	1836.00	1836.00	1836.00	1836.00

[*]Mortar type S

Table D-8 Values of $(EI)_{eff}$ (N-mm^2 x 10^9) for Reinforced Masonry 250 Block Wall[*]
Unit Strength = 20 MPa

Vertical Reinforcement Area (mm^2)	Number of Grouted Cores/m	Eccentricity e (mm)								
		0.1t	0.2t	0.3t	0.4t	0.5t	0.6t	0.7t	0.8t	$\geq$ 0.9t
400	1	2326.71	2326.71	2239.32	1943.80	1648.28	1352.76	1057.25	761.73	728.37
	2	2382.13	2382.13	2117.75	1752.67	1387.58	1022.50	720.36	720.36	720.36
	3	2422.84	2422.68	1994.84	1567.01	1139.17	711.82	711.82	711.82	711.82
	4	2443.96	2351.66	1870.20	1388.73	907.27	702.71	702.71	702.71	702.71
	5	2448.00	2272.49	1745.98	1219.46	692.95	692.95	692.95	692.95	692.95
500	1	2326.71	2326.71	2246.76	1976.41	1706.06	1435.71	1165.36	895.01	864.49
	2	2382.13	2382.13	2139.01	1803.28	1467.55	1131.82	853.97	853.97	853.97
	3	2422.84	2422.69	2027.60	1632.52	1237.43	842.79	842.79	842.79	842.79
	4	2443.96	2358.45	1912.43	1466.40	1020.37	830.87	830.87	830.87	830.87
	5	2448.00	2285.01	1796.05	1307.08	818.12	818.12	818.12	818.12	818.12
600	1	2326.71	2326.71	2253.64	2006.57	1759.49	1512.41	1265.33	1018.26	990.37
	2	2382.13	2382.13	2158.63	1849.99	1541.36	1232.72	977.30	977.30	977.30
	3	2422.84	2422.70	2057.78	1692.85	1327.93	963.42	963.42	963.42	963.42
	4	2443.96	2364.70	1951.24	1537.78	1124.32	948.65	948.65	948.65	948.65
	5	2448.00	2296.49	1841.95	1387.42	932.88	932.88	932.88	932.88	932.88
800	1	2326.71	2326.71	2266.06	2060.95	1855.85	1650.75	1445.65	1240.55	1217.40
	2	2382.13	2382.13	2193.93	1934.04	1674.15	1414.26	1199.18	1199.18	1199.18
	3	2422.84	2422.72	2111.93	1801.13	1490.34	1179.89	1179.89	1179.89	1179.89
	4	2443.96	2375.87	2020.69	1665.50	1310.32	1159.41	1159.41	1159.41	1159.41
	5	2448.00	2316.96	1923.84	1530.72	1137.60	1137.60	1137.60	1137.60	1137.60
1000	1	2326.71	2326.71	2277.04	2109.07	1941.10	1773.13	1605.16	1437.19	1418.24
	2	2382.13	2382.13	2225.07	2008.18	1791.28	1574.39	1394.90	1394.90	1394.90
	3	2422.84	2422.74	2159.54	1896.34	1633.14	1370.24	1370.24	1370.24	1370.24
	4	2443.96	2385.66	2081.55	1777.43	1473.32	1344.11	1344.11	1344.11	1344.11
	5	2448.00	2334.84	1995.35	1655.86	1316.36	1316.36	1316.36	1316.36	1316.36
1500	1	2326.71	2326.71	2299.98	2209.60	2119.21	2028.83	1938.45	1848.06	1837.86
	2	2382.13	2382.13	2289.86	2162.44	2035.02	1907.61	1802.16	1802.16	1802.16
	3	2422.84	2422.78	2258.18	2093.59	1928.99	1764.59	1764.59	1764.59	1764.59
	4	2443.96	2405.85	2207.05	2008.24	1809.44	1724.97	1724.97	1724.97	1724.97
	5	2448.00	2371.51	2142.04	1912.57	1683.10	1683.10	1683.10	1683.10	1683.10
2000	1	2326.71	2326.71	2318.40	2290.31	2262.22	2234.13	2206.04	2177.95	2174.78
	2	2382.13	2382.13	2341.62	2285.69	2229.76	2173.83	2127.54	2127.54	2127.54
	3	2422.84	2422.81	2336.58	2250.35	2164.12	2077.99	2077.99	2077.99	2077.99
	4	2443.96	2421.80	2306.22	2190.64	2075.05	2025.94	2025.94	2025.94	2025.94
	5	2448.00	2400.31	2257.26	2114.20	1971.15	1971.15	1971.15	1971.15	1971.15
2500	1	2454.53	2454.53	2454.53	2454.53	2454.53	2454.53	2454.53	2454.53	2326.71
	2	2396.61	2396.61	2396.61	2396.61	2396.61	2396.61	2382.13	2382.13	2382.13
	3	2422.84	2422.83	2401.13	2379.43	2357.73	2336.05	2336.05	2336.05	2336.05
	4	2443.96	2434.88	2387.50	2340.13	2292.75	2272.63	2272.63	2272.63	2272.63
	5	2448.00	2423.81	2351.23	2278.65	2206.07	2206.07	2206.07	2206.07	2206.07
3500	1	2897.38	2897.38	2897.38	2897.38	2897.38	2897.38	2897.38	2897.38	2326.71
	2	2820.55	2820.55	2820.55	2820.55	2820.55	2820.55	2382.13	2382.13	2382.13
	3	2740.58	2740.58	2740.58	2740.58	2740.58	2422.84	2422.84	2422.84	2422.84
	4	2657.22	2657.22	2657.22	2657.22	2657.22	2443.96	2443.96	2443.96	2443.96
	5	2570.20	2570.20	2570.20	2570.20	2448.00	2448.00	2448.00	2448.00	2448.00

[*]Mortar type S

Table D-9 Values of $(EI)_{eff}$ (N-mm^2 x 10^9) for Reinforced Masonry 250 Block Wall[*]

Unit Strength = 30 MPa

Vertical Reinforcement Area (mm^2)	Number of Grouted Cores/m	Eccentricity e (mm)								
		0.1t	0.2t	0.3t	0.4t	0.5t	0.6t	0.7t	0.8t	≥ 0.9t
400	1	3133.55	3133.55	3004.57	2568.39	2132.22	1696.05	1259.88	823.70	774.47
	2	3209.81	3209.81	2821.20	2284.55	1747.89	1211.24	767.11	767.11	767.11
	3	3266.51	3266.27	2639.34	2012.42	1385.49	759.27	759.27	759.27	759.27
	4	3297.04	3162.07	2458.05	1754.03	1050.00	750.88	750.88	750.88	750.88
	5	3304.80	3048.51	2279.64	1510.76	741.89	741.89	741.89	741.89	741.89
500	1	3133.55	3133.55	3012.81	2604.53	2196.24	1787.96	1379.68	971.39	925.31
	2	3209.81	3209.81	2844.82	2340.78	1836.74	1332.70	915.57	915.57	915.57
	3	3266.51	3266.28	2675.85	2085.41	1494.97	905.20	905.20	905.20	905.20
	4	3297.04	3169.67	2505.25	1840.83	1176.42	894.13	894.13	894.13	894.13
	5	3304.80	3062.55	2335.79	1609.03	882.27	882.27	882.27	882.27	882.27
600	1	3133.55	3133.55	3020.52	2638.30	2256.07	1873.85	1491.63	1109.40	1066.26
	2	3209.81	3209.81	2866.85	2393.24	1919.63	1446.02	1054.07	1054.07	1054.07
	3	3266.51	3266.30	2709.84	2153.39	1596.93	1041.10	1041.10	1041.10	1041.10
	4	3297.04	3176.73	2549.13	1921.53	1293.93	1027.28	1027.28	1027.28	1027.28
	5	3304.80	3075.57	2387.88	1700.19	1012.50	1012.50	1012.50	1012.50	1012.50
800	1	3133.55	3133.55	3034.61	2700.04	2365.47	2030.90	1696.33	1361.76	1324.00
	2	3209.81	3209.81	2907.06	2488.97	2070.88	1652.78	1306.78	1306.78	1306.78
	3	3266.51	3266.32	2771.73	2277.14	1782.54	1288.51	1288.51	1288.51	1288.51
	4	3297.04	3189.54	2628.80	2068.06	1507.32	1269.07	1269.07	1269.07	1269.07
	5	3304.80	3099.15	2482.22	1865.28	1248.34	1248.34	1248.34	1248.34	1248.34
1000	1	3133.55	3133.55	3047.28	2755.55	2463.82	2172.09	1880.36	1588.63	1555.71
	2	3209.81	3209.81	2943.11	2574.81	2206.50	1838.20	1533.39	1533.39	1533.39
	3	3266.51	3266.34	2827.07	2387.81	1948.54	1509.77	1509.77	1509.77	1509.77
	4	3297.04	3200.97	2699.85	2198.72	1697.59	1484.68	1484.68	1484.68	1484.68
	5	3304.80	3120.12	2566.07	2012.02	1457.97	1457.97	1457.97	1457.97	1457.97
1500	1	3133.55	3133.55	3074.37	2874.23	2674.10	2473.97	2273.83	2073.70	2051.11
	2	3209.81	3209.81	3019.91	2757.67	2495.43	2233.19	2016.17	2016.17	2016.17
	3	3266.51	3266.39	2944.52	2622.66	2300.80	1979.30	1979.30	1979.30	1979.30
	4	3297.04	3225.13	2849.98	2474.84	2099.70	1940.32	1940.32	1940.32	1940.32
	5	3304.80	3164.22	2742.48	2320.74	1898.99	1898.99	1898.99	1898.99	1898.99
2000	1	3133.55	3133.55	3096.73	2972.21	2847.70	2723.19	2598.68	2474.16	2460.11
	2	3209.81	3209.81	3083.05	2907.99	2732.93	2557.87	2412.99	2412.99	2412.99
	3	3266.51	3266.42	3040.61	2814.80	2588.99	2363.43	2363.43	2363.43	2363.43
	4	3297.04	3244.79	2972.20	2699.61	2427.02	2311.20	2311.20	2311.20	2311.20
	5	3304.80	3199.92	2885.29	2570.66	2256.03	2256.03	2256.03	2256.03	2256.03
2500	1	3133.55	3133.55	3115.72	3055.45	2995.18	2934.91	2874.64	2814.36	2807.56
	2	3209.81	3209.81	3136.48	3035.22	2933.95	2832.69	2748.88	2748.88	2748.88
	3	3266.51	3266.45	3121.63	2976.81	2831.98	2687.33	2687.33	2687.33	2687.33
	4	3297.04	3261.29	3074.81	2888.33	2701.85	2622.63	2622.63	2622.63	2622.63
	5	3304.80	3229.77	3004.67	2779.58	2554.48	2554.48	2554.48	2554.48	2554.48
3500	1	3372.93	3372.93	3372.93	3372.93	3372.93	3372.93	3372.93	3372.93	3133.55
	2	3293.06	3293.06	3293.06	3293.06	3293.06	3293.06	3209.81	3209.81	3209.81
	3	3266.51	3266.50	3252.28	3238.05	3223.82	3209.61	3209.61	3209.61	3209.61
	4	3297.04	3287.78	3239.46	3191.15	3142.83	3122.30	3122.30	3122.30	3122.30
	5	3304.80	3277.40	3195.20	3112.99	3030.79	3030.79	3030.79	3030.79	3030.79

[*]Mortar type S

Table D-10 Values of $(EI)_{\text{eff}}$ (N-mm^2 x 10^9) for Reinforced Masonry 250 Block Wall[*]
Unit Strength $\geq$ 40 MPa

Vertical Reinforcement Area (mm^2)	Number of Grouted Cores/m	Eccentricity e (mm)								
		$0.1t$	$0.2t$	$0.3t$	$0.4t$	$0.5t$	$0.6t$	$0.7t$	$0.8t$	$\geq 0.9t$
400	1	3940.39	3940.39	3769.10	3189.86	2610.62	2031.37	1452.13	872.89	807.51
	2	4037.50	4037.50	3522.55	2811.42	2100.30	1389.17	800.65	800.65	800.65
	3	4110.18	4109.86	3280.50	2451.13	1621.77	793.34	793.34	793.34	793.34
	4	4150.13	3971.77	3041.44	2111.11	1180.78	785.52	785.52	785.52	785.52
	5	4161.60	3823.15	2807.81	1792.46	777.11	777.11	777.11	777.11	777.11
500	1	3940.39	3940.39	3777.94	3228.59	2679.25	2129.90	1580.55	1031.20	969.20
	2	4037.50	4037.50	3547.91	2871.81	2195.71	1519.60	960.07	960.07	960.07
	3	4110.18	4109.88	3319.77	2529.66	1739.56	950.35	950.35	950.35	950.35
	4	4150.13	3979.96	3092.33	2204.70	1317.08	939.95	939.95	939.95	939.95
	5	4161.60	3838.32	2868.48	1898.65	928.81	928.81	928.81	928.81	928.81
600	1	3940.39	3940.39	3786.26	3265.05	2743.84	2222.63	1701.42	1180.21	1121.38
	2	4037.50	4037.50	3571.74	2928.56	2285.37	1642.19	1109.90	1109.90	1109.90
	3	4110.18	4109.89	3356.62	2603.36	1850.09	1097.67	1097.67	1097.67	1097.67
	4	4150.13	3987.63	3140.00	2292.38	1444.75	1084.62	1084.62	1084.62	1084.62
	5	4161.60	3852.51	2925.22	1997.94	1070.65	1070.65	1070.65	1070.65	1070.65
800	1	3940.39	3940.39	3801.62	3332.34	2863.06	2393.79	1924.51	1455.23	1402.26
	2	4037.50	4037.50	3615.65	3033.11	2450.56	1868.01	1385.90	1385.90	1385.90
	3	4110.18	4109.92	3424.37	2738.83	2053.28	1368.52	1368.52	1368.52	1368.52
	4	4150.13	4001.69	3227.45	2453.20	1678.95	1350.00	1350.00	1350.00	1350.00
	5	4161.60	3878.46	3029.04	2179.62	1330.21	1330.21	1330.21	1330.21	1330.21
1000	1	3940.39	3940.39	3815.58	3393.51	2971.44	2549.38	2127.31	1705.24	1657.60
	2	4037.50	4037.50	3655.48	3127.93	2600.38	2072.83	1636.23	1636.23	1636.23
	3	4110.18	4109.94	3485.67	2861.40	2237.13	1613.57	1613.57	1613.57	1613.57
	4	4150.13	4014.39	3306.35	2598.32	1890.29	1589.47	1589.47	1589.47	1589.47
	5	4161.60	3901.82	3122.46	2343.11	1563.76	1563.76	1563.76	1563.76	1563.76
1500	1	3940.39	3940.39	3845.91	3526.40	3206.89	2887.38	2567.87	2248.36	2212.30
	2	4037.50	4037.50	3741.71	3333.25	2924.78	2516.32	2178.28	2178.28	2178.28
	3	4110.18	4109.99	3617.93	3125.88	2633.82	2142.32	2142.32	2142.32	2142.32
	4	4150.13	4041.67	3475.97	2910.27	2344.57	2104.23	2104.23	2104.23	2104.23
	5	4161.60	3951.82	3322.46	2693.11	2063.76	2063.76	2063.76	2063.76	2063.76
2000	1	3940.39	3940.39	3871.43	3638.25	3405.07	3171.89	2938.71	2705.53	2679.21
	2	4037.50	4037.50	3814.01	3505.39	3196.77	2888.14	2632.73	2632.73	2632.73
	3	4110.18	4110.03	3728.35	3346.67	2964.99	2583.74	2583.74	2583.74	2583.74
	4	4150.13	4064.35	3616.93	3169.51	2722.09	2531.99	2531.99	2531.99	2531.99
	5	4161.60	3993.16	3487.84	2982.51	2477.19	2477.19	2477.19	2477.19	2477.19
2500	1	3940.39	3940.39	3893.47	3734.82	3576.17	3417.51	3258.86	3100.21	3082.30
	2	4037.50	4037.50	3876.22	3653.51	3430.79	3208.08	3023.76	3023.76	3023.76
	3	4110.18	4110.07	3823.02	3535.98	3248.93	2962.21	2962.21	2962.21	2962.21
	4	4150.13	4083.72	3737.32	3390.93	3044.53	2897.36	2897.36	2897.36	2897.36
	5	4161.60	4028.33	3628.51	3228.69	2828.87	2828.87	2828.87	2828.87	2828.87
3500	1	3940.39	3940.39	3930.04	3895.06	3860.08	3825.10	3790.11	3755.13	3751.18
	2	4037.50	4037.50	3979.04	3898.30	3817.57	3736.83	3670.02	3670.02	3670.02
	3	4110.18	4110.13	3978.81	3847.49	3716.17	3585.00	3585.00	3585.00	3585.00
	4	4150.13	4115.44	3934.52	3753.59	3572.67	3495.80	3495.80	3495.80	3495.80
	5	4161.60	4085.64	3857.77	3629.90	3402.02	3402.02	3402.02	3402.02	3402.02

[*]Mortar type S

Table D-11 Values of $(EI)_{eff}$ (N-mm^2 x 10^9) for Reinforced Masonry 300 Block Wall[*]
Unit Strength = 10 MPa

Vertical Reinforcement Area (mm^2)	Number of Grouted Cores/m	Eccentricity e (mm)								
		0.1t	0.2t	0.3t	0.4t	0.5t	0.6t	0.7t	0.8t	≥ 0.9t
400	1	1948.58	1948.58	1899.66	1715.03	1530.40	1345.77	1161.14	976.51	938.64
	2	2027.31	2027.31	1851.80	1609.69	1367.58	1125.48	925.70	925.70	925.70
	3	2089.64	2088.21	1793.08	1497.95	1202.82	911.98	911.98	911.98	911.98
	4	2133.12	2065.81	1723.23	1380.65	1038.06	897.39	897.39	897.39	897.39
	5	2159.00	2030.92	1647.58	1264.24	881.82	881.82	881.82	881.82	881.82
500	1	1948.58	1948.58	1907.46	1752.25	1597.04	1441.83	1286.62	1131.41	1099.58
	2	2027.31	2027.31	1876.84	1669.28	1461.71	1254.15	1082.88	1082.88	1082.88
	3	2089.64	2088.40	1831.67	1574.94	1318.21	1065.21	1065.21	1065.21	1065.21
	4	2133.12	2073.93	1772.67	1471.41	1170.16	1046.45	1046.45	1046.45	1046.45
	5	2159.00	2045.43	1705.51	1365.59	1026.48	1026.48	1026.48	1026.48	1026.48
600	1	1948.58	1948.58	1914.51	1785.94	1657.37	1528.79	1400.22	1271.65	1245.28
	2	2027.31	2027.31	1899.46	1723.10	1546.73	1370.37	1224.85	1224.85	1224.85
	3	2089.64	2088.56	1866.43	1644.29	1422.16	1203.25	1203.25	1203.25	1203.25
	4	2133.12	2081.23	1817.10	1552.97	1288.84	1180.38	1180.38	1180.38	1180.38
	5	2159.00	2058.42	1757.40	1456.38	1156.08	1156.08	1156.08	1156.08	1156.08
800	1	1948.58	1948.58	1926.90	1845.07	1763.23	1681.40	1599.57	1517.74	1500.96
	2	2027.31	2027.31	1939.03	1817.26	1695.48	1573.70	1473.22	1473.22	1473.22
	3	2089.64	2088.86	1927.05	1765.25	1603.45	1444.00	1444.00	1444.00	1444.00
	4	2133.12	2093.90	1894.30	1694.70	1495.10	1413.13	1413.13	1413.13	1413.13
	5	2159.00	2080.92	1847.25	1613.58	1380.47	1380.47	1380.47	1380.47	1380.47
1000	1	1948.58	1948.58	1937.51	1895.71	1853.91	1812.12	1770.32	1728.53	1719.95
	2	2027.31	2027.31	1972.81	1897.62	1822.44	1747.25	1685.22	1685.22	1685.22
	3	2089.64	2089.10	1978.60	1868.10	1757.60	1648.70	1648.70	1648.70	1648.70
	4	2133.12	2104.64	1959.68	1814.73	1669.77	1610.25	1610.25	1610.25	1610.25
	5	2159.00	2099.90	1923.01	1746.13	1569.66	1569.66	1569.66	1569.66	1569.66
1500	1	2157.37	2157.37	2157.37	2157.37	2157.37	2157.37	2157.37	2157.37	1948.58
	2	2106.59	2106.59	2106.59	2106.59	2106.59	2106.59	2027.31	2027.31	2027.31
	3	2089.64	2089.60	2080.54	2071.48	2062.42	2053.50	2053.50	2053.50	2053.50
	4	2133.12	2125.75	2088.26	2050.76	2013.27	1997.87	1997.87	1997.87	1997.87
	5	2159.00	2136.99	2071.11	2005.23	1939.50	1939.50	1939.50	1939.50	1939.50
2000	1	2490.12	2490.12	2490.12	2490.12	2490.12	2490.12	2490.12	2490.12	1948.58
	2	2425.31	2425.31	2425.31	2425.31	2425.31	2425.31	2027.31	2027.31	2027.31
	3	2357.79	2357.79	2357.79	2357.79	2357.79	2089.64	2089.64	2089.64	2089.64
	4	2287.36	2287.36	2287.36	2287.36	2287.36	2133.12	2133.12	2133.12	2133.12
	5	2213.78	2213.78	2213.78	2213.78	2159.00	2159.00	2159.00	2159.00	2159.00
2500	1	2754.64	2754.64	2754.64	2754.64	2754.64	2754.64	2754.64	2754.64	1948.58
	2	2677.52	2677.52	2677.52	2677.52	2677.52	2677.52	2027.31	2027.31	2027.31
	3	2597.43	2597.43	2597.43	2597.43	2597.43	2089.64	2089.64	2089.64	2089.64
	4	2514.17	2514.17	2514.17	2514.17	2514.17	2133.12	2133.12	2133.12	2133.12
	5	2427.48	2427.48	2427.48	2427.48	2159.00	2159.00	2159.00	2159.00	2159.00
3500	1	3152.68	3152.68	3152.68	3152.68	3152.68	3152.68	3152.68	3152.68	1948.58
	2	3055.06	3055.06	3055.06	3055.06	3055.06	3055.06	2027.31	2027.31	2027.31
	3	2954.19	2954.19	2954.19	2954.19	2954.19	2089.64	2089.64	2089.64	2089.64
	4	2849.85	2849.85	2849.85	2849.85	2849.85	2133.12	2133.12	2133.12	2133.12
	5	2741.82	2741.82	2741.82	2741.82	2159.00	2159.00	2159.00	2159.00	2159.00

[*]Mortar type S

Table D-12 Values of $(EI)_{eff}$ (N-mm^2 x 10^9) for Reinforced Masonry 300 Block Wall[*]

Unit Strength = 15 MPa

Vertical Reinforcement Area (mm^2)	Number of Grouted Cores/m	Eccentricity e (mm)								
		0.1t	0.2t	0.3t	0.4t	0.5t	0.6t	0.7t	0.8t	≥0.9t
400	1	2935.45	2935.45	2843.68	2497.38	2151.07	1804.77	1458.47	1112.16	1041.14
	2	3051.28	3051.28	2729.07	2284.61	1840.16	1395.70	1028.97	1028.97	1028.97
	3	3141.92	3139.34	2606.57	2073.80	1541.03	1016.00	1016.00	1016.00	1016.00
	4	3203.70	3083.80	2473.45	1863.11	1252.76	1002.14	1002.14	1002.14	1002.14
	5	3238.50	3012.74	2337.05	1661.36	987.28	987.28	987.28	987.28	987.28
500	1	2935.45	2935.45	2852.97	2541.73	2230.49	1919.24	1608.00	1296.76	1232.93
	2	3051.28	3051.28	2759.03	2355.89	1952.76	1549.63	1216.99	1216.99	1216.99
	3	3141.92	3139.57	2652.92	2166.27	1679.62	1200.04	1200.04	1200.04	1200.04
	4	3203.70	3093.59	2533.10	1972.61	1412.12	1181.97	1181.97	1181.97	1181.97
	5	3238.50	3030.32	2407.26	1784.20	1162.63	1162.63	1162.63	1162.63	1162.63
600	1	2935.45	2935.45	2861.53	2582.59	2303.66	2024.72	1745.78	1466.84	1409.64
	2	3051.28	3051.28	2786.57	2421.44	2056.31	1691.17	1389.89	1389.89	1389.89
	3	3141.92	3139.77	2695.44	2251.11	1806.79	1368.91	1368.91	1368.91	1368.91
	4	3203.70	3102.55	2587.70	2072.85	1558.00	1346.58	1346.58	1346.58	1346.58
	5	3238.50	3046.38	2471.37	1896.37	1322.73	1322.73	1322.73	1322.73	1322.73
800	1	2935.45	2935.45	2876.90	2655.95	2435.01	2214.06	1993.11	1772.17	1726.86
	2	3051.28	3051.28	2835.90	2538.80	2241.70	1944.60	1699.46	1699.46	1699.46
	3	3141.92	3140.14	2771.37	2402.61	2033.84	1670.44	1670.44	1670.44	1670.44
	4	3203.70	3118.51	2684.90	2251.29	1817.67	1639.62	1639.62	1639.62	1639.62
	5	3238.50	3074.86	2585.12	2095.38	1606.80	1606.80	1606.80	1606.80	1606.80
1000	1	2935.45	2935.45	2890.42	2720.49	2550.56	2380.63	2210.69	2040.76	2005.92
	2	3051.28	3051.28	2879.15	2641.72	2404.29	2166.86	1970.95	1970.95	1970.95
	3	3141.92	3140.46	2837.74	2535.03	2232.32	1934.00	1934.00	1934.00	1934.00
	4	3203.70	3132.42	2769.56	2406.71	2043.86	1894.86	1894.86	1894.86	1894.86
	5	3238.50	3099.58	2683.82	2268.06	1853.28	1853.28	1853.28	1853.28	1853.28
1500	1	2935.45	2935.45	2918.44	2854.27	2790.11	2725.94	2661.77	2597.60	2584.44
	2	3051.28	3051.28	2968.44	2854.18	2739.92	2625.66	2531.38	2531.38	2531.38
	3	3141.92	3141.11	2974.12	2807.12	2640.12	2475.55	2475.55	2475.55	2475.55
	4	3203.70	3160.84	2942.65	2724.47	2506.28	2416.69	2416.69	2416.69	2416.69
	5	3238.50	3149.85	2884.52	2619.19	2354.50	2354.50	2354.50	2354.50	2354.50
2000	1	3044.58	3044.58	3044.58	3044.58	3044.58	3044.58	3044.58	3044.58	2935.45
	2	3051.28	3051.28	3039.10	3022.29	3005.48	2988.68	2974.81	2974.81	2974.81
	3	3141.92	3141.63	3081.42	3021.21	2961.01	2901.67	2901.67	2901.67	2901.67
	4	3203.70	3183.07	3078.04	2973.01	2867.98	2824.86	2824.86	2824.86	2824.86
	5	3238.50	3188.91	3040.50	2892.08	2744.02	2744.02	2744.02	2744.02	2744.02
2500	1	3423.70	3423.70	3423.70	3423.70	3423.70	3423.70	3423.70	3423.70	2935.45
	2	3338.63	3338.63	3338.63	3338.63	3338.63	3338.63	3051.28	3051.28	3051.28
	3	3249.72	3249.72	3249.72	3249.72	3249.72	3141.92	3141.92	3141.92	3141.92
	4	3203.70	3201.14	3188.09	3175.04	3161.99	3156.63	3156.63	3156.63	3156.63
	5	3238.50	3220.50	3166.62	3112.75	3059.00	3059.00	3059.00	3059.00	3059.00
3500	1	4018.43	4018.43	4018.43	4018.43	4018.43	4018.43	4018.43	4018.43	2935.45
	2	3906.53	3906.53	3906.53	3906.53	3906.53	3906.53	3051.28	3051.28	3051.28
	3	3790.13	3790.13	3790.13	3790.13	3790.13	3141.92	3141.92	3141.92	3141.92
	4	3668.88	3668.88	3668.88	3668.88	3668.88	3203.70	3203.70	3203.70	3203.70
	5	3542.39	3542.39	3542.39	3542.39	3238.50	3238.50	3238.50	3238.50	3238.50

[*]Mortar type S

Table D-13 Values of $(EI)_{\text{eff}}$ (N-mm^2 x 10^9) for Reinforced Masonry 300 Block Wall[*]
Unit Strength =20 MPa

Vertical Reinforcement Area (mm^2)	Number of Grouted Cores/m	Eccentricity e (mm)								
		0.1t	0.2t	0.3t	0.4t	0.5t	0.6t	0.7t	0.8t	≥ 0.9t
400	1	3897.17	3897.17	3762.00	3251.89	2741.78	2231.68	1721.57	1211.46	1106.85
	2	4054.63	4054.63	3583.19	2932.88	2282.58	1632.27	1095.68	1095.68	1095.68
	3	4179.28	4175.52	3399.77	2624.01	1848.26	1083.77	1083.77	1083.77	1083.77
	4	4266.24	4092.21	3206.40	2320.59	1434.78	1071.04	1071.04	1071.04	1071.04
	5	4318.00	3991.01	3012.36	2033.71	1057.39	1057.39	1057.39	1057.39	1057.39
500	1	3897.17	3897.17	3772.29	3301.04	2829.78	2358.52	1887.26	1416.00	1319.36
	2	4054.63	4054.63	3616.48	3012.09	2407.70	1803.32	1304.62	1304.62	1304.62
	3	4179.28	4175.77	3451.43	2727.09	2002.74	1288.92	1288.92	1288.92	1288.92
	4	4266.24	4103.17	3273.12	2443.07	1613.02	1272.17	1272.17	1272.17	1272.17
	5	4318.00	4010.75	3091.18	2171.61	1254.23	1254.23	1254.23	1254.23	1254.23
600	1	3897.17	3897.17	3781.88	3346.79	2911.71	2476.62	2041.53	1606.45	1517.22
	2	4054.63	4054.63	3647.42	3085.71	2524.00	1962.30	1498.81	1498.81	1498.81
	3	4179.28	4176.00	3499.36	2822.71	2146.06	1479.25	1479.25	1479.25	1479.25
	4	4266.24	4113.31	3334.88	2556.46	1778.03	1458.38	1458.38	1458.38	1458.38
	5	4318.00	4028.98	3163.99	2299.01	1436.07	1436.07	1436.07	1436.07	1436.07
800	1	3897.17	3897.17	3799.32	3430.06	3060.80	2691.53	2322.27	1953.01	1877.28
	2	4054.63	4054.63	3703.59	3219.38	2735.17	2250.95	1851.41	1851.41	1851.41
	3	4179.28	4176.42	3586.16	2995.90	2405.64	1823.96	1823.96	1823.96	1823.96
	4	4266.24	4131.63	3446.46	2761.29	2076.13	1794.77	1794.77	1794.77	1794.77
	5	4318.00	4061.83	3295.16	2528.49	1763.64	1763.64	1763.64	1763.64	1763.64
1000	1	3897.17	3897.17	3814.91	3504.49	3194.07	2883.66	2573.24	2262.82	2199.16
	2	4054.63	4054.63	3753.68	3338.55	2923.43	2508.30	2165.77	2165.77	2165.77
	3	4179.28	4176.79	3663.33	3149.87	2636.41	2130.42	2130.42	2130.42	2130.42
	4	4266.24	4147.87	3545.35	2942.83	2340.31	2092.90	2092.90	2092.90	2092.90
	5	4318.00	4090.85	3411.02	2731.18	2052.97	2052.97	2052.97	2052.97	2052.97
1500	1	3897.17	3897.17	3847.98	3662.36	3476.74	3291.12	3105.50	2919.88	2881.81
	2	4054.63	4054.63	3859.50	3590.35	3321.19	3052.03	2829.94	2829.94	2829.94
	3	4179.28	4177.58	3825.72	3473.86	3122.00	2775.25	2775.25	2775.25	2775.25
	4	4266.24	4181.88	3752.51	3323.14	2893.76	2717.45	2717.45	2717.45	2717.45
	5	4318.00	4151.35	3652.58	3153.80	2656.22	2656.22	2656.22	2656.22	2656.22
2000	1	3897.17	3897.17	3875.01	3791.42	3707.83	3624.24	3540.64	3457.05	3439.91
	2	4054.63	4054.63	3945.62	3795.25	3644.88	3494.51	3370.43	3370.43	3370.43
	3	4179.28	4178.21	3957.21	3736.20	3515.20	3297.41	3297.41	3297.41	3297.41
	4	4266.24	4209.28	3919.37	3629.46	3339.55	3220.50	3220.50	3220.50	3220.50
	5	4318.00	4199.80	3846.03	3492.26	3139.33	3139.33	3139.33	3139.33	3139.33
2500	1	3910.20	3910.20	3910.20	3910.20	3910.20	3910.20	3910.20	3910.20	3897.17
	2	4054.63	4054.63	4017.91	3967.26	3916.61	3865.96	3824.16	3824.16	3824.16
	3	4179.28	4178.74	4067.14	3955.55	3843.95	3733.97	3733.97	3733.97	3733.97
	4	4266.24	4232.09	4058.27	3884.46	3710.64	3639.27	3639.27	3639.27	3639.27
	5	4318.00	4239.94	4006.31	3772.68	3539.61	3539.61	3539.61	3539.61	3539.61
3500	1	4668.03	4668.03	4668.03	4668.03	4668.03	4668.03	4668.03	4668.03	3897.17
	2	4551.97	4551.97	4551.97	4551.97	4551.97	4551.97	4054.63	4054.63	4054.63
	3	4430.86	4430.86	4430.86	4430.86	4430.86	4179.28	4179.28	4179.28	4179.28
	4	4304.26	4304.26	4304.26	4304.26	4304.26	4266.24	4266.24	4266.24	4266.24
	5	4318.00	4303.33	4259.43	4215.52	4171.73	4171.73	4171.73	4171.73	4171.73

[*]Mortar type S

Table D-14 Values of $(EI)_{eff}$ (N-mm^2 x 10^9) for Reinforced Masonry 300 Block Wall[*]
Unit Strength = 30 MPa

Vertical Reinforcement Area (mm²)	Number of Grouted Cores/m	Eccentricity e (mm)								
		0.1t	0.2t	0.3t	0.4t	0.5t	0.6t	0.7t	0.8t	≥ 0.9t
400	1	5248.60	5248.60	5051.07	4305.60	3560.13	2814.66	2069.20	1323.73	1170.85
	2	5463.44	5463.44	4777.89	3832.24	2886.60	1940.95	1160.66	1160.66	1160.66
	3	5634.57	5629.12	4505.21	3381.29	2257.38	1149.79	1149.79	1149.79	1149.79
	4	5755.39	5503.92	4223.87	2943.83	1663.78	1138.16	1138.16	1138.16	1138.16
	5	5829.30	5357.59	3945.83	2534.07	1125.66	1125.66	1125.66	1125.66	1125.66
500	1	5248.60	5248.60	5062.37	4359.57	3656.76	2953.96	2251.15	1548.35	1404.22
	2	5463.44	5463.44	4814.53	3919.44	3024.34	2129.25	1390.67	1390.67	1390.67
	3	5634.57	5629.40	4562.23	3495.06	2427.89	1376.23	1376.23	1376.23	1376.23
	4	5755.39	5516.04	4297.72	3079.40	1861.07	1360.79	1360.79	1360.79	1360.79
	5	5829.30	5379.51	4033.35	2687.19	1344.23	1344.23	1344.23	1344.23	1344.23
600	1	5248.60	5248.60	5073.00	4410.30	3747.60	3084.90	2422.21	1759.51	1623.60
	2	5463.44	5463.44	4848.93	4001.29	3153.64	2305.99	1606.57	1606.57	1606.57
	3	5634.57	5629.65	4615.66	3601.67	2587.68	1588.43	1588.43	1588.43	1588.43
	4	5755.39	5527.39	4366.80	3206.22	2045.64	1569.07	1569.07	1569.07	1569.07
	5	5829.30	5399.98	4115.08	2830.17	1548.33	1548.33	1548.33	1548.33	1548.33
800	1	5248.60	5248.60	5092.59	4503.80	3915.01	3326.22	2737.43	2148.64	2027.90
	2	5463.44	5463.44	4912.20	4151.82	3391.45	2631.07	2003.65	2003.65	2003.65
	3	5634.57	5630.13	4713.74	3797.35	2880.97	1977.90	1977.90	1977.90	1977.90
	4	5755.39	5548.16	4493.31	3438.46	2383.61	1950.46	1950.46	1950.46	1950.46
	5	5829.30	5437.37	4264.36	3091.35	1921.13	1921.13	1921.13	1921.13	1921.13
1000	1	5248.60	5248.60	5110.36	4588.63	4066.91	3545.18	3023.45	2501.73	2394.74
	2	5463.44	5463.44	4969.47	4288.10	3606.72	2925.35	2363.12	2363.12	2363.12
	3	5634.57	5630.55	4802.30	3974.05	3145.80	2329.59	2329.59	2329.59	2329.59
	4	5755.39	5566.87	4607.24	3647.61	2687.98	2293.93	2293.93	2293.93	2293.93
	5	5829.30	5470.94	4398.40	3325.87	2255.89	2255.89	2255.89	2255.89	2255.89
1500	1	5248.60	5248.60	5148.86	4772.43	4396.01	4019.58	3643.16	3266.73	3189.54
	2	5463.44	5463.44	5093.15	4582.37	4071.59	3560.81	3139.35	3139.35	3139.35
	3	5634.57	5631.47	4992.86	4354.24	3715.63	3086.30	3086.30	3086.30	3086.30
	4	5755.39	5606.96	4851.42	4095.88	3340.34	3030.09	3030.09	3030.09	3030.09
	5	5829.30	5542.59	4684.51	3826.43	2970.39	2970.39	2970.39	2970.39	2970.39
2000	1	5248.60	5248.60	5181.16	4926.64	4672.13	4417.61	4163.10	3908.58	3856.39
	2	5463.44	5463.44	5196.49	4828.26	4460.03	4091.80	3787.96	3787.96	3787.96
	3	5634.57	5632.24	5151.39	4670.55	4189.71	3715.85	3715.85	3715.85	3715.85
	4	5755.39	5640.16	5053.62	4467.08	3880.54	3639.68	3639.68	3639.68	3639.68
	5	5829.30	5601.63	4920.22	4238.82	3559.03	3559.03	3559.03	3559.03	3559.03
2500	1	5248.60	5248.60	5208.97	5059.42	4909.86	4760.31	4610.75	4461.20	4430.53
	2	5463.44	5463.44	5285.16	5039.25	4793.34	4547.43	4344.52	4344.52	4344.52
	3	5634.57	5632.89	5286.93	4940.98	4595.02	4254.10	4254.10	4254.10	4254.10
	4	5755.39	5668.44	5225.82	4783.20	4340.58	4158.83	4158.83	4158.83	4158.83
	5	5829.30	5651.69	5120.12	4588.55	4058.24	4058.24	4058.24	4058.24	4058.24
3500	1	5380.11	5380.11	5380.11	5380.11	5380.11	5380.11	5380.11	5380.11	5248.60
	2	5463.44	5463.44	5431.22	5386.78	5342.34	5297.89	5261.22	5261.22	5261.22
	3	5634.57	5633.96	5509.20	5384.44	5259.67	5136.72	5136.72	5136.72	5136.72
	4	5755.39	5714.58	5506.86	5299.14	5091.42	5006.12	5006.12	5006.12	5006.12
	5	5829.30	5732.98	5444.71	5156.44	4868.85	4868.85	4868.85	4868.85	4868.85

[*]Mortar type S

Table D-15 Values of $(EI)_{eff}$ (N-mm^2 x 10^9) for Reinforced Masonry 300 Block Wall[*]
Unit Strength $\geq$ 40 MPa

Vertical Reinforcement Area (mm²)	Number of Grouted Cores/m	Eccentricity e (mm)								
		0.1t	0.2t	0.3t	0.4t	0.5t	0.6t	0.7t	0.8t	≥ 0.9t
400	1	6600.04	6600.04	6339.25	5355.06	4370.87	3386.68	2402.49	1418.31	1216.47
	2	6872.25	6872.25	5969.62	4724.55	3479.47	2234.39	1207.03	1207.03	1207.03
	3	7089.85	7082.70	5605.89	4129.09	2652.28	1196.94	1196.94	1196.94	1196.94
	4	7244.55	6914.58	5235.00	3555.41	1875.82	1186.13	1186.13	1186.13	1186.13
	5	7340.60	6722.23	4871.52	3020.82	1174.51	1174.51	1174.51	1174.51	1174.51
500	1	6600.04	6600.04	6351.30	5412.56	4473.82	3535.08	2596.35	1657.61	1465.10
	2	6872.25	6872.25	6008.73	4817.59	3626.46	2435.32	1452.47	1452.47	1452.47
	3	7089.85	7082.99	5666.85	4250.70	2834.56	1438.99	1438.99	1438.99	1438.99
	4	7244.55	6927.57	5314.09	3700.60	2087.12	1424.57	1424.57	1424.57	1424.57
	5	7340.60	6745.76	4965.46	3185.16	1409.09	1409.09	1409.09	1409.09	1409.09
600	1	6600.04	6600.04	6362.69	5466.96	4571.24	3675.51	2779.78	1884.06	1700.37
	2	6872.25	6872.25	6045.68	4905.52	3765.36	2625.20	1684.41	1684.41	1684.41
	3	7089.85	7083.27	5724.36	4365.46	3006.56	1667.40	1667.40	1667.40	1667.40
	4	7244.55	6939.81	5388.60	3837.40	2286.20	1649.22	1649.22	1649.22	1649.22
	5	7340.60	6767.88	5053.81	3339.73	1629.73	1629.73	1629.73	1629.73	1629.73
800	1	6600.04	6600.04	6383.88	5568.09	4752.31	3936.53	3120.75	2304.97	2137.67
	2	6872.25	6872.25	6114.25	5068.68	4023.10	2977.52	2114.77	2114.77	2114.77
	3	7089.85	7083.78	5830.89	4578.00	3325.10	2090.42	2090.42	2090.42	2090.42
	4	7244.55	6962.42	5526.33	4090.23	2654.14	2064.43	2064.43	2064.43	2064.43
	5	7340.60	6808.69	5216.74	3624.79	2036.63	2036.63	2036.63	2036.63	2036.63
1000	1	6600.04	6600.04	6403.29	5660.79	4918.30	4175.80	3433.30	2690.80	2538.53
	2	6872.25	6872.25	6176.98	5217.92	4258.86	3299.81	2508.45	2508.45	2508.45
	3	7089.85	7084.25	5928.11	4771.98	3615.84	2476.51	2476.51	2476.51	2476.51
	4	7244.55	6983.01	5651.72	4320.44	2989.15	2442.48	2442.48	2442.48	2442.48
	5	7340.60	6845.74	5364.70	3883.66	2406.14	2406.14	2406.14	2406.14	2406.14
1500	1	6600.04	6600.04	6445.99	5864.62	5283.26	4701.89	4120.52	3539.15	3419.93
	2	6872.25	6872.25	6314.48	5545.09	4775.70	4006.31	3371.46	3371.46	3371.46
	3	7089.85	7085.27	6140.56	5195.84	4251.12	3320.13	3320.13	3320.13	3320.13
	4	7244.55	7027.84	5924.77	4821.69	3718.62	3265.66	3265.66	3265.66	3265.66
	5	7340.60	6926.13	5685.66	4445.19	3207.68	3207.68	3207.68	3207.68	3207.68
2000	1	6600.04	6600.04	6482.46	6038.73	5595.01	5151.28	4707.56	4263.83	4172.83
	2	6872.25	6872.25	6431.50	5823.53	5215.56	4607.59	4105.94	4105.94	4105.94
	3	7089.85	7086.14	6320.65	5555.15	4789.66	4035.29	4035.29	4035.29	4035.29
	4	7244.55	7065.69	6155.25	5244.81	4334.37	3960.51	3960.51	3960.51	3960.51
	5	7340.60	6993.67	5955.34	4917.02	3881.16	3881.16	3881.16	3881.16	3881.16
2500	1	6600.04	6600.04	6514.34	6190.91	5867.48	5544.05	5220.62	4897.20	4830.87
	2	6872.25	6872.25	6533.46	6066.14	5598.82	5131.50	4745.89	4745.89	4745.89
	3	7089.85	7086.90	6477.04	5867.19	5257.34	4656.35	4656.35	4656.35	4656.35
	4	7244.55	7098.44	6354.69	5610.95	4867.20	4561.80	4561.80	4561.80	4561.80
	5	7340.60	7051.89	6187.81	5323.74	4461.72	4461.72	4461.72	4461.72	4461.72
3500	1	6600.04	6600.04	6568.04	6447.27	6326.51	6205.74	6084.98	5964.21	5939.45
	2	6872.25	6872.25	6704.58	6473.31	6242.03	6010.75	5819.91	5819.91	5819.91
	3	7089.85	7088.16	6738.45	6388.75	6039.05	5694.43	5694.43	5694.43	5694.43
	4	7244.55	7152.94	6686.60	6220.27	5753.94	5562.45	5562.45	5562.45	5562.45
	5	7340.60	7148.33	6572.87	5997.42	5423.34	5423.34	5423.34	5423.34	5423.34

[*]Mortar type S

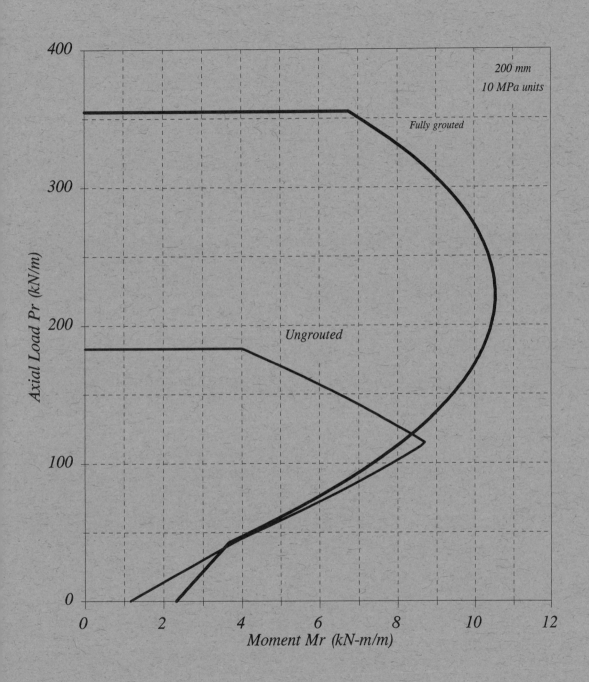

200 mm
10 MPa units

Fully grouted

Ungrouted

Figure E-1 Unreinforced Wall Interaction Diagram
200 Block, 10 MPa Unit Strength

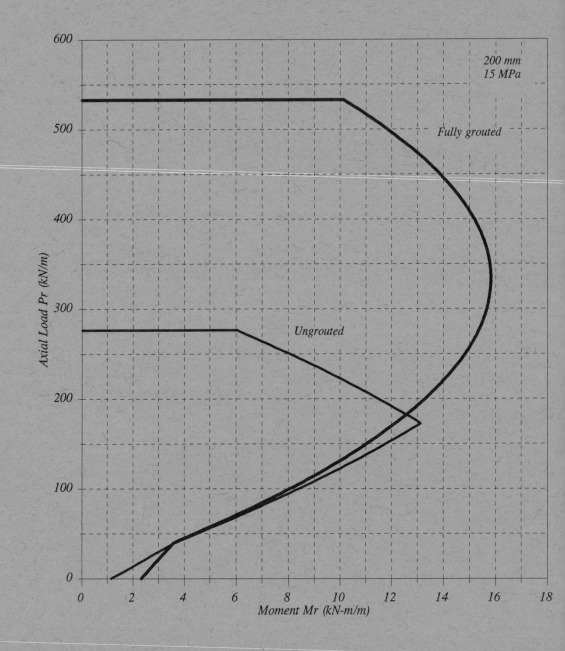

Figure E-2 Unreinforced Wall Interaction Diagram
200 Block, 15 MPa Unit Strength

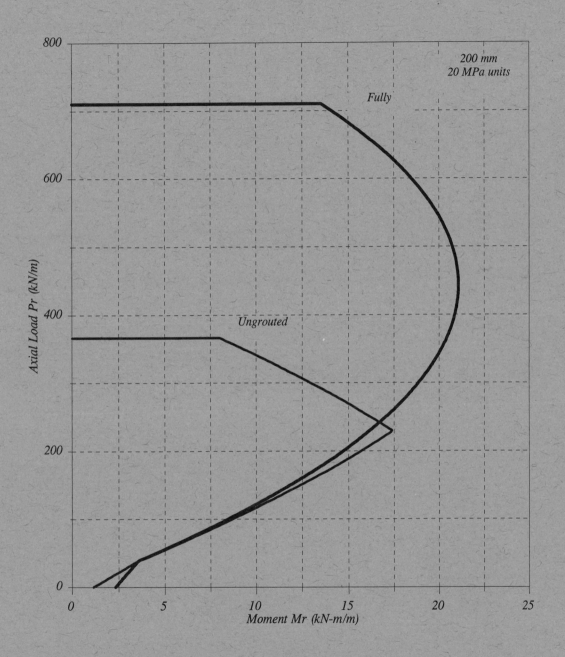

Figure E-3 Unreinforced Wall Interaction Diagram
200 Block, 20 MPa Unit Strength

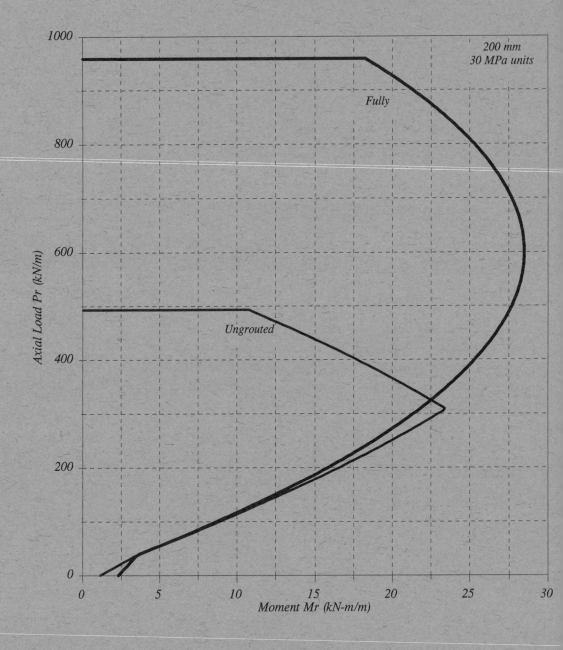

Figure E-4 Unreinforced Wall Interaction Diagram
200 Block, 30 MPa Unit Strength

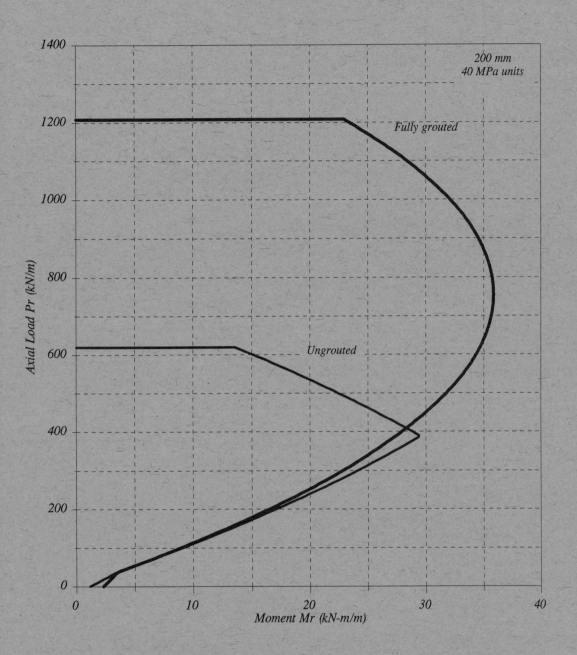

Figure E-5 Unreinforced Wall Interaction Diagram
200 Block, 40 MPa Unit Strength

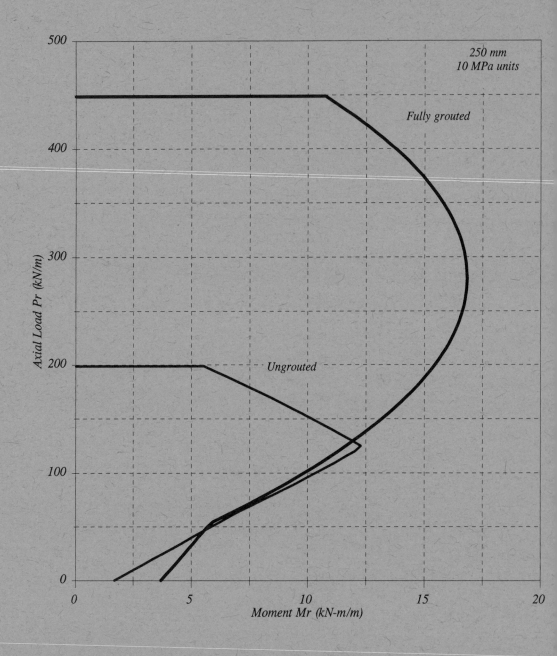

Figure E-6 Unreinforced Wall Interaction Diagram
250 Block, 10 MPa Unit Strength

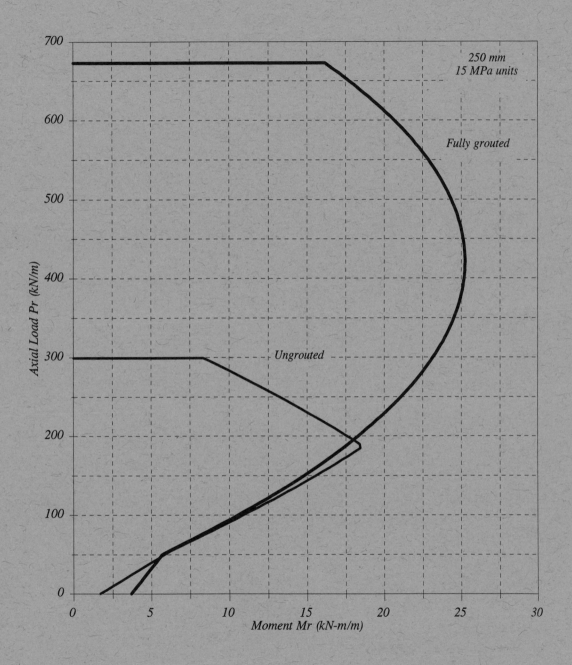

Figure E-7 Unreinforced Wall Interaction Diagram
250 Block, 15 MPa Unit Strength

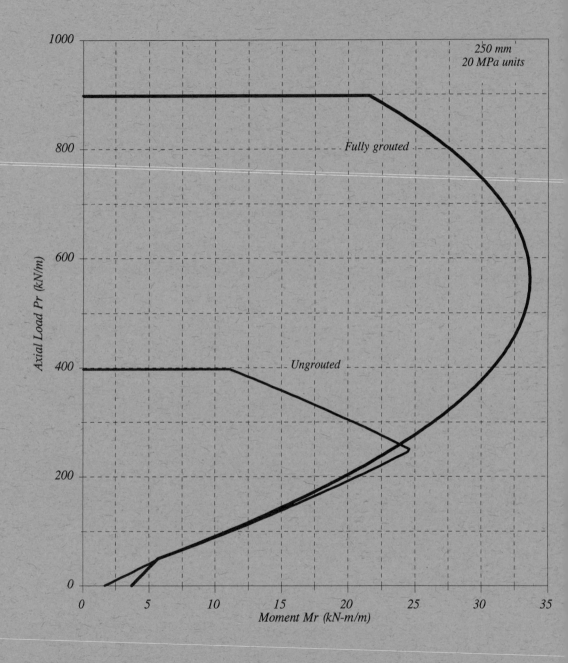

Figure E-8 Unreinforced Wall Interaction Diagram
250 Block, 20 MPa Unit Strength

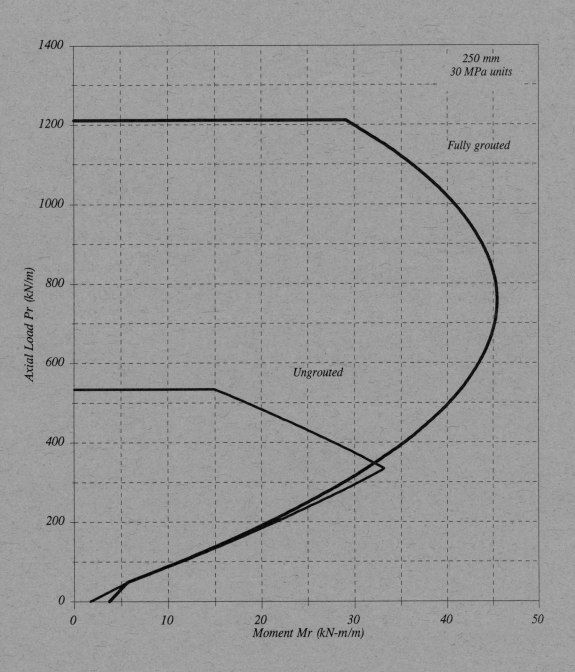

Figure E-9 Unreinforced Wall Interaction Diagram
250 Block, 30 MPa Unit Strength

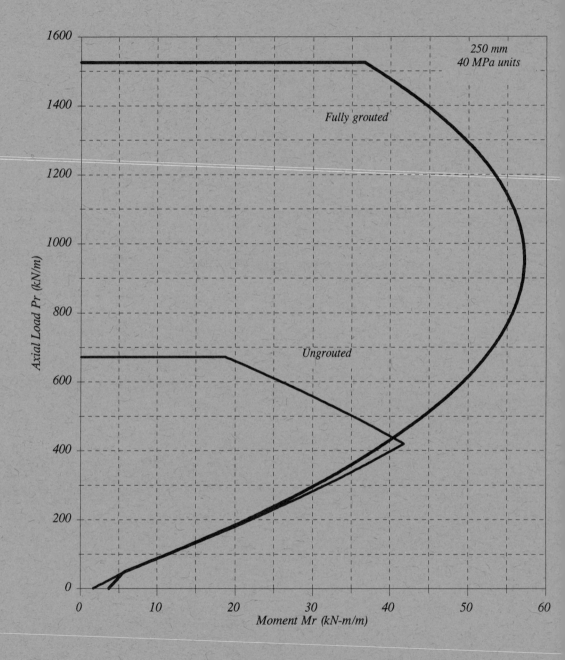

Figure E-10 Unreinforced Wall Interaction Diagram
250 Block, 40 MPa Unit Strength

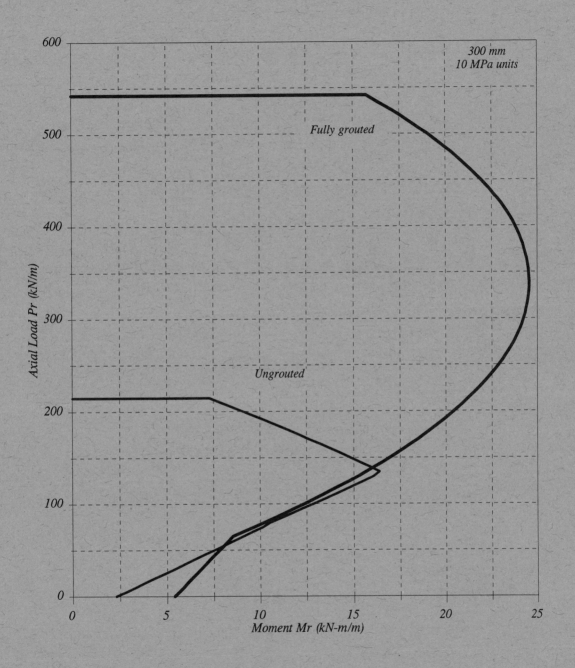

Figure E-11 Unreinforced Wall Interaction Diagram
300 Block, 10 MPa Unit Strength

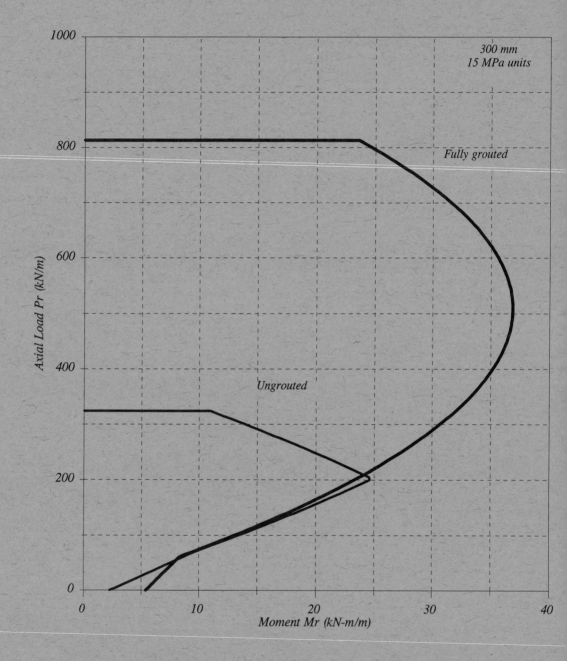

Figure E-12 Unreinforced Wall Interaction Diagram
300 Block, 15 MPa Unit Strength

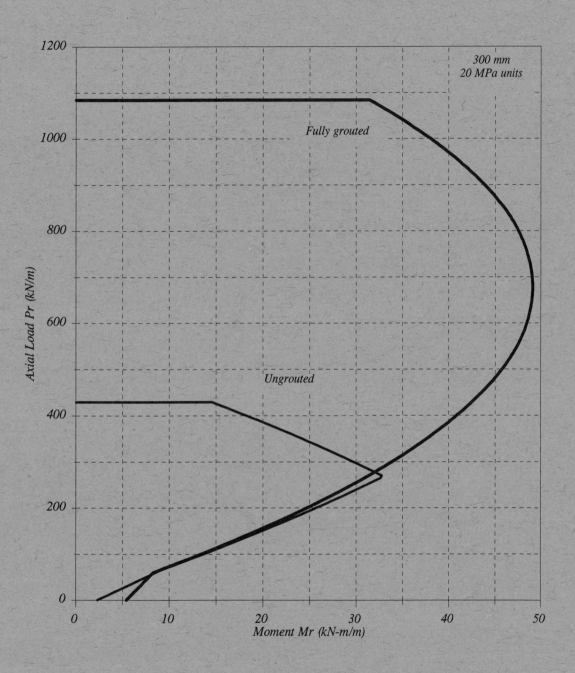

Figure E-13 Unreinforced Wall Interaction Diagram
300 Block, 20 MPa Unit Strength

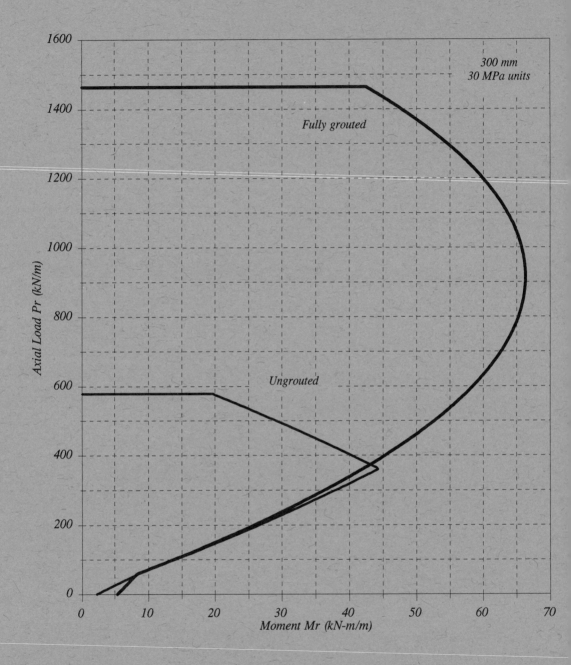

Figure E-14 Unreinforced Wall Interaction Diagram
300 Block, 30 MPa Unit Strength

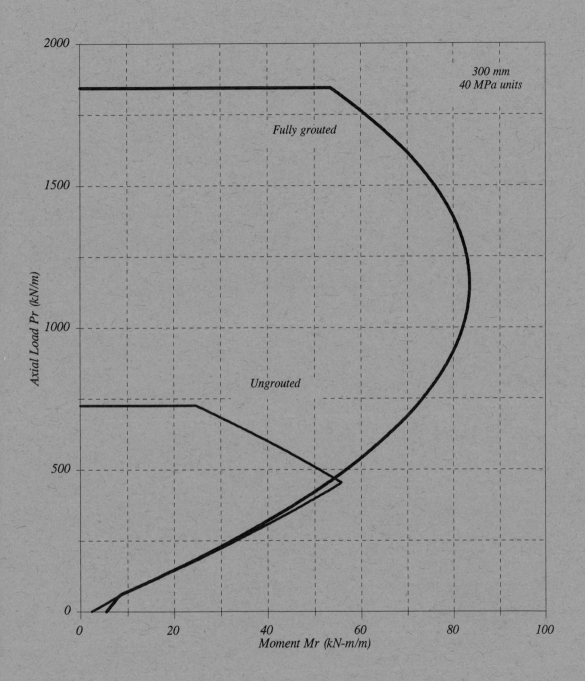

Figure E-15 Unreinforced Wall Interaction Diagram
300 Block, 40 MPa Unit Strength

REINFORCED MASONRY WALLS

Axial Load and Out-of-Plane Bending

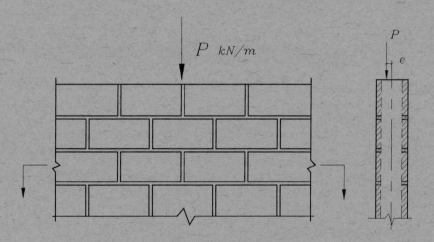

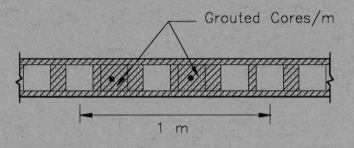

Grouted Cores/m

1 m

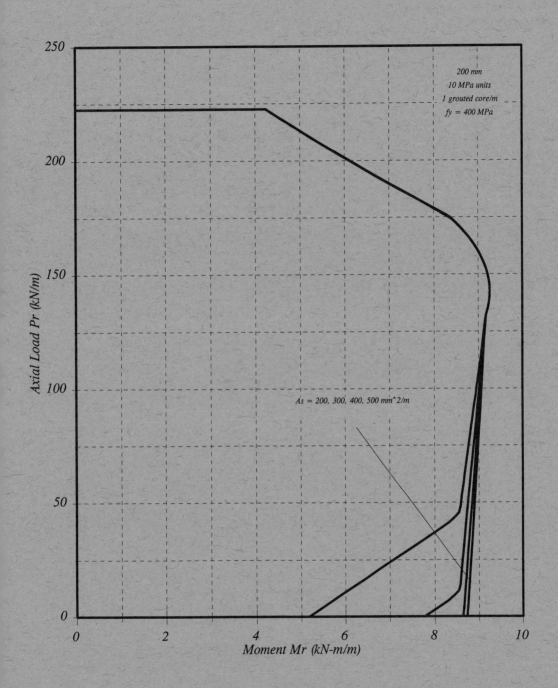

Figure F-1 Reinforced Wall Interaction Diagram
200 Block, 1 Grouted Core/m, 10 MPa Unit Strength

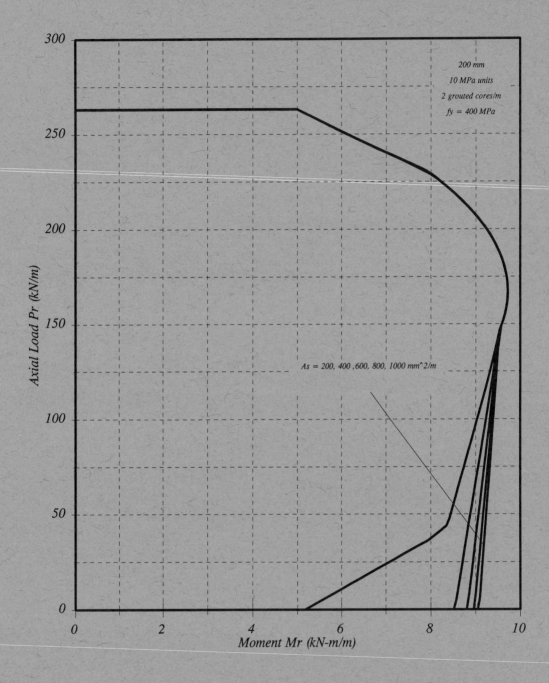

Figure F-2 Reinforced Wall Interaction Diagram
200 Block, 2 Grouted Cores/m, 10 MPa Unit Strength

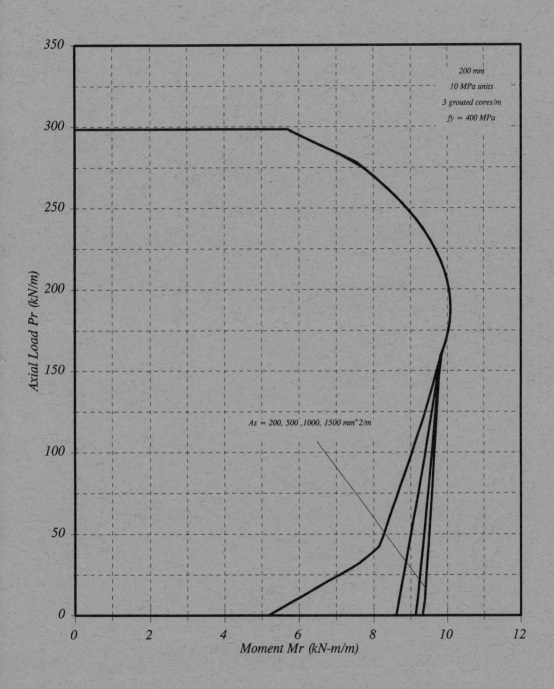

Figure F-3 Reinforced Wall Interaction Diagram
200 Block, 3 Grouted Cores/m, 10 MPa Unit Strength

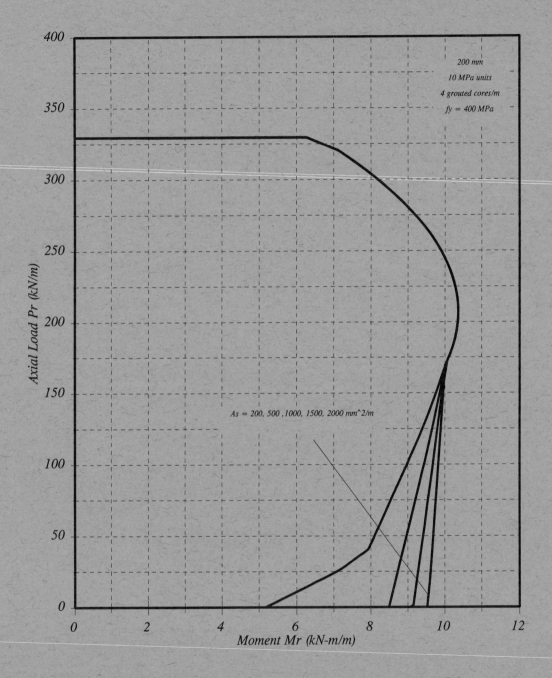

Figure F-4 Reinforced Wall Interaction Diagram
200 Block, 4 Grouted Cores/m, 10 MPa Unit Strength

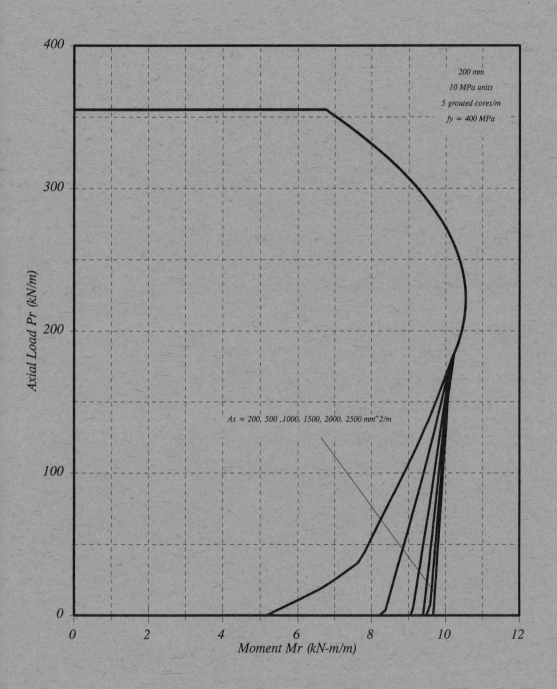

Figure F-5 Reinforced Wall Interaction Diagram
200 Block, 5 Grouted Cores/m, 10 MPa Unit Strength

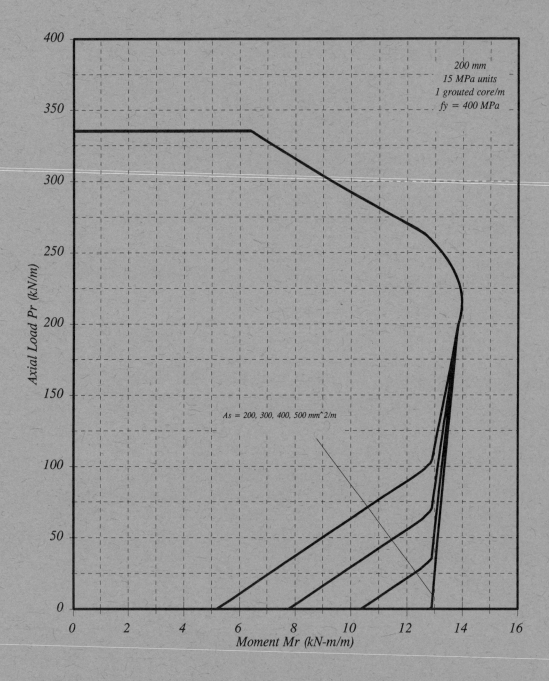

Figure F-6 Reinforced Wall Interaction Diagram
200 Block, 1 Grouted Core/m, 15 MPa Unit Strength

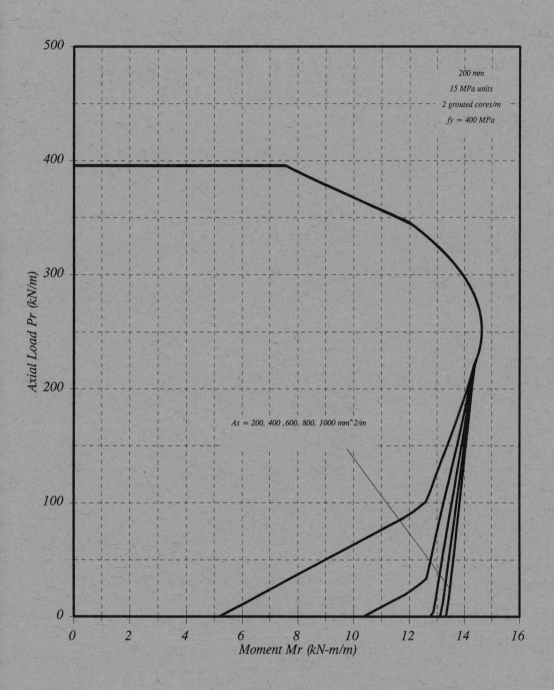

Figure F-7 Reinforced Wall Interaction Diagram
200 Block, 2 Grouted Cores/m, 15 MPa Unit Strength

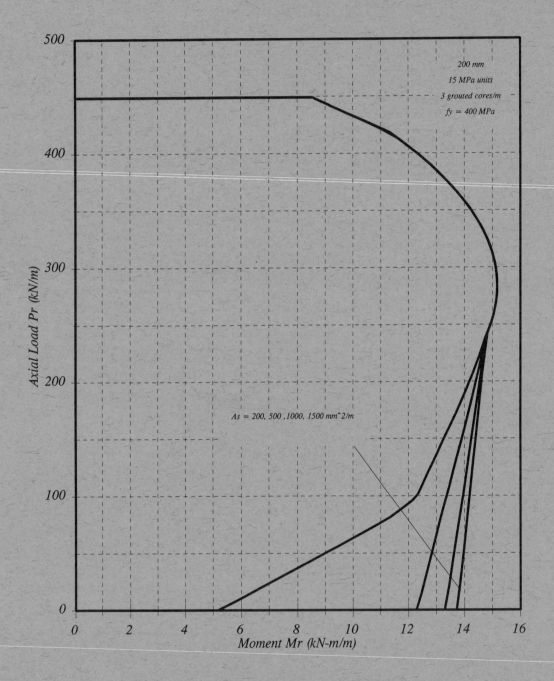

Figure F-8 Reinforced Wall Interaction Diagram
200 Block, 3 Grouted Cores/m, 15 MPa Unit Strength

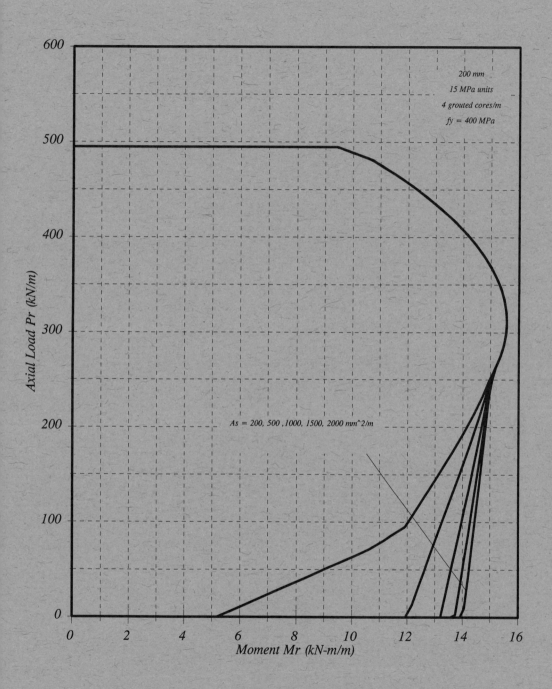

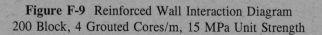

Figure F-9 Reinforced Wall Interaction Diagram
200 Block, 4 Grouted Cores/m, 15 MPa Unit Strength

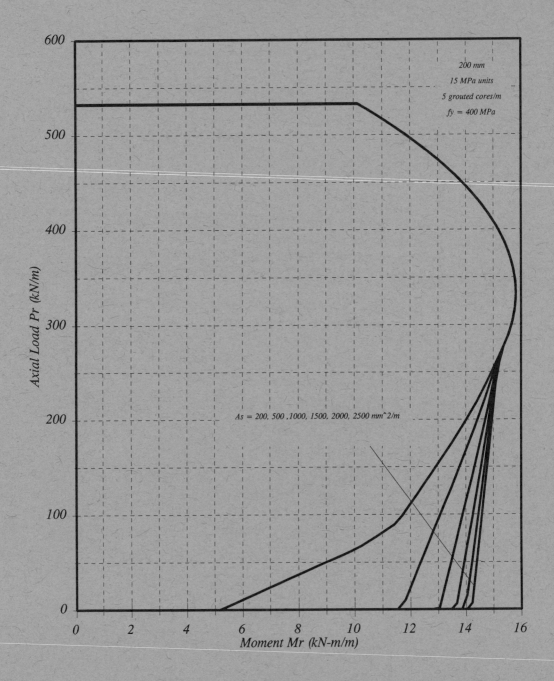

200 mm
15 MPa units
5 grouted cores/m
fy = 400 MPa

As = 200, 500 ,1000, 1500, 2000, 2500 mm^2/m

Figure F-10 Reinforced Wall Interaction Diagram
200 Block, 5 Grouted Cores/m, 15 MPa Unit Strength

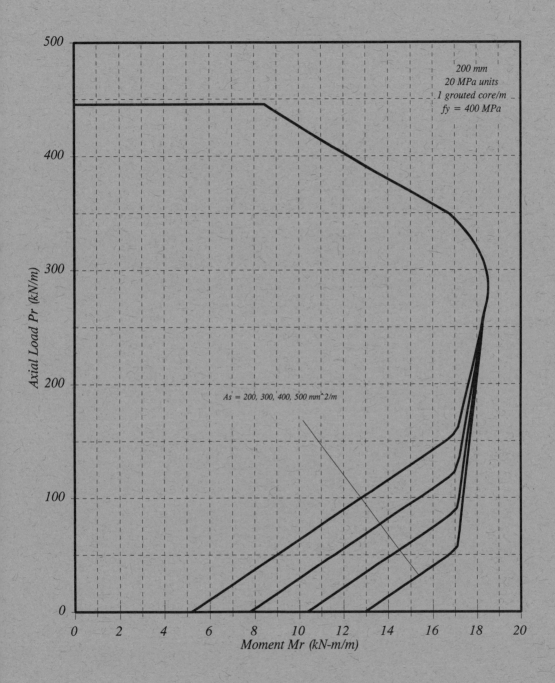

200 mm
20 MPa units
1 grouted core/m
fy = 400 MPa

As = 200, 300, 400, 500 mm^2/m

Figure F-11 Reinforced Wall Interaction Diagram
200 Block, 1 Grouted Core/m, 20 MPa Unit Strength

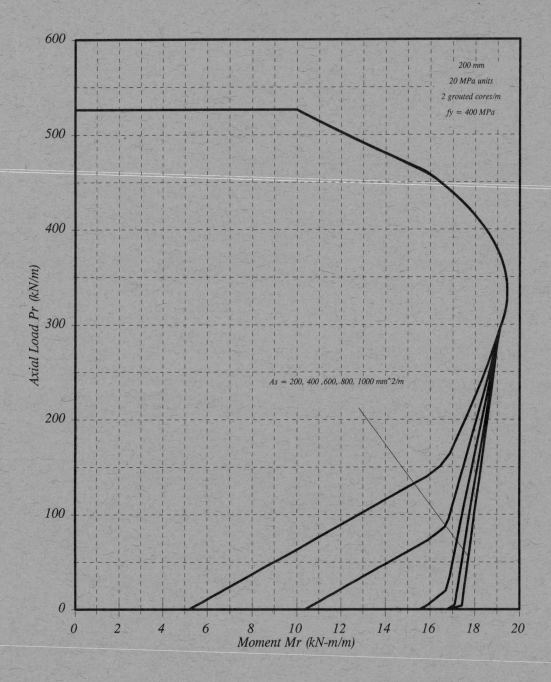

Figure F-12 Reinforced Wall Interaction Diagram
200 Block, 2 Grouted Cores/m, 20 MPa Unit Strength

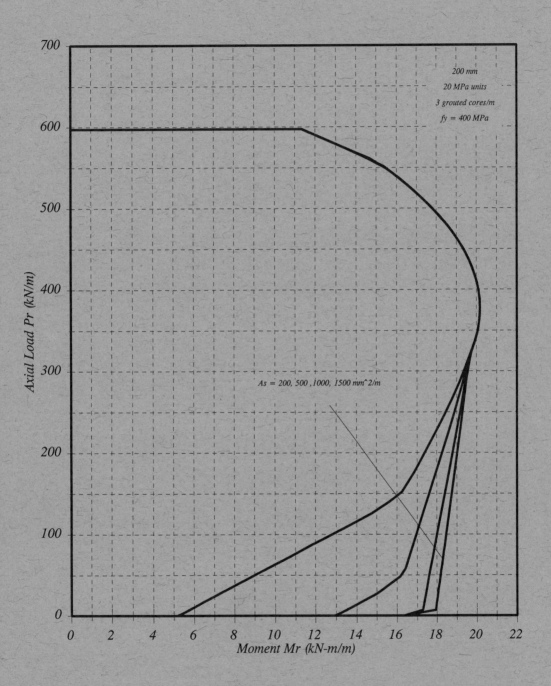

Figure F-13 Reinforced Wall Interaction Diagram
200 Block, 3 Grouted Cores/m, 20 MPa Unit Strength

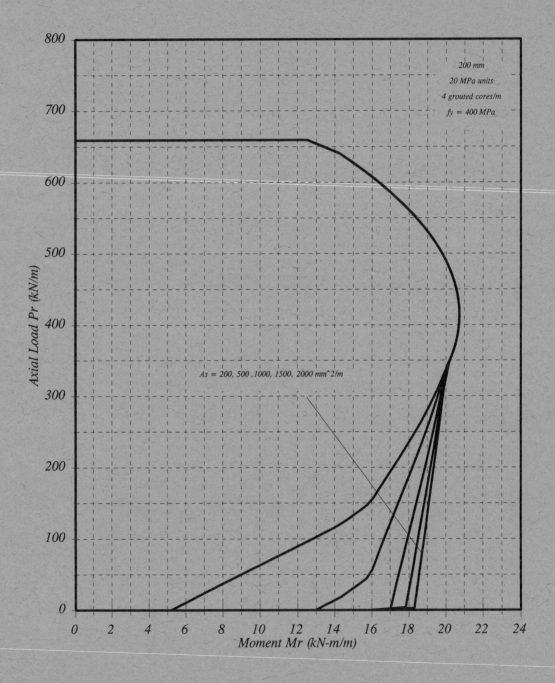

Figure F-14 Reinforced Wall Interaction Diagram
200 Block, 4 Grouted Cores/m, 20 MPa Unit Strength

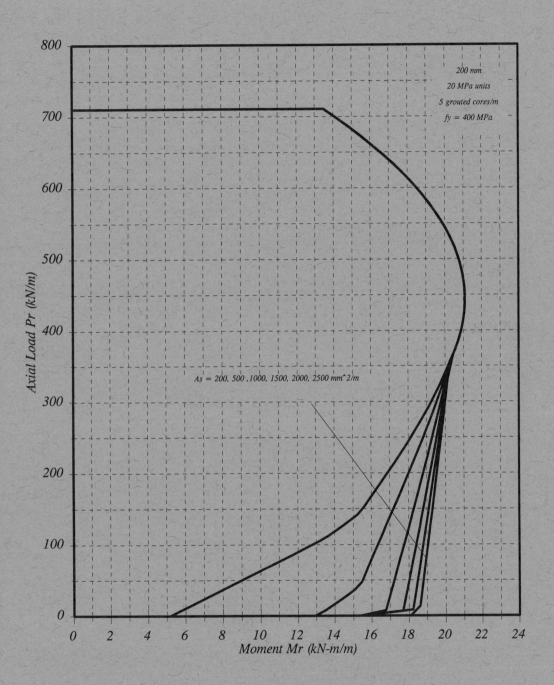

Figure F-15 Reinforced Wall Interaction Diagram
200 Block, 5 Grouted Cores/m, 20 MPa Unit Strength

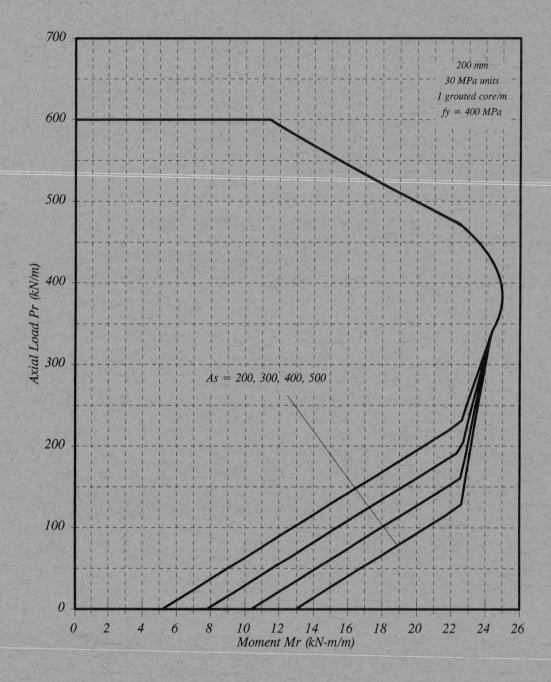

Figure F-16 Reinforced Wall Interaction Diagram
200 Block, 1 Grouted Core/m, 30 MPa Unit Strength

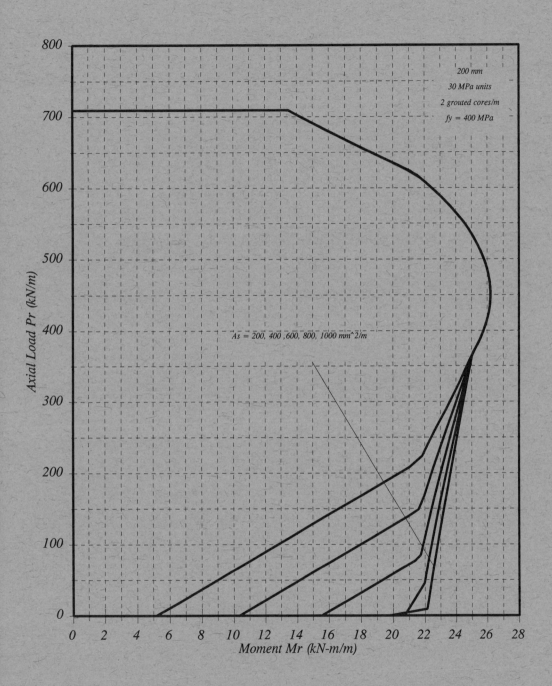

Figure F-17 Reinforced Wall Interaction Diagram
200 Block, 2 Grouted Cores/m, 30 MPa Unit Strength

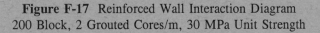

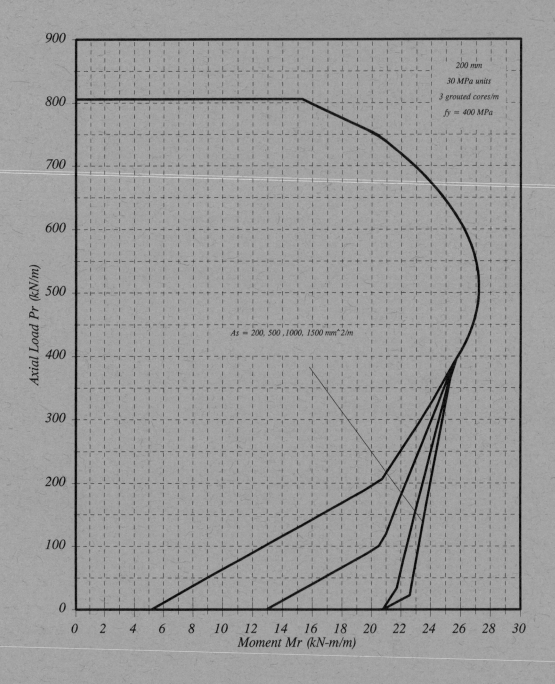

Figure F-18 Reinforced Wall Interaction Diagram
200 Block, 3 Grouted Cores/m, 30 MPa Unit Strength

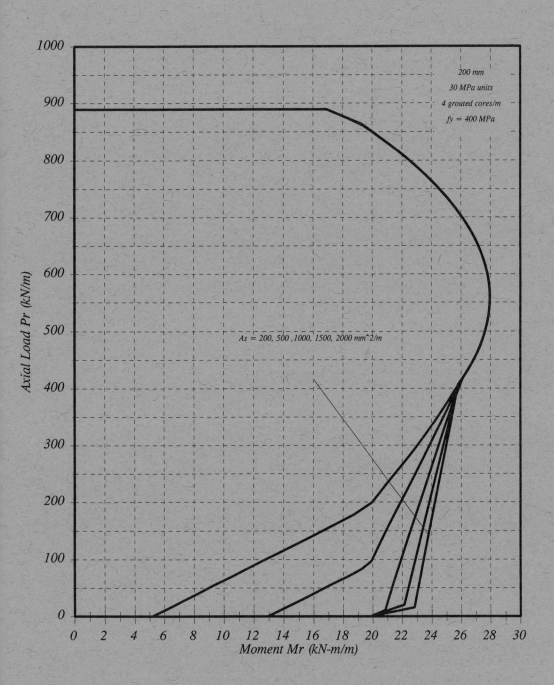

Figure F-19 Reinforced Wall Interaction Diagram
200 Block, 4 Grouted Cores/m, 30 MPa Unit Strength

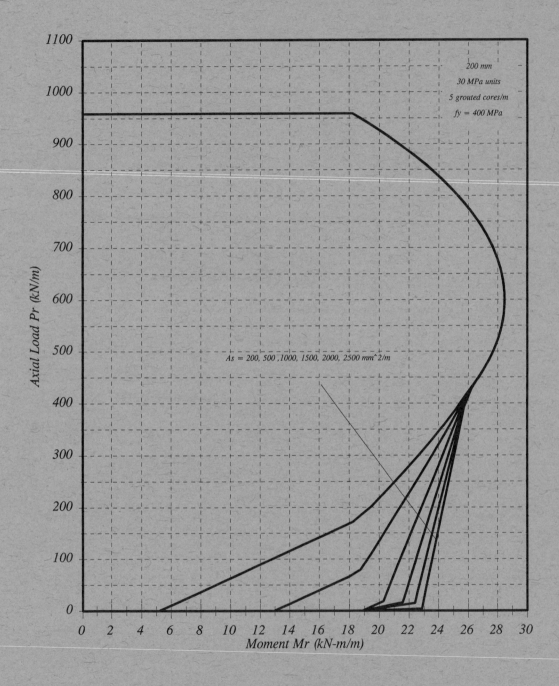

Figure F-20 Reinforced Wall Interaction Diagram
200 Block, 5 Grouted Cores/m, 30 MPa Unit Strength

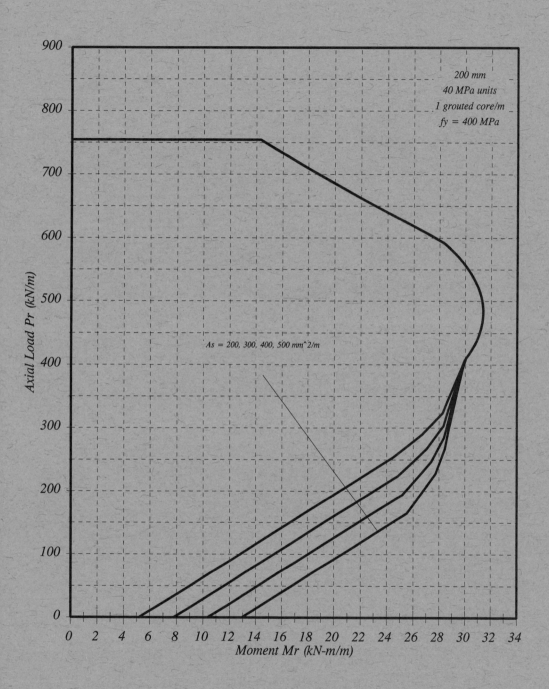

200 mm
40 MPa units
1 grouted core/m
fy = 400 MPa

As = 200, 300, 400, 500 mm^2/m

Figure F-21 Reinforced Wall Interaction Diagram
200 Block, 1 Grouted Core/m, 40 MPa Unit Strength

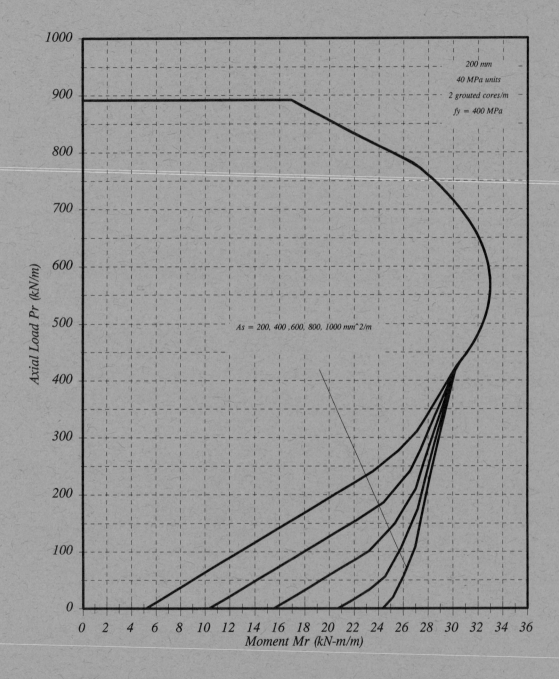

Figure F-22 Reinforced Wall Interaction Diagram
200 Block, 2 Grouted Cores/m, 40 MPa Unit Strength

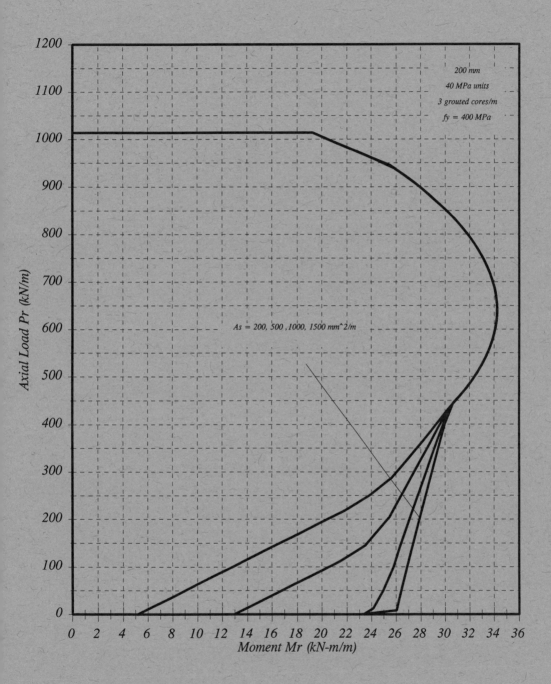

Figure F-23 Reinforced Wall Interaction Diagram
200 Block, 3 Grouted Cores/m, 40 MPa Unit Strength

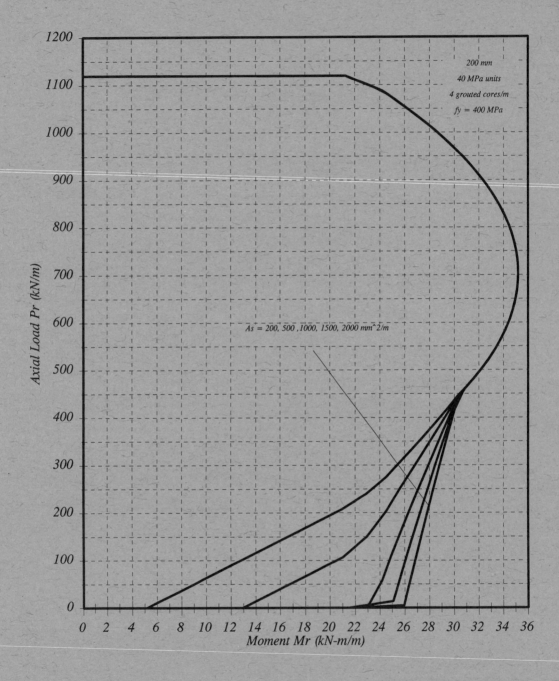

Figure F-24 Reinforced Wall Interaction Diagram
200 Block, 4 Grouted Cores/m, 40 MPa Unit Strength

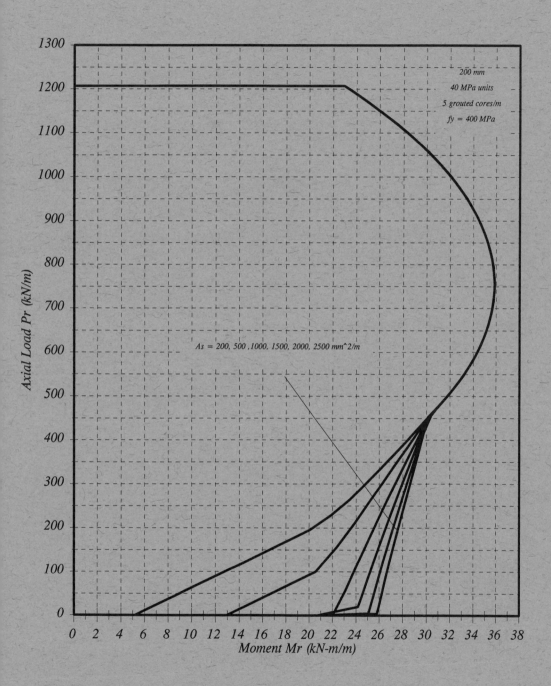

Figure F-25 Reinforced Wall Interaction Diagram
200 Block, 5 Grouted Cores/m, 40 MPa Unit Strength

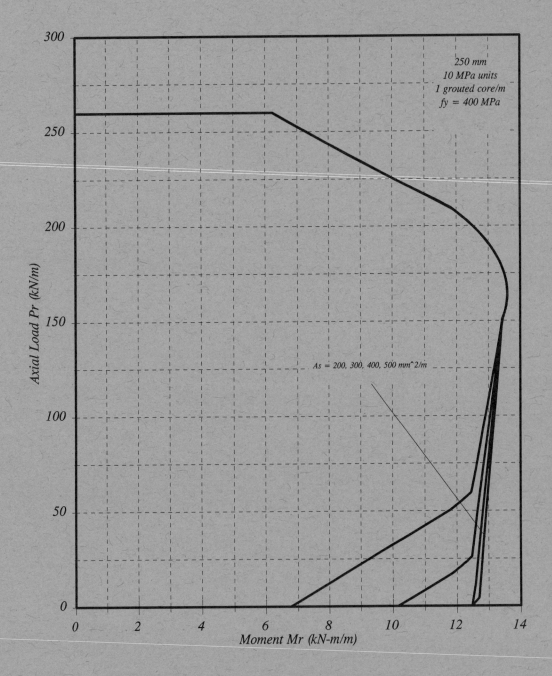

Figure F-26 Reinforced Wall Interaction Diagram
250 Block, 1 Grouted Core/m, 10 MPa Unit Strength

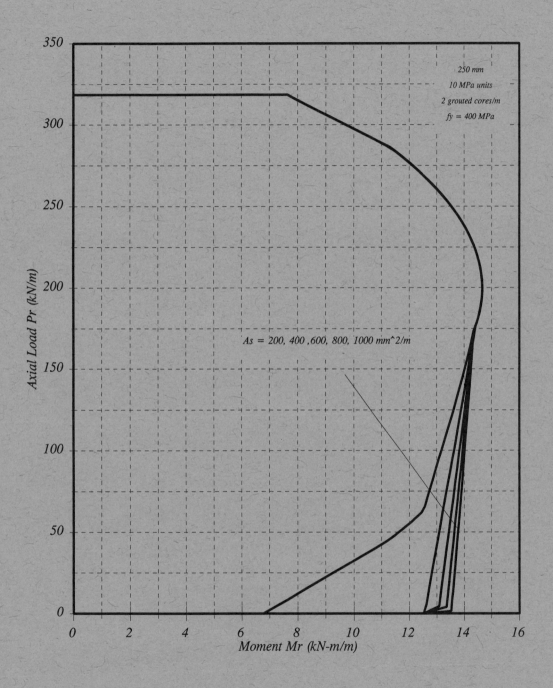

Figure F-27 Reinforced Wall Interaction Diagram
250 Block, 2 Grouted Cores/m, 10 MPa Unit Strength

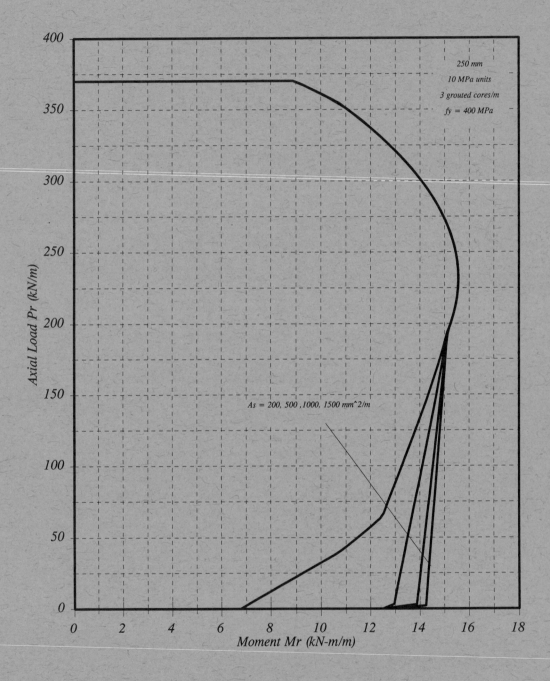

250 mm
10 MPa units
3 grouted cores/m
fy = 400 MPa

As = 200, 500 ,1000, 1500 mm^2/m

Figure F-28 Reinforced Wall Interaction Diagram
205 Block, 3 Grouted Cores/m, 10 MPa Unit Strength

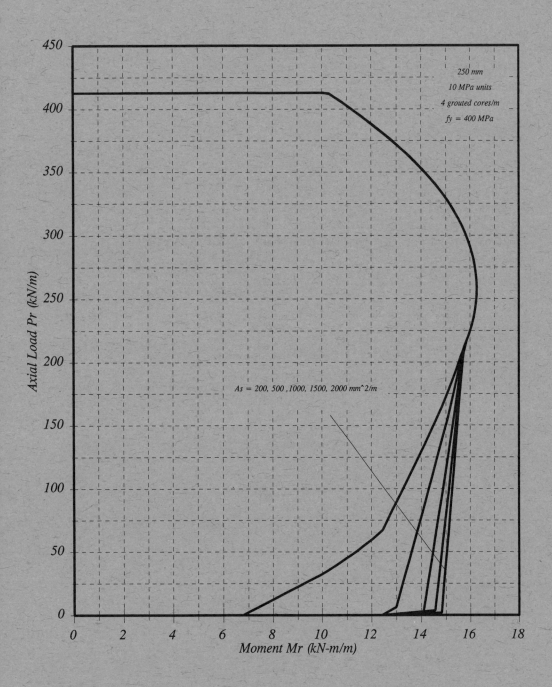

Figure F-29 Reinforced Wall Interaction Diagram
250 Block, 4 Grouted Cores/m, 10 MPa Unit Strength

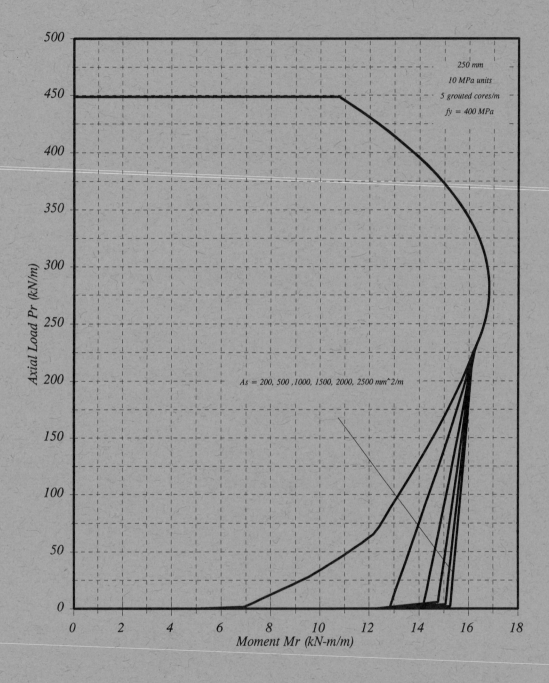

Figure F-30 Reinforced Wall Interaction Diagram
250 Block, 5 Grouted Cores/m, 10 MPa Unit Strength

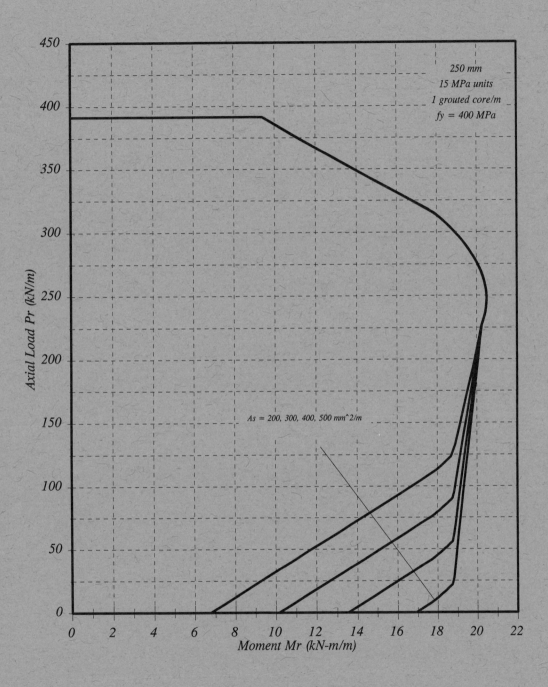

250 mm
15 MPa units
1 grouted core/m
fy = 400 MPa

As = 200, 300, 400, 500 mm^2/m

Figure F-31 Reinforced Wall Interaction Diagram
250 Block, 1 Grouted Core/m, 15 MPa Unit Strength

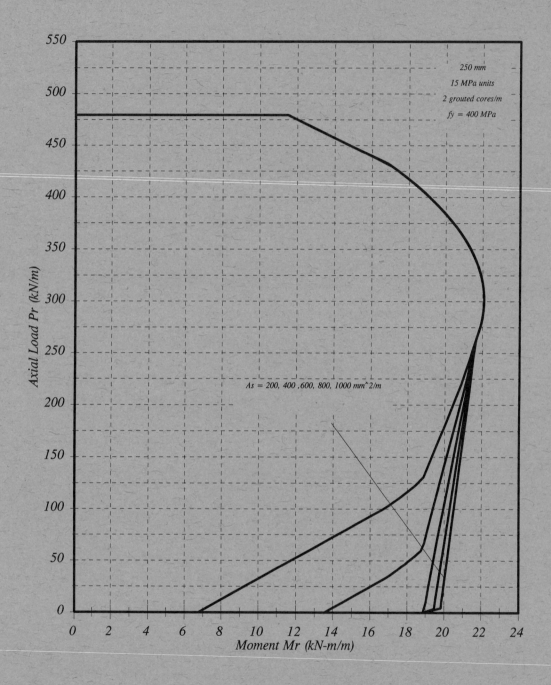

250 mm
15 MPa units
2 grouted cores/m
fy = 400 MPa

As = 200, 400 ,600, 800, 1000 mm^2/m

Figure F-32 Reinforced Wall Interaction Diagram
250 Block, 2 Grouted Cores/m, 15 MPa Unit Strength

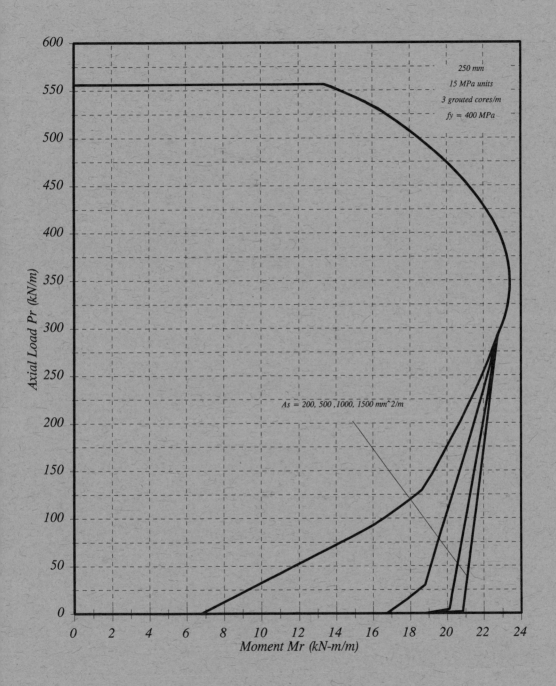

Figure F-33 Reinforced Wall Interaction Diagram
250 Block, 3 Grouted Cores/m, 15 MPa Unit Strength

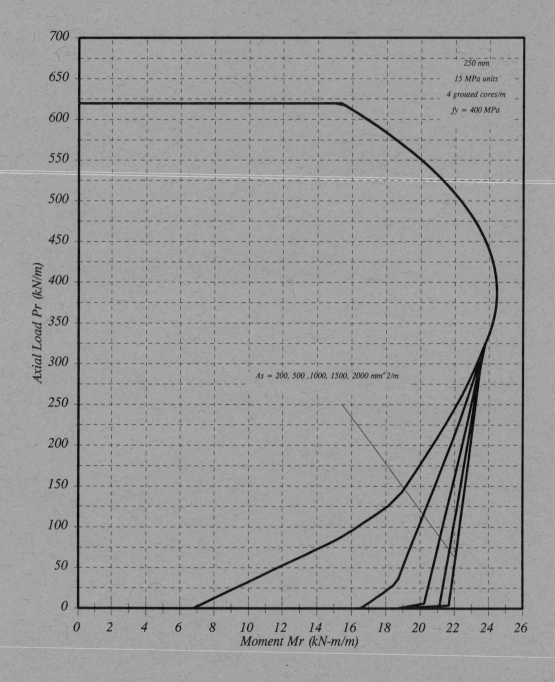

Figure F-34 Reinforced Wall Interaction Diagram
250 Block, 4 Grouted Cores/m, 15 MPa Unit Strength

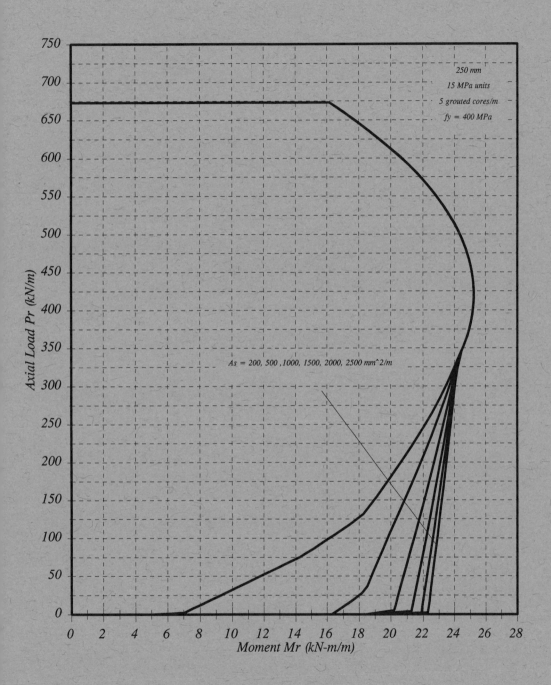

Figure F-35 Reinforced Wall Interaction Diagram
250 Block, 5 Grouted Cores/m, 15 MPa Unit Strength

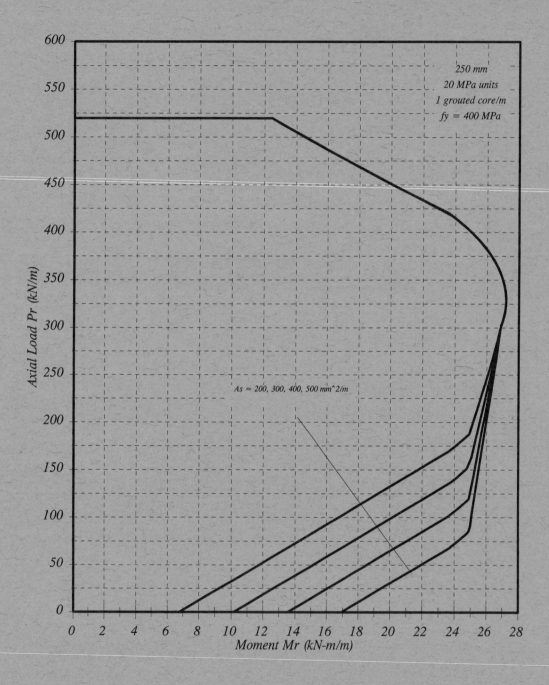

Figure F-36 Reinforced Wall Interaction Diagram
250 Block, 1 Grouted Core/m, 20 MPa Unit Strength

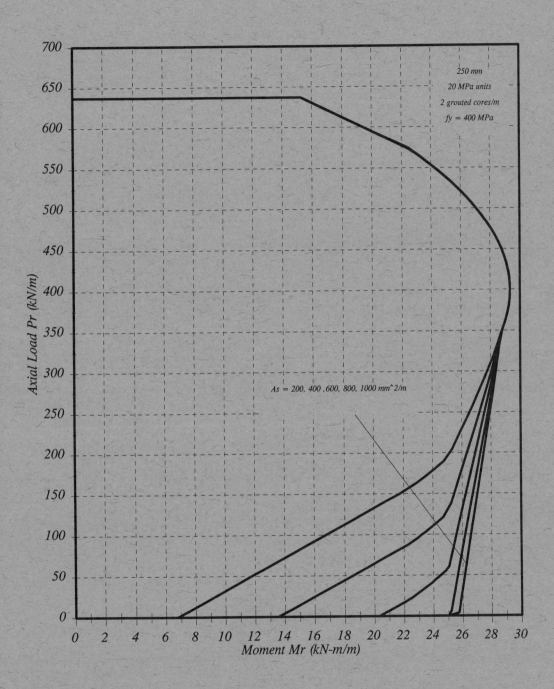

Figure F-37 Reinforced Wall Interaction Diagram
250 Block, 2 Grouted Cores/m, 20 MPa Unit Strength

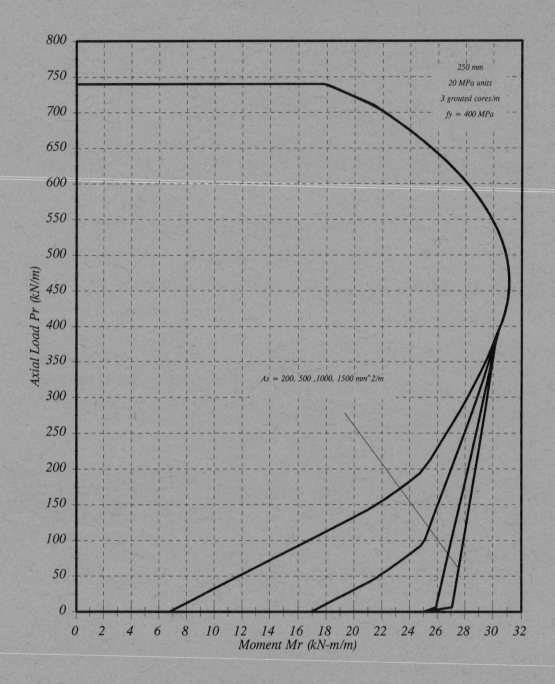

Figure F-38 Reinforced Wall Interaction Diagram
250 Block, 3 Grouted Cores/m, 20 MPa Unit Strength

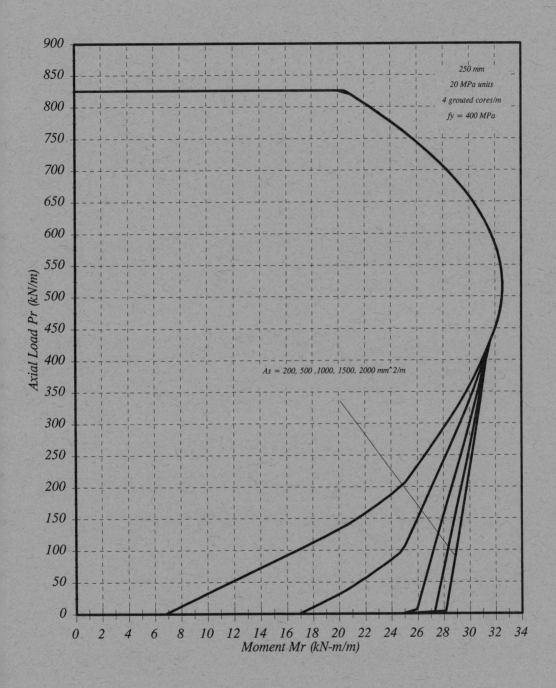

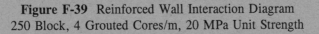

Figure F-39 Reinforced Wall Interaction Diagram
250 Block, 4 Grouted Cores/m, 20 MPa Unit Strength

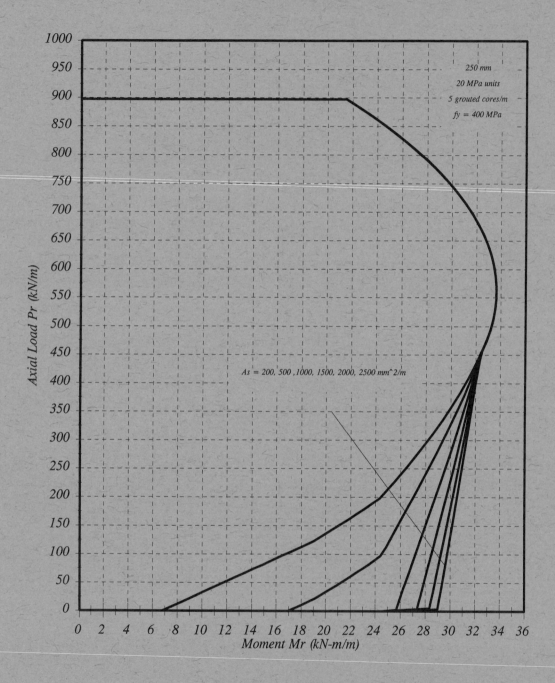

Figure F-40 Reinforced Wall Interaction Diagram
250 Block, 5 Grouted Cores/m, 20 MPa Unit Strength

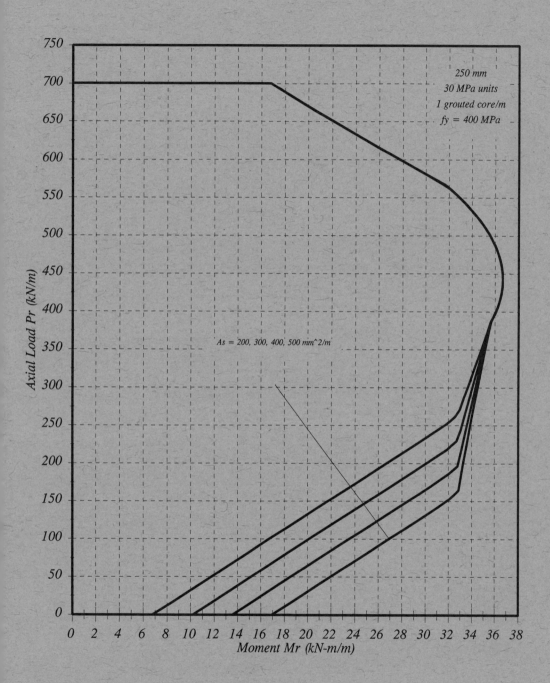

250 mm
30 MPa units
1 grouted core/m
fy = 400 MPa

As = 200, 300, 400, 500 mm^2/m

Figure F-41 Reinforced Wall Interaction Diagram
250 Block, 1 Grouted Core/m, 30 MPa Unit Strength

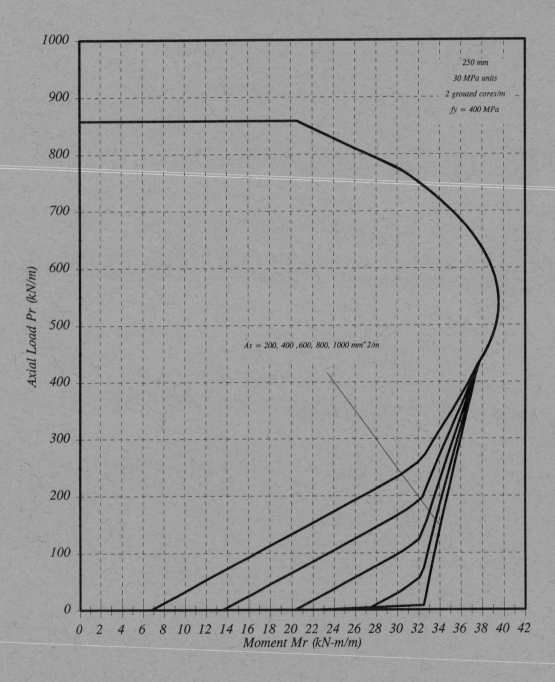

250 mm
30 MPa units
2 grouted cores/m
fy = 400 MPa

As = 200, 400 ,600, 800, 1000 mm^2/m

Figure F-42 Reinforced Wall Interaction Diagram
250 Block, 2 Grouted Cores/m, 30 MPa Unit Strength

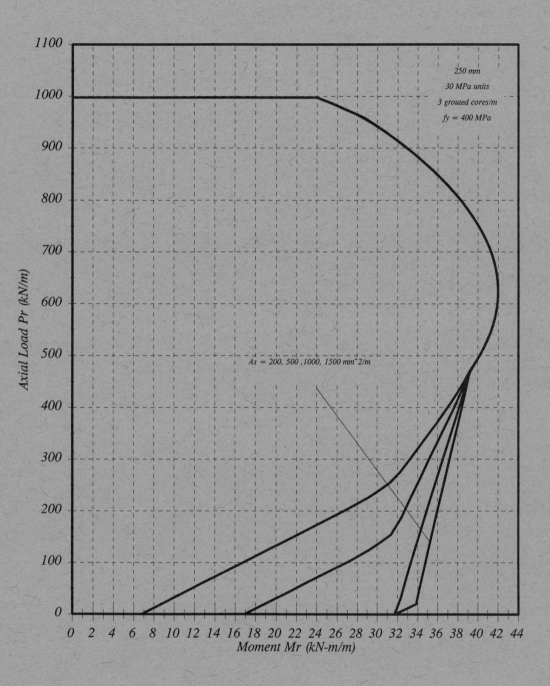

250 mm
30 MPa units
3 grouted cores/m
fy = 400 MPa

As = 200, 500 ,1000, 1500 mm^2/m

Axial Load Pr (kN/m)

Moment Mr (kN-m/m)

Figure F-43 Reinforced Wall Interaction Diagram
250 Block, 3 Grouted Cores/m, 30 MPa Unit Strength

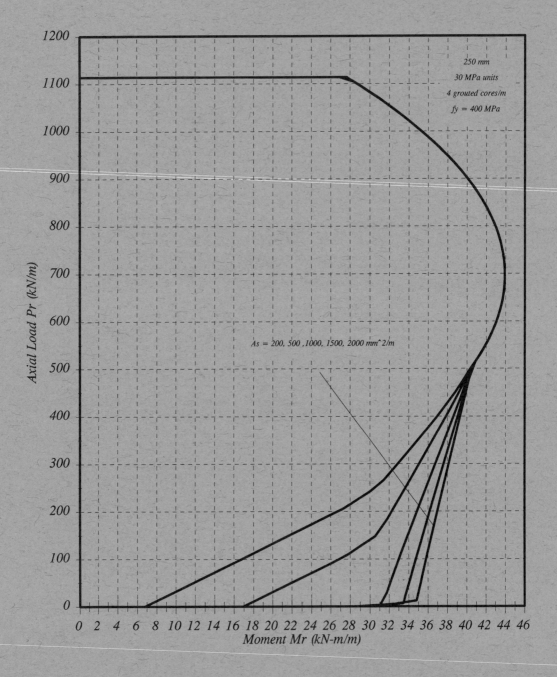

Figure F-44 Reinforced Wall Interaction Diagram
250 Block, 4 Grouted Cores/m, 30 MPa Unit Strength

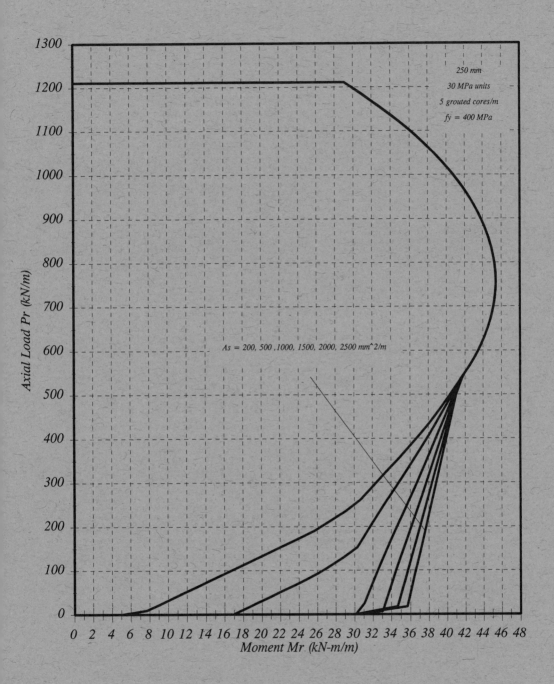

Figure F-45 Reinforced Wall Interaction Diagram
250 Block, 5 Grouted Cores/m, 30 MPa Unit Strength

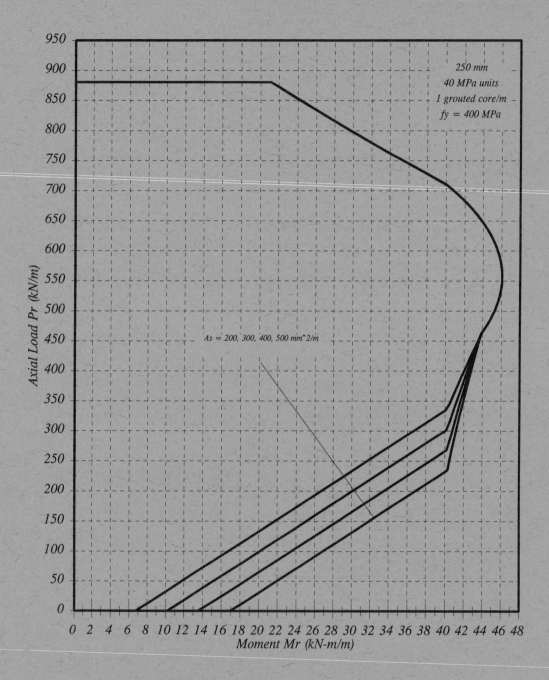

Figure F-46 Reinforced Wall Interaction Diagram
250 Block, 1 Grouted Core/m, 40 MPa Unit Strength

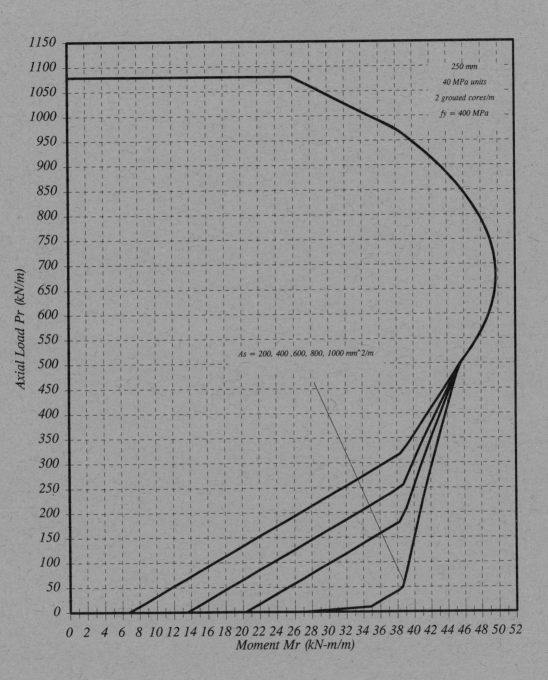

Figure F-47 Reinforced Wall Interaction Diagram
250 Block, 2 Grouted Cores/m, 40 MPa Unit Strength

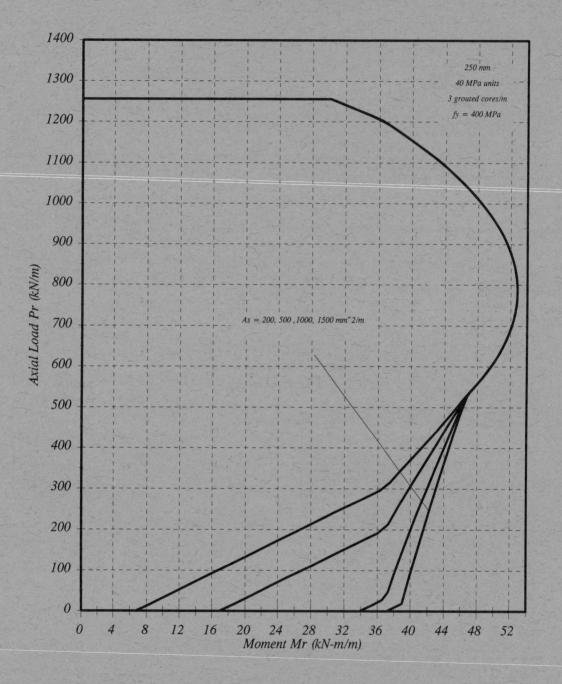

Figure F-48 Reinforced Wall Interaction Diagram
250 Block, 3 Grouted Cores/m, 40 MPa Unit Strength

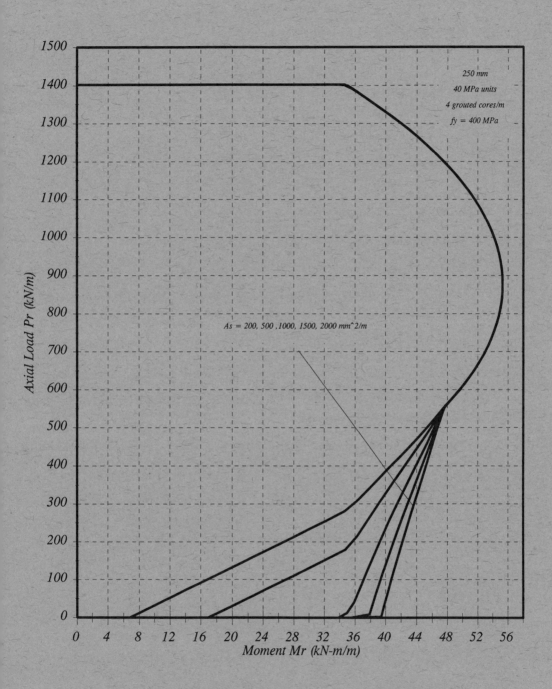

Figure F-49 Reinforced Wall Interaction Diagram
250 Block, 4 Grouted Cores/m, 40 MPa Unit Strength

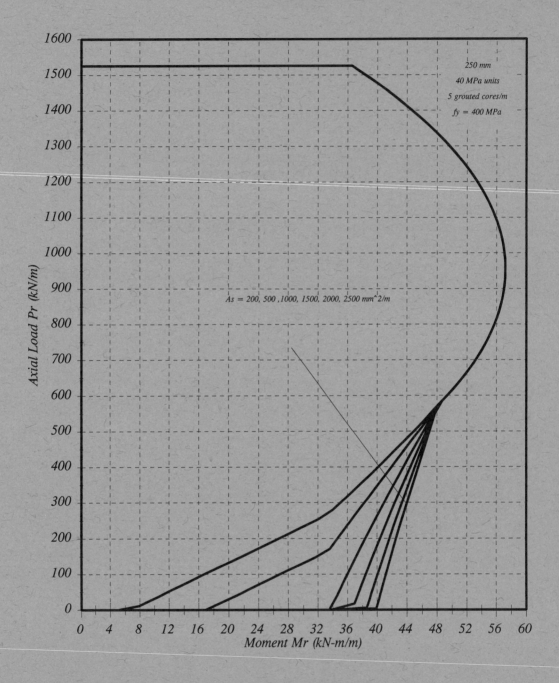

Figure F-50 Reinforced Wall Interaction Diagram
250 Block, 5 Grouted Cores/m, 40 MPa Unit Strength

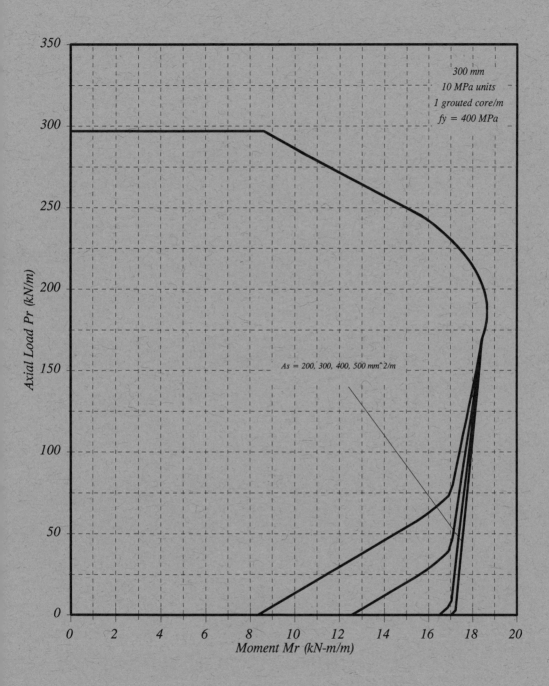

Figure F-51 Reinforced Wall Interaction Diagram
300 Block, 1 Grouted Core/m, 10 MPa Unit Strength

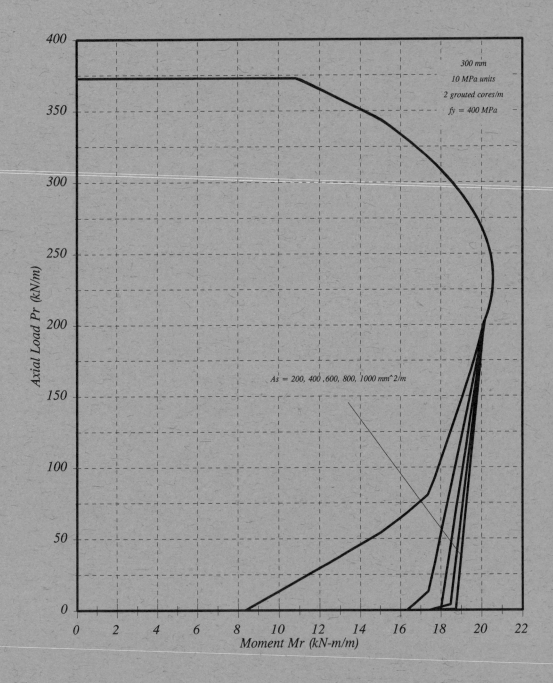

Figure F-52 Reinforced Wall Interaction Diagram
300 Block, 2 Grouted Cores/m, 10 MPa Unit Strength

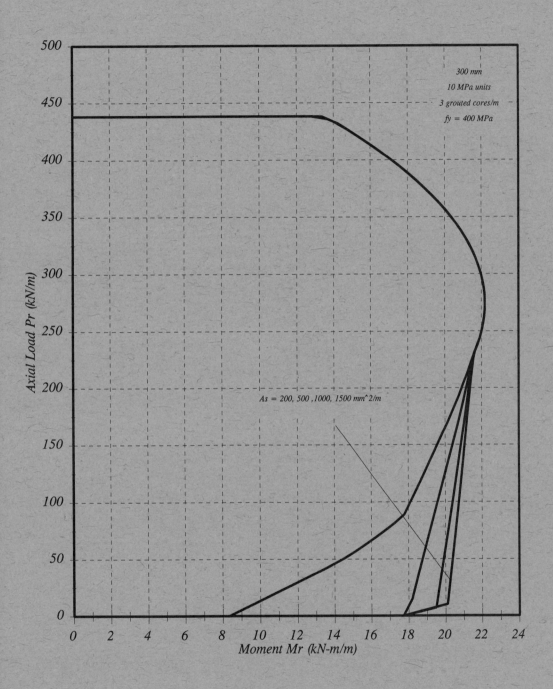

Figure F-53 Reinforced Wall Interaction Diagram
300 Block, 3 Grouted Cores/m, 10 MPa Unit Strength

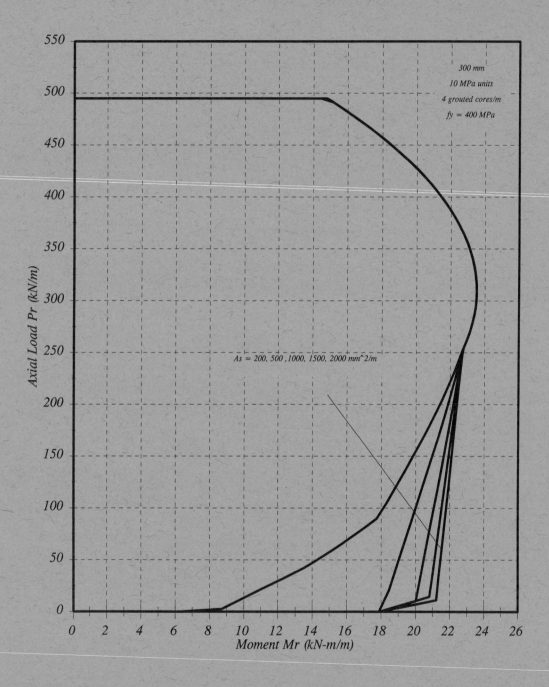

Figure F-54 Reinforced Wall Interaction Diagram
300 Block, 4 Grouted Cores/m, 10 MPa Unit Strength

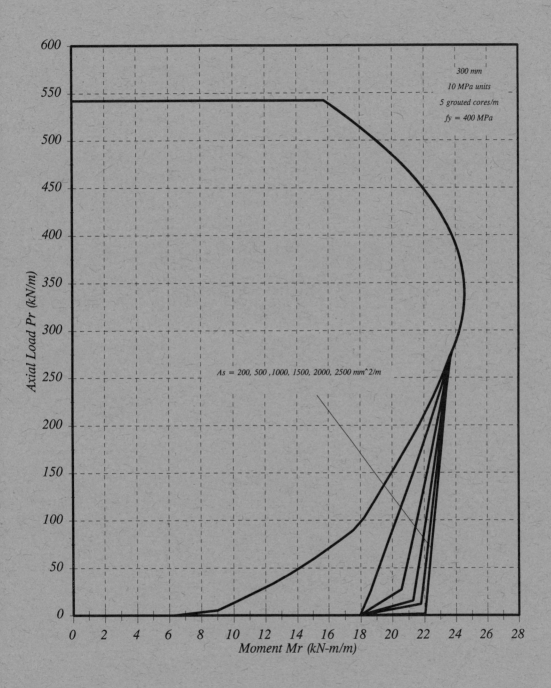

Figure F-55 Reinforced Wall Interaction Diagram
300 Block, 5 Grouted Cores/m, 10 MPa Unit Strength

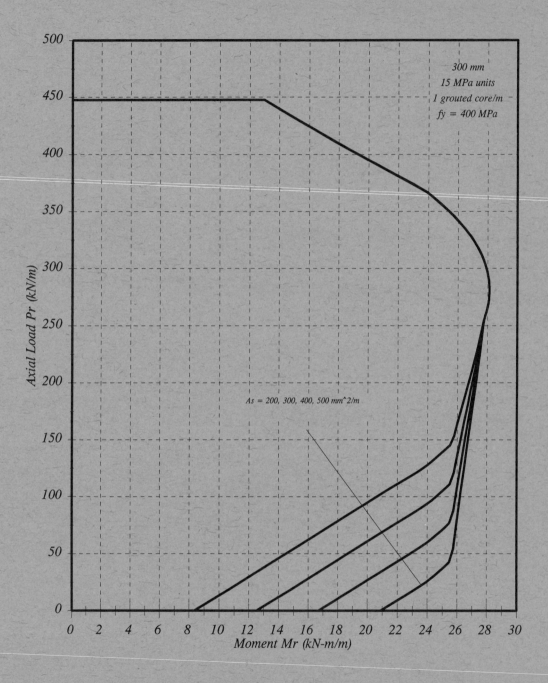

Figure F-56 Reinforced Wall Interaction Diagram
300 Block, 1 Grouted Core/m, 15 MPa Unit Strength

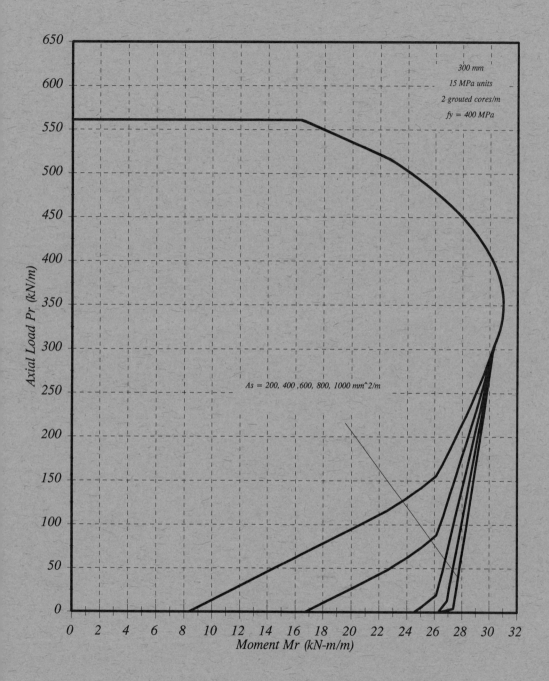

300 mm
15 MPa units
2 grouted cores/m
fy = 400 MPa

As = 200, 400 ,600, 800, 1000 mm^2/m

Figure F-57 Reinforced Wall Interaction Diagram
300 Block, 2 Grouted Cores/m, 15 MPa Unit Strength

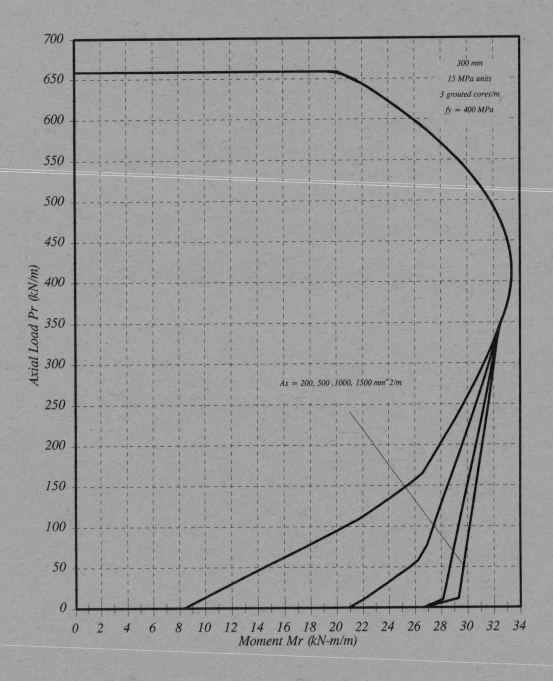

Figure F-58 Reinforced Wall Interaction Diagram
300 Block, 3 Grouted Cores/m, 15 MPa Unit Strength

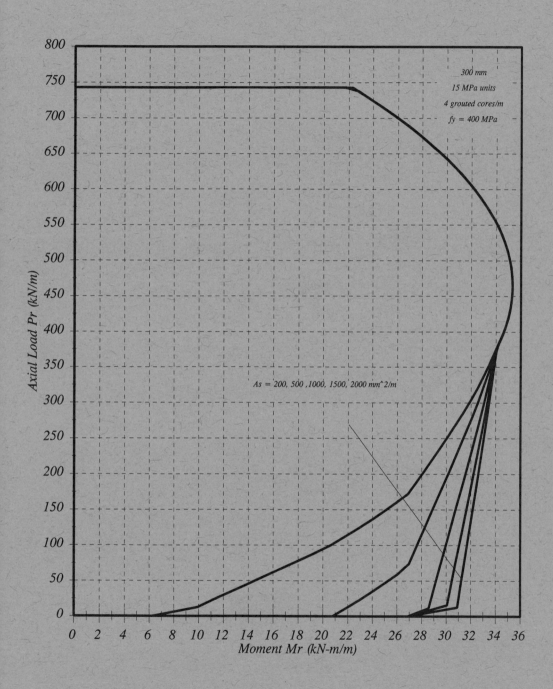

Figure F-59 Reinforced Wall Interaction Diagram
300 Block, 4 Grouted Cores/m, 15 MPa Unit Strength

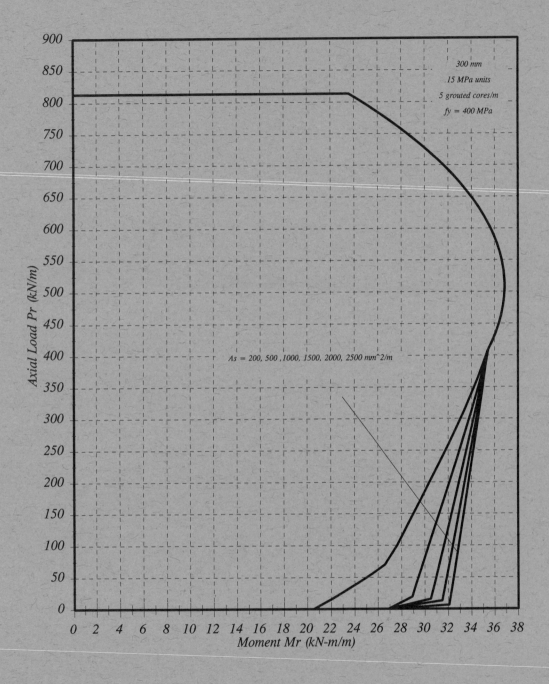

Figure F-60 Reinforced Wall Interaction Diagram
300 Block, 5 Grouted Cores/m, 15 MPa Unit Strength

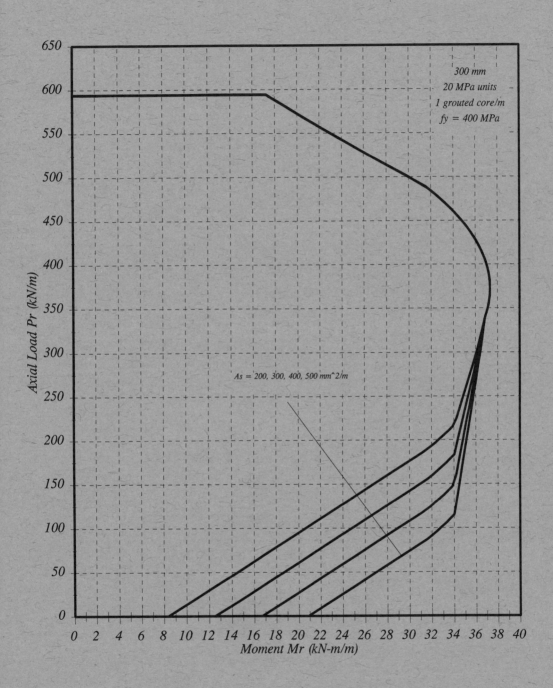

Figure F-61 Reinforced Wall Interaction Diagram
300 Block, 1 Grouted Core/m, 20 MPa Unit Strength

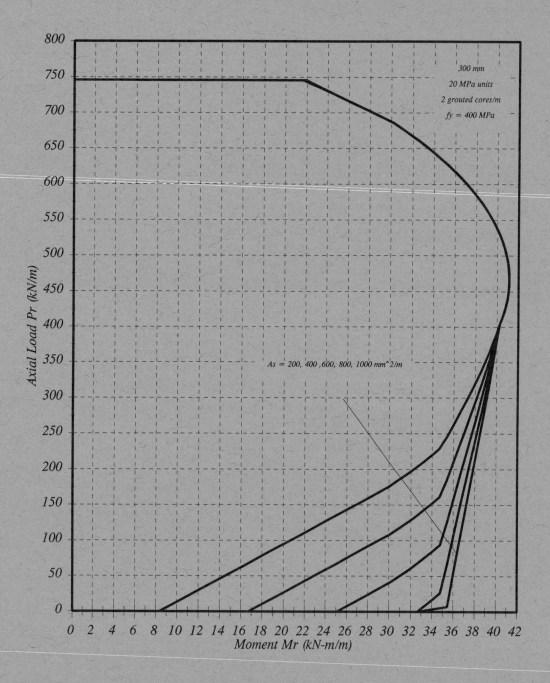

Figure F-62 Reinforced Wall Interaction Diagram
300 Block, 2 Grouted Cores/m, 20 MPa Unit Strength

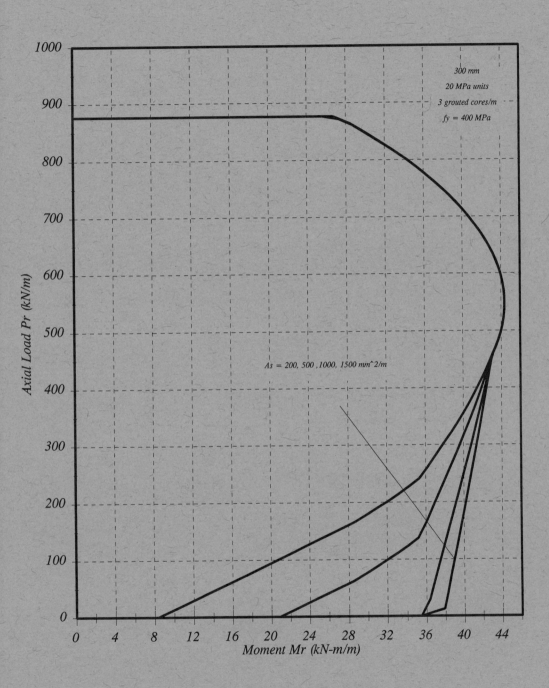

Figure F-63 Reinforced Wall Interaction Diagram
300 Block, 3 Grouted Cores/m, 20 MPa Unit Strength

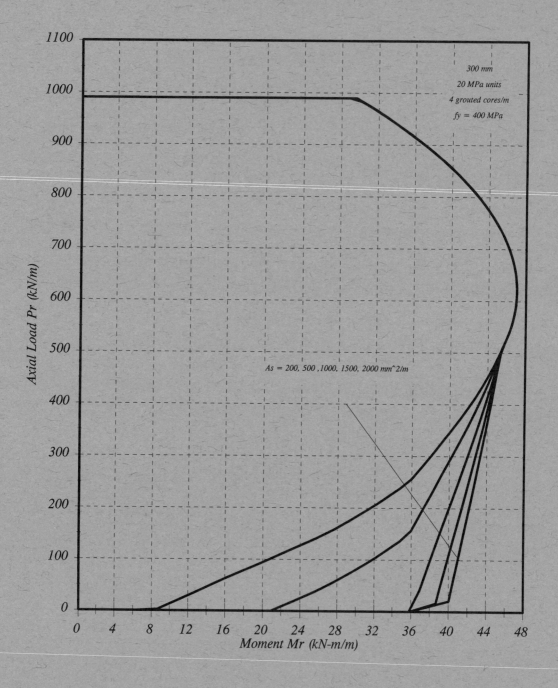

Figure F-64 Reinforced Wall Interaction Diagram
300 Block, 4 Grouted Cores/m, 20 MPa Unit Strength

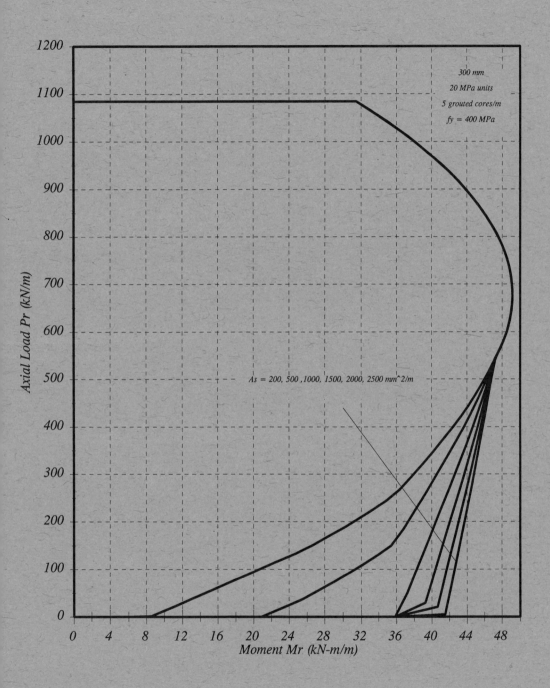

Figure F-65 Reinforced Wall Interaction Diagram
300 Block, 5 Grouted Cores/m, 20 MPa Unit Strength

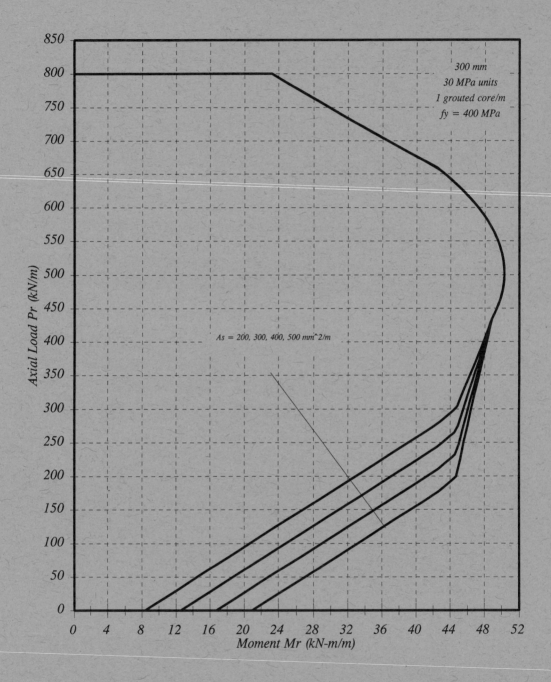

Figure F-66 Reinforced Wall Interaction Diagram
300 Block, 1 Grouted Core/m, 30 MPa Unit Strength

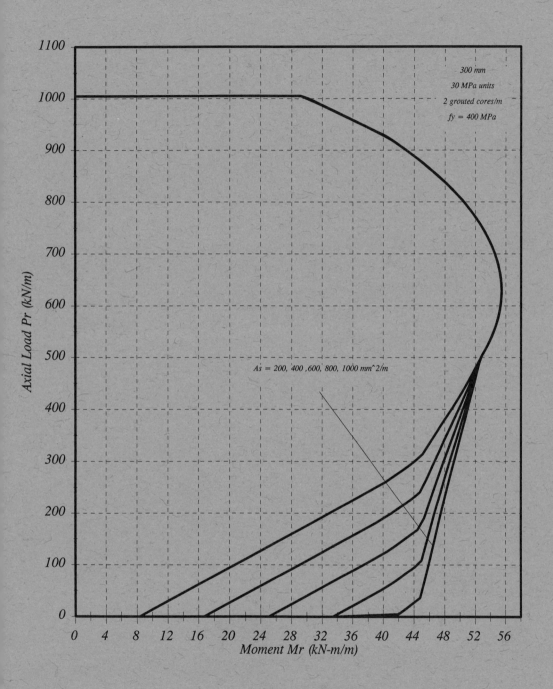

300 mm
30 MPa units
2 grouted cores/m
fy = 400 MPa

As = 200, 400 ,600, 800, 1000 mm^2/m

Figure F-67 Reinforced Wall Interaction Diagram
300 Block, 2 Grouted Cores/m, 30 MPa Unit Strength

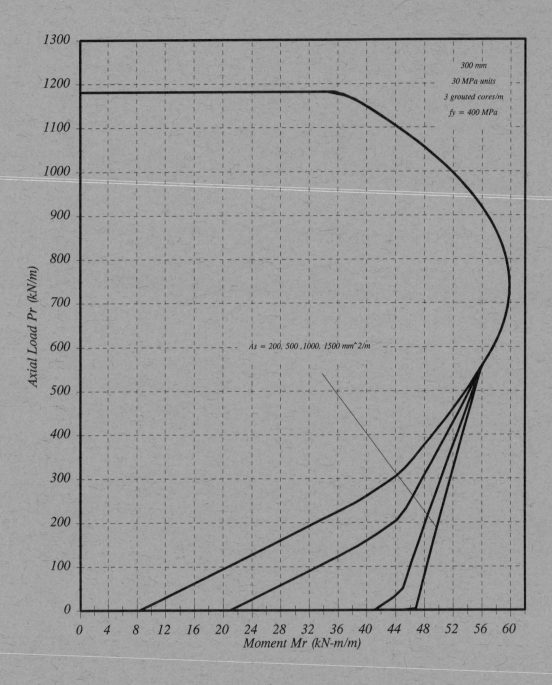

Figure F-68 Reinforced Wall Interaction Diagram
300 Block, 3 Grouted Cores/m, 30 MPa Unit Strength

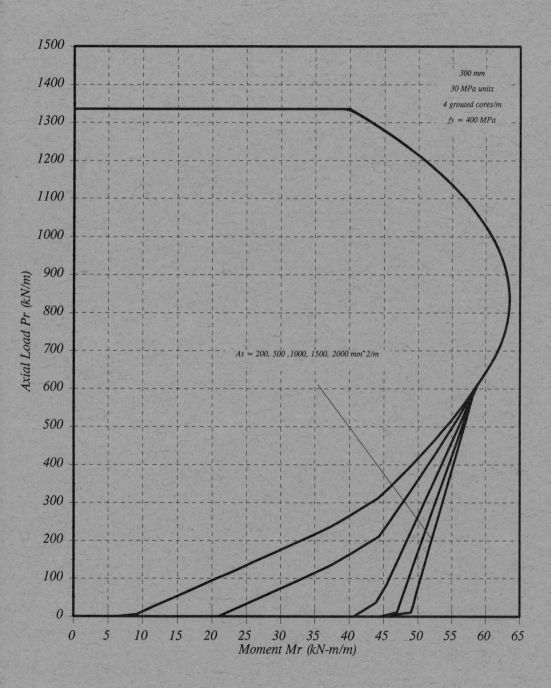

Figure F-69 Reinforced Wall Interaction Diagram
300 Block, 4 Grouted Cores/m, 30 MPa Unit Strength

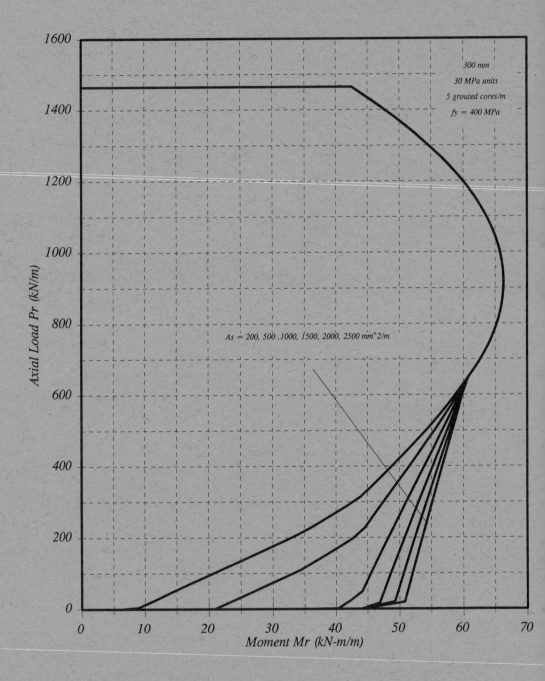

Figure F-70 Reinforced Wall Interaction Diagram
300 Block, 5 Grouted Cores/m, 30 MPa Unit Strength

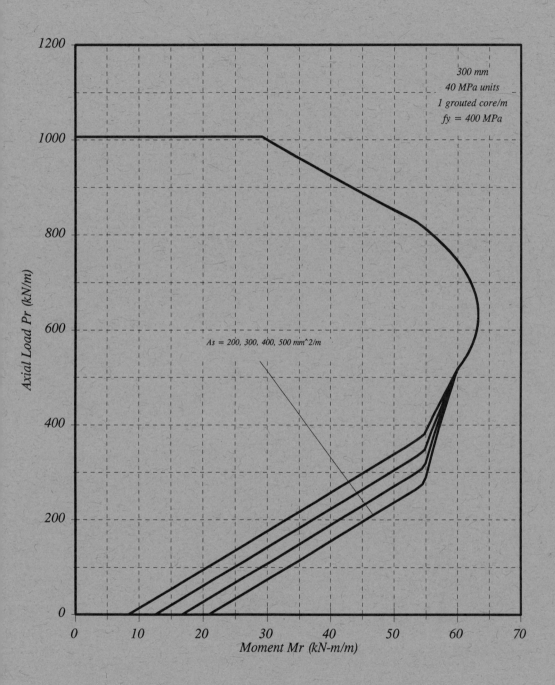

Figure F-71 Reinforced Wall Interaction Diagram
300 Block, 1 Grouted Core/m, 40 MPa Unit Strength

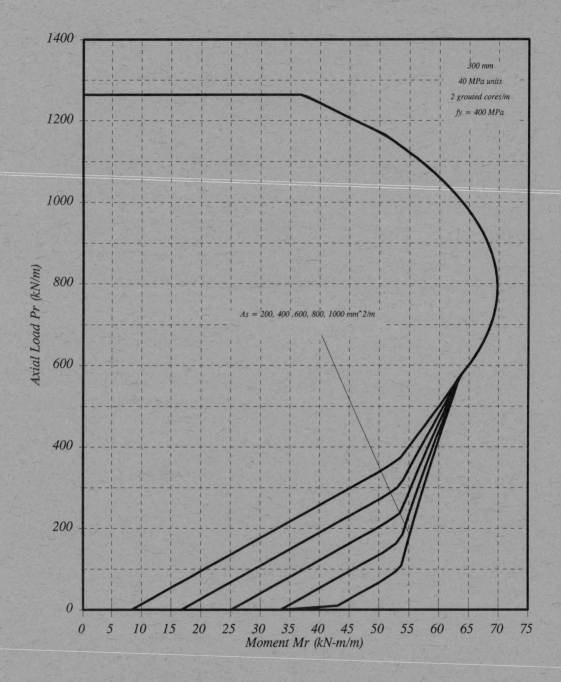

Figure F-72 Reinforced Wall Interaction Diagram
300 Block, 2 Grouted Cores/m, 40 MPa Unit Strength

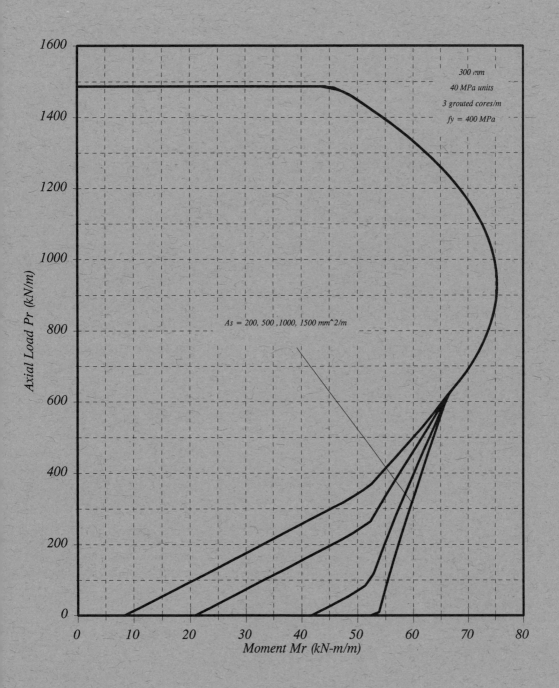

Figure F-73 Reinforced Wall Interaction Diagram
300 Block, 3 Grouted Cores/m, 40 MPa Unit Strength

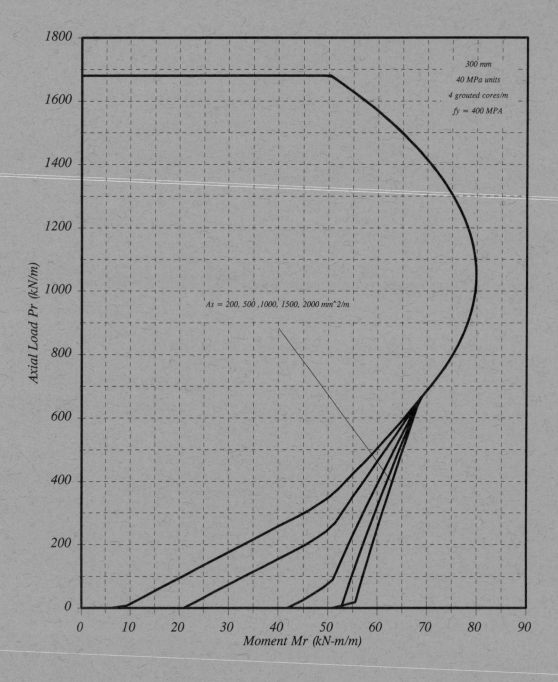

Figure F-74 Reinforced Wall Interaction Diagram
300 Block, 4 Grouted Cores/m, 40 MPa Unit Strength

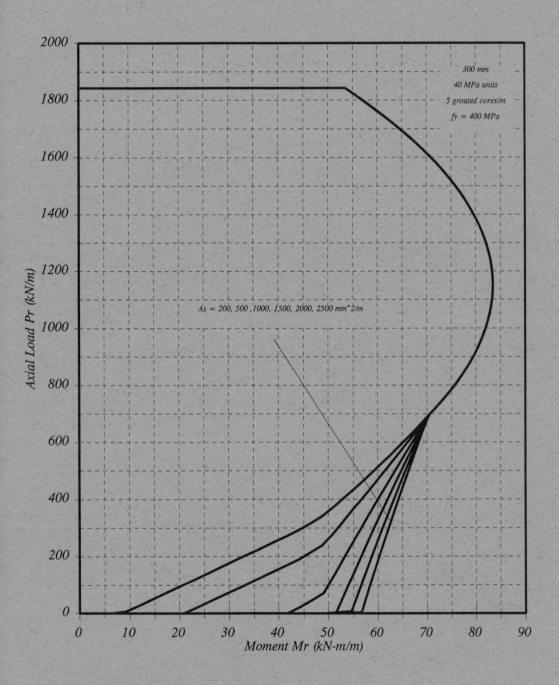

Figure F-75 Reinforced Wall Interaction Diagram
300 Block, 5 Grouted Cores/m, 40 MPa Unit Strength

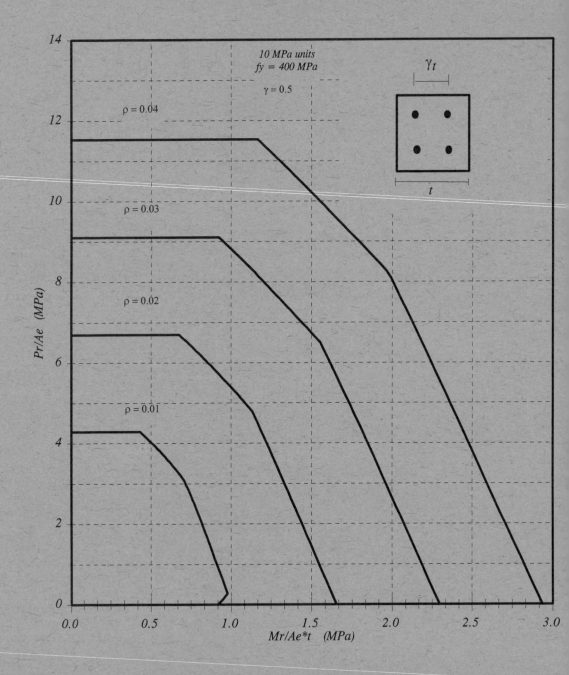

Figure G-1 Masonry Column Interaction Diagram
$\gamma = 0.5$, 10 MPa Unit Strength

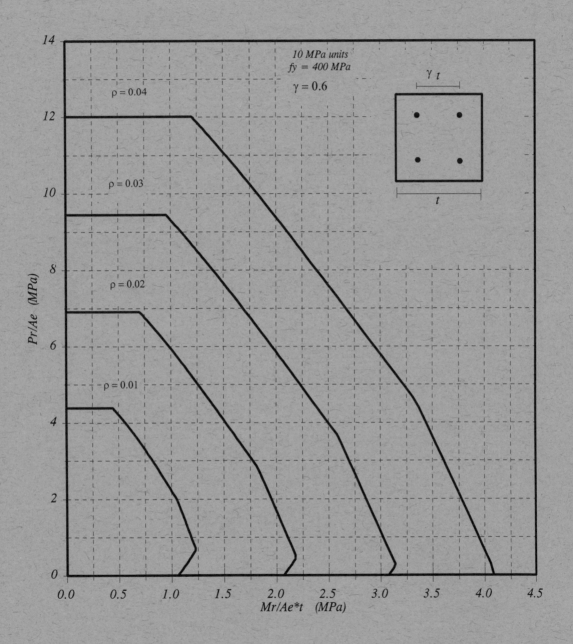

Figure G-2 Masonry Column Interaction Diagram
$\gamma = 0.6$, 10 MPa Unit Strength

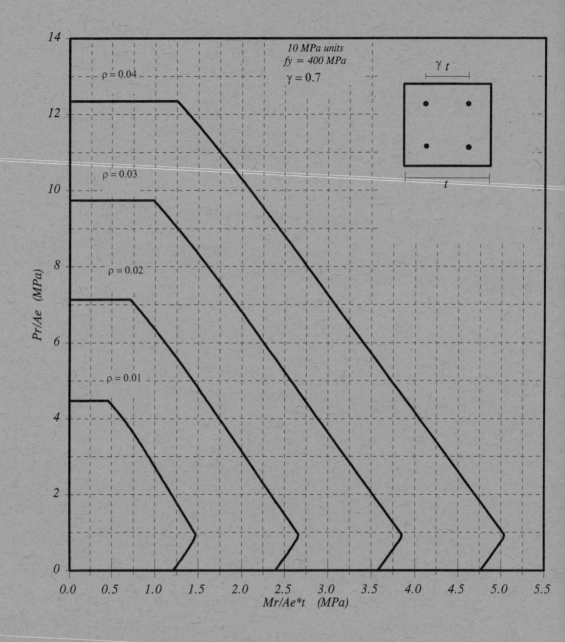

Figure G-3 Masonry Column Interaction Diagram
$\gamma = 0.7$, 10 MPa Unit Strength

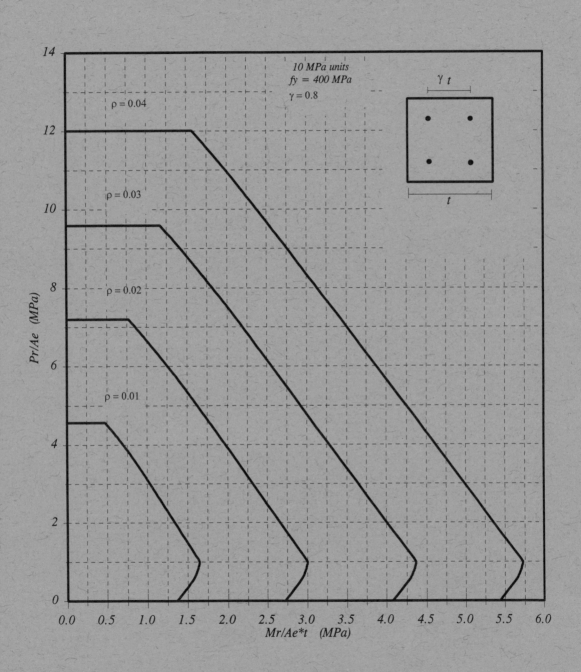

Figure G-4 Masonry Column Interaction Diagram
$\gamma = 0.8$, 10 MPa Unit Strength

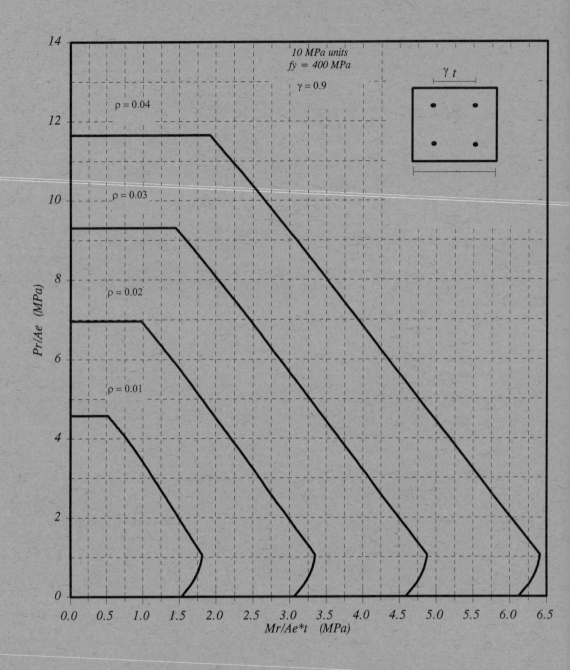

Figure G-5 Masonry Column Interaction Diagram
$\gamma = 0.9$, 10 MPa Unit Strength

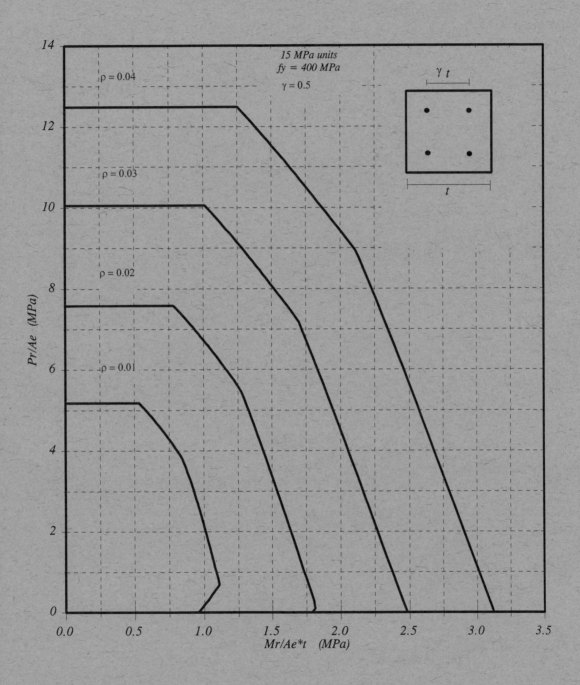

Figure G-6 Masonry Column Interaction Diagram
$\gamma = 0.5$, 15 MPa Unit Strength

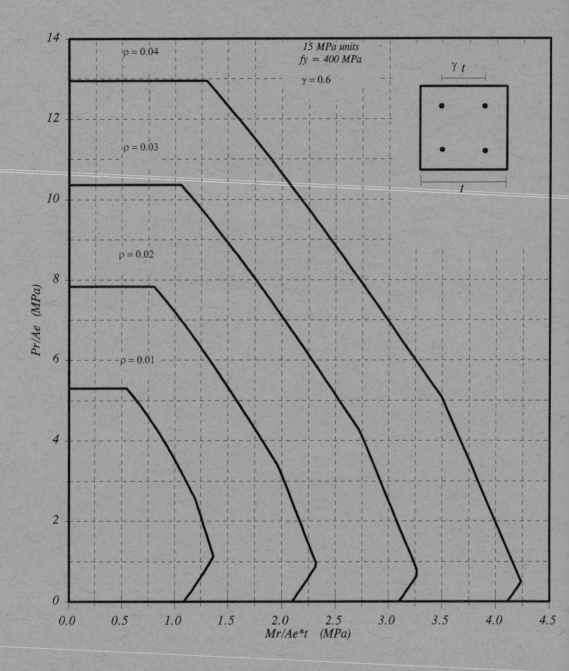

Figure G-7 Masonry Column Interaction Diagram
$\gamma = 0.6$, 15 MPa Unit Strength

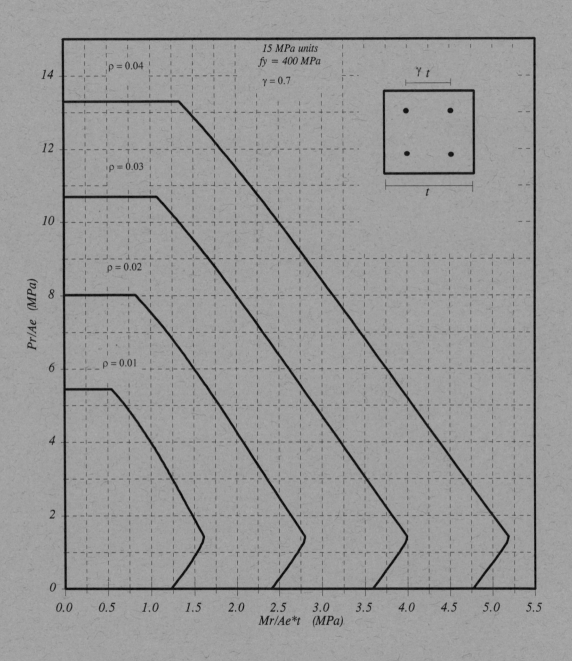

Figure G-8 Masonry Column Interaction Diagram
$\gamma = 0.7$, 15 MPa Unit Strength

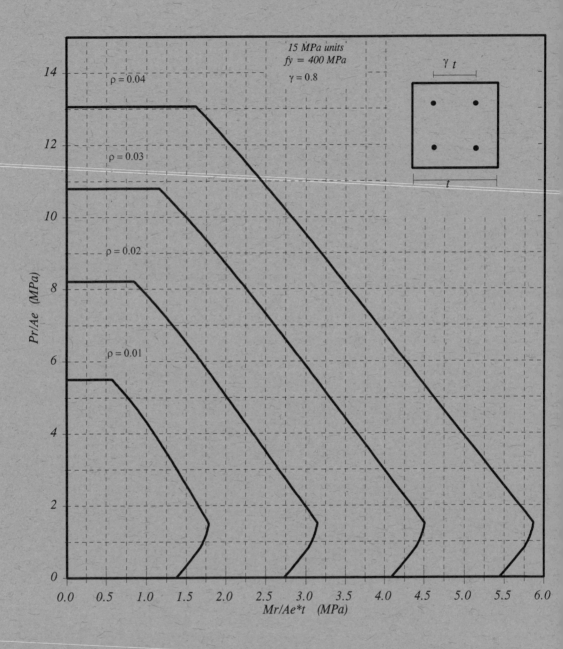

Figure G-9 Masonry Column Interaction Diagram
$\gamma = 0.8$, 15 MPa Unit Strength

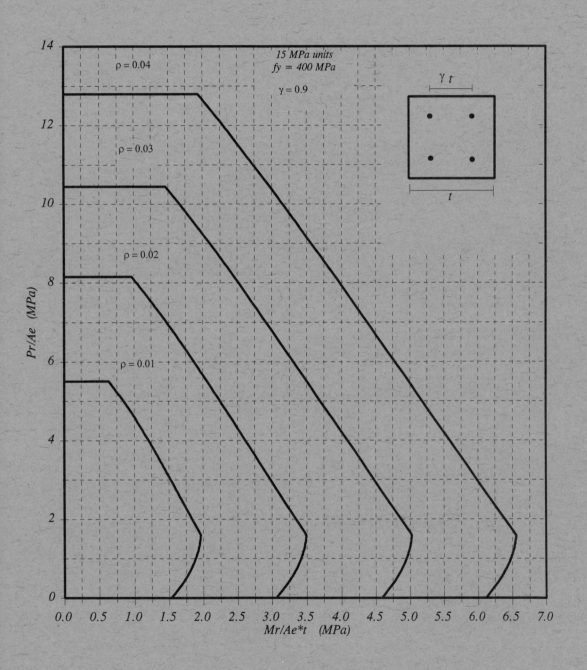

Figure G-10 Masonry Column Interaction Diagram
γ = 0.9, 15 MPa Unit Strength

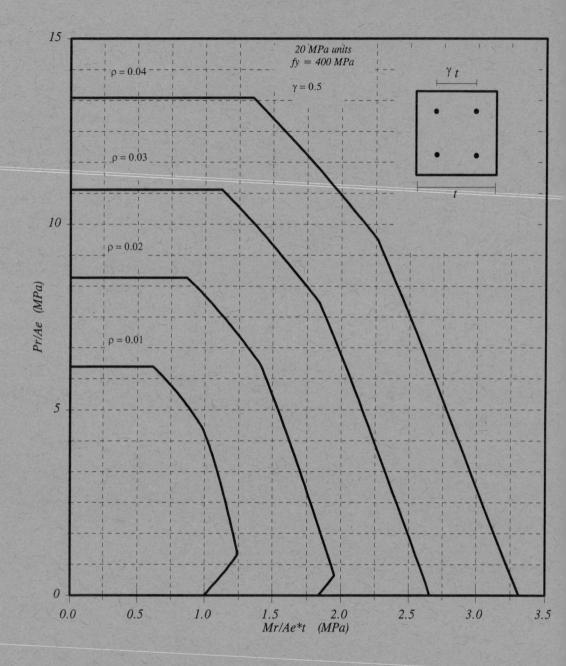

Figure G-11 Masonry Column Interaction Diagram
$\gamma = 0.5$, 20 MPa Unit Strength

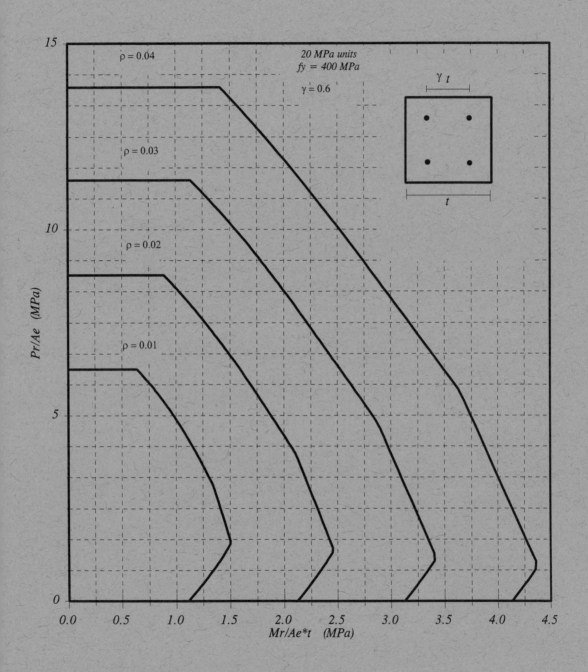

Figure G-12 Masonry Column Interaction Diagram
$\gamma = 0.6$, 20 MPa Unit Strength

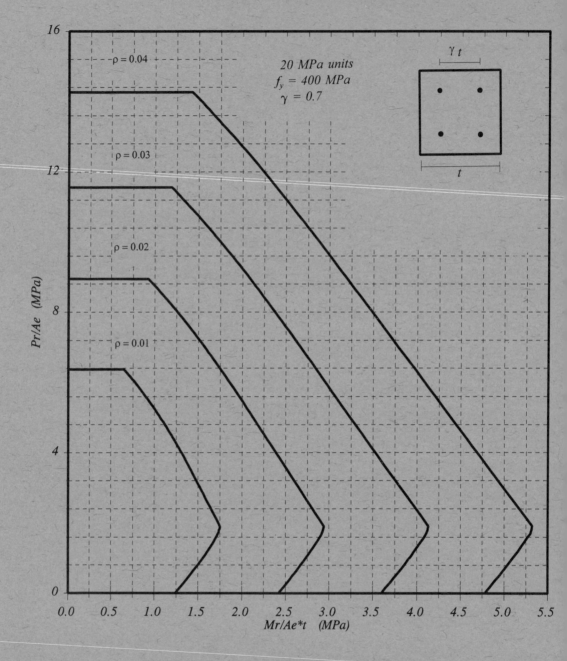

Figure G-13 Masonry Column Interaction Diagram
$\gamma = 0.7$, 20 MPa Unit Strength

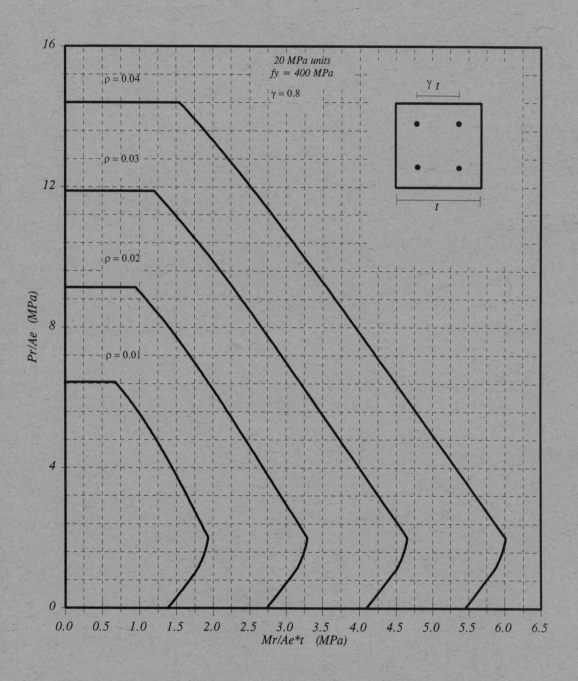

Figure G-14 Masonry Column Interaction Diagram
γ = 0.8, 20 MPa Unit Strength

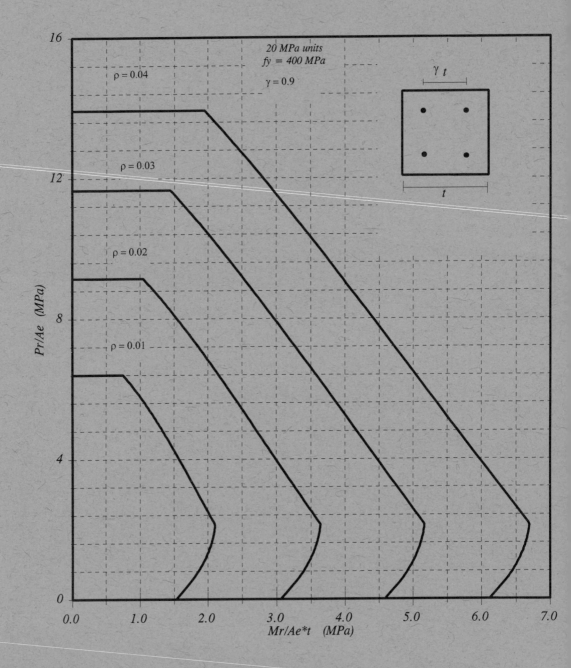

Figure G-15 Masonry Column Interaction Diagram
$\gamma = 0.9$, 20 MPa Unit Strength

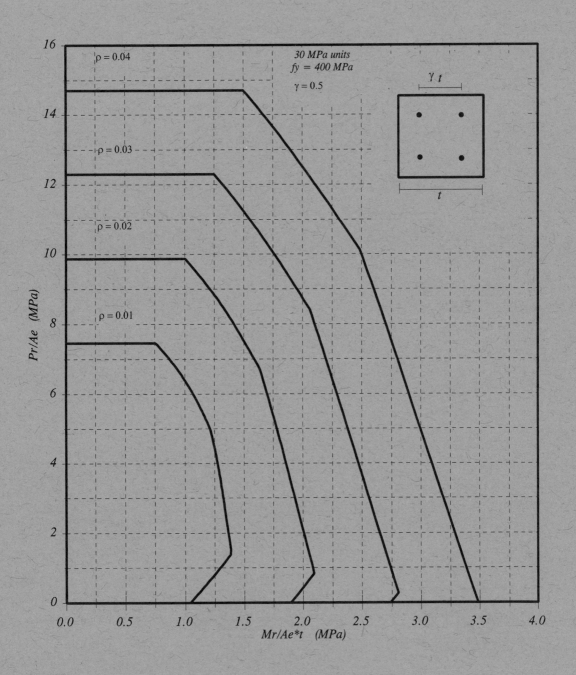

Figure G-16 Masonry Column Interaction Diagram
$\gamma = 0.5$, 30 MPa Unit Strength

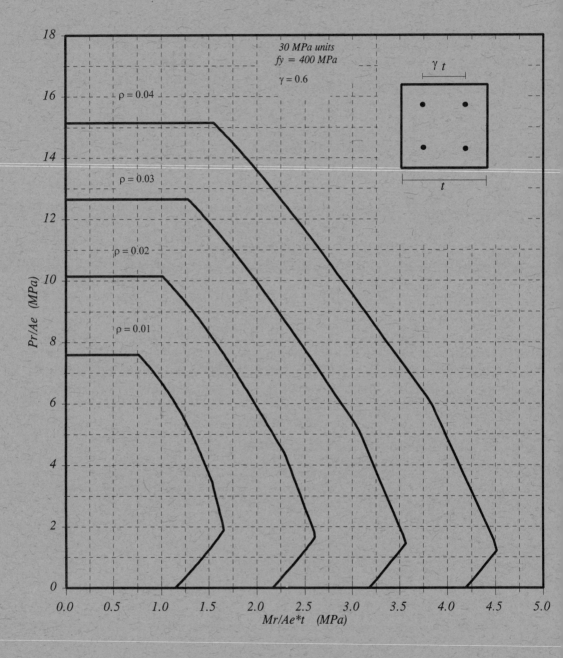

Figure G-17 Masonry Column Interaction Diagram
$\gamma = 0.6$, 30 MPa Unit Strength

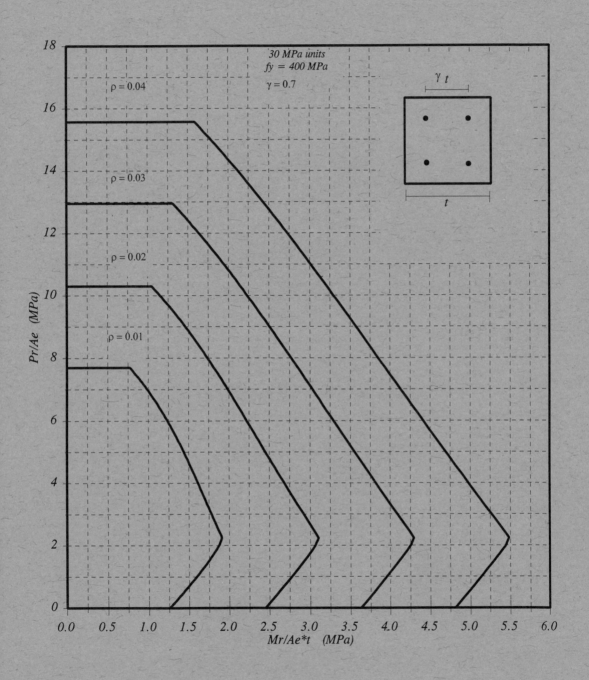

Figure G-18 Masonry Column Interaction Diagram
$\gamma = 0.7$, 30 MPa Unit Strength

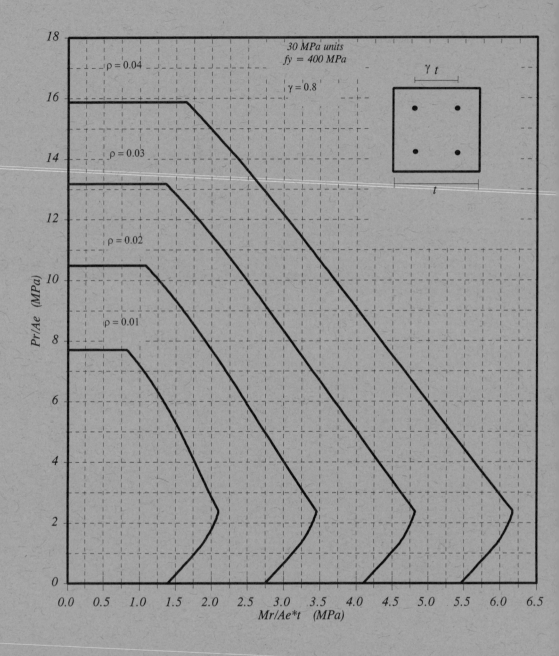

Figure G-19 Masonry Column Interaction Diagram
γ = 0.8, 30 MPa Unit Strength

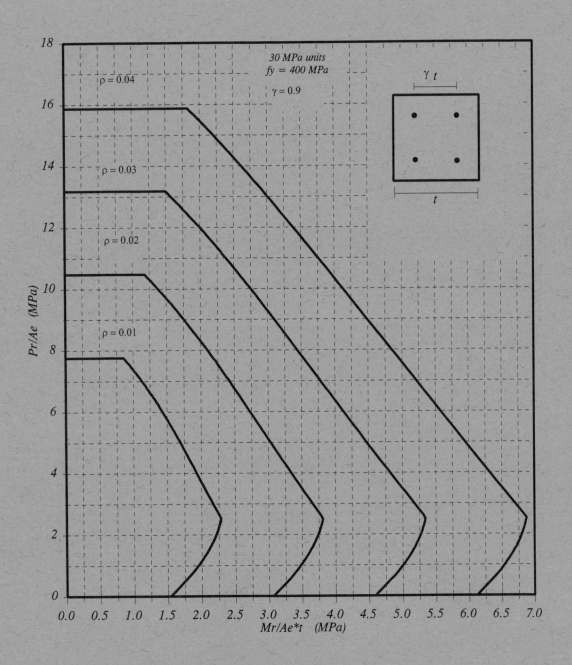

Figure G-20 Masonry Column Interaction Diagram
$\gamma = 0.9$, 30 MPa Unit Strength

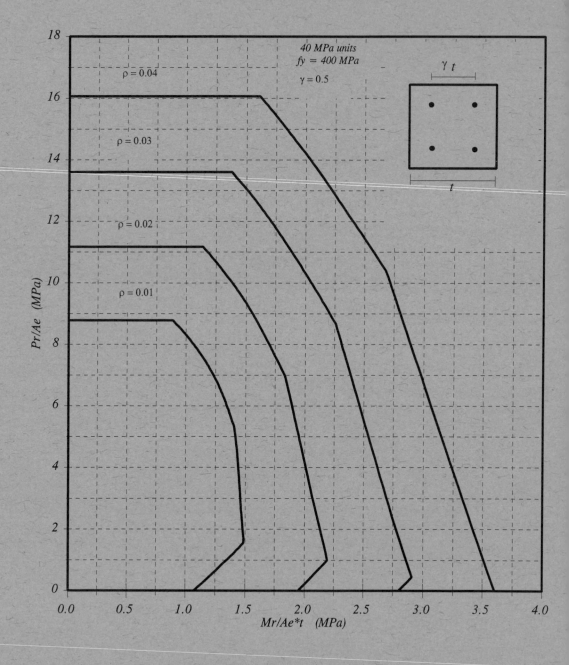

Figure G-21 Masonry Column Interaction Diagram
$\gamma = 0.5$, 40 MPa Unit Strength

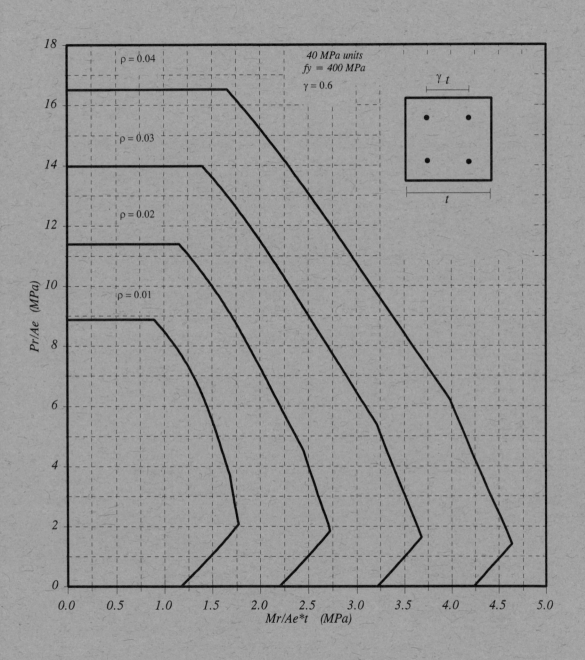

Figure G-22 Masonry Column Interaction Diagram
$\gamma = 0.6$, 40 MPa Unit Strength

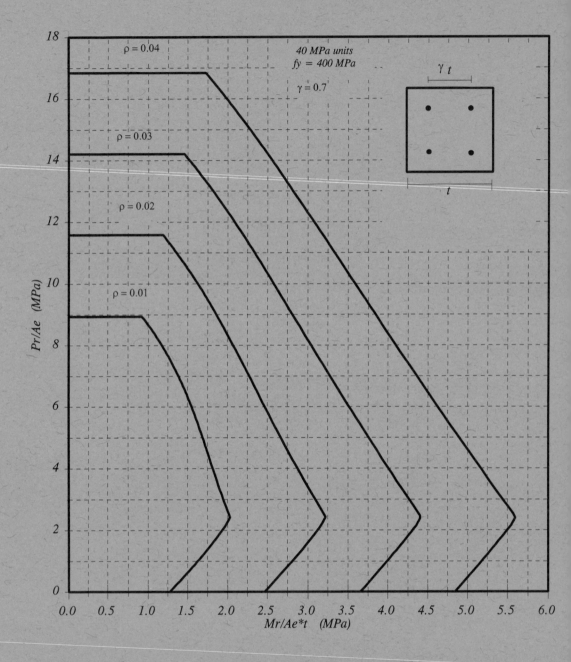

Figure G-23 Masonry Column Interaction Diagram
$\gamma = 0.7$, 40 MPa Unit Strength

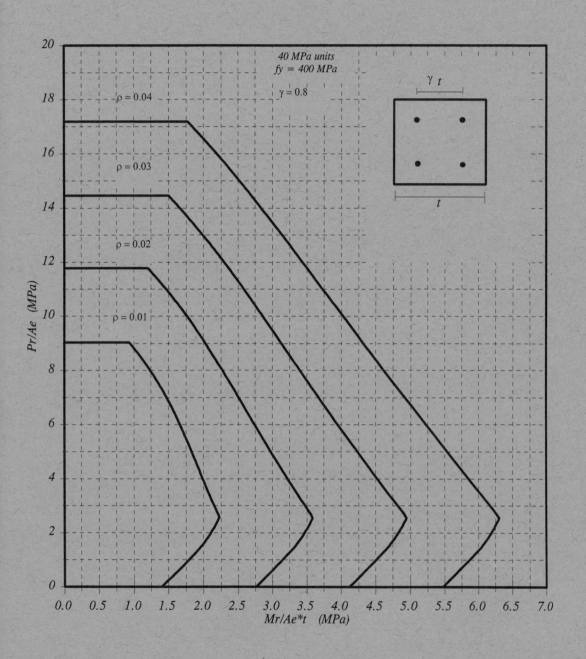

Figure G-24 Masonry Column Interaction Diagram
$\gamma = 0.8$, 40 MPa Unit Strength

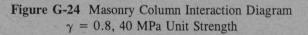

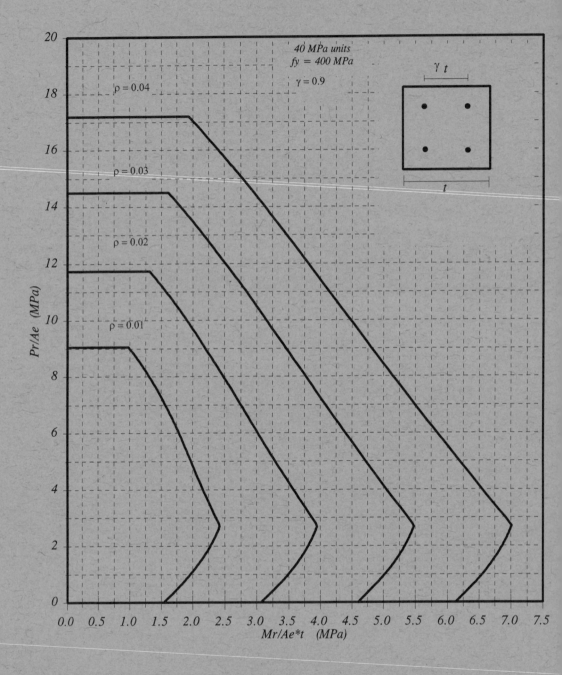

Figure G-25 Masonry Column Interaction Diagram
γ = 0.9, 40 MPa Unit Strength

Dead loads of floors, ceilings, roofs, and walls

Floorings	Force (kN/m²)
Normal density concrete topping, per 10 mm of thickness	0.24
Semi-low density (1900 kg/m³) concrete topping, per 10 mm	0.19
Low density (1500 kg/m³) concrete topping, per 10 mm	0.15
22 mm hardwood floor on sleepers clipped to concrete without fill	0.24
40 mm terrazzo floor finish directly on slab	0.95
40 mm terrazzo floor finish on 25 mm mortar bed	1.49
25 mm terrazzo finish on 50 mm concrete bed	1.79
20 mm ceramic or quarry tile on 12 mm mortar bed	0.80
20 mm ceramic or quarry tile on 25 mm mortar bed	1.06
8 mm linoleum or asphalt tile directly on concrete	0.06
8 mm linoleum or asphalt tile on 25 mm mortar bed	0.59
20 mm mastic floor	0.45
Hardwood flooring, 22 mm thick	0.19
Subflooring (soft wood), 20 mm thick	0.13
Asphaltic concrete, 40 mm thick	0.90

Ceilings	
12.7 mm gypsum board	0.10
15.9 mm gypsum board	0.12
20 mm plaster directly on concrete	0.26
20 mm plaster on metal lath furring	0.40
Suspended ceilings	
Acoustical tile	0.10
Acoustical tile on wood furring strips	0.05
	0.15

Roofs	
Five-ply felt and gravel (or slag)	0.31
Three-ply felt and gravel (or slag)	0.27
Five-ply felt composition roof, on gravel	0.20
Three-ply felt composition roof, on gravel	0.15
Asphalt strip shingles	0.15
Rigid insulation, per 100 mm (glass fibre)	0.07
Gypsum, per 10 mm of thickness	0.08
Insulating concrete, per 10 mm	0.06

	Unplastered	One side paltered	Both sides plastered
Walls			
100 mm brick wall	1.86	2.10	2.33
200 mm brick wall	3.77	4.00	4.24
300 mm brick wall	5.59	5.83	6.06
100 mm hollow normal density concrete block	1.37	1.61	1.84
150 mm hollow normal density concrete block	1.67	1.90	2.14
200 mm hollow normal density concrete block	2.11	2.34	2.58
300 mm hollow normal density concrete block	2.94	3.18	3.39
100 mm hollow low density block or tile	1.08	1.31	1.55
150 mm hollow low density block or tile	1.28	1.51	1.75
200 mm hollow low density block or tile	1.62	1.85	2.09
300 mm hollow low density block or tile	2.26	2.49	2.73
100 mm brick 100 mm hollow normal density block backing	3.24	3.47	3.71
100 mm brick 200 mm hollow normal density block backing	3.97	4.21	4.4
100 mm brick 300 mm hollow normal density block backing	4.81	5.04	5.28
100 mm brick 100 mm hollow low density block or tile backing	2.94	3.18	3.41
100 mm brick 200 mm hollow low density block or tile backing	3.48	3.72	3.95
100 mm brick 300 mm hollow low density block or tile backing	4.12	4.35	4.59
Windows, glass, frame and sash	0.38		
100 mm stone	2.59		
Steel or wood stud, lath, 20 mm plaster	0.86		
Steel or wood studs, lath, 15.9 mm gypsum board each side	0.28		
Steel or wood studs, 2 layers 12.7 mm gypsum board each side	0.44		

Recommended minimum floor or roof live loads*

Uniformly Distributed Loads	
Use of Area of Floor or Roof	Minimum Specified Load kN/m²
Apartments (see residential)	
Assembly halls and other places of assembly:	
Fixed seats	2.4
Movable seats	4.8
Platforms (assembly)	4.8
Balconies (exterior and interior):	
Residential, not used as passage ways	1.9
Other types	4.8
Bowling alleys, poolrooms, and similar recreational areas	3.6
Corridors:	
First floor	4.8
Other floors, same as occupancy served except as indicated	
Dance halls and ballrooms	4.8
Dining rooms and restaurants	4.8
Dwellings (see residential)	
Fire escapes and exits	4.8
Garages:	
Passenger cars	2.4
Unloaded buses and light trucks	6.0
Loaded buses and trucks and all other trucking spaces	12.0
Grandstands (see reviewing stands)	
Gymnasiums, main floors and balconies	4.8
Hospitals:	
Operating rooms, laboratories	3.6
Private rooms	1.9
Wards	1.9
Hotels (see residential)	
Libraries:	
Reading rooms	2.9
Stack rooms	7.2
Manufacturing	6.0
Office Buildings:	
Offices: (basement and first floor)	4.8
Floors above the first floor	2.4
Corridors, above the first floor	4.8
File and computer rooms require heavier loads based upon anticipated occupancy	
Penal institutions:	
Cell blocks	1.9
Corridors	4.8
Residential:	
Multifamily houses:	
Private apartments	1.9
public rooms	4.8
Dwellings:	
First floor	1.9
Bed rooms and habitable attics	1.4
Uninhabitable attics	0.5
Hotels:	
Guest rooms	1.9
Public rooms	4.8
Corridors serving public rooms	4.8
Corridors, same as occupancy served except as indicated	
Reviewing stands and bleachers	4.8

Uniformly Distributed Loads	
Use of Area of Floor or Roof	Minimum Specified Load kN/m²
Schools:	
Classrooms	2.4
Corridors	4.8
Sidewalks, vehicular driveways, and yards, subject to trucking	12.0
Skating rinks	4.8
Stairs and exitways	4.8
Storage warehouses	4.8
Stores:	
Retail and wholesale areas	4.8
Theatres:	
Aisles, corridors, and lobbies	4.8
Orchestra floors	4.8
Balconies	4.8
Stage floors	4.8
Yards and terraces, pedestrians	4.8

Concentrated Loads

The specified load due to possible concentrations of load resulting from the use of an area of floor or roof shall not be less than that listed below applied over an area of 750 mm by 750 mm located so as to cause maximum effects.

Area of Floor or Roof	Minimum Specified Concentrated load, kN
Roof surface	1.3
Floors of classrooms	4.5
Floors of offices, manufacturing buildings, hospital wards and stages	9.0
Floors and areas used by passenger cars	11
Floors and areas used by vehicles not exceeding 3600 kg gross weight	18
Floors and areas used by vehicles exceeding 3600 kg but not exceeding 9000 kg gross weight	36
Floors and areas used by vehicles exceeding 9000 kg gross weight	54
Driveways and sidewalks over area-ways and basement	54

Bleacher seats shall be designed for a uniformly distributed load of 1.75 kN for each linear metre or for a concentrated load of 2.2 kN distributed over a length of 0.75 m, whichever produces the greatest effect on the supporting members.

Helicopter landing areas on roofs shall be constructed in conformance with the regulation for heliports established by transport Canada.

Where the use of an area of floor is not provided for above, the specified live loads due to the use and occupancy of the area shall be determined from an analysis of the loads resulting from

  (a) the weight of the probable assembly of persons,

  (b) the weight of the probable accumulation of equipment and furnishings, and

  (c) the weight of the probable storage of materials.

* source National Building Code of Canada, 1995

Beam design equations and diagrams

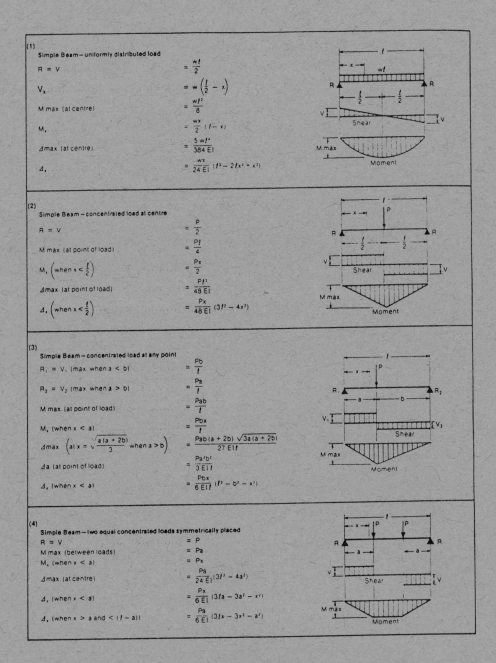

(1) Simple Beam – uniformly distributed load

$$R = V = \frac{wl}{2}$$

$$V_x = w\left(\frac{l}{2} - x\right)$$

$$M \text{ max (at centre)} = \frac{wl^2}{8}$$

$$M_x = \frac{wx}{2}(l - x)$$

$$\Delta \text{max (at centre)} = \frac{5\,wl^4}{384\,EI}$$

$$\Delta_x = \frac{wx}{24\,EI}(l^3 - 2lx^2 + x^3)$$

(2) Simple Beam – concentrated load at centre

$$R = V = \frac{P}{2}$$

$$M \text{ max (at point of load)} = \frac{Pl}{4}$$

$$M_x \left(\text{when } x < \frac{l}{2}\right) = \frac{Px}{2}$$

$$\Delta \text{max (at point of load)} = \frac{Pl^3}{48\,EI}$$

$$\Delta_x \left(\text{when } x < \frac{l}{2}\right) = \frac{Px}{48\,EI}(3l^2 - 4x^2)$$

(3) Simple Beam – concentrated load at any point

$$R_1 = V_1 \text{ (max when } a < b) = \frac{Pb}{l}$$

$$R_2 = V_2 \text{ (max when } a > b) = \frac{Pa}{l}$$

$$M \text{ max (at point of load)} = \frac{Pab}{l}$$

$$M_x \text{ (when } x < a) = \frac{Pbx}{l}$$

$$\Delta \text{max} \left(\text{at } x = \sqrt{\frac{a(a + 2b)}{3}} \text{ when } a > b\right) = \frac{Pab(a + 2b)\sqrt{3a(a + 2b)}}{27\,EIl}$$

$$\Delta a \text{ (at point of load)} = \frac{Pa^2b^2}{3\,EIl}$$

$$\Delta_x \text{ (when } x < a) = \frac{Pbx}{6\,EIl}(l^2 - b^2 - x^2)$$

(4) Simple Beam – two equal concentrated loads symmetrically placed

$$R = V = P$$

$$M \text{ max (between loads)} = Pa$$

$$M_x \text{ (when } x < a) = Px$$

$$\Delta \text{max (at centre)} = \frac{Pa}{24\,EI}(3l^2 - 4a^2)$$

$$\Delta_x \text{ (when } x < a) = \frac{Px}{6\,EI}(3la - 3a^2 - x^2)$$

$$\Delta_x \text{ (when } x > a \text{ and } < (l - a)) = \frac{Pa}{6\,EI}(3lx - 3x^2 - a^2)$$

Beam design equations and diagrams

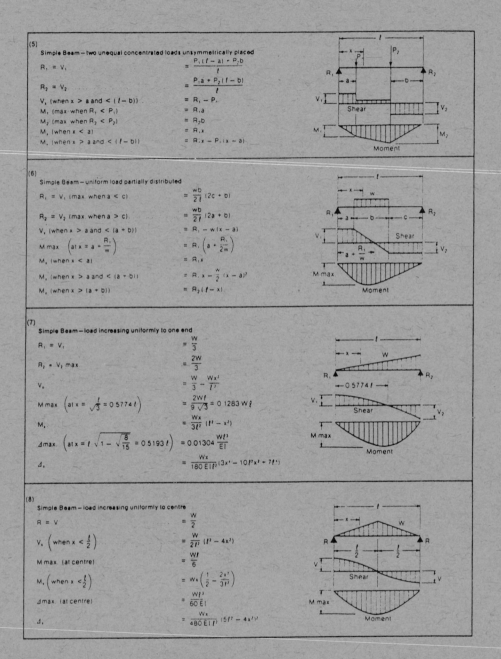

(5)

Simple Beam — two unequal concentrated loads unsymmetrically placed

$$R_1 = V_1 \qquad = \frac{P_1(l-a) + P_2 b}{l}$$

$$R_2 = V_2 \dots \qquad = \frac{P_1 a + P_2(l-b)}{l}$$

$$V_x \ (\text{when } x > a \text{ and} < (l-b)) \qquad = R_1 - P_1$$

$$M_1 \ (\text{max when } R_1 < P_1) \qquad = R_1 a$$

$$M_2 \ (\text{max when } R_2 < P_2) \qquad = R_2 b$$

$$M_x \ (\text{when } x < a) \qquad = R_1 x$$

$$M_x \ (\text{when } x > a \text{ and} < (l-b)) \qquad = R_1 x - P_1(x-a)$$

(6)

Simple Beam — uniform load partially distributed

$$R_1 = V_1 \ (\text{max when } a < c) \qquad = \frac{wb}{2l}(2c+b)$$

$$R_2 = V_2 \ (\text{max when } a > c) \qquad = \frac{wb}{2l}(2a+b)$$

$$V_x \ (\text{when } x > a \text{ and} < (a+b)) \qquad = R_1 - w(x-a)$$

$$M \text{ max} \ \left(\text{at } x = a + \frac{R_1}{w}\right) \qquad = R_1\left(a + \frac{R_1}{2w}\right)$$

$$M_x \ (\text{when } x < a) \qquad = R_1 x$$

$$M_x \ (\text{when } x > a \text{ and} < (a+b)) \qquad = R_1 x - \frac{w}{2}(x-a)^2$$

$$M_x \ (\text{when } x > (a+b)) \qquad = R_2(l-x)$$

(7)

Simple Beam — load increasing uniformly to one end

$$R_1 = V_1 \qquad = \frac{W}{3}$$

$$R_2 = V_2 \text{ max} \qquad = \frac{2W}{3}$$

$$V_x \qquad = \frac{W}{3} - \frac{Wx^2}{l^2}$$

$$M \text{ max} \ \left(\text{at } x = \frac{l}{\sqrt{3}} = 0.5774 l\right) \qquad = \frac{2Wl}{9\sqrt{3}} = 0.1283 \, Wl$$

$$M_x \qquad = \frac{Wx}{3l^2}(l^2 - x^2)$$

$$\Delta \text{max} \ \left(\text{at } x = l\sqrt{1 - \sqrt{\tfrac{8}{15}}} = 0.5193 l\right) \qquad = 0.01304 \frac{Wl^3}{EI}$$

$$\Delta_x \qquad = \frac{Wx}{180 \, EI l^2}(3x^4 - 10l^2 x^2 + 7l^4)$$

(8)

Simple Beam — load increasing uniformly to centre

$$R = V \qquad = \frac{W}{2}$$

$$V_x \ \left(\text{when } x < \frac{l}{2}\right) \qquad = \frac{W}{2l^2}(l^2 - 4x^2)$$

$$M \text{ max} \ (\text{at centre}) \qquad = \frac{Wl}{6}$$

$$M_x \ \left(\text{when } x < \frac{l}{2}\right) \qquad = Wx\left(\frac{1}{2} - \frac{2x^2}{3l^2}\right)$$

$$\Delta \text{max} \ (\text{at centre}) \qquad = \frac{Wl^3}{60 \, EI}$$

$$\Delta_x \qquad = \frac{Wx}{480 \, EI l^2}(5l^2 - 4x^2)^2$$

Beam design equations and diagrams

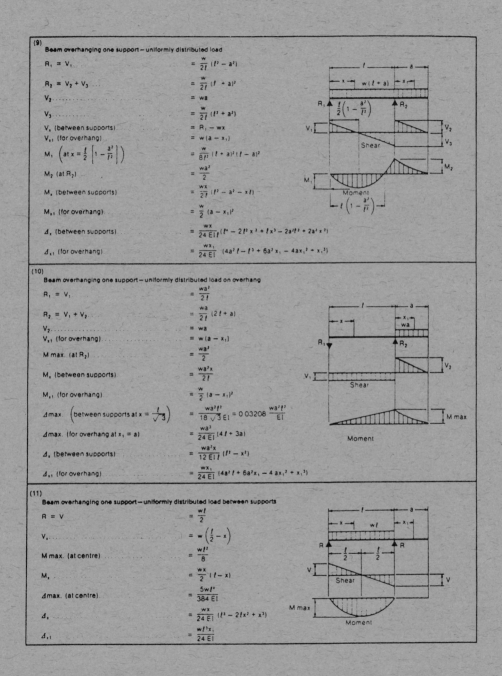

(9)

Beam overhanging one support – uniformly distributed load

$R_1 = V_1 \qquad = \dfrac{w}{2l}(l^2 - a^2)$

$R_2 = V_2 + V_3 \qquad = \dfrac{w}{2l}(l + a)^2$

$V_2 \qquad = wa$

$V_3 \qquad = \dfrac{w}{2l}(l^2 + a^2)$

$V_x \ (\text{between supports}) \qquad = R_1 - wx$

$V_{x1} \ (\text{for overhang}) \qquad = w(a - x_1)$

$M_1 \left(\text{at } x = \dfrac{l}{2}\left[1 - \dfrac{a^2}{l^2}\right]\right) \qquad = \dfrac{w}{8l^2}(l + a)^2(l - a)^2$

$M_2 \ (\text{at } R_2) \qquad = \dfrac{wa^2}{2}$

$M_x \ (\text{between supports}) \qquad = \dfrac{wx}{2l}(l^2 - a^2 - xl)$

$M_{x1} \ (\text{for overhang}) \qquad = \dfrac{w}{2}(a - x_1)^2$

$\Delta_x \ (\text{between supports}) \qquad = \dfrac{wx}{24\,EIl}(l^4 - 2l^2 x^2 + l x^3 - 2a^2 l^2 + 2a^2 x^2)$

$\Delta_{x1} \ (\text{for overhang}) \qquad = \dfrac{wx_1}{24\,EI}(4a^2 l - l^3 + 6a^2 x_1 - 4ax_1^2 + x_1^3)$

(10)

Beam overhanging one support – uniformly distributed load on overhang

$R_1 = V_1 \qquad = \dfrac{wa^2}{2l}$

$R_2 = V_1 + V_2 \qquad = \dfrac{wa}{2l}(2l + a)$

$V_2 \qquad = wa$

$V_{x1} \ (\text{for overhang}) \qquad = w(a - x_1)$

$M \text{ max. } (\text{at } R_2) \qquad = \dfrac{wa^2}{2}$

$M_x \ (\text{between supports}) \qquad = \dfrac{wa^2 x}{2l}$

$M_{x1} \ (\text{for overhang}) \qquad = \dfrac{w}{2}(a - x_1)^2$

$\Delta \text{ max. } \left(\text{between supports at } x = \dfrac{l}{\sqrt{3}}\right) \qquad = \dfrac{wa^2 l^2}{18\sqrt{3}\,EI} = 0.03208\,\dfrac{wa^2 l^2}{EI}$

$\Delta \text{ max. } (\text{for overhang at } x_1 = a) \qquad = \dfrac{wa^3}{24\,EI}(4l + 3a)$

$\Delta_x \ (\text{between supports}) \qquad = \dfrac{wa^2 x}{12\,EIl}(l^2 - x^2)$

$\Delta_{x1} \ (\text{for overhang}) \qquad = \dfrac{wx_1}{24\,EI}(4a^2 l + 6a^2 x_1 - 4ax_1^2 + x_1^3)$

(11)

Beam overhanging one support – uniformly distributed load between supports

$R = V \qquad = \dfrac{wl}{2}$

$V_x \qquad = w\left(\dfrac{l}{2} - x\right)$

$M \text{ max. } (\text{at centre}) \qquad = \dfrac{wl^2}{8}$

$M_x \qquad = \dfrac{wx}{2}(l - x)$

$\Delta \text{ max. } (\text{at centre}) \qquad = \dfrac{5wl^4}{384\,EI}$

$\Delta_x \qquad = \dfrac{wx}{24\,EI}(l^3 - 2lx^2 + x^3)$

$\Delta_{x1} \qquad = \dfrac{wl^3 x_1}{24\,EI}$

Beam design equations and diagrams

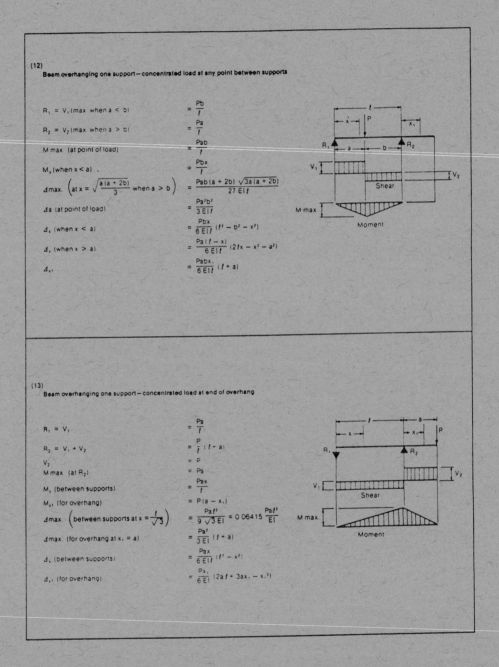

(12)

Beam overhanging one support — concentrated load at any point between supports

$R_1 = V_1$ (max when $a < b$) $= \dfrac{Pb}{l}$

$R_2 = V_2$ (max when $a > b$) $= \dfrac{Pa}{l}$

M max (at point of load) $= \dfrac{Pab}{l}$

M_x (when $x < a$) $= \dfrac{Pbx}{l}$

Δ max. $\left(\text{at } x = \sqrt{\dfrac{a(a+2b)}{3}} \text{ when } a > b\right) = \dfrac{Pab(a+2b)\sqrt{3a(a+2b)}}{27\,EIl}$

Δa (at point of load) $= \dfrac{Pa^2b^2}{3EIl}$

Δ_x (when $x < a$) $= \dfrac{Pbx}{6EIl}(l^2 - b^2 - x^2)$

Δ_x (when $x > a$) $= \dfrac{Pa(l-x)}{6EIl}(2lx - x^2 - a^2)$

$\Delta_{x_1} = \dfrac{Pabx_1}{6EIl}(l+a)$

(13)

Beam overhanging one support — concentrated load at end of overhang

$R_1 = V_1$ $= \dfrac{Pa}{l}$

$R_2 = V_1 + V_2$ $= \dfrac{P}{l}(l+a)$

V_2 $= P$

M max (at R_2) $= Pa$

M_x (between supports) $= \dfrac{Pax}{l}$

M_{x_1} (for overhang) $= P(a - x_1)$

Δ max. $\left(\text{between supports at } x = \dfrac{l}{\sqrt 3}\right) = \dfrac{Pal^2}{9\sqrt3\,EI} = 0.06415\,\dfrac{Pal^2}{EI}$

Δ max. (for overhang at $x_1 = a$) $= \dfrac{Pa^2}{3EI}(l+a)$

Δ_x (between supports) $= \dfrac{Pax}{6EIl}(l^2 - x^2)$

Δ_{x_1} (for overhang) $= \dfrac{Px_1}{6EI}(2al + 3ax_1 - x_1^2)$

Beam design equations and diagrams

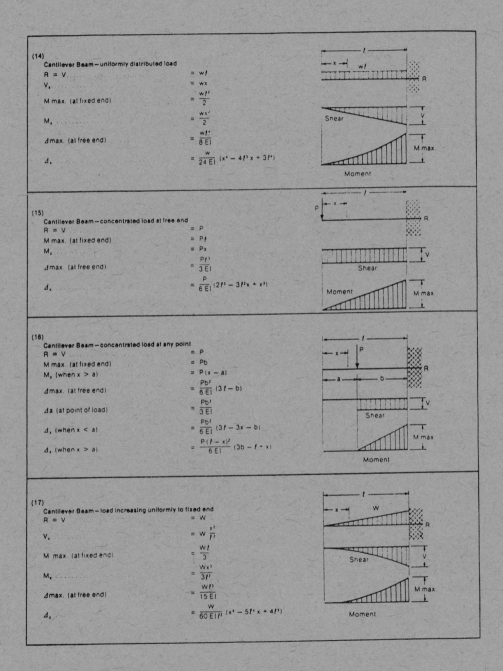

(14)
Cantilever Beam — uniformly distributed load

$R = V$ .... $= wl$

V_x .... $= wx$

M max. (at fixed end) $= \dfrac{wl^2}{2}$

M_x .... $= \dfrac{wx^2}{2}$

Δ max. (at free end) $= \dfrac{wl^4}{8\,EI}$

Δ_x .... $= \dfrac{w}{24\,EI}\,(x^4 - 4l^3 x + 3l^4)$

(15)
Cantilever Beam — concentrated load at free end

$R = V$ $= P$

M max. (at fixed end) $= Pl$

M_x .... $= Px$

Δ max. (at free end) $= \dfrac{Pl^3}{3\,EI}$

Δ_x .... $= \dfrac{P}{6\,EI}\,(2l^3 - 3l^2 x + x^3)$

(16)
Cantilever Beam — concentrated load at any point

$R = V$ .... $= P$

M max. (at fixed end) $= Pb$

M_x (when $x > a$) $= P(x - a)$

Δ max. (at free end) $= \dfrac{Pb^2}{6\,EI}\,(3l - b)$

Δa (at point of load) $= \dfrac{Pb^3}{3\,EI}$

Δ_x (when $x < a$) $= \dfrac{Pb^2}{6\,EI}\,(3l - 3x - b)$

Δ_x (when $x > a$) $= \dfrac{P(l - x)^2}{6\,EI}\,(3b - l + x)$

(17)
Cantilever Beam — load increasing uniformly to fixed end

$R = V$ $= W$

V_x .... $= W\,\dfrac{x^2}{l^2}$

M max. (at fixed end) $= \dfrac{Wl}{3}$

M_x .... $= \dfrac{Wx^3}{3l^2}$

Δ max. (at free end) $= \dfrac{Wl^3}{15\,EI}$

Δ_x .... $= \dfrac{W}{60\,EI\,l^2}\,(x^5 - 5l^4 x + 4l^5)$

Beam design equations and diagrams

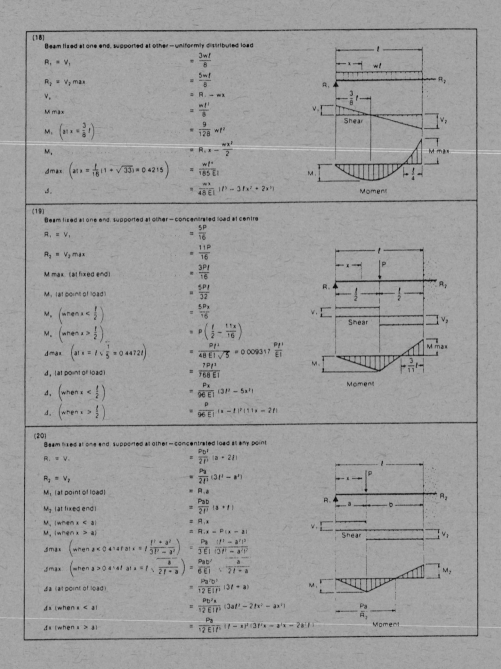

(18)
Beam fixed at one end, supported at other—uniformly distributed load

$$R_1 = V_1 = \frac{3wl}{8}$$

$$R_2 = V_2\,max = \frac{5wl}{8}$$

$$V_x = R_1 - wx$$

$$M\,max = \frac{wl^2}{8}$$

$$M_1 \left(at\ x = \frac{3}{8}l\right) = \frac{9}{128}wl^2$$

$$M_x = R_1 x - \frac{wx^2}{2}$$

$$\Delta max \left(at\ x = \frac{l}{16}(1 + \sqrt{33}) = 0.4215\right) = \frac{wl^4}{185\,EI}$$

$$\Delta_x = \frac{wx}{48\,EI}(l^3 - 3lx^2 + 2x^3)$$

(19)
Beam fixed at one end, supported at other—concentrated load at centre

$$R_1 = V_1 = \frac{5P}{16}$$

$$R_2 = V_2\,max = \frac{11P}{16}$$

$$M\,max\ (at\ fixed\ end) = \frac{3Pl}{16}$$

$$M_1\ (at\ point\ of\ load) = \frac{5Pl}{32}$$

$$M_x \left(when\ x < \frac{l}{2}\right) = \frac{5Px}{16}$$

$$M_x \left(when\ x > \frac{l}{2}\right) = P\left(\frac{l}{2} - \frac{11x}{16}\right)$$

$$\Delta max \left(at\ x = l\sqrt{\frac{1}{5}} = 0.4472l\right) = \frac{Pl^3}{48\,EI\sqrt{5}} = 0.009317\frac{Pl^3}{EI}$$

$$\Delta_x\ (at\ point\ of\ load) = \frac{7Pl^3}{768\,EI}$$

$$\Delta_x \left(when\ x < \frac{l}{2}\right) = \frac{Px}{96\,EI}(3l^2 - 5x^2)$$

$$\Delta_x \left(when\ x > \frac{l}{2}\right) = \frac{P}{96\,EI}(x - l)^2(11x - 2l)$$

(20)
Beam fixed at one end, supported at other—concentrated load at any point

$$R_1 = V_1 = \frac{Pb^2}{2l^3}(a + 2l)$$

$$R_2 = V_2 = \frac{Pa}{2l^3}(3l^2 - a^2)$$

$$M_1\ (at\ point\ of\ load) = R_1 a$$

$$M_2\ (at\ fixed\ end) = \frac{Pab}{2l^2}(a + l)$$

$$M_x\ (when\ x < a) = R_1 x$$

$$M_x\ (when\ x > a) = R_1 x - P(x - a)$$

$$\Delta max \left(when\ a < 0.414l\ at\ x = l\frac{l^2 + a^2}{3l^2 - a^2}\right) = \frac{Pa}{3\,EI}\frac{(l^2 - a^2)^2}{(3l^2 - a^2)^2}$$

$$\Delta max \left(when\ a > 0.414l\ at\ x = l\sqrt{\frac{a}{2l + a}}\right) = \frac{Pab^2}{6\,EI}\sqrt{\frac{a}{2l + a}}$$

$$\Delta a\ (at\ point\ of\ load) = \frac{Pa^2 b^3}{12\,EI l^3}(3l + a)$$

$$\Delta x\ (when\ x < a) = \frac{Pb^2 x}{12\,EI l^3}(3al^2 - 2lx^2 - ax^2)$$

$$\Delta x\ (when\ x > a) = \frac{Pa}{12\,EI l^3}(l - x)^2(3l^2 x - a^2 x - 2a^2 l)$$

Beam design equations and diagrams

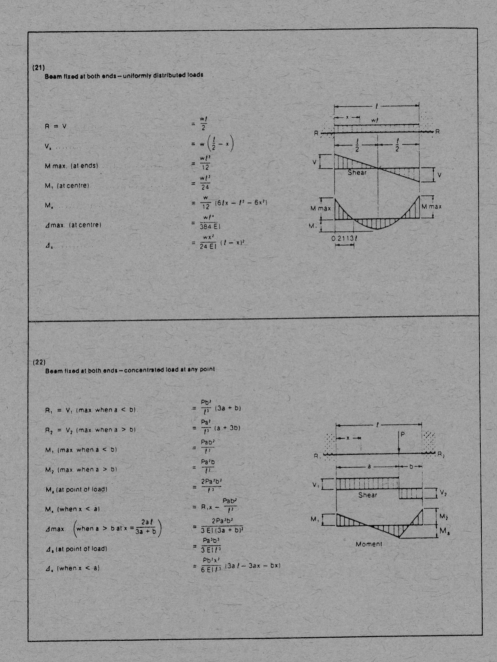

(21)
Beam fixed at both ends — uniformly distributed loads

$$R = V = \frac{wl}{2}$$

$$V_x = w\left(\frac{l}{2} - x\right)$$

$$M \text{ max. (at ends)} = \frac{wl^2}{12}$$

$$M_1 \text{ (at centre)} = \frac{wl^2}{24}$$

$$M_x = \frac{w}{12}(6lx - l^2 - 6x^2)$$

$$\Delta \text{ max. (at centre)} = \frac{wl^4}{384\,EI}$$

$$\Delta_x = \frac{wx^2}{24\,EI}(l - x)^2$$

(22)
Beam fixed at both ends — concentrated load at any point

$$R_1 = V_1 \text{ (max when } a < b) = \frac{Pb^2}{l^3}(3a + b)$$

$$R_2 = V_2 \text{ (max when } a > b) = \frac{Pa^2}{l^3}(a + 3b)$$

$$M_1 \text{ (max when } a < b) = \frac{Pab^2}{l^2}$$

$$M_2 \text{ (max when } a > b) = \frac{Pa^2 b}{l^2}$$

$$M_a \text{ (at point of load)} = \frac{2Pa^2 b^2}{l^3}$$

$$M_x \text{ (when } x < a) = R_1 x - \frac{Pab^2}{l^2}$$

$$\Delta \text{ max } \left(\text{when } a > b \text{ at } x = \frac{2al}{3a + b}\right) = \frac{2Pa^3 b^2}{3\,EI(3a + b)^2}$$

$$\Delta_a \text{ (at point of load)} = \frac{Pa^3 b^3}{3\,EI\,l^3}$$

$$\Delta_x \text{ (when } x < a) = \frac{Pb^2 x^2}{6\,EI\,l^3}(3al - 3ax - bx)$$

CONVERSION FACTORS - METRIC/IMPERIAL

Metric units	Imperial equivalents		Imperial units	Metric equivalents	
Length					
1 millimetre (mm)	= 0.039 370 1	inch	1 inch	= 25.4	mm
1 metre (m)	= 39.370 1	inches		= 0.025 4	m
	= 3.280 84	feet	1 foot	= 0.304 8	m
1 kilometre (km)	= 0.621 371	mile	1 mile	= 1.609 34	km
Length/time					
1 metre per second (m/s)	= 3.280 84	feet per sec.	1 foot per sec.	= 0.304 8	m/s
1 kilometre per hour (km/h)	= 0.621 371	mile per hour	1 mile per hour	= 1.609 34	km/h
Area					
1 square millimetre (mm^2)	= 0.001 550	square inch	1 square inch	= 645.16	mm^2
1 square metre (m^2)	= 10.763 9	square foot	1 square foot	= 0.092 903 0	m^2
1 hectare (ha)	= 2.471 05	acres	1 acre	= 0.404 686	ha
1 square Kilometre (km^2)	= 0.386 102	square mile	1 square mile	= 2.589 99	km^2
Volume					
1 cubic millimetre (mm^3)	= 0.000 061 0237	cubic inch	1 cubic inch	= 16 387.1	mm^3
1 cubic metre (m^3)	= 35.314 7	cubic feet	1 cubic foot	= 0.028 316 8	m^3
	= 1.307 95	cubic yard	1 cubic yard	= 0.764 555	m^3
1 millilitre (mL)	= 0.035 195 1	fluid ounce	1 fluid ounce	= 28.413 1	mL
1 litre (L)	= 0.219 969	gallon	1 gallon	= 4.546 09	L
Mass					
1 gram (g)	= 0.035 274 0	ounce	1 ounce	= 28.349 5	g
1 kilogram (kg)	= 2.204 62	pounds	1 pound	= 0.453 592	kg
1 tonne (t) (=1,000 kg)	= 1.102 31	tons (2,000 lbs)	1 ton (2,000 lbs)	= 0.907 185	t
	= 2 204.62	pounds	1 pond	= 0.000 453 9	t
Mass/Volume					
1 kilogram per cubic meter (kg/m^3)	= 0.062 428 0	pound per cubic foot	1 pcf	= 16.018 5	kg/m^3
Force					
1 newton (N)	= 0.224 809	pound-force	1 pound	= 4.448 22	N
Stress					
1 megapascal (MPa) (=1 N/mm^2)	= 145.038	pounds-force per sq.in	1 psi	= 0.006 894 76	MPa
Loading					
1 kilonewton per sq. metre (kN/m^2)	= 20.885 4	pounds-force per sq. ft	1 psf	= 0.047 880 3	kN/m^2
1 kilonewton per metre (kN/m) (=1 n/mm)	= 68.521 8	pounds-force	1 p/f	= 0.014 593 9	kN/m
Moment					
1 kilonewton-metre (kN.m)	= 737.562	pound-ft	1 pound-foot	= 0.001 355 82	kN.m
Temperature					
1 degree Celsius ($^\circ$C)	= 32 + 1.8 ($^\circ$C)	degrees fahrenheit	1 degree fahrenheit	= ($^\circ$F - 32)/1.8 ($^\circ$C)	

NOTES

NOTES

NOTES

NOTES

PART 3

CSA STANDARD S304.1-94
Masonry Design for Buildings

The following reprint of the S304.1-94 standard has been included in this book with permission from the Canadian Standards Association. This copy is a photographic reduction to 77% of its original size. To be placed on the mailing list for any future amendments the reader should contact the Canadian Standards Association.

S304.1-94

Masonry Design for Buildings (Limit States Design)

Structures (Design)

ISSN 0317-5669
Published in December 1994
by
Canadian Standards Association
178 Rexdale Boulevard
Etobicoke, Ontario, Canada
M9W 1R3

Technical Editor: Bill Glover
Managing Editor: Gary Burford

Contents

Technical Committee on Masonry Design for Buildings

N.T. Loomis	Pittsburgh Corning Corporation, Pittsburgh, Pennsylvania, USA	*Associate*
D.A. Lutes	National Research Council of Canada, Ottawa, Ontario	*Associate*
A.H.P. Maurenbrecher	National Research Council of Canada, Ottawa, Ontario	
R.J. McGrath	Canadian Portland Cement Association, Ottawa, Ontario	
R. Pacholok	Fero Holdings Limited, Edmonton, Alberta	
M.A. Patamia	Canadian Concrete Masonry Producers Association, Downsview, Ontario	*Associate*
B.W. Peter	Canadian Masonry Contractors Association, Burnaby, British Columbia,	
R.J. Primeau	Metro Separate School Board, Islington, Ontario	
M.J. Rosseker	RSD Engineering Inc., Edmonton, Alberta	*Associate*
N. Shrive	University of Calgary, Calgary, Alberta	
M. Spencer	Maitland Spencer Engineering Limited, Milton, Ontario	
G.R. Sturgeon	Masonry Council of Canada, Calgary, Alberta	*Associate*
G.T. Suter	Carleton University, Ottawa, Ontario	
C.J. Turkstra	Hamilton, Ontario	*Associate*
W.L. Glover	Canadian Standards Association, Etobicoke, Ontario	*Administrator*

S304.1-94
Masonry Design for Buildings (Limit States Design)

1. Scope

1.1
This Standard provides requirements for the engineered design of unreinforced, reinforced, and prefabricated masonry structures in accordance with the limit states design method of the *National Building Code of Canada*. In addition, this Standard provides requirements for the empirical design of unreinforced masonry.
Note: *The* National Building Code of Canada *requires that certain reviews be carried out during construction by the designer or another suitably qualified person to determine conformance with the design.*

1.2
Requirements for masonry construction and masonry connectors are specified in CSA Standards A371 and A370, respectively. Both of these Standards include requirements that affect the design and are required for use with this Standard.

1.3
Clauses 1 through 3 and Clauses 6.3.4, 6.3.5, 6.4.1, and 6.4.2 apply to both the engineered design of masonry and the empirical design of masonry. Clauses 4 through 15 apply to the engineered design of masonry while Clause 16 covers the requirements for the empirical design of masonry.

2. Definitions and Standard Notation

2.1 Definitions
The following definitions apply in this Standard:

Anchor—a device used to connect masonry walls and stone facings at their intersections or to attach them to their supports or to other structural members or systems.

Beam, masonry—a horizontal masonry member supporting vertical loads. The flexural forces are applied horizontally against the mortar in the head joints between the masonry units and against any grout in the spaces in and between the units.

Bearing support—a structural member or system of structural members supporting masonry and resisting all applied loads.

Bond—the
(a) arrangement of masonry units having a regular pattern and intended to increase the strength or enhance the appearance of a construction;
(b) overlap of units across the collar joint of a multi-wythe masonry wall system so as to increase its strength;
(c) adhesion between units and mortar or grout.

Bond beam—a course or courses of a masonry wall grouted and reinforced in the horizontal direction. A bond beam may serve as a horizontal wall tie, a bearing course for structural members, or as a beam.

Building height (in storeys)—the number of storeys contained between the roof and the floor of the first storey.

Cavity wall—a construction of masonry units laid up with a cavity between the wythes. The wythes are tied together with metal ties or bonding units and are relied on to act together in resisting lateral loads.

Clay masonry unit—a masonry unit made of fired clay as specified in CSA Standards A82.1 and A82.8.

Concrete masonry unit—a masonry unit made of natural or synthetic aggregates, portland cement and other cementitious materials as specified in CSA Standard A165.

Column—a vertical masonry member having a height >5 t and a length <3 t supporting vertical and sometimes horizontal loads. The flexural forces are applied vertically against the mortar in the bed joints between the units and against any grout in and between the units.

Composite wall—a multi-wythe wall in which the wythes are tied together by connectors, filled collar joints, bonding units, or other means to ensure shear transfer between wythes and effective composite action.
Note: *See Clause 11.2.2.*

Connector—a general term for ties, anchors, and fasteners.

Control joint—term no longer used; see Movement joint.

Cross-sectional area—the area of masonry on a plane parallel to the bearing surface of a masonry unit.

   Effective cross-sectional area—the area of masonry based on the area that includes the mortar bedded area and the area of voids filled with grout.
Note: *See Clause 10.2.1.1.*

   Gross cross-sectional area—the area of masonry on a plane parallel to the bearing surface of a masonry unit, calculated by multiplying the actual length by the actual thickness.

   Net cross-sectional area—the solid area of masonry in a plane parallel to the bearing surface of a masonry unit.

Designer—the person responsible for the structural design.

Factored load—the product of a specified load and its load factor.

Factored resistance—the product of the calculated resistance and the appropriate resistance factor or factors.

Grout—a mixture of cementitious material and aggregate of a consistency suitable for pouring or pumping without segregation of the constituents.

Hollow unit—a unit that has a net cross-sectional area in any plane parallel to the bearing surface of less than 75% of its gross cross-sectional area measured in the same plane.

Importance factor, γ —a factor in Clause 7.4 applied to the factored loads other than dead load to take into account the consequences of collapse as related to the use and occupancy of the building.

Lateral support—a structural member or system of structural members resisting the horizontal component of loads applied to masonry.

Loadbearing—a term which indicates the presence of loads on a building component in addition to its dead load.

Load combination factor, ψ —a factor in Clause 7.3, applied to the factored loads other than dead load to take into account the reduced probability of a number of loads from different sources acting simultaneously.

Load factor, α —a factor in Clause 7.2 applied to a specified load which, for the limit states under consideration, takes into account the variability of the loads and load patterns and analysis of their effects.

Masonry—a construction of masonry units laid up with mortar or other bonding methods.

Masonry unit—materials usually shaped to a rectangular prism; usually of a size and mass that can be hand-placed into position (see also clay masonry unit and concrete masonry unit).

Mortar—a mixture of cementitious material or materials, aggregate, and water used for bedding, jointing, and bonding of masonry or other structural units.

Mortar bedded area—the horizontal area of mortar in a bed joint that is in full contact with both the masonry unit above and the masonry unit below (also called net mortar bedded area).

Movement joint—a continuous joint in the structure, used to regulate the location and amount of cracking and to accommodate closure or separation resulting from relative movements such as those caused by temperature or moisture changes.

Panel wall—an exterior nonloadbearing wall wholly supported at each storey.

Partition—an interior nonloadbearing dividing wall of one storey or part of one storey in height.

Plain masonry—see Unreinforced masonry.

Prism—a small assemblage of masonry units and mortar used as a test specimen for determining the strength of masonry.

Reinforced masonry—masonry with reinforcing steel, grout, and/or mortar which act together in resisting forces.

Resistance—the maximum load that a member, connection, or structure can sustain at a limit state, calculated in accordance with this Standard from the geometry, the material properties, and actual dimensions.

Resistance factor, ϕ—a factor applied to a specified material property or to the resistance of a member, connection, or structure which, for the limit state under consideration, takes into account the variability of dimensions and material properties, workmanship, type of failure, and uncertainty in the prediction of resistance.

Solid masonry—masonry of solid or hollow units that does not have cavities or unfilled collar joints between the wythes.

Solid unit—a unit that has a net cross-sectional area in planes parallel to the bearing surface of at least 75% of the gross cross-sectional area measured in the same plane.

Stack pattern—the arrangement in which the head joints form continuous vertical lines. (Also called checkerboard bond or stack bond.)

Strength—the characteristic ultimate material stress or connector force at failure measured in accordance with appropriate test Standards.

Structural backing—the masonry or system of structural members to which masonry veneer is tied. The backing is designed to resist the applied lateral loads.

Tie—a device for connecting two or more wythes or for connecting a masonry veneer to its structural backing.

Toothed joint—the construction of the end of a masonry wall so that the end stretchers of every alternate course project for bonding to future work.

Transformed section—a derived section of one material similar to and having the same elastic properties as a section composed of two materials having different elastic properties.

Unreinforced masonry—masonry bonded without the use of steel reinforcement other than that required for bonding or for material dimensional change control; also commonly referred to as plain masonry.

Veneer—a nonloadbearing masonry facing attached to and supported by the structural backing.

Virtual eccentricity—the eccentricity of the axial load calculated by dividing the total moment at the section by the axial load.

Wall—a vertical masonry member supporting vertical and horizontal loads. The flexural forces are usually applied vertically against the mortar in the bed joints between the units and against any grout in and between the units.

4

Wythe—a continuous vertical section of a masonry wall, one unit in thickness.

2.2 Standard Notation

2.2.1
Throughout this Standard the subscript "f" ($_f$) denotes a factored load and the subscript "r" ($_r$) denotes a factored resistance.

2.2.2
The following notations apply to this Standard. Deviations and additions are noted where they are used.

a = depth of the equivalent rectangular stress block, mm (see Clause 10.2.3.1.7)

A = effective tension area of masonry surrounding the flexural tension reinforcement and extending from the extreme tension fibre to the centroid of the flexural tension reinforcement and an equal distance past that centroid, divided by the number of bars, mm^2. When the flexural reinforcement consists of bars of different sizes, the number of bars used to compute A shall be taken as the total area of reinforcement divided by the area of the largest bar used

A_b = area of bar, mm^2;

A_1 = bearing area, mm^2

A_e = the effective cross-sectional area used for design, mm^2 (see Clause 10.2.1)

A_g = gross cross-sectional area, mm^2

A_p = area of prestressed reinforcement, mm^2

A_s = area of nonprestressed tension reinforcement, mm^2

A'_s = area of nonprestressed compression reinforcement, mm^2

A_{st} = the total area of longitudinal reinforcement, mm^2

A_v = cross-sectional area of web reinforcement, mm^2

b = width of rectangular beam or column, or width of flange of a T-beam, mm

b_w = web width of beam or flanged wall, mm

c = distance from extreme compression fibre to the neutral axis in a flexural member, mm

d = distance from extreme compression fibre to centroid of tension reinforcement, mm

d_b = nominal diameter of reinforcing bar or wire, mm

d_c = thickness of masonry cover measured from extreme tension fibre to the centre of the longitudinal bar located closest thereto, mm

e = virtual eccentricity, mm

e_1 = the smaller virtual eccentricity occurring at the top or bottom of a vertical member at lateral supports, mm

e_2 = the larger virtual eccentricity occurring at the top or bottom of a vertical member at lateral supports, mm

E_m = modulus of elasticity of masonry, MPa

E_s = modulus of elasticity of steel, MPa

f_{cs} = axial compressive stress, P/A_e, due to factored dead loads, MPa

f'_m = compressive strength of masonry at 28 days, MPa

f_t = flexural tensile strength of masonry (also called the modulus of rupture or the flexural bond strength), MPa

f_v = stress in web reinforcement, MPa

f_y = yield strength of reinforcement, MPa

h = unsupported height of a wall or column, mm

I_{cr} = the moment of inertia of the compression zone and the transformed area of the tension steel about the centroidal axis of the cracked section when subjected to a yield moment and, in most cases, no axial load, mm^4. The transformed area of the reinforcement in the compression zone shall not be included unless the reinforcement is tied in accordance with Clause 5.2.5.

I_o = moment of inertia of the effective area section about its centroidal axis, mm^4

k = effective height factor for compression members

ℓ_d = development length of reinforcement bar or wire, mm

ℓ_W = length of a masonry wall, mm

M_1 = the smaller factored end moment in a compression member associated with the same loading case as M_2: positive if member is bent in single curvature, negative if bent in double curvature, N•mm

M_2 = the larger factored end moment in a compression member, always positive, N•mm

M_a = maximum moment due to specified loads

6

M_f = factored moment at section, N•mm

M_r = factored moment resistance, calculated using the assumptions in Clauses 9 and 10 and the resistance factors given in Clause 7, N•mm

P_f = factored vertical load, N

$P•\delta$ = secondary moments due to axial loads and member displacements caused by primary and secondary moments, N•mm

r = radius of gyration of a section $\sqrt{I_o/A_e}$, mm

s = spacing of shear reinforcement measured parallel to the longitudinal axis of the member, mm

t = actual thickness of a wall or column, mm

v_m = shear strength of masonry, MPa (see Clause 11.5.3)

v_r = shear resistance stress in reinforced masonry having shear reinforcement designed to resist the entire shear in accordance with Clause 8.6.6, MPa

V_f = shear under factored loads, N

V_m = factored shear resistance of masonry members provided by the masonry, N

V_r = factored shear resistance, N

V_s = factored shear resistance provided by shear reinforcement, N

y_t = distance from neutral axis to the extreme tension fibre of the section, mm

z = quantity limiting distribution of flexural reinforcement, kN/mm (see Clause 12.2.3.2)

α = load factor defined in Clause 7.2, or
= reinforcement distribution factor in Clause 5.2.2.2

β_b = ratio of area of cut off reinforcement to total area of tension reinforcement at a section

β_d = ratio of factored dead load moment to total factored moment

β_1 = ratio of depth of rectangular compression block to depth to the neutral axis

γ = importance factor defined in Clause 7.4

δ = lateral displacement of walls or columns due to end moments, lateral loads, and secondary moments, mm

ρ = ratio of the area of non-prestressed tensile reinforcement, A_s, to effective masonry area between the extreme compression fibre and the centroid of the tensile reinforcement

ρ' = ratio of the area of non-prestressed compression reinforcement, A'_s, to effective masonry area between the extreme compression fibre and the centroid of the tensile reinforcement

ρ_g = ratio of effective cross-sectional area of reinforcement, A_s, to the gross cross-sectional area, A_g

λ = factor to account for low density concrete masonry units (see Clause 12.3.4)

ε_s = strain in reinforcing steel

ϕ_e = resistance factor for member (see Clause 11)

ϕ_m = resistance factor for masonry (see Clause 7)

ϕ_p = resistance factor for prestressing tendons (see Clause 7)

ϕ_s = resistance factor for reinforcing bars (see Clause 7)

χ = factor defined in Clause 10.2.3.1.7

ψ = load combination factor

3. General Requirements

3.1 Design Methods
Engineered masonry design under this Standard shall be carried out in conformance with Clauses 4 through 15. Empirical masonry design under this Standard shall conform to Clauses 6.3.4, 6.3.5, 6.4.1, 6.4.2 and 16.

3.2 Other Design Methods

3.2.1 Special Designs
A rational design based on theory, tests or analysis and engineering practice acceptable to the regulatory authority, may be used in lieu of the formulae and rules provided in this Standard. In such cases the design shall provide for nominal levels of safety and serviceability at least equal to those implied by the provisions of this Standard.

3.2.2 Working Stress Design
The requirements of CSA Standard S304, shall not be used in conjunction with this Standard.

3.3 Drawings and Related Documents

In addition to the information required by the *National Building Code of Canada*, the drawings and related documents for structures designed in accordance with this Standard shall include, where appropriate, the

(a) material to be used in masonry;
(b) details and location of movement joints;
(c) specified compressive strength of masonry;
(d) specified flexural tensile strength of masonry;
(e) specified compressive strength of masonry units;
(f) specified strength or grade of reinforcement;
(g) specified mortar type;
(h) specified grout type, slumps, proportions or compressive strength;
(i) position, location, type, spacing and size of ties, anchors, lifting devices, and other supports;
(j) classification of corrosion protection of metal components including those in prefabricated masonry;
(k) governing set of forces required for the preparation of shop or detail drawings;
alternatively, such information may be provided by supplementary material to the drawings and specifications;
(l) size and spacing of reinforcement;
(m) types of mortar joints;
(n) dimensions of masonry;
(o) details of bonding, tying, and anchorage of masonry; and
(p) details and location of chases and recesses.

3.4 Materials

3.4.1 Masonry

Materials used in masonry construction shall conform to the requirements of CSA Standard A371.

Note: *Although referenced indirectly through CSA Standard A371, CSA Standards A179 and A370 contain design provisions and are of particular importance to the designer.*

3.5 Reference Publications

This Standard refers to the following publications and where such reference is made it shall be considered to refer to the latest edition and any amendments published thereto:

CSA Standards
A23.1-94,
Concrete Materials and Methods of Concrete Construction;

A23.3-94,
Design of Concrete Structures;

A23.4-94,
Precast Concrete — Materials and Construction;

CAN/CSA-A82.1-M87 (R1992),
Burned Clay Brick (Solid Masonry Units Made from Clay or Shale);

CAN3-A82.2-M78 (R1992),
Methods of Sampling and Testing Brick;

CAN3-A82.8-M78 (R1992),
Hollow Clay Brick;

A165 Series-94,
CSA Standards on Concrete Masonry Units;

A179-94,
Mortar and Grout for Unit Masonry;

CAN/CSA-A369.1-M90,
Method of Test for Compressive Strength of Masonry Prisms;

A370-94,
Connectors for Masonry;

A371-94,
Masonry Construction for Buildings;

G30.14-M1983 (R1991),
Deformed Steel Wire for Concrete Reinforcement;

G30.15-M1983 (R1991),
Welded Deformed Steel Wire Fabric for Concrete Reinforcement;

CAN/CSA-G30.18-M92
Billet-Steel Bars for Concrete Reinforcement;

CAN3-S304-M84,
Masonry Design for Buildings;

S478-95 (under preparation),
Guideline on Durability in Buildings;

W186-M1990,
Welding of Reinforcing Bars in Reinforced Concrete Construction.

ASTM* Standards
C1072-86,
Method for Measurement of Masonry Flexural Bond Strength;

E72-80,
Method for Conducting Strength Tests of Panels for Building Construction;

National Research Council of Canada
National Building Code of Canada, 1995;

Supplement to the National Building Code of Canada, 1995.

UBC† Standard
21-30,
Standard Test Method for Flexural Bond Strength of Mortar Cement.

* *American Society for Testing and Materials.*
† *Uniform Building Code.*

4. Field Control Tests

4.1 Masonry Unit Testing

4.1.1
At least three masonry units shall be selected and tested in conformance with Clause 9.2.3.3 for each 500 m² of wall or portion thereof for each unit type and for each storey. The number of tests shall be doubled for concrete masonry units with specified strength higher than 15 MPa, and for clay masonry units with specified strengths greater than 25 MPa.

4.1.2
Where the specified f'_m used for design is not greater than 10 MPa, the testing requirements may be waived if the producer of the masonry units provides satisfactory test data.

4.2 Prism Method Tests
When the masonry compressive strength used in the design has been determined in accordance with the method described in Clause 9.2.2, the average of any compressive test referred to in Clause 4.1.1 shall not be lower than the unit strength required to obtain the specified prism strength, and no individual test result shall be less than 0.80 of that strength.

4.3 Unit and Mortar Method Tests
When the masonry compressive strength used in the design has been determined in accordance with the method described in Clause 9.2.3, the average of any compressive test referred to in clause 4.1.1 shall not be lower than the compressive strength of the units used in the selection of f'_m as provided in either Clause 9.2.3.4.1 or Clause 9.2.3.4.2.

4.4 Mortar Testing

4.4.1 Tests

4.4.1.1 Proportion Specification Mortars
Mortars specified under the proportion specifications of CSA Standard A179 shall be sampled and tested to determine the ratio of aggregate to cementitious material, in accordance with the procedure set forth in CSA Standard A179, except that:
(a) these testing requirements may be waived where satisfactory evidence is provided prior to commencement of the work to demonstrate that the quantities of correct ingredients are being batched and mixed as specified. Thereafter batching and mixing procedures should be reviewed periodically, as work progresses, to establish a measure of quality assurance; or
(b) a compressive strength test in accordance with Clause 4.4.1.2, may be used as the measure of quality control for proportion specification mortar, or as a supplement to testing for the ratio of aggregate to cementitious material provided that a control value for the compressive strength of the proportioned mortar (containing the correct ingredients and

quantities, mixed and batched as specified, and of consistency suitable for laying the masonry units to be used) has been previously established.

4.4.1.2 Property Specification Mortars

Mortars specified under the property specifications of CSA Standard A179 shall be sampled and tested to determine the cube compressive strength, in accordance with the procedures set forth in CSA Standard A179.

Alternatively, a test for the ratio of aggregate to cementitious material may be used as the measure of quality control for property specification mortar (where the test is applicable to the type of ingredients used), or as a supplement to testing for compressive strength, provided that a control value for the ratio of the aggregate to cementitious material of the mortar (containing the correct ingredients and quantities, mixed and batched as specified) has been previously established.

4.4.1.3

Except as provided in Clause 4.4.1.4, compressive strength tests of mortar cubes shall be made at an age of 28 days.

4.4.1.4

Compressive strength tests of mortar cubes may be made at an age of 1 day, and 7 days, provided that the relationship between the test age and 28 days strength of the mortar has been established by previous tests, or where the relationship has not been established, the compressive strengths obtained from the 1 day and 7 days shall be assumed to be 40% and 90% respectively, of the 28 days value.

Note: *Ready-mixed mortar (set retarded mortar) should be tested only at 28 days.*

4.4.2 Test Frequency

4.4.2.1

Mortar used for concrete block or hollow clay brick masonry shall be tested in accordance with the requirements of Clause 4.4.1:
(a) for each 500 m^2 of masonry or portion thereof, for a project having more than 500 m^2 of masonry;
(b) for each 250 m^2 of masonry or portion thereof, for a project having less than 500 m^2 of masonry.

4.4.2.2

Mortar used for brick masonry shall be tested in accordance with the requirements of Clause 4.4.1:
(a) for each 250 m^2 of masonry or portion thereof, for a project having more than 250 m^2 of masonry; and
(b) for each 125 m^2 of masonry or portion thereof, for a project having less than 250 m^2 of masonry.

4.4.3 Acceptance

4.4.3.1 Ratio of Aggregate to Cementitious Material

The ratio of aggregate to cementitious material determined in accordance with Clause 4.4.1.1 shall be:
(a) greater than 0.85 R; and
(b) less than 1.15 R;

where R is the control value for the ratio of aggregate to cementitious material for the mortar being tested, determined in accordance with the procedures set forth in CSA Standard A179.

4.4.3.2 Compressive Strength
The average mortar cube compressive strength determined from 7 days and 28 days field control tests, in accordance with Clause 4.4.1.2, shall satisfy the compressive strength criteria set forth for property specification mortars in CSA Standard A179.

4.5 Grout Testing

4.5.1 Tests

4.5.1.1 Proportion Specification Grouts
Where compressive strength tests are specified by the designer, the compressive strength of grout specified under the proportion specifications shall be determined in accordance with the procedures set forth in CSA Standard A179.

Note: *These testing requirements can be waived where satisfactory evidence is provided prior to commencement of the work to demonstrate that the quantities of correct ingredients are being batched and mixed as specified. Thereafter batching and mixing procedures should be reviewed periodically, as work progresses, to establish a measure of quality assurance.*

4.5.1.2 Property Specification Grouts
The compressive strength of grout specified under the property specifications shall be determined by tests in accordance with the procedures set forth in CSA Standard A179.

4.5.2 Test Frequency
Grout shall be tested in accordance with the requirements of Clause 4.5.1
(a) for each 20 m^3 of grout poured or portion thereof, for a project having more than 20 m^3 of grout; and
(b) for each 10 m^3 of grout poured or portion thereof, for a project having less than 20 m^3 of grout.

4.5.3 Acceptance
Grout shall satisfy the compressive strength criteria set forth in CSA Standard A179, as applicable for grout specified under either the property specifications or the proportion specifications options.

4.6 Flexural Tensile Strength
Where required by the designer, the flexural tensile strength of masonry shall be determined by test in accordance with one of the following standard tests:
(a) ASTM E72;
(b) ASTM C1072; or
(c) UBC No. 21-30.

Notes:
(1) *Flexural tensile strength determined by methods (b) and (c) should not be interpreted as the flexural tensile strength of a wall constructed with the same materials.*
(2) *Guidance on prequalification, preconstruction, and construction testing for flexural tensile strength is provided in CSA Standard A179.*
(3) *Flexural tensile strength is also called the flexural bond strength or the modulus of rupture.*

5. Reinforcement: Details, Development and Splices

5.1 General

5.1.1
Reinforcement shall be detailed and located taking into account
(a) the sequence of masonry construction;
(b) the geometry and clearance of reinforced cells, cores, and spaces;
(c) thickness of mortar joints; and
(d) anchorage and splices in reinforcement.

5.1.2
The maximum size of deformed reinforcement used in masonry shall be No. 30. The maximum size of smooth reinforcement shall be 6.3 mm.

5.1.3
The diameter of reinforcement shall not exceed one-half of the least clear dimension of the cell, core, bond beam or collar joint in which it is placed.

5.1.4
The diameter of joint reinforcement shall be not less than 3.0 mm and shall not exceed one-half the joint thickness or 5 mm whichever is less.
Note: *Caution should be used in specifying joint reinforcement over 4.1 mm in diameter because it is difficult to install.*

5.1.5
Parallel reinforcing bars bundled in contact to act as a unit shall be limited to two in any one bundle.

5.1.6
Reinforcement used in masonry construction shall be detailed, fabricated, and installed in accordance with CSA Standards A370 and A371, and the requirements of Clause 5.

5.2 Reinforcement in Walls and Columns

5.2.1 Minimum Requirements for Reinforced Walls

5.2.1.1
Where reinforcement is required to resist flexural tensile stresses, the minimum vertical reinforcement shall be determined in accordance with Clauses 5.2.1.2 and 10.2.3.4 and shall be
(a) continuous between lateral supports;
(b) spaced at not more than 2400 mm along the wall;
(c) provided at each side of each opening over 1200 mm long;
(d) provided at each side of each movement joint; and
(e) provided at corners and ends.

5.2.1.2
For reinforced loadbearing walls and reinforced sections of locally reinforced loadbearing walls, the minimum vertical reinforcement shall be not less than $0.00133A_g$. The term A_g in

this case shall be taken as the thickness of the wall, t, times a dimension equal to the lesser of 4t or one-half the distance to adjacent reinforcement on either side of the bar(s).

5.2.1.3
Where reinforcement is required to resist flexural tensile stresses, the minimum horizontal reinforcing shall be determined in accordance with Clause 10.2.3.4 and shall be
(a) continuous between lateral supports;
(b) spaced not more than 2400 mm on centre over the height of the wall;
(c) provided above and below each opening over 1200 mm high; and
(d) provided at the top of the wall.

5.2.1.4
Where reinforcement is required to resist flexural tensile stresses, reinforcing bars shall be placed so as to remain in their specified positions and to ensure grout cover completely encircles the bars. Reinforcing installed such that each bar extends the full height (between lateral supports) of the wall or column, has cleanouts provided at the bottom of each bar, is securely positioned top and bottom, and has the cavities containing the bars grouted bottom-to-top may be deemed to satisfy this requirement. Reinforcing bars that are provided in less-than-full-height lengths shall be installed using spacers or positioners to maintain their specified positioning and grout cover.

5.2.2 Minimum Seismic Reinforcement for Walls

5.2.2.1
Where required by Clauses 6.2 and 6.3.3, walls shall be reinforced to resist design seismic forces. Not less than the reinforcement specified in Clauses 5.2.2.2 to 5.2.2.4 shall be provided.

5.2.2.2
Loadbearing walls and shear walls in velocity- or acceleration-related seismic zones 2 and higher shall be reinforced horizontally and vertically with steel having a minimum total area of $0.002 \, A_g$ distributed as follows:
(a) $A_v = 0.002 \, A_g \, \alpha$; and
(b) $A_h = 0.002 \, A_g \, (1 - \alpha)$
where
A_v = area of vertical steel
A_h = area of horizontal steel
α = distribution factor between 0.33 and 0.67, at the discretion of the designer.
  Reinforcement shall be spaced at not more than 6 times the wall thickness or 1.2 m.
  Reinforcement equivalent to at least one No. 15 bar shall be provided around each masonry panel and around each opening exceeding 1000 mm in width or height. Such reinforcement shall be detailed to develop the yield strength of the bars at corners and splices.

5.2.2.3
Nonloadbearing walls in velocity- or acceleration-related seismic zones 4 and higher shall be reinforced in two directions with reinforcing steel having a minimum total area of $0.001 \, A_g$. The areas of steel shall be allocated using the distribution rules in Clause 5.2.2.2.
  The spacing shall not exceed
(a) 400 mm where joint reinforcement is used; and
(b) 1200 mm for vertical reinforcement and where bond beams are used.

5.2.2.4

Nonloadbearing walls in velocity- or acceleration-related seismic zones 2 and 3 shall be reinforced in one or more directions with reinforcing steel having a minimum total area of $0.0005 A_g$.

The spacing shall not exceed

(a) 400 mm where joint reinforcement is used; and

(b) 1200 mm where reinforced bond beams are used.

The reinforcement may be placed in one direction provided that it is continuous between lateral supports and is located to adequately reinforce the wall against lateral loads.

5.2.3 Maximum Reinforcement for Walls

Vertical reinforcement in walls shall not exceed 2% of the gross area of the wall.

5.2.4 Horizontal Joint Reinforcement in Walls

Horizontal wire reinforcement in the mortar joints may be considered as horizontal steel where it is continuous and spliced in accordance with the requirement of Clause 5.5.

5.2.5 Reinforced Columns

5.2.5.1

The cross-sectional area of vertical reinforcement in columns shall be at least 1% and not more than 4.0% of the effective cross-sectional area of the column, except where a column is stressed to less than one-half its factored capacity when its reinforcement may be reduced to not less than 0.5%.

5.2.5.2

Reinforced masonry columns shall have at least four vertical bars.

5.2.5.3 Lateral Ties

5.2.5.3.1

Lateral ties shall be not less than 3.8 mm diameter (No. 9 ASWG) and the tie spacing shall be the least of

(a) 16 bar diameters;

(b) 48 tie diameters; or

(c) the least dimension of the section.

5.2.5.3.2

Lateral ties shall terminate in a standard hook, in accordance with Clause 5.4. Lap length for circular ties shall be not less than 48 tie diameters.

5.2.5.3.3

At the top and bottom of each column, lateral ties shall be located vertically not more than 1/2 tie spacing from each end.

5.2.5.3.4

Where beams or brackets frame into a column from four directions, lateral ties may be terminated not more than 75 mm below the lowest reinforcement in the shallowest of such beams or brackets.

5.2.5.4
Ties may be placed in horizontal mortar joints, or in grout, except for velocity- or acceleration-related seismic zones 4 and higher, where the ties shall be in the grout.

5.2.5.5
The ties shall be so arranged that every corner and intermediate bar is laterally supported by a tie forming an included angle of not more than 135° at the bar, except that
(a) an intermediate bar that is not more than 150 mm from a laterally supported bar need not be supported; and
(b) a circular tie may be used where the bars are located around the periphery of a circle.

5.3 Reinforcement in Masonry Beams
Flexural reinforcement requirements for masonry beams shall be as specified in Clauses 10 and 12.

5.4 Hooks and Bends
Standard hooks, stirrups and tie hooks, and other than standard hooks shall conform to CSA Standard A23.1. Nonstandard hooks or bends shall be detailed on the drawings.

5.5 Development and Splices of Reinforcement

5.5.1 Development of Reinforcement, General
The calculated tension or compression in the reinforcement at each section shall be developed on each side of that section by embedment length, hook, mechanical device or a combination thereof. Hooks may be used in the development of tension reinforcement only.

5.5.2 Development in Tension

5.5.2.1 Deformed Bars and Deformed Wire
The development length, ℓ_d of deformed bars and deformed wire in tension shall be computed as the product of the basic development length, ℓ_{db}, determined by Clause 5.5.2.3, and the applicable modification factor(s) of Clauses 5.5.2.4 and 5.5.2.5, but shall be not less than the minimum length specified in Clause 5.5.2.6.

5.5.2.2 Smooth Bars and Smooth Wire
The development length, ℓ_d, for smooth bars and smooth wire in tension shall be 2.0 times the length determined by Clause 5.5.2.1 for deformed material, but shall be not less than the minimum length specified in Clause 5.5.2.6.

5.5.2.3 Basic Tension Development Length
The basic development length, ℓ_{db} (mm), shall be: *max $L/2$*
(a) deformed bars $0.004d_b^2f_y$ *bar diameter*
(b) deformed wire
  (i) embedded in grout $0.10d_bf_y$
  (ii) embedded in mortar $0.14d_bf_y$

5.5.2.4 Modification Factors Greater Than 1.0
The basic development length, ℓ_{db} (mm), shall be multiplied by the factor
(a) 1.3, for top bars, defined as horizontal reinforcement bars with more than 300 mm of grout placed below them; and

(b) 1.6, for two or more bars in a layer spaced less than 75 mm centre-to-centre.

5.5.2.5 Modification Factors less Than 1.0

The basic development length, ℓ_{db}, multiplied by the appropriate factors of Clause 5.5.2.4, may be multiplied by the following reduction factors, as applicable:

(a) 0.7 when reinforcement bars are spaced laterally at least 150 mm apart and located at least 60 mm from the face of the member to the edge bar; and

(b) $A_{s(required)}/A_{s(provided)}$ when reinforcement bars in flexural members, and deformed wire, are present in excess of that required by analysis.

Where both factors are applied, the combined factor shall be not less than 0.6.

5.5.2.6 Minimum Tension Development Length

The development length, ℓ_d, shall be not less than

(a) 300 mm for deformed bars;
(b) 150 mm for deformed wire;
(c) 600 mm for smooth bars; or
(d) 300 mm for smooth wire;

except when calculating lap splices in Clause 5.5.10.3 and development of web reinforcement by Clause 5.5.9.

5.5.3 Development in Compression

5.5.3.1 Deformed Bars and Deformed Wire

The development length, ℓ_d, of deformed bars and deformed wire in compression shall be computed as the product of the basic development length, ℓ_{db}, determined by Clause 5.5.3.3, and the applicable modification factor(s) of Clauses 5.5.3.4 and 5.5.3.5 but shall be not less than the minimum length specified in Clause 5.5.3.6.

5.5.3.2 Smooth Bars and Smooth Wire

The development length, ℓ_d, of smooth bars and smooth wire in compression shall be 2.0 times the length determined by Clause 5.5.3.1 for deformed material, but shall be not less than the minimum length specified in Clause 5.5.3.6.

5.5.3.3 Basic Compression Development Length

The basic compression development length, ℓ_{db} (mm), shall be

(a) deformed bars $0.07d_bf_y$
(b) deformed wire
  (i)   embedded in grout $0.10d_bf_y$
  (ii) embedded in mortar $0.14d_bf_y$

5.5.3.4 Modification Factors Greater Than 1.0

The basic development length, ℓ_{db}, shall be multiplied by 1.3 when two or more bars are present in a layer with bars spaced less than 75 mm centre-to-centre.

5.5.3.5 Modification Factors Less Than 1.0

The basic development length, ℓ_{db}, modified by the factor of Clause 5.5.3.4 where appropriate may be reduced by application of the factor calculated from $A_{s(required)}/A_{s(provided)} \geq 0.6$ when reinforcement bars and wire are present in excess of that required.

5.5.3.6 Minimum Compression Development Length
Except when calculating lap splices in accordance with Clause 5.5.10.4, the development length, ℓ_d, shall be not less than
(a) 200 mm for deformed bars;
(b) 150 mm for deformed wire;
(c) 400 mm for smooth bars; or
(d) 300 mm for smooth wire.

5.5.4 Development of Standard Hook in Tension

5.5.4.1 Compression Bars
Hooks shall not be considered effective in developing bars in compression.

5.5.4.2 Hooked Bar Development Length
The development length, ℓ_{dh}, for deformed bars in tension terminating in a standard hook, in accordance with Clause 5.4, measured along a bar from a perpendicular line tangent to the outside end of the hook, shall be computed as the product of the hook basic development length, ℓ_{hb}, of Clause 5.5.4.3 and the applicable modification factor(s) of Clause 5.5.4.4 but ℓ_{dh} shall not be less than the greater of 8 d_b and 150 mm.

5.5.4.3 Hook Basic Development Length
The basic development length, ℓ_{hb}, for a hooked bar with f_y = 400 MPa shall be 25 d_b.

5.5.4.4 Modification Factors for Hook Development Length
The hook basic development length, ℓ_{hb}, shall be multiplied by the following factor(s), as applicable:
(a) $f_y/400$, for bars with f_y other than 400 MPa;
(b) 0.7, for bars where the side cover (normal to the plane of the hook) is not less than 60 mm and for 90° hooks where the cover on the bar extension beyond the hook is not less than 50 mm;
(c) 0.8, for bars where the hook is enclosed horizontally or vertically within at least three ties or stirrup ties spaced along a length at least equal to the inside diameter of the hook, at spacing not exceeding $3d_b$, where d_b is the diameter of the hooked bar, and provided the side and top cover over the hook is at least 60 mm; and
(d) $A_{s(required)}/A_{s(provided)}$ for reinforcement in excess of that required by analysis.

5.5.4.5 Hooks at Non-Continuous Ends of Members
For bars to be developed by a standard hook at the ends of members, where both the side cover and the top (or bottom) cover over the hook is less than 60 mm, the hook shall be enclosed with at least three ties or stirrup ties spaced along a length at least equal to the inside diameter of the hook at a spacing not greater than 3 d_b where d_b is the diameter of the hooked bar. For this case, the modification factor of Clause 5.5.4.4(c) shall not apply.

5.5.4.6
Hooks shall not be permitted in the tension portion of any beam, except at the ends of simple cantilever beams or at the freely supported end of continuous or restrained beams.

5.5.5 Mechanical Anchors

5.5.5.1
Any mechanical device demonstrated by test to be capable of developing the yield strength of reinforcement without damage to the masonry may be used as an anchor.

5.5.5.2
The development of reinforcement may consist of a combination of mechanical anchorage plus additional embedment length of reinforcement between the point of maximum bar stress and the mechanical anchor.

5.5.6 Development of Flexural Reinforcement—General

5.5.6.1
Tension reinforcement may be anchored into the compression zone by bending it across the web and making it continuous with the reinforcement on the opposite face of the member or anchoring it there.

5.5.6.2
Critical sections for development of reinforcement in flexural members are at points of maximum stress and at points within the span where adjacent reinforcement terminates or is bent. The location of the points of maximum stress and the points at which reinforcement is no longer required to resist flexure shall be derived from the factored bending moment diagram.

5.5.6.3
Reinforcement shall extend beyond the point at which it is no longer required to resist flexure for a distance equal to the effective depth of the member or 12 d_b, whichever is greater, except at supports of simple spans, at the free end of cantilevers, and at the exterior supports of continuous spans.

5.5.6.4
Continuing reinforcement shall have an embedment length of not less than the development length, ℓ_d, plus the effective depth of the member or 12 d_b, whichever is greater, beyond the point where bent or terminated tension reinforcement is no longer required to resist flexure.

5.5.6.5
Flexural reinforcement shall not be terminated in a tension zone unless one of the following conditions is satisfied:
(a) the shear at the cut-off point does not exceed two-thirds of that permitted, including the shear strength of the shear reinforcement provided; or
(b) stirrup area in excess of that required for shear and tension is provided along each terminated bar or wire over a distance from the termination point equal to three-fourths of the effective depth of the member. The excess stirrup area, A_v, shall be not less than $b_w s/(3 f_y)$. The spacing s, shall not exceed $d/(8\beta_b)$; or
(c) the continuing reinforcement provides double the area required for flexure at the cut-off point and the shear does not exceed three fourths of that permitted.

5.5.6.6
Special attention shall be given to the provision of adequate anchorage for tension reinforcement in flexural members such as brackets, and deep beams, or members in which the tension reinforcement is not parallel to the compression face.

5.5.7 Development of Positive Moment Reinforcement

5.5.7.1
At least one-third of the total reinforcement required for positive moment in simple spans or at the simply supported end of continuous spans, and at least one-quarter of the total reinforcing required for positive moment in a continuous beam, shall extend along the same face of the beam at least 150 mm past the face of the support.

5.5.7.2
Where a flexural member is part of a primary lateral load resisting system, the positive moment reinforcement required by Clause 5.5.7.1 to be extended into the support, shall be anchored to develop the specified yield strength f_y, in tension at the face of the support.

5.5.7.3
Except as permitted in Clause 5.5.7.4, at simple supports and at points of inflection, the positive moment tension reinforcement shall be limited in diameter or increased in area such that ℓ_d, calculated in accordance with Clause 5.5.2, satisfies the equation

$$\frac{M_r}{V_f} + \ell_a \geq \ell_d$$

where
(a) at a support, ℓ_a shall be the embedment length beyond the centre of the support;
(b) at a point of inflection, ℓ_a shall be limited to the effective depth of the member or 12 d_b, whichever is greater.
   The calculated value of M_r/V_f may be increased by 30% when the ends of the reinforcement are confined by a compression reaction.

5.5.7.4
The requirement of Clause 5.5.7.3 need not be satisfied for reinforcement terminating by a standard hook extending ℓ_{dh} beyond the centreline of simple supports or mechanical anchorage at least equivalent to a standard hook.

5.5.8 Development of Negative Moment Reinforcement

5.5.8.1
Negative moment reinforcement in a continuous restrained or cantilever member, or in any member of a rigid frame, shall be anchored in, or through, the supporting member by embedment length, hooks, or mechanical anchorage.

5.5.8.2
Negative moment reinforcement shall have an embedment length into the span as required by Clauses 5.5.1 and 5.5.6.3.

5.5.8.3

At least one-third of the total tension reinforcement provided for negative moment at a support shall have an embedment length beyond the point of inflection of not less than the effective depth of the member, $12d_b$, or 1/16 the clear span, whichever is greater.

5.5.9 Development of Web Reinforcement

5.5.9.1

Web reinforcement shall be carried as close to the compression and tension surfaces of a member as cover requirements and proximity of other reinforcement will permit.

5.5.9.2

The ends of the legs of stirrups shall be anchored by one of the following means:
(a) by a standard hook plus an embedment of $0.5\ell_d$. The $0.5\ell_d$ embedment of a stirrup leg shall be taken as the distance between the mid-depth of the member, d/2, and the start of the hook (point of tangency). The standard hook shall be placed around the longitudinal reinforcement; or
(b) for No. 15 bars and smaller bars, by bending around the longitudinal reinforcement through at least 135 degrees, plus, for stirrups with design stress exceeding 300 MPa, an embedment of $0.33\ell_d$. The $0.33\ell_d$ embedment of a stirrup leg shall be taken as the distance between the mid-depth of the member, d/2, and the start of the hook (point of tangency).

5.5.9.3

Between anchored ends, each bend in the continuous portion of a stirrup shall enclose a longitudinal bar.

5.5.9.4

Longitudinal bars bent to act as shear reinforcement, if extended into a region of tension, shall be continuous with the longitudinal reinforcement and if extended into a region of compression, shall be developed beyond the mid-depth d/2.

5.5.9.5

Pairs of U stirrups or ties so placed as to form a closed unit shall be considered properly spliced when the length of the laps are $1.7\ell_d$. In members at least 450 mm deep, such splices where $A_b f_y$ is not more than 40 KN per leg, may be considered adequate if the stirrup legs extend the full available depth of the member.

5.5.10 Splices in Reinforcement

5.5.10.1 Noncontact Lap Splices
Bars spliced by noncontact lap splices in flexural members shall not be spaced transversely further apart than 1/5 of the required lap splice length nor more than 200 mm.

5.5.10.2 Welded Splices and Mechanical Connections
Welded splices and other mechanical connections may be used.

5.5.10.2.1 Welding
All welding shall conform to CSA Standard A23.1 or A23.4, as applicable.

5.5.10.2.2 Weld Strength
Except as provided in Clause 5.5.10.3.4.2 for tension lap splices, a full welded splice shall have bars welded to develop in tension, at least 125% of the specified yield strength, f_y, of the bar.

5.5.10.2.3 Mechanical Connection Strength
Except as provided by Clause 5.5.10.3.4.2 for tension lap splices, a full mechanical connection shall develop, in tension or compression as required, at least 125% of the specified yield strength, f_y, of the bar.

5.5.10.3 Splices of Deformed Bars and Deformed Wire in Tension

5.5.10.3.1 Lap Lengths

5.5.10.3.1.1 Deformed Bars and Deformed Wire
The lap length for tension lap splices shall be as required for a Class A, B, or C splice in Clause 5.5.10.3.2 but shall be not less than the minimum length specified in Clause 5.5.10.3.3:
(a) Class A splice—$1.0\ell_d$;
(b) Class B splice—$1.3\ell_d$;
(c) Class C splice—$1.7\ell_d$;
where
ℓ_d is the tensile development length for the specified yield strength, f_y, in accordance with Clause 5.5.2.1.

5.5.10.3.1.2 Smooth Bars and Smooth Wire
The lap length for tension lap splices shall be 2.0 times the length determined by Clause 5.5.10.3.1.1 for deformed material, but shall be not less than the minimum length specified in Clause 5.5.10.3.3.

5.5.10.3.2 Classification of Tension Lap Splices
Lap splices of deformed bars and deformed wire in tension shall conform to the following:

Tension Lap Splices

	Maximum percent of A_s, spliced within required lap length		
$A_{s(provided)}/A_{s(required)}$*	50	75	100
2 or greater	Class A	Class A	Class B
Less than 2	Class B	Class C	Class C

*Ratio of area of reinforcement provided to area of reinforcement required by analysis at splice location.

5.5.10.3.3 Minimum Tension Lap Lengths
The minimum length of lap for tension lap splices shall be not less than
(a) 300 mm for deformed bars;
(b) 150 mm for deformed wire;
(c) 600 mm for smooth bars; or
(d) 300 mm for smooth wire.

5.5.10.3.4 Welded Splices and Mechanical Connections

5.5.10.3.4.1
Welded splices or mechanical connections, used where the area of reinforcement provided is less than twice that required by analysis, shall meet the requirements of Clause 5.5.10.2.2 and 5.5.10.2.3.

5.5.10.3.4.2
Welded splices or mechanical connections, used where the area of reinforcement provided is at least twice that required by analysis, shall meet the following requirements:
(a) whenever possible, splices shall be staggered by at least 600 mm and in such a manner as to develop, at every section, at least twice the factored tensile force at that section, but not less than 140 MPa for the total area of reinforcement provided; and
(b) in computing the tensile resistance developed at each section, spliced reinforcement may be rated at the specified splice strength. Unspliced reinforcement shall be rated at that fraction of f_y defined by the ratio of the shorter actual development length to the development length, ℓ_d, required to develop the specified yield strength, f_y.

5.5.10.3.5 Splices in Tension Tie Members
Splices in tension tie members shall be made with a full welded splice or a full mechanical connection in accordance with Clauses 5.5.10.2 and splices in adjacent bars shall be staggered by at least 750 mm.

5.5.10.4 Splices of Deformed Bars and Deformed Wire in Compression

5.5.10.4.1 Compression Lap Splices
The lap length for compression lap splices for both deformed and smooth material shall be calculated as the product of $1.35\ell_d$ and the applicable modification factor(s) of Clauses 5.5.10.4.3 and 5.5.10.4.4, where ℓ_d is the development length in compression determined in accordance with Clause 5.3, but the lap length shall be not less than the minimum length specified in Clause 5.5.10.4.6.

5.5.10.4.2 Compression Splices of Different Sized Bars
When compression bars of different sizes are lap spliced, the lap length shall be the larger of the development length of the large bar or the splice length of the smaller bar.

5.5.10.4.3 Compression Splices Confined by Ties
In tied reinforced compression members, where ties throughout the lap splice length have an effective area of not less than 0.0015 ts, the lap splice length as computed by Clause 5.5.10.4.1 may be multiplied by 0.83. Tie legs perpendicular to the dimension, t, shall be used in determining the effective area.

5.5.10.4.4 Compression Splices Confined by Spirals
In spirally reinforced compression members, the lap splice length of bars within a spiral as computed by Clause 5.5.10.4.1 may be multiplied by 0.75.

5.5.10.4.5 Welded and Mechanical Compression Splices
Welded splices or mechanical connections used in compression shall meet the requirements of Clause 5.5.10.2.

5.5.10.4.6 Minimum Compression Lap Lengths

The lap length for compression lap splices shall be not less than

(a) 300 mm for deformed bars;
(b) 150 mm for deformed wire;
(c) 600 mm for smooth bars; or
(d) 300 mm for smooth wire.

5.5.10.4.7 End Bearing Compression Splices

5.5.10.4.7.1

In bars required for compression only, the compressive stress may be transmitted by the bearing of square cut ends held in concentric contact by a suitable device.

5.5.10.4.7.2

Bar ends shall terminate in flat surfaces within 1-1/2° of a right angle to the axis of the bars and shall be fitted to within 3° of full bearing after assembly.

5.5.10.4.7.3

End bearing splices shall be used only in members containing closed ties, stirrups, or spirals.

6. Design Requirements

6.1 Safety and Serviceability Criteria

6.1.1 Limit States

Masonry structures and elements shall be designed to be safe and serviceable in accordance with Clauses 6.1.2 and 6.1.3, respectively.

Note: *Limit states define the various types of collapse and unserviceability that are to be avoided; those concerning safety are called ultimate limit states (eg, strength, overturning and sliding) and those concerning serviceability are called serviceability limit states (eg, deflections and crack control). The object of limit states design calculations is to keep the probability of a limit state being reached below a certain value previously established for the given type of structure. This is achieved in this Standard by the use of load factors applied to the specified loads (see Clauses 7.1 to 7.4) and resistance factors applied to the specific resistances of the various components (see Clause 7.5).*

The various limit states are set out in this Clause. Some of these relate to the specified loads and others to the factored loads. Deflections and provisions for dimensional changes are further design requirements related to serviceability. In addition there is the requirement for durability which is primarily a serviceability limit state (local damage) but can also be an ultimate limit state.

6.1.2 Strength Requirements Under Factored Loads

A building and its structural components shall be designed to resist the forces resulting from the application of factored loads acting in the most critical combination to satisfy the condition

factored resistance $\geq$ effects of factored loads

in which specified loads and calculated resistances have been modified by the load factors, combination factors, importance factors, and resistance factors in this Standard.

6.1.3 Serviceability Requirements Under Specified Loads

A building and its structural components shall be checked for serviceability limit states when the specified loads in this Standard are applied in the most critical combination.

6.2 Engineered Masonry Design

6.2.1 Unreinforced Masonry

Except as permitted in Clause 6.3.3.1(c), unreinforced masonry design shall be used only in velocity- or acceleration-related seismic zones 0 and 1.

6.2.2 Locally Reinforced Masonry

Where unreinforced masonry requires local reinforcement such as at openings, the design shall consider the effects of flexural cracking in the reinforced section on the tensile strength of adjacent unreinforced sections. Reinforcement shall be provided in any such adjacent sections that require tensile stresses for adequate resistance.

6.2.3 Unreinforced Shearwalls

Unreinforced shearwalls shall not be combined with reinforced shearwalls in a lateral load-resisting system.

6.3 Safety

6.3.1 Structural Integrity

The general arrangement of the structural system and the interconnection of its members shall be designed to provide resistance to widespread collapse due to local failure.

Notes:

(1) *The requirements of this Standard generally provide a satisfactory level of structural integrity for most masonry structures for buildings.*

(2) *Supplementary provisions may be required for masonry structures with precast floors or where accidental loads such as vehicle impact or explosion are likely to occur. For further guidance see Chapter 4, Commentary C of the* Supplement to the National Building Code of Canada, *and particularly reference (4) M. Fintel and G. Annamalai,* Philosophy of structural integrity of multi-storey loadbearing concrete masonry structures.

6.3.2 Stability

When walls are dependent upon structural members or diaphragms for their lateral support, provision shall be made in the building to transfer the lateral forces to the ground. When buttresses or cross walls are relied upon for lateral support, they shall have sufficient strength and rigidity to resist the lateral forces and sufficient redundancy to satisfy the requirements of Clause 6.3.1

6.3.3 Seismic Design

6.3.3.1

In velocity- or acceleration-related seismic zones of 2 and higher, reinforcement conforming to Clause 5.2.2 shall be provided for masonry construction in

(a) loadbearing and lateral load-resisting masonry;

(b) masonry enclosing elevator shafts and stairways, or used as exterior cladding; and

(c) masonry partitions except for partitions which do not exceed

   (i)   200 kg/m^2 in mass; and

   (ii)   3 m in height and are laterally supported at the top.

6.3.3.2 Shear Walls with Nominal Ductility
Masonry shear walls capable of displaying limited displacement ductility without collapse and designed for seismic loadings corresponding to R = 2.0 shall be classified as nominally ductile shear walls that shall be designed in accordance with Appendix A unless a more comprehensive analysis is performed.

6.3.4 Fire Resistance
Masonry elements shall satisfy the required fire resistance ratings. Materials or structures supporting masonry shall have a fire resistance rating at least equivalent to that required for the masonry.

6.3.5 Bearing and Lateral Support

6.3.5.1 Rigidity Requirements
A structural element designed to support masonry shall have a rigidity compatible with the stiffness of the masonry.

Notes:
(1) *Roof diaphragms, beams supporting infill walls, girts providing lateral support, cross walls, and structural frames are examples of supports to be designed to have rigidities compatible with the masonry they support.*
(2) *Elements supporting masonry should be limited to elastic deflections under load of L/600 or less and longterm deflection under sustained load of L/480 or less.*

6.3.5.2 Support of Masonry

6.3.5.2.1
The bearing support for any masonry
(a) shall have lateral stability; and
(b) shall be noncombustible material, except for the support of minor masonry decorative features, and except as permitted by Clause 6.3.5.2.2; and
(c) shall meet the requirements of Clause 6.3.4.

6.3.5.2.2
For wood structures of four storeys or less, non-loadbearing masonry cladding may be supported by wood or by shelf angles supported by wood, provided the cladding and its support are designed in conformance with Clauses 1 to 15 of this Standard and Part 4 of the *National Building Code of Canada.*

Notes:
(1) *Wood structures may undergo significant longterm shrinkage and creep, (see Clause 6.4.1). The designer should take such movement into account when considering, for example, movement joints, wall ties, and flashing details around openings and at parapet level.*
(2) *The designer should take into account any expected rotation of the cladding support.*
(3) *Wood in contact with the masonry or in contact with the shelf angle supporting the masonry should be protected from moisture or otherwise be resistant to the effects of moisture.*

6.3.5.3 Anchorage at Bearing Supports
Unless friction or bond are shown to provide adequate anchorage at bearing supports, the connection shall be designed to have positive mechanical connection.

6.3.5.4 Anchorage at Lateral Supports
Masonry walls and partitions shall be anchored to their lateral supports by interlocking bond of masonry units in accordance with CSA Standard A371 or by anchors in accordance with Clause 6.3.6.

6.3.6 Anchors

Anchors shall resist all loads prescribed in Clause 4.1, *Structural Loads and Procedures*, of the *National Building Code of Canada*, and shall conform to the requirements of CSA Standard A370.

6.4 Serviceability

6.4.1 Differential Movements and Dimensional Changes

6.4.1.1 Structural Considerations

Consideration shall be given to the structural effects of differential movements, both within a masonry member and between the masonry member and adjacent structural members, due to elastic deformation, creep, moisture changes, and temperature changes.

Notes:

(1) *The provision of horizontal and vertical movement joints should be carefully considered by the designer.*

(2) *Further information may be obtained from Part 4 of the* National Building Code of Canada, *Commentary D, Effects of Deformations in Building Components.*

(3) *In the absence of more specific information regarding the actual properties of materials used, the values for thermal coefficients, moisture movement, creep movement and coefficient of friction in Tables 1 and 2 may be used.*

6.4.1.2 Long Term Effects

Consideration shall be given to the effect of long term differential movement in composite walls, veneer walls, and cavity walls where the wythes are of different materials or serve under different exposure.

6.4.1.3 Horizontally Aligned Movement Joint Requirements for Veneer

In concrete-masonry and reinforced concrete buildings clad with clay-masonry supported by shelf angles and plates rigidly attached to the structure, horizontal joints to allow for vertical movement shall be provided under the angles or plates and at points where the veneer or outer wythe extends beneath rigid parts of the structure, such as at balconies and recessed windows.

Note: *Other types of structures and masonry also may require these provisions.*

6.4.2 Displacements

Masonry members shall be proportioned so that displacements are within acceptable limits for the nature of the application. In the absence of more detailed information, the provisions of CSA Standard A23.3 and Commentary A of Chapter 4 of the *Supplement to the National Building Code of Canada* shall apply.

6.4.3 Crack Control

6.4.3.1

Masonry members shall be designed to ensure that cracking is within limits acceptable for their intended use. For beams, the requirements of Clause 12.2.3.2 shall apply. For walls and columns, the requirements of Clause 11.9 shall apply.

6.4.3.2

For all masonry members, the build-up of movement-related stresses and cracking shall be controlled through the requirements of Clause 6.4.1.

6.5 Durability

6.5.1 General
Masonry and its components shall be designed for durability.

Notes:
(1) *Masonry material should be selected and masonry elements should be designed*
(a) to satisfy their function;
(b) to achieve their performance requirements; and
(c) to resist the loads, acting alone or in combination, to which they will be subjected within their anticipated service environment for their design service life.
(2) Masonry structures designed in accordance with this Standard and constructed in accordance with CSA Standard A371 are considered to have met the requirements of Note (1).
(3) For special structures, or structures exposed to unusual environmental conditions, the application of additional durability measures may be warranted.
(4) A major factor influencing the durability of masonry is its moisture content. For example, excessive moisture may lead to freeze-thaw damage and accelerated corrosion of metal components. The use of durable materials and design details which reduce water ingress into the wall will reduce the likelihood of damage.
(5) Further guidance is provided in CSA Standard S478, Guideline on Durability in Buildings.

6.5.2 Masonry Units and Mortars
Masonry units and mortar shall conform to the requirements in Clause 3. Reclaimed or previously used units shall meet the applicable requirements for new masonry units of the same material for their intended use.

6.5.3 Corrosion Protection of Metal Components

6.5.3.1 Ties and Anchors
Connectors in exterior masonry walls shall be provided with not less than the minimum corrosion protection specified in CSA Standard A370.

6.5.3.2 Reinforcement in Mortar
Steel reinforcement located within the mortar bed joints of exterior wythes and veneers shall be provided with not less than the corrosion protection specified for ties in CSA Standard A370.

6.5.3.3 Reinforcement in Grout
Steel reinforcement contained within grouted cavities or cores shall have a minimum cover of 15 mm of grout. Where this cover is not achieved, the steel shall be provided with not less than the corrosion protection for anchors specified in CSA Standard A370.

6.5.3.4 Prestressing Tendons in Grout

6.5.3.4.1 Grouted Tendons
Prestressing tendons placed in grouted cavities or cores shall have a minimum cover of 20 mm of grout. Where the minimum cover is not achieved, they shall be provided with not less than the corrosion protection specified in CSA Standard A370.

6.5.3.4.2 Unbonded Tendons
Unbonded prestressing tendons shall be sheathed in extruded polyethylene tubes completely filled with corrosion inhibiting grease. Suitable grease fittings and vents shall be provided at the anchorages to facilitate the injection of grease after tensioning. Anchorages shall be completely filled with grease and permanently sealed by threaded caps before the anchorage grout pockets are filled.

Note: *Tendon sheathing must be carefully supported and inspected for damage before the concrete is placed. It must not be damaged while the grout is being placed. A damaged sheath and loss of corrosion inhibiting grease will greatly increase the probability of tendon failure within a few years.*

6.5.3.5 Shelf Angles And Related Supports
Shelf angles, lintels, plates and related supports shall be provided with not less than the corrosion protection specified for connectors in CSA Standard A370.

7. Loads and Factored Resistance

7.1 Loads

7.1.1 Specified Loads
The following specified loads, forces, and effects shall be considered in the design of a building and its structural members and connections:

D - dead loads as provided for in Part 4 of the *National Building Code of Canada*;

E - live load due to earthquake;

L - live load due to static and inertial forces arising from intended use and occupancy (includes loads due to cranes); snow, ice and rain; and earth and hydrostatic pressure;

T - loads due to contraction or expansion caused by temperature changes, shrinkage, moisture changes, creep in component materials, movement due to differential settlement or combination thereof; and

W - live load due to wind.

7.1.2 Load Combinations

7.1.2.1 Combinations Not Including Earthquake
For load combinations not including earthquake, the effect of factored loads is the structural effect due to the specified loads multiplied by load factors, α, in Clause 7.2, a load combination factor, Ψ, in Clauses 7.3.1 and 7.3.2 and an importance factor, γ, in Clause 7.4, and the factored load combination shall be taken as

$$\alpha_D D + \gamma \Psi (\alpha_L L + \alpha_W W + \alpha_T T)$$

7.1.2.2 Dynamic Effects
Minimum specified values of these loads, as set forth in Subsections 4.1.5 to 4.1.10 of the *National Building Code of Canada*, shall be increased to account for dynamic effects where applicable.

7.1.2.3 Loads Not Listed
Where a building or structural member is expected to be subjected to the effects of loads or forces that are not listed in Clause 7.1.1, such effects shall be included in the design based on the most appropriate information available.

7.1.2.4 Combinations Including Earthquake
For load combinations including earthquake, the factored load combinations shall be taken as
(a) $1.0D + \gamma (1.0E)$; and either
(b) for storage and assembly occupancies, $1.0D + \gamma (1.0L + 1.0E)$; or
(c) for all other occupancies, $1.0D + \gamma (0.5L + 1.0E)$.

7.2 Load Factors

The load factors, α, shall be equal to

(a) $\alpha_D = 1.25$, except that when the dead load resists overturning, uplift, and reversal of load effect, $\alpha_D = 0.85$;

(b) $\alpha_L = 1.5$;

(c) $\alpha_W = 1.5$; and

(d) $\alpha_T = 1.25$.

7.3 Load Combination Factors

7.3.1 Factor

The load combination factor, Ψ, to be used in Clause 7.1.2.1 shall be equal to

(a) 1.0 when only 1 of the loads L, W, and T in Clause 7.1.1 acts;

(b) 0.70 when 2 of the loads L, W, and T in Clause 7.1.1 act; and

(c) 0.60 when all of the loads, L, W, and T in Clause 7.1.1 act.

7.3.2 Most Unfavourable Effect

The most unfavourable effect shall be determined by considering the loads L, W, and T acting alone with $\Psi = 1.0$ or in combination with $\Psi = 0.70$ or 0.60, according to Clause 7.3.1.

7.3.3 Anchorage

In cases of overturning, uplift and sliding, anchorage is required if the effect of loads tending to cause overturning, uplift or sliding, multiplied by load factors given in Clause 7.2 is greater than the stabilizing effect of dead load multiplied by the load factor $\alpha = 0.85$, also given in Clause 7.2.

7.4 Importance Factor

The importance factor, γ, shall be not less than 1.0 for all buildings, except that for buildings where it can be shown that collapse is not likely to cause injury or other serious consequences, it shall be not less than 0.8.

7.5 Factored Resistance

7.5.1 General

The factored resistance of a member, its cross-section and its connections to other members shall be taken as the resistance calculated in accordance with the requirements and assumptions of this Standard, using the material strengths specified in Clause 9 multiplied by resistance factors in accordance with Clause 7.5.2.

7.5.2 Factored Material Strengths

7.5.2.1 Masonry

The resistance factor to be used in checking ultimate limit states for compression, tension, shear and bearing in masonry shall be taken as $\phi_m = 0.55$.

7.5.2.2 Reinforcement and Prestressing Steel

The factored force in reinforcement and prestressing steel shall be taken as $\phi_s A_s f_s$ and $\phi_p A_p f_s$ as specified in other Clauses of this Standard

where

f_s = the stress in the reinforcement determined by a strain compatibility analysis, $\leq f_y$.

$f_s \leq f_y$ not yielding steel.

— ϕ_s = 0.85 for reinforcing bars,
— ϕ_p = 0.90 for prestressing steel

7.5.2.3 Connectors
The factored resistance of connectors shall be calculated in accordance with CSA Standard A370.

8. Analysis of the Structure

8.1 General

8.1.1 Safety and Serviceability
In proportioning the structure to meet the design requirements of Clause 6, the methods of analysis given in this Clause shall be used. The distribution of internal forces and bending moments shall be determined both under specified loads, to satisfy the requirements of serviceability, and under factored loads to satisfy the requirements of safety.

8.1.2 Methods of Analysis
Except as permitted in Clause 8.1.3, under a particular loading combination, the forces and moments throughout all or part of the structure shall be determined by an analysis that assumes that the various individual members behave elastically.

8.1.3 Alternate Methods
Alternate methods of analysis shall be permitted provided that they conform to recognized engineering principles and satisfy the requirements for serviceability and safety.

8.2 Secondary Effects
The analysis shall account for the effects of displacements due to elastic deformation and creep on the moments in axially loaded members. Creep effects in masonry may be accounted for by multiplying the value of $(EI)_{eff}$ by the creep adjustment factor $1/(1+0.5\beta_d)$.

8.3 Member Stiffness

8.3.1 Modulus of Elasticity

8.3.1.1
The modulus of elasticity of steel reinforcement, E_s, may be taken as 200 000 MPa.

8.3.1.2
The modulus of elasticity, E_m, of masonry made of concrete or clay units shall be determined in accordance with Clause 8.3.1.4 or may be taken as $E_m = 850 f'_m$ MPa but not greater than 20 000 MPa.

8.3.1.3
The modulus of elasticity, E_m, of masonry made of stone or other types of units shall be determined in accordance with Clause 8.3.1.4.

32

8.3.1.4
The modulus of elasticity of masonry determined experimentally shall be based on the secant modulus of at least five prisms tested in accordance with CSA Standard CAN/CSA-A369.1. The modulus shall be measured over a stress range extending from 0.05 to 0.33 of the measured mean prism compressive strength. The modulus shall be based on the average value.

8.3.2 Effective Moment of Inertia for Deflection Calculations at Specified Loads

8.3.2.1
The effective moment of inertia, I_{eff}, to be used in deflection calculations for reinforced and unreinforced walls and columns and for reinforced beams shall be calculated in accordance with Clauses 8.3.2.2 to 8.3.2.4.

Note: *For the determination of the effective moment of inertia for very slender walls, see Clause 11.2.4.3.3.*

8.3.2.2
Unless stiffness values are obtained by a more comprehensive analysis, immediate deflection shall be calculated using the modulus of elasticity for masonry, E_m, specified in Clause 8.3.1 and the effective moment of inertia, I_{eff}, determined as follows, except that I_{eff} shall not be greater than I_o:

$$I_{eff} = \left(\frac{M_{cr}}{M_a}\right)^3 I_o + \left[1 - \left(\frac{M_{cr}}{M_a}\right)^3\right] I_{cr}$$

where

$$M_{cr} = \frac{(\phi_m f_t + f_{cs}) I_o}{y_t}$$

and
f_t = the appropriate flexural tensile strength value from Table 6
f_{cs} = unfactored axial load, P, divided by A_e
M_a = maximum moment due to specified loads.

I_{cr} may be calculated with the effects of axial loads included.

8.3.2.3
For continuous spans, I_{eff} may be taken as the average of the values from Clause 8.3.2.2 for the critical positive and negative moment sections. For prismatic members, I_{eff} may be taken as the value obtained from Clause 8.3.2.2 at midspan for simple spans and at the support for cantilevers.

8.3.2.4
Unless values are obtained by a more comprehensive analysis, the total immediate-plus-longterm deflection for flexural members shall be obtained by multiplying the immediate deflection (caused by the sustained load) by the factor calculated from

$$\left[1 + \frac{S}{1 + 50\rho'}\right]$$

where
ρ' = the value at midspan for simple and continuous spans and at the support for cantilevers.

The time dependent factor, S, may be taken as equal to

(a) 1.0 for a sustained load of 5 years or more;

(b) 0.7 for a sustained load of 12 months;

(c) 0.6 for a sustained load of 6 months; and

(d) 0.5 for a sustained load of 3 months.

8.3.3 Composite Members

Where a member is constructed of two or more types or grades of unit or mortar, the member properties shall be calculated using a transformed section analysis.

Note: *Differential movement considerations are discussed in Clause 6.4.1.*

8.3.4 Cavity Walls

8.3.4.1 Lateral Loads

Unless otherwise indicated by rational analysis, for lateral load effects the cavity wall stiffness shall be taken as the sum of the stiffnesses of the two wythes acting noncompositely, the ties acting as struts, forcing the two wythes into similar curvatures, but transferring no shear across the cavity.

8.3.4.2 Axial Load and Bending

Unless otherwise indicated by rational analysis, each wythe shall be considered to act independently and the effective thickness of each wythe shall be assumed as its actual thickness.

9. Material Strengths

9.1 General

The material strengths used in determining member resistance shall be as specified in Clause 9.

9.2 Masonry Compressive Strength

9.2.1 Design Strength

The compressive strength f_m' used in design, shall be determined by the test methods of Clause 9.2.2 or 9.2.3.

9.2.2 Prism Test

9.2.2.1

The specified compressive strength, f_m', used in design shall be confirmed in advance of construction by tests of specimens that conform to CSA Standard CAN/CSA-A369.1.

9.2.2.2

At least five prisms shall be tested in accordance with the procedures prescribed in CSA Standard CAN/CSA-A369.1 and the prism compressive strength, f_m', shall be obtained by multiplying the resulting average compressive strength so determined by

$$\left[1 - \frac{1.5}{\overline{x}} \sqrt{\frac{\Sigma \, (x - \overline{x})^2}{n - 1}} \right]$$

where

x = an individual test result
$\overline{x}$ = the average of individual test results
n = the number of prisms
Note: *Ten prisms should be tested if the coefficient of variation of the first five tests exceeds 15%.*

9.2.2.3
At least five masonry units selected from the same batch used to construct the prisms in Clause 9.2.2.2 shall be tested in accordance with the procedures prescribed in CSA Standard CAN/CSA-A369.1 and the unit compressive strength obtained by multiplying the resulting average compressive strength so determined by

$$\left[1 - \frac{1.5}{\overline{x}} \sqrt{\frac{\Sigma \, (x - \overline{x})^2}{n - 1}} \right]$$

where

x = an individual test result
$\overline{x}$ = the average of the individual test results
n = the number of units
Note: *Ten units should be tested if the coefficient of variation of the first five tests exceeds 15%.*

9.2.2.4
The specified strength for masonry units shall be
(a) the same or greater than the unit compressive strength determined in accordance with Clause 9.2.2.3; or
(b) less than the compressive unit strength determined in accordance with Clause 9.2.2.3, provided that the prism strength used for design is not taken to be greater than
$\gamma \, f'_m$

where

γ = specified unit strength/tested unit compressive strength, ≤ 1.
f'_m = the tested prism strength from Clause 9.2.2.2.

9.2.2.5
At least six mortar cubes shall be tested in conformance with Clause 9.2.2.1. The mortar compressive strength shall be the average compressive strength of the specimens.

9.2.2.6
At least six grout test specimens shall be tested in conformance with Clause 9.2.2.1. The grout compressive strength shall be the average compressive strength of the specimens.

9.2.2.7
The prism strength shall be calculated by dividing the test load by the effective cross-sectional area, A_e. The mortar bedding in the prism shall be similar to that in the completed masonry.

9.2.2.8
The prism strength shall not be taken greater than the strength of the masonry units as determined in Clause 9.2.2.3.

9.2.3 Unit and Mortar Tests

9.2.3.1 General

9.2.3.1.1
The compressive strength of masonry, f'_m, shall be established on the basis of mortar type, and the compressive strength of the masonry unit.

9.2.3.1.2
In masonry constructed of different kinds or grades of units or mortars, the value of f'_m used in design shall correspond to the weakest combination of units and mortars of which the member or element is constructed, except that in a cavity wall or a composite wall where only one wythe supports the vertical load, the value of f'_m shall be appropriate for the materials in the loaded wythe.

9.2.3.2 Mortar
Mortar Type for engineered masonry shall be Type S or N, and shall be determined in accordance with the requirements of CSA Standard A179.

Note: *CSA Standard A179 permits the designer to specify mortar either by the property specification or the proportion specification. The property specification is a performance-type specification, and requires mortar testing to establish mortar type. The proportion specification is a prescription-type specification and requires no mortar strength testing to establish mortar type, since acceptance is based on the known properties and proportions of the constituent materials.*

9.2.3.3 Unit

9.2.3.3.1
Test for the compressive strength of masonry units shall be carried out in accordance with the following CSA Standards, as applicable:
(a) A82.2;
(b) A165.1; and
(c) A165.2.

9.2.3.3.2
At least five masonry units shall be tested and the compressive strength shall be obtained by multiplying the average compressive strength of the specimens by

$$\left[1 - \frac{1.5}{\overline{x}} \sqrt{\frac{\Sigma\, (x - \overline{x})^2}{n - 1}} \right]$$

where
x = an individual test result
$\overline{x}$ = the average of individual test results
n = the number of specimens

Note: *Ten units should be tested if the coefficient of variation of the first five tests exceeds 15%.*

9.2.3.3.3
The compressive strength of concrete block and hollow clay brick masonry units shall be based on the net cross-sectional area measured at mid-height of the units.

9.2.3.4 Determining Masonry Compressive Strength

9.2.3.4.1 Clay, Shale, Concrete or Calcium Silicate Brick
The value of the compressive strength, f'_m, to be used in the design of clay, shale, concrete, or calcium silicate brick masonry shall conform to Table 3.

9.2.3.4.2 Concrete Block
The value of the compressive strength, f'_m, to be used in the design of masonry constructed with solid or hollow concrete blocks, or hollow concrete blocks filled with grout conforming to CSA Standard A179 shall conform to Table 5.
Notes:
(1) *The value to be used for partially grouted masonry may be interpolated. Averaging will be appropriate if the grout cells are uniformly spaced.*
(2) *For out-of-plane bending, the f'_m value for masonry of hollow units may be used if the grouted area is not included in the calculations.*

9.2.3.4.3 Hollow Clay Brick
The value of the compressive strength, f'_m, to be used in the design of masonry constructed with hollow clay bricks or hollow clay bricks filled with grout conforming to CSA Standard A179 shall be determined in accordance with Clause 9.2.2.
Notes:
(1) *The value to be used for partially grouted masonry may be interpolated. Averaging will be appropriate if the grout cells are uniformly spaced.*
(2) *For out-of-plane bending, the f'_m value for masonry of hollow units may be used if the grouted area is not included in the calculations.*

9.3 Masonry Flexural Tensile Strength
The design flexural tensile strength, f_t, for unreinforced masonry shall be as specified in Table 6.
Note: *The tensile strength of unreinforced masonry in direct (axial) tension is assumed to be zero.*

9.4 Masonry Shear Strengths

9.4.1 Walls and Columns
The design shear strength for walls and columns shall be as specified in Clause 11.5.

9.4.2 Beams
The design shear strength of masonry beams shall be as specified in Clauses 12.3.5 and 12.3.6.

9.5 Masonry Bearing Strength
Direct bearing resistance shall be as specified in Clause 10.4.

9.6 Reinforcing Steel Yield Strength
The yield strength, f_y, in reinforcing steel shall be as specified in CSA Standards CAN/CSA-G30.18, G30.14, and G30.15. The yield strength used for design shall not exceed 400 MPa for non-prestressed masonry.

9.7 Connector Strength

The strength of masonry connectors shall be as specified in CSA Standard A370.

10. Factored Resistance

10.1 General

10.1.1

The factored resistance of masonry members shall be determined in accordance with the provisions of Clauses 7.2, 9, and 10 and the applicable provisions of Clauses 11 and 12.

10.2 Flexure and Axial Loads

10.2.1 Effective Cross-Sectional Area

10.2.1.1 A_e for Walls and Columns

The effective cross-sectional area, A_e, to be used in the design of masonry walls and columns shall include the mortar bedded area and the area of voids filled with grout. It shall take into account raked joints, voids, chases, and recesses in the section.

 No reduction in area is required for

(a) voids that do not exceed 25% of the area of cored units; and

(b) concave tooling of mortar joints to a depth not exceeding 3 mm.

10.2.1.2 A_e for Beams

The effective cross-sectional area, A_e, to be used in the design of masonry beams shall be based on the minimum cross-sectional area in a plane perpendicular to the span. In grouted masonry with noncontinuous grout across head joints, the effective area for compression shall be reduced to account for voids due to incomplete filling of the joint by mortar or grout.

Note: *Noncontinuous (partially filled) grouted head joints may also exist in beams constructed of solid units.*

10.2.2 Unreinforced Walls and Columns

10.2.2.1

For the critical combination of factored loads, unreinforced masonry walls and columns shall be designed to remain uncracked when the eccentricity resulting from bending about either the major or minor axis exceeds 0.33 times the dimension of the section perpendicular to the axis about which moments are being computed.

Note:

(1) *The eccentricity of the axial load on an unreinforced masonry section should be carefully evaluated based on the effects of short- and long-term gravity loads, the short- and long-term relative stiffness of the roof/floor/wall/column frame members, and the type of roof/floor member bearings to be used (eg, rocker, soft strip, or rigid).*

(2) *For non-rectangular sections the maximum eccentricity should not exceed 0.5 times the distance from the centroid of the section to the extreme compression fibre in the direction of bending unless the section is designed to remain uncracked.*

10.2.2.2

Stresses in unreinforced sections which are designed to remain uncracked when subjected to tensile stresses shall be calculated using a linear elastic analysis. The maximum tensile stress shall not exceed $\phi_m f_t$ and the maximum compressive stress shall not exceed $\phi_m f'_m$.

10.2.2.3
Unreinforced sections entirely in compression or sections allowed to be cracked may be designed using the rectangular stress block in accordance with the methods described in Clause 10.2.3.2 but excluding Clause 10.2.3.2.4.

10.2.3 Reinforced Masonry

10.2.3.1 Factored Flexural Resistance

10.2.3.1.1
The factored moment resistance, M_r, of members shall be based on the assumptions given in Clauses 10.2.3.1.2 and 10.2.3.1.3, the satisfaction of the applicable conditions of equilibrium and compatibility of strains, and the resistance factors given in Clause 7.5.2.

10.2.3.1.2 Plane Sections Assumption
Strain in reinforcement and masonry shall be assumed directly proportional to the distance from the neutral axis, except for deep flexural members as defined in Clause 10.2.3.6.

10.2.3.1.3 Maximum Usable Masonry Strain
Maximum usable strain at the extreme masonry compression fibre shall be assumed to be equal to 0.003. ε_m

10.2.3.1.4 Reinforcement Stress-Strain Relationships
The factored force in the reinforcement shall be calculated as ϕ_s for reinforcing bars and ϕ_p for tendons, times the force determined from strain compatibility based on a stress-strain curve representative of the steel.
  For reinforcement with a specified yield strength of 400 MPa or less the following assumptions may be used: $f_s = 0.003(d-c/c)E_s$ $\varepsilon_s = 0.003(d-c/c) < \varepsilon_y$
(a) for strains less than the yield strain, f_y/E_s, the force in the reinforcement shall be taken as $\phi_s(E_s\varepsilon_s A_s)$; and
(b) for strains greater than the yield strain, the force in the reinforcement shall be taken as $\phi_s f_y A_s$. T

10.2.3.1.5 Tensile Strength of Masonry
The tensile strength of masonry shall be neglected in the calculation of the factored flexural resistance of reinforced and prestressed masonry members.

10.2.3.1.6 Masonry Stress-Strain Relationship
The relationship between the masonry's compressive stress and masonry strain may be assumed to be parabolic, trapezoidal or any other shape that results in prediction of strength in substantial agreement with results of comprehensive tests.

→ **10.2.3.1.7 Equivalent Rectangular Masonry Stress Block**
The requirements of Clause 10.2.3.1.6 may be satisfied by an equivalent rectangular masonry stress block defined by a masonry stress assumed uniformly distributed over a compression zone bounded by edges of the cross-section and a straight line located parallel to the neutral axis at a distance $a = \beta_1 c$ from the fibre of maximum compressive strain and calculated as $0.85\phi_m \chi f'_m$. C
  (ba)

where

c = the distance from the fibre of maximum strain to the neutral axis measured in a direction perpendicular to that axis; and

β_1 = 0.8 for masonry strengths f'_m up to and including 20 MPa; and

= 0.8 minus (0.1 for each 10 MPa of strength in excess of 20 MPa);

χ = the factor to account for the direction of flexural compressive stresses relative to the direction used in prism testing

= 0.5 for compressive forces applied horizontally and normal to the head joints; and

= 1.0 for compressive forces applied vertically and normal to the bed joint

Note: *Care should be taken to ensure that splitter blocks are not used in the construction of masonry beams as the split void in the centre web of these units will result in a reduced moment capacity.*

10.2.3.2 Maximum Reinforcement in Flexural Members

For flexural members having no axial load, the area of tension reinforcement shall be such that the following inequality is satisfied for the section:

$$\frac{c}{d} \le \frac{600}{600 + f_y}$$

– under reinforced

10.2.3.3 Compression Reinforcement

The compressive resistance of reinforcement shall not be included unless the reinforcement is tied as required by Clauses 5.2.5 and 12.2.3.4.

10.2.3.4 Minimum Reinforcement of Flexural Members

10.2.3.4.1

At any section of a flexural member, except as provided in Clause 10.2.3.4.2 where reinforcement is required by analysis, the ratio, ρ, provided shall not be less than that given by

$$\rho_{min} = \frac{0.8}{f_y}$$

< As

10.2.3.4.2

Alternatively, the area of reinforcement provided at every section shall be at least one-third greater than that required by analysis.

10.2.3.5 Maximum Factored Axial Load Resistance

10.2.3.5.1

Except as permitted in Clause 10.2.3.5.2, the factored axial load resistance, P_r, of compression members shall not be taken greater than

$$P_{r(max)} = 0.80[0.85\phi_m f'_m A_e]$$

10.2.3.5.2

Where compression reinforcement is tied in accordance with the requirements of Clause 5.2.5, the factored axial load resistance, P_r, of compression members shall not be taken greater than

$$P_{r(max)} = 0.80[0.85\phi_m f'_m (A_e - A_{st}) + \phi_s f_y A_{st}]$$

10.2.3.6 Deep Sections
Masonry members having span to depth ratios less than 1.5 or cantilever lengths to depth ratios less than 0.75 shall be designed as deep beams having a reduced moment arm between the compression zone and the tensile reinforcement. For these members the effective depth, d, may be taken as 0.67 of the section depth but not greater than 0.7 times the span or 0.35 times the cantilever length.

10.3 Factored Shear Resistance

10.3.1 Walls and Columns
The factored shear resistance of walls and columns shall be as specified in Clause 11.5.

10.3.2 Masonry Beams
The factored shear resistance of masonry beams shall be as specified in Clause 12.3.

10.4 Concentrated Load Bearing Resistance

10.4.1 Factored Bearing Resistance
The factored bearing resistance of masonry, B_r, shall be calculated as

$$B_r = 0.85 \phi_m f'_m A_1$$

10.4.2 Dispersion of Concentrated Load
Concentrated loads shall be assumed to disperse downward and outward from the outer edges of the bearing plate at an angle of 45° for solid unit brick masonry and an angle of 30° to the vertical for all other masonry. The dispersion downward shall not extend
(a) into the dispersion zone of an adjacent concentrated load on the member; or
(b)· beyond the end face or a movement joint in the member; or
(c) beyond a continuous vertical mortar joint in the member unless there is sufficient tying or bonding across the joint to ensure transfer of compressive loads to the adjacent masonry.

11. Design of Walls and Columns

11.1 Geometric Considerations

11.1.1 Effective Cross-sectional Area
The design of masonry walls and columns shall be based on the effective cross-sectional area, A_e, determined in accordance with Clause 10.2.1.

11.1.2 Wall Height

11.1.2.1
The effective height, kh, of a wall or column shall be established on the basis of recognized principles of structural analysis. In no case however shall the value of "k" used for design be less than 0.80. Walls and columns not laterally supported at the top shall have k = 2.
Note: *Additional information on effective length "k" values is contained in Appendix B.*

11.1.2.2
Where a masonry wall is provided with lateral supports at more than one level, the height h, between supports may be assumed to be the clear distance between such supports.
Note: *Care should be taken to ensure that the lateral supports are sufficiently stiff to justify the assumption permitted by this Clause.*

11.1.2.3
Where vertical lateral supports are provided for a nonloadbearing wall, the height, h, may be taken as the clear horizontal distance between vertical supports.

11.1.3 Effective Compression Zone Width

11.1.3.1
In walls and columns the width of section acting with a single reinforcing bar shall be taken as the lesser of the spacing between bars and either 4 times the wall thickness for running bond or the length of the reinforced unit for stack pattern. $b_{eff} = 4t/s$

11.1.3.2 Shearwall Flange Width
In shearwalls the effective overhanging width of flange on each side of webs in flanged I, T and L sections shall be taken as the least of
(a) half the distance to the next web;
(b) 6 times the flange thickness; and
(c)
 (i) 1/12 the distance from the section to the top of I or T shaped shearwalls, or
 (ii) 1/16 the distance from the section to the top of L shaped shearwalls.
The effects of chases and openings in flanges shall be considered in the design.

11.2 Minor Axis Flexure and Axial Loads

11.2.1 Cavity Walls
For cavity walls, each wythe shall be considered to act independently in resisting the loads applied to each wythe.

11.2.2 Composite Walls
For composite walls where shear transfer between wythes is assured by connectors and filled collar joints, or by other mechanical means, consideration shall be given to the compressive strengths and related properties of the constituent wythes in a rational analysis. The shear transfer system shall be designed with adequate strength and rigidity to ensure effective composite action.

11.2.3 Minimum Primary Moment
The minimum primary moment to be used for determination of secondary effects and for design shall be that produced by the axial load applied to produce single curvature at an eccentricity of 0.10t at each end.

11.2.4 Section Total Moment Effects

11.2.4.1
The design of masonry walls and columns shall be based on forces and moments determined by a rational analysis of the structure. This analysis shall account for the effects of axial loads, creep and cracking on member stiffness used in determination of primary moments in the

building frame, and displacements in the member and may make allowance for the restraining effect of the floor system on end joint rotations.

Section total moment effects at all sections along a member shall be calculated for

(a) primary end moments M_1 and M_2;

(b) lateral load primary moment; and

(c) secondary moment, $P \cdot \delta$, due to the axial load and the displacements caused by the primary and secondary moments.

Notes:

(1) *Where zero or very small moments or transverse loads occur, minimum end eccentricities or load path curvature should be included to ensure structural integrity.*

(2) *More than one cycle of $P \cdot \delta$ calculations may be required to ensure that the member is stable and that all significant $P \cdot \delta$ effects have been included. Increasing moments increase the extent of member cracking, reducing I_{eff} and can trigger instability if the I_o / I_{cr} ratio is high.*

11.2.4.2

Where vertical lateral supports are provided for load-bearing masonry, the secondary effects on the moments in the masonry of the displacements in the axial load paths shall be included in the design. The calculations shall consider

(a) the displacements in the lateral supports;

(b) the displacements in the horizontal span of the masonry member between the supports; and

(c) the effects of these combined displacements on the forces and stresses in the member.

11.2.4.3 Slenderness Limits

11.2.4.3.1 Slenderness Ignored

The effects of slenderness can be neglected when the ratio of effective wall height to wall thickness (slenderness ratio), kh/t, is less than $(10 - 3.5(e_1 / e_2))$.

Note: *See Clause 11.1.2.1 for information on the factor "k".*

11.2.4.3.2 Slender Walls or Columns with kh/t ≤ 30

Except as provided in Clause 11.2.4.3.1, if the slenderness ratio, kh/t, does not exceed 30, the procedures of either Clause 11.2.5.2 or 11.2.5.3 shall be applied.

11.2.4.3.3 Very Slender Walls with kh/t > 30

If the slenderness ratio, kh/t, of a wall is greater than 30, the design procedures and requirements of Clause 11.2.5.6 may be applied.

11.2.5 Design Methods

11.2.5.1 Effective Stiffness For Consideration of Slenderness

In the determination of slenderness effects, the effective stiffness, $(EI)_{eff}$, shall be determined as follows:

(a) in lieu of more accurate calculations, $(EI)_{eff}$ shall be determined in accordance with Clause 11.2.5.4; or

(b) where $EI_{(eff)}$ is determined by alternate methods, the analysis shall take into account the influence of axial loads, variable moments of inertia, and the effects of creep.

11.2.5.2 P•δ (Load Displacement) Method

The secondary moment may be calculated directly as the product of the axial load, P, and the displacement of the section centroid from the centroidal plane through the wall ends calculated using the rigidity coefficient

$\boxed{\phi_e (EI)_{eff} / (1+0.5\beta_d).}$

11.2.5.3 Moment Magnifier Method

For walls and columns with $kh/t \leq 30$, the section total moment, M_{tot} may be determined from the moment magnifier expression:

$$M_{tot} = M_P \frac{C_{m\,(1)}}{\left(1 - \dfrac{P_f}{P_{cr}}\right)}$$

where

M_p = the factored primary moment at the section due to the end factored moments and lateral loads

C_m = is determined in accordance with Clause 11.2.5.5

P_{cr} = $\pi^2 \phi_e (EI)_{eff} / [(1+0.5\beta_d)(kh)^2]$ in which $(EI)_{eff}$ is calculated in accordance with Clause 11.2.5.4

ϕ_e = 0.65

11.2.5.4 Effective Stiffness, $(EI)_{eff}$

The effective stiffness of walls and columns shall be calculated

(a) for unreinforced masonry, from

$$(EI)_{eff} = 0.4\, E_m I_o$$

where

I_o = moment of inertia of the effective cross-sectional area.

E_m = 850 f'_m

(b) for reinforced masonry, from

$$(EI)_{eff} = E_m \left(0.25 I_o - (0.25 I_o - I_{cr}) \left(\frac{(e - e_k)}{(2 e_k)} \right) \right)$$

where

$(EI)_{eff}$ shall not be taken greater than $0.25 E_m I_o$, but need not be taken as less than $E_m I_{cr}$.

E_m = 850 f'_m

I_o = moment of inertia of the effective area of a section about its centroidal axis.

e = M_p / P_f

e_k = S / A_e

S = section modulus

Notes: $n = E_y / E_m$

(1) I_{cr} *is calculated ignoring the effects of axial load.* = $bkd^3/3 + nA_s(d-kd)^2$

(2) *Where reinforcement is not taken into account in the calculation of the wall or column resistance, $(EI)_{eff}$ for unreinforced masonry may be conservatively used.*

11.2.5.5 Moment Diagrams Factor, C_m

In Clause 11.2.5.3, C_m may be taken as

$C_m = 0.6 + 0.4\, M_1/M_2$

but not less then 0.4.

The ratio M_1/M_2 shall be determined either

(a) when calculated end eccentricities are less than 0.1t, by calculating end moments; or

(b) if calculations show that there is essentially no moment at both ends of a compression member, by taking the ratio M_1/M_2 equal to 1.0.

Where lateral loads occur between the ends of the member such that they contribute more than 50% of the factored moment at the critical section, the ratio of M_1/M_2 should be taken equal to 1.0.

11.2.5.6 Very Slender Reinforced Walls Under Low Axial Load

11.2.5.6.1

Reinforced walls having slenderness ratio kh/t > 30 shall be designed using the provisions of Clauses 11.2.5.6.2 to 11.2.5.6.7.

11.2.5.6.2

$\checkmark t > ?$

Walls shall be constructed with masonry units 140 mm or more in actual thickness. Raked joints shall not be permitted.

11.2.5.6.3

Eccentric pin end conditions at each end of the member, inducing symmetrical single curvature, shall be assumed.

11.2.5.6.4 $\checkmark$

The axial load, P_f, shall not exceed $0.1\phi_m f_m A_e$. P_{max}

11.2.5.6.5

The maximum area of reinforcement provided shall be less than or equal to 80% of that provided by the condition $As_{max} \leq 0.8 As_b$

$$\frac{c}{d} \leq \frac{600}{600 + f_y}$$ $\frac{P.C/S}{d}$

Minimum vertical reinforcement shall be provided in accordance with Clause 5.2.1.2.

11.2.5.6.6

The mid-height displacement under unfactored lateral and vertical loads shall not exceed the requirements of Clause 11.8.3. The midheight deflection under service loads, Δ_s, shall be calculated using

(a) for $M_s < M_{cr}$, $$\Delta_s = \frac{5M_s h^2}{48 E_m I_o}$$

(b) for $M_{cr} < M_s < M_n$, $$\Delta_s = \frac{5 M_{cr} h^2}{48 E_m I_o} + \frac{5(M_s - M_{cr})h^2}{48 E_m I_{cr}}$$

where

h = unsupported height of wall

M_s = service moment at the midheight of the panel, including P•δ effects

M_n = nominal moment strength of the masonry wall calculated with material resistance factors set equal to 1.0

I_o = the gross moment of inertia of the section using the effective area A_e

I_{cr} is calculated ignoring the effects of axial load $bkd^2/2 = nAs(d-kd)$

$$M_{cr} = \frac{(\phi_m f_t + f_{cs})}{y_t} I_o$$

f_{cs} = the axial stress on the masonry imposed by service dead loads $0.85D/A_e$ $t(2)(1000)$

f_t = the appropriate flexural tensile strength value obtained from Table 6

11.2.5.6.7
The factored moment, M_{tot}, shall be determined at the midheight of the wall and shall be calculated from

$$M_{tot}^3 = (w_f h^2/8) + P_{tf}(e/2) + (P_{wf} + P_{tf})\Delta_f + \left(P_{DL} \Delta max \right)$$
$$\left(P_{DL} \frac{L}{180} \right)$$

where

w_f = factored wind load on the wall

h = height of wall between points of support.

Δ_f = horizontal deflection at midheight under factored lateral and axial loads; P•δ effects shall be included in deflection calculation.

P_{wf} = factored weight of wall tributary to and above design section.

P_{tf} = factored load from tributary roof or floor area.

e = eccentricity of P_{tf}.

$= M_c - 1.5WL(h)^2/8 \rightarrow M_f / 7.3e_k$

11.3 Major Axis Bending of Walls

11.3.1 Design of Compression Zone
The design of shearwall compression zones shall provide for the effects of
(a) major axis flexural compression, including secondary effects, if any;
(b) concurrent gravity loads; and
(c) concurrent minor axis bending and secondary effects.

11.4 Masonry Columns

11.4.1 Axial Load and Single Axis Bending
Columns subjected to load and bending about one axis only shall be designed in accordance with Clause 8.2 to provide adequate resistance in both directions. The minimum eccentricity specified in Clause 11.2.3 shall be checked about both major axes of the section. Masonry columns designed to the requirements of Clause 11.2.5 shall be deemed to have met the requirements of Clause 8.2.

11.4.2 Axial Load and Biaxial Bending
Columns subjected to axial load and biaxial bending shall be designed to satisfy Clause 8.2 and to satisfy the condition

$$\frac{M_x}{M_{rx}} + \frac{M_y}{M_{ry}} \leq 1.0$$

$Mr = C\left(\frac{t}{2} - \frac{B.c}{2}\right) + T\left(d - \frac{t}{2}\right) + Cs\left(\frac{t}{2} - d'\right)$ beam $(T)(d - \frac{B.c}{2})$ $T(d-d')$

where

M_x, M_y are concurrent total factored moments in each direction including the effects of slenderness; and

M_{rx}, M_{ry} are factored moment resistances in each direction obtained from the associated interaction diagrams at the ordinate corresponding to the concurrent factored axial load.

11.5 Shear in Walls and Columns

11.5.1 General
The factored shear resistance shall be such that

$$V_r \geq V_f$$

where V_r is determined in accordance with Clause 11.5.3.

11.5.2 Calculation of Factored Shear Resistance
In calculating the factored shear resistance, flanges or projections formed by intersecting walls shall be neglected.

11.5.3 Factored In-Plane Shear Resistance

11.5.3.1 General
The factored shear resistance, V_r, shall be taken as

$$V_r = \phi_m(v_m\, b_w d + 0.25P)\gamma_g + \phi_s\left(0.60A_v\, f_y\, \frac{d}{s}\right)$$

but not greater than

$$\phi_m(0.4)\sqrt{f'_m}\ b_w d\gamma_g$$

where
v_m = shear strength attributed to the masonry and given in Clause 11.5.3.2
d = effective depth which need not be taken less than $0.8\ell_w$ for walls or columns with flexure reinforcement distributed along the length or for unreinforced masonry
γ_g = factor to account for partially grouted walls or columns
  = 1 for fully grouted walls or columns
  = $A_e/A_g \leq 0.5$ for partially grouted walls or columns
A_g = gross cross-sectional area
P = axial compressive load on the section under consideration, based on 0.85 times dead load plus any axial load arising from bending in coupling beams.

11.5.3.2 Low Aspect Ratio Walls or Columns
The factored shear resistance of low aspect ratio walls or columns $(h_w/\ell_w < 1)$ is greater than that given in Clause 11.5.3; however care must be taken that the distribution of shear input to the wall would not lead to failure of a portion of the wall or column. If such care is taken, then the maximum factored shear resistance may be increased to

$$V_r < \phi_m(0.4)\sqrt{f'_m}\ b_w d\ \gamma_g\ [2-(h_w/\ell_w)]$$

where h_w/ℓ_w shall not be taken less than 0.5 but need not be taken as more than 1

h_w = total wall height
ℓ_w = wall length

11.5.3.3 Masonry Shear Strength

Shear strength contributed by masonry, v_m, shall be as given by

$$v_m = 0.16 \left(2 - \frac{M_f}{V_f d}\right)\sqrt{f'_m}$$

where

$\dfrac{M_f}{V_f d}$ need not be taken more than 1 nor less than 0.25

M_f and V_f are the concurrent factored moment and factored shear at the section under consideration.

11.5.4 Factored Out-of-Plane Shear Resistance

The factored out-of-plane shear resistance, V_r, shall be taken as

(a) for unreinforced walls or columns,

$$V_r = \phi_m[v_m A_e + 0.25P]$$

but not greater than

$$\phi_m (0.4)\sqrt{f'_m} \; A_e$$

(b) for walls or columns reinforced for out-of-plane bending,

$$V_r = \phi_m[v_m \, bd + 0.25P]$$

but not greater than

$$\phi_m(0.4)\sqrt{f'_m} \; bd$$

where
v_m is given by Clause 11.5.3.2, and
b = width of webs and grouted cells within a length not greater than four times the wall thickness around each vertical bar for running bond, and within the length of the reinforced unit for stack pattern.

11.5.5 Stack Pattern Factored Shear Resistance

The maximum vertical shear stress shall not exceed that corresponding to the shear friction resistance of the continuous horizontal reinforcing used to tie the wall together at the continuous head joints. Such reinforcing shall be spaced at not more than 800 mm for bond beam reinforcing and 400 mm for wire joint reinforcing. Shear friction resistance shall be based on a friction coefficient of 0.7 and the factored resistance of the reinforcement.

11.5.6 Factored Sliding Shear Resistance of Masonry Walls

The factored sliding shear resistance, V_r, across a horizontal section shall be calculated using the shear friction concept,

$$V_r = \phi_m \mu C$$

where

C = compressive force in the masonry acting normal to the sliding plane; normally taken as P plus the factored yield strength of the vertical reinforcement

μ = 1.0 for a masonry to masonry or masonry to roughened concrete slide plane

= 0.7 otherwise.

11.6 Intersections

11.6.1

Where wall intersections are bonded so that at least 50% of the units of one wall are embedded at least 90 mm in the other wall, the factored vertical shear at the intersection shall not exceed the factored shear resistance specified in Clause 11.5.3 for shear walls.

11.6.2

Toothed joints shall not be used in shear walls.

11.6.3

Where wall intersections are bonded by concrete or grout completely filling vertical keyways, recesses, or a combination of these, to provide a bond at least equivalent to the masonry in Clause 11.6.1, the vertical factored shear resistance at the intersection shall not exceed either that specified in Clause 11.5.3 for shear walls or the shear friction resistance of the joint. The compressive strength of concrete or grout used to bond the intersection shall be not less than 10 MPa. The minimum horizontal reinforcement across the vertical intersection shall be at least equivalent in strength to two 3.8 mm diameter steel wires spaced 400 mm vertically. The factored shear friction resistance of the joint shall be based on a friction coefficient of 1.0 and the factored tensile resistance in the reinforcement.

11.6.4

Rigid steel connectors such as anchors, rods, or bolts, may be utilized to bond wall intersections except in portions of reinforced masonry shear walls in which the flanges contain tensile steel and are subject to axial tension under load.

11.6.5

Where rigid steel connectors described in Clause 11.6.4 are used

(a) connectors shall be embedded in mortar or grout, as specified in CSA Standard A370;

(b) vertical masonry joints at the intersections shall be completely filled with mortar or grout;

(c) the bearing stress of steel connectors on masonry shall not exceed the factored bearing resistance calculated in accordance with Clause 10.4 due to the action of the vertical shear at the intersection. In determining this bearing stress, the eccentricity of the shear loads shall be provided for in the design;

(d) adequate anchorage shall be provided by hooks or rigid cross pieces that are fully embedded in mortar or grout in the horizontal joints or vertical voids in the masonry where the embedment length is limited or where there is not sufficient thickness of masonry to develop the connector; and

(e) the vertical spacing of steel connectors shall not exceed 600 mm.

11.7 Factored Connector Resistance
The factored resistance of connectors shall be as specified in CSA Standard A370.

11.8 Deflections

11.8.1
When walls or columns are reinforced to resist lateral loads, the deflection due to lateral loads shall be checked when spans exceed 25 d.

11.8.2
Deflections may be calculated in accordance with Clause 8.3. The effects of axial loads may be included.

11.8.3
Wind load deflection of reinforced walls and columns shall not exceed
(a) where masonry veneers are attached—span/720;
(b) where brittle finishes are attached—span/360; and
(c) otherwise—span/180. △

11.9 Crack Control
When walls or columns are reinforced to resist lateral loads, cross-sections at locations of maximum positive and negative moments shall be so proportioned that the quantity, z, given by

$$z = f_s \sqrt[3]{d_c A} \times 10^{-3}$$

does not exceed the following:
(a) 25 kN/mm for exterior exposure except that cracking due to wind loading shall not exceed 50 kN/mm; and
(b) 30 kN/mm for interior exposure except that cracking due to wind loading shall not exceed 60 kN/mm.

The calculated stress in reinforcement at the specified load, f_s (MPa), shall be computed as the unfactored moment divided by the product of the tension steel area and the internal moment arm. In lieu of such computations, f_s may be taken as 60% of the specified yield strength, f_y. $f_s = 0.6 f_y$

$A = 2 \times b \times d_c$

12. Design of Masonry Beams

12.1 Applicability
This Clause applies to the design of reinforced masonry beams
(a) built in running bond; and of either
(b) fully grouted hollow units; or
(c) solid units.

12.2 Beams—Flexure

12.2.1 Effective Cross-sectional Area
The flexural design of masonry beams shall be in accordance with Clause 10 and shall be based on the effective cross-sectional area A_e, calculated in accordance with Clause 10.2.1.

12.2.2 Distance Between Lateral Supports of Beams

12.2.2.1
Unless a stability analysis, including the effects of torsional loading, is carried out, beams shall comply with the limits specified in Clauses 12.2.2.2, 12.2.2.3, and 12.2.2.4.

12.2.2.2
Effects of lateral eccentricity of load shall be taken into account in determining spacing of lateral supports.

12.2.2.3
For a simply supported or continuous beam the distance between points at which lateral support is provided shall not exceed the smaller of 30b or $120b^2/d$.

12.2.2.4
For a cantilever beam having lateral restraint at the support, the distance between the support and the end of the cantilever shall not exceed the smaller of 15b or $60b^2/d$.

12.2.3 Distribution of Flexural Reinforcement in Beams

12.2.3.1 Crack Control
To control cracking in beams, flexural tension reinforcement shall be well distributed within maximum flexural tension zones of a member's cross-section, as required by Clause 12.2.3.2.

12.2.3.2 Crack Control Parameter
Cross-sections of maximum positive and negative moments shall be so proportioned that the quantity, z, given by

$$z = f_s \sqrt[3]{d_c A} \times 10^{-3}$$

does not exceed 30 kN/mm for interior exposure and 25 kN/mm for exterior exposure. The calculated stress in reinforcement at specified load, f_s (MPa), shall be computed as the moment divided by the product of the steel area and the internal moment arm. In lieu of such computations, f_s may be taken as 60% of the specified yield strength, f_y.

Note: *These provisions may not be sufficient for structures subject to very aggressive exposure or designed to be watertight. For such structures, special investigations and precautions will be required.*

12.2.3.3 Intermediate Reinforcement
Where the height, h, exceeds 600 mm, longitudinal reinforcement shall be uniformly distributed over the height of the beam. No. 15 bars at 400 mm spacing for beams up to 240 mm wide and No. 15 bars each side for wider beams shall be provided.

12.2.3.4 Compression Reinforcement

Where compression steel is required in beams, it shall be anchored by ties or stirrups not less than 6 mm in diameter, spaced not more than 16 bar diameters or 48 tie diameters apart, whichever is less. Such ties or stirrups shall be used throughout the distance where compression steel is required.

12.2.4 Deep Beams

12.2.4.1

Beams with overall depth to clear span ratios greater than 1/3 for continuous spans or 2/3 for simple spans shall be designed as deep beams taking into account nonlinear distribution of strain, lateral buckling, and the increased anchorage requirements in such members.

Note: *See also Clauses 10.2.3.6 and 12.2.3.*

12.2.4.2

The minimum flexural tension reinforcement in deep beams shall conform to Clause 10.2.3.5 and 10.2.3.6.

12.2.4.3

Minimum horizontal and vertical reinforcement in the side faces of deep beams shall satisfy the requirements of Clause 12.3.6.

12.3 Beams—Shear

12.3.1 Scope

Provisions of Clause 11 shall apply to the design of structural elements subject to shear.

12.3.2 General Principles and Requirements

12.3.2.1 Design Methods and Design Considerations

12.3.2.1.1

Beams shall be designed for shear, in accordance with Clauses 12.3.2 through 12.3.6.

12.3.2.1.2

For deep beams, the special provisions of Clause 12.3.6 shall apply.

12.3.2.1.3

In determining shear resistance, the effects of axial tension due to creep, shrinkage, and thermal effects in restrained members shall be considered wherever applicable.

12.3.2.1.4

For variable depth members, the components of flexural compression and tension in the direction of the applied shear shall be taken into account if their effect is unfavourable and may be taken into account if their effect is favourable.

12.3.2.1.5

In determining shear resistance, V_r, the effect of any openings in members shall be considered.

12.3.3 Shear Reinforcement Details

12.3.3.1 Type of Shear Reinforcement
Transverse reinforcement provided for shear shall consist of stirrups perpendicular to the axis of the member.

12.3.3.2 Anchorage of Shear Reinforcement
Stirrups and other bars or wires used as shear reinforcement shall be anchored at both ends according to Clause 5.5.9 to develop the design yield strength of the reinforcement.

12.3.3.3 Yield Strength of Shear Reinforcement
The yield strength used in design calculations of shear transverse reinforcement shall not exceed 400 MPa.

12.3.4 Low and Normal Density Concrete Masonry Units
Values of the modification factor, λ, to account for the type of concrete shall be
$\lambda = 1.00$ for concrete units with density over 2000 kg/m^3.
$\lambda = 0.85$ for concrete units with density not less than 1800 kg/m^3.
$\lambda = 0.75$ for concrete units with density not less than 1700 kg/m^3.

12.3.5 Shear Design

12.3.5.1 Required Shear Reinforcement
Transverse reinforcement required for shear shall be determined from

$$V_r \geq V_f$$

12.3.5.2 Factored Shear Resistance
The factored shear resistance shall be determined from

$$V_r = V_m + V_s$$

where
V_m is determined in accordance with
(a) Clause 12.3.5.4 for beams of continuously grouted hollow masonry units; and
(b) Clause 12.3.5.5 for beams of solid masonry units; and
V_s is determined in accordance with Clause 12.3.5.6.

12.3.5.3 Calculation of V_f in Regions Near Supports
Sections located less than d from the face of a support for non-prestressed beams, or h/2 from the face of support for prestressed beams, may be designed for the same V_f as that computed at distance d if the following conditions are satisfied:
(a) the support reaction, in the direction of the applied shear, produces compression in the end region of the member; and
(b) no concentrated load occurs within a distance d from the face of the support.

12.3.5.4 Calculation of V_m
The factored shear resistance of beams of continuously* grouted hollow block masonry, V_m, shall be calculated as follows:

$$V_m = \phi_m \, 0.2\lambda\sqrt{f'_m} \left(1.0 - \frac{(d-400)}{1500}\right) b_w d \quad \text{, but not greater than} \quad \phi_m \, 0.2\lambda\sqrt{f'_m} \, b_w d$$

V_m need not be taken as less than $\phi_m \, 0.12\lambda\sqrt{f'_m} \, b_w d$ $= 0.16 \left[2 - Mf/V_{fd} \right] \sqrt{f_m}$

If the masonry beam is not continuously* grouted then the capacity derived from the above equation shall be multiplied by 0.6.

*The term *continuously grouted* in this sense means a beam formed with lintel or U shaped blocks such that the grout is uninterrupted by block webs for the entire length of the beam.

If the beam is subjected to axial tension, V_m shall be multiplied by the factor

$$R_t = 1 - N_f/N_r$$

where
N_f is positive for axial tension
$N_r = \phi_m f_t b_w d$
f_t is from Table 6.

12.3.5.5 Calculation of V_m for Solid Masonry Units
The factored shear resistance of beams of solid masonry units, V_m, shall be calculated using

$$V_m = \phi_m \chi \, 0.08\sqrt{f'_m} \, b_w d$$

but not greater than $\phi_m \, \chi 32 \sqrt{f'_m} \, b_w$

Note: *For value of χ see Clause 10.2.3.1.7.*

12.3.5.6 Calculation of V_s
The factored resistance, V_s, of shear reinforcement perpendicular to the flexural reinforcement in the member shall be calculated as

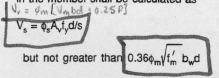

$V_r = \phi_m \left[V_m \, b d + 0.25 P \right]$

$$V_s = \phi_s A_v f_y d/s$$

but not greater than $0.36\phi_m\sqrt{f'_m} \, b_w d$

12.3.5.7 Minimum Shear Reinforcement

12.3.5.7.1
A minimum area of shear reinforcement shall be provided in all regions of beams where the factored shear force, V_f exceeds $0.5V_m$. This requirement may be waived for beams with a total depth of not greater than 200 mm. $V_f > V_m/2$ - stirrups

12.3.5.7.2
Where shear reinforcement is required by Clause 12.3.5.7.1 or by calculation, the minimum area of shear reinforcement shall be computed by

$$A_v = 0.35\frac{b_w s}{f_y}$$

12.3.5.8 Spacing Limits for Shear Reinforcement

Where shear reinforcement is required, the maximum spacing of shear reinforcement placed perpendicular to the member shall be the lesser of d/2 or 600 mm.

12.3.5.9 Calculation of V_m—Prestressed Members

The shear resistance attributed to prestressed masonry beams shall be that used for non-prestressed masonry beams unless justification is presented for the use of alternate values.

12.3.5.10 Calculation of V_s in Prestressed Members

When shear reinforcement perpendicular to the axis of a member is used

$$V_s = \frac{\phi_s A_v f_y d}{s}$$

12.3.6 Special Provisions for Deep Shear Spans

12.3.6.1

The provisions of this Clause shall apply for those parts of members in which
(a) the effective depth, d, exceeds 400 mm and the distance from the point of zero shear to the face of the support is less than 2d; or
(b) a load causing more than 50% of the shear at a support is located less than 2d from the face of the support.

12.3.6.2

Shear design of deep shear spans shall be in accordance with a recognized design method, and modified in accordance with Clause 12.3.6.3.

Note: *Special attention must be given to the anchorage of longitudinal reinforcement in deep beams.*

12.3.6.3 Minimum Shear Reinforcement Requirements for Deep Shear Spans

12.3.6.3.1

The area of transverse shear reinforcement, A_v, shall not be less than $0.002b_w s$, and s shall not exceed d/5 nor 300 mm.

12.3.6.3.2

Longitudinal reinforcing bars shall be distributed over the depth of the beam. The cross-sectional area of each layer of bars, with one bar near each face, shall be not less than $0.002b_w$ times the spacing between layers of bars. This spacing shall not exceed d/3 nor 300 mm.

12.4 Beams—Deflection

12.4.1

Deflections of beams shall be checked when the clear span exceeds 15d.

12.4.2
Immediate deflections shall be computed using the modulus of elasticity, E_m, for masonry as specified in Clause 8.3.1 and the effective moment of inertia of Clause 8.3.2.

12.4.3
The total immediate plus long-term deflection may be determined in accordance with Clause 8.3.

12.4.4
Total immediate plus long-term deflection of beams shall not exceed span/480.

13. Unit Masonry Veneer

13.1 Minimum Thickness
The minimum thickness of the masonry veneer shall be 75 mm.
Note: *Joint reinforcing is required in stack pattern veneer in accordance with CSA Standard A371.*

13.2 Ties

13.2.1
The design of ties shall conform to CSA Standard A370. Ties shall be spaced not more than 800 mm apart horizontally and 600 mm apart vertically. Tie spacing shall not be staggered.

13.2.2
Ties shall be designed to transfer the lateral load on the veneer to the backup.

13.2.3
With flexible backup systems as defined by Clause 13.3.2, all ties shall be designed for 40% of the tributary lateral load on a vertical line of ties, but not less than double the tributary lateral load on the tie, unless otherwise calculated by detailed stiffness analysis considering the tie forces before and after cracking of the veneer. For stiffer backup systems, each tie shall be designed for the lateral load on its tributary area.

13.3 Structural Backing

13.3.1
The structural backing shall be designed to resist the lateral load applied to the wall system.

13.3.2
Flexible structural backing systems are defined as having stiffness, EI, less than 2.5 times the uncracked stiffness of the veneer. For reinforced masonry structural backing walls, the stiffness shall be based on the cracked moment of inertia.

13.3.3
For flexible structural backing systems the total deflection of the veneer due to specified lateral wind loads shall not exceed the span of the structural backing system divided by 600.
Notes:
(1) *The reason for limiting the total deflection of the veneer is to limit the crack width in the veneer and thereby limit the water penetration.*

(2) *The requirement of this Clause is deemed to have been met provided that both the following criteria are met:*
(a) The bending deflection of the structural backing does not exceed the span of the structural backing divided by 720; and
(b) The tie deflection due to one half of the total mechanical play plus a tension or compression load of 0.45 kN does not exceed 1.0 mm.
(3) *For more information refer to* Exterior Wall Construction in High-Rise Buildings: Brick Veneer on Concrete Masonry or Steel Stud Wall Systems *by R.G. Drysdale and G.T. Suter, published by Canada Mortgage and Housing Corp. and to Canadian Sheet Steel Building Institute publications S5-90* Guide Specification for Wind Bearing Studs *and 51M-91* Lightweight Steel Framing Design Manual.

13.4 Thin Masonry Veneer
The requirements for thin masonry veneer shall be as specified in CSA Standard A371.

14. Prefabricated Masonry

14.1
The provisions of Clause 6.3.5.4 do not apply to prefabricated masonry.

14.2
All details of jointing, inserts, anchors, and openings shall be shown on the drawings.

14.3
Lifting devices designed for 100% impact shall be provided in prefabricated masonry sections and the material used in the lifting device shall
(a) not be brittle; and
(b) be capable of resisting all forces that might arise during the process of erection.

14.4
The effects of loads introduced during storage, transport, and placing shall be accounted for in the design.
Notes:
(1) *Instructions for handling, and temporary and permanent support should be provided by the fabricator.*
(2) *Instructions for temporary support and bracing, and for proper alignment during erection should be provided by the fabricator.*

14.5
Design and detailing of all joints and bearings shall be based on the forces to be resisted and the effects of dimensional changes due to shrinkage, elastic deformation, creep, and temperature.

14.6
Joints and connections shall be detailed to allow sufficient tolerances for manufacture and erection of the elements.

14.7
Bearings shall be detailed to provide for stress concentrations, rotations, and the possible development of horizontal forces by friction or other restraints.

15. Glass Block Masonry

15.1 General

15.1.1
Glass Block masonry shall
(a) be nonloadbearing;
(b) be isolated from adjacent construction by movement joints to prevent or relieve stress due to differential movement; and
(c) have a minimum thickness of 75 mm at the mortar joint.

15.1.2
Joint reinforcement shall be placed in glass block masonry panels, and shall
(a) be not less than conventional continuous-welded ladder reinforcing, in accordance with CSA Standard A370;
(b) be spaced at not more than
  (i)   every other mortar joint where the courses are not greater than 205 mm in height, and
  (ii) every mortar joint where the courses are greater than 205 mm in height.
(c) be installed in accordance with CSA Standard A371.

15.2 Design Requirements

15.2.1 Serviceability

15.2.1.1
Members supporting the weight of glass block masonry and members laterally supporting glass block masonry shall not deflect more than their span divided by 600, under specified loads.

15.2.1.2
For exterior walls the maximum length of glass block walls between movement joints shall be 7600 mm, and the maximum height of glass block walls between movement joints shall be 6100 mm.

15.2.1.3
Where anchors are used to secure glass block masonry panels to their lateral supports, they shall allow in-plane movement of the masonry.

15.2.2 Material Strength
The modulus of rupture of glass block masonry, f'_{gm}, shall be determined by test in accordance with ASTM E72.
Notes:
(1) *ASTM E72 tests should be used as prequalification guidance for the manufacturer of glass block for the development of data necessary for engineered designs. Test panels should be representative of the materials and workmanship to be used in the construction.*
(2) *At least five test replicates should be tested, and if the coefficient of variation of the first five tests exceeds 15%, at least ten replicates should be tested. The modulus of rupture, f'_{gm}, should be calculated as the arithmetic mean of the strengths determined from the test replicates.*

15.2.3 Analysis
Analysis of glass block masonry shall be based on elastic plate theory.

15.2.4 Safety

15.2.4.1
Glass block masonry shall be laterally supported such that the factored moments due to lateral loads do not result in flexural tensile stresses in the masonry exceeding $\phi_m f'_{gm}$.

15.2.4.2
Anchors shall conform to CSA Standard A370.

16. Empirical Design for Unreinforced Masonry

16.1 General

16.1.1 Design
Where permitted by Clause 6.2.1, Clause 16 applies to the design of unreinforced masonry where the design is based on a simplified analysis of the structural effects of the loads and forces acting on the structure, and in accordance with the principles of working stress design.

16.1.2 Limitations for Empirical Design
Clause 16 shall not be used for
(a) loadbearing walls where they exceed the overall height limits set in Clause 16.3.2.;
(b) nonloadbearing exterior walls which are higher than 20 m above grade or in areas where the 1 in 30 years hourly wind pressure exceeds 0.5 kN/m²;
(c) foundation walls subjected to lateral loads;
(d) cases in which applied loads other than wind loads cause a lateral force on a masonry structure or where the resultant vertical force of a gravity load on a masonry element falls outside the central third of the actual thickness of the masonry; or
(e) design of structures for use in velocity- or acceleration-related seismic zones 2 and higher.

16.1.3 Dimensions
Dimensions of masonry units or masonry are actual dimensions.

16.1.4 Roof Anchorage
Anchorage for roofs shall extend down to engage sufficient factored dead loads to resist twice the wind load.

16.1.5 Allowable Masonry Stresses

16.1.5.1
Except as provided in Clause 16.1.6.2, the compressive stresses in masonry walls and columns shall not exceed the values set forth in Table 7.

16.1.5.2
The stresses shall be calculated by dividing the gravity load on a section by
(a) the gross cross-sectional area when it is solid masonry of hollow or solid units; or
(b) the gross cross-sectional area of the loaded wythe or wythes when it is a cavity wall.
Note: *Where the inner and outer wythes of a cavity wall are not the same material type, it is recommended that the cavity wall be loaded on one wythe.*

16.1.5.3
The calculated load on masonry shall include all tributary gravity loads including the dead load of masonry itself.

16.1.5.4
In masonry constructed of different kinds or grades of units or mortar, the allowable stress in Table 7 used in design shall correspond to the weakest combination of units and mortar of which the member is constructed, except that in a cavity wall where only one wythe supports the vertical load, the allowable stress shall be appropriate for the materials in the loaded wythe.

16.1.5.5
Where a type of masonry unit or a type of mortar is not provided for in Table 7, the allowable compressive stress of the masonry shall be 15% of the ultimate compressive strength of the masonry and determined by tests in accordance with ASTM Standard E72.

16.1.6 Support of Loads

16.1.6.1
Where masonry supports uniform loads the contact bearing pressure, assuming uniform pressure distribution on the masonry, shall not exceed the allowable compressive stresses specified in Table 7.

16.1.6.2
Where masonry supports concentrated loads, the contact pressure directly under the bearing, assuming uniform pressure distribution, shall not exceed the allowable compressive stresses in Table 7 by more than 25%.

16.1.6.3
Where any wall of masonry supports a continuous load such as a slab, a deck, or wood joists spaced not more than 760 mm on-centre, the
(a) support shall be continuous and shall be of either solid units to a depth of at least 57 mm measured down from the bearing surface, or a course of hollow units filled solidly to a depth of 190 mm with concrete having a compressive strength of at least 15 MPa; and
(b) bearing shall extend at least 75 mm into the masonry.

16.1.6.4
Where masonry supports a load applied other than provided for in Clause 16.1.6.3, the support shall be of solid units or units with voids filled with grout having a compressive strength of at least 15 MPa to a depth of at least 190 mm measured down from the bearing surface. The bearing for such loads shall extend at least 90 mm into the masonry.

16.1.7 Change in Thickness of Wall

16.1.7.1
When changes in wall thickness are required for structural purposes, these changes shall occur only at lines of lateral supports.

16.1.7.2
Where a change in thickness of masonry occurs, a height of 190 mm of the thicker portion at the change shall be of solid units or filled hollow units.

16.2 Spacing of Lateral Supports

16.2.1 General
Masonry walls shall have lateral supports at either vertical or horizontal intervals spaced so that the allowable slenderness ratio specified in Table 8 is not exceeded for the type of masonry being used.

16.2.2 Effective Thickness of a Cavity Wall
The effective thickness of a cavity wall used to determine the height or length to thickness ratio shall be taken as two-thirds of the sum of the thickness of the wythes, but not less than the thickness of either wythe. The effective thickness calculation is independent of the loading of the wythes. Where raked mortar joints are used the effective thickness of the wythe shall be reduced by the depth of the raking.

16.2.3 Wall Not Supported at Top

16.2.3.1
Except as provided in Clause 16.2.3.2, where a wall of masonry does not have lateral support along its top, and if its height exceeds four times its thickness, it shall have vertical lateral supports at horizontal intervals spaced in accordance with Clause 16.2.1.

16.2.3.2
The portion of a wall extending from the sill of a window to the floor immediately below shall be laterally supported along its top, or have vertical lateral supports at horizontal intervals spaced in accordance with Clause 16.2.1 where
(a) its height exceeds three times its thickness; and
(b) the length of the wall below the window exceeds the limits given in Clause 16.2.1.

16.3 Height and Thickness of Solid Masonry

16.3.1 General
Where a solid masonry wall is made up of two or more wythes, the thickness of the wall shall not include any wythes less than 90 mm in thickness for loadbearing masonry walls or 75 mm in thickness for nonloadbearing walls.

16.3.2 Loadbearing Walls

16.3.2.1
Except as provided in Clause 16.3.4, the minimum thickness of a loadbearing wall of solid masonry above the floor of the first storey (excluding basement or cellar walls) shall be as set forth in Table 8.

16.3.2.2
Except as provided in Clause 16.3.4, the maximum height of a loadbearing wall above the floor of the first storey shall be 11 m.

16.3.3 Nonloadbearing Exterior Walls

16.3.3.1
Except as provided in Clause 16.3.4, the minimum thickness of a nonloadbearing exterior wall of solid masonry above the floor of the first storey (excluding basement or cellar walls) shall be as set forth in Table 8.

16.3.3.2
Nonloadbearing exterior walls of solid masonry of solid units not less than 140 mm in thickness may be built to a height not exceeding 3 m provided Type S mortar is used.

16.3.4 Gable Walls
Gable walls of solid units 140 mm in thickness may be built to a height not exceeding 2.8 m at the eave and 4.6 m at the peak of a gable
(a) in one storey buildings; and
(b) for the top storey of two-storey buildings where the wall of the first storey is permitted to be 190 mm.

16.3.5 Partitions

16.3.5.1
Except as provided in Clause 16.3.5.2, the minimum thickness of a partition shall conform to the value given in Table 8.
Note: *Partitions likely to be subjected to wind loading should be designed as exterior walls.*

16.3.5.2
Where lateral support of a partition is provided by walls or columns spaced at horizontal intervals not exceeding 36 times the partition thickness, the height of a partition shall not exceed 72 times its thickness.

16.4 Height and Thickness of Cavity Walls

16.4.1
Except as provided in Clause 16.4.4, a cavity wall shall not be built to a height greater than 11 m above its bearing support.

16.4.2
Except as provided in Clause 16.4.4, the minimum thickness of a wythe in a cavity wall shall be in accordance with the values given in Table 8.

16.4.3
The width of a cavity in a cavity wall shall not be more than 150 mm.

16.4.4
Where both the facing and backing wythes are composed of solid masonry units the thickness of the lesser wythe may be reduced to 75 mm, but the total wall height shall not exceed 6 m above the floor of the first storey. The maximum spacing between lateral supports for construction covered by this Clause is 2400 mm.

16.4.5
Raked mortar joints shall not be used in cavity walls except when the wythes are at least 90 mm in thickness.

16.5 Height of Shaft and Penthouse Walls
Loadbearing masonry walls not more than 3.6 m in height above the main roof level, which enclose mechanical rooms, elevators, or stairway penthouses having an aggregate area not exceeding 15% of the roof area, need not be considered in computing the height of other walls in the building.

16.6 Chases and Recesses

16.6.1
The width of a vertical chase or recess shall be taken as its maximum horizontal width, and that of a sloping chase shall be taken as the horizontal distance between vertical lines through its extremities.

16.6.2
Except where a chase or recess is designed as an opening in accordance with Clause 16.7, chases and recesses shall not
(a) be cut into walls made with hollow units after the masonry units are in place;
(b) exceed 500 mm in width; the sum of the widths of chases and recesses in a wall shall not exceed 25% of its length;
(c) be less than four times the wall thickness apart and not less than 600 mm away from any structural member that provides lateral support; and
(d) exceed one-third of the thickness of the wall in depth.

16.7 Allowable Openings

16.7.1 General
Evidence shall be provided to show that openings do not cause stresses in the wall greater than the values given in Table 7.

16.7.2 Effect of Openings on Lateral Support Spacings

16.7.2.1
This Clause applies to exterior walls which are laterally supported top and bottom.

16.7.2.2
The length of the wall between openings shall not be less than the centre-to-centre distance between adjacent openings, multiplied by the percentage values given in Table 9 for various h/t ratios.

16.7.2.3
The length of the wall between an opening and the end or return of a wall shall not be less than the distance from the centre of the opening to the end of the wall multiplied by the percentage values given in Table 9 for various h/t ratios.

16.7.2.4
In no case shall the length of the wall between openings, or between an opening and the end of the wall, be less than three times the wall thickness, unless it is designed as a column.

16.8 Columns

16.8.1
Every masonry column shall be constructed of solid masonry of solid units or hollow units filled with grout or concrete.

16.8.2
A masonry column shall be laterally supported in each direction with the distance between lateral supports not exceeding 10 times the thickness of the column in the same direction.

16.9 Veneer

16.9.1
Veneer shall not be considered to be part of a wall when computing the strength or effective thickness of the wall.

16.9.2
Veneer shall be tied to its backing in accordance with CSA Standard A370.

16.9.3
The structural backing for veneer shall be concrete or shall be masonry conforming to the empirical rules.
Note: *Refer to Clause 13 for other types of structural backing.*

16.9.4
Masonry veneer more than 11 m above the top of the foundation wall shall bear on masonry, concrete, or other noncombustible bearing supports spaced not more than 3.6 m vertically.

16.10 Glass Block Walls

16.10.1
Glass block masonry shall
(a) be nonloadbearing;
(b) be isolated from adjacent construction by movement joints to prevent or relieve stress due to differential movement; and
(c) have a minimum thickness of 75 mm at the mortar joint.

16.10.2
Joint reinforcement shall be placed in glass block masonry panels, and shall be
(a) not less than conventional continuous-welded ladder reinforcing, in accordance with CSA Standard A370;
(b) spaced at not more than
  (i)   every other mortar joint where the courses are not greater than 205 mm in height, and
  (ii) every mortar joint where the courses are greater than 205 mm in height.
(c) installed in accordance with CSA Standard A371.

16.10.3
Where anchors are used to secure glass block masonry panels to their lateral supports, they shall allow in-plane movement of the masonry and shall be in accordance with CSA Standard A370.

16.10.4
Members supporting the weight of glass block masonry and members laterally supporting glass block masonry shall be of sufficient stiffness to avoid excessive or harmful deflections.

16.10.5
For exterior walls the maximum length of glass block walls between movement joints shall be 7600 mm, and the maximum height of glass block walls between movement joints shall be 6100 mm.

16.10.6
For exterior walls, the area of each individual panel shall not be more than 8.5 m^2.

16.10.7
Movement joints shall accommodate volume change of glass block walls and deflection of adjacent structure.

16.10.8
The allowable slenderness ratio of a glass block wall shall conform to the requirements for nonloadbearing walls in Table 8.

Table 1
Masonry Dimensional Properties

Type of masonry units	Thermal movement mm/m/100°C	Moisture movement mm/m		Initial elastic modulus, GPa	Long-term strain/ initial strain
		Reversible	Permanent		
Concrete					
- aerated (autoclaved cellular)	0.8	0.2–0.3	0.5–0.9*	3–8	4
- normal weight aggregate	0.6–1.2	0.2–0.4	0.2–0.4*	10–25	3–4
- lightweight aggregate	0.8–1.2	0.3–0.6	0.2–0.6*	4–16	4–5
Calcium silicate	0.8–1.4	0.1–0.5	0.1–0.4*	14–18	3–4
Clay					
- horizontal	0.5–0.6	0.2	0.2–0.7†	4–26	2–3
- vertical	0.7–0.9	0.2	0.2–0.7†	4–26	2–4

*shrinkage.
†expansion.

Notes:

(1) The above numbers are given for general guidance only. Actual movement in a wall is affected by age and degree of wetness of the unit at the time of construction, temperature and humidity to which the wall is exposed, age of wall when it is loaded and the degree of restraint at the boundaries to the wall.

(2) Movements due to temperature and moisture are usually not additive. For example a wet wall under an increasing temperature may lead to drying shrinkage which counteracts the expansion due to temperature.

(3) The values for moisture movement are extremes representing the range completely wet to completely dry.

(4) Permanent moisture expansion of clay bricks is caused by reactions between moisture (humid air is sufficient) and ceramic constituents. The magnitude of the expansion depends on the raw material and the degree of firing. Much of it occurs early in the life of the unit. Thus potential movement in a wall will also depend on the age of the brick at the time of construction.

Table 2
Coefficient of Friction for Serviceability

	Dry	Wet
Masonry against masonry	0.7	0.6
Masonry against concrete	0.7	0.6
Masonry against steel	0.45	0.35
Masonry against wood	0.6	0.5

Table 3
Value of f′$_m$ for Solid Brick Masonry

Compressive strength of units, MPa* (gross area)	Compressive strength, f′$_m$ of brick masonry, MPa	
	Type S mortar	Type N mortar
90	25	21
80	23	19
70	20	17
55	16	14
40	13	11
25	8.8	7.5
15	6.8	6.0

Linear interpolation is permitted.
Note: *See CSA Standards A82.1 and A165.2 for requirements pertaining to clay and concrete brick masonry units, respectively.*

Table 4
Value of f′$_m$ for Hollow Clay Brick Masonry

(Reserved)

Table 5
Value of f'_m for Concrete Block Masonry

Compressive strength of unit, MPa (net area)*	Compressive strength, f'_m, of concrete block masonry			
	Type S mortar		Type N mortar	
	Hollow	Solid or grouted	Hollow	Solid or grouted
>40	22	17	14	10.5
30	17.5	13.5	12	9
20	13	10	10	7.5
15	9.8	7.5	8	6
10	6.5	5	6	4.5

*Linear interpolation is permitted.
Note: Requirements for concrete block masonry units are included in CSA Standards A165.1 and A165.3.

Table 6
Flexural Tensile Strength, f_t

Unit Type	Normal to bed joints, MPa (vertical span)		Parallel to bed joints, MPa (horizontal span)	
	Mortar type		Mortar type	
	S	N	S	N
Clay brick, solid	0.70	0.50	1.4	1.0
Clay brick, hollow	0.30	0.20	0.60	0.40
Concrete brick & block	0.45	0.30	0.90	0.60
Calcium silicate brick	0.45	0.30	0.90	0.60
Grouted hollow block & brick	0.70	0.50	0.90	0.60

Notes:
(1) The stresses in this table do not apply to free-standing cantilever walls (no support at the top or sides). In such cases the strength shall be limited to 0.1 MPa.
(2) At locations where flashings go through the wall, the flexural tensile stress shall be taken as zero, unless shown otherwise by tests.
(3) The stresses listed in the table may not be achieved for all types and combinations of masonry unit and mortar. For example, reductions of strength may occur if masonry units with very low or high initial rates of water absorption, or mortars with excessive amounts of entrained air, are used.

Table 7
Maximum Allowable Compressive Stress for Unreinforced Masonry
(See Clause 16.)

Maximum allowable compressive stress, based on gross cross-sectional area, MPa

		Type of mortar	
Type of masonry	Type of masonry units (strength based on gross cross-sectional area)	S	N
Solid masonry or single-wythe masonry	Rubble stone	0.8	0.7
	Ashlar granite	5.0	4.4
	Ashlar limestone and marble	3.1	2.8
	Ashlar sandstone and cast-stone	2.5	2.2
	Solid units (except concrete block) with an ultimate compressive strength of		
	over 70 MPa	3.1	2.4
	55–70 MPa	2.4	2.1
	42–55 MPa	1.9	1.7
	30–42 MPa	1.5	1.4
	18–30 MPa	1.1	1.0
	10–18 MPa	0.8	0.7
	Solid concrete block		
	20 MPa and over	1.6	1.4
	12.5–20 MPa	1.1	1.0
	8.0–12.5 MPa	0.8	0.7
	Hollow load-bearing units		
	7.5 MPa and over	0.7	0.6
	5.0–7.5 MPa	0.5	0.5
Cavity walls*	Solid units (except concrete block) with an ultimate compressive strength of		
	18 MPa and over	0.9	0.8
	10–18 MPa	0.6	0.5
	Solid concrete block		
	12.5 MPa and over	0.9	0.8
	8–12.5 MPa	0.6	0.5
	Hollow loadbearing units		
	7.5 MPa and over	0.5	0.4

*See Clause 16.1.5.2.

Table 8
Allowable Slenderness Ratio and Minimum Thickness of Masonry Walls
(See Clause 16.)

Type of masonry	Allowable slenderness ratio of unsupported height or length to masonry thickness*	Minimum thickness masonry, mm
Load-bearing walls		
Cavity wall†‡	20	90 (per wythe)
Solid masonry of hollow or solid units	20	190
Solid masonry of rubble stone	14	290
Nonloadbearing walls		
Exterior cavity walls†,‡	20	90 (per wythe)
Exterior solid masonry of solid units	20	140
Exterior solid masonry of hollow units	20	190
Partitions	36	75

*Values for exterior walls shall be reduced according to Clause 16.7.
†See Clause 16.6.2 for thickness of cavity walls.
‡Except for Clause 16.4.4.

Table 9
Percentage of Masonry Wall with Openings Remaining to Resist Wind Loading
(See Clause 16.7.)

(h/t)*	Percentage of wall remaining to resist wind loading
20	85
18	70
16	55
14	40
12	30
10 or less	20 minimum

*h = height of wall between horizontal lateral supports
t = effective thickness

Appendix A
Seismic Design of Shear Walls with Nominal Ductility

Note: *This Appendix is not a mandatory part of this Standard but is written in mandatory language to accommodate its adoption by anyone wishing to do so.*

A1. Scope
This Appendix sets out requirements for seismic design of masonry cantilever shear walls classified as nominally ductile as defined in Clause 6.3.3.2.

A2. Notations
c = distance from the extreme compression fibre to the neutral axis
h_w = total height of wall from the base
ℓ_w = horizontal length of wall
ℓ_p = length of plastic hinge region

A3. Definitions
Plastic hinge means a region of a member where inelastic flexural curvatures occur.

A4. General Requirements

A4.1
The provisions of Clauses 1 through 11 shall apply except as modified by the provisions of this Appendix.

A4.2
Structures designed in accordance with the provisions of this Appendix are required to be of reinforced masonry.

A4.3
Redistribution of design moments obtained from elastic analysis is not permitted unless it can be demonstrated that the ductility capacity of affected members is not exceeded.

A4.4
Nominally ductile walls shall be designed to resist a shear force greater than the shear that is present when the wall develops a plastic hinge mechanism.

A5. Plastic Hinge Region

A5.1 Plastic Hinge Length
The extent of the plastic hinge region above the base of the wall shall be

ℓ_p = greater of ℓ_w or $h_w/6$

A5.2
The unsupported height of the section of the wall that contains the plastic hinge should be such that the height to thickness ratio of the wall in the compression zone satisfies $h/b_w \leq 14$.

A5.3 .
Masonry within the plastic hinge region shall be solidly grouted, and constructed of open-ended blocks if the masonry is laid in stack pattern.

A6. Factored Shear Resistance

A6.1

The factored shear resistance shall be based on Clause 11.5.3, except that, within the potential plastic hinge region, the factored shear resistance contributed by the masonry and the axial compressive load shall be reduced by one-half.

A6.2 Factored Sliding Shear Strength

The factored sliding shear strength shall be based on Clause 11.5.6, except that within the potential hinge region the masonry compressive force, C, should be reduced by the compressive yield force of the reinforcement in the compression zone.

Note: *The compressive reinforcement is assumed to have yielded in tension in a previous moment cycle and is now exerting a compressive force across the shear plane as it yields in compression.*

A7. Ductility Requirement

A7.1

The maximum compressive strain in the masonry in the plastic hinge zone shall be shown to not exceed 0.0025 at the desired ductility level.

A7.2

For walls having a height to length ratio less than 3, the limiting strain requirement of Clause A.7.1 is satisfied when $c < 0.2\ \ell_w$.

A8. Reinforcement

A8.1

Vertical and horizontal reinforcement shall be provided.

A8.2

Vertical reinforcement shall be uniformly distributed over the length of the wall, and shall be spaced not more than one-quarter of the wall effective depth, six times the wall thickness nor 1200 mm, whichever is less.

A8.3

At any section within the plastic hinge region, no more than half of the area of vertical reinforcement can be lapped.

A8.4

Horizontal reinforcement shall be continuous to the ends of the wall, and have 180° hooks around vertical reinforcing bars.

A8.5

Horizontal reinforcement shall not be lapped within 600 mm or the neutral axis depth c, whichever is greater, from the end of the wall.

Appendix B
Effective Length Factors

Note: *This Appendix is not a mandatory part of this Standard.*

Table B1
Effective Length Factors, k, For Walls and Columns
Laterally Supported Top and Bottom
(See Clause 11.1.2.1.)

		k			
Top	Hinged	0.81	0.91	0.95	1.00
	Elastic	0.80	0.86	0.90	0.95
	Elastic	0.80	0.83	0.86	0.91
	Stiff	0.80	0.80	0.80	0.81
		Stiff	Elastic	Elastic	Hinged
		Bottom			

NOTES

NOTES

NOTES

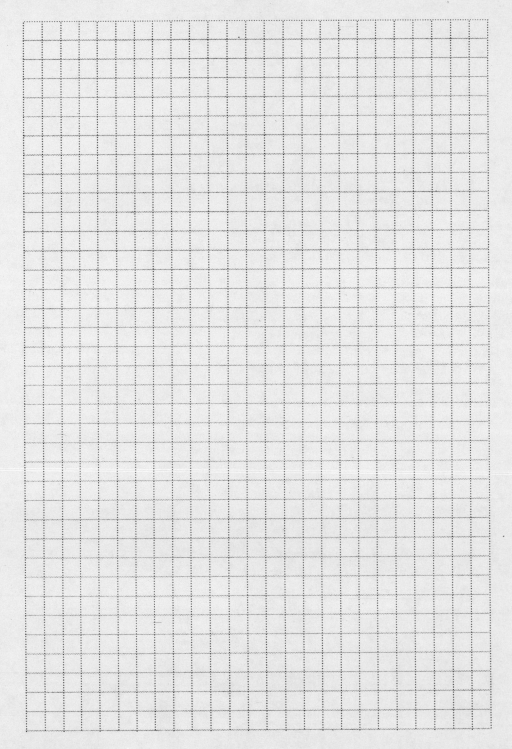